Beginning T-SQL

Third Edition

Kathi Kellenberger
Scott Shaw

Apress®

Beginning T-SQL

ISBN-13 (pbk): 978-1-4842-0047-6

ISBN-13 (electronic): 978-1-4842-0046-9

Publisher: Heinz Weinheimer
Lead Editor: Jonathan Gennick
Technical Reviewer: Louis Davidson
Editorial Board: Steve Anglin, Mark Beckner, Ewan Buckingham, Gary Cornell, Louise Corrigan, Jim DeWolf, Jonathan Gennick, Jonathan Hassell, Robert Hutchinson, Michelle Lowman, James Markham, Matthew Moodie, Jeff Olson, Jeffrey Pepper, Douglas Pundick, Ben Renow-Clarke, Dominic Shakeshaft, Gwenan Spearing, Matt Wade, Steve Weiss
Coordinating Editor: Jill Balzano
Copy Editor: Mary Bearden
Compositor: SPi Global
Indexer: SPi Global
Artist: SPi Global
Cover Designer: Anna Ishchenko

Distributed to the book trade worldwide by Springer Science+Business Media New York, 233 Spring Street, 6th Floor, New York, NY 10013. Phone 1-800-SPRINGER, fax (201) 348-4505, e-mail orders-ny@springer-sbm.com, or visit www.springeronline.com. Apress Media, LLC is a California LLC and the sole member (owner) is Springer Science + Business Media Finance Inc (SSBM Finance Inc). SSBM Finance Inc is a Delaware corporation.

For information on translations, please e-mail rights@apress.com, or visit www.apress.com.

Apress and friends of ED books may be purchased in bulk for academic, corporate, or promotional use. eBook versions and licenses are also available for most titles. For more information, reference our Special Bulk Sales–eBook Licensing web page at www.apress.com/bulk-sales.

Any source code or other supplementary material referenced by the author in this text is available to readers at www.apress.com. For detailed information about how to locate your book's source code, go to www.apress.com/source-code.

For my new little guy, Wyatt.

Contents at a Glance

About the Authors.. xxiii

About the Technical Reviewer xxv

Acknowledgments xxvii

Foreword xxix

■Chapter 1: Getting Started 1

■Chapter 2: Exploring Database Concepts 19

■Chapter 3: Writing Simple *SELECT* Queries 31

■Chapter 4: Using Built-In Functions and Expressions 59

■Chapter 5: Joining Tables 101

■Chapter 6: Building on Subqueries, Common Table Expressions, and Unions.............127

■Chapter 7: Grouping and Summarizing Data 147

■Chapter 8: Discovering Windowing Functions 169

■Chapter 9: Advanced *WHERE* Clauses...193

■Chapter 10: Manipulating Data..211

■Chapter 11: Writing Advanced Queries...241

■Chapter 12: Understanding T-SQL Programming Logic 275

■Chapter 13: Managing Transactions...309

■Chapter 14: Implementing Logic in the Database 325

■**Chapter 15: Working with XML**..**379**

■**Chapter 16: Expanding on Data Type Concepts** **403**

■**Chapter 17: Running SQL Server in the Cloud** **433**

■**Chapter 18: Where to Go Next?**..**449**

Index...**453**

Contents

About the Authors.. xxiii

About the Technical Reviewer xxv

Acknowledgments xxvii

Foreword xxix

■Chapter 1: Getting Started...1

Installing SQL Server Express Edition 1

Installing Books Online..10

Using Books Online 11

Using SQL Server Management Studio 12

    Launching SQL Server Management Studio 12

Installing the Sample Databases...14

Get Started with SSMS...15

Summary..18

■Chapter 2: Exploring Database Concepts 19

What Is SQL Server?..19

Databases in the Cloud 20

Service vs. Application 20

Database as Container 21

Data Is Stored in Tables...23

Data Types 23

Normalization 25

Understanding Indexes...27

Database Schemas..28

Summary..29

■Chapter 3: Writing Simple *SELECT* Queries.....................................31

Using the *SELECT* Statement...31

    Selecting a Literal Value 31

    Retrieving from a Table...32

    Generating a Select-List 34

    Mixing Literals and Column Names 35

Filtering Data...37

    Adding a *WHERE* Clause 37

    Using *WHERE* Clauses with Alternate Operators 38

    Using *BETWEEN*...40

    Using *BETWEEN* with *NOT* 42

    Filtering on Date and Time...43

Using *WHERE* Clauses with Two Predicates 45

    Using the *IN* Operator 47

Working with *NULL*...48

Sorting Data 50

Thinking About Performance...52

    Taking Advantage of Indexes 52

    Viewing Execution Plans...54

Summary..56

Answers to the Exercises 56

    Solutions to Exercise 3-1: Using the *SELECT* Statement 56

    Solutions to Exercise 3-2: Filtering Data 56

    Solutions to Exercise 3-3: Using WHERE Clauses with Two Predicates...............57

    Solutions to Exercise 3-4: Working with *NULL*..58

    Solutions to Exercise 3-5: Sorting Data...58

■Chapter 4: Using Built-In Functions and Expressions 59

Expressions Using Operators 59

Concatenating Strings 59

Concatenating Strings and *NULL* 60

CONCAT 61

ISNULL and *COALESCE* 62

Concatenating Other Data Types to Strings 63

Using Mathematical Operators 65

Using String Functions 67

RTRIM and LTRIM 67

LEFT and RIGHT 68

LEN and DATALENGTH 69

CHARINDEX 69

SUBSTRING 70

CHOOSE 71

REVERSE 71

UPPER and LOWER 72

REPLACE 72

Nesting Functions 74

Using Date and Time Functions 75

GETDATE and SYSDATETIME 75

DATEADD 75

DATEDIFF 77

DATENAME and DATEPART 77

DAY, MONTH, and YEAR 78

CONVERT 79

FORMAT 80

DATEFROMPARTS 81

EOMONTH 81

Using Mathematical Functions 82

    ABS 82

    POWER 82

    SQUARE and *SQRT* 83

    ROUND 83

    RAND 84

Logical Functions and Expressions 85

    The *CASE* Expression 85

    IIF 88

    COALESCE 89

Administrative Functions 89

Using Functions in the *WHERE* and *ORDER BY* Clauses 90

The *TOP* Keyword 92

Thinking About Performance 93

Summary 95

Answers to the Exercises 96

    Solutions to Exercise 4-1: Expressions Using Operators 96

    Solutions to Exercise 4-2: Using Mathematical Operators 96

    Solution to Exercise 4-3: Using Functions 97

    Solution to Exercise 4-4: Using Date and Time Functions 98

    Solution to Exercise 4-5: Using Mathematical Functions 99

    Solution to Exercise 4-6: Using Logical and System Functions 99

    Solution to Exercise 4-7: Using Functions in the *WHERE* and *ORDER BY* Clauses 100

■ **Chapter 5: Joining Tables** **101**

Using *INNER JOIN* 101

    Joining Two Tables 101

    Avoiding an Incorrect Join Condition 103

    Joining on a Different Column Name 104

    Joining on More Than One Column 105

    Joining Three or More Tables 106

Using *OUTER JOIN* 108

    Using *LEFT OUTER JOIN* 108

    Using *RIGHT OUTER JOIN* 109

    Using *OUTER JOIN* to Find Rows with No Match 110

    Adding a Table to the Right Side of a *LEFT JOIN* 111

    Adding a Table to the Main Table of a *LEFT JOIN* 113

    FULL OUTER JOIN 114

    CROSS JOIN 115

    Self-Joins 117

Thinking About Performance 119

    Merge Join 119

    Nested Loop 120

    Hash Match 122

Summary 123

Answers to the Exercises 123

    Solutions to Exercise 5-1: Using INNER JOIN 123

    Solutions to Exercise 5-2: Using OUTER JOIN 125

■Chapter 6: Building on Subqueries, Common Table Expressions, and Unions 127

Writing Subqueries 127

    Using a Subquery in an *IN* List 127

    Using a Subquery and *NOT IN* 128

    Using a Subquery Containing *NULL* with *NOT IN* 129

    Using *EXISTS* 130

    Using *CROSS APPLY* and *OUTER APPLY* 131

    Writing *UNION* Queries 132

    Using *EXCEPT* and *INTERSECT* 135

Using Derived Tables and Common Table Expressions 136

    Using Derived Tables 136

    Using Common Table Expressions 138

    Using a Common Table Expression to Solve a Complicated Join Problem 139

Thinking About Performance 142

Summary 144

Answers to the Exercises 144

    Solutions to Exercise 6-1: Using Subqueries 145

    Solutions to Exercise 6-2: Using Derived Tables and Common Table Expressions 146

■Chapter 7: Grouping and Summarizing Data 147

Aggregate Functions 147

The *GROUP BY* Clause 149

    Grouping on Columns 149

    Grouping on Expressions 151

The *ORDER BY* Clause 153

The *WHERE* Clause 154

The *HAVING* Clause 155

DISTINCT Keyword 158

    Using *DISTINCT* vs. *GROUP BY* 158

    DISTINCT Within an Aggregate Expression 159

Aggregate Queries with More Than One Table 160

Aggregate Functions and *NULL* 161

Thinking About Performance 162

Summary 165

Answers to the Exercises 165

    Solutions to Exercise 7-1: Aggregate Functions 165

    Solutions to Exercise 7-2: The *GROUP BY* Clause 166

    Solutions to Exercise 7-3: The *HAVING* Clause 166

    Solutions to Exercise 7-4: *DISTINCT* Keyword 167

    Solutions to Exercise 7-5: Aggregate Queries with More Than One Table 168

■Chapter 8: Discovering Windowing Functions 169

What Is a Windowing Function? 169

Ranking Functions 169

Defining the Window 170

Dividing the Window into Partitions 171

Using *NTILE* 172

Summarizing Results with Window Aggregates 174

Defining the Window with Framing 175

Calculating Running Totals 176

Understanding the Difference Between *ROWS* and *RANGE* 177

Using Window Analytic Functions 178

LAG and *LEAD* 179

FIRST_VALUE and *LAST_VALUE* 180

PERCENT_RANK and *CUME_DIST* 181

PERCENTILE_CONT and *PERCENTILE_DISC* 182

Applying Windowing Functions 184

Removing Duplicates 184

Solving an Islands Problem 186

Thinking About Performance 187

Indexing 187

The Trouble with Window Aggregates 187

Framing 188

Summary 189

Answers to the Exercises 189

Solutions to Exercise 8-1: Ranking Functions 189

Solutions to Exercise 8-2: Summarizing Results with Window Aggregates 189

Solutions to Exercise 8-3: Understanding the Difference Between *ROWS* and *RANGE* .. 190

Solutions to Exercise 8-4: Using Window Analytic Functions 190

■Chapter 9: Advanced *WHERE* Clauses 193

Pattern Matching 193

Using *LIKE* 193

Restricting the Characters in Pattern Matches...195

Searching for Wildcards 196

Combining Wildcards...196

Using *PATINDEX*..198

Using *WHERE* Clauses with Three or More Predicates 199

Using *NOT* with Parentheses 201

Performing a Full-Text Search...202

Using *CONTAINS* 203

Using Multiple Terms with *CONTAINS*..203

Searching Multiple Columns..204

Using *FREETEXT* 205

Thinking About Performance...206

Summary..207

Answers to the Exercises 208

Solutions to Exercise 9-1: Using *LIKE*..208

Solution to Exercise 9-2: Using *WHERE* Clauses with Three or More Predicates 209

Solution to Exercise 9-3: Performing a Full-Text Search 209

■Chapter 10: Manipulating Data...211

Inserting New Rows 211

Adding One Row with Literal Values...212

Avoiding Common Insert Errors..213

Inserting Multiple Rows with One Statement 215

Inserting Rows from Another Table...216

Inserting Missing Rows 217

Creating and Populating a Table in One Statement 218

Inserting Rows into Tables with Default Column Values..220

Inserting Rows into Tables with Automatically Populating Columns 221

Deleting Rows 224

    Using *DELETE* 224

    Deleting from a Table Using *EXISTS* 227

    Truncating..229

Updating Existing Rows...230

    Using the *UPDATE* Statement 230

    Updating Data with Expressions and Columns 231

    Updating with a Join...233

Thinking About Performance 234

    Database Cleanup...236

Summary..237

Answers to the Exercises 238

    Solution to Exercise 10-1: Inserting New Rows...238

    Solution to Exercise 10-2: Deleting Rows...240

    Solution to Exercise 10-3: Updating Existing Rows 240

■Chapter 11: Writing Advanced Queries...241

Advanced CTE Queries 241

    Alternate CTE Syntax 241

    Using Multiple CTEs..242

    Referencing a CTE Multiple Times 246

    Joining a CTE to Another CTE 247

    Writing a Recursive Query...248

    Data Manipulation with CTEs...251

Isolating Aggregate Query Logic 252

    Correlated Subqueries in the SELECT list 252

    Using Derived Tables 253

    Common Table Expressions 254

    Using *CROSS APPLY* and *OUTER APPLY*...255

The *OUTPUT* Clause 256

    Using *OUTPUT* to View Data 256

    Saving *OUTPUT* Data to a Table 259

The *MERGE* Statement 260

GROUPING SETS 263

CUBE and *ROLLUP* 264

Pivoted Queries 266

    Pivoting Data with *CASE* 266

    Using the *PIVOT* Function 267

    Using the *UNPIVOT* Function 269

Paging 271

Summary 273

■**Chapter 12: Understanding T-SQL Programming Logic** **275**

Variables 275

    Declaring and Initializing a Variable 275

    Using Expressions and Functions with Variables 277

    Using Variables in *WHERE* and *HAVING* Clauses 279

The *IF . . . ELSE* Construct 281

    Using *IF* 281

    Using *ELSE* 283

    Using Multiple Conditions 284

    Nesting *IF . . . ELSE* 285

    Using *IF* with a Query 286

WHILE 288

    Using a *WHILE* Loop 288

    Nesting *WHILE* Loops 289

    Exiting a Loop Early 290

    Using *CONTINUE* 291

Temporary Tables and Table Variables..293

Creating Local Temp Tables 293

Creating Global Temp Tables 295

Creating Table Variables 295

Using a Temp Table or Table Variable...296

Using a Temp Table or Table Variable Like an Array 298

Using a Cursor 299

Thinking About Performance 301

Summary 304

Answers to the Exercises 304

Solutions to Exercise 12-1: Variables 304

Solutions to Exercise 12-2: The *IF ... ELSE* Construct...305

Solutions to Exercise 12-3: *WHILE*...306

Solutions to Exercise 12-4: Temporary Tables and Table Variables 307

■Chapter 13: Managing Transactions 309

ACID Properties 309

Writing an Explicit Transaction 310

Rolling Back a Transaction 311

Using the *XACT_ABORT* Setting..312

Error Handling 314

Using *TRY ... CATCH*...314

Viewing Untrappable Errors...316

Using *RAISERROR* 317

Using *TRY ... CATCH* with Transactions 318

Using *THROW* Instead of *RAISERROR* 319

Thinking About Performance 321

Summary 322

Answers to the Exercises 323

Solutions to Exercise 13-1: Writing an Explicit Transaction..323

Solutions to Exercise 13-2: Error Handling 324

■Chapter 14: Implementing Logic in the Database 325

Tables 325

Adding Check Constraints to a Table 326

Adding *UNIQUE* Constraints 328

Adding a Primary Key to a Table 330

Creating Foreign Keys 333

Creating Foreign Keys with Delete and Update Rules 335

Defining Automatically Populated Columns 339

Views 342

Creating Views 343

Avoiding Common Problems with Views 345

Manipulating Data with Views 347

User-Defined Functions 350

Creating User-Defined Scalar Functions 351

Using Table-Valued User-Defined Functions 353

Stored Procedures 355

Using Default Values with Parameters 358

Using the *OUTPUT* Parameter 359

Saving the Results of a Stored Procedure in a Table 360

Using a Logic in Stored Procedures 362

User-Defined Data Types 364

Table Types 365

Triggers 367

CLR Integration 368

Thinking About Performance 368

Database Cleanup 369

Summary 371

Answers to the Exercises 371

    Solutions to Exercise 14-1: Tables..371

    Solution to Exercise 14-2: Views 373

    Solution to Exercise 14-3: User-Defined Functions 374

    Solution to Exercise 14-4: Stored Procedures 376

■Chapter 15: Working with XML..379

The Parts of XML 379

Converting XML Using *OPENXML* 380

Retrieving Data as XML Using the *FOR XML* Clause 383

    FOR XML RAW..383

    FOR XML AUTO..385

    FOR XML EXPLICIT..386

    FOR XML PATH..388

The XML Data Type 391

XML Methods 392

    The *QUERY* Method...393

    The *VALUE* Method...395

    The *EXIST* Method..396

    The *MODIFY* Method...397

    The *NODES* Method..398

Namespaces...399

Splitting a String 400

Summary..401

■Chapter 16: Expanding on Data Type Concepts 403

Large-Value String Data Types (MAX)...403

Large-Value Binary Data Types...405

    Creating *VARBINARY(MAX)* Data 405

    Using FILESTREAM 406

    FileTables..413

Enhanced Date and Time...415

    Using *DATE, TIME*, and *DATETIME2*...415

    Using *DATETIMEOFFSET*..416

HIERARCHYID...417

    Viewing *HIERARCHYID*..417

    Creating a Hierarchy..418

    Using Stored Procedures to Manage Hierarchical Data...420

Spatial Data Types..422

    Using *GEOMETRY*..423

    Using *GEOGRAPHY*..424

    Viewing the Spatial Results Tab...425

    Circular Arcs...426

Sparse Columns...428

Thinking About Performance..430

Summary..431

■ **Chapter 17: Running SQL Server in the Cloud**..**433**

Procuring a Microsoft Azure Account..433

The Azure Dashboard..434

Windows Azure Virtual Machines..435

Azure SQL Database...440

    Throttling...446

    Database Size Limitations...446

    Pricing...446

Summary..447

■**Chapter 18: Where to Go Next?** **449**

Online Resources 449

Conferences 450

User Groups...450

Vendors 451

Books 451

Classes 451

SQL Server Documentation 451

Practice, Practice, and More Practice...451

Teach Someone Else 452

Index..**453**

About the Authors

Kathi Kellenberger, known as Aunt Kathi to the SQL Server community, is a business intelligence consultant and a former DBA with 17 years of SQL Server experience. She loves writing, teaching, and speaking about SQL Server and will talk about SQL Server to just about anyone who will listen. Kathi talks about SQL Server so much that she received the MVP award for SQL Server in 2013. Kathi loves karaoke just about as much as SQL Server. Have you heard about all the karaoke parties after SQL Saturdays and at PASS Summit? Kathi and three friends started the first SQL karaoke event the week of PASS Summit in 2006. You can't blame her for how big and crazy it has become, but you can blame her for getting karaoke started in the SQL Server community to begin with. There is one more thing that is very important to Kathi and that is family. Even though she goes by Aunt Kathi in the computing world, she is the proud mother of two and grandmother of four.

Scott Shaw has over a decade of experience in data management. Scott is a frequent speaker at local and national community events. He teaches Pig, Hive, Hadoop, SQL Server, and Microsoft BI-related courses. He is currently working on a book titled *Practical Hive for Apress*. He lives in St. Louis, Missouri, and is a solutions engineer for Hortonworks.

About the Technical Reviewer

Louis Davidson has over 19 years as a corporate database developer and architect. Currently he is the data architect for the Christian Broadcasting Network in Nashville, Tennessee. Nearly all of Louis's professional experience has been with Microsoft SQL Server, from the early days to whatever is the latest version currently in beta. Louis has been the principal author of several books, including one on DMVs and five editions of a book on database design, including one for SQL Server 2012. Louis's primary areas of interest are database architecture and coding in T-SQL, with experience designing many databases and writing thousands of stored procedures and triggers throughout the years. Louis blogs at simple-talk.com with an ongoing series of posts regarding "What Counts for a DBA." He also has a blog at SQLblog.com, where he writes about technical issues and upcoming presentations, including previewing the thought process that goes into a blog. On his web site, drsql.org, Louis includes his professional activity calendar, book descriptions, code samples, utilities, as well as code and slides from all of the presentations he has done throughout the years.

Acknowledgments

Until you actually write a book, you have no idea how much work it is and how many people it takes to make it happen. I want to thank Jonathan Gennick, Scott Shaw, Louis Davidson, Jill Balzano, and Mary Bearden for their roles in making this a better book.

I also need to thank my husband, Dennis, for his love and support and for putting up with all the time I spent writing and reviewing. To my parents, kids, grandkids, siblings, and entire extended family, thank you for your patience as I often had to miss out on spending time with you so I could meet my many deadlines.

But the most important person to thank is you, the person who is learning T-SQL from this book. Without you, there is no reason for this book at all. Be sure to say hello if you happen to be at a SQL Server event or user group meeting and see me there!

Foreword

We all have to start somewhere, and we start different things at different stages in our lives. There are a few skills that come naturally to us and a few we need to learn.

Let's look at a quick example—we learn how to walk with very little help when we are children, but we need help when we start to learn swimming. Both of the activities have almost the same kind of body behavior—we move our hands, legs, and head in a systematic rhythm to achieve our goal. However, swimming is a skill we needed to learn and walking was a natural process.

Learning new technology is a very complicated affair. Although computers are a part of our lives and have blended into our daily routines, the behind-the-scene situation is still mysterious. Just like we needed training to learn how to swim, we also need comprehensive training to master technology. It is equally important that the trainer also understands the importance of training. My father always told me "An expert is not necessarily a good teacher, but a teacher must be an expert."

If you ask a hundred database experts how they started to work with databases, the most common answer you will get is accidently. It is true that most database professionals were not trained for databases, but rather they started with databases accidently. The reasons for this accident can be different, but the fact remains that we all ended up working with databases when we are not expecting it.

My own story is that I was working as a software developer when one fine day I was asked to manage the database until a new administrator for our database could be found. I was happy to take on the challenge of managing the database, but the real challenge for me was to learn database administration overnight. I ran to a nearby bookstore and purchased five database books. For the next five days, I was up every night until four in the morning reading different books.

As I started to read, I learned a lot about databases. But I also learned that a good educational book will give support to the learner. Instead of testing the user early, the book places challenges at strategic intervals. It is extremely important that a book presents the experience of learning naturally. If a technology book can teach us a complicated subject with the same ease as learning to walk, the book is capable of changing how we progress in our professional lives.

Of the five books I purchased, I found one book that taught me the complicated subject of SQL Server in simple words. The book was capable of intriguing me to learn and practice more. I instantly felt connected with the book and the book's author. The book was authored by Kathi Kellenberger. Since that time, I have read every single one of her books. It gives me great confidence that I have made a right choice for my personal learning when I see these books as part of SQL curriculums across the world.

I have been working with databases for over 10 years now, and I am no longer a beginner. I think I am way beyond the basics, but when I read this book while writing this foreword, I realized that every new version of SQL Server introduces new concepts. I will admit that while reading this book, I learned about Azure database and the newly introduced features related to SQL performance. I also learned how T-SQL has been enhanced from version 2008 to 2012 and from 2012 to 2014. It was interesting to see how the author explains a concept of performance across various chapters. She even explicitly called out a few mistakes to avoid while working with SQL Server.

I am delighted that this book is in our hands now so we can all learn T-SQL from an industry expert who also is a great teacher.

—Pinal Dave
SQLAuthority.com

CHAPTER 1

Getting Started

If you are reading this book, you probably already know something about T-SQL. T-SQL, also known as Transact-SQL, is Microsoft's implementation of the Structured Query Language (SQL) for SQL Server. T-SQL is the language that is most often used to extract or modify data stored in an SQL Server database, regardless of which application or tool you use. SQL Server 2014 T-SQL is based on standards created by the American National Standards Institute (ANSI), but Microsoft has added several functionality enhancements. You will find that T-SQL is a very versatile and powerful programming language.

T-SQL consists of Data Definition Language (DDL), Data Manipulation Language (DML), and control-of-flow statements. Although the book focuses primarily on the DML statements, which you will use to retrieve and manipulate data, this book covers DDL statements and programming logic as well.

This chapter will explain how to install a free edition of SQL Server and get it ready for running the example code and performing the exercises in the rest of this book. This chapter also gives you a quick tour of SQL Server Management Studio.

Installing SQL Server Express Edition

Microsoft makes SQL Server 2014 available in several editions. If you don't have access to SQL Server, you can download and install the free SQL Server Express edition from Microsoft's web site at http://msdn.microsoft.com/en-us/library/dn434042.aspx. To fully take advantage of all the concepts covered in this book, download SQL Server 2014 Express with Advanced Services. This will give you the database engine and SQL Server Management Studio. You will be able to run all of the queries demonstrated in this book, including Full Text Search queries. Be sure to choose either the 64-bit or 32-bit download according to the operating system you are running. The Express with Advanced Services edition will run on the following operating systems available at the time of this writing: Windows Server 2012, Windows Server 2012 R2, Windows Server 2008 R2 SP1 or SP2, Windows 8.1, Windows 8, and Windows 7 SP1.

Note　SP is shorthand for service pack, so SP2 refers to Service Pack 2. A *service pack* is an update to the operating system or to other software that fixes bugs and security issues.

The .NET Framework 3.5.1 is required before installing SQL Server 2014. If this is not enabled, you will see an error message during the SQL Server installation process. The instructions are different depending on the operating system you are running, so be sure to use your favourite search engine to learn how to do this on your computer.

The order of the installation steps are slightly different if an instance of SQL Server has already been installed on your computer. These instructions assume that this is the first install.

Here are the steps to follow to install SQL Server Express:

1. Once you have downloaded the SQL Server 2014 Express with Advanced Services installation file from Microsoft's site, double-click the file to extract and start up the SQL Server Installation Center. Figure 1-1 shows the Planning pane of the SQL Server Installation Center once the extraction has completed. You may need to click Planning in the left-hand side to see these options.

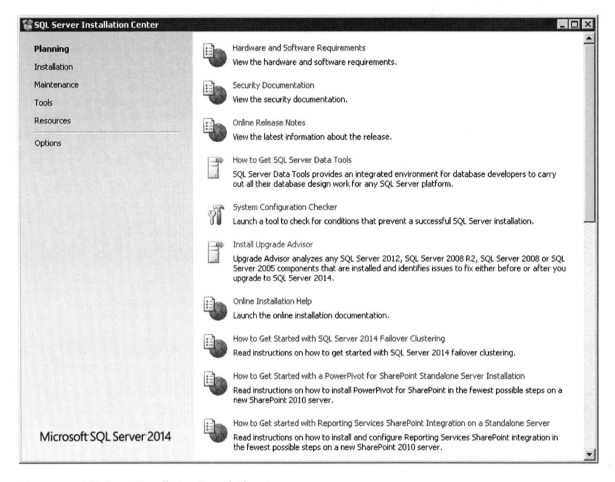

Figure 1-1. *SQL Server Installation Center's Planning pane*

2. To make sure your system meets all the requirements to install SQL Server Express with Advanced Services, click the System Configuration Checker link, which opens the Global Rules screen (Figure 1-2). Click Show details to see more information if the system does not meet the requirements. Click OK to dismiss the screen when you are done or the screen may close on its own if there are no issues.

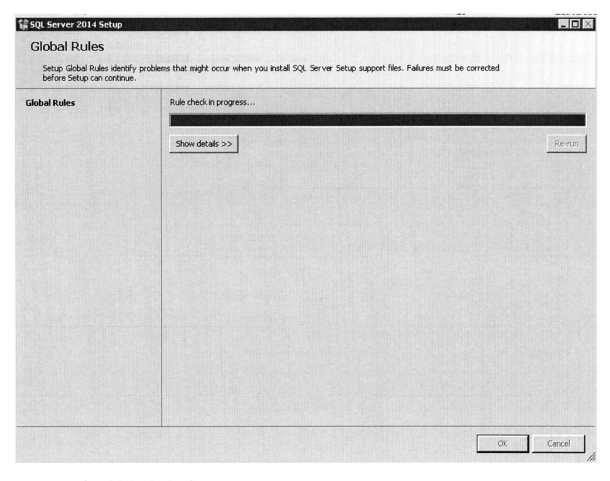

Figure 1-2. *The Global Rules details page*

3. If your system doesn't meet the requirements, click the Hardware and Software Requirements link on the Planning pane of the SQL Server Installation Center, which will take you to a web page on Microsoft's web site. Be sure to scroll down the web page to find the information for the Express edition. The hardware requirements are not difficult to meet with today's PCs.

4. Once you are certain that your computer meets all the requirements, switch to the Installation pane, shown in Figure 1-3, and click New SQL Server stand-alone installation or add features to an existing installation.

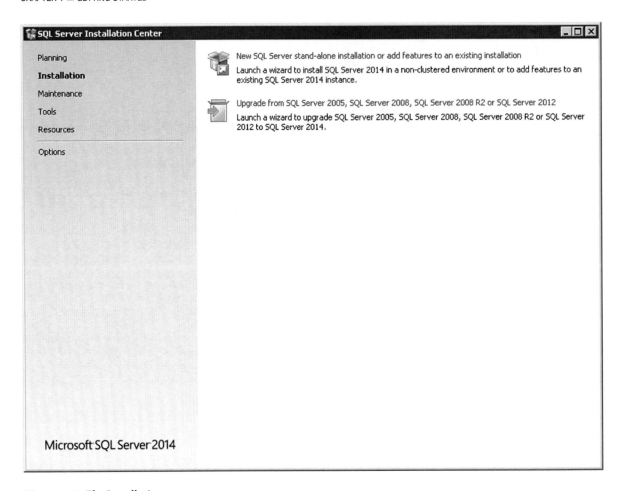

Figure 1-3. *The Installation pane*

5. Once the installation wizard starts up, read and accept the license terms. Click Next.

6. On the Microsoft Update screen, check if you wish to get automatic updates for SQL Server. Click Next.

7. Several screens checking for product updates, installing setup files, and checking rules will quickly display. If there are no problems, these screens will advance to the Feature Selection screen shown in Figure 1-4. Be sure to select the Database Engine Services, Full Text, the Documentation Components, and the Management Tools. Click Next.

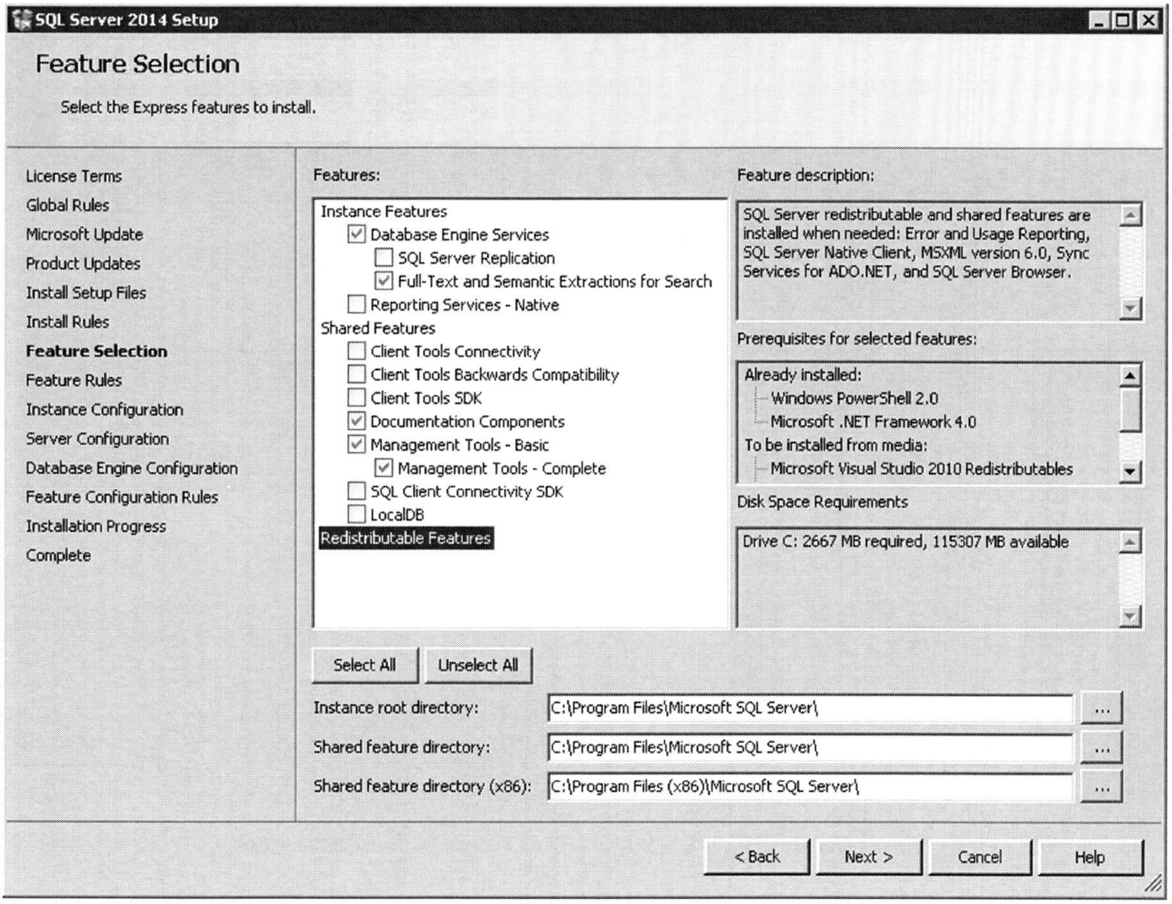

Figure 1-4. *Select the Installation Type*

8.   On the Instance Configuration screen (Figure 1-5), you can choose a Default instance or a Named instance. When installing SQL Server Express edition, it will be named SQLEXPRESS unless you change it. Write down what you decide to do on this screen because you will need this information when connecting to SQL Server later. Click Next.

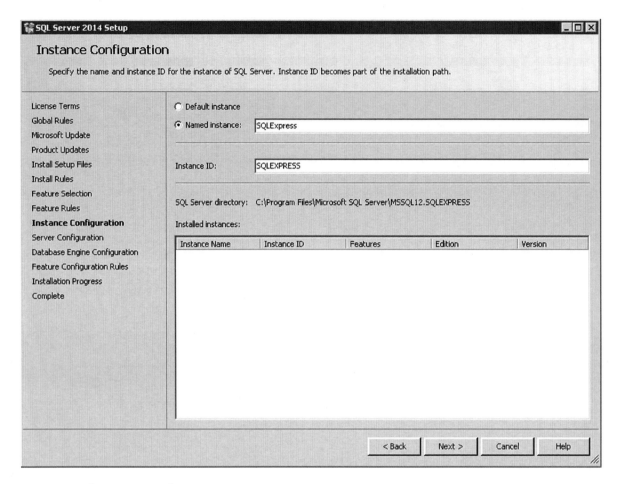

Figure 1-5. *The Instance Configuration screen*

■ **Named Instances** Multiple SQL Server installations can run on one computer. Each installation is called an *instance*. You may have only one default instance on a computer. Any additional instances must be named. When connecting to named instances, use the computer name plus the instance name: computer*Name\instanceName*.

---

9. On the Service Configuration screen, you must specify accounts under which SQL Server will run. If you are setting up SQL Server for a production environment, you may want to have a special service account to make sure that the installation is secure. Installing a secure SQL Server instance is beyond the scope of this book. Because you are just installing the Express edition for learning purposes here, choose the defaults for all the services and click Next.

10. On the Database Engine Configuration screen's Server Configuration tab (Figure 1-6), you will either select the Windows authentication mode option or the Mixed Mode option. For the purposes of this book, you can leave the authentication mode as "Windows authentication mode." Click the Add Current User button near the bottom of the page to make sure that the account you are using is added as an administrator.

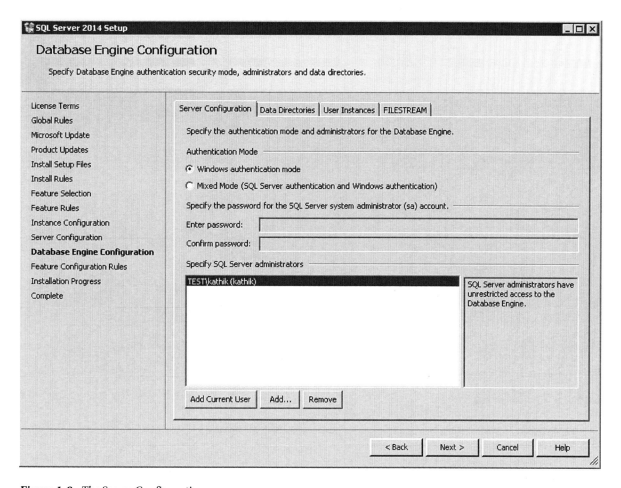

Figure 1-6. *The Server Configuration screen*

11. Click the FILESTREAM tab on the current screen to enable FILESTREAM functionality, as shown in Figure 1-7. FILESTREAM was introduced in SQL Server 2008 and I will explain that in more detail in Chapter 16. Click Next.

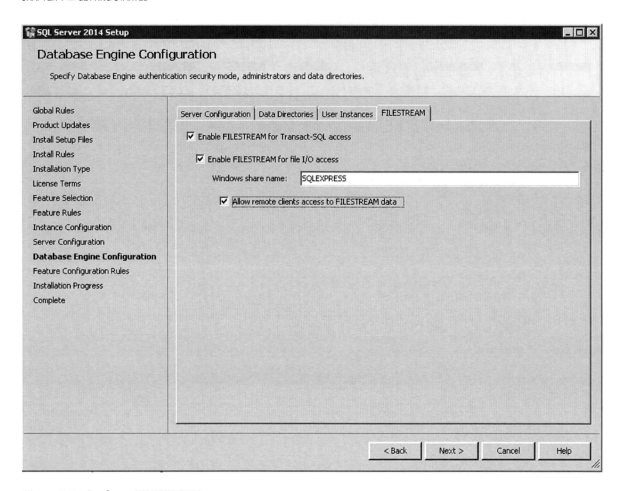

Figure 1-7. *Configure FILESTREAM*

12. The installation will perform additional rule checks based on the components you chose to install. If the requirements are met, the installation will immediately begin. Figure 1-8 shows the Installation Progress screen.

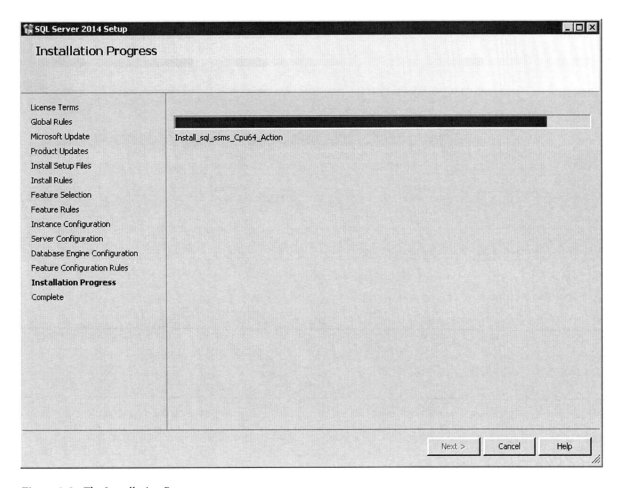

Figure 1-8. *The Installation Progress screen*

13. Once the install is complete, you can view a report to help you solve any issues with the installation. Figure 1-9 shows the report from a successful installation.

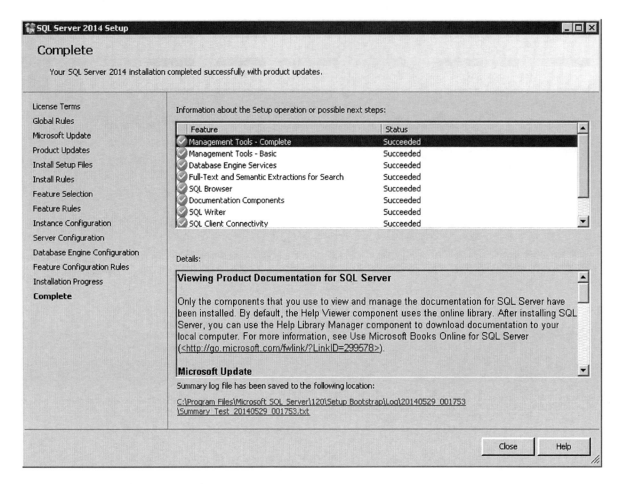

Figure 1-9. *The installation is complete*

14. Click the Close button. Congratulations! You have just installed SQL Server Express.

After the installation completes, the SQL Server Installation Center displays once more. You may be interested in viewing some of the resources available in this application at a later time. Luckily, you don't have to start the install again. You can run the Installation Center by selecting Start ➤ All Programs ➤ Microsoft SQL Server 2014 ➤ Configuration Tools ➤ SQL Server Installation Center at any time.

Installing Books Online

You have the choice of accessing Books Online via the Internet or locally. When you first install SQL Server, you have the option to install the Books Online components. These components allow for better integration with the web-based documentation. The online components allow for updates to Books Online on the Internet to be applied to your local installation. Follow these steps to install Books Online locally:

1. Open the SQL Server Management Studio and select Help from the menu. Under Help, select Manage Help Settings.

2. If you are prompted for a location, accept the default and click OK.

3. A window will pop up with a list of items. Select Install Content from Online.

4. Scroll down until you find the entry for SQL Server 2014 Books Online and click Add, as shown in Figure 1-10, and then click Update.

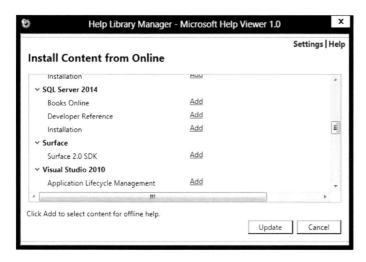

Figure 1-10. *Installing Books Online*

Using Books Online

Once SQL Server Books Online is installed, you can launch it by opening SQL Server Management Studio and selecting Help from the top menu. Under the Help menu, select View Help.

Books Online is now part of the standardized Help Viewer. The screen for Microsoft Help Viewer is divided into two sections, as shown in Figure 1-11. The contents are displayed in the left pane. You can expand each entry to see the sections and click a topic to view each article on the right.

Figure 1-11. *The two panes of Microsoft Help Viewer*

In the top right corner there is a search bar. Type in a term, such as query, to see the results found in the local help system and any articles posted online.

You will learn how to write T-SQL from reading this book, but I recommend that you check Books Online frequently to learn even more!

Using SQL Server Management Studio

Now that you have SQL Server and SQL Server Books Online, it's time to get acquainted with SQL Server Management Studio (SSMS). SSMS is the tool that ships with most editions of SQL Server, and you can use it to manage SQL Server and the databases as well as write T-SQL code. If you have installed SQL Server Express with Advanced Services as outlined earlier, you should be able to find SSMS by selecting Start ➤ All Programs ➤ Microsoft SQL Server 2014 ➤ SQL Server Management Studio. If you are using Windows 8.X or Windows Server 2012, just type SSMS in the search box. SSMS is your window into SQL Server. You can manage your database, create scripts, and, most importantly, execute T-SQL code and see the results.

Launching SQL Server Management Studio

Launch SSMS. After the splash screen displays, you will be prompted to connect to an instance of SQL Server, as shown in Figure 1-12.

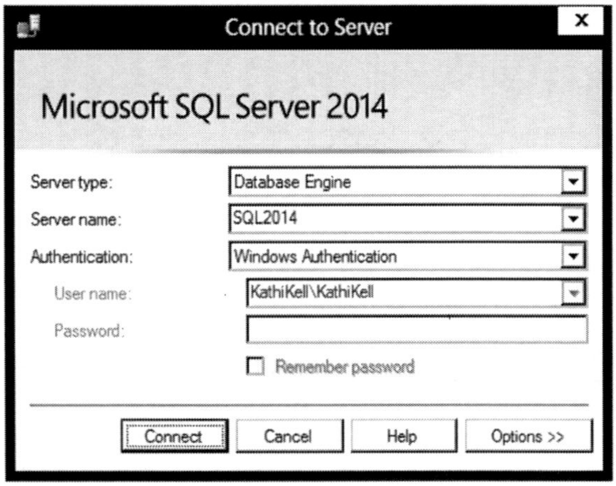

Figure 1-12. *Connect to Server dialog box*

Notice in this example that the Server (computer) name is SQL2014, which is a default instance. If you installed a named instance, you will need to type in the computer name followed by a backward slash (\) and then the instance name. You can also use (local), Localhost, or a period (.) instead of the computer name as long as you are logged on locally and not trying to connect to a remote SQL Server. Make sure that the appropriate Server name is filled in, and click Connect. If you installed SQL Server Express edition, your instance name probably will be SQLEXPRESS.

Once connected to an instance of SQL Server, you can view the databases and all the objects in the Object Explorer. The Object Explorer is located on the left side of the screen by default. You can expand each item to see other items underneath. For example, once you expand the Databases folder, you can expand one of the databases. Then you can expand the Tables folder for that database. You can expand a table name and drill down to see the columns, indexes, and other properties. In the right pane, you can see a list of some additional details such as the Create Date for the selected item. If you don't see the details, press the F7 key. Figure 1-13 shows the Object Explorer window and details.

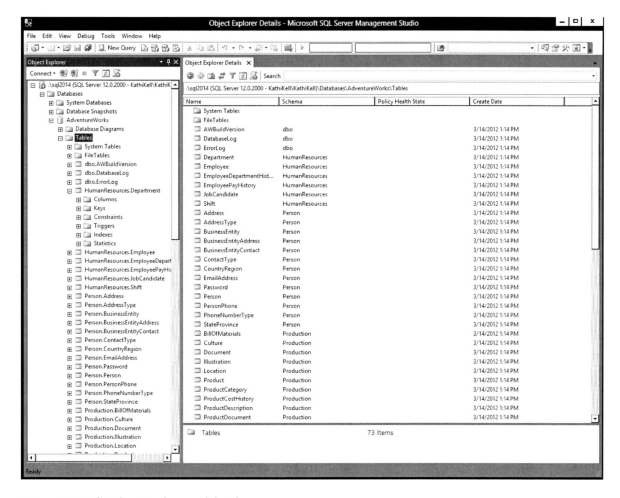

Figure 1-13. *The Object Explorer and details*

One SSMS feature that you will use extensively during this book is the Query Editor. In this window you will type and run queries as you learn about T-SQL. The following steps will guide you through writing your first query in the Query Editor.

1. Make sure your SQL Server instance is selected in the Object Explorer, and click New Query, which is located right above the Object Explorer, to open the Query Editor window.

2. Type the following code in the Query Editor window on the right. It's a list of all the databases on the SQL Server.

```
SELECT * FROM sys.databases;
```

3. You will notice as you type that IntelliSense (Figure 1-14) is available in the Query Editor window. IntelliSense helps you by eliminating keystrokes to save you time. It also validates the code before the code is compiled. It doesn't work when connecting to versions earlier than SQL Server 2008.

SQLQuery3.sql - loc...Kell\KathiKell (52))*   ✕   SQLQuery2.sql - not connected*   SQLQuery1.sql - not connected*

```
SELECT * FROM sys.databases
```

databases
[x] availability_databases_cluster
[x] change_tracking_databases
view master.sys.databases   [x] databases
[x] sysdatabases

Figure 1-14. IntelliSense

4.   Click Execute or press the F5 key to see the results.

Installing the Sample Databases

Sample databases are very useful to help beginners practice writing code. Several databases, such as Pubs, Northwind, and AdventureWorks, have been available for this purpose over the many releases of SQL Server. You can download the sample databases from the CodePlex samples web site at `www.codeplex.com`. Because the link will change frequently as updated samples become available, search for SQL Server Database Product Samples. At the time of this writing, a regular version of the database was not available specifically for SQL Server 2014. There is a special version available for the new In-Memory OLTP (online transaction processing) features. For this book, you will need the traditional AdventureWorks database, and it will work for all examples in this book.

Make sure you are downloading the latest version of the sample databases. Figure 1-15 shows a portion of the download page that was current the day this section was written.

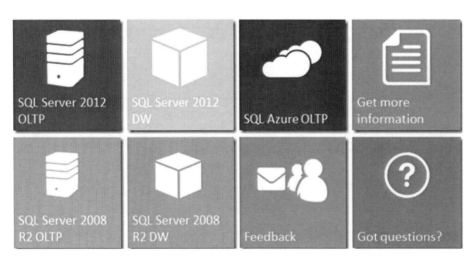

Figure 1-15. The source for the AdventureWorks databases

The following steps will guide you through installing the sample databases:

1. Click the link for SQL Server 2012 OLTP.

2. Click the link for AdventureWorks2012 Data file.

3. Click Save to download the files.

4. Navigate to a location that you will remember, and click Save.

5. Once the download completes, open SQL Server Management Studio and start a new query. In the query windows, execute the command shown in Listing 1-1. You will need to change the path to match the location where you downloaded the AdventureWorks2012 data file. Figure 1-16 shows how your screen should look.

Listing 1-1. Script to Create the AdventureWorks2012 Database

```
CREATE DATABASE AdventureWorks ON (FILENAME = '<drive>:\<file path>\AdventureWorks2012_Data.mdf')
FOR ATTACH_REBUILD_LOG ;
```

```
CREATE DATABASE AdventureWorks ON
(FILENAME = 'C:\Data\AdventureWorks2012_Data.mdf')
 FOR ATTACH_REBUILD_LOG ;
```

```
100 %  ▼ ◄
Messages
File activation failure. The physical file name "C:\Program File
New log file 'C:\Data\AdventureWorks_log.ldf' was created.
Converting database 'AdventureWorks' from version 705 to the cu:
Database 'AdventureWorks' running the upgrade step from version
```

Figure 1-16. *The sample database install*

You should now have the AdventureWorks database installed on your SQL Server instance. All of the examples in this book assume that you have named the database AdventureWorks, not AdventureWorks2012 or with any other version year. The error message, File activation failure, appears in the message if the file is not in the folder SQL Server expects it to be in.

Get Started with SSMS

SSMS has several scripting features to help you write code. Follow these steps to learn how to create a query without typing:

1. Make sure that the Tables folder is expanded, and select the HumanResources.Employee table, as in Figure 1-17.

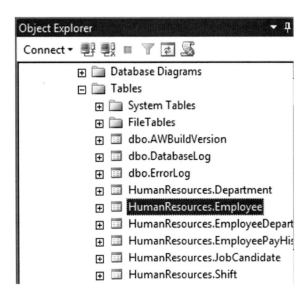

Figure 1-17. The HumanResources.Employee table

2. Right-click the HumanResources.Employee table, and select Script Table as ➤ Select To ➤ New Query Editor Window.

3. A new window will automatically open with some code (Figure 1-18). Click Execute.

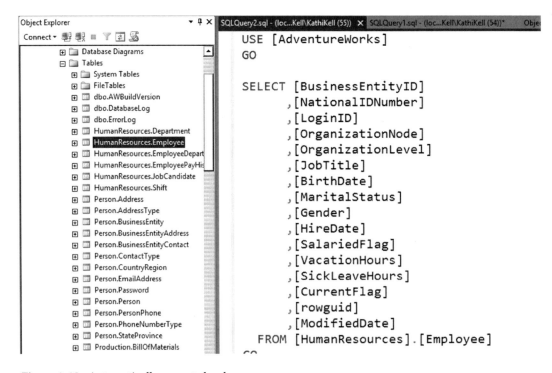

Figure 1-18. Automatically generated code

16

Sometimes you will end up with multiple statements in one Query Editor Window. To run only some of the statements in the window, select what you want to run, and click Execute or press F5. Figure 1-19 shows an example. When you execute, only the first query will run.

Figure 1-19. *Selected code*

Sections of code can be collapsed to get them out of your way by clicking the minus sign to the left of the code. You can search and replace just like a regular text editor, and, of course, you have IntelliSense to help you write the code.

Results can be saved to text files by clicking the Results to File icon shown in Figure 1-20 before you execute the code. You can also select and copy the results for pasting into Excel or Notepad.

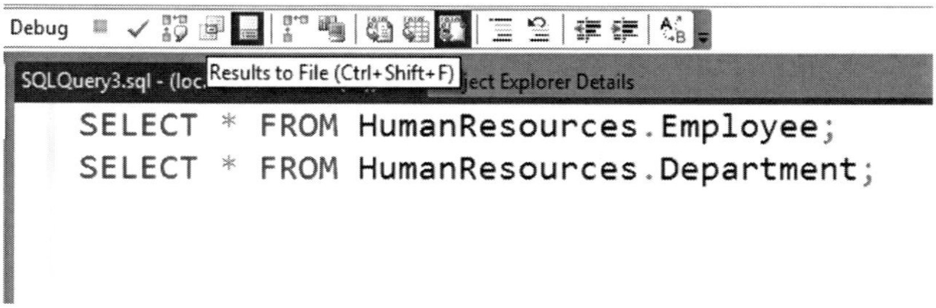

Figure 1-20. *Results to File icon*

You can add documentation to your code or just keep code from running by adding comments. To comment a section of code, begin the section with /* and end the section with */. You can comment out a line of code or the end of a line of code with two hyphens (--). To automatically comment out code, select the lines you want to comment, and click the Comment button circled in Figure 1-21. Uncomment code by selecting commented lines and clicking the Uncomment button next to the Comment button.

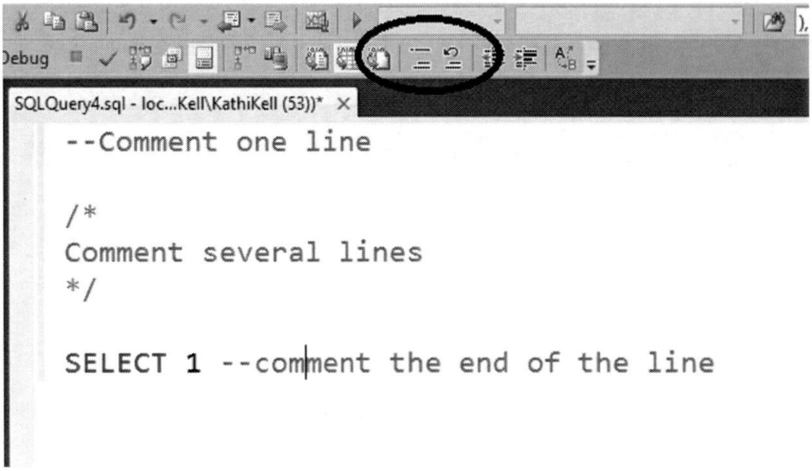

Figure 1-21. *Commented code*

The Object Explorer allows you to manage the databases, security, maintenance jobs, and other aspects of SQL Server. Most of the tasks that can be performed are within the realm of database administrators, so I will not explore them in this book.

Summary

This chapter provided the information you need to install SQL Server Express Edition with Advanced Services on your local computer and get the sample database set up. You also got a quick tour of SSMS, which you will use to interact with SQL Server in this book and beyond.

Chapter 2 provides an introduction of databases and the objects that make them up. You will need this background knowledge when you begin writing your own queries in Chapter 3.

CHAPTER 2

■ ■ ■

Exploring Database Concepts

This chapter will explain just what SQL Server is, what a database is, and describe the objects that make up those databases. You will learn how data is stored in a database, and you'll learn about objects, called *indexes*, that help SQL Server return the results of your queries quickly.

What Is SQL Server?

SQL Server is Microsoft's relational database management system (RDBMS). An RDBMS stores data in tables according to the relational model. The relational model is beyond the scope of this book, but you can learn more about it by reading *Beginning Relational Data Modeling*, second edition, by Sharon Allen and Evan Terry (Apress, 2005).

Microsoft makes SQL Server available in many editions, including a free edition called Express, that can be distributed with applications or used to learn about SQL Server and several expensive, full-featured editions (Standard, Business Intelligence, and Enterprise) that are used to store terabytes of data in the most demanding enterprises. There is even a version that lives in the cloud calls Microsoft Azure SQL Database and one that is meant for mobile devices called Compact. Review the article "Features Supported by the Editions of SQL Server 2014" found at http://msdn.microsoft.com/en-us/library/cc645993(v=sql.120).aspx for more information about the editions and features of each. Table 2-1 gives an overview of the editions available. Core T-SQL features and version differences have been around since early versions of SQL Server. Many new versions of SQL Server contain added T-SQL functionality.

Table 2-1. *SQL Server 2014 Editions*

Edition	Usage	Expense
Compact	Occasionally connected systems including mobile devices.	Free
Express	Great for learning SQL Server and can be distributed with applications. Has limitations to database size, memory, and number of processors used.	Free
Developer	Full featured but used for development only.	Inexpensive
Standard	Complete data platform with some high-availability and business intelligence features. Some limitations to memory and CPU usage.	Expensive
Enterprise	All available features.	Very expensive
Business Intelligence	Used in both large and small companies to deploy comprehensive Business Intelligence solutions. Has limitations to memory and CPU usage.	Expensive
Microsoft Azure SQL Database	Cloud version of SQL Server database.	Pay-as-you-go model

Many well-known companies trust SQL Server with their data. To read case studies about how some of these companies use SQL Server, visit www.microsoft.com/en-in/SQLserver/default.aspx.

Databases in the Cloud

Cloud computing is becoming more popular as companies and consumers begin storing data "in the cloud." For example, most smartphones allow backing up data, such as photos, automatically to the cloud. You may be wondering just what the cloud is. I always imagine servers floating around in the sky, but cloud computing actually means that a vendor such as Microsoft supplies computing services via the Internet. Microsoft owns several data centers around the world with thousands of servers supplying these services. Some of the services Microsoft offers for consumers are e-mail (Outlook.com), storage (OneDrive), and Office. For commercial use, they offer Azure hosted storage, web services, virtual machines, databases, and more.

This model allows companies to use only the services and resources they need without investing in hardware and with decreased maintenance and administration. It is also possible to scale out their solutions very quickly. One of the early adopters of Azure services is the company Blue Book. If you would like to read more about how they are using Azure databases, take a look at this case study: www.slideshare.net/msitpro/microsoft-windows-azure-kelly-blue-book-case-study.

There are two ways Microsoft can host your database in the cloud. The first is by installing SQL Server on an Azure virtual machine. Except that the server is hosted by Microsoft, you will work with the SQL Server in the same ways that you do when it is installed on your own server in your own data center. The second way is by creating a Microsoft Azure SQL Database. In this case, you don't manage the instance at all, just the database(s). There is built-in high availability and disaster recovery. Except for some missing administrative commands and some advanced features, the T-SQL language is mostly the same. An interesting aspect of Microsoft Azure SQL Database is that Microsoft can push out updates and new features on a frequent basis, much more frequently than the traditional SQL Server. You will learn more about Microsoft Azure SQL Database in Chapter 17.

Service vs. Application

SQL Server is a service, not just an application. Even though you can install some of the editions on a regular workstation, it generally runs on a dedicated server and will run when the server starts; in other words, usually no one needs to manually start the SQL Server. To minimize or practically eliminate downtime for critical systems, SQL Server boasts high-availability features such as clustering, log shipping, database mirroring, and Availability Groups. Think about your favorite shopping web site. You expect it to be available any time day or night and every day. Behind the scenes, a database server, possibly a SQL Server instance, must be running and performing well at all times. Even during necessary maintenance—when applying security patches, for example—administrators must keep downtime to a minimum.

SQL Server is feature rich, providing a complete business intelligence suite, impressive management tools, sophisticated data replication features, and much more. These features are well beyond the scope of this book, but I invite you to visit www.apress.com to find books to help you learn about these other topics if you are interested.

SQL Server doesn't come with a data-entry interface for regular users or even a way to create a web site or a Windows application. To do that, you will most likely use a programming language such as Visual Basic .NET or C#. Calls to the SQL Server via T-SQL can be made within your application code or through a middle tier such as a web service. Regardless of your application architecture, at some point you'll use T-SQL. SQL Server does have a very nice reporting tool called Reporting Services that is part of the business intelligence suite. Otherwise, you will have to use another programming language to create your user interface outside of the management tools.

Figure 2-1 shows the architecture of a typical web application. The web server requests data from the database server. The clients communicate with the web server.

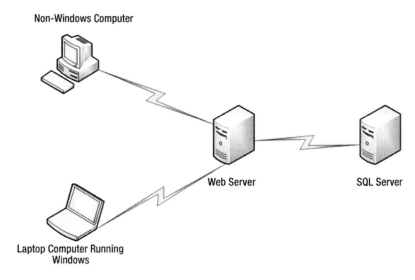

Figure 2-1. *The architecture of a typical web application*

Database as Container

A database in SQL Server is basically a container that holds several types of objects and data in an organized fashion. Generally, one database is used for a particular application or purpose, though this is not a hard and fast rule. For example, some systems have one database for all the enterprise applications required to run a business. On the other hand, one application could access more than one database.

Start SQL Server Management Studio if it is not already running and connect to the SQL Server instance you installed in Chapter 1. Expand the Databases folder to see the databases installed on the SQL Server. You should be able to see the AdventureWorks database, as shown in Figure 2-2.

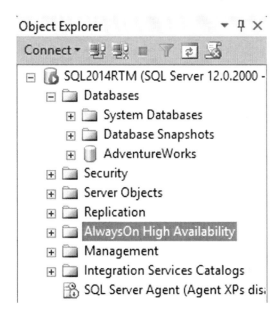

Figure 2-2. *The databases*

Within a database, you will find several ~~objects,~~ but only one type of object, the table, holds the data that we usually think about. In addition to tables, a database can contain other objects, as listed in Table 2-2. Later chapters in this book will cover most of the other objects that are used to make up a database. You'll find an introduction to indexes later in this chapter.

Table 2-2. *The Database Objects*

Object Type	Purpose
Views	A stored query definition that can be used to simplify writing T-SQL statements or to control security to data.
Stored procedures	A stored T-SQL script that can include queries, data definition statements (DDL) that create or modify objects, and programming logic. Stored procedures can return tabular data results.
User-defined functions	A user-defined function is similar to a stored procedure but with several differences. They can return tabular data or a single value, but they cannot affect anything outside the function.
Indexes	A structured that assists the database engine when locating rows.
Constraints	Rules controlling the behavior of the table and columns and the data that can be stored in a column.
Triggers	A trigger is a special type of stored procedure that fires when something happens in the database such as a row is inserted or an object is created.
Types	Each column in a database has rules governing what type of data the column can contain. It is possible to create custom types to help organize the database.
Rules and defaults	These features are no longer recommended and are only available for backward compatibility.
Plan guides	This is an advanced feature used to override SQL Server's behavior for a particular query. It is well beyond the scope of this book.
Sequences	Sequences are containers holding incrementing numbers.
Synonyms	Synonyms are nicknames or aliases for database objects.
Assemblies	Assemblies are references to database objects created in a .Net language. This functionality is called common language runtime (CLR) integration.

SQL SERVER FILES

A SQL Server database must comprise at least two files. One is the data file with the default extension .mdf, and the other is the log file with the default extension .ldf. Additional data files, if they are used, will usually have the extension .ndf. Technically, the .mdf, .ldf, and .ndf files can have any given extension name, though it is not recommended to change them from the defaults. Data files can be organized into multiple file groups. File groups are useful for strategically backing up only portions of the database at a time or to store the data on different drives for increased performance. This is just a quick introduction to files and file groups. There are also other files and file groups that are beyond the scope of this book.

The ~~log file in SQL~~ Server stores *transactions*, or changes to the data, to ensure data consistency. Database administrators can, as required, take frequent backups of the log files to allow the database to be restored to a point in time in case of data corruption, disk failure, or other disaster.

Data Is Stored in Tables

The most important ~~objects~~ in a database are ~~tables~~ because the tables are the objects that store the data and allow you to retrieve the data in an organized fashion. You can represent a table as a grid with ~~columns~~ and ~~rows.~~ The terminology used to describe the data in a database varies depending on the system, but in this book, I will stick with the terms *table, row,* and *column.* The following is an example of a table created to hold data about store owners:

(primary key)

```
CustomerID  Title  FirstName  MiddleName  LastName  Suffix  CompanyName
1           Mr.    Orlando    N.          Gee       NULL    A Bike Store
2           Mr.    Keith      NULL        Harris    NULL    Progressive Sports
3           Ms.    Donna      F.          Carreras  NULL    Advanced Bike Components
4           Ms.    Janet      M.          Gates     NULL    Modular Cycle Systems
```

In a ~~normalized database~~, each table holds information about one type of entity. An entity type might be a student, customer, or vehicle, for example. ~~Each row in a table contains the information about one instance of the entity represented by that table.~~ For example, a row will represent one student, one customer, or one vehicle. Each column in the table will contain one piece of information about the entity. In the ~~vehicle table~~, there might be a VIN column, a make column, a model column, a color column, and a year column, among others.

Each column within a table has a definition specifying a data type along with rules, called *constraints*, that enforce the values that can be stored. Constraints include whether a column can be left empty, whether its values must be unique from other rows, whether it is limited to a certain range of values, and so on. You will learn more about constraints in Chapter 14.

In a ~~normalized database~~, ~~each table~~ will have ~~a primary key~~ that is used to ~~uniquely identify each row.~~ In the previous example, the primary key is `CustomerID`.

■ **Note**   You will learn what NULL means in Chapter 3.

Data Types

SQL Server has a rich assortment of data types for storing strings, numbers, money, XML, binary, and temporal data. ~~Start SQL Server Management Studio~~ if it is not running already, and connect to the SQL Server you installed in the "Installing SQL Server Express Edition" section of Chapter 1. Expand the Databases section. Expand the AdventureWorks database and the Tables section. Locate the HumanResources.Employee table, and expand the Columns section. View the properties as shown in Figure 2-3.

☐ ▦ HumanResources.Employee
   ☐ 🗀 Columns
       🔑 BusinessEntityID (PK, FK, int, not null)
       ▤ NationalIDNumber (nvarchar(15), not null)
       ▤ LoginID (nvarchar(256), not null)
       ▤ OrganizationNode (hierarchyid, null)
       ▦ OrganizationLevel (Computed, smallint, null)
       ▤ JobTitle (nvarchar(50), not null)
       ▤ BirthDate (date, not null)
       ▤ MaritalStatus (nchar(1), not null)
       ▤ Gender (nchar(1), not null)
       ▤ HireDate (date, not null)
       ▤ SalariedFlag (Flag(bit), not null)
       ▤ VacationHours (smallint, not null)
       ▤ SickLeaveHours (smallint, not null)
       ▤ CurrentFlag (Flag(bit), not null)
       ▤ rowguid (uniqueidentifier, not null)
       ▤ ModifiedDate (datetime, not null)

Figure 2-3. *The properties of the* `HumanResources.Employee` *table*

The HumanResources.Employee table contains columns with a variety of data types and one column, `OrganizationalLevel`, is a computed column defined by a formula. This is designated by the word **Computed** and the data type returned by the formula, **smallint.**

`SalariedFlag` and `CurrentFlag` have the `Flag` user-defined data type, which is defined within the database. Developers can create user-defined data types to simplify table creation and to ensure consistency. For example, the AdventureWorks database has a Phone data type used whenever a column contains phone numbers. To see the Phone data type definition, expand the Programmability section, the Type section, and the User Defined Data Types section. Locate and double-click the Phone data type to see the properties (see Figure 2-4).

General	
Schema:	dbo
Name:	Phone
Data type:	nvarchar
Length:	25
☑ Allow NULLs	
Storage:	50 bytes
Binding	
Default:	
Rule:	

Figure 2-4. *The properties of the Phone user-defined data type*

Developers can create custom data types, called *CLR data types*, with multiple properties and methods using a .NET language such as C#. Chapter 16 covers three built-in CLR data types: HIERARCHYID, GEOMETRY, and GEOGRAPHY. The OrganizationNode column is a HIERARCHYID. You will find a wealth of information about data types in SQL Server Books Online by searching for the data type that interests you.

Normalization

Normalization is the process of designing database tables in a way that makes for efficient use of disk space and that allows the efficient manipulation and updating of the data. Generally, normalization allows each piece of information to be stored only once. Normalization is especially important in online transaction processing (OLTP) databases, such as those used in e-commerce. Database architects usually design reporting-only databases in a less normalized manner, often using different design patterns known as *dimensional modeling*. This allows easier and quicker retrieval of information for reporting because the data is not often updated.

The process of normalization is beyond the scope of this book, but it is helpful to understand why databases are normalized. To learn more about normalization, see *Pro SQL Server 2012 Relational Database Design and Implementation* by Louis Davidson and Jessica Moss (Apress, 2012).

Figure 2-5 shows how a database design might look before it is normalized. The example is of an order-entry database. There is one table, and that table consists of data about both customers and orders. One problem that you can probably see straightaway is that there is room for only three items per order and only three orders per customer.

CustomerOrders

| CustomerID |
| Title |
| FirstName |
| LastName |
| CompanyName |
| AddressLine1 |
| AddressLine2 |
| City |
| State_Province |
| Country |
| PostalCode |
| OrderID1 |
| OrderDate1 |
| OrderItem1_1 |
| OrderQty1_1 |
| OrderItem1_2 |
| OrderQty1_2 |
| OrderItem1_3 |
| OrderQty1_3 |
| OrderItem2_1 |
| OrderQty2_1 |
| OrderItem2_2 |
| OrderQty2_2 |
| OrderItem2_3 |
| OrderQty2_3 |
| OrderItem3_1 |
| OrderQty3_1 |
| OrderItem3_2 |
| OrderQty3_2 |
| OrderItem3_3 |

Figure 2-5. *The denormalized database*

Figure 2-6 shows how the database might look once it is normalized. In this case, the database contains a table to hold information about the customer and a table to contain information about the order, such as the order date. The database contains a separate table to hold the items ordered. The order table contains a CustomerID that determines the customer instead of repeating all the customer information in the Order table. The OrderDetail table allows as many items as needed per order. The OrderDetail table contains the OrderID column to specify the correct order.

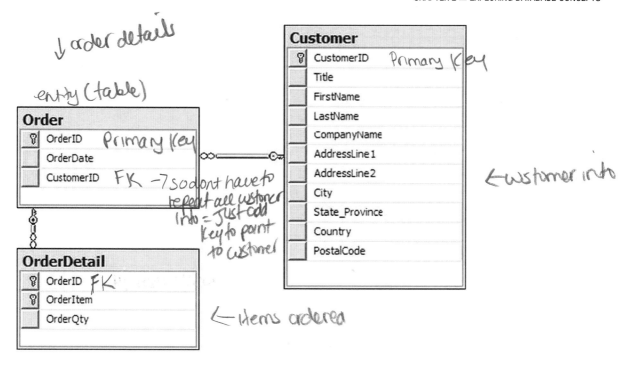

↓ order details

entity (table)

Primary Key (Order, OrderID)

Primary Key (Customer, CustomerID)

FK → so dont have to repeat all customer info = just add key to point to customer

FK (OrderDetail, OrderID)

← customer info

← items ordered

Figure 2-6. *The normalized database*

It may seem like a lot of trouble to properly define a database upfront. However, it is well worth the effort to do so. I was called in once to help create reports on one of the most poorly designed databases I have ever seen. This was a small Microsoft Access database that was used to record information from interviewing users at a medium-sized company about the applications that the employees used. Each time a new application was entered into the database, a new Yes/No column for that application was created, and the data-entry form had to be modified. The developer, who should have known better, told me that she just didn't have time to create a properly normalized database. Much more time was spent fighting with this poor design than would have been spent properly designing the database up front.

Understanding Indexes

When a user runs a query to retrieve a portion of the rows from a table, how does the database engine determine which rows to return? If the table has indexes defined on it, SQL Server may use the indexes to find the appropriate rows.

There are several types of indexes, but this section covers two types: clustered and nonclustered. A *clustered index* stores and organizes the table. A *nonclustered index* is defined on one or more columns of the table, but it is a separate structure that points to the actual table. Both types of indexes are optional, but they can greatly improve the performance of queries when properly designed and maintained. A couple of analogies will help explain how indexes work.

A printed phone directory is a great example of a clustered index. Each entry in the directory represents one row of the table. A table can have only one clustered index. That is because a clustered index is the actual table organized in order of the cluster key. At first glance, you might think that inserting a new row into the table would require all the rows after the inserted row to be moved on the disk. Luckily, this is not the case. The row will have to be inserted into the correct data page. A list of pointers maintains the order between the pages, so the rows in other pages will not have to actually move.

The primary key of the phone directory is the phone number. Usually the primary key is used as the clustering key as well, but this is not the case in our example. The cluster key in the phone directory is a combination of the last name and first name. How would you find a friend's phone number if you knew the last and first name? Easy—you would open the book approximately to the section of the book that contains the entry. If your friend's last name starts with an *F*, you search near the beginning of the book; if it starts with an *S*, you search toward the back. You can use the names printed at the top of the page to quickly locate the page with the listing. You then drill down to the section of the correct page until you find the last name of your friend. Now you can use the first name to choose the correct listing. The phone number is right there next to the name. It probably takes more time to describe the process than to actually do it. Using the last name plus the first name to find the number is called a *clustered index seek.*

The index in the back of a book is an example of a nonclustered index. A nonclustered index has the indexed columns and a pointer or bookmark pointing to the actual row. In the case of our example, it contains a page number. Another example could be a search done on Google, Bing, or another search engine. The results on the page contain links to the original web pages. The thing to remember about nonclustered indexes is that you may have to retrieve part of the required information from the rows in the table. When using a book index, you will probably have to turn to the page of the book. When searching on Google, you will probably have to click the link to view the original page. If all the information you need is included in the index, you have no need to visit the actual data.

Although you can have only one clustered index per table, you can have up to 999 nonclustered indexes per table. If you ever need that many, you might have a design problem! An important thing to keep in mind is that although indexes can improve the performance of queries, indexes take up disk space and require resources to maintain. If a table has four nonclustered indexes, every write to that table may require four additional writes to keep the indexes up to date.

I just mentioned that 999 nonclustered indexes is too many. When talking about databases, an answer I hear all the time to the question of how many is too many is "It depends." The number of indexes allowed per table increased with the release of SQL Server 2008 to take advantage of a couple of new features: sparse columns and filtered indexes. You will learn more about sparse columns in Chapter 16.

Database Schemas

A *schema* is a container that you can use to organize database objects. A schema is a way to organize the tables and object within the database. For example, the AdventureWorks database contains several schemas based on the purpose: HumanResources, Person, Production, Purchasing, and Sales. Each table or other object belongs to one of the schemas.

■ **Note**   SQL Server 2000 and earlier did not have schemas. Instead the prefix of the object referred to the owner of the object.

A user can have a default schema. When accessing an object in the default schema, the user doesn't have to specify the schema name; however, it's a good practice to do so. If the user has permission to create new objects, the objects will belong to the user's default schema unless specified otherwise. To access objects outside the default schema, the schema name must be used. Table 2-3 shows several objects along with the schema.

Table 2-3. *Schemas Found in AdventureWorks*

Name	Schema	Object
HumanResources.Employee	HumanResources	Employee
Sales.SalesOrderDetail	Sales	SalesOrderDetail
Person.Address	Person	Address

Summary

This chapter provided a quick tour of SQL Server. You learned how databases are structured and designed; you also learned how SQL Server uses indexes to efficiently return data. In Chapter 3, you will get a chance to write your own queries, and you'll learn about the SELECT statement, the next step in your journey to T-SQL mastery.

■ ■ ■

CHAPTER 3

Writing Simple *SELECT* Queries

Chapter 1 had you prepare your computer by installing SQL Server and the AdventureWorks sample database. You learned how to get around in SQL Server Management Studio and a few tips to help make writing queries easier. In Chapter 2, you learned about databases, tables, and the other objects that make up a database.

Now that you're ready, it's time to learn how to retrieve data from an SQL Server database, which you will do by using the SELECT statement, starting with the simplest syntax. This chapter will cover the different parts, called *clauses*, of the SELECT statement so that you will be able to not only retrieve data but also filter and order it. The ultimate goal is to get exactly the data you need from your database—no more, no less.

Beginning in this chapter, you will find many code examples. Even though all the code is available from this book's catalog pages at www.apress.com, you will probably find that by typing the examples yourself you will learn more quickly. As they say, practice makes perfect! In addition, exercises follow many of the sections so that you can practice using what you have just learned. You can find the answers for each set of exercises at the end of the chapter.

■ **Note**   If you take a look at SQL Server Books Online, you will find the syntax displayed for each kind of statement. Books Online displays every possible parameter and option, which is not always helpful when learning about a new concept for the first time. In this book, you will find only the syntax that applies to the topic being discussed at the time.

Using the *SELECT* Statement

You use the SELECT statement to retrieve data from SQL Server. T-SQL requires only the word SELECT followed by at least one item in what is called a *select-list*.

If SQL Server Management Studio is not running, go ahead and start it. When prompted to connect to SQL Server, enter the name of the SQL Server instance you installed in Chapter 1 or the name of your development SQL Server. You will need the AdventureWorks sample databases installed to follow along with the examples and to complete the exercises. You will find instructions for installing the sample databases in Chapter 1.

Selecting a Literal Value

Perhaps the simplest form of a SELECT statement is that used to return a literal value. A *literal value* is one that you specify exactly. It is not data that come from the database. Begin by clicking New Query to open a new query window. Listing 3-1 shows two SELECT statements that each return a literal value. Notice the single quote marks that are used to designate the string value. It is recommended that all T-SQL statements be followed with a semicolon (;). At this point, the semicolons are not required, but it is a good practice to get in the habit of using them so you will be ready once they are required. Type each line of the code from Listing 3-1 into your query window.

Listing 3-1. Statements Returning Literal Values

```
SELECT 1;
SELECT 'ABC';
```

After typing the code in the query window, press F5 or click Execute to run the code. You will see the results displayed in two windows at the bottom of the screen, as shown in Figure 3-1. Because you just ran two statements, two sets of results are displayed.

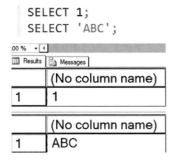

Figure 3-1. *The results of running your first T-SQL statements*

■ Tip By highlighting one or more statements in the query window, you can run just a portion of the code. For example, you may want to run one statement at a time. Use the mouse to select the statements you want to run, and press F5. You can also click the Execute icon or press CTRL+E.

Notice the Messages tab next to the Results tab. Click Messages, and you will see the number of rows affected by the statements as well as any error or informational messages. In this case, the rows affected are actually just outputted. If an error occurs, you will see the Messages tab selected by default instead of the Results tab when the statement execution completes. You can then find the results, if any, by clicking the Results tab.

Retrieving from a Table

You will usually want to retrieve data from a table instead of literal values. After all, if you already know what value you want, you probably don't need to execute a query to get that value.

In preparation for retrieving data from a table, either delete the current code or open a new query window. Change to the example database by typing Use AdventureWorks and executing or by selecting the AdventureWorks database from the drop-down list, as shown in Figure 3-2.

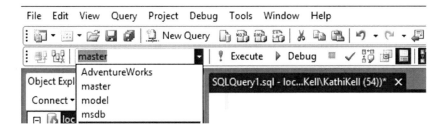

Figure 3-2. *Choosing the AdventureWorks database*

You use the FROM clause to specify a table name in a SELECT statement. The FROM clause is the first part of the statement that the database engine evaluates and processes. Here is the syntax for the SELECT statement with a FROM clause:

```
SELECT <column1>, <column2> FROM <schema>.<table>;
```

■ **Note**   There are many versions of the AdventureWorks database with the SQL Server version appended to the name. Throughout this book, the generic name "AdventureWorks" will be used instead of any specific version.

Type in and execute the code in Listing 3-2 to learn how to retrieve data from a table.

Listing 3-2. Writing a Query with a FROM Clause

```
USE AdventureWorks;
GO
SELECT BusinessEntityID, JobTitle
FROM HumanResources.Employee;
```

The first statement in Listing 3-2 switches the connection to the AdventureWorks database if it's not already connected to it. The word GO doesn't really do anything except divide the code up into separate distinct code batches. You'll learn more about the reasons for using batches in Chapter 12.

When retrieving from a table, you still have a select-list as shown in Listing 3-1; however, your select-list typically contains column names from a table. The select-list in Listing 3-2 requests data from the BusinessEntityID and JobTitle columns, which are both found in the Employee table. The Employee table is in turn found in the HumanResources schema.

Figure 3-3 shows the output from executing the code in Listing 3-2. There is only one set of results, because there is only one SELECT statement.

	BusinessEntityID	JobTitle
1	1	Chief Executive Officer
2	2	Vice President of Engineering
3	3	Engineering Manager
4	4	Senior Tool Designer
5	5	Design Engineer
6	6	Design Engineer
7	7	Research and Development Manager
8	8	Research and Development Engineer
9	9	Research and Development Engineer
10	10	Research and Development Manager

Figure 3-3. *The partial results of running a query with a FROM clause*

Notice that the FROM clause in Listing 3-2 specifies the table name in two parts: HumanResources.Employee. The first part—HumanResources—is a schema name. In SQL Server, groups of related tables can be organized together as schemas. You don't always need to provide those schema names, but it's the best practice to do so. Two schemas can potentially each contain a table named Employee, and those would be different tables with different structures and data. Specifying the schema name as part of your table reference eliminates a source of potential confusion and error.

To retrieve all the columns from a table, you can use the * symbol, also known as *asterisk*, *star*, or *splat*. Run the following statement to try this shortcut: SELECT * FROM HumanResources.Employee. You will see that all the columns from the table are returned.

The asterisk technique is useful for performing a quick query, but you should avoid it in a production application, report, or process. Retrieving more data than you really need may have a negative impact on performance. Why retrieve all the columns from a table and pull more data across the network when you need only a few columns? Besides performance, application code may break if an additional column is added to or removed from the table. Additionally, there might be security reasons for returning only some of the columns. The best practice is to write select-lists specifying exactly the columns that you need and return only the rows you need.

Generating a Select-List

You might think that typing all the required columns for a select-list is tedious work. Luckily, SQL Server Management Studio provides a shortcut for writing good SELECT statements. Follow these instructions to learn the shortcut:

1. In the Object Explorer, expand Databases.

2. Expand the AdventureWorks database.

3. Expand Tables.

4. Right-click the HumanResources.Employee table.

5. Select **Script Table as....** ➤ **SELECT To** ➤ **New Query Editor Window**.

6. Run the code.

You now have a properly formed SELECT statement, as shown in Listing 3-3, that retrieves all the columns from the HumanResources.Employee table. You can also easily remove any unneeded columns from the query.

Listing 3-3. A Scripted SELECT Statement

```
USE [AdventureWorks]
GO

SELECT [BusinessEntityID]
      ,[NationalIDNumber]
      ,[LoginID]
      ,[OrganizationNode]
      ,[OrganizationLevel]
      ,[JobTitle]
      ,[BirthDate]
      ,[MaritalStatus]
      ,[Gender]
      ,[HireDate]
      ,[SalariedFlag]
      ,[VacationHours]
      ,[SickLeaveHours]
      ,[CurrentFlag]
      ,[rowguid]
      ,[ModifiedDate]
  FROM [HumanResources].[Employee]
GO
```

Notice the brackets around the names in Listing 3-3. Column and table names need to follow specific naming rules so that SQL Server's parser can recognize them. When a table, column, or database has a name that doesn't follow those rules, you can still use that name, but you must enclose it within square brackets ([]). Automated tools often enclose *all* names within square brackets as a just-in-case measure.

▨ **Note** Another shortcut to typing all the column names is to click and drag the column(s) from the left side of Management Studio into the query window. For example, if you click the Columns folder and drag it to the query window, SQL Server will list all the columns.

Mixing Literals and Column Names

You can mix literal values and column names in one statement. Listing 3-4 shows an example. SQL Server allows you to create or rename a column within a query by using what is known as an *alias*. You use the keyword AS to specify an alias for the column. This is especially useful when using literal values where you create a column name in the T-SQL statement that doesn't exist in the table.

Listing 3-4. Mixing Literal Values and Column Names

```
SELECT 'A Literal Value' AS "Literal Value",
    BusinessEntityID AS EmployeeID,
    LoginID JobTitle
FROM HumanResources.Employee;
```

Now execute the query in Listing 3-4. You should see results similar to those shown in Figure 3-4. Notice the column names in your results. The column names are the aliases that you specified in your query. You can alias any column, giving you complete control over the headers for your result sets.

	Literal Value	EmployeeID	JobTitle
1	A Literal Value	225	adventure-works\alan0
2	A Literal Value	193	adventure-works\alejandro0
3	A Literal Value	163	adventure-works\alex0
4	A Literal Value	109	adventure-works\alice0
5	A Literal Value	287	adventure-works\amy0
6	A Literal Value	214	adventure-works\andreas0
7	A Literal Value	47	adventure-works\andrew0
8	A Literal Value	164	adventure-works\andrew1
9	A Literal Value	149	adventure-works\andy0
10	A Literal Value	115	adventure-works\angela0

Figure 3-4. *The partial results of using aliases*

The keyword AS is optional. You can specify an alias name immediately following a column name. If an alias contains a space or is a reserved word, you can surround the alias with square brackets, single quotes, or double quotes. If the alias follows the rules for naming objects, the quotes or square brackets are not required.

Be aware that any word listed immediately after a column within the SELECT list is treated as an alias. If you forget to add the comma between two column names, the second column name will be used as the alias for the first. Omitting this comma is a common error. Look carefully at the query in Listing 3-4 and you'll see that the intent is to display the LoginID and JobTitle columns. Because the comma was left out between those two column names, the name of the LoginID column was changed to JobTitle. JobTitle was treated as an alias rather than as an additional column. Watch for and avoid this common mistake.

Reading about T-SQL and typing in code examples are wonderful ways to learn. The best way to learn, however, is to figure out the code for yourself. Imagine learning how to swim by reading about it instead of jumping into the water. Practice now with what you have learned so far. Follow the instructions in Exercise 3-1, and write a few queries to test what you know.

EXERCISE 3-1

For this exercise, switch to the AdventureWorks database. You can find the solutions to this exercise at the end of the chapter.

Remember that you can expand the tables in the Object Explorer to see the list of table names and then expand the column section of the table to see the list of column names.

Now, try your hand at the following tasks:

1. Write a SELECT statement that lists the customers along with their ID numbers. Include the StoreID and the AccountNumber from the Sales.Customers table.

2. Write a SELECT statement that lists the name, product number, and color of each product from the Production.Product table.

3. Write a SELECT statement that lists the customer ID numbers and sales order ID numbers from the Sales.SalesOrderHeader table.

4. Answer this question: Why should you specify column names rather than an asterisk when writing the select-list? Give at least two reasons.

Filtering Data

Usually an application requires only a fraction of the rows from a table at any given time. For example, an order-entry application that shows the order history will often need to display the orders for only one customer at a time. There might be millions of orders in the database, but the operator of the software will view only a handful of rows instead of the entire table. Filtering data is a very important part of T-SQL.

Adding a *WHERE* Clause

To filter the rows returned from a query, you will add a WHERE clause to your SELECT statement. The database engine processes the WHERE clause second, right after the FROM clause. The WHERE clause will contain expressions, called *predicates,* that can be evaluated to TRUE, FALSE, or UNKNOWN. You will learn more about UNKNOWN in the "Working with *NULL*" section later in the chapter. The WHERE clause syntax is as follows:

```
SELECT <column1>,<column2>
FROM <schema>.<table>
WHERE <column> = <value>;
```

Listing 3-5 shows the syntax and some examples demonstrating how to compare a column to a literal value. The following examples are from the AdventureWorks database. Be sure to type each query into the query window and execute the statement to see how it works. Make sure you understand how the expression in the WHERE clause affects the results returned by each query. Notice that tick marks, or single quotes, have been used around literal strings and dates.

Listing 3-5. How to Use the WHERE Clause

```
--1
SELECT CustomerID, SalesOrderID
FROM Sales.SalesOrderHeader
WHERE CustomerID = 11000;

--2
SELECT CustomerID, SalesOrderID
FROM Sales.SalesOrderHeader
WHERE SalesOrderID = 43793;

--3
SELECT CustomerID, SalesOrderID, OrderDate
FROM Sales.SalesOrderHeader
WHERE OrderDate = '2005-07-02';

--4
SELECT BusinessEntityID, LoginID, JobTitle
FROM HumanResources.Employee
WHERE JobTitle = 'Chief Executive Officer';
```

Each query in Listing 3-5 returns rows that are filtered by the expression in the WHERE clause. Be sure to check the results of each query to make sure that the expected rows are returned (see Figure 3-5). Each query returns only the information specified in that query's WHERE clause.

	CustomerID	SalesOrderID
1	11000	43793
2	11000	51522
3	11000	57418

	CustomerID	SalesOrderID
1	11000	43793

	CustomerID	SalesOrderID	OrderDate
1	27645	43702	2005-07-02 00:00:00.000
2	16624	43703	2005-07-02 00:00:00.000
3	11005	43704	2005-07-02 00:00:00.000
4	11011	43705	2005-07-02 00:00:00.000

	BusinessEntityID	LoginID	JobTitle
1	1	adventure-works\ken0	Chief Executive Officer

Figure 3-5. *The results of using the WHERE clause*

■ **Note** Throughout this book you will see many comments in the code. Comments are not processed by SQL Server and will help make your code more readable. To create a one-line comment, type in two dashes (--). To comment out several lines begin the section with a slash and asterisk (/*) and end the section with an asterisk and slash (*/).

Using *WHERE* Clauses with Alternate Operators

Within WHERE clause expressions, you can use many comparison operators, not just the equals sign. Books Online lists the following operators:

> *(greater than)*

< *(less than)*

= *(equals)*

<= *(less than or equal to)*

>= *(greater than or equal to)*

!= *(not equal to)*

<> *(not equal to)*

!< *(not less than)*

!> *(not greater than)*

Type in and execute the queries in Listing 3-6 to practice using these additional operators in the WHERE clause.

Listing 3-6. *Using Operators with the WHERE Clause*

```
--Using a DateTime column
--1
SELECT CustomerID, SalesOrderID, OrderDate
FROM Sales.SalesOrderHeader
WHERE OrderDate > '2005-07-05';
```

```
--2
SELECT CustomerID, SalesOrderID, OrderDate
FROM Sales.SalesOrderHeader
WHERE OrderDate < '2005-07-05';


--3
SELECT CustomerID, SalesOrderID, OrderDate
FROM Sales.SalesOrderHeader
WHERE OrderDate >= '2005-07-05';


--4
SELECT CustomerID, SalesOrderID, OrderDate
FROM Sales.SalesOrderHeader
WHERE OrderDate <> '2005-07-05';


--5
SELECT CustomerID, SalesOrderID, OrderDate
FROM Sales.SalesOrderHeader
WHERE OrderDate != '2005-07-05';

--Using a number column
--6
SELECT SalesOrderID, SalesOrderDetailID, OrderQty
FROM Sales.SalesOrderDetail
WHERE OrderQty > 10;


--7
SELECT SalesOrderID, SalesOrderDetailID, OrderQty
FROM Sales.SalesOrderDetail
WHERE OrderQty <= 10;


--8
SELECT SalesOrderID, SalesOrderDetailID, OrderQty
FROM Sales.SalesOrderDetail
WHERE OrderQty <> 10;


--9
SELECT SalesOrderID, SalesOrderDetailID, OrderQty
FROM Sales.SalesOrderDetail
WHERE OrderQty != 10;

--Using a string column
--10
SELECT BusinessEntityID, FirstName
FROM Person.Person
WHERE FirstName <> 'Catherine';


--11
SELECT BusinessEntityID, FirstName
FROM Person.Person
WHERE FirstName != 'Catherine';
```

```
--12
SELECT BusinessEntityID, FirstName
FROM Person.Person
WHERE FirstName > 'M';

--13
SELECT BusinessEntityID, FirstName
FROM Person.Person
WHERE FirstName !> 'M';
```

Take a look at the results of each query to make sure that the results make sense and that you understand why you are getting them. Remember that both != and <> mean "not equal to" and are interchangeable. Using either operator should return the same results if all other aspects of a query are the same.

You may find the results of query 12 interesting. At first glance, you may think that only rows with the first name beginning with the letter *N* or later in the alphabet should be returned. However, if any FirstName value begins with *M* followed by at least one additional character, the value is greater than *M*, so the row will be returned. For example, *Ma* is greater than *M*.

Query 13 is also an interesting example that you will probably not see often. This means that the FirstName is not greater than *M*. That means that it could be *M* or anything in the alphabet before *M*.

Using *BETWEEN*

BETWEEN is another useful operator you can use in the WHERE clause to specify an inclusive range of values. It is frequently used with dates but can be used with string and numeric data as well. Here is the syntax for BETWEEN:

```
SELECT <column1>,<column2>
FROM <schema>.<table>
WHERE <column> BETWEEN <value1> AND <value2>;
```

Type in and execute the code in Listing 3-7 to learn how to use BETWEEN.

Listing 3-7. Using BETWEEN

```
--1
SELECT CustomerID, SalesOrderID, OrderDate
FROM Sales.SalesOrderHeader
WHERE OrderDate BETWEEN '2005-07-02' AND '2005-07-04';

--2
SELECT CustomerID, SalesOrderID, OrderDate
FROM Sales.SalesOrderHeader
WHERE CustomerID BETWEEN 25000 AND 25005;

--3
SELECT BusinessEntityID, JobTitle
FROM HumanResources.Employee
WHERE JobTitle BETWEEN 'C' and 'E';
```

```
--4 An illogical BETWEEN expression
SELECT CustomerID, SalesOrderID, OrderDate
FROM Sales.SalesOrderHeader
WHERE CustomerID BETWEEN 25005 AND 25000;
```

Pay close attention to the results of Listing 3-7 shown in Figure 3-6. Query 1 returns all orders placed on the two dates specified in the query as well as the orders placed between the dates. You will see the same behavior from the second query—all orders placed by customers with customer IDs within the range specified. What can you expect from query 3? You will see all job titles that start with C or D. You will not see the job titles beginning with E, however. A job title composed of *only* the letter E would be returned in the results. Any job title beginning with E and at least one other character is greater than E and therefore not within the range. For example, the *Ex* in *Executive* is greater than just E, so any job titles beginning with *Executive* get eliminated.

	CustomerID	SalesOrderID	OrderDate
1	27645	43702	2005-07-02 00:00:00.000
2	16624	43703	2005-07-02 00:00:00.000
3	11005	43704	2005-07-02 00:00:00.000
4	11011	43705	2005-07-02 00:00:00.000

	CustomerID	SalesOrderID	OrderDate
1	25000	73018	2008-06-15 00:00:00.000
2	25001	61662	2008-01-08 00:00:00.000
3	25002	61397	2008-01-03 00:00:00.000
4	25003	60269	2007-12-18 00:00:00.000

	BusinessEntityID	JobTitle
1	1	Chief Executive Officer
2	5	Design Engineer
3	6	Design Engineer
4	15	Design Engineer

	CustomerID	SalesOrderID	OrderDate

Figure 3-6. *The partial results of queries with BETWEEN*

Query 4 returns no rows at all because the values listed in the BETWEEN expression are switched. No values meet the qualification of being greater than or equal to 25005 and also less than or equal to 25000. Make sure you always list the lower value first and the higher value second when using BETWEEN. Another thing to notice about the results is that all of the datetime values do not contain times. When time values are recorded, then the expressions in the WHERE clause must take this into account. You'll see an example of this later in this chapter in the section "Filtering on Date and Time."

Using *BETWEEN* with *NOT*

To find values outside a particular range of values, you write the WHERE clause expression using BETWEEN along with the NOT keyword. In this case, the query returns any rows outside the range. Try the examples in Listing 3-8, and compare them to the results from Listing 3-7.

Listing 3-8. Using NOT BETWEEN

```
--1
SELECT CustomerID, SalesOrderID, OrderDate
FROM Sales.SalesOrderHeader
WHERE OrderDate NOT BETWEEN '2005-07-02' AND '2005-07-04';

--2
SELECT CustomerID, SalesOrderID, OrderDate
FROM Sales.SalesOrderHeader
WHERE CustomerID NOT BETWEEN 25000 AND 25005;

--3
SELECT BusinessEntityID, JobTitle
FROM HumanResources.Employee
WHERE JobTitle NOT BETWEEN 'C' and 'E';

--4 An illogical BETWEEN expression
SELECT CustomerID, SalesOrderID, OrderDate
FROM Sales.SalesOrderHeader
WHERE CustomerID NOT BETWEEN 25005 AND 25000;
```

Query 1 displays all orders placed before July 2, 2005 (2005-07-02) or after July 4, 2005 (2005-07-04)—in other words, any orders placed outside the range specified (see Figure 3-7). Query 2 displays the orders placed by customers with customer IDs less than 25000 or greater than 25005. When using the NOT operator with BETWEEN, the values specified in the BETWEEN expression don't show up in the results. Query 3 returns all job titles beginning with *A* and *B*. It also displays any job titles beginning with *E* and at least one more character, as well as any job titles starting with a letter greater than *E*. If a title consists of just the letter *E*, it will not show up in the results. This is just the opposite of what you saw in Listing 3-7.

	CustomerID	SalesOrderID	OrderDate
1	11000	43793	2005-07-22 00:00:00.000
2	11000	51522	2007-07-22 00:00:00.000
3	11000	57418	2007-11-04 00:00:00.000
4	11001	43767	2005-07-18 00:00:00.000

	CustomerID	SalesOrderID	OrderDate
1	11000	43793	2005-07-22 00:00:00.000
2	11000	51522	2007-07-22 00:00:00.000
3	11000	57418	2007-11-04 00:00:00.000
4	11001	43767	2005-07-18 00:00:00.000

	BusinessEntityID	JobTitle
1	2	Vice President of Engineering
2	3	Engineering Manager
3	4	Senior Tool Designer
4	7	Research and Developmen...

	CustomerID	SalesOrderID	OrderDate
1	11000	43793	2005-07-22 00:00:00.000
2	11000	51522	2007-07-22 00:00:00.000
3	11000	57418	2007-11-04 00:00:00.000
4	11001	43767	2005-07-18 00:00:00.000

Figure 3-7. *The partial results of queries with NOT BETWEEN*

Query 4 with the illogical BETWEEN expression returns all the rows in the table. Because no customer ID values can be less than or equal to 25005 and also be greater than or equal to 25000, no rows meet the criteria in the BETWEEN expression. By adding the NOT operator, every row ends up in the results, which is probably not the original intent.

Filtering on Date and Time

Some temporal data columns store the time as well as the date. If you attempt to filter on such a column specifying only the date, you may retrieve incomplete results. Type in and run the code in Listing 3-9 to create and populate a temporary table that will be used to illustrate this issue. Don't worry about trying to understand the table creation code at this point.

Listing 3-9. Table Setup for Date/Time Example

```
CREATE TABLE #DateTimeExample(
    ID INT NOT NULL IDENTITY PRIMARY KEY,
    MyDate DATETIME2(0) NOT NULL,
    MyValue VARCHAR(25) NOT NULL
);
GO
INSERT INTO #DateTimeExample
    (MyDate,MyValue)
VALUES ('2009-01-02 10:30','Bike'),
    ('2009-01-03 13:00','Trike'),
    ('2009-01-03 13:10','Bell'),
    ('2009-01-03 17:35','Seat');
```

Now that the table is in place, type in and execute the code in Listing 3-10 to see what happens when filtering on the MyDate column.

Listing 3-10. Filtering on Date and Time Columns

```
--1
SELECT ID, MyDate, MyValue
FROM #DateTimeExample
WHERE MyDate = '2009-01-03';

--2
SELECT ID, MyDate, MyValue
FROM #DateTimeExample
WHERE MyDate BETWEEN '2009-01-03 00:00:00' AND '2009-01-03 23:59:59';
```

Figure 3-8 shows the results of the two queries. Suppose you want to retrieve a list of entries from January 3, 2009 (2009-01-03). Query 1 tries to do that but returns no results. Results will be returned only for entries where the MyDate value is precisely 2009-01-03 00:00:00, and there are no such entries. The second query returns the expected results— all values where the date is 2009-01-03. It does that by taking the time of day into account. To be even more accurate, the query could be written using two expressions: one filtering for dates greater than or equal to 2009-01-03 and another filtering for dates less than 2009-01-04. You will learn more about data types in Chapter 16, but this example will only work because of the specific data type datetime2(0) that was used. You will learn how to write WHERE clauses with two expressions in the next section, which will have an example that is actually a better way to handle filtering on date and time data types.

	ID	MyDate	MyValue

	ID	MyDate	MyValue
1	2	2009-01-03 13:00:00	Trike
2	3	2009-01-03 13:10:00	Bell
3	4	2009-01-03 17:35:00	Seat

Figure 3-8. *Results of filtering on a date and time column*

So what would happen if you formatted the date differently? Will you get the same results if slashes (/), are used or if the month is spelled out (in other words, as January 3, 2009)? SQL Server does not store the date using any particular character-based format but rather as an integer representing the number of days between 1900-01-01 and the date specified. If the data type holds the time, the time is stored as the number of clock ticks past midnight. As long as you pass a date in an appropriate format based on the localization settings of the server where SQL Server is installed, the value will be recognized as a date, but as a best practice always use the 'YYYY-MM-DD' format.

Writing a WHERE clause is a very important skill. Take the time to practice what you have learned so far by completing Exercise 3-2.

EXERCISE 3-2

Use the AdventureWorks database to complete this exercise. Be sure to run each query and check the results. You can go back and review the examples in the section if you don't remember how to write the queries. You can find the solutions at the end of the chapter.

1. Write a query using a WHERE clause that displays all the employees listed in the HumanResources.Employee table who have the job title Research and Development Engineer. Display the business entity ID number, the login ID, and the title for each one.

2. Write a query using a WHERE clause that displays all the names in Person.Person with the middle name *J*. Display the first, last, and middle names along with the ID numbers.

3. Write a query displaying all the columns of the Production.ProductCostHistory table from the rows in which the standard cost is between the values of $10 and $13. Be sure to use one of the features in SQL Server Management Studio to help you write this query.

4. Rewrite the query you wrote in question 1, changing it so the employees who do not have the title Research and Development Engineer are displayed.

5. Explain why a WHERE clause should be used in many of your T-SQL queries.

Using *WHERE* Clauses with Two Predicates

So far, the examples have shown only one condition or predicate in the WHERE clause, but the WHERE clause can be much more complex. They can have multiple predicates by using the logical operators AND and OR. Type in and execute the code in Listing 3-11 that demonstrates how to use AND and OR to combine two predicates.

Listing 3-11. How to Use AND and OR

```
--1
SELECT BusinessEntityID, FirstName, MiddleName, LastName
FROM Person.Person
WHERE FirstName = 'Ken' AND LastName = 'Myer';


--2
SELECT BusinessEntityID, FirstName, MiddleName, LastName
FROM Person.Person
WHERE LastName = 'Myer' OR LastName = 'Meyer';


--3
IF OBJECT_ID('tempdb..#DateTimeExample') IS NOT NULL BEGIN
        DROP TABLE #DateTimeExample;
END;
GO
CREATE TABLE #DateTimeExample(
    ID INT NOT NULL IDENTITY PRIMARY KEY,
    MyDate DATETIME2(0) NOT NULL,
    MyValue VARCHAR(25) NOT NULL
);
```

```
GO
INSERT #DateTimeExample (ID, MyDate, MyValue)
VALUES ('2009-01-01 10:30','Bike'),
    ('2009-01-01 11:30','Bike'),
    ('2009-01-02 13:00','Trike'),
    ('2009-01-03 13:10','Bell'),
    ('2009-01-03 17:35','Seat'),
    ('2009-01-04 00:00','Bike');

--4
SELECT ID, MyDate, MyValue
FROM #DateTimeExample
WHERE MyDate >= '2009-01-02' AND MyDate < '2009-01-04';
```

Figure 3-9 shows the results. Query 1 returns any rows with the first name *Ken* and the last name *Myer* because both expressions must evaluate to TRUE. Query 2 returns any rows with either the last name *Myer* or the last name *Meyer* because only one of the expressions must evaluate to TRUE. Query 3 demonstrates the best way to deal with datetime data types. This query returns all rows where MyDate is any time on 2009-01-02 or 2009-01-03. By using greater than or equal to the lower date and less than one more than the upper date, you will get the expected results. Using more than two predicates, especially when including OR along with AND, can get quite complex. You will learn more about this in Chapter 9.

	BusinessEntityID	FirstName	MiddleName	LastName
1	1525	Ken	NULL	Myer
2	203	Ken	L	Myer

	BusinessEntityID	FirstName	MiddleName	LastName
1	1459	Deanna	NULL	Meyer
2	1455	Eric	B.	Meyer
3	1457	Helen	M.	Meyer
4	2140	Ken	NULL	Meyer
5	1523	Dorothy	J.	Myer
6	1525	Ken	NULL	Myer
7	203	Ken	L	Myer
8	2319	Linda	NULL	Myer

	ID	MyDate	MyValue
1	2	2009-01-03 13:00:00	Trike
2	3	2009-01-03 13:10:00	Bell
3	4	2009-01-03 17:35:00	Seat

Figure 3-9. *The results of queries with two predicates in the WHERE clause*

Using the *IN* Operator

The IN operator is very useful when a set of multiple values must be compared to the same column. Query 2 in Listing 3-11 could have been written using the IN operator. Follow the IN operator with a list of possible values for a column within parentheses. Here is the syntax:

```
SELECT <column1>,<column2>
FROM <schema>.<table>
WHERE <column> IN (<value1>,<value2>);
```

Type in and execute the code from Listing 3-12. The queries in this listing demonstrate how to use the IN operator. Review the results to be sure that you understand them.

Listing 3-12. Using the IN Operator

```
--1
SELECT BusinessEntityID,FirstName,MiddleName,LastName
FROM Person.Person
WHERE FirstName = 'Ken' AND
    LastName IN ('Myer','Meyer');

--2
SELECT TerritoryID, Name
FROM Sales.SalesTerritory
WHERE TerritoryID IN (2,2,1,4,5);

--3
SELECT TerritoryID, Name
FROM Sales.SalesTerritory
WHERE TerritoryID NOT IN (2,1,4,5);
```

You will probably find that the operator IN can simplify many queries when you have multiple values to compare. Query 1 requires that the first name must be *Ken* and the last name can be either *Myer* or *Meyer*. You can also use IN with numbers and dates and most data types. Query 2 returns all rows with TerritoryID *2, 1, 4,* or *5*. Notice that *2* was listed twice. This doesn't cause the row to be returned twice, however. By using NOT, query 3 returns the opposite results. Figure 3-10 shows the results of the three queries from Listing 3-12.

	BusinessEntityID	FirstName	MiddleName	LastName
1	2140	Ken	NULL	Meyer
2	1525	Ken	NULL	Myer
3	203	Ken	L	Myer

	TerritoryID	Name
1	1	Northwest
2	2	Northeast
3	4	Southwest
4	5	Southeast

	TerritoryID	Name
1	9	Australia
2	6	Canada
3	3	Central
4	7	France
5	8	Germany
6	10	United Kingdom

Figure 3-10. *The results of queries using the IN operator*

As the WHERE clause becomes more complicated, it becomes very easy to make a mistake. You will spend more time learning about the WHERE clause in Chapter 9. Complete Exercise 3-3 to practice writing WHERE clauses with multiple predicates and the IN operator.

EXERCISE 3-3

Use the AdventureWorks database to complete this exercise. Be sure to check your results to ensure that they make sense. You can find the solutions at the end of the chapter.

1. Write a query displaying the order ID, order date, and total due from the Sales.SalesOrderHeader table. Retrieve only those rows where the order was placed during the month of September 2005.

2. Write a query with the same columns as question 1. Include rows where the Total Due is $10,000 or more or the SalesOrderID is less than 43000.

3. Explain when it makes sense to use the IN operator.

Working with *NULL*

Probably nothing causes more aggravation to T-SQL developers than NULL values. NULL means that a value has not been entered for a particular column in a row. Suppose you have an e-commerce application that requires the customer to fill in information such as name and address. In this example, the phone number is optional. What does it mean if the customer does not enter a phone number and the table ends up with NULL in the PhoneNumber column of the Customer table? Does it mean that the customer does not have a phone? That's one possibility. Another is that the customer has at least one phone number but chose not to supply it because it was not required. Either way, the end result is that you do not know if a phone number exists or not.

Think about what would happen if you had a list of 1 million phone numbers and tried to figure out whether any of the phone numbers belonged to this particular customer. Even if you compared each phone number to the customer's row, one by one, you would never know whether any of the phone numbers were the right one. You would never know because you would be comparing 1 million values to an unknown value. Conversely, can you guarantee that every one of your 1 million phone numbers is not the missing phone number? No, you can't do that either, because the customer's phone number is unknown and one of those numbers might actually be correct.

This example should give you an idea about the challenges of working with NULL values. Type in and execute the code in Listing 3-13 to work on some examples using real data.

Listing 3-13. An Example Illustrating NULL

```
--1 Returns 19,972 rows
SELECT MiddleName
FROM Person.Person;

--2 Returns 291 rows
SELECT MiddleName
FROM Person.Person
WHERE MiddleName = 'B';

--3 Returns 11,182 but 19,681 were expected
SELECT MiddleName
FROM Person.Person
WHERE MiddleName != 'B';

--4 Returns 19,681
SELECT MiddleName
FROM Person.Person
WHERE MiddleName IS NULL
    OR MiddleName !='B';
```

Query 1 with no WHERE clause returns 19,972 rows, the total number of rows in the table. Query 2 returns 291 rows with the middle name B. Logic follows that query 3 will return the difference of the two numbers: 19,681 rows. When you check the results of query 3, you will find that more than 8,000 rows are not accounted for. That is because the rows with NULL values can't be found by the expression containing not equal. Comparing NULL to B returns UNKNOWN, so the rows are not returned. You must specifically check for NULL values by using the IS NULL operator, as shown in query 4, which returns the correct number of rows.

Usually comparing the data in a column to a value or comparing the values from two columns returns either TRUE or FALSE. If the expression in the WHERE clause evaluates to TRUE, then the row is returned. If the expression evaluates to FALSE, then the row is not returned. If a value in the expression contains NULL, then the expression is resolved to UNKNOWN. In some ways, the behavior is like FALSE. When an expression resolves to UNKNOWN, the row is not returned. The problems begin when using any operator except for equal to (=). The opposite of FALSE is TRUE, but the opposite of UNKNOWN is still UNKNOWN.

■ **Note** Be aware that NULL is not a value so it can't equal itself or any other value. T-SQL instead provides specific expressions and functions to test for NULL values. To test for a NULL value you will want to use the IS [NOT] NULL expression (http://msdn.microsoft.com/en-us/library/ms188795(v=SQL.120).aspx). Additionally, you may want to change a NULL value to a value like an empty string (''). The function ISNULL will replace a NULL value with another value specified in the query (see Chapter 4).

Neglecting to take possible NULL values into consideration can often cause incomplete results. Always remember to think about NULL values, especially when writing any expression containing NOT. Do the NULL values belong in the results? If so, you will have to check for NULL. You will also need to keep NULL values in mind when using the less than (<) operator. NULL values will be left out of those results as well. Chapter 4 will show you some other options for working with NULL.

Understanding how NULL values can affect the results of your queries is one of the most important skills you will learn. Even experienced T-SQL developers struggle from time to time when working with NULL values. You have covered a lot of ground about the WHERE clause in these sections, but there is much more to learn. You will spend time in Chapter 9 learning even more on this subject. Be sure to complete Exercise 3-4 to practice what you have just learned.

EXERCISE 3-4

Use the AdventureWorks database to complete this exercise. Make sure you consider how NULL values will affect your results. You can find the solutions at the end of the chapter.

1. Write a query displaying the ProductID, Name, and Color columns from rows in the Production.Product table. Display only those rows where no color has been assigned.

2. Write a query displaying the ProductID, Name, and Color columns from rows in the Production.Product table. Display only those rows in which the color is *known* not to be blue.

3. Write a query displaying ProductID, Name, Style, Size, and Color from the Production.Product table. Include only the rows where at least one of the Size or Color columns contains a value.

Sorting Data

So far, you have learned how to retrieve a list of columns from a table and filter the results. This section covers how to sort the data that are retrieved using the ORDER BY clause. The ORDER BY clause is the last part of the SELECT statement that the database engine will process.

You can specify one or more columns in the ORDER BY clause separated by commas. The sort order is ascending by default, but you can specify descending order by using the keyword DESCENDING or DESC after the column name. You can also specify ASCENDING or ASC if you wish, but the sort order is ascending by default. Here is the syntax for ORDER BY:

```
SELECT <column1>,<column2>
FROM <schema>.<tablename>
ORDER BY <column1>[<sort direction>],<column2> [<sort direction>]
```

Type in and execute the code in Listing 3-14 to learn how to use the ORDER BY clause.

Listing 3-14. How to Use ORDER BY

```
--1
SELECT ProductID, LocationID
FROM Production.ProductInventory
ORDER BY LocationID;

--2
SELECT ProductID, LocationID
FROM Production.ProductInventory
ORDER BY ProductID, LocationID DESC;
```

Figure 3-11 shows the partial results. The rows from query 1 display in order of LocationID. Query 2 returns the results ordered first by ProductID, and then the results are further sorted by LocationID in descending order.

	ProductID	LocationID
1	1	1
2	2	1
3	3	1
4	4	1
5	317	1
6	318	1
7	319	1

	ProductID	LocationID
1	1	50
2	1	6
3	1	1
4	2	50
5	2	6
6	2	1
7	3	50
8	3	6
9	3	1

Figure 3-11. The results when using the ORDER BY clause

When NULL values are part of the results, they will show up first when sorting in an ascending manner. This reminds me of the secretarial skills class I took in high school. When learning about filing, the teacher said to remember "Nothing before something." Except for learning how to type on an electric typewriter, which I haven't done in years, that was the most important thing I learned in the class. Another interesting thing you can do is use aliases from the SELECT clause in the ORDER BY clause. Here is an example that actually causes a problem because the same column name is used in the SELECT list.

```
SELECT BusinessEntityID, 1 as LastName, LastName, FirstName, MiddleName
FROM Person.Person
ORDER BY LastName DESC, FirstName DESC, MiddleName DESC;

Msg 209, Level 16, State 1, Line 11 Ambiguous column name 'LastName'
```

You may find the ORDER BY clause easy to use, but you should still practice what you have learned about sorting the results of your queries by completing Exercise 3-5.

EXERCISE 3-5

Use the AdventureWorks database to complete this exercise and practice sorting the results of your queries. You can find the solutions at the end of the chapter.

1. Write a query that returns the business entity ID and name columns from the Person.Person table. Sort the results by LastName, FirstName, and MiddleName.

2. Modify the query written in question 1 so that the data is returned in the opposite order.

Thinking About Performance

Reading this book and performing the exercises found in each chapter will enable you to become a proficient T-SQL programmer. You will learn how to write the queries, often in more than one way, to get results. Frequently, T-SQL developers don't learn the best way to write a query, and the performance of their applications and reports suffers. As a result, several chapters of this book, beginning with this chapter, feature a section on performance to get you thinking about how the statements you write can affect performance.

Taking Advantage of Indexes

Indexes help the database engine locate the rows that must be returned by a query. In fact, the database engine, if possible, will retrieve all the required columns from the index instead of accessing the table. I am not advocating creating an index on every column, but strategically designed indexes immensely improve the performance of queries.

When a table contains an index on a column, the database engine will usually use that index to find the rows for the results if the column appears in the WHERE clause. For example, the Person.Person table contains an index called IX_Person_LastName_FirstName_MiddleName, which consists of the LastName, FirstName, and MiddleName columns. To see the index properties, follow these steps:

1. Using SQL Server Management Studio, connect to your SQL Server instance if you aren't connected already.

2. Expand Databases.

3. Expand AdventureWorks.

4. Expand Tables.

5. Expand Person.Person.

6. Expand Indexes.

7. Locate the IX_Person_LastName_FirstName_MiddleName index, and double-click it to view the properties.

View the index properties in Figure 3-12. Notice that the LastName column appears first in the list. To take full advantage of this index, the WHERE clause must filter on LastName. Imagine searching a phone book by first name when you don't know the last name! SQL Server must do the same thing, looking at each entry in the index, when the query filters on FirstName but not LastName.

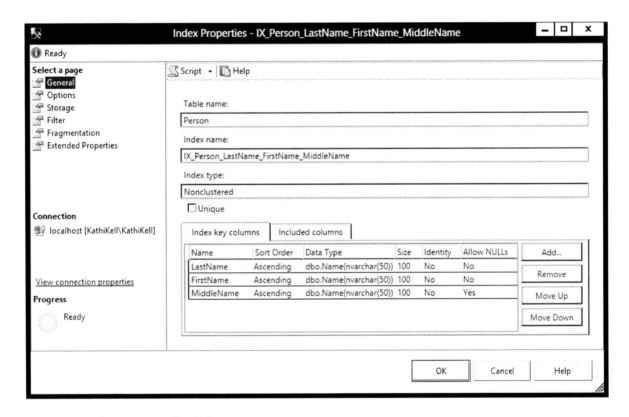

Figure 3-12. *The properties of an index*

What happens when you filter on only a nonindexed column? The database engine must check the value of the column in each row of the table to find the rows meeting the criteria. Again, I'm not advocating creating an index for every query, and index creation and tuning are both well beyond the scope of this book. I just want to make you aware that the indexes defined on the table will affect the performance of your queries.

Viewing Execution Plans

By using execution plans, you can determine whether the database engine utilizes an index to return the rows in the query. You can also compare the performance of two or more queries to see which one performs the best. Again, this book doesn't intend to make you an expert on execution plans but instead just gets you started using them to help you understand how your query performs.

■ **Note**   To learn more about execution plans, see the book *SQL Server 2008 Query Performance Tuning Distilled* by Grant Fritchey and Sajal Dam (Apress, 2009).

While you have a query window open, click the Include Actual Execution Plan icon (see Figure 3-13) to turn on this feature for the current session. The setting must be toggled on for each query window; it is not a permanent setting.

Figure 3-13. *Clicking the Include Actual Execution Plan icon*

Listing 3-15 contains three queries to demonstrate the differences in performance found depending on whether SQL Server can take advantage of an index to return the results. Type in and execute the code in Listing 3-15.

Listing 3-15. Learning How to View Execution Plans

```
--1
SELECT LastName, FirstName
FROM Person.Person
WHERE LastName = 'Smith';

--2
SELECT LastName, FirstName
FROM Person.Person
WHERE FirstName = 'Ken';

--3
SELECT ModifiedDate
FROM Person.Person
WHERE ModifiedDate BETWEEN '2005-01-01' and '2005-01-31';
```

Once the query execution completes, click the Execution Plan tab. Figure 3-14 shows the graphical execution plans for the three queries. First, take a look at the query cost for each query shown at the top of each section. The query cost gives you an estimated weight of each query compared to the total. The numbers should add up to approximately 100 percent.

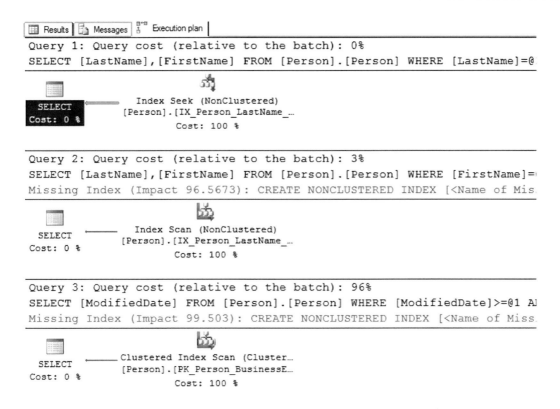

Figure 3-14. The actual execution plans generated from Listing 3-15

Query 1, which has a relative query cost of 0 percent, filters the results on the LastName column. Recall that an index comprised of the LastName, FirstName, and MiddleName columns exists on the Person.Person table. Because the query filters on the first column in the index, the database engine can take full advantage of the index; it performs an *index seek* without scanning the entire index. This is similar to looking at the phone book when you know the last name; you don't need to look at every page or every entry to find the name you are looking for. Query 2, which has a relative query cost of 3 percent, filters the results on the FirstName column. The table has an index that contains the FirstName column, but because it appears second in the index, SQL Server must perform an *index scan*. This means that the database engine must compare the string *Ken* to every FirstName value in the index. The query was able to take advantage of the index but not to the fullest extent. Because the index contains both columns found in the results, the database engine didn't have to touch the actual table, pulling all the needed data from the much smaller index. Because the index has less data in it than the table, SQL Server can do less work when retrieving from the index. The execution plan also suggests a new index that will make this query perform better.

Query 3, which has a relative query cost of 96 percent, filters the results on the ModifiedDate column. The table doesn't have an index containing this column. To filter the rows, the database engine must perform a *clustered index scan*. The *clustered index* is the actual table. In this case, the database engine had to look at each row of the table to retrieve the results. Scanning the table is much more work for SQL Server than scanning the nonclustered index or searching either type. Review the "Understanding Indexes" section in Chapter 2 to learn more about clustered indexes and indexes in general.

Viewing and understanding execution plans will help you learn how writing queries will affect the performance of your applications and reports. Don't rush to your database administrator demanding changes to the database indexes in your production database; this section doesn't intend to teach index tuning. Think of execution plans as another tool you can use to write better code.

Summary

The SELECT statement is used to retrieve data from tables stored in SQL Server databases. The statement can be broken down into several parts called *clauses*. The FROM clause specifies the table where the data is stored. The SELECT clause contains a list of columns to be retrieved. To filter the data, use the WHERE clause. To sort the data, use the ORDER BY clause.

This chapter covered a lot of ground, especially many nuances of the WHERE clause. Make sure you really understand the material covered in the chapter before continuing in this book. Everything you learn throughout the rest of the book will depend on a thorough knowledge of the basics. The next chapter explores many of the built-in functions you can use to make data retrieval even more interesting.

Answers to the Exercises

This section provides solutions to the exercises found on writing simple SELECT queries.

Solutions to Exercise 3-1: Using the *SELECT* Statement

Use the AdventureWorks database to complete this exercise.

1. Write a SELECT statement that lists the customers along with their ID numbers. Include the StoreID and the AccountNumber from the Sales.Customers table.

    ```
    SELECT CustomerID, StoreID, AccountNumber
    FROM Sales.Customer;
    ```

2. Write a SELECT statement that lists the name, product number, and color of each product from the Production.Product table.

    ```
    SELECT Name, ProductNumber, Color
    FROM Production.Product;
    ```

3. Write a SELECT statement that lists the customer ID numbers and sales order ID numbers from the Sales.SalesOrderHeader table.

    ```
    SELECT CustomerID, SalesOrderID
    FROM Sales.SalesOrderHeader;
    ```

4. Answer this question: Why should you specify column names rather than an asterisk when writing the select-list? Give at least two reasons.

    You would do this to decrease the amount of network traffic and increase the performance of the query, retrieving only the columns needed for the application or report. You can also keep users from seeing confidential information by retrieving only the columns they should see.

Solutions to Exercise 3-2: Filtering Data

Use the AdventureWorks database to complete this exercise.

1. Write a query using a WHERE clause that displays all the employees listed in the HumanResources.Employee table who have the job title Research and Development Engineer. Display the business entity ID number, the login ID, and the title for each one.

```
SELECT BusinessEntityID, JobTitle, LoginID
FROM HumanResources.Employee
WHERE JobTitle = 'Research and Development Engineer';
```

2. Write a query using a WHERE clause that displays all the names in Person.Person with the middle name *J*. Display the first, last, and middle names along with the ID numbers.

```
SELECT FirstName, MiddleName, LastName, BusinessEntityID
FROM Person.Person
WHERE MiddleName = 'J';
```

3. Write a query displaying all the columns of the Production.ProductCostHistory table from the rows in which the standard cost is between the values of $10 and $13. Be sure to use one of the features in SQL Server Management Studio to help you write this query.

    In SQL Server Management Studio, expand the AdventureWorks database. Expand Tables. Right-click the Production.ProductionCostHistory table and choose "Script Table as," "SELECT to," and "New Query Editor Window." Then type in the WHERE clause.

```
USE [AdventureWorks]
GO
SELECT [ProductID]
      ,[StartDate]
      ,[EndDate]
      ,[StandardCost]
      ,[ModifiedDate]
FROM [Production].[ProductCostHistory]
WHERE StandardCost BETWEEN 10 and 13;
GO
```

4. Rewrite the query you wrote in question 1, changing it so that the employees who do not have the title Research and Development Engineer are displayed.

```
SELECT BusinessEntityID, JobTitle, LoginID
FROM HumanResources.Employee
WHERE JobTitle <> 'Research and Development Engineer';
```

5. Explain why a WHERE clause should be used in many of your T-SQL queries.

    Most of the time the application or report will not require all the rows. The query should be filtered to include only the required rows to cut down on network traffic and increase SQL Server performance because returning a smaller number of rows is usually more efficient.

Solutions to Exercise 3-3: Using WHERE Clauses with Two Predicates

Use the AdventureWorks database to complete this exercise.

1. Write a query displaying the order ID, order date, and total due from the Sales.SalesOrderHeader table. Retrieve only those rows where the order was placed during the month of September 2005.

```
SELECT SalesOrderID, OrderDate, TotalDue
FROM Sales.SalesOrderHeader
WHERE OrderDate >= '2005-09-01'
      AND OrderDate < '2005-10-01';
```

2. Write a query with the same columns as question 1. Include rows where the Total Due is $10,000 or more or the SalesOrderID is less than 43000.

```
SELECT SalesOrderID, OrderDate, TotalDue
FROM Sales.SalesOrderHeader
WHERE TotalDue >=10000 OR SalesOrderID < 43000;
```

3. Explain when it makes sense to use the IN operator.

You will want to use the IN operator when you have a small number of literal values to compare to one column.

Solutions to Exercise 3-4: Working with *NULL*

Use the AdventureWorks database to complete this exercise.

1. Write a query displaying the ProductID, Name, and Color columns from rows in the Production.Product table. Display only those rows where no color has been assigned.

```
SELECT ProductID, Name, Color
FROM Production.Product
WHERE Color IS NULL;
```

2. Write a query displaying the ProductID, Name, and Color columns from rows in the Production.Product table. Display only those rows in which the color is *known* not to be blue.

```
SELECT ProductID, Name, Color
FROM Production.Product
WHERE Color <>'BLUE ';
```

3. Write a query displaying ProductID, Name, Style, Size, and Color from the Production.Product table. Include only the rows where at least one of the Size or Color columns contains a value.

```
SELECT ProductID, Name, Color
FROM Production.Product
WHERE Color IS NOT NULL

    OR Size IS NOT NULL;
```

Solutions to Exercise 3-5: Sorting Data

Use the AdventureWorks database to complete this exercise.

1. Write a query that returns the business entity ID and name columns from the Person.Person table. Sort the results by LastName, FirstName, and MiddleName.

```
SELECT BusinessEntityID, LastName, FirstName, MiddleName
FROM Person.Person
ORDER BY LastName, FirstName, MiddleName;
```

2. Modify the query written in question 1 so that the data is returned in the opposite order.

```
SELECT BusinessEntityID, LastName, FirstName, MiddleName
FROM Person.Person
ORDER BY LastName DESC, FirstName DESC, MiddleName DESC;
```

■ ■ ■

Using Built-In Functions and Expressions

Now that you have the knowledge to write simple SELECT statements, it is time to explore some of the other features of T-SQL that allow you to manipulate how the data is displayed, filtered, or ordered. To create expressions in T-SQL, you use functions and operators along with literal values and columns. The reasons for using expressions in T-SQL code are many. For example, you may want to display only the year of a column of the DATETIME data type on a report, or you may need to calculate a discount based on the order quantity in an order-entry application. Any time the data must be displayed, filtered, or ordered in a way that is different from how they are stored, you can use expressions and functions to manipulate the results.

You will find a very rich and versatile collection of functions and operators available to create expressions that manipulate strings and dates and much more. You can use expressions in the SELECT, WHERE, and ORDER BY clauses as well as in other clauses you will learn about in Chapter 7.

Expressions Using Operators

You learned how to use several comparison operators in the WHERE clause in Chapter 3. In this section, you will learn how to use operators to concatenate strings and perform mathematical calculations in T-SQL queries.

Concatenating Strings

The concatenation operator (+) allows you to connect two strings. The syntax is simple: <string or column name> + <string or column name>. Start up SQL Server Management Studio if it is not already running, and connect to your development server. Open a new query window, and type in and execute the code in Listing 4-1.

Listing 4-1. Concatenating Strings

```
--1
SELECT 'ab' + 'c';

--2
SELECT BusinessEntityID, FirstName + ' ' + LastName AS "Full Name"
FROM Person.Person;

--3
SELECT BusinessEntityID, LastName + ', ' + FirstName AS "Full Name"
FROM Person.Person;
```

Figure 4-1 shows the partial results of running Listing 4-1. Query 1 shows that you can concatenate two strings. Queries 2 and 3 demonstrate concatenating the LastName and FirstName columns along with either a space or a comma and space. Notice that you specified the alias, Full Name, to provide a column header for the result of the expressions combining FirstName and LastName. If you did not provide the alias, the column header would be (No column name), as in query 1. In reality, it doesn't have a name at all, so it is very important that you always alias expressions.

	(No column name)
1	abc

	BusinessEntityID	Full Name
1	285	Syed Abbas
2	293	Catherine Abel
3	295	Kim Abercrombie
4	2170	Kim Abercrombie

	BusinessEntityID	Full Name
1	285	Abbas, Syed
2	293	Abel, Catherine
3	295	Abercrombie, K...
4	2170	Abercrombie, K...

Figure 4-1. *The partial results of queries concatenating strings*

Concatenating Strings and *NULL*

In Chapter 3 you learned about the challenges when working with NULL in WHERE clause expressions. When concatenating a string with a NULL, NULL is returned. Listing 4-2 demonstrates this problem. Type the code in Listing 4-2 into a new query window and execute it.

Listing 4-2. Concatenating Strings with NULL Values

```
SELECT BusinessEntityID, FirstName + ' ' + MiddleName +
    ' ' + LastName AS "Full Name"
FROM Person.Person;
```

Figure 4-2 shows the results of Listing 4-2. The query combines the FirstName, MiddleName, and LastName columns into a Full Name column. The MiddleName column is optional; that is, NULL values are allowed. Only the rows where the MiddleName value has been entered show the expected results. The rows where MiddleName is NULL return NULL. You will learn how to fix this problem later in this chapter.

	BusinessEntityID	Full Name
1	285	Syed E Abbas
2	293	Catherine R. Abel
3	295	NULL
4	2170	NULL
5	38	Kim B Abercrombie
6	211	Hazem E Abolrous
7	2357	NULL
8	297	NULL
9	291	NULL
10	299	NULL

Figure 4-2. *The results of concatenating a string with NULL*

CONCAT

SQL Server 2012 introduced another powerful tool for concatenating strings and even nonstring values. The CONCAT function takes any number of values as arguments and automatically concatenates them together. The values can be passed to the CONCAT function as variables, columns or as literal values. The output is always implicitly converted to a string data type. Run the code in Listing 4-3 to see how to use the CONCAT function.

Listing 4-3. CONCAT Examples

```
--1 Simple CONCAT function
SELECT CONCAT ('I ', 'love', ' writing', ' T-SQL') AS RESULT;

--2 Using variable with CONCAT
DECLARE @a VARCHAR(30) = 'My birthday is on '
DECLARE @b DATE = '1980/08/25'
SELECT CONCAT (@a, @b) AS RESULT;

--3 Using CONCAT with table rows
SELECT CONCAT (AddressLine1, PostalCode) AS Address
FROM Person.Address;

--4 Using CONCAT with NULL
SELECT CONCAT ('I',' ','love', ' ', 'using',' ','CONCAT',' ',
    'because',' ','NULL',' ','values',
    ' ','vanish',' ','SEE:',NULL,'!') AS RESULT;
```

Query 1 command simply concatenates four separate string values. Query 2 declares two variables and then concatenates those into a single result. Query 3 uses the CONCAT function in a SELECT clause to concatenate table rows. The final example, query 4, shows that NULL values are ignored when using CONCAT. Figure 4-3 shows the output. I've only showed the partial results for the third example.

	RESULT
1	I love writing T-SQL

	RESULT
1	My birthday is on 1980-08-25

	Address
1	#500-75 O'Connor StreetK4B 1S2
2	#9900 2700 Production WayV5A 4X1
3	00, rue Saint-Lazare59140
4	02, place de Fontenoy91370

	RESULT
1	I love using CONCAT because NULL values vanish SEE:!

Figure 4-3. *Partial results of CONCAT functions*

ISNULL and *COALESCE*

Two functions are available to replace NULL values with another value. The first function, ISNULL, requires two parameters: the value to check and the replacement for NULL values. COALESCE works a bit differently. COALESCE will take any number of parameters and return the first non-NULL value. T-SQL developers often prefer COALESCE over ISNULL because COALESCE meets ANSI (American National Standards Institute) standards, while ISNULL does not. Also, COALESCE is more versatile. Here is the syntax for the two functions:

```
ISNULL(<value>,<replacement>)
COALESCE(<value1>,<value2>,…,<valueN>)
```

Type in and execute the code in Listing 4-4 to learn how to use ISNULL and COALESCE.

Listing 4-4. Using the ISNULL and COALESCE Functions

```
--1
SELECT BusinessEntityID, FirstName + ' ' + ISNULL(MiddleName,'') +
    ' ' + LastName AS "Full Name"
FROM Person.Person;

--2
SELECT BusinessEntityID, FirstName + ISNULL(' ' + MiddleName,'') +
    ' ' + LastName AS "Full Name"
FROM Person.Person;

--3
SELECT BusinessEntityID, FirstName + COALESCE(' ' + MiddleName,'') +
    ' ' + LastName AS "Full Name"
FROM Person.Person;
```

Figure 4-4 shows the partial result of running the code. Query 1 uses the ISNULL function to replace any missing MiddleName values with an empty string in order to build Full Name. Notice in the results that whenever MiddleName is missing, you end up with two spaces between FirstName and LastName. Line 3 in the results of query 1 contains two spaces between Kim and Ambercrombie because a space is added both before and after the ISNULL function. To correct this problem, move the space inside the ISNULL function instead of before it: ISNULL(' ' + MiddleName,''). Concatenating a space (or anything really) with NULL returns NULL. When the MiddleName value is NULL, the space is eliminated and no extra spaces show up in your results. Instead of ISNULL, query 3 contains the COALESCE function. If MiddleName is NULL, the next non-NULL value, the empty string, is returned.

	BusinessEntityID	Full Name
1	285	Syed E Abbas
2	293	Catherine R. Abel
3	295	Kim Abercrombie
4	2170	Kim Abercrombie

	BusinessEntityID	Full Name
1	285	Syed E Abbas
2	293	Catherine R. Abel
3	295	Kim Abercrombie
4	2170	Kim Abercrombie

	BusinessEntityID	Full Name
1	285	Syed E Abbas
2	293	Catherine R. Abel
3	295	Kim Abercrombie
4	2170	Kim Abercrombie

Figure 4-4. *The partial results of using ISNULL and COALESCE when concatenating strings*

Concatenating Other Data Types to Strings

To concatenate nonstring values to strings, the nonstring value must be converted to a string. If the string value can be implicitly converted to a number, the values will be added together instead. Run this statement to see what happens: SELECT 1 + '1';. If the desired result is 11 instead of 2, the numeric value must be explicitly converted to a string using either the CAST or CONVERT function. If you attempt to concatenate a nonnumeric string and a number without converting, you will receive an error message. Run this example to see the error: SELECT 1 + 'a';. This is because integers have higher precedence than strings.

■ **Note**   Instead of using CAST or CONVERT to convert to string data types when concatenating, use the CONCAT function. This function was introduced with SQL Server 2012 and automatically converts other data types to strings.

Use one of the functions, CAST or CONVERT, to convert a number or date value to a string. Here is the syntax:

```
CAST(<value> AS <new data type>)
CONVERT(<new data type>,<value>)
```

Listing 4-5 demonstrates how to use these functions. Type in and execute the code in a query window.

Listing 4-5. Using CAST and CONVERT

```
--1
SELECT CAST(BusinessEntityID AS NVARCHAR) + ': ' + LastName
    + ', ' + FirstName AS ID_Name
FROM Person.Person;

--2
SELECT CONVERT(NVARCHAR(10),BusinessEntityID) + ': ' + LastName
    + ', ' + FirstName AS ID_Name
FROM Person.Person;

--3
SELECT BusinessEntityID, BusinessEntityID + 1 AS "Adds 1",
    CAST(BusinessEntityID AS NVARCHAR(10)) + '1'AS "Appends 1"
FROM Person.Person;
```

Figure 4-5 shows the partial results of running the code. The functions in queries 1 and 2 have very different syntaxes, but they accomplish the same result. They both change the BusinessEntityID values from integers into a string data type (NVARCHAR) so that it can be concatenated to a string. Many programmers prefer CAST over CONVERT because CAST is compliant with the ANSI SQL-99 standard. Query 1 specifies just NVARCHAR as the data type without a size. By default, the maximum length will be 30 characters. If you need to cast to a value more than 30 characters, you must specify a length argument greater than 30. As a best practice, always specify the length. Query 3 demonstrates the difference between converting the numeric value and not converting it. For more information about CONVERT, take a look at the "*CONVERT*" section later in the chapter.

	ID_Name
1	285: Abbas, Syed
2	293: Abel, Catherine
3	295: Abercrombie, Kim
4	2170: Abercrombie, Kim

	ID_Name
1	285: Abbas, Syed
2	293: Abel, Catherine
3	295: Abercrombie, Kim
4	2170: Abercrombie, Kim

	BusinessEntityID	Adds 1	Appends 1
1	16496	16497	164961
2	12506	12507	125061
3	11390	11391	113901
4	10798	10799	107981

Figure 4-5. *The partial results of using CAST and CONVERT*

Developers must often concatenate strings for reports or for loading data from one system to another. Now practice what you have learned about concatenating strings within a T-SQL query by completing Exercise 4-1.

EXERCISE 4-1

Use the AdventureWorks database to complete this exercise. You can find the solutions at the end of the chapter.

1. Write a query that returns data from the Person.Address table in this format AddressLine1 (City PostalCode) from the Person.Address table.

2. Write a query using the Production.Product table displaying the product ID, color, and name columns. If the color column contains a NULL value, replace the color with *No Color*.

3. Modify the query written in question 2 so that the description of the product is returned formatted as Name: Color. Make sure that all rows display a value even if the Color value is missing.

4. Write a query using the Production.Product table displaying a description with the ProductID: Name format. Hint: You will need to use a function to write this query.

5. Explain the difference between the ISNULL and COALESCE functions.

Using Mathematical Operators

You can use several operators to perform simple mathematical operations on numeric values. Use the plus symbol (+) to perform addition, the hyphen (–) to perform subtraction, the asterisk (*) to perform multiplication, and the slash (/) to perform division. One operator that may be new to you is the modulo (%) operator, which returns the remainder when division is performed on the two values. For example, 5 % 2 returns 1 because 1 is the remainder when you divide 5 by 2. One common use for modulo is to determine whether a number is odd or even when the second value in the expression is 2. If the result is 1, then the value is odd; if the result is 0, then the value is even. Listing 4-6 shows how to use some of the mathematical operators. Type in and execute the code to see the results.

Listing 4-6. Using Mathematical Operators

```
--1
SELECT 1 + 1 AS ADDITION, 10.0 / 3 AS DIVISION, 10 / 3 AS [Integer Division], 10 % 3 AS MODULO;

--2
SELECT OrderQty, OrderQty * 10 AS Times10
FROM Sales.SalesOrderDetail;

--3
SELECT OrderQty * UnitPrice * (1.0 - UnitPriceDiscount)
    AS Calculated, LineTotal
FROM Sales.SalesOrderDetail;

--4
SELECT SpecialOfferID,MaxQty,DiscountPct,
    DiscountPct * ISNULL(MaxQty, 1000) AS MaxDiscount
FROM Sales.SpecialOffer;
```

Take a look at the results shown in Figure 4-6. Query 1 shows how to perform calculations on literal values. Note that 10 / 3 does not equal 3.333. Because the two operators in that expression are integers, the result is also an integer. Query 2 shows the result of multiplying the values stored in the OrderQty column by 10.

	ADDITION	DIVISION	Integer DIVISION	MODULO
1	2	3.333333	3	1

	OrderQty	Times10
1	1	10
2	3	30
3	1	10
4	1	10

	Calculated	LineTotal
1	2024.994000	2024.994000
2	6074.982000	6074.982000
3	2024.994000	2024.994000
4	2039.994000	2039.994000

	SpecialOfferID	MaxQty	DiscountPct	MaxDiscount
1	1	NULL	0.00	0.00
2	2	14	0.02	0.28
3	3	24	0.05	1.20
4	4	40	0.10	4.00

Figure 4-6. *The partial results of using mathematical operators*

Query 3 replicates the precalculated LineTotal column by calculating the value by using an expression. The LineTotal column is a "computed column." The actual formula used in the table definition looks a bit more complicated than the one I used since it checks for NULL values. The simplified formula I used requires parentheses to enforce the logic, causing subtraction to be performed before multiplication. Because multiplication has a higher precedence than subtraction, use parentheses to enforce the intended logic. Query 4 shows how to use the ISNULL function to substitute the value 1000 when the MaxQty is NULL before multiplying by the DiscountPct value.

Practice what you have learned about mathematical operators to complete Exercise 4-2.

EXERCISE 4-2

Use the AdventureWorks database to complete this exercise. You can find the solutions at the end of the chapter.

1. Write a query using the Sales.SpecialOffer table. Display the difference between the MinQty and MaxQty columns along with the SpecialOfferID and Description columns.

2. Write a query using the Sales.SpecialOffer table. Multiply the MinQty column by the DiscountPct column. Include the SpecialOfferID and Description columns in the results.

3. Write a query using the Sales.SpecialOffer table that multiplies the MaxQty column by the DiscountPct column. If the MaxQty value is NULL, replace it with the value 10. Include the SpecialOfferID and Description columns in the results.

4. Describe the difference between division and modulo.

When using operators, you must keep the data types of the values in mind. When performing an operation that involves two different data types, the expression will return values for the data type with the highest precedence if possible. What value can be rolled into the other value? For example, an INT can be converted to a BIGINT, but not the other way around. In other words, if a value can be a valid INT, it is also a valid BIGINT. However, many valid BIGINT values are too big to be converted to INT. Therefore, when an operation is performed on a BIGINT and an INT, the result will be a BIGINT.

It is not always possible to convert the lower precedence data type to the higher precedence data type. A character can't always be converted to a numeric value. This is why the expression 1 + 'a' fails. For a list of possible data types in order of precedence, see the article "Data Type Precedence" in SQL Server's help system, Books Online.

Using String Functions

You will find a very rich set of T-SQL functions for manipulating strings. You often have a choice of where a string will be manipulated. If the manipulation will occur on one of the columns in the select-list, it might make sense to utilize the client to do the work if the manipulation is complex, but it is possible to do quite a bit of manipulation with T-SQL. You can use the string functions to clean up data before loading them into a database. This section covers many of the commonly used string functions. You can find many more in Books Online.

RTRIM and LTRIM

The RTRIM and LTRIM functions remove spaces from the right side (RTRIM) or left side (LTRIM) of a string data types, respectively. You may need to use these functions when working with fixed-length data types (CHAR and NCHAR) or to clean up flat-file data before it is loaded from a staging database into a data warehouse. The syntax is simple:

```
RTRIM(<string>)
LTRIM(<string>)
```

Type in and execute the code in Listing 4-7. The first part of the code creates and populates a temporary table. Don't worry about understanding that part of the code at this point.

Listing 4-7. Using the RTRIM and LTRIM Functions

```
--Create the temp table
CREATE TABLE #trimExample (COL1 VARCHAR(10));
GO
--Populate the table
INSERT INTO #trimExample (COL1)
VALUES ('a'),('b '),(' c'),(' d ');

--Select the values using the functions
SELECT COL1, '*' + RTRIM(COL1) + '*' AS "RTRIM",
    '*' + LTRIM(COL1) + '*' AS "LTRIM"
FROM #trimExample;

--Clean up
DROP TABLE #trimExample;
```

Figure 4-7 shows the results of the code. The INSERT statement added four rows to the table with no spaces (a), spaces on the right (b), spaces on the left (c), and spaces on both (d). Inside the SELECT statement, you will see that asterisks surround the values to make it easier to see the spaces in the results. The RTRIM function removed the spaces from the right side; the LTRIM function removed the spaces from the left side. T-SQL doesn't contain a native function that removes the spaces from both sides of the string, but you will learn how to get around this problem in the section "Nesting Functions" later in the chapter.

	COL1	RTRIM	LTRIM
1	a	*a*	*a*
2	b	*b*	*b *
3	c	* c*	*c*
4	d	* d*	*d *

Figure 4-7. *The results of using RTRIM and LTRIM*

LEFT and RIGHT

The LEFT and RIGHT functions return a specified number of characters on the left or right side of a string, respectively. Developers use these functions to parse strings. For example, you may need to retrieve the three-character extension from file path data by using RIGHT. Take a look at the syntax:

```
LEFT(<string>,<number of characters>)
RIGHT(<string>,<number of characters>)
```

Listing 4-8 demonstrates how to use these functions. Type in and execute the code.

Listing 4-8. Using the LEFT and RIGHT Functions

```
SELECT LastName,LEFT(LastName,5) AS "LEFT",
    RIGHT(LastName,4) AS "RIGHT"
FROM Person.Person
WHERE BusinessEntityID IN (293,295,211,297,299,3057,15027);
```

Figure 4-8 shows the results. Notice that even if the value contains fewer characters than the number specified in the second parameter, the function still works to return as many characters as possible.

	LastName	LEFT	RIGHT
1	Abolrous	Abolr	rous
2	Abel	Abel	Abel
3	Abercrombie	Aberc	mbie
4	Acevedo	Aceve	vedo
5	Ackerman	Acker	rman
6	Alexander	Alexa	nder
7	Bell	Bell	Bell

Figure 4-8. *The results of using LEFT and RIGHT*

LEN and DATALENGTH

Use LEN to return the number of characters in a string. Developers sometimes use another function, DATALENGTH, incorrectly in place of LEN. DATALENGTH returns the number of bytes in a string. DATALENGTH returns the same value as LEN when the string is a CHAR or VARCHAR data type, which takes one byte per character. The problem occurs when using DATALENGTH on NCHAR or NVARCHAR data types, which take two bytes per character. In this case, the DATALENGTH value is two times the LEN value. This is not incorrect; the two functions measure different things. The syntax is very simple:

```
LEN(<string>)
DATALENGTH(<string>)
```

Type in and execute the code in Listing 4-9 to learn how to use LEN and DATALENGTH.

Listing 4-9. Using the LEN and DATALENGTH Functions

```
SELECT LastName,LEN(LastName) AS "Length",
    DATALENGTH(LastName) AS "Internal Data Length"
FROM Person.Person
WHERE BusinessEntityID IN (293,295,211,297,299,3057,15027);
```

Figure 4-9 shows the results. The Length column displays a count of the characters, while the Internal Data Length column displays the number of bytes.

	LastName	Length	Internal Data Length
1	Abolrous	8	16
2	Abel	4	8
3	Abercrombie	11	22
4	Acevedo	7	14
5	Ackerman	8	16
6	Alexander	9	18
7	Bell	4	8

Figure 4-9. *The results of using LEN and DATALENGTH*

CHARINDEX

Use CHARINDEX to find the numeric starting position of a search string inside another string. By checking to see whether the value returned by CHARINDEX is greater than zero, you can use the function to just determine whether the search string exists inside the second value. Developers often use CHARINDEX to locate a particular character, such as the at symbol (@) in an e-mail address column, along with other functions when parsing strings. You will learn more about this in the "Nesting Functions" section later in the chapter. The CHARINDEX function requires two parameters: the search string and the string to be searched. An optional parameter, the start location, instructs the function to ignore a given number of characters at the beginning of the string to be searched. The following is the syntax; remember that the third parameter is optional (square brackets surround optional parameters in the syntax):

```
CHARINDEX(<search string>,<target string>[,<start location>])
```

Listing 4-10 demonstrates how to use CHARINDEX. Type in and execute the code to learn how to use this function.

Listing 4-10. Using the CHARINDEX Function

```
SELECT LastName, CHARINDEX('e',LastName) AS "Find e",
    CHARINDEX('e',LastName,4) AS "Skip 3 Characters",
    CHARINDEX('be',LastName) AS "Find be",
    CHARINDEX('Be',LastName) AS "Find Be"
FROM Person.Person
WHERE BusinessEntityID IN (293,295,211,297,299,3057,15027);
```

Figure 4-10 shows the results. The Find e column in the results displays the first location of the letter *e* in the LastName value. The Skip 3 Characters column displays the first location of the letter *e* when the first three characters of the LastName value are ignored. Finally, the Find be column demonstrates that you can use the function with search strings that are more than one character in length. There are many versions of AdventureWorks available and some of those are case sensitive. If you are using a case-sensitive version, your results will be slightly different. You'll see different values returned when searching for *be* and *Be*.

	LastName	Find e	Skip 3 Characters	Find be	Find Be
1	Abolrous	0	0	0	0
2	Abel	3	0	2	2
3	Abercrombie	3	11	2	2
4	Acevedo	3	5	0	0
5	Ackerman	4	4	0	0
6	Alexander	3	8	0	0
7	Bell	2	0	1	1

Figure 4-10. *The results of using CHARINDEX*

SUBSTRING

Use SUBSTRING to return a portion of a string starting at a given position and for a specified number of characters. In some ways, it is just a more powerful LEFT function. For example, an order-entry application may assign a customer ID based on the first seven letters of the customer's last name plus digits 4 to 9 of the phone number. The SUBSTRING function requires three parameters: the string, a starting location, and the number of characters to retrieve. If the number of characters to retrieve is greater than the length of the string, the function will return as many characters as possible. If the start location is past the end of the string, then an empty string, not a NULL, will be returned. Here is the syntax of SUBSTRING:

```
SUBSTRING(<string>,<start location>,<length>)
```

Type in and execute the code in Listing 4-11 to learn how to use SUBSTRING.

Listing 4-11. Using the SUBSTRING Function

```
SELECT LastName, SUBSTRING(LastName,1,4) AS "First 4",
    SUBSTRING(LastName,5,50) AS "Characters 5 and later"
FROM Person.Person
WHERE BusinessEntityID IN (293,295,211,297,299,3057,15027);
```

Notice in the results shown in Figure 4-11 that if the starting point is located after the available characters (Abel and Bell), an empty string is returned. Otherwise, in this example, the FirstName column is divided into two strings.

	LastName	First 4	Characters 5 and later
1	Abolrous	Abol	rous
2	Abel	Abel	
3	Abercrombie	Aber	crombie
4	Acevedo	Acev	edo
5	Ackerman	Acke	rman
6	Alexander	Alex	ander
7	Bell	Bell	

Figure 4-11. *The results of using SUBSTRING*

CHOOSE

CHOOSE is a function new with SQL Server 2012 that allows you to select a value in an array based on an index. The CHOOSE function requires an index value and list of values for the array. Here is the basic syntax for the CHOOSE function:

```
CHOOSE ( index, val_1, val_2 [, val_n ] )
```

The index simply points to the position in the array that you want to return. Listing 4-12 shows a basic example.

Listing 4-12. Using the CHOOSE Function

```
SELECT CHOOSE (4, 'a', 'b', 'c', 'd', 'e', 'f', 'g', 'h', 'i');
```

Figure 4-12 shows the results of running the CHOOSE function. Keep in mind that the results take the highest data type precedence. This means if there is an integer in the list, the CHOOSE function will try to convert any results to an integer. If the value is a string, the CHOOSE command will throw an error. You will need to convert any integer values in the array to VARCHAR to avoid this error. If the position doesn't exist, a NULL value will be returned.

	(No column name)
1	d

Figure 4-12. *Result from the CHOOSE Function*

REVERSE

REVERSE returns a string in reverse order. I often use it along with the CHARINDEX and RIGHT functions to find a file name from the file's path. I use CHARINDEX on the reversed string to find the last backslash in the path, which then tells me how many characters, minus 1, on the right side of the string I need to grab. The same method can be used to parse an e-mail address. To see how to do this, see the example in the "Nesting Functions" later in the chapter. Type in and execute this code to learn how to use REVERSE:

```
SELECT REVERSE('!dlroW ,olleH')
```

UPPER and LOWER

Use UPPER and LOWER to change a string to either uppercase or lowercase. You may need to display all uppercase data in a report, for example. The syntax is very simple:

```
UPPER(<string>)
LOWER(<string>)
```

Type in and execute the code in Listing 4-13 to learn about using UPPER and LOWER.

Listing 4-13. Using the UPPER and LOWER Functions

```
SELECT LastName, UPPER(LastName) AS "UPPER",
    LOWER(LastName) AS "LOWER"
FROM Person.Person
WHERE BusinessEntityID IN (293,295,211,297,299,3057,15027);
```

Take a look at the results in Figure 4-13. All LastName values appear in uppercase in the UPPER column, while they appear in lowercase in the LOWER column.

	LastName	UPPER	LOWER
1	Abolrous	ABOLROUS	abolrous
2	Abel	ABEL	abel
3	Abercrombie	ABERCROMBIE	abercrombie
4	Acevedo	ACEVEDO	acevedo
5	Ackerman	ACKERMAN	ackerman
6	Alexander	ALEXANDER	alexander
7	Bell	BELL	bell

Figure 4-13. *The partial results of using UPPER and LOWER*

■ **Note** You may think that you will use UPPER or LOWER often in the WHERE clause to make sure that the case of the value does not affect the results, but usually you don't need to do this. By default, searching in T-SQL is case insensitive. The collation of the column determines whether the search will be case sensitive. This is defined at the server, but you can specify a different collation of the database, table, or column. See "Working with Collations" in Books Online for more information.

REPLACE

Use REPLACE to substitute one string value inside another string value. REPLACE has three required parameters, but it is very easy to use. Use REPLACE to clean up data; for example, you may need to replace slashes (/) in a phone number column with hyphens (-) for a report. Here is the syntax:

```
REPLACE(<string value>,<string to replace>,<replacement>)
```

Type in and execute the code in Listing 4-14 to learn how to use REPLACE.

Listing 4-14. Using the REPLACE Function

```
--1
SELECT LastName, REPLACE(LastName,'A','Z') AS "Replace A",
    REPLACE(LastName,'A','ZZ') AS "Replace with 2 characters",
    REPLACE(LastName,'ab','') AS "Remove string"
FROM Person.Person
WHERE BusinessEntityID IN (293,295,211,297,299,3057,15027);

--2
SELECT BusinessEntityID,LastName,MiddleName,
    REPLACE(LastName,'a',MiddleName) AS "Replace with MiddleName",
    REPLACE(LastName,MiddleName,'a') AS "Replace MiddleName"
FROM Person.Person
WHERE BusinessEntityID IN (285,293,10314);
```

Notice in the results shown in Figure 4-14 that the REPLACE function replaces every instance of the string to be replaced. It doesn't matter if the strings in the second and third parameter are not the same length, as shown in the column Replace with 2 characters. The Remove string column shows a convenient way to remove a character or characters from a string by replacing them with an empty string represented by two single quotes. Because the last name *Bell* doesn't contain any of the values to be replaced, the value doesn't change.

	LastName	Replace A	Replace with 2 characters	Remove string
1	Abolrous	Zbolrous	ZZbolrous	olrous
2	Abel	Zbel	ZZbel	el
3	Abercrombie	Zbercrombie	ZZbercrombie	ercrombie
4	Acevedo	Zcevedo	ZZcevedo	Acevedo
5	Ackerman	ZckermZn	ZZckermZZn	Ackerman
6	Alexander	ZlexZnder	ZZlexZZnder	Alexander
7	Bell	Bell	Bell	Bell

	BusinessEntityID	LastName	MiddleName	Replace with MiddleName	Replace MiddleName
1	285	Abbas	E	EbbEs	Abbas
2	293	Abel	R.	R.bel	Abel
3	10314	Adams	M	MdMms	Adaas

Figure 4-14. *The partial results of using REPLACE*

Query 2 demonstrates that the second and third parameters don't have to be literal values by using the MiddleName column either as the string to replace in the Replace MiddleName column or as the replacement in the Replace with MiddleName column.

Nesting Functions

The previous sections showed how to use one function at a time to manipulate strings. If the results of one expression must be used as a parameter of another function call, you can nest functions. For example, you can nest the LTRIM and RTRIM functions to remove the spaces from the beginning and ending of a string like this: LTRIM(RTRIM(' test ')). Keep in mind when writing nested functions that you work from the inside out. The inner-most function is executed first and the outer functions execute against the results. Let's look at some examples. Type in and execute the example shown in Listing 4-15 to display the domains in a list of e-mail addresses and the file name from a list of file paths.

Listing 4-15. Nesting Functions

```
--1
SELECT EmailAddress,
    SUBSTRING(EmailAddress,CHARINDEX('@',EmailAddress) + 1,50) AS DOMAIN
FROM Production.ProductReview;

--2
SELECT physical_name,
    RIGHT(physical_name,CHARINDEX('\',REVERSE(physical_name))-1) AS FileName
FROM sys.database_files;
```

Figure 4-15 shows the results of running this code. Query 1 first uses the CHARINDEX function to find the location of the at symbol (@). The results of that expression are used a parameter to the outer SUBSTRING function. To display the characters after the @ symbol, add 1 to the position of the @ symbol.

	EmailAddress	DOMAIN
1	john@fourthcoffee.com	fourthcoffee.com
2	david@graphicdesigninstitute.com	graphicdesigninstitute.com
3	jill@margiestravel.com	margiestravel.com
4	laura@treyresearch.net	treyresearch.net

	physical_name	FileName
1	C:\Program Files\Microsoft SQL Server\MSSQL11.MSS...	AdventureWorks2012_Data.mdf
2	C:\Program Files\Microsoft SQL Server\MSSQL11.MSS...	AdventureWorks2012_log.ldf

Figure 4-15. The results of using nested functions

Query 2 finds the file name in a list of file paths. The query performs a SELECT command from the system view sys.database_files. After the SELECT command the inner REVERSE function reverses the string value. Then the outer CHARINDEX finds the location of the backslash (\) symbol and subtracts one character to remove it from the results. By using that result as the second parameter of the RIGHT function, the query returns the file name. When writing a query like this, take it a step at a time and work from the inside out. You may have to experiment a bit to get it right.

This section covered a sample of the many functions available to manipulate strings in T-SQL. Complete Exercise 4-3 to practice using these functions.

EXERCISE 4-3

Use the AdventureWorks database to complete this exercise. If you need help, refer to the discussion of the functions to help you figure out which ones to use. You can find the solutions to these questions at the end of the chapter.

1. Write a query that displays the first 10 characters of the AddressLine1 column in the Person.Address table.

2. Write a query that displays characters 10 to 15 of the AddressLine1 column in the Person.Address table.

3. Write a query displaying the first and last names from the Person.Person table all in uppercase.

4. The ProductNumber in the Production.Product table contains a hyphen (-). Write a query that uses the SUBSTRING function and the CHARINDEX function to display the characters in the product number following the hyphen. Note: There is also a second hyphen in many of the rows; ignore the second hyphen for this question. Hint: Try writing this statement in two steps, the first using the CHARINDEX function and the second adding the SUBSTRING function.

Using Date and Time Functions

Just as T-SQL features a rich set of functions for working with string data, it also boasts an impressive list of functions for working with date and time data types. In this section, you'll take a look at some of the most commonly used functions for date and time data.

GETDATE and SYSDATETIME

Use GETDATE or SYSDATETIME to return the current date and time of the server. The difference is that SYSDATETIME returns seven decimal places after the second, the datetime2(7) data type, while GETDATE returns only three places, the DATETIME data type.

GETDATE and SYSDATETIME are *nondeterministic* functions. This means that they return different values each time they are called. Most of the functions in this chapter are *deterministic*, which means that a function always returns the same value when called with the same parameters and database settings. For example, the code CHARINDEX('B','abcd') will always return 2 if the collation of the database is case insensitive. In a case-sensitive database, the expression will return 0.

Run this code several times to see how these functions work:

```
SELECT GETDATE(), SYSDATETIME();
```

DATEADD

Use DATEADD to add a number of time units to a date. The function requires three parameters: the date part, the number, and a date. T-SQL doesn't have a DATESUBTRACT function, but you can use a negative number to accomplish the same thing. You might use DATEADD to calculate an expiration date or a date that a payment is due, for example. Table 4-1 from Books Online lists the possible values for the date part parameter in the DATEADD function and other date functions. Here is the syntax for DATEADD:

```
DATEADD(<date part>,<number>,<date>)
```

Table 4-1. *The Values for the Date Part Parameter*

Date Part	Abbreviation
Year	yy, yyyy
Quarter	qq, q
Month	mm, m
Dayofyear	dy, y
Day	dd, d
Week	wk, ww
Weekday	Dw
Hour	Hh
Minute	mi, n
Second	ss, s
Millisecond	Ms
Microsecond	Mcs
Nanosecond	Ns

Type in and execute the code in Listing 4-16 to learn how to use the DATEADD function.

Listing 4-16. Using the DATEADD Function

```
--1
SELECT OrderDate, DATEADD(year,1,OrderDate) AS OneMoreYear,
    DATEADD(month,1,OrderDate) AS OneMoreMonth,
    DATEADD(day,-1,OrderDate) AS OneLessDay
FROM Sales.SalesOrderHeader
WHERE SalesOrderID in (43659,43714,60621);

--2
SELECT DATEADD(month,1,'1/29/2009') AS FebDate;
```

Figure 4-16 shows the results of Listing 4-16. In query 1, the DATEADD function adds exactly the time unit specified in each expression to the OrderDate column from the Sales.SalesOrderHeader table. Notice in the results of query 2 that because there is no 29th day of February 2009, adding one month to January 29, 2009, returns February 28, the last possible day in February that year.

	OrderDate	OneMoreYear	OneMoreMonth	OneLessDay
1	2005-07-01 00:00:00.000	2006-07-01 00:00:00.000	2005-08-01 00:00:00.000	2005-06-30 00:00:00.000
2	2005-07-05 00:00:00.000	2006-07-05 00:00:00.000	2005-08-05 00:00:00.000	2005-07-04 00:00:00.000
3	2007-12-23 00:00:00.000	2008-12-23 00:00:00.000	2008-01-23 00:00:00.000	2007-12-22 00:00:00.000

	FebDate
1	2009-02-28 00:00:00.000

Figure 4-16. *The results of using the DATEADD function*

DATEDIFF

The DATEDIFF function allows you to find the difference between two dates. The function requires three parameters: the date part and the two dates. The DATEDIFF function might be used to calculate how many days have passed since unshipped orders were taken, for example. Here is the syntax:

```
DATEDIFF(<datepart>,<early date>,<later date>)
```

See Table 4-1 for the list of possible date parts. Listing 4-17 demonstrates how to use DATEDIFF. Be sure to type in and execute the code.

Listing 4-17. Using the DATEDIFF Function

```
--1
SELECT OrderDate, GETDATE() CurrentDateTime,
    DATEDIFF(year,OrderDate,GETDATE()) AS YearDiff,
    DATEDIFF(month,OrderDate,GETDATE()) AS MonthDiff,
    DATEDIFF(d,OrderDate,GETDATE()) AS DayDiff
FROM Sales.SalesOrderHeader
WHERE SalesOrderID in (43659,43714,60621);

--2
SELECT DATEDIFF(year,'12/31/2008','1/1/2009') AS YearDiff,
    DATEDIFF(month,'12/31/2008','1/1/2009') AS MonthDiff,
    DATEDIFF(d,'12/31/2008','1/1/2009') AS DayDiff;
```

Figure 4-17 shows the results. Your results from query 1 will be different from mine because the query uses GETDATE(), a nondeterministic function, instead of hard-coded dates or dates from a table. Remember that you can use the date part name or abbreviate it. The examples abbreviate "day" with "d." Even though query 2 compares the difference between two dates that are just one day apart, the differences in years and months are both 1. The DATEDIFF rounds up the result to the nearest integer and doesn't display decimal results.

	OrderDate	CurrentDateTime	YearDiff	MonthDiff	DayDiff
1	2005-07-01 00:00:00.000	2014-02-20 21:01:04.270	9	103	3156
2	2005-07-05 00:00:00.000	2014-02-20 21:01:04.270	9	103	3152
3	2007-12-23 00:00:00.000	2014-02-20 21:01:04.270	7	74	2251

	YearDiff	MonthDiff	DayDiff
1	1	1	1

Figure 4-17. *The results of using DATEDIFF*

DATENAME and DATEPART

The DATENAME and DATEPART functions return the part of the date specified. Developers use the DATENAME and DATEPART functions to display just the year or month on reports, for example. DATEPART always returns an integer value. DATENAME returns a character string, the actual name when the date part is the month or the day of the week. Again, you can find the possible date parts in Table 4-1. The syntax for the two functions is similar:

```
DATENAME(<datepart>,<date>)
DATEPART(<datepart>,<date>)
```

Type in and execute the code in Listing 4-18 to learn how to use DATENAME and DATEPART.

Listing 4-18. Using the DATENAME and DATEPART Functions

```
--1
SELECT OrderDate, DATEPART(year,OrderDate) AS OrderYear,
    DATEPART(month,OrderDate) AS OrderMonth,
    DATEPART(day,OrderDate) AS OrderDay,
    DATEPART(weekday,OrderDate) AS OrderWeekDay
FROM Sales.SalesOrderHeader
WHERE SalesOrderID in (43659,43714,60621);

--2
SELECT OrderDate, DATENAME(year,OrderDate) AS OrderYear,
    DATENAME(month,OrderDate) AS OrderMonth,
    DATENAME(day,OrderDate) AS OrderDay,
    DATENAME(weekday,OrderDate) AS OrderWeekDay
FROM Sales.SalesOrderHeader
WHERE SalesOrderID in (43659,43714,60621);
```

Figure 4-18 displays the results. You will see that the results are the same except for spelling out the month and weekday in query 2. One other thing to keep in mind is that the value returned from DATEPART is always an integer, while the value returned from DATENAME is always a string, even when the expression returns a number.

	OrderDate	OrderYear	OrderMonth	OrderDay	OrderWeekDay
1	2005-07-01 00:00:00.000	2005	7	1	6
2	2005-07-05 00:00:00.000	2005	7	5	3
3	2007-12-23 00:00:00.000	2007	12	23	1

	OrderDate	OrderYear	OrderMonth	OrderDay	OrderWeekDay
1	2005-07-01 00:00:00.000	2005	July	1	Friday
2	2005-07-05 00:00:00.000	2005	July	5	Tuesday
3	2007-12-23 00:00:00.000	2007	December	23	Sunday

Figure 4-18. *Results of using DATENAME and DATEPART*

DAY, MONTH, and YEAR

The DAY, MONTH, and YEAR functions work just like DATEPART. These functions are just alternate ways to get the day, month, or year from a date. Here is the syntax:

```
DAY(<date>)
MONTH(<date>)
YEAR(<date>)
```

Type in and execute the code in Listing 4-19 to see that this is just another way to get the same results as using the DATEPART function.

Listing 4-19. Using the DAY, MONTH, and YEAR Functions

```
SELECT OrderDate, YEAR(OrderDate) AS OrderYear,
    MONTH(OrderDate) AS OrderMonth,
    DAY(OrderDate) AS OrderDay
FROM Sales.SalesOrderHeader
WHERE SalesOrderID in (43659,43714,60621);
```

Figure 4-19 displays the results of the code from Listing 4-19. If you compare the results of query 1 from Listing 4-18 to that when the DATEPART function was used, you will see that they are the same.

	OrderDate	OrderYear	OrderMonth	OrderDay
1	2005-07-01 00:00:00.000	2005	7	1
2	2005-07-05 00:00:00.000	2005	7	5
3	2007-12-23 00:00:00.000	2007	12	23

Figure 4-19. *The result of using YEAR, MONTH, and DAY*

CONVERT

You learned about CONVERT earlier in the chapter when I talked about concatenating strings. To append a number or a date to a string, the number or date must first be cast to a string. The CONVERT function has an optional parameter called style that can be used to format a date or number.

I have frequently seen code that used the DATEPART function to break a date into its parts and then cast the parts into strings and concatenate them back together to format the date. It is so much easier just to use CONVERT to accomplish the same thing! Here is the syntax:

```
CONVERT(<data type, usually varchar>,<date>,<style>)
```

Type in and execute the code in Listing 4-20 to compare both methods of formatting dates. Take a look at the SQL Server Books Online article "CAST and CONVERT" for a list of all the possible formats.

Listing 4-20. Using CONVERT to Format a Date/Time Value

```
--1 The hard way!
SELECT CAST(DATEPART(YYYY,GETDATE()) AS VARCHAR) + '/' +
    CAST(DATEPART(MM,GETDATE()) AS VARCHAR) +
    '/' + CAST(DATEPART(DD,GETDATE()) AS VARCHAR) AS DateCast;

--2 The easy way!
SELECT CONVERT(VARCHAR,GETDATE(),111) AS DateConvert;

--3
SELECT CONVERT(VARCHAR,OrderDate,1) AS "1",
    CONVERT(VARCHAR,OrderDate,101) AS "101",
    CONVERT(VARCHAR,OrderDate,2) AS "2",
    CONVERT(VARCHAR,OrderDate,102) AS "102"
FROM Sales.SalesOrderHeader
WHERE SalesOrderID in (43659,43714,60621);
```

Figure 4-20 shows the results of Listing 4-20. Notice in query 1 that you not only had to use DATEPART three times, but you also had to cast each result to a VARCHAR in order to concatenate the pieces back together. Query 2 shows the easy way to accomplish the same thing. This method is often used to remove the time from a DATETIME data type. Query 3 demonstrates four different formats. Notice that the three-digit formats always produce four-digit years.

	DateCast
1	2014/2/20

	DateConvert
1	2014/02/20

	1	101	2	102
1	07/01/05	07/01/2005	05.07.01	2005.07.01
2	07/05/05	07/05/2005	05.07.05	2005.07.05
3	12/23/07	12/23/2007	07.12.23	2007.12.23

Figure 4-20. *The results of formatting dates*

FORMAT

SQL Server 2012 introduced the FORMAT function. The primary purpose is to simplify the conversion of date/time values as string values. Another purpose of the format function is to convert date/time values to their cultural equivalencies. This function is easy to use and is similar to other programming languages. If performance is important, however, you will want to stick with using the CONVERT function as covered earlier in the chapter. Here is the syntax:

```
FORMAT(value, format [, culture ])
```

The FORMAT function greatly simplifies how date/time values are converted, and it should be used for date/time values instead of the CAST or CONVERT functions. Listing 4-21 shows some examples.

Listing 4-21. FORMAT Function Examples

```
DECLARE @d DATETIME = GETDATE();

SELECT FORMAT( @d, 'dd', 'en-US' ) AS Result;
SELECT FORMAT( @d, 'yyyy-M-d') AS Result;
SELECT FORMAT( @d, 'MM/dd/yyyy', 'en-US' ) AS Result;
```

Figure 4-21 shows the results. Keep in mind the letters for each part of the date are case sensitive. For example, if you switch mm for MM you will get back minutes instead of months.

	Result
1	02

	Result
1	2014-3-2

	Result
1	03/02/2014

Figure 4-21. *FORMAT function results*

DATEFROMPARTS

SQL Server 2012 also introduced a simple method to derive a date, time, or date and time from a list of values. The primary function is called DATEFROMPARTS but there is also a version of the function for each date or time data type. Listing 4-22 shows some examples.

Listing 4-22. DATEFROMPARTS Examples

```
SELECT DATEFROMPARTS(2012, 3, 10) AS RESULT;
SELECT TIMEFROMPARTS(12, 10, 32, 0, 0) AS RESULT;
SELECT DATETIME2FROMPARTS (2012, 3, 10, 12, 10, 32, 0, 0) AS RESULT;
```

Figure 4-22 shows the results from each function. The first function returns only the date. The TIMEFROMPARTS function returns a time. Finally, the DATETIME2FROMPARTS returns both a date and a time. If a value is out of the range of either a date or time (for example, if you were to type 13 for the month value), the function will throw an error.

	RESULT
1	2012-03-10

	RESULT
1	12:10:32

	RESULT
1	2012-03-10 12:10:32

Figure 4-22. *Results from DATEFROMTIME functions*

EOMONTH

One of the most useful functions introduced with SQL Server 2012 is the EOMONTH function. It returns the date of the last day of the supplied month argument. You can also supply an offset to return the end of the month for another month. Here is an example that you can run to see how EOMONTH works:

```
SELECT EOMONTH(GETDATE()) AS [End of this month],
    EOMONTH(GETDATE(),1) AS [End of next month],
    EOMONTH('2009-01-01') AS [Another month];
```

This section covered a sample of the functions available for manipulating dates. Practice what you have learned by completing Exercise 4-4.

EXERCISE 4-4

Use the AdventureWorks database to complete this exercise. You can find the solutions to the questions at the end of the chapter.

1. Write a query that calculates the number of days between the date an order was placed and the date that it was shipped using the Sales.SalesOrderHeader table. Include the SalesOrderID, OrderDate, and ShipDate columns.

2. Write a query that displays only the date, not the time, for the order date and ship date in the Sales.SalesOrderHeader table.

3. Write a query that adds six months to each order date in the Sales.SalesOrderHeader table. Include the SalesOrderID and OrderDate columns.

4. Write a query that displays the year of each order date and the numeric month of each order date in separate columns in the results. Include the SalesOrderID and OrderDate columns.

5. Change the query written in question 4 to display the month name instead.

Using Mathematical Functions

You can use several mathematical functions on numeric values. These include trigonometric functions such as SIN and TAN and logarithmic functions that are not used frequently in business applications. This section discusses some of the more commonly used mathematical functions.

ABS

The ABS function returns the absolute value of the number—the distance between the number and zero. Type in and execute this code to see how to use ABS:

```
SELECT ABS(2) AS "2", ABS(-2) AS "-2"
```

POWER

The POWER function returns the power of one number to another number. The syntax is simple:

```
POWER(<number>,<power>)
```

There may not be many uses for POWER in business applications, but you may use it in scientific or academic applications. Type in and execute the code in Listing 4-23.

Listing 4-23. Using the POWER Function

```
SELECT POWER(10,1) AS "Ten to the First",
    POWER(10,2) AS "Ten to the Second",
    POWER(10,3) AS "Ten to the Third";
```

Figure 4-23 displays the results. The POWER function returns a FLOAT value. Caution must be taken, however, with this function. The results will increase in size very quickly and can cause an overflow error. Try finding the value of 10 to the 10th power to see what can happen.

	Ten to the First	Ten to the Second	Ten to the Third
1	10	100	1000

Figure 4-23. *The results of using the POWER function*

SQUARE and *SQRT*

The SQUARE function returns the square of a number, or the number multiplied to itself. The SQRT function returns the opposite, the square root of a number. Type in and execute the code in Listing 4-24 to see how to use these functions.

Listing 4-24. Using the SQUARE and SQRT Functions

```
SELECT SQUARE(10) AS "Square of 10",
    SQRT(10) AS "Square Root of 10",
    SQRT(SQUARE(10)) AS "The Square Root of the Square of 10";
```

Figure 4-24 shows the results. Notice that the third expression in the query is a nested function that squares 10 and then takes the square root of that result.

	Square of 10	Square Root of 10	The Square Root of the Square of 10
1	100	3.16227766016838	10

Figure 4-24. *The results of using SQUARE and SQRT functions*

ROUND

The ROUND function allows you to round a number to a given precision. The ROUND function is used frequently to display only the number of decimal places required in the report or application. The ROUND function requires two parameters, the number and the length, which can be either positive or negative. It also has an optional third parameter that causes the function to just truncate instead of rounding if a nonzero value is supplied. Here is the syntax:

```
ROUND(<number>,<length>[,<function>])
```

Type in and execute the code in Listing 4-25 to learn how to use ROUND.

Listing 4-25. Using the ROUND Function

```
SELECT ROUND(1234.1294,2) AS "2 places on the right",
    ROUND(1234.1294,-2) AS "2 places on the left",
    ROUND(1234.1294,2,1) AS "Truncate 2",
    ROUND(1234.1294,-2,1) AS "Truncate -2";
```

You can view the results in Figure 4-25. When the expression contains a negative number as the second parameter, the function rounds on the left side of the decimal point. Notice the difference when 1 is used as the third parameter, causing the function to truncate instead of rounding. When rounding 1234.1294, the expression returns 1234.1300. When truncating 1234.1294, the expression returns 1234.1200. It doesn't round the value; it just changes the specified digits to zero.

	2 places on the right	2 places on the left	Truncate 2	Truncate -2
1	1234.1300	1200.0000	1234.1200	1200.0000

Figure 4-25. *The results of using the ROUND function*

RAND

RAND returns a float value between 0 and 1. RAND can be used to generate a random value. This might be used to generate data for testing an application, for example. The RAND function takes one optional integer parameter, @seed. When the RAND expression contains the seed value, the function returns the same value each time. If the expression doesn't contain a seed value, SQL Server randomly assigns a seed, effectively providing a random number. Type in and execute the code in Listing 4-26 to generate a random number.

Listing 4-26. Using the RAND Function

```
SELECT CAST(RAND() * 100 AS INT) + 1 AS "1 to 100",
    CAST(RAND()* 1000 AS INT) + 900 AS "900 to 1900",
    CAST(RAND() * 5 AS INT)+ 1 AS "1 to 5";
```

Because the function returns a float value, multiply by the size of the range and add the lower limit (see Figure 4-26). The first expression returns random numbers between 1 and 100. The second expression returns random numbers between 900 and 1900. The third expression returns random values between 1 and 5.

	1 to 100	900 to 1900	1 to 5
1	5	1730	2

Figure 4-26. *The results of generating random numbers with the RAND function*

If you supply a seed value to one of the calls to RAND within a batch of statements, that seed affects the other calls. The value is not the same, but the values are predictable. Run this statement several times to see what happens when a seed value is used:

```
SELECT RAND(3),RAND(),RAND();
```

If you leave out the seed, you will see different results each time. Another interesting thing is that, even though you see different values in each column, you will see the same values in each row. Run this statement multiple times to see what happens:

```
SELECT RAND(),RAND(),RAND(),RAND()
FROM sys.objects;
```

Just like strings and dates, you will find several functions that manipulate numbers. Practice using these functions by completing Exercise 4-5.

EXERCISE 4-5

Use the AdventureWorks database to complete this exercise. You can find the solutions to the questions at the end of the chapter.

1. Write a query using the Sales.SalesOrderHeader table that displays the `SubTotal` rounded to two decimal places. Include the SalesOrderID column in the results.

2. Modify the query from question 1 so that the SubTotal is rounded to the nearest dollar but still displays two zeros to the right of the decimal place.

3. Write a query that calculates the square root of the SalesOrderID value from the Sales.SalesOrderHeader table.

4. Write a statement that generates a random number between 1 and 10 each time it is run.

Logical Functions and Expressions

T-SQL contains a number of functions and the CASE expression that allow you to add conditional expressions to a query. You can return a value that depends on another value or the results of an expression. These techniques are similar to using IF...THEN, CASE or SWITCH in other programming languages.

The *CASE* Expression

Use the CASE expression to evaluate a list of expressions and return the first one that evaluates to true. For example, a report may need to display the season of the year based on one of the date columns in the table. CASE is similar to Select Case or Switch used in other programming languages, but it is used inside the statement.

There are two ways to write a CASE expression: simple or searched. The following sections will explain the differences and how to use them.

Simple CASE

To write the simple CASE expression, come up with an expression that you want to evaluate, often a column name, and a list of possible values. Here is the syntax:

```
CASE <test expression>
    WHEN <comparison expression1> THEN <return value1>
    WHEN <comparison expression2> THEN <return value2>
    [ELSE <value3>] END
```

Type in and execute the code in Listing 4-27 to learn how to use the simple version of CASE.

Listing 4-27. Using Simple CASE

```
SELECT Title,
    CASE Title
    WHEN 'Mr.' THEN 'Male'
    WHEN 'Ms.' THEN 'Female'
    WHEN 'Mrs.' THEN 'Female'
    WHEN 'Miss' THEN 'Female'
    ELSE 'Unknown' END AS Gender
FROM Person.Person
WHERE BusinessEntityID IN (1,5,6,357,358,11621,423);
```

Figure 4-27 shows the results. Even though the CASE expression took up a lot of room in the query, it is producing only one column in the results. For each row returned, the expression evaluates the Title column to see whether it matches any of the possibilities listed and returns the appropriate value. If the value from Title doesn't match or is NULL, then whatever is in the ELSE part of the expression is returned. If no ELSE exists, the expression returns NULL.

	Title	Gender
1	NULL	Unknown
2	Ms.	Female
3	Mr.	Male
4	Ms.	Female
5	Sr.	Unknown
6	Mrs.	Female

Figure 4-27. *The results of using simple CASE*

Searched CASE

Developers often use the searched CASE syntax when the expression is too complicated for the simple CASE syntax. For example, you might want to compare the value from a column to several values in an IN list or use greater-than or less-than operators. The CASE expression returns the first expression that returns true. This is the syntax for the searched CASE:

```
CASE WHEN <test expression1> THEN <value1>
[WHEN <test expression2> THEN <value2>]
[ELSE <value3>] END
```

Type in and execute the code in Listing 4-28 to learn how to use this more flexible method of CASE.

Listing 4-28. Using Searched CASE

```
SELECT Title,
    CASE WHEN Title IN ('Ms.','Mrs.','Miss') THEN 'Female'
    WHEN Title = 'Mr.' THEN 'Male'
    ELSE 'Unknown' END AS Gender
FROM Person.Person
WHERE BusinessEntityID IN (1,5,6,357,358,11621,423);
```

This query returns the same results (see Figure 4-28) as the results shown in Listing 4-27. The CASE expression evaluates each WHEN expression independently until finding the first one that returns true. It then returns the appropriate value. If none of the expressions returns true, the function returns the value from the ELSE part or NULL if no ELSE is available.

	Title	Gender
1	NULL	Unknown
2	Ms.	Female
3	Mr.	Male
4	Ms.	Female
5	Sr.	Unknown
6	Mrs.	Female

Figure 4-28. *The results of using searched CASE*

One very important note about using CASE is that the return values must be of compatible data types. For example, you can't have one part of the expression returning an integer while another part returns a nonnumeric string. Precedence rules apply as with other operations. Type in and run this example to see what happens:

```
SELECT Title,
    CASE WHEN Title IN ('Ms.','Mrs.','Miss') THEN 1
    WHEN Title = 'Mr.' THEN 'Male'
    ELSE '1' END AS Gender
FROM Person.Person
WHERE BusinessEntityID IN (1,5,6,357,358,11621,423);
```

Listing a Column as the Return Value

It is also possible to list a column name instead of hard-coded values in the THEN part of the CASE expression. This means that you can display one column for some of the rows and another column for other rows. Type in and execute the code in Listing 4-29 to see how this works.

Listing 4-29. Returning a Column Name in CASE

```
SELECT VacationHours,SickLeaveHours,
    CASE WHEN VacationHours > SickLeaveHours THEN VacationHours
    ELSE SickLeaveHours END AS 'More Hours'
FROM HumanResources.Employee;
```

In this example (see Figure 4-29), if there are more VacationHours than SickLeaveHours, the query displays the VacationHours column from the HumanResources.Employee table in the More Hours column. Otherwise, the query returns the SickLeaveHours.

	VacationHours	SickLeaveHours	More Hours
1	99	69	99
2	1	20	20
3	2	21	21
4	48	80	80
5	5	22	22
6	6	23	23
7	61	50	61
8	62	51	62
9	63	51	63
10	16	64	64

Figure 4-29. *The partial results of returning a column from CASE*

IIF

SQL Server 2012 introduced one easier method of writing a simple CASE expression. Starting with SQL Server 2012 you can now use an IIF function to return a result based on whether a Boolean expression is true or false. To create an expression with the IFF function, you need a Boolean expression and the values to return based on the results. Here is the basic syntax for the IIF function:

```
IIF ( boolean_expression, true_value, false_value )
```

Execute the code in Listing 4-30. The first IIF function is a simple execution, while the second IFF shows how you can introduce variables into the statement.

Listing 4-30. Using the IIF Function

```
--1 IIF function without variables
SELECT IIF (50 > 20, 'TRUE', 'FALSE') AS RESULT;

--2 IIF function with variables
DECLARE @a INT = 50
DECLARE @b INT = 25
SELECT IIF (@a > @b, 'TRUE', 'FALSE') AS RESULT;
```

Figure 4-30 shows the results. Keep in mind that all rules that apply to CASE expressions also apply to IIF functions.

	RESULT
1	TRUE

	RESULT
1	TRUE

Figure 4-30. *Results of using the IFF function*

COALESCE

You learned about COALESCE earlier in the chapter in the "Concatenating Strings and NULL" section. You can use COALESCE with other data types as well and with any number of arguments to return the first non-NULL value. You can use the COALESCE function in place of ISNULL. If a list of values must be evaluated instead of one value, you must use COALESCE instead of ISNULL. COALESCE may be used when concatenating strings or any time that a replacement for NULL must be found. Type in and execute the code in Listing 4-31 to learn more about COALESCE.

Listing 4-31. Using the COALESCE Function

```
SELECT ProductID,Size, Color,
    COALESCE(Size, Color,'No color or size') AS 'Description'
FROM Production.Product
where ProductID in (1,2,317,320,680,706);
```

Figure 4-31 displays the results. The COALESCE function first checks the Size value and then the Color value to find the first non-NULL value. If both values are NULL, then the string No color or size is returned.

	ProductID	Size	Color	Description
1	1	NULL	NULL	No color or size
2	2	NULL	NULL	No color or size
3	317	NULL	Black	Black
4	320	NULL	Silver	Silver
5	680	58	Black	58
6	706	58	Red	58

Figure 4-31. *The results of using the COALESCE function*

Administrative Functions

T-SQL contains many administrative functions that are useful for developers. SQL Server also has many functions that help database administrators manage SQL Server; these functions are beyond the scope of this book. Listing 4-32 shows a few examples of functions that return information about the current connection, such as the database name and application.

Listing 4-32. A Few System Functions

```
SELECT DB_NAME() AS "Database Name",
    HOST_NAME() AS "Host Name",
    CURRENT_USER AS "Current User",
    SUSER_NAME() AS "Login",
    USER_NAME() AS "User Name",
    APP_NAME() AS "App Name";
```

Take a look at Figure 4-32 for my results; your results will probably be different. When I ran the query, I was connected to the AdventureWorks database on a computer named KATHIKELL as the dbo (database owner) user while using Management Studio.

	Database Name	Host Name	Current User	Login	User Name	App Name
1	AdventureWorks	KATHIKELL	dbo	KathiKell\KathiKell	dbo	Microsoft SQL Server Management Studio - Query

Figure 4-32. *The results of using administrative system functions*

In addition to the functions used to manipulate strings, dates, and numbers, you will find many system functions. Some of these work on different types of data, such as CASE, while others provide information about the current connection. Administrators can manage SQL Server using dozens of system functions not covered in this book. Complete Exercise 4-6 to practice using the logical and system functions covered in the previous sections.

EXERCISE 4-6

Use the AdventureWorks database to complete this exercise. You can find the solutions to the questions at the end of the chapter.

1. Write a query using the HumanResources.Employee table to display the BusinessEntityID column. Also include a CASE expression that displays "Even" when the BusinessEntityID value is an even number or "Odd" when it is odd. Hint: Use the modulo operator.

2. Write a query using the Sales.SalesOrderDetail table to display a value ("Under 10" or "10–19" or "20–29" or "30–39" or "40 and over") based on the OrderQty value by using the CASE expression. Include the SalesOrderID and OrderQty columns in the results.

3. Using the Person.Person table, build the full names using the Title, FirstName, MiddleName, LastName, and Suffix columns. Check the table definition to see which columns allow NULL values and use the COALESCE function on the appropriate columns.

4. Look up the SERVERPROPERTY function in Books Online. Write a statement that displays the edition, instance name, and machine name using this function.

Using Functions in the *WHERE* and *ORDER BY* Clauses

So far you have seen functions used in the SELECT list. You may also use functions in the WHERE and ORDER BY clauses. Take a look at Listing 4-33 for several examples.

Listing 4-33. Using Functions in WHERE and ORDER BY

```
--1
SELECT FirstName
FROM Person.Person
WHERE CHARINDEX('ke',FirstName) > 0;

--2
SELECT LastName,REVERSE(LastName)
FROM Person.Person
ORDER BY REVERSE(LastName);
```

```
--3
SELECT BirthDate
FROM HumanResources.Employee
ORDER BY YEAR(BirthDate);
```

Figure 4-33 shows the results of Listing 4-34. Even though it is very easy to use a function on a column in the WHERE clause, it is important to note that performance may suffer. If the database designer created an index on the searched column, the database engine must evaluate each row one at a time when a function is applied to a column. It still may search the column in the index, one value at a time, which could still be better than searching every row of the table.

	FirstName
1	Blake
2	Kevin
3	Luke
4	Mackenzie

	LastName	(No column name)
1	Skjønaa	aanøjkS
2	Lyeba	abeyL
3	Vaca	acaV
4	Okada	adakO

	BirthDate
1	1945-11-17
2	1946-06-13
3	1946-10-29
4	1946-04-03

Figure 4-33. *The results of using functions in the WHERE and ORDER BY clauses*

Practice using functions in the WHERE and ORDER by clauses by completing Exercise 4-7.

EXERCISE 4-7

Use the AdventureWorks database to complete this exercise. You will find the solutions to the questions at the end of the chapter.

1. Write a query using the Sales.SalesOrderHeader table to display the orders placed during 2005 by using a function. Include the SalesOrderID and OrderDate columns in the results.

2. Write a query using the Sales.SalesOrderHeader table listing the sales in order of the month the order was placed and then the year the order was placed. Include the SalesOrderID and OrderDate columns in the results.

3. Write a query that displays the PersonType and the name columns from the Person.Person table. Sort the results so that rows with a PersonType of IN, SP, or SC sort by LastName. The other rows should sort by FirstName. Hint: Use the CASE expression.

The *TOP* Keyword

Use the TOP keyword to limit the number or percentage of rows returned from a query. Here is the syntax:

```
SELECT TOP(<number>) [PERCENT] [WITH TIES] <col1>,<col2>
FROM <table1> [ORDER BY <col1>]
```

The ORDER BY clause is optional, but most of the time, you will use it to determine which rows the query returns when using TOP. Sometimes you will see the same rows returned over and over even when not using an ORDER BY. This doesn't mean that there is any guarantee about the rows returned. It rarely makes sense to request the TOP N rows without ordering. Usually one sorts by some criteria in order to get the TOP N rows in that sequence.

The WITH TIES option means that if there are rows that have identical values in the ORDER BY clause, the results will include all the rows even though you now end up with more rows than you expect. Type in and execute the code in Listing 4-34 to learn how to use TOP.

Listing 4-34. Limiting Results with TOP

```
--1
DECLARE @Rows INT = 2;
SELECT TOP(@Rows) PERCENT CustomerID, OrderDate, SalesOrderID
FROM Sales.SalesOrderHeader
ORDER BY SalesOrderID;

--2
SELECT TOP(2) CustomerID, OrderDate, SalesOrderID
FROM Sales.SalesOrderHeader
ORDER BY OrderDate;

--3
SELECT TOP(2) WITH TIES CustomerID, OrderDate, SalesOrderID
FROM Sales.SalesOrderHeader
ORDER BY OrderDate;

--4
SELECT TOP(2) CustomerID, OrderDate, SalesOrderID
FROM Sales.SalesOrderHeader
ORDER BY NEWID();
```

Figure 4-34 shows the results. Query 1 shows that you can use a variable along with TOP. This has been possible since version 2005 of SQL Server. It also demonstrates the use of the PERCENT option. Query 2 is a typical example returning just two rows. Query 3 demonstrates the WITH TIES option. Otherwise, it is identical to Query 2. It returns many more rows because there are many orders placed on the same date. Query 4 demonstrates a trick to get random rows. If you sort by the NEWID function, you will get different rows each time you run the query.

	CustomerID	OrderDate	SalesOrderID
1	29825	2005-07-01 00:00:00.000	43659
2	29672	2005-07-01 00:00:00.000	43660
3	29734	2005-07-01 00:00:00.000	43661
4	29994	2005-07-01 00:00:00.000	43662

	CustomerID	OrderDate	SalesOrderID
1	29734	2005-07-01 00:00:00.000	43661
2	29672	2005-07-01 00:00:00.000	43660

	CustomerID	OrderDate	SalesOrderID
1	29825	2005-07-01 00:00:00.000	43659
2	29672	2005-07-01 00:00:00.000	43660
3	29734	2005-07-01 00:00:00.000	43661
4	29994	2005-07-01 00:00:00.000	43662

	CustomerID	OrderDate	SalesOrderID
1	14903	2007-10-16 00:00:00.000	56205
2	26934	2007-12-13 00:00:00.000	59977

Figure 4-34. *The partial results of using TOP*

■ **Note** Microsoft recommends using the OFFSET and FETCH clauses, introduced with SQL Server 2008, instead of TOP as a paging solution and to limit the amount of data sent to a client. OFFSET and FETCH also allow more options, including the use of variables. OFFSET and FETCH are covered in Chapter 11.

Thinking About Performance

In Chapter 3 you learned how to use execution plans to compare two or more queries and determine which query uses the least resources or, in other words, performs the best. In this chapter, you have seen how using functions can affect performance. Review the "Thinking About Performance" section in Chapter 3 if you need to take another look at how to use execution plans or to brush up on how SQL Server uses indexes.

Functions can be used in the WHERE clause to filter out unneeded rows. Although I am not saying that you should never include a function in the WHERE clause, you need to realize that including a function that operates on a column may cause a decrease in performance.

The Sales.SalesOrderHeader table does not contain an index on the OrderDate column. Run the following code to create an index on the column. Don't worry about trying to understand the code at this point.

```
--Add an index
IF  EXISTS (SELECT * FROM sys.indexes WHERE object_id =
    OBJECT_ID(N'[Sales].[SalesOrderHeader]')
    AND name = N'DEMO_SalesOrderHeader_OrderDate')
```

```
DROP INDEX [DEMO_SalesOrderHeader_OrderDate]
    ON [Sales].[SalesOrderHeader] WITH ( ONLINE = OFF );
GO

CREATE NONCLUSTERED INDEX [DEMO_SalesOrderHeader_OrderDate]
    ON [Sales].[SalesOrderHeader]
([OrderDate] ASC);
```

Toggle on the Include Actual Execution Plan setting before typing and executing the code in Listing 4-35.

Listing 4-35. Compare the Performance When Using a Function in the WHERE Clause

```
--1
SELECT SalesOrderID, OrderDate
FROM Sales.SalesOrderHeader
WHERE OrderDate >= '2005-01-01 00:00:00'
    AND OrderDate <= '2006-01-01 00:00:00';


--2
SELECT SalesOrderID, OrderDate
FROM Sales.SalesOrderHeader
WHERE YEAR(OrderDate) = 2005;
```

Query 1 finds all the orders placed in 2005 without using a function. Query 2 uses the YEAR function to return the same results. When looking at performance differences of queries against the AdventureWorks database, keep in mind that it is a very small database and the queries may seem quick. In real life, tables can contain millions of rows where you will experience performance differences more realistically.

Take a look at the execution plans in Figure 4-35 to see that query 1 performs much better with a relative query cost of 7 percent. When executing query 2, the database engine performs a scan of the entire index to see whether the result of the function applied to each value meets the criteria. The database engine performs a seek of the index in query 1 because it only has to compare the actual values, not the results of the function, for each value.

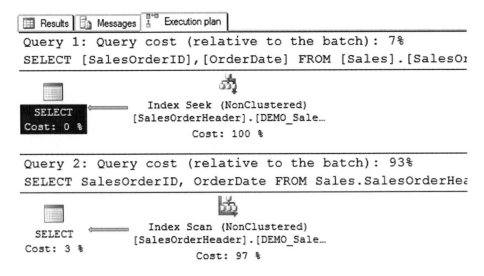

Figure 4-35. *The execution plans showing that using a function in the WHERE clause can affect performance*

Remove the index you created for this demonstration by running this code:

```
IF  EXISTS (SELECT * FROM sys.indexes WHERE object_id =
    OBJECT_ID(N'[Sales].[SalesOrderHeader]')
    AND name = N'DEMO_SalesOrderHeader_OrderDate')
DROP INDEX [DEMO_SalesOrderHeader_OrderDate]
    ON [Sales].[SalesOrderHeader] WITH ( ONLINE = OFF );
```

Run Listing 4-35 again now that the index is gone. Figure 4-36 shows that with no index on the OrderDate column, the performance is almost identical. Now the database engine must perform a scan of the table (in this case, the clustered index) to find the correct rows in both of the queries. Notice that the execution plan suggests an index to help the performance of query 1. It doesn't suggest an index for query 2 because an index won't help.

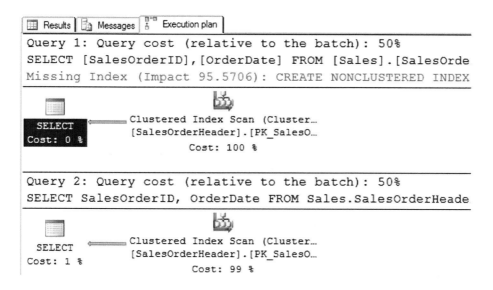

Figure 4-36. *The execution plans after removing the index*

You can see from these examples that writing queries is more than just getting the correct results; performance is important, too.

Summary

Using expressions in T-SQL with the built-in functions and operators can be very convenient. There is a rich collection of functions for string and date manipulation as well as mathematical and system functions and more. It's possible to use expressions and functions in the SELECT, WHERE, and ORDER BY clauses. You must use caution when using functions in the WHERE clause; it is possible to decrease performance.

Answers to the Exercises

This section provides solutions to the exercises found on writing queries with expressions.

Solutions to Exercise 4-1: Expressions Using Operators

Use the AdventureWorks database to complete this exercise.

1. Write a query that returns data from the `Person.Address` table in this format AddressLine1 (City PostalCode) from the `Person.Address` table.

```
SELECT AddressLine1 + '  (' + City + ' ' + PostalCode + ') '
FROM Person.Address;
```

2. Write a query using the `Production.Product` table displaying the product ID, color, and name columns. If the color column contains a NULL value, replace the color with *No Color*.

```
SELECT ProductID, ISNULL(Color, 'No Color') AS Color, Name
FROM Production.Product;
```

3. Modify the query written in question 2 so that the description of the product is returned formatted as Name: Color. Make sure that all rows display a value even if the `Color` value is missing.

```
SELECT ProductID, Name + ISNULL(': ' + Color,'') AS Description
FROM Production.Product;
```

4. Write a query using the `Production.Product` table displaying a description with the ProductID: Name format. Hint: You will need to use a function to write this query.

   Here are two possible answers:

```
SELECT CAST(ProductID AS VARCHAR) + ': ' +  Name AS IDName
FROM Production.Product;
```

```
SELECT CONVERT(VARCHAR, ProductID) + ': ' + Name AS IDName
FROM Production.Product;
```

5. Explain the difference between the ISNULL and COALESCE functions.

   You can use ISNULL to replace a NULL value or column with another value or column. You can use COALESCE to return the first non-NULL value from a list of values or columns.

Solutions to Exercise 4-2: Using Mathematical Operators

Use the AdventureWorks database to complete this exercise.

1. Write a query using the `Sales.SpecialOffer` table. Display the difference between the MinQty and MaxQty columns along with the `SpecialOfferID` and `Description` columns.

```
SELECT SpecialOfferID, Description,
    MaxQty - MinQty AS Diff
FROM Sales.SpecialOffer;
```

2. Write a query using the `Sales.SpecialOffer` table. Multiply the `MinQty` column by the `DiscountPct` column. Include the `SpecialOfferID` and `Description` columns in the results.

    ```
    SELECT SpecialOfferID, Description, MinQty * DiscountPct AS Discount
    FROM Sales.SpecialOffer;
    ```

3. Write a query using the `Sales.SpecialOffer` table that multiplies the `MaxQty` column by the `DiscountPct` column. If the `MaxQty` value is NULL, replace it with the value 10. Include the `SpecialOfferID` and `Description` columns in the results.

    ```
    SELECT SpecialOfferID, Description,
        ISNULL(MaxQty,10) * DiscountPct AS Discount
    FROM Sales.SpecialOffer;
    ```

4. Describe the difference between division and modulo.

When performing division, you divide two numbers, and the result, the quotient, is the answer. If you are using modulo, you divide two numbers, but the reminder is the answer. If the numbers are evenly divisible, the answer will be zero.

Solution to Exercise 4-3: Using Functions

Use the AdventureWorks database to complete this exercise. If you need help, refer to the discussion of the functions to help you figure out which ones to use.

1. Write a query that displays the first 10 characters of the `AddressLine1` column in the `Person.Address` table.

    Here are two possible solutions:

    ```
    SELECT LEFT(AddressLine1,10) AS Address10
    FROM Person.Address;
    ```

    ```
    SELECT SUBSTRING(AddressLine1,1,10) AS Address10
    FROM Person.Address;
    ```

2. Write a query that displays characters 10 to 15 of the AddressLine1 column in the `Person.Address` table.

    ```
    SELECT SUBSTRING(AddressLine1,10,6) AS Address10to15
    FROM Person.Address;
    ```

3. Write a query displaying the first and last names from the `Person.Person` table all in uppercase.

    ```
    SELECT UPPER(FirstName) AS FirstName,
        UPPER(LastName) AS LastName
    FROM Person.Person;
    ```

4. The ProductNumber in the `Production.Product` table contains a hyphen (-). Write a query that uses the SUBSTRING function and the CHARINDEX function to display the characters in the product number following the hyphen. Note: There is also a second hyphen in many of the rows; ignore the second hyphen for this question. Hint: Try writing this statement in two steps, the first using the CHARINDEX function and the second adding the SUBSTRING function.

```
--Step 1
SELECT ProductNumber, CHARINDEX('-',ProductNumber)
FROM Production.Product;

--Step 2
SELECT ProductNumber,
    SUBSTRING(ProductNumber,CHARINDEX('-',ProductNumber)+1,25) AS ProdNumber
FROM Production.Product;
```

Solution to Exercise 4-4: Using Date and Time Functions

Use the AdventureWorks database to complete this exercise.

1. Write a query that calculates the number of days between the date an order was placed and the date that it was shipped using the Sales.SalesOrderHeader table. Include the SalesOrderID, OrderDate, and ShipDate columns.

```
SELECT SalesOrderID, OrderDate, ShipDate,
    DATEDIFF(day,OrderDate,ShipDate) AS NumberOfDays FROM Sales.SalesOrderHeader;
```

2. Write a query that displays only the date, not the time, for the order date and ship date in the Sales.SalesOrderHeader table.

```
SELECT CONVERT(VARCHAR(12),OrderDate,111) AS OrderDate,
    CONVERT(VARCHAR(12), ShipDate,111) AS ShipDate
FROM Sales.SalesOrderHeader;
```

3. Write a query that adds six months to each order date in the Sales.SalesOrderHeader table. Include the SalesOrderID and OrderDate columns.

```
SELECT SalesOrderID, OrderDate,
    DATEADD(m,6,OrderDate) AS Plus6Months
FROM Sales.SalesOrderHeader;
```

4. Write a query that displays the year of each order date and the numeric month of each order date in separate columns in the results. Include the SalesOrderID and OrderDate columns. Here are two possible solutions:

```
SELECT SalesOrderID, OrderDate, YEAR(OrderDate) AS OrderYear,
    MONTH(OrderDate) AS OrderMonth
FROM Sales.SalesOrderHeader;

SELECT SalesOrderID, OrderDate, DATEPART(yyyy,OrderDate) AS OrderYear,
    DATEPART(m,OrderDate) AS OrderMonth
FROM Sales.SalesOrderHeader;
```

5. Change the query written in question 4 to display the month name instead.

```
SELECT SalesOrderID, OrderDate,
     DATEPART(yyyy,OrderDate) AS OrderYear,
     DATENAME(m,OrderDate) AS OrderMonth
FROM Sales.SalesOrderHeader;
```

Solution to Exercise 4-5: Using Mathematical Functions

Use the AdventureWorks database to complete this exercise.

1. Write a query using the `Sales.SalesOrderHeader` table that displays the `SubTotal` rounded to two decimal places. Include the `SalesOrderID` column in the results.

   ```
   SELECT SalesOrderID, ROUND(SubTotal,2) AS SubTotal
   FROM Sales.SalesOrderHeader;
   ```

2. Modify the query from question 1 so that the `SubTotal` is rounded to the nearest dollar but still displays two zeros to the right of the decimal place.

   ```
   SELECT SalesOrderID, ROUND(SubTotal,0) AS SubTotal
   FROM Sales.SalesOrderHeader;
   ```

3. Write a query that calculates the square root of the `SalesOrderID` value from the `Sales.SalesOrderHeader` table.

   ```
   SELECT SQRT(SalesOrderID) AS OrderSQRT
   FROM Sales.SalesOrderHeader;
   ```

4. Write a statement that generates a random number between 1 and 10 each time it is run.

   ```
   SELECT CAST(RAND() * 10 AS INT) + 1;
   ```

Solution to Exercise 4-6: Using Logical and System Functions

Use the AdventureWorks database to complete this exercise.

1. Write a query using the `HumanResources.Employee` table to display the `BusinessEntityID` column. Also include a `CASE` expression that displays "Even" when the `BusinessEntityID` value is an even number or "Odd" when it is odd. Hint: Use the modulo operator.

   ```
   SELECT BusinessEntityID,
       CASE BusinessEntityID % 2
       WHEN 0 THEN 'Even' ELSE 'Odd' END
   FROM HumanResources.Employee;
   ```

2. Write a query using the `Sales.SalesOrderDetail` table to display a value ("Under 10" or "10-19" or "20-29" or "30-39" or "40 and over") based on the `OrderQty` value by using the `CASE` expression. Include the SalesOrderID and OrderQty columns in the results.

   ```
   SELECT SalesOrderID, OrderQty,
       CASE WHEN OrderQty BETWEEN 0 AND 9
               THEN 'Under 10'
           WHEN OrderQty BETWEEN 10 AND 19
               THEN '10-19'
           WHEN OrderQty BETWEEN 20 AND 29
               THEN '20-29'
           WHEN OrderQty BETWEEN 30 AND 39
               THEN '30-39'
           ELSE '40 and over' end AS range
   FROM Sales.SalesOrderDetail;
   ```

3. Using the `Person.Person` table, build the full names using the `Title`, `FirstName`, `MiddleName`, `LastName`, and `Suffix` columns. Check the table definition to see which columns allow `NULL` values and use the `COALESCE` function on the appropriate columns.

```
SELECT COALESCE(Title + ' ','') + FirstName +
    COALESCE(' ' + MiddleName,'') + ' ' + LastName +
    COALESCE(', ' + Suffix,'')
FROM Person.Person;
```

4. Look up the `SERVERPROPERTY` function in Books Online. Write a statement that displays the edition, instance name, and machine name using this function.

```
SELECT SERVERPROPERTY('Edition'),
    SERVERPROPERTY('InstanceName'),
    SERVERPROPERTY('MachineName');
```

Solution to Exercise 4-7: Using Functions in the *WHERE* and *ORDER BY* Clauses

Use the AdventureWorks database to complete this exercise.

1. Write a query using the `Sales.SalesOrderHeader` table to display the orders placed during 2005 by using a function. Include the `SalesOrderID` and `OrderDate` columns in the results.

```
--one possible solution.
SELECT SalesOrderID, OrderDate
FROM Sales.SalesOrderHeader
WHERE YEAR(OrderDate) = 2005;
```

2. Write a query using the `Sales.SalesOrderHeader` table listing the sales in order of the month the order was placed and then the year the order was placed. Include the `SalesOrderID` and `OrderDate` columns in the results.

```
SELECT SalesOrderID, OrderDate
FROM Sales.SalesOrderHeader
ORDER BY MONTH(OrderDate), YEAR(OrderDate);
```

3. Write a query that displays the `PersonType` and the name columns from the `Person.Person` table. Sort the results so that rows with a `PersonType` of IN, SP, or SC sort by `LastName`. The other rows should sort by `FirstName`. Hint: Use the CASE expression.

```
SELECT PersonType, FirstName, MiddleName, LastName
FROM Person.Person
ORDER BY CASE WHEN PersonType IN ('IN','SP','SC')
    THEN LastName ELSE FirstName END;
```

Joining Tables

Now that you know how to write simple queries using one table and how to use functions and expressions in queries, it is time to learn how to write queries involving two or more tables. In a properly designed relational database, a table contains data about one thing or entity. For example, an order-entry application will have a table storing customer information, a table containing data about orders, and a table containing detail information about each item ordered. The order table has a column, called a *foreign key*, which refers to a row in the customer table. The detail table has a foreign key column that refers to the order table. By using *joins*, you can link these tables together within the query so you can display columns from each table in the same result set.

You can also think about joining two tables in terms of a parent-child relationship. The parent row has one or more matching rows in the child table. The child table matches back to just one row in the parent table. In the previous example, the customer table is a parent to the orders table and the orders table is a parent to the details table.

Learning how to join tables is a critical skill for T-SQL developers because it allows you to combine the relational data stored in multiple tables and present it as a single result set. There are also multiple types of joins. You will start this chapter learning about the most common type, the INNER JOIN. Make sure you understand all the example code and complete the exercises in this chapter before moving on to the next chapter.

Using *INNER JOIN*

Most of the time, to join tables together, you will use INNER JOIN. When connecting two tables with INNER JOIN, only the rows from the tables that match on the joining columns will show up in the results. If you join the customer and order tables, the query will return only the customers who have placed orders, along with the orders that have been placed. Only the rows where the customer ID is common in both tables will show up in the results.

Joining Two Tables

To join tables together, it might seem like another major clause would need to be added to the SELECT statement. This is not the case. Instead, the FROM clause contains information about how the tables join together. Here is the syntax for joining two tables (the keyword INNER is optional):

```
SELECT <select list>
FROM <table1>
[INNER] JOIN <table2> ON <table1>.<col1> = <table2>.<col2>
```

Figure 5-1 shows how the Sales.SalesOrderHeader and Sales.SalesOrderDetail tables connect and shows some of the columns in the tables. You will see these tables joined in the first example query, so make sure you understand how they connect before typing the code in Listing 5-1.

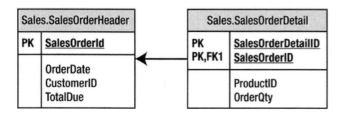

Figure 5-1. *The Sales.SalesOrderHeader and Sales.SalesOrderDetail tables*

The Sales.SalesOrderHeader table has a primary key called SalesOrderID. The Sales.SalesOrderDetail table has a composite primary key, one that is made up of more than one column, consisting of SalesOrderDetailID and SalesOrderID. The SalesOrderID column in the Sales.SalesOrderDetail table is also a foreign key pointing back to the Sales.SalesOrderHeader table. The arrow points from the foreign key in the Sales.SalesOrderDetail table to the primary key in the Sales.SalesOrderHeader table.

Take a look at the code in Listing 5-1. Type in and execute the code to learn how to join the two tables.

Listing 5-1. Joining Two Tables

```
SELECT s.SalesOrderID, s.OrderDate, s.TotalDue, d.SalesOrderDetailID,
    d.ProductID, d.OrderQty
FROM Sales.SalesOrderHeader AS s
INNER JOIN Sales.SalesOrderDetail AS d ON s.SalesOrderID = d.SalesOrderID;
```

Figure 5-2 displays the partial results. The SELECT list may contain columns from either of the tables. In the FROM clause, you list one of the tables followed by the words INNER JOIN and the second table name. To define how the two tables join together, use the keyword ON and an equality expression. Each Sales.OrderHeader row contains a unique SalesOrderID. Each Sales.SalesOrderDetail row contains a SalesOrderID column that determines to which order the detail belongs. When you join these two tables together, the query displays every row from the Sales.SalesOrderHeader table that matches one or more rows in the Sales.SalesOrderDetail table.

	SalesOrderID	OrderDate	TotalDue	SalesOrderDetailID	ProductID	OrderQty
1	43659	2005-07-01 00:00:00.000	23153.2339	1	776	1
2	43659	2005-07-01 00:00:00.000	23153.2339	2	777	3
3	43659	2005-07-01 00:00:00.000	23153.2339	3	778	1
4	43659	2005-07-01 00:00:00.000	23153.2339	4	771	1
5	43659	2005-07-01 00:00:00.000	23153.2339	5	772	1
6	43659	2005-07-01 00:00:00.000	23153.2339	6	773	2
7	43659	2005-07-01 00:00:00.000	23153.2339	7	774	1
8	43659	2005-07-01 00:00:00.000	23153.2339	8	714	3
9	43659	2005-07-01 00:00:00.000	23153.2339	9	716	1
10	43659	2005-07-01 00:00:00.000	23153.2339	10	709	6
11	43659	2005-07-01 00:00:00.000	23153.2339	11	712	2

Figure 5-2. *The partial results of joining two tables*

Take a look at the data from the Sales.SalesOrderHeader columns in the query results. The information from the Sales.SalesOrderHeader table repeats for each matching row in the Sales.SalesOrderDetail table. If a row exists in the Sales.SalesOrderHeader table with no matches in the Sales.SalesOrderDetail table, the Sales.SalesOrderHeader row will not show up in the results.

Because the column name, SalesOrderID, is the same in both tables, it must be fully qualified with the table name anywhere it is used in the query. To save typing, use an alias for each table. Notice that the query uses the table alias for all the columns in the SELECT list. Fully qualifying the column name is not required except for the columns with the same name; however, fully qualifying all of the column names will make the query more readable. Six months after you write a query, you can immediately see which table each column came from without spending a lot of time trying to figure it out. There are many schools of thought represented here. Some recommend aliasing even one table query so you don't have to go back to fix it if another table is added later. You will also see recommendations to use abbreviations for each table name. The worst recommendation I have seen in the real world is lettering tables, such as "A," "B," "C," and so on. These letters mean nothing in regard to your tables.

Avoiding an Incorrect Join Condition

Although you must specify join criteria with ON in the FROM clause when using INNER JOIN, nothing can prevent you from writing the join incorrectly. Take a look at Listing 5-2. If you decide to run the code, you may have to click the red square Cancel Executing Query icon to the right of the Execute icon to stop query execution, or the query will run for several minutes and return almost 4 billion rows. Not only is this a waste of your time, but it also affects all other operations on the SQL Server.

Listing 5-2. Writing an Incorrect Query

```
SELECT s.SalesOrderID, OrderDate, TotalDue, SalesOrderDetailID,
    d.ProductID, d.OrderQty
FROM Sales.SalesOrderHeader AS s
INNER JOIN Sales.SalesOrderDetail d ON 1 = 1;
```

Figure 5-3 displays a portion of the results after scrolling down more than 3,000 rows. When comparing the results to those in Figure 5-2, you will see that the rows from Sales.SalesOrderHeader join inappropriate rows from Sales.SalesOrderDetail. Both sets of results show SalesOrderID 43659, but the results are correct only in Figure 5-2. Because 1 = 1 is always true, *every* row from the first table joins *every* row from the second table to produce these incorrect results, which is also called a *Cartesian product*.

	SalesOrderID	OrderDate	TotalDue	SalesOrderDetailID	ProductID	OrderQty
3826	43659	2005-07-01 00:00:00.000	23153.2339	3826	708	2
3827	43659	2005-07-01 00:00:00.000	23153.2339	3827	756	2
3828	43659	2005-07-01 00:00:00.000	23153.2339	3828	711	2
3829	43659	2005-07-01 00:00:00.000	23153.2339	3829	761	6
3830	43659	2005-07-01 00:00:00.000	23153.2339	3830	754	3
3831	43659	2005-07-01 00:00:00.000	23153.2339	3831	725	1
3832	43659	2005-07-01 00:00:00.000	23153.2339	3832	750	4
3833	43659	2005-07-01 00:00:00.000	23153.2339	3833	738	4
3834	43659	2005-07-01 00:00:00.000	23153.2339	3834	732	3
3835	43659	2005-07-01 00:00:00.000	23153.2339	3835	769	1

Figure 5-3. *The partial results of an incorrect join*

Whenever you write a query with INNER JOIN, make sure you understand the relation between the two tables. For example, you could join the OrderQty column from the Sales.SalesOrderDetail table to the SalesOrderID column in the Sales.SalesOrderHeader table. The query would run, but the results would not make any sense at all.

Joining on a Different Column Name

In the previous two examples, the key column names happen to be the same, but this is not a requirement. The Person.Person table contains information about people from several tables in the AdventureWorks database. Figure 5-4 shows how the Person.Person and the Sales.Customer table connect. The PersonID from the Sales.Customer table joins to the BusinessEntityID in the Person.Person table. The PersonID column in the Sales.Customer table is the foreign key.

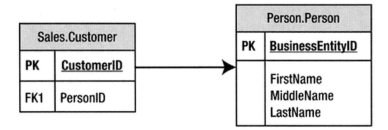

Figure 5-4. *How to connect the Sales.Customer and Person.Person tables*

Listing 5-3 shows an example that joins these two tables.

Listing 5-3. Joining Two Tables with Different Column Names

```
SELECT c.CustomerID, c.PersonID, p.BusinessEntityID, p.LastName
FROM Sales.Customer AS c
INNER JOIN Person.Person AS p ON c.PersonID = p.BusinessEntityID;
```

Figure 5-5 shows the partial results. The Person.Person table contains information about people from several tables in the database. In this case, the columns joining the two tables have different names. The PersonID from the Sales.Customer table joins to the BusinessEntityID in the Person.Person table. This works even though the columns have different names.

	CustomerID	PersonID	BusinessEntityID	LastName
1	29485	293	293	Abel
2	29486	295	295	Abercrombie
3	29487	297	297	Acevedo
4	29484	291	291	Achong
5	29488	299	299	Ackerman
6	28866	16867	16867	Adams
7	13323	16901	16901	Adams
8	21139	16724	16724	Adams
9	29170	10263	10263	Adams
10	19419	10312	10312	Adams

Figure 5-5. *The partial results of joining tables with different key column names*

Joining on More Than One Column

Although a JOIN frequently involves joining a column from one table to a column from another table, sometimes you must join multiple columns. The AdventureWorks database contains only one example in which multiple columns must be used in a single JOIN: Sales.SalesOrderDetail to Sales.SpecialOfferProduct. Figure 5-6 shows how these two tables connect.

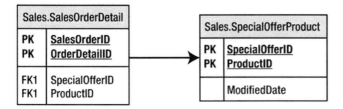

Figure 5-6. *How to connect the Sales.SalesOrderDetail table to the Sales.SpecialOfferProduct table*

The Sales.SpecialOfferProduct table has a composite primary key composed of SpecialOfferID plus ProductID. To identify a row in this table, you must use both columns. When joining Sales.SalesOrderDetail to the Sales.SpecialOfferProduct table, you specify both columns in the join. Here is the syntax for joining more than one column:

```
SELECT <SELECT list>
FROM <table1>
[INNER] JOIN <table2> ON <table1>.<col1> = <table2><col2>
    AND <table1>.<col3> = <table2>.<col4>
```

Type in and execute the code in Listing 5-4 to learn how to join two columns.

Listing 5-4. Joining Two Columns

```
SELECT sod.SalesOrderID, sod.SalesOrderDetailID,
    so.ProductID, so.SpecialOfferID, so.ModifiedDate
FROM Sales.SalesOrderDetail AS sod
INNER JOIN Sales.SpecialOfferProduct AS so
    ON so.ProductID = sod.ProductID AND
    so.SpecialOfferID = sod.SpecialOfferID
WHERE sod.SalesOrderID IN (51116,51112);
```

Take a look at the results (see Figure 5-7). Two columns, ProductID and SpecialOfferID, comprise the join condition. To determine which row matches the rows from Sales.SalesOrderDetail, both columns are used in the join condition. If the join contained only one of the columns, the results would be similar to the incorrect results presented earlier in the section "Avoiding an Incorrect Join Condition." If the join contained only the ProductID, the results would show every possible SpecialOfferID row for each ProductID, not just the correct rows. Try modifying the join yourself by leaving out one of the conditions to see what happens.

	SalesOrderID	SalesOrderDetailID	ProductID	SpecialOfferID	ModifiedDate
1	51112	36341	956	14	2007-06-01 00:00:00.000
2	51112	36342	965	13	2007-06-01 00:00:00.000
3	51112	36343	885	1	2005-05-02 00:00:00.000
4	51112	36344	948	1	2005-05-02 00:00:00.000
5	51112	36345	960	13	2007-06-01 00:00:00.000
6	51112	36346	886	1	2005-05-02 00:00:00.000
7	51112	36347	994	1	2005-05-02 00:00:00.000
8	51112	36348	966	1	2005-05-02 00:00:00.000
9	51112	36349	959	13	2007-06-01 00:00:00.000
10	51112	36350	978	13	2007-06-01 00:00:00.000

Figure 5-7. *The partial results of joining on two columns*

Joining Three or More Tables

Sometimes you will need to join only two tables together in a query, but more frequently, you will need to join three or more tables. You will often join three tables when there is a *many-to-many* relationship between two of the tables. For example, suppose you have a table listing college courses and a table listing students. You would need a third table that records which students take which courses. To join courses to students, your query will join all three tables.

In the AdventureWorks database, you will find many reasons to join more than two tables in one query. For example, suppose you want to see a list of the product names for each order, along with the OrderDate column. This query requires the Sales.SalesOrderHeader, Sales.SalesOrderDetail, and Production.Product tables. Figure 5-8 shows how to connect these three tables.

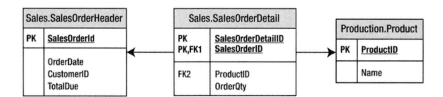

Figure 5-8. *How to join Sales.SalesOrderDetail to Production.Product and Sales.SalesOrderHeader*

To add a third or more tables, just continue the FROM clause. Take a look at the syntax:

```
SELECT <SELECT list> FROM <table1>
[INNER] JOIN <table2> ON <table1>.<col1> = <table2>.<col2>
[INNER] JOIN <table3> ON <table2>.<col2> = <table3>.<col3>
```

Type in and execute the query in Listing 5-5 to learn how to join more than two tables in one query.

Listing 5-5. Joining Three Tables

```
SELECT soh.SalesOrderID, soh.OrderDate, p.ProductID, p.Name
FROM Sales.SalesOrderHeader as soh
INNER JOIN Sales.SalesOrderDetail AS sod ON soh.SalesOrderID = sod.SalesOrderID
INNER JOIN Production.Product AS p ON sod.ProductID = p.ProductID
ORDER BY soh.SalesOrderID;
```

Figure 5-9 shows the results. Notice that even though the query joins three tables, the query displays columns from only two of the tables. To get from Sales.SalesOrderHeader to the names of the products ordered in the Production.Product table, the query must include the Sales.SalesOrderDetail table to connect the other two tables. Depending on the goal of the query, you may want to include columns from all tables involved in the query.

	SalesOrderID	OrderDate	ProductID	Name
1	43659	2005-07-01 00:00:00.000	711	Sport-100 Helmet, Blue
2	43659	2005-07-01 00:00:00.000	714	Long-Sleeve Logo Jersey, M
3	43659	2005-07-01 00:00:00.000	716	Long-Sleeve Logo Jersey, XL
4	43659	2005-07-01 00:00:00.000	778	Mountain-100 Black, 48
5	43659	2005-07-01 00:00:00.000	771	Mountain-100 Silver, 38
6	43659	2005-07-01 00:00:00.000	709	Mountain Bike Socks, M
7	43659	2005-07-01 00:00:00.000	774	Mountain-100 Silver, 48
8	43659	2005-07-01 00:00:00.000	772	Mountain-100 Silver, 42
9	43659	2005-07-01 00:00:00.000	712	AWC Logo Cap
10	43659	2005-07-01 00:00:00.000	777	Mountain-100 Black, 44

Figure 5-9. *The partial results of joining three tables*

Take another look at the FROM clause. The Sales.SalesOrderHeader table joins to the Sales.SalesOrderDetail table on the SalesOrderID column. Then the Sales.SalesOrderDetail table joins the Production.Product table on the ProductID column. If you have trouble figuring out how to join the tables, take it a step at a time. Join two tables first, and then add the third table.

Joining tables is a very important skill for T-SQL developers. Before you move on to the next section, make sure you are comfortable with what the chapter has covered so far by completing Exercise 5-1.

EXERCISE 5-1

Use the AdventureWorks database to complete this exercise. You can find the solutions at the end of the chapter.

1. The HumanResources.Employee table does not contain the employee names. Join that table to the Person.Person table on the BusinessEntityID column. Display the job title, birth date, first name, and last name.

2. The customer names also appear in the Person.Person table. Join the Sales.Customer table to the Person.Person table. The BusinessEntityID column in the Person.Person table matches the PersonID column in the Sales.Customer table. Display the CustomerID, StoreID, and TerritoryID columns along with the name columns.

3. Extend the query written in question 2 to include the Sales.SalesOrderHeader table. Display the SalesOrderID column along with the columns already specified. The Sales. SalesOrderHeader table joins the Sales.Customer table on CustomerID.

4. Write a query that joins the Sales.SalesOrderHeader table to the Sales.SalesPerson table. Join the BusinessEntityID column from the Sales.SalesPerson table to the SalesPersonID column in the Sales.SalesOrderHeader table. Display the SalesOrderID along with the SalesQuota and Bonus.

5. Add the name columns to the query written in question 4 by joining on the Person.Person table. See whether you can figure out which columns will be used to write the join.

6. The catalog description for each product is stored in the Production.ProductModel table. Display the columns that describe the product such as the color and size, along with the catalog description for each product.

7. Write a query that displays the names of the customers along with the product names they have purchased. Hint: Five tables will be required to write this query!

Using *OUTER JOIN*

When joining two tables with INNER JOIN, there must be an exact match between the two tables for a row to show up in the results. Occasionally, you'll need to retrieve all the rows from one of the tables even if the other table doesn't contain a match for every row. For example, you may want to display all the customers along with their orders, including the customers who have not placed orders yet. By using OUTER JOIN, you can retrieve all the rows from one table along with any rows that match from the other table.

Using *LEFT OUTER JOIN*

When writing OUTER JOIN, you must specify either LEFT or RIGHT. If the main table, the table you want to see all the rows from even if there is not a match, is on the left side of the join, you will specify LEFT. Figure 5-10 shows how the Sales.Customer and Sales.SalesOrderHeader tables connect when using LEFT OUTER JOIN so that all customers show up in the results even if they have not placed any orders. The tan area of the Venn diagram illustrates how all the CustomerID values in the Sales.Customer table will be returned whether or not there is a matching CustomerID value in the Sales.SalesOrderHeader table. Additionally, all matching CustomerID values (this is where the circles intersect in the diagram) will also be returned.

Sales.Customer   **Sales.SalesOrderHeader**

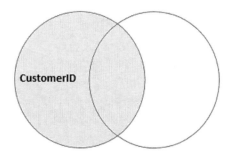

Figure 5-10. *How to perform LEFT OUTER JOIN*

Here is the syntax for LEFT OUTER JOIN:

```
SELECT <SELECT list>
FROM <table1>
LEFT [OUTER] JOIN <table2> ON <table1>.<col1> = <table2>.<col2>
```

Type in and execute the code in Listing 5-6 to learn how to write a LEFT OUTER JOIN query. Note that the word OUTER is optional.

Listing 5-6. Using LEFT OUTER JOIN

```
SELECT c.CustomerID, s.SalesOrderID, s.OrderDate
FROM Sales.Customer AS c
LEFT OUTER JOIN Sales.SalesOrderHeader AS s ON c.CustomerID = s.CustomerID
WHERE c.CustomerID IN (11028,11029,1,2,3,4);
```

Figure 5-11 displays the results. Just like INNER JOIN, you must determine which column or columns from one table join the column or columns from the other table. All the rows from the table on the left side of the join, the Sales. Customer table, that meet the criteria in the WHERE clause show up in the results. The query returns rows from the right side of the join, the Sales.SalesOrderHeader table, only if they match on CustomerID. All of the columns from the Sales.SalesOrderHeader rows that don't match return NULL values. The query returns the customers along with the orders for customers with no orders (customers 1–4).

	CustomerID	SalesOrderID	OrderDate
1	1	NULL	NULL
2	2	NULL	NULL
3	3	NULL	NULL
4	4	NULL	NULL
5	11028	43831	2005-07-29 00:00:00.000
6	11028	57943	2007-11-14 00:00:00.000
7	11028	67961	2008-04-09 00:00:00.000
8	11029	43794	2005-07-22 00:00:00.000
9	11029	57294	2007-11-02 00:00:00.000
10	11029	70593	2008-05-14 00:00:00.000

Figure 5-11. *The results of using LEFT OUTER JOIN*

Using OUTER JOIN is not difficult, but it seems to be confusing when someone first tries to use it. If the tables have the primary and foreign keys defined, the table joining with the primary key will usually be the table on the left side in a LEFT OUTER JOIN. Figure out which table must have rows returned even if there is not a match. That table must show up on the left side of a LEFT OUTER JOIN.

Using *RIGHT OUTER JOIN*

RIGHT OUTER JOIN differs from LEFT OUTER JOIN in just the location of the tables. If the main table, the table in which you want to see all the rows, even if there is not a match, is on the right side of the join, you will specify RIGHT. Here is the syntax:

```
SELECT <SELECT list>
FROM <table2>
RIGHT [OUTER] JOIN <table1> ON <table1>.<col1> = <table2>.<col2>
```

Type in and execute the code in Listing 5-7 to learn how to write a query using RIGHT OUTER JOIN. This query is just like the query in Listing 5-6, only the position of the tables has been switched.

Listing 5-7. Using RIGHT OUTER JOIN

```
SELECT c.CustomerID, s.SalesOrderID, s.OrderDate
FROM Sales.SalesOrderHeader AS s
RIGHT OUTER JOIN Sales.Customer AS c ON c.CustomerID = s.CustomerID
WHERE c.CustomerID IN (11028,11029,1,2,3,4);
```

Figure 5-12 shows the results; they are identical to the results shown in Figure 5-11. The only difference between this query and the one from Listing 5-6 is the order of the tables within the FROM clause and the direction keyword. Again, all of the customers who meet the criteria are displayed along with any orders that were placed. For customers with no orders, NULL values are returned in the SalesOrderID and OrderDate columns.

	CustomerID	SalesOrderID	OrderDate
1	1	NULL	NULL
2	2	NULL	NULL
3	3	NULL	NULL
4	4	NULL	NULL
5	11028	43831	2005-07-29 00:00:00.000
6	11028	57943	2007-11-14 00:00:00.000
7	11028	67961	2008-04-09 00:00:00.000
8	11029	43794	2005-07-22 00:00:00.000
9	11029	57294	2007-11-02 00:00:00.000
10	11029	70593	2008-05-14 00:00:00.000

Figure 5-12. *Result of using RIGHT OUTER JOIN*

Using *OUTER JOIN* to Find Rows with No Match

Sometimes it's useful to find all the rows in one table that don't have corresponding rows in another table. For example, you may want to find all the customers who have never placed an order. Because the columns from the nonmatching rows contain NULL values, you can use OUTER JOIN to find rows with no match by checking for NULL. The syntax is as follows:

```
SELECT <SELECT list>
FROM <table1>
LEFT [OUTER] JOIN <table2> ON <table1>.<col1> = <table2>.<col2>
WHERE <col2> IS NULL
```

Type in and execute the code in Listing 5-8 to see how this works.

Listing 5-8. Using LEFT OUTER JOIN to Find the Rows with No Matches

```
SELECT c.CustomerID, s.SalesOrderID, s.OrderDate
FROM Sales.Customer AS c
LEFT OUTER JOIN Sales.SalesOrderHeader AS s ON c.CustomerID = s.CustomerID
WHERE s.SalesOrderID IS NULL;
```

Figure 5-13 shows the partial results. The query in Listing 5-8 returns a list of all customers who have not placed an order. After you run the query, scroll down to see that every row in the results contains NULL in the SalesOrderID column. Actually, the SalesOrderID and OrderDate columns are not needed in the results and can decrease the performance of this query. In this case, I have left them in the query so that you can verify the NULL values.

	CustomerID	SalesOrderID	OrderDate
1	215	NULL	NULL
2	46	NULL	NULL
3	169	NULL	NULL
4	507	NULL	NULL
5	630	NULL	NULL
6	338	NULL	NULL
7	229	NULL	NULL
8	567	NULL	NULL
9	461	NULL	NULL
10	398	NULL	NULL

Figure 5-13. *The partial results of finding rows with no match*

The LEFT JOIN returns all rows from Sales.Customer even if the customer has no orders. The customer rows with no orders contain NULL in the SalesOrderID and OrderDate columns. By checking for NULL, the customers with no orders show up in the results. Again, this might be complicated to understand at first. Just take it a step at a time when writing your own queries. You will learn another way to find rows with no match in Chapter 6.

Adding a Table to the Right Side of a *LEFT JOIN*

The next step is to understand what to do when additional tables are added to the query. For example, you might want to display all the customers and their orders even if an order has not been placed, along with the ProductID from those orders that were placed. To keep the customers with no orders from dropping out of the results, you must continue to use LEFT JOIN. Figure 5-14 shows how these three tables can be joined to produce the correct results. Notice the Venn diagram shows the SalesOrderHeader and the SalesOrderDetail tables joining on the SalesOrderID. Those results are matched with the CustomerID to get a result set that includes all of the customers in the Customer table including those without orders. The diagram in Figure 5-14 shows the SalesOrderHeader as the circle linking the CustomerID and SalesOrderDetail together because it is the only table containing both the CustomerID and the SalesOrderID. These types of linking tables are normally referred to as *junction* tables, which allow you to combine in a single query output SalesOrderDetail and Customer data.

Sales.Customer　　　　　　**Sales.SalesOrderHeader**

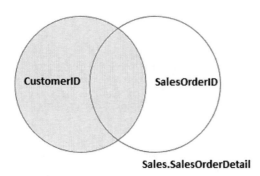

Sales.SalesOrderDetail

Figure 5-14. *How to connect the tables with two LEFT OUTER JOINs*

Take a look at the syntax:

```
SELECT <SELECT list>
FROM <table1> LEFT [OUTER]JOIN <table2> ON <table1>.<col1> = <table2>.<col2>
LEFT [OUTER] JOIN <table3> ON <table2>.<col3> = <table3>.<col4>
```

Listing 5-9 contains an example query. Type in and execute the code to learn how to write this type of join.

Listing 5-9. Joining Three Tables with LEFT OUTER JOIN

```
SELECT C.CustomerID, SOH.SalesOrderID, SOD.SalesOrderDetailID, SOD.ProductID
FROM Sales.Customer AS C
LEFT OUTER JOIN Sales.SalesOrderHeader AS SOH ON C.CustomerID = SOH.CustomerID
LEFT OUTER JOIN Sales.SalesOrderDetail AS SOD ON SOH.SalesOrderID = SOD.SalesOrderID
WHERE C.CustomerID IN (11028,11029,1,2,3,4);
```

Figure 5-15 shows the results. Because the columns from the nonmatching rows from Sales.SalesOrderHeader contain NULL, they can't join to the Sales.SalesOrderDetail table. If you must join another table to the Sales.SalesOrderHeader table, you must use LEFT OUTER JOIN because you can't join on the NULL values. On your own, change the query by removing the words LEFT OUTER in the join between Sales.SalesOrderHeader and Sales.SalesOrderDetail. The customers with no orders will drop out of the results.

	CustomerID	SalesOrderID	SalesOrderDetailID	ProductID
1	1	NULL	NULL	NULL
2	2	NULL	NULL	NULL
3	3	NULL	NULL	NULL
4	4	NULL	NULL	NULL
5	11028	43831	487	776
6	11028	57943	65072	779
7	11028	57943	65073	930
8	11028	57943	65074	873
9	11028	67961	98619	962
10	11029	43794	450	774
11	11029	57294	63489	779
12	11029	57294	63490	711
13	11029	57294	63491	882
14	11029	70593	107626	962
15	11029	70593	107627	872
16	11029	70593	107628	870

Figure 5-15. *The results of querying multiple tables with* LEFT OUTER JOIN

I prefer listing the main, or parent, table first and using LEFT JOIN over RIGHT JOIN. In fact, this always makes the query more readable regardless of the type of join. If you list the main table first and you start down the LEFT OUTER JOIN path, you can continue to use LEFT. If you start out with RIGHT, you may have to switch to LEFT when you add more tables, which can be confusing.

Adding a Table to the Main Table of a *LEFT JOIN*

You may be wondering what kind of join you would use if you wanted to join another table to the main table of a left join. To be on the safe side, use LEFT OUTER JOIN to ensure that you will not lose any rows from the main table. In some cases it will not matter if you use INNER JOIN or LEFT OUTER JOIN, and the following example is one of those cases. Because the Territory table is joining directly to the Customer table and every customer must have a territory, you won't lose any rows with an INNER JOIN. With more experience, you will know when it is safe to use INNER JOIN with situations like these.

Listing 5-10 shows an example query that joins another table to the main table. Type in and execute the code.

Listing 5-10. *Adding Another Table to the Left Side of the Join*

```
SELECT C.CustomerID, SOH.SalesOrderID, SOD.SalesOrderDetailID,
    SOD.ProductID, T.Name
FROM Sales.Customer AS C
LEFT OUTER JOIN Sales.SalesOrderHeader AS SOH ON C.CustomerID = SOH.CustomerID
LEFT OUTER JOIN Sales.SalesOrderDetail AS SOD ON SOH.SalesOrderID = SOD.SalesOrderID
LEFT OUTER JOIN Sales.SalesTerritory AS T ON C.TerritoryID = T.TerritoryID
WHERE C.CustomerID IN (11028,11029,1,2,3,4);
```

Figure 5-16 shows the partial results. The Sales.SalesTerritory table joins the Sales.Customer table on TerritoryID.

	CustomerID	SalesOrderID	SalesOrderDetailID	ProductID	Name
1	1	NULL	NULL	NULL	Northwest
2	2	NULL	NULL	NULL	Northwest
3	3	NULL	NULL	NULL	Southwest
4	4	NULL	NULL	NULL	Southwest
5	11028	43831	487	776	Australia
6	11028	57943	65072	779	Australia
7	11028	57943	65073	930	Australia
8	11028	57943	65074	873	Australia
9	11028	67961	98619	962	Australia
10	11029	43794	450	774	Australia
11	11029	57294	63489	779	Australia
12	11029	57294	63490	711	Australia
13	11029	57294	63491	882	Australia
14	11029	70593	107626	962	Australia
15	11029	70593	107627	872	Australia
16	11029	70593	107628	870	Australia

Figure 5-16. *The partial results of joining to the left side of LEFT OUTER JOIN*

FULL OUTER JOIN

FULL OUTER JOIN is similar to LEFT OUTER JOIN and RIGHT OUTER JOIN, but in this case, all the rows from each side of the join are returned. In other words, all rows from the left side of the join, even if there is not a match, and all rows from the right side, even if there is not a match, show up in the results. This type of join is rare and could indicate some problems with the database design or the data. For example, this type of join might be necessary if the Sales. SalesOrderHeader table contains orders with invalid CustomerID values. Here is the syntax:

```
SELECT <column list>
FROM <table1>
FULL [OUTER] JOIN <table2> ON <table1>.<col1>  = <table2>.<col2>
```

Because no good example exists in the AdventureWorks database, Listing 5-11 includes a script that creates and populates a table of colors that can be used in the Production.Product table. After populating the table, it contains colors that don't appear in the Production.Product table, and it is missing a color that should be there. Don't worry about understanding the table creation and population part of the script at this point.

Listing 5-11. FULL OUTER JOIN Demonstration

```
IF OBJECT_ID('Production.ProductColor') IS NOT NULL BEGIN
    DROP TABLE Production.ProductColor;
END
CREATE table Production.ProductColor
    (Color nvarchar(15) NOT NULL PRIMARY KEY);
GO
--Insert most of the existing colors
INSERT INTO Production.ProductColor
SELECT DISTINCT Color
FROM Production.Product
WHERE Color IS NOT NULL and Color <> 'Silver';
```

```
--Insert some additional colors
INSERT INTO Production.ProductColor
VALUES ('Green'),('Orange'),('Purple');

--Here is the query:
SELECT c.Color AS "Color from list", p.Color, p.ProductID
FROM Production.Product AS p
FULL OUTER JOIN Production.ProductColor AS c ON p.Color = c.Color
ORDER BY p.ProductID;
```

Figure 5-17 displays the results. When colors from the Production.ProductColor table have no matches in the Production.Product table, the query returns NULL values in the second and third columns, which are from Production. Product (rows 1–3). When colors from the Production.Product table don't match the Production.ProductColor table (in this case, silver) or no color for a product is specified, the query returns NULL values in the first column, which is from Production.ProductColor (row 12). Finally, when a product has a color that matches one found in the Production.ProductColor table, the query returns all non-NULL values (rows 9–11). A query like this might be used to find problems in data so that it can be cleaned up before loading it into a production system or data warehouse.

	Color from list	Color	ProductID
1	Purple	NULL	NULL
2	Green	NULL	NULL
3	Orange	NULL	NULL
4	NULL	NULL	1
5	NULL	NULL	2
6	NULL	NULL	3
7	NULL	NULL	4
8	NULL	NULL	316
9	Black	Black	317
10	Black	Black	318
11	Black	Black	319
12	NULL	Silver	320

Figure 5-17. *The partial results of using FULL OUTER JOIN*

CROSS JOIN

Another type of rarely used join is CROSS JOIN. This is actually the same as the Cartesian product mentioned earlier in the section "Avoiding an Incorrect Join Condition." In this case, use CROSS JOIN when you intend to multiply two tables together—every row from one table matched to every row from another table. You might write a CROSS JOIN query to populate a table for a special purpose such as an inventory worksheet. You may need a list of every product in every possible location to create forms for the inventory crew. Here is the syntax:

```
SELECT <SELECT list> FROM <table1> CROSS JOIN <table2>
```

Notice that the FROM clause doesn't contain a join condition. Every possible row from one table joins every possible row from another table, so you don't have to specify a join condition. Listing 5-12 demonstrates how to write this type of query. Type in and execute the code.

Listing 5-12. A CROSS JOIN

```
--1
SELECT p.ProductID, l.LocationID
FROM Production.Product AS p
CROSS JOIN Production.Location AS l
ORDER BY ProductID;

--2
SELECT p.ProductID, l.LocationID
FROM Production.Product AS p
CROSS JOIN Production.Location AS l
ORDER BY LocationID;
```

Figure 5-18 shows the partial results. These queries, just sorted differently, each produce a row for every possible product and every possible location. Query 1 shows that product 1 displays along with every location. Query 2 shows that location 1 displays along with every product.

	ProductID	LocationID
1	1	1
2	1	2
3	1	3
4	1	4
5	1	5
6	1	6
7	1	7
8	1	10

	ProductID	LocationID
1	980	1
2	365	1
3	771	1
4	404	1
5	977	1
6	818	1
7	474	1
8	748	1

Figure 5-18. *The partial results of a CROSS JOIN*

Self-Joins

A self-join is a special type of query that joins a table back to itself. In this example, you will first create a temporary table named #Employee. Normally the EmployeeID would be a primary key column and the ManagerID would be a foreign key pointing back to the same table. This would ensure that only an existing EmployeeID could be added to the ManagerID column. Every employee, except for one, has a manager—another employee appearing in the same table. The one employee with no manager is the CEO of Adventure Works. The SQL Server team chose to eliminate the self-join when creating recent versions of AdventureWorks in favor of a new feature first introduced with SQL Server 2008, the HIERARCHYID data type. You will learn about HIERARCHYID in Chapter 16.

You can actually join any table to itself even if it doesn't have a foreign key pointing back to the primary key. This relationship is called a *unary relationship*. Here is the syntax for a self-join:

```
SELECT <a.col1>, <b.col1>
FROM <table1> AS a
LEFT [OUTER] JOIN <table1> AS b ON a.<col1> = b.<col2>
```

Listing 5-13 demonstrates how to write a self-join by creating and populating a temporary table. Type in and execute the code to learn about this.

Listing 5-13. Using Self-Join

```
CREATE TABLE #Employee (
EmployeeID  int,
ManagerID int,
Title nvarchar(50));

INSERT INTO #Employee
VALUES (1, NULL, 'Chief Executive Officer');
INSERT INTO #Employee
VALUES (2, 1, 'Engineering Manager');
INSERT INTO #Employee
VALUES (3, 2, 'Senior Tool Designer');
INSERT INTO #Employee
VALUES (4, 2, 'Design Engineer');
INSERT INTO #Employee
VALUES (5, 2, 'Research and Development');
INSERT INTO #Employee
VALUES (6, 1, 'Marketing Manager');
INSERT INTO #Employee
VALUES (7, 6, 'Marketing Specialist');

SELECT a.EmployeeID AS Employee,
    a.Title AS EmployeeTitle,
    b.EmployeeID AS ManagerID,
    b.Title AS ManagerTitle
FROM #Employee AS a
LEFT OUTER JOIN #Employee AS b ON a.ManagerID = b.EmployeeID;

DROP TABLE #Employee;
```

Take a look at the results shown in Figure 5-19. Each employee, except for one, has a manager who is also an employee listed in the same table. The table has ManagerID, which points back to the Employee. Because employee 1 doesn't have a manager, the query uses LEFT OUTER JOIN. Be sure to keep track of which table each column is supposed to come from. Even though the query uses the same table twice, it has two separate roles.

	Employee	EmployeeTitle	ManagerID	ManagerTitle
1	1	Chief Executive Officer	NULL	NULL
2	2	Engineering Manager	1	Chief Executive Officer
3	3	Senior Tool Designer	2	Engineering Manager
4	4	Design Engineer	2	Engineering Manager
5	5	Research and Development	2	Engineering Manager
6	6	Marketing Manager	1	Chief Executive Officer
7	7	Marketing Specialist	6	Marketing Manager

Figure 5-19. *The results of using a self-join*

The important thing to remember is that one table is used twice in the query. At least one of the table names must be aliased; this is not optional because you can't have two tables with the same name in the query. You will have to qualify all the column names, so you may want to alias both table names to save typing.

This section covered several advanced joining techniques. Understanding how the techniques work and when to use them are very important skills. Practice what you have learned by completing Exercise 5-2.

EXERCISE 5-2

Use the AdventureWorks database to complete this exercise. You can find the solutions at the end of the chapter.

1. Write a query that displays all the products along with the SalesOrderID even if an order has never been placed for that product. Join to the Sales.SalesOrderDetail table using the ProductID column.

2. Change the query written in question 1 so that only products that have not been ordered show up in the query.

3. Write a query that returns all the rows from the Sales.SalesPerson table joined to the Sales.SalesOrderHeader table along with the SalesOrderID column even if no orders match. Include the SalesPersonID, SalesYTD and SalesOrderID columns in the results.

4. Change the query written in question 3 so that the salesperson's name also displays from the Person.Person table.

5. The Sales.SalesOrderHeader table contains foreign keys to the Sales.CurrencyRate and Purchasing.ShipMethod tables. Write a query joining all three tables, and make sure it contains all rows from Sales.SalesOrderHeader. Include the CurrencyRateID, AverageRate, SalesOrderID, and ShipBase columns.

6. Write a query that returns the BusinessEntityID column from the Sales.SalesPerson table along with every ProductID from the Production.Product table.

Thinking About Performance

When joining two tables, the database engine can choose from three ways to join the tables: Merge Join, Hash Match, and Nested Loop. There is no one way that is the best; SQL Server will select the best choice for each situation. The component of SQL Server that chooses a good execution plan for each query is called the *optimizer*. To learn more about this topic, view the Technet article found at http://technet.microsoft.com/en-us/library/ms191426(v=sql.105).aspx.

Merge Join

The Merge Join operator will be used when the optimizer estimates that a relatively large number of rows will be returned from both sides of the join, and the data on each side is sorted by the join key. In the AdventureWorks database, the Sales.SalesOrderHeader table joins to the Sales.SalesOrderDetail table on SalesOrderID. This column is the primary key of the Sales.SalesOrderHeader table and the first column of the primary key of the Sales.SalesOrderDetail table. The primary keys are also used as the clustered index keys, therefore, each of those tables is sorted by the SalesOrderID column. The query in Listing 5-14 uses a Merge Join.

Listing 5-14. Query Using a Merge Join

```
SELECT SOH.SalesOrderID, SOD.OrderQty, SOD.ProductID
FROM Sales.SalesOrderHeader AS SOH
INNER JOIN Sales.SalesOrderDetail AS SOD
ON SOH.SalesOrderID = SOD.SalesOrderID;
```

Figure 5-20 shows the execution plan for this query with the Merge Join operator. As this query is processed, the SalesOrderID of the two sides is compared. When there is a match, the combined row is returned as part of the results.

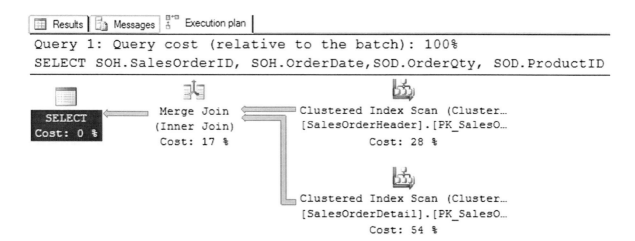

Figure 5-20. *The execution plan showing a Merge Join*

Figure 5-21 illustrates how this works. The two inputs are sorted. In step 1 the first two values are compared and they match. Now the first value of the top input is compared to the second value of the bottom input in step 2 for another match. In step three, the first value of the top row is compared to the third value of the bottom input. In this case, it is not a match. Now the process can move to the second value of the top input in step 4 where there is another match. In step 5, the inputs do not match so the process moves to the last two items in step 6.

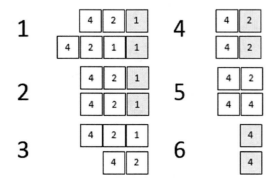

Figure 5-21. *How a Merge Join works*

Nested Loop

If the optimizer *estimates* that one side of the join has a small number of rows to join, it may choose to use a Nested Loop. It doesn't matter if the two sides of the join are sorted. With a Nested Loop, SQL Server will loop through all the rows from the small side of the join looking for a match in the rows of the larger side. Listing 5-15 will produce a Nested Loop.

Listing 5-15. Query Using a Nested Loop

```
SELECT SOH.SalesOrderID, SOD.OrderQty, SOD.ProductID
FROM Sales.SalesOrderHeader AS SOH
INNER JOIN Sales.SalesOrderDetail AS SOD
ON SOH.SalesOrderID = SOD.SalesOrderID
WHERE SOH.CustomerID = 11000;
```

Figure 5-22 shows the execution plan featuring Nested Loop. In this case, the database engine will loop through the clustered index of the Sales.SalesOrderDetail table for every row found in the IX_SalesOrderHeader_CustomerID index. Even if there is not an index on the joining columns, the optimizer may select this type of join.

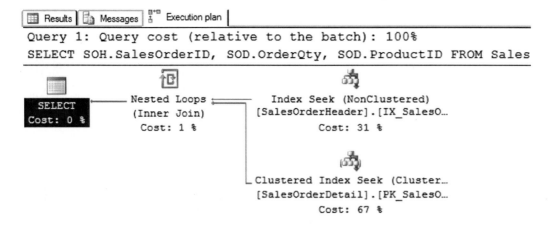

Figure 5-22. *The execution plan showing a Nested Loop*

To see the estimated and actual number of rows, mouse-over the Seek or Scan operators to see the properties and read the values. Figure 5-23 shows the properties of the seek of the SalesOrderHeader index.

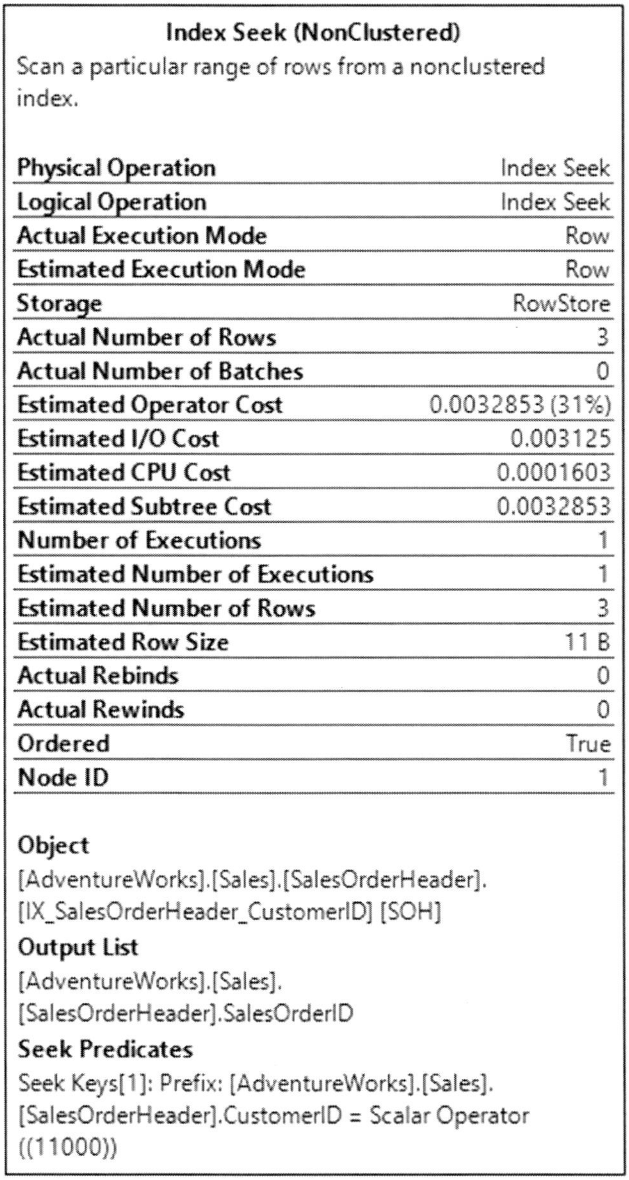

Index Seek (NonClustered)
Scan a particular range of rows from a nonclustered index.

Physical Operation	Index Seek
Logical Operation	Index Seek
Actual Execution Mode	Row
Estimated Execution Mode	Row
Storage	RowStore
Actual Number of Rows	3
Actual Number of Batches	0
Estimated Operator Cost	0.0032853 (31%)
Estimated I/O Cost	0.003125
Estimated CPU Cost	0.0001603
Estimated Subtree Cost	0.0032853
Number of Executions	1
Estimated Number of Executions	1
Estimated Number of Rows	3
Estimated Row Size	11 B
Actual Rebinds	0
Actual Rewinds	0
Ordered	True
Node ID	1

Object
[AdventureWorks].[Sales].[SalesOrderHeader].
[IX_SalesOrderHeader_CustomerID] [SOH]
Output List
[AdventureWorks].[Sales].
[SalesOrderHeader].SalesOrderID
Seek Predicates
Seek Keys[1]: Prefix: [AdventureWorks].[Sales].
[SalesOrderHeader].CustomerID = Scalar Operator
((11000))

Figure 5-23. *The properties of the index seek*

To illustrate this join operator, take a look at Figure 5-24. In a Nested Loop, the process loops through the smaller side of the join, comparing each value to the values of the larger side of the join. The process loops through the smaller input one time, but loops through the larger input one time for each iteration of the small loop. Notice that this process takes 12 steps compared with only six steps in the Merge Join example because the data doesn't have to be sorted in this type of operation.

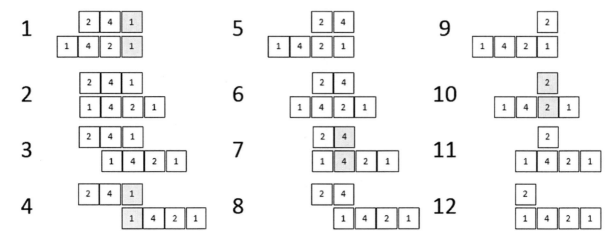

Figure 5-24. *How a Nested Loop works*

Hash Match

Finally, the optimizer may select the Hash Match join type. This type of join is used when the optimizer estimates that a large number of rows will be returned from each side of the join and the input is not sorted on the joining columns. The database engine actually creates hash tables in memory to get this to work. Listing 5-16 shows a query that uses a Hash Match.

Listing 5-16. Query Using Hash Match

```
SELECT C.CustomerID, TotalDue
FROM Sales.Customer AS C
JOIN Sales.SalesOrderHeader S
ON C.CustomerID = S.CustomerID;
```

Figure 5-25 shows the execution plan. Because there is not an index on the Sales.SalesOrderHeader table containing both the CustomerID and the TotalDue, the optimizer decides to use Sales.SalesOrderHeader's clustered index (table). It is sorted by SalesOrderID so a Merge Join can't be used because CustomerID is the joining column. If TotalDue was added to the IX_SalesOrderHeader_CustomerID index, then the query could perform much better and also use a Merge Join instead. There are two ways the TotalDue column could be added to the index: either as a key column or as an included column. The included column doesn't help with ordering or searching, but it would allow the index to be used instead of the actual table.

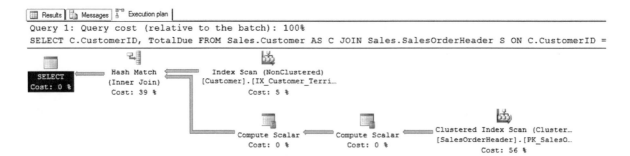

Figure 5-25. *The execution plan showing a Hash Match*

The Hash Match join type builds one or more hash tables, like buckets, with the smaller input. Then the larger input probes the hash table looking for matches. The process will loop through the larger input once, and it will be efficient to find the matches in the hash table.

Indexes can affect the performance of queries joining more than one table. Although this book is not meant to teach index tuning, it is a best practice to add indexes to foreign keys. To learn more about index tuning, see *Expert Performance Indexing for SQL Server 2012* by Jason Strate and Ted Kruger (Apress 2012).

Summary

For the data to make sense in reports and applications, tables must be joined together. As you can see from the number of topics in this chapter, there are many ways to do this. Most queries will use the INNER JOIN syntax, but for returning all the rows, even if there is not a match, use an OUTER JOIN. For queries using INNER JOIN, there must be a match on columns from both sides of the join, usually in a parent–child relationship. The OUTER JOIN syntax allows you to join tables when there is not a match in some cases. In Chapter 6 you will learn even more ways to use more than two tables in a query, such as common table expressions and subqueries.

Answers to the Exercises

This section provides solutions to the exercises found on writing queries joining tables.

Solutions to Exercise 5-1: Using INNER JOIN

Use the AdventureWorks database to complete this exercise.

1. The HumanResources.Employee table does not contain the employee names. Join that table to the Person.Person table on the BusinessEntityID column. Display the job title, birth date, first name, and last name.

    ```
    SELECT E.JobTitle, E.BirthDate, P.FirstName, P.LastName
    FROM HumanResources.Employee AS E
    INNER JOIN Person.Person AS P ON
        E.BusinessEntityID = P.BusinessEntityID;
    ```

2. The customer names also appear in the Person.Person table. Join the Sales.Customer table to the Person.Person table. The BusinessEntityID column in the Person.Person table matches the PersonID column in the Sales.Customer table. Display the CustomerID, StoreID, and TerritoryID columns along with the name columns.

    ```
    SELECT C.CustomerID, C.StoreID, C.TerritoryID,
        P.FirstName, P.MiddleName, P.LastName
    FROM Sales.Customer AS C
    INNER JOIN Person.Person AS P
        ON C.PersonID = P.BusinessEntityID;
    ```

3. Extend the query written in question 2 to include the Sales.SalesOrderHeader table. Display the SalesOrderID column along with the columns already specified. The Sales.SalesOrderHeader table joins the Sales.Customer table on CustomerID.

```
SELECT C.CustomerID, C.StoreID, C.TerritoryID,
    P.FirstName, P.MiddleName,
    P.LastName, S.SalesOrderID
FROM Sales.Customer AS C
INNER JOIN Person.Person AS P
    ON C.PersonID = P.BusinessEntityID
INNER JOIN Sales.SalesOrderHeader AS S
    ON S.CustomerID = C.CustomerID;
```

4. Write a query that joins the Sales.SalesOrderHeader table to the Sales.SalesPerson table. Join the BusinessEntityID column from the Sales.SalesPerson table to the SalesPersonID column in the Sales.SalesOrderHeader table. Display the SalesOrderID along with the SalesQuota and Bonus.

```
SELECT S.SalesOrderID, SP.SalesQuota, SP.Bonus
FROM Sales.SalesOrderHeader AS S
INNER JOIN Sales.SalesPerson AS SP
    ON S.SalesPersonID = SP.BusinessEntityID;
```

5. Add the name columns to the query written in question 4 by joining on the Person.Person table. See whether you can figure out which columns will be used to write the join.

```
SELECT SalesOrderID, SalesQuota, Bonus, FirstName,
    MiddleName, LastName
FROM Sales.SalesOrderHeader AS S
INNER JOIN Sales.SalesPerson AS SP
    ON S.SalesPersonID = SP.BusinessEntityID
INNER JOIN Person.Person AS P
    ON SP.BusinessEntityID = P.BusinessEntityID;
```

6. The catalog description for each product is stored in the Production.ProductModel table. Display the columns that describe the product such as the color and size, along with the catalog description for each product.

```
SELECT PM.CatalogDescription, P.Color, P.Size
FROM Production.Product AS P
INNER JOIN Production.ProductModel AS PM
    ON P.ProductModelID = PM.ProductModelID;
```

7. Write a query that displays the names of the customers along with the product names that they have purchased. Hint: Five tables will be required to write this query!

```
SELECT FirstName, MiddleName, LastName, Prod.Name
FROM Sales.Customer AS C
INNER JOIN Person.Person AS P
    ON C.PersonID = P.BusinessEntityID
INNER JOIN Sales.SalesOrderHeader AS SOH
    ON C.CustomerID = SOH.CustomerID
INNER JOIN Sales.SalesOrderDetail AS SOD
    ON SOH.SalesOrderID = SOD.SalesOrderID
INNER JOIN Production.Product AS Prod
    ON SOD.ProductID = Prod.ProductID;
```

Solutions to Exercise 5-2: Using OUTER JOIN

Use the AdventureWorks database to complete this exercise.

1. Write a query that displays all the products along with the SalesOrderID even if an order has never been placed for that product. Join to the Sales.SalesOrderDetail table using the ProductID column.

    ```
    SELECT SalesOrderID, P.ProductID, P.Name
    FROM Production.Product AS P
    LEFT OUTER JOIN Sales.SalesOrderDetail
        AS SOD ON P.ProductID = SOD.ProductID;
    ```

2. Change the query written in question 1 so that only products that have not been ordered show up in the query.

    ```
    SELECT SalesOrderID, P.ProductID, P.Name
    FROM Production.Product AS P
    LEFT OUTER JOIN Sales.SalesOrderDetail
        AS SOD ON P.ProductID = SOD.ProductID
    WHERE SalesOrderID IS NULL;
    ```

3. Write a query that returns all the rows from the Sales.SalesPerson table joined to the Sales.SalesOrderHeader table along with the SalesOrderID column even if no orders match. Include the SalesPersonID, SalesYTD and SalesOrderID columns in the results.

    ```
    SELECT SalesOrderID, SalesPersonID, SalesYTD, SOH.SalesOrderID
    FROM Sales.SalesPerson AS SP
    LEFT OUTER JOIN Sales.SalesOrderHeader AS SOH
        ON SP.BusinessEntityID = SOH.SalesPersonID;
    ```

4. Change the query written in question 3 so that the salesperson's name also displays from the Person.Person table.

    ```
    SELECT SalesOrderID, SalesPersonID, SalesYTD, SOH.SalesOrderID,
        FirstName, MiddleName, LastName
    FROM Sales.SalesPerson AS SP
    LEFT OUTER JOIN Sales.SalesOrderHeader AS SOH
        ON SP.BusinessEntityID = SOH.SalesPersonID
    LEFT OUTER JOIN Person.Person AS P
        ON P.BusinessEntityID = SP.BusinessEntityID;
    ```

5. The Sales.SalesOrderHeader table contains foreign keys to the Sales.CurrencyRate and Purchasing.ShipMethod tables. Write a query joining all three tables, and make sure it contains all rows from Sales.SalesOrderHeader. Include the CurrencyRateID, AverageRate, SalesOrderID, and ShipBase columns.

```
SELECT CR.CurrencyRateID, CR.AverageRate,
    SM.ShipBase, SalesOrderID
FROM Sales.SalesOrderHeader AS SOH
LEFT OUTER JOIN Sales.CurrencyRate AS CR
    ON SOH.CurrencyRateID = CR.CurrencyRateID
LEFT OUTER JOIN Purchasing.ShipMethod AS SM
    ON SOH.ShipMethodID = SM.ShipMethodID;
```

6. Write a query that returns the BusinessEntityID column from the Sales.SalesPerson table along with every ProductID from the Production.Product table.

```
SELECT SP.BusinessEntityID, P.ProductID
FROM Sales.SalesPerson AS SP
CROSS JOIN Production.Product AS P;
```

CHAPTER 6

Building on Subqueries, Common Table Expressions, and Unions

The most common way to use more than one table in a query is by joining them, which you learned about in Chapter 5. This chapter will explain several other ways to combine tables in a query. *Subqueries* and *common table expressions* (CTE) allow you to isolate the logic of complex queries. *Union queries* allow you to combine the results of two independent queries into one result set. The first thing you will learn in this chapter is how to substitute a query for a hard-coded IN list.

Writing Subqueries

This section demonstrates using subqueries in the WHERE clause. A *subquery* is a nested query—a query within a query. One reason to use a subquery is to find the rows in one table that match the rows in another table without actually joining the second table. For example, without actually joining the order table, you could use a subquery to display a list of the customers who have placed an order.

Using a Subquery in an *IN* List

Using a subquery in an IN list is similar to the hard-coded IN list you learned to use in a WHERE clause in Chapter 3. Here is the syntax:

```
SELECT <select list> FROM <table1>
WHERE <col1> IN (SELECT <col2> FROM <table2>)
```

Listing 6-1 demonstrates this technique. Type in and execute the code.

Listing 6-1. Using a Subquery in the IN List

```
SELECT CustomerID, AccountNumber
FROM Sales.Customer
WHERE CustomerID IN (SELECT CustomerID FROM Sales.SalesOrderHeader);
```

This query returns a list of the customers who have placed an order (see Figure 6-1). The difference between this example and the examples in Chapter 5 that join these tables is that the columns from the Sales.SalesOrderHeader table don't show up in the results. Each customer displays only once in the results, not once for each order placed. The subquery produces a list of possible values from one, and only one, column. The outer query compares a column to that list.

127

	CustomerID	AccountNumber
1	11000	AW00011000
2	11001	AW00011001
3	11002	AW00011002
4	11003	AW00011003
5	11004	AW00011004
6	11005	AW00011005
7	11006	AW00011006
8	11007	AW00011007
9	11008	AW00011008
10	11009	AW00011009

Figure 6-1. *The partial results of using a subquery in an IN list*

Using a Subquery and *NOT IN*

A subquery in the WHERE clause can also be used to find rows that don't match the values from another table by adding the NOT operator. You can find the customers who have not placed an order by adding the word NOT to the previous query. Type in and execute the code in Listing 6-2, which demonstrates using NOT IN.

Listing 6-2. A Subquery with NOT IN

```
SELECT CustomerID, AccountNumber
FROM Sales.Customer
WHERE CustomerID NOT IN
    (SELECT CustomerID FROM Sales.SalesOrderHeader);
```

This query returns the opposite results of Listing 6-1 (see Figure 6-2). The subquery returns a list of all the CustomerID values found in Sales.SalesOrderHeader. By using NOT IN, the query returns all the rows from Sales. Customer that don't match.

	CustomerID	AccountNumber
1	1	AW00000001
2	2	AW00000002
3	3	AW00000003
4	4	AW00000004
5	5	AW00000005
6	6	AW00000006
7	7	AW00000007
8	8	AW00000008
9	9	AW00000009
10	10	AW00000010

Figure 6-2. *The partial results of using a subquery with NOT IN*

Using a Subquery Containing *NULL* with *NOT IN*

Recall that you will often get unexpected results if you don't take NULL values into account. If the subquery contains any NULL values, using NOT IN will incorrectly produce no rows. This is not a bug in SQL Server; you simply must take NULL values into account. For example, the values returned by a subquery are NULL, 1, 2, and 3. The values from the outer query (1, 2, and 10) must each be compared with that list. The database engine can tell that 10 is not 1, 2, or 3, but it can't tell whether it is the same as NULL. The intended result is 10 because it doesn't match any of the values from the subquery, but because of the NULL, the comparison returns no results at all. Type in and execute the code in Listing 6-3, which shows unexpected results and how to correct the problem.

Listing 6-3. A Subquery with NOT IN

```
--1
SELECT CurrencyRateID, FromCurrencyCode, ToCurrencyCode
FROM Sales.CurrencyRate
WHERE CurrencyRateID NOT IN
    (SELECT CurrencyRateID
     FROM Sales.SalesOrderHeader);

--2
SELECT CurrencyRateID, FromCurrencyCode, ToCurrencyCode
FROM Sales.CurrencyRate
WHERE CurrencyRateID NOT IN
    (SELECT CurrencyRateID
     FROM Sales.SalesOrderHeader
     WHERE CurrencyRateID IS NOT NULL);
```

Figure 6-3 shows the results. Query 1 does not return any results because NULL values exist in the values returned by the subquery. Because any value from CurrencyRateID compared to NULL returns UNKNOWN, it is impossible to know whether any of the values meet the criteria. Query 2 corrects the problem by adding a WHERE clause to the subquery that eliminates NULL values.

	CurrencyRateID	FromCurrencyCode	ToCurrencyCode

	CurrencyRateID	FromCurrencyCode	ToCurrencyCode
1	1	USD	ARS
2	3	USD	BRL
3	5	USD	CNY
4	6	USD	DEM
5	7	USD	EUR
6	9	USD	GBP
7	10	USD	JPY
8	11	USD	MXN

Figure 6-3. *The results of code that corrects the NULL problem with NOT IN*

Using a subquery in the WHERE clause is a very popular technique. Just make sure you always eliminate the possibility of NULL values in the subquery.

Using *EXISTS*

Another way to find rows that are included or missing from another table is by using a subquery along with EXISTS. This usually performs better as well. Instead of comparing one column to the results of a subquery, this technique joins the subquery with the outer query in the WHERE clause. If a row is returned when using EXISTS, the subquery returns TRUE and the outer row is returned. Conversely, if no rows are returned, NOT EXISTS returns TRUE and the row from the outer query is returned. Listing 6-4 shows how to write queries using this method.

Listing 6-4. Using the EXISTS Subquery

```
--1
SELECT CustomerID, AccountNumber
FROM Sales.Customer
WHERE EXISTS
    (SELECT* FROM Sales.SalesOrderHeader AS SOH
    WHERE SOH.CustomerID = Customer.CustomerID);

--2
SELECT CustomerID, AccountNumber
FROM Sales.Customer
WHERE NOT EXISTS
    (SELECT * FROM Sales.SalesOrderHeader AS SOH
    WHERE SOH.CustomerID = Customer.CustomerID);
```

Figure 6-4 shows the results. Notice that the subquery uses the asterisk instead of a list of columns. In this case, it is perfectly fine to do so because no actual data is returned from the subquery. In the WHERE clause, the subquery joins to the outer query on the CustomerID. The outer query table name must be specified. You will learn about other ways to use correlated subqueries in Chapter 10.

	CustomerID	AccountNumber
1	11000	AW00011000
2	11001	AW00011001
3	11002	AW00011002
4	11003	AW00011003

	CustomerID	AccountNumber
1	1	AW00000001
2	2	AW00000002
3	3	AW00000003
4	4	AW00000004

Figure 6-4. *The partial results of using the NOT EXISTS technique*

Using *CROSS APPLY* and *OUTER APPLY*

Two more techniques for joining subqueries are CROSS APPLY and OUTER APPLY. These work similarly to functions that join the results to the left side of the query. The inner query runs once for each input of the outer query. The difference between the two is that OUTER APPLY returns all rows from the left side even if there is not a match. You'll see some more advanced examples of these techniques in Chapter 14, but for now take a look at the simple examples in Listing 6-5.

Listing 6-5. Using CROSS APPLY and OUTER APPLY

```
--1
SELECT CustomerID, AccountNumber, SalesOrderID
FROM Sales.Customer AS Cust
CROSS APPLY(SELECT  SalesOrderID
FROM Sales.SalesOrderHeader AS SOH
WHERE Cust.CustomerID = SOH.CustomerID) AS A;


--2
SELECT CustomerID, AccountNumber, SalesOrderID
FROM Sales.Customer AS Cust
OUTER APPLY(SELECT  SalesOrderID
FROM Sales.SalesOrderHeader AS SOH
WHERE Cust.CustomerID = SOH.CustomerID) AS A;
```

Figure 6-5 shows the results. Query 1 returns the customers along with the orders. Query 2 is similar to a LEFT OUTER JOIN. All customers are returned even if the customer has not placed an order.

	CustomerID	AccountNumber	SalesOrderID
1	11000	AW00011000	43793
2	11000	AW00011000	51522
3	11000	AW00011000	57418
4	11001	AW00011001	43767

	CustomerID	AccountNumber	SalesOrderID
1	1	AW00000001	NULL
2	2	AW00000002	NULL
3	3	AW00000003	NULL
4	4	AW00000004	NULL

Figure 6-5. *Using CROSS APPLY and OUTER APPLY*

Writing *UNION* Queries

A UNION query is not really a join, but it is a way to combine the results of two queries with the same structure together. I like to think of it as "folding" one set of results into another set of results. One reason for using a UNION query is to view data with one query that combines data from a production table along with data that has been archived into another table. A UNION query combines two queries, and the results are returned in one result set. Here is the syntax:

```
SELECT <col1>, <col2>,<col3>
FROM <table1>
UNION [ALL]
SELECT <col4>,<col5>,<col6>FROM <table2>
```

Figure 6-6 shows a diagram of how two UNION queries might look. In this case there are three queries combined with two UNION operators. Each individual query must contain the same number of columns and be of compatible data types. For example, you could have an INT column and a VARCHAR column line up as long as the VARCHAR column contains only numbers. There is an optional keyword, ALL, that actually performs better than without. When the word ALL is left out, the database engine must expend resources removing duplicate rows.

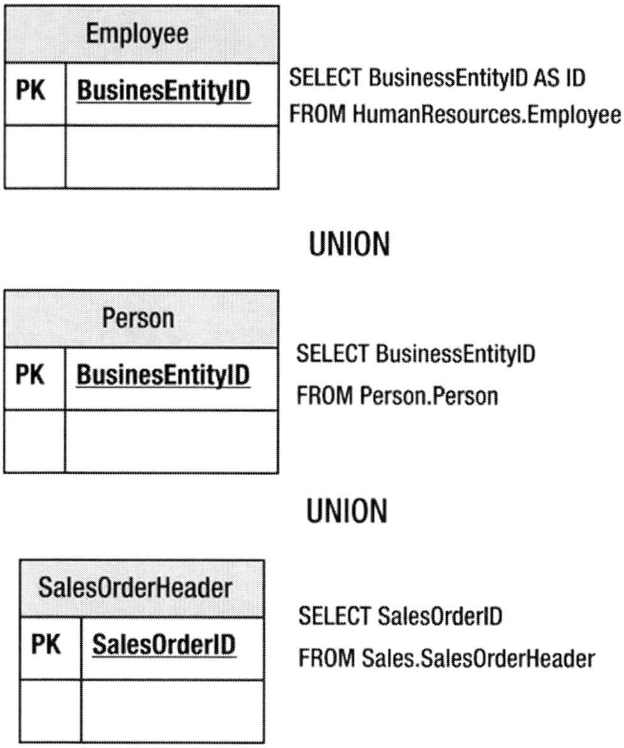

Employee
PK | BusinesEntityID

SELECT BusinessEntityID AS ID
FROM HumanResources.Employee

UNION

Person
PK | BusinesEntityID

SELECT BusinessEntityID
FROM Person.Person

UNION

SalesOrderHeader
PK | SalesOrderID

SELECT SalesOrderID
FROM Sales.SalesOrderHeader

Figure 6-6. *The diagram of a UNION query*

Type in and execute the code in Listing 6-6 to learn how to use UNION.

Listing 6-6. Using UNION

```
--1
SELECT BusinessEntityID AS ID
FROM HumanResources.Employee
UNION
SELECT BusinessEntityID
FROM Person.Person
UNION
SELECT SalesOrderID
FROM Sales.SalesOrderHeader
ORDER BY ID;
```

133

```
--2
SELECT BusinessEntityID AS ID
FROM HumanResources.Employee
UNION ALL
SELECT BusinessEntityID
FROM Person.Person
UNION ALL
SELECT SalesOrderID
FROM Sales.SalesOrderHeader
ORDER BY ID;
```

Notice the difference in the two queries in Listing 6-6. Figure 6-7 shows the results. Query 2 uses UNION ALL, which returns all rows, even if they are duplicates. Leaving out the keyword ALL eliminates the duplicates. If at all possible, include the keyword ALL because of the performance benefits. For example, if you are certain that there will not be duplicates, don't make SQL Server do the work of eliminating duplicates that don't exist. The first query in the UNION query determines the number of columns and the name of each column. When using a UNION query, only one ORDER BY clause can be used, and it will be located at the end of the statement.

	ID
1	1
2	2
3	3
4	4
5	5

	ID
1	1
2	1
3	2
4	2
5	3

Figure 6-7. *The results of UNION queries*

A UNION query is often used to combine the results of two tables so that they look the same. For example, a database has separate customer tables for each division of the company. By using a UNION query, the customers can be displayed together as if they were in the same table. It is also possible to write UNION queries using the same table.

When writing a UNION query, you must make sure that both queries contain the same number of columns in the results and that the data types are compatible. The first query sets the number of columns and the name of each column. The second and later queries must match up to the first query. The data type of each column follows precedence rules, so you can't allow one query to return an integer where the other query returns a string unless the string can be implicitly converted to an integer. Run these practice queries to see what happens when a UNION query doesn't follow these rules:

```
--Incompatible types
SELECT 1
UNION ALL
```

```
SELECT 'a'
--Number of columns don't match up
SELECT 1
UNION ALL
SELECT 1,2
```

This section covered some alternate ways to utilize more than one table within a query. Practice these techniques by completing Exercise 6-1.

EXERCISE 6-1

Use the AdventureWorks database to complete this exercise. You can find the solutions at the end of the chapter.

1. Using a subquery, display the product names and product ID numbers from the Production. Product table that have been ordered.

2. Change the query written in question 1 to display the products that have not been ordered.

3. If the Production.ProductColor table is not part of the AdventureWorks database, run the code in Listing 5-11 to create it. Write a query using a subquery that returns the rows from the Production.ProductColor table that are not being used in the Production.Product table. Use the NOT EXISTS technique.

4. Write a query that displays the colors used in the Production.Product table that are not listed in the Production.ProductColor table using a subquery. Use the keyword DISTINCT before the column name to return each color only once.

5. Write a query that combines the ModifiedDate from Person.Person and the HireDate from HumanResources.Employee with no duplicates in the results.

Using *EXCEPT* and *INTERSECT*

Two query types that are similar to UNION are the EXCEPT and INTERSECT queries. Instead of combining the data, queries written with EXCEPT return rows from the left side that do not match the right side. Queries written with INTERSECT will return rows that are found in both sides. Listing 6-7 shows an example of each query.

Listing 6-7. Using EXCEPT and INTERSECT

```
--1
SELECT BusinessEntityID AS ID
FROM HumanResources.Employee
EXCEPT
SELECT BusinessEntityID
FROM Person.Person;

--2
SELECT BusinessEntityID AS ID
FROM HumanResources.Employee
INTERSECT
SELECT BusinessEntityID
FROM Person.Person;
```

Figure 6-8 shows the partial results. There are no BusinessEntityID values found in `HumanResources.Employee` that do not exist in Person.Person, so no rows are returned by query 1. Query 2 returns rows that exist in both of these tables.

	ID

	ID
1	263
2	78
3	242
4	125

Figure 6-8. *The partial results of using EXCEPT and INTERSECT*

Using Derived Tables and Common Table Expressions

Derived tables and CTEs are techniques used to create a temporary set of results that is used within a query. It's a way to isolate part of the logic from the rest of the query. Using derived tables and CTEs allows T-SQL developers to solve some complicated query problems. You will find these techniques useful as you learn about aggregate queries (see Chapter 7) and updating data (see Chapter 10). With only the skills you have learned so far, using these techniques does not actually make writing queries any easier, but you will appreciate having learned about them before you progress to more advanced skills.

Using Derived Tables

A *derived table* is a subquery that appears in the FROM clause of a query. Derived tables allow developers to join to queries instead of tables so that the logic of the query is isolated. At this point, I just want you to learn how to write a query using a derived table. This technique will be very useful as you learn to write more advanced queries. Here is the syntax:

```
SELECT * FROM (SELECT <select list> FROM <table>) AS <alias>

SELECT <select list> FROM <table1>
[INNER] JOIN (SELECT <select list>
              FROM <table2>) AS <alias> ON <table1>.<col1> = <alias>.<col2>
```

The first syntax example shows that you can just have any query as a subquery in the FROM clause and select from it in the outer query. The second syntax example shows INNER JOIN, but this could also be done with OUTER JOIN as well. Figure 6-9 shows a diagram representing a LEFT OUTER JOIN query joining the Sales.Customer table to a query of the Sales.SalesOrderHeader table as a derived table. One interesting thing about derived tables is that they must *always* be aliased.

Sales.Customer

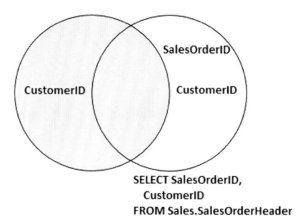

Figure 6-9. *The diagram of a derived query*

Listing 6-8 demonstrates how to use a derived table. Type in and execute the code. Make sure you take the time to understand how this works with these simple examples even though a regular join makes more sense at this point.

Listing 6-8. Using a Derived Table

```
SELECT c.CustomerID, s.SalesOrderID
FROM Sales.Customer AS c
INNER JOIN (SELECT SalesOrderID, CustomerID
            FROM Sales.SalesOrderHeader) AS s ON c.CustomerID = s.CustomerID;
```

Obviously, you could write this query using a regular INNER JOIN. Figure 6-10 shows the results. Keep in mind these rules when using derived tables. First, any columns that will be needed outside the derived table must be included in its SELECT list. Even though only SalesOrderID from the derived table appears in the main SELECT list, CustomerID is required for joining. Second, the derived table requires an alias. Use the alias to refer to columns from the derived table in the outer query. Finally, the derived table may contain multiple tables, a WHERE clause, and even another derived table. You can use an ORDER BY clause in the derived table only if you use TOP. A derived table cannot contain a CTE, which you will learn about in the next section.

	CustomerID	SalesOrderID
1	11000	43793
2	11000	51522
3	11000	57418
4	11001	43767
5	11001	51493
6	11001	72773
7	11002	43736
8	11002	51238
9	11002	53237
10	11003	43701

Figure 6-10. *The partial results of a query with a virtual table*

Using Common Table Expressions

Microsoft introduced the CTE feature with SQL Server 2005. This gives developers another way to separate out the logic of part of the query. When writing a CTE, you define one or more queries upfront, which you can then immediately use. This technique will come in handy when learning more advanced skills. For simple problems, there is no advantage over derived tables, but CTEs have several advanced features, which will be covered in Chapter 11, that are not available with derived table subqueries. There are two ways to write CTEs, one of which specifies alias columns names upfront. Here is the syntax:

```
WITH <CTE Name> AS (SELECT <select list FROM <table>)
SELECT * FROM <CTE Name>

WITH <CTE Name> AS (SELECT <select list> FROM <table1>)
SELECT <select list> FROM <table2>
[INNER] JOIN <CTE Name> ON <table2>.<col1> = <CTE Name>.<col2>

WITH <CTE Name> [(<colname1>,<colname2>,...<colnameN>)]
AS (SELECT <select list> FROM <table1>)
SELECT <select list> FROM <table2>
[INNER] JOIN <CTE Name> ON <table2>.<col1> = <CTE Name>.<col2>
```

Type in and execute the code in Listing 6-9. Again, these examples are very simple but they should help you learn the technique.

Listing 6-9. Using Common Table Expressions

```
--1
;WITH orders AS (
    SELECT SalesOrderID, CustomerID, TotalDue + Freight AS Total
```

```
    FROM Sales.SalesOrderHeader
    )
SELECT c.CustomerID, orders.SalesOrderID, Orders.Total
FROM Sales.Customer AS c
INNER JOIN orders ON c.CustomerID = orders.CustomerID;

--2
;WITH orders ([Order ID],[Customer ID], Total)
AS (SELECT SalesOrderID, CustomerID, TotalDue + Freight
    FROM Sales.SalesOrderHeader )
SELECT c.CustomerID, orders.[Order ID], Orders.Total
FROM Sales.Customer AS c
INNER JOIN orders ON c.CustomerID = orders.[Customer ID];
```

You can see the partial results in Figure 6-11. The CTE begins with the word WITH. Because WITH is a keyword in several T-SQL commands, it must be either the first word in the batch, as in this example, or it must be preceded by a semicolon. Because the semicolon is not required yet at the end of T-SQL statements, you may want to get in the habit of staring the common table expression with a semicolon. Supply the CTE name followed by the definition in query 1. In query 2, the column aliases are defined before the AS keyword. In this case, it is required because the expression TotalDue + Frieght doesn't have an alias. If aliases are defined upfront, they will be used instead of the column names. The main query immediately follows the CTE definition in both cases. Treat the CTE as a regular table in the main query. Once the query completes executing, the CTE goes out of scope and can no longer be used.

	CustomerID	SalesOrderID	Total
1	29825	43659	23769.3323
2	29672	43660	1496.1564
3	29734	43661	37851.3542
4	29994	43662	33342.1713

	CustomerID	Order ID	Total
1	29825	43659	23769.3323
2	29672	43660	1496.1564
3	29734	43661	37851.3542
4	29994	43662	33342.1713

Figure 6-11. *The results of a query using a CTE*

Using a Common Table Expression to Solve a Complicated Join Problem

The examples in Chapter 5 on joining tables demonstrated very simple join conditions; one or two columns from one table equal to the same number of columns in another table. Join conditions may be much more complicated. For example, suppose you wanted to produce a list of all customers along with the orders, if any, placed on a certain date. Figure 6-12 shows a diagram of this query. The left-hand circle represents the Customer table in the AdventureWorks database, while the right-hand circle represents the CTE. The Customer table is then joined to the results of the CTE query.

Sales.Customer

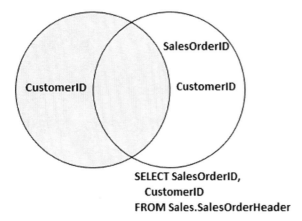

Figure 6-12. *A diagram of a CTE query*

Listing 6-10 demonstrates the problem and how to solve it with a CTE.

Listing 6-10. Using a CTE to Solve a Problem

```
--1
SELECT c.CustomerID, s.SalesOrderID, s.OrderDate
FROM Sales.Customer AS c
LEFT OUTER JOIN Sales.SalesOrderHeader AS s ON c.CustomerID = s.CustomerID
WHERE s.OrderDate = '2005/07/01';

--2
;WITH orders AS (
    SELECT SalesOrderID, CustomerID, OrderDate
    FROM Sales.SalesOrderHeader
    WHERE OrderDate = '2005/07/01'
    )
SELECT c.CustomerID, orders.SalesOrderID, orders.OrderDate
FROM Sales.Customer AS c
LEFT OUTER JOIN orders ON c.CustomerID = orders.CustomerID
ORDER BY orders.OrderDate DESC;
```

Take a look at the results in Figure 6-13. Query 1 returns only the 43 rows with the specified order date. The nonmatching rows dropped out of the query because of the NULLs and values other than 2005/07/01 in the OrderDate column. If you want to show all customers even if there is not an order placed on the specified date, then by adding the WHERE clause to the CTE instead, the NULL values and other OrderDate values do not cause any problems, and the correct results are returned.

37	29958	43695	2005-07-01 00:00:00.000
38	29849	43696	2005-07-01 00:00:00.000
39	21768	43697	2005-07-01 00:00:00.000
40	28389	43698	2005-07-01 00:00:00.000
41	25863	43699	2005-07-01 00:00:00.000
42	14501	43700	2005-07-01 00:00:00.000
43	11003	43701	2005-07-01 00:00:00.000

	CustomerID	SalesOrderID	OrderDate
39	29761	43679	2005-07-01 00:00:00.000
40	29824	43677	2005-07-01 00:00:00.000
41	29994	43662	2005-07-01 00:00:00.000
42	29734	43661	2005-07-01 00:00:00.000
43	29912	43684	2005-07-01 00:00:00.000
44	29945	NULL	NULL
45	29740	NULL	NULL
46	29750	NULL	NULL
47	29755	NULL	NULL

Figure 6-13. *The results of using a CTE to solve a tricky query*

Another way to solve this when joining two tables with a LEFT OUTER JOIN is to move any conditions affecting the right table to the join criteria. This works fine when dealing with just two tables. Once more than two tables are involved, this technique can fall apart and a CTE or derived table is a better choice.

This section demonstrated how to use derived tables and CTEs. The examples, except for the last one, covered queries that could have easily been written using joins. In Chapter 11, you will learn about the advanced features of CTEs. Practice writing queries with derived tables and CTEs by completing Exercise 6-2.

EXERCISE 6-2

Use the AdventureWorks database to complete this exercise. You can find the solutions at the end of the chapter.

1. Using a derived table, join the Sales.SalesOrderHeader table to the Sales.SalesOrderDetail table. Display the SalesOrderID, OrderDate, and ProductID columns in the results. The Sales.SalesOrderDetail table should be inside the derived table query.

2. Rewrite the query in question 1 with a common table expression.

3. Write a query that displays all customers along with the orders placed in 2005. Use a common table expression to write the query and include the CustomerID, SalesOrderID, and OrderDate columns in the results.

Thinking About Performance

The section on UNION queries stated that you will see better performance when using UNION ALL in place of UNION. If you are certain that there are no duplicate rows in the results, you can easily use UNION ALL with no issues.

Compare the performance of the two queries shown in Listing 6-11. Be sure to toggle on the Include Actual Execution Plan setting before running the queries.

Listing 6-11. Compare UNION to UNION ALL

```
--1
SELECT SalesOrderDetailID
FROM Sales.SalesOrderDetail
WHERE SalesOrderDetailID <= 59549
UNION
SELECT SalesOrderDetailID
FROM Sales.SalesOrderDetail
WHERE SalesOrderDetailID > 59549;

--2
SELECT SalesOrderDetailID
FROM Sales.SalesOrderDetail
WHERE SalesOrderDetailID <= 59549
UNION ALL
SELECT SalesOrderDetailID
FROM Sales.SalesOrderDetail
WHERE SalesOrderDetailID > 59549;
```

Because the SalesOrderDetailID column makes the Sales.SalesOrderDetail table rows unique, there are no duplicates in the results. The database engine will not know that, however, and will expend resources attempting to eliminate duplicates anyway. Figure 6-14 shows that query 1 using UNION takes 77 percent of the resources. The amount of the difference will vary from query to query. Most of the resources in query 1 are used by the Hash Match operator, which you will always see when using UNION without the ALL keyword.

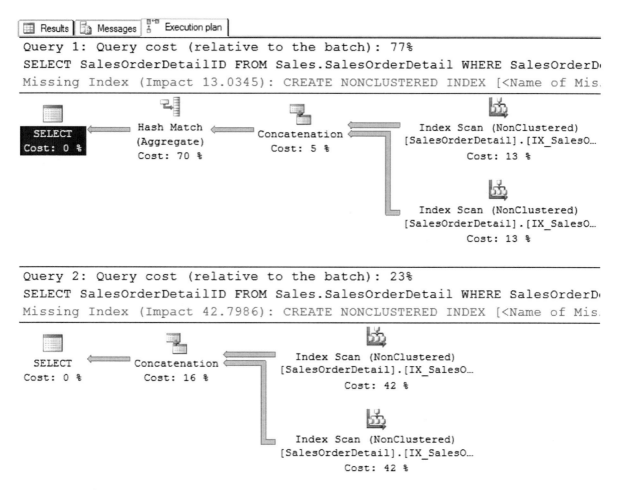

Figure 6-14. *The execution plans of UNION queries*

It seems logical that nesting the UNION ALL query inside a CTE or derived table subquery and then selecting with DISTINCT in the outer query should increase performance and eliminate duplicates at the same time. The optimizer doesn't work that way, however, and processes the query as if you had used UNION without the ALL keyword. Listing 6-12 shows an example.

Listing 6-12. An Attempt to Get Better Performance and Eliminate Duplicates

```
SELECT DISTINCT SalesOrderDetailID
FROM (
SELECT SalesOrderDetailID
FROM Sales.SalesOrderDetail
WHERE SalesOrderDetailID <= 59549
UNION ALL
SELECT SalesOrderDetailID
FROM Sales.SalesOrderDetail
WHERE SalesOrderDetailID > 59549
) AS SOD;
```

Figure 6-15 shows the execution plan, which is identical to the plan for query 1 in Listing 6-11. There was no improvement in the performance with this technique over using UNION without ALL. This also demonstrates that the optimizer can change the query around behind the scenes and still return the same results.

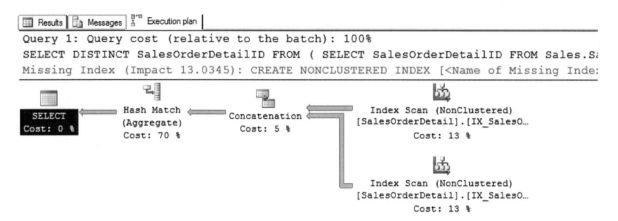

Figure 6-15. *The execution plan when combining UNION ALL and a subquery*

If you know that there are duplicates within each of the queries, but there are no duplicate rows that span both queries, you can use DISTINCT in the individual queries along with UNION ALL. Just keep in mind that you should use UNION ALL whenever possible to improve performance. Another interesting thing about UNION queries is that they use the Hash Match operator. The Hash Match operator can be used to eliminate duplicates. See Chapter 5 to learn more about join operators.

Summary

This chapter covered several ways to involve multiple tables in a query besides joins: subqueries, common table expressions, and union. You can use subqueries in a WHERE clause or to isolate part of the query logic. Starting with SQL Server 2005, you can use common table expressions in place of many subqueries, especially derived tables. Finally, you learned about union queries, which combine the results of multiple queries into one set of results.

The examples shown in this chapter were simple, but it is important to understand these techniques as you progress to more advanced material. In Chapter 7 you will learn how to group and summarize data.

Answers to the Exercises

This section provides solutions to the exercises found on writing queries with subqueries, CTEs, and unions.

Solutions to Exercise 6-1: Using Subqueries

Use the AdventureWorks database to complete this exercise.

1. Using a subquery, display the product names and product ID numbers from the
   Production.Product table that have been ordered.

   ```
   SELECT ProductID, Name
   FROM Production.Product
   WHERE ProductID IN
        (SELECT ProductID FROM Sales.SalesOrderDetail);
   ```

2. Change the query written in question 1 to display the products that have not been ordered.

   ```
   SELECT ProductID, Name
   FROM Production.Product
   WHERE ProductID NOT IN (
        SELECT ProductID FROM Sales.SalesOrderDetail
        WHERE ProductID IS NOT NULL);
   ```

3. If the Production.ProductColor table is not part of the AdventureWorks database, run the
   code in Listing 5-11 to create it. Write a query using a subquery that returns the rows from
   the Production.ProductColor table that are not being used in the Production.Product table.

   ```
   SELECT Color
   FROM Production.ProductColor
   WHERE Color NOT IN (
        SELECT Color FROM Production.Product
        WHERE Color IS NOT NULL);
   ```

4. Write a query that displays the colors used in the Production.Product table that are not
   listed in the Production.ProductColor table using a subquery. Use the keyword DISTINCT
   before the column name to return each color only once. Use the NOT EXISTS method in
   this query.

   ```
   SELECT DISTINCT Color
   FROM Production.Product AS P
   WHERE NOT EXISTS (
        SELECT Color FROM Production.ProductColor AS PC
        WHERE P.Color = PC.Color);
   ```

5. Write a query that combines the ModifiedDate from Person.Person and the HireDate
   from HumanResources.Employee with no duplicates in the results.

   ```
   SELECT ModifiedDate
   FROM Person.Person
   UNION
   SELECT HireDate
   FROM HumanResources.Employee;
   ```

Solutions to Exercise 6-2: Using Derived Tables and Common Table Expressions

Use the AdventureWorks database to complete this exercise.

1. Using a derived table, join the `Sales.SalesOrderHeader` table to the
   `Sales.SalesOrderDetail` table. Display the SalesOrderID, OrderDate, and ProductID
   columns in the results. The `Sales.SalesOrderDetail` table should be inside the derived
   table query.

```
SELECT SOH.SalesOrderID, SOH.OrderDate, ProductID
FROM Sales.SalesOrderHeader AS SOH
INNER JOIN (
    SELECT SalesOrderID, ProductID
    FROM Sales.SalesOrderDetail) AS SOD
    ON SOH.SalesOrderID = SOD.SalesOrderID;
```

2. Rewrite the query in question 1 with a common table expression.

```
;WITH SOD AS (
    SELECT SalesOrderID, ProductID
    FROM Sales.SalesOrderDetail)
SELECT SOH.SalesOrderID, SOH.OrderDate, ProductID
FROM Sales.SalesOrderHeader AS SOH
INNER JOIN SOD ON SOH.SalesOrderID = SOD.SalesOrderID;
```

3. Write a query that displays all customers along with the orders placed in 2005. Use a
   common table expression to write the query and include the CustomerID, SalesOrderID,
   and OrderDate columns in the results.

```
WITH SOH AS (
    SELECT SalesOrderID, OrderDate, CustomerID
    FROM Sales.SalesOrderHeader
    WHERE OrderDate BETWEEN '1/1/2005' AND '12/31/2005'
    )
SELECT C.CustomerID, SalesOrderID, OrderDate
FROM Sales.Customer AS C
LEFT OUTER JOIN SOH ON C.CustomerID = SOH.CustomerID;
```

CHAPTER 7

■ ■ ■

Grouping and Summarizing Data

So far, you have learned to write simple queries that include filtering and ordering. You can also work with expressions built with operators and functions. Chapters 5 and 6 taught you how to write queries with multiple tables so that the data makes sense in applications and reports. Now it's time to learn about a special type of query, *aggregate queries*, used to group and summarize data. You may find that writing aggregate queries is more challenging than the other queries you have learned so far, but by taking a step-by-step approach, you will see that they are not difficult to write at all. Be sure to take the time to understand the examples and complete all the exercises before moving on to the next section.

Aggregate Functions

You use aggregate functions to summarize data in queries. The functions that you worked with in Chapter 4 operate on one value at a time. These functions operate on sets of values from multiple rows all at once. For example, you may need to supply information about how many orders were placed and the total amount ordered for a report. Here are the most commonly used aggregate functions:

- COUNT: Counts the number of rows or the number of non-NULL values in a column.

- SUM: Adds up the values in numeric or money data.

- AVG: Calculates the average in numeric or money data.

- MIN: Finds the lowest value in the set of values. This can be used on string data as well as numeric, money, or date data.

- MAX: Finds the highest value in the set of values. This can be used on string data as well as numeric, money, or date data.

Keep the following in mind when working with these aggregate functions:

- The functions AVG and SUM will operate only on numeric and money data columns.

- The functions MIN, MAX, and COUNT will work on numeric, money, string, and temporal data columns.

- The aggregate functions will not operate on TEXT, NTEXT, and IMAGE columns. These data types are deprecated, meaning that they may not be supported in future versions of SQL Server. If you are stuck with these data types for now, you may be able to cast to a supported data type.

- The aggregate functions will not operate on some special data types like HierarchyID and spatial.

- The aggregate functions will not work on BIT columns except for COUNT. You can always cast a BIT to an INT if you need to.

- COUNT can be used with an asterisk (*) to give a count of all the rows.

- The aggregate functions ignore NULL values except for the case of COUNT(*). Using the typical settings, you will see a warning about NULLs.

- Once any aspect of aggregate queries are used in a query, the query becomes an aggregate query.

Here is the syntax for the simplest type of aggregate query where the aggregate function is used in the SELECT list:

```
SELECT <aggregate function>(<col1>)
FROM <table>
```

Listing 7-1 shows an example of using aggregate functions. Type in and execute the code to learn how these functions are used over the entire result set.

Listing 7-1. Using Aggregate Functions

```
--1
SELECT COUNT(*) AS CountOfRows,
    MAX(TotalDue) AS MaxTotal,
    MIN(TotalDue) AS MinTotal,
    SUM(TotalDue) AS SumOfTotal,
    AVG(TotalDue) AS AvgTotal
FROM Sales.SalesOrderHeader;

--2
SELECT MIN(Name) AS MinName,
    MAX(Name) AS MaxName,
    MIN(SellStartDate) AS MinSellStartDate
FROM Production.Product;

--3
SELECT COUNT(*) AS CountOfRows,
    COUNT(Color) AS CountOfColor,
        COUNT(DISTINCT Color) AS CountOfDistinctColor
FROM Production.Product;
```

Take a look at the results of running this in Figure 7-1. The aggregate functions operate on all the rows in the Sales.SalesOrderHeader table in query 1 and return just one row of results. The first expression, CountOfRows, uses an asterisk (*) to count all the rows in the table. The other expressions perform calculations on the TotalDue column. Query 2 demonstrates using the MIN and MAX functions on string and date columns. Query 3 demonstrates the three ways to use COUNT. You can count the rows, count the non-NULL value of a column, or count the distinct values of a column. In these examples, the SELECT clause lists only aggregate expressions. You will learn how to add columns that are not part of aggregate expressions in the next section.

	CountOfRows	MaxTotal	MinTotal	SumOfTotal	AvgTotal
1	31465	187487.825	1.5183	123216786.1159	3915.9951

	MinName	MaxName	MinSellStartDate
1	Adjustable Race	Women's Tights, S	2002-06-01 00:00:00.000

	CountOfRows	CountOfColor	CountOfDistinctColor
1	504	256	9

Figure 7-1. *The results of using aggregate functions*

Now that you know how to use aggregate functions to summarize a result set, practice what you have learned by completing Exercise 7-1.

EXERCISE 7-1

Use the AdventureWorks database to complete this exercise. You can find the solutions at the end of the chapter.

1. Write a query to determine the number of customers in the Sales.Customer table.

2. Write a query that retrieves the total number of products ordered. Use the OrderQty column of the Sales.SalesOrderDetail table and the SUM function.

3. Write a query to determine the price of the most expensive product ordered. Use the UnitPrice column of the Sales.SalesOrderDetail table.

4. Write a query to determine the average freight amount in the Sales.SalesOrderHeader table.

5. Write a query using the Production.Product table that displays the minimum, maximum, and average ListPrice.

The *GROUP BY* Clause

The previous example queries and exercise questions listed only aggregate expressions in the SELECT list. The aggregate functions operated on the entire result set in each query. By adding more nonaggregated columns to the SELECT list, you add grouping levels to the query, which requires the use of the GROUP BY clause. The aggregate functions then operate on the grouping levels instead of on the entire set of results. This section covers grouping on columns and grouping on scalar expressions.

Grouping on Columns

You can use the GROUP BY clause to group data so the aggregate functions apply to groups of values instead of the entire result set. For example, you may want to calculate the count and sum of the orders placed, grouped by order date or grouped by customer. Here is the syntax for the GROUP BY clause:

```
SELECT <aggregate function>(<col1>), <col2>
FROM <table>
GROUP BY <col2>
```

One big difference you will notice once the query contains a GROUP BY clause is that additional nonaggregated columns may be included in the SELECT list. Once nonaggregated columns are in the SELECT list, you must add the GROUP BY clause and include all the nonaggregated columns. Run this code example and you will see an error message:

```
SELECT CustomerID,SUM(TotalDue) AS TotalPerCustomer
FROM Sales.SalesOrderHeader;
```

Figure 7-2 shows the error message. To get around this error, add the GROUP BY clause and include nonaggregated columns in that clause. Make sure that the SELECT list includes only those columns you really need in the results, because the SELECT list directly affects which columns will be required in the GROUP BY clause and the results of the query.

```
Messages
 Msg 8120, Level 16, State 1, Line 1
 Column 'Sales.SalesOrderHeader.CustomerID' is invalid in the select list because
 it is not contained in either an aggregate function or the GROUP BY clause.
```

Figure 7-2. The error message that results when the required GROUP BY clause is missing

Type in and execute the code in Listing 7-2, which demonstrates how to use GROUP BY.

Listing 7-2. Using the GROUP BY Clause

```
--1
SELECT CustomerID,SUM(TotalDue) AS TotalPerCustomer
FROM Sales.SalesOrderHeader
GROUP BY CustomerID;

--2
SELECT TerritoryID,AVG(TotalDue) AS AveragePerTerritory
FROM Sales.SalesOrderHeader
GROUP BY TerritoryID;
```

Take a look at the results of running this code in Figure 7-3. Query 1 displays every customer with orders along with the sum of the TotalDue for each customer. The results are grouped by the CustomerID, and the sum is applied over each group of rows. Query 2 returns the average of the TotalDue values grouped by the TerritoryID. In each case, the nonaggregated column in the SELECT list must appear in the GROUP BY clause.

	CustomerID	TotalPerCustomer
1	14324	5659.1783
2	22814	5.514
3	11407	59.659
4	28387	645.2869

	TerritoryID	AveragePerTerritory
1	9	1726.4907
2	3	23151.4266
3	6	4523.956
4	7	3038.8283

Figure 7-3. *The partial results of using the GROUP BY clause*

Any columns listed that are not part of an aggregate expression must be used to group the results. Those columns must be included in the GROUP BY clause. If you don't want to group on a column, don't list it in the SELECT list. This is where developers struggle when writing aggregate queries, so I can't stress this enough.

Grouping on Expressions

The previous examples demonstrated how to group on columns, but it is possible to also group on scalar expressions. You must include the exact expression from the SELECT list in the GROUP BY clause. Listing 7-3 demonstrates how to avoid this mistake caused by adding a column instead of the expression to the GROUP BY clause.

Listing 7-3. How to Group on an Expression

```
--1
SELECT COUNT(*) AS CountOfOrders, YEAR(OrderDate) AS OrderYear
FROM Sales.SalesOrderHeader
GROUP BY OrderDate;


--2
SELECT COUNT(*) AS CountOfOrders, YEAR(OrderDate) AS OrderYear
FROM Sales.SalesOrderHeader
GROUP BY YEAR(OrderDate);
```

You can find the results of this code in Figure 7-4. Notice that query 1 will run, but instead of returning one row per year, the query returns multiple rows with unexpected values. Because the GROUP BY clause contains OrderDate, the grouping is on OrderDate. The CountOfOrders expression is the count by OrderDate, not OrderYear. The expression in the SELECT list just changes how the data displays; it doesn't affect the calculations.

	CountOfOrders	OrderYear
1	12	2006
2	10	2007
3	52	2008
4	7	2006
5	9	2007
6	63	2007
7	57	2008
8	10	2006

	CountOfOrders	OrderYear
1	12443	2007
2	13951	2008
3	1379	2005
4	3692	2006

Figure 7-4. Using an expression in the GROUP BY clause

Query 2 fixes this problem by including the exact expression from the SELECT list in the GROUP BY clause. Query 2 returns only one row per year, and CountOfOrders is correctly calculated.

You use aggregate functions along with the GROUP BY clause to summarize data over groups of rows. Be sure to practice what you have learned by completing Exercise 7-2.

EXERCISE 7-2

Use the AdventureWorks database to complete the exercise. You can find the solutions at the end of the chapter.

1. Write a query that shows the total number of items ordered for each product. Use the Sales. SalesOrderDetail table to write the query.

2. Write a query using the Sales.SalesOrderDetail table that displays a count of the detail lines for each SalesOrderID.

3. Write a query using the Production.Product table that lists a count of the products in each product line.

4. Write a query that displays the count of orders placed by year for each customer using the Sales.SalesOrderHeader table.

The *ORDER BY* Clause

You already know how to use the ORDER BY clause, but special rules exist for using the ORDER BY clause in aggregate queries. If a nonaggregate column appears in the ORDER BY clause, it must also appear in the GROUP BY clause, just like the SELECT list. Here is the syntax:

```
SELECT <aggregate function>(<col1>),<col2>
FROM <table1>
GROUP BY <col2>
ORDER BY <col2>
```

Type in the following code to see the error that results when a column included in the ORDER BY clause is missing from the GROUP BY clause:

```
SELECT CustomerID,SUM(TotalDue) AS TotalPerCustomer
FROM Sales.SalesOrderHeader
GROUP BY CustomerID
ORDER BY TerritoryID;
```

Figure 7-5 shows the error message that results from running the code. To avoid this error, make sure you add only those columns to the ORDER BY clause that you intend to be grouping levels.

```
Messages
 Msg 8127, Level 16, State 1, Line 4
 Column "Sales.SalesOrderHeader.TerritoryID" is invalid in the
 ORDER BY clause because it is not contained in either an
 aggregate function or the GROUP BY clause.
```

Figure 7-5. *The error message resulting from including a column in the ORDER BY clause that is not a grouping level*

Listing 7-4 demonstrates how to use the ORDER BY clause within an aggregate query. Be sure to type in and execute the code.

Listing 7-4. Using ORDER BY

```
--1
SELECT CustomerID,SUM(TotalDue) AS TotalPerCustomer
FROM Sales.SalesOrderHeader
GROUP BY CustomerID
ORDER BY CustomerID;

--2
SELECT CustomerID,SUM(TotalDue) AS TotalPerCustomer
FROM Sales.SalesOrderHeader
GROUP BY CustomerID
ORDER BY MAX(TotalDue) DESC;
```

```
--3
SELECT CustomerID,SUM(TotalDue) AS TotalPerCustomer
FROM Sales.SalesOrderHeader
GROUP BY CustomerID
ORDER BY TotalPerCustomer DESC;
```

View the results of Listing 7-4 in Figure 7-6. As you can see, the ORDER BY clause follows the same rules as the SELECT list. Query 1 queries the results in the order of the nonaggregated column that is listed in the GROUP BY clause. Query 2 displays the results in order of the maximum order per customer, an expression not even listed in the SELECT list. As long as it is an aggregate expression, it will work in the ORDER BY clause. Query 3 shows a nice shortcut. If you want to sort by one of the aggregate expressions in the SELECT list, you can list the alias instead of the expression.

	CustomerID	TotalPerCustomer
1	11000	9115.1341
2	11001	7054.1875
3	11002	8966.0143
4	11003	8993.9155

	CustomerID	TotalPerCustomer
1	29641	606819.6087
2	29614	901346.856
3	30103	725867.1659
4	29701	841866.5522

	CustomerID	TotalPerCustomer
1	29818	989184.082
2	29715	961675.8596
3	29722	954021.9235
4	30117	919801.8188

Figure 7-6. Partial results of using ORDER BY

The *WHERE* Clause

The WHERE clause in an aggregate query may contain anything allowed in the WHERE clause in any other query type. It may not, however, contain an aggregate expression. You use the WHERE clause to eliminate rows before the groupings and aggregates are applied. To filter after the groupings are applied, you will use the HAVING clause. You'll learn about HAVING in the next section. Type in and execute the code in Listing 7-5, which demonstrates using the WHERE clause in an aggregate query.

Listing 7-5. Using the WHERE Clause

```
SELECT CustomerID,SUM(TotalDue) AS TotalPerCustomer
FROM Sales.SalesOrderHeader
WHERE TerritoryID in (5,6)
GROUP BY CustomerID;
```

The results shown in Figure 7-7 contain only those rows where the TerritoryID is either 5 or 6. The query eliminates the rows before the grouping is applied. Notice that TerritoryID doesn't appear anywhere in the query except for the WHERE clause. The WHERE clause may contain any of the columns in the table as long as it doesn't contain an aggregate expression.

	CustomerID	TotalPerCustomer
1	11739	5257.6232
2	18237	2562.4508
3	26040	3335.2547
4	18546	32.5754
5	29761	68068.6803
6	30093	111168.3274
7	28101	87.2729
8	17026	288.836
9	18523	177.8388
10	18855	1276.8054

Figure 7-7. *The partial results of using the WHERE clause in an aggregate query*

The *HAVING* Clause

To eliminate rows based on an aggregate expression, use the HAVING clause. The HAVING clause may contain aggregate expressions that may or may not appear in the SELECT list. For example, you could write a query that returns the sum of the total due for customers who have placed at least ten orders. The count of the orders doesn't have to appear in the SELECT list. Alternately, you could include only those customers who have spent at least $10,000 (sum of total due), which does appear in the list.

You can also include nonaggregated columns in the HAVING clause as long as the columns appear in the GROUP BY clause. In other words, you can eliminate some of the groups with the HAVING clause. Behind the scenes, however, the database engine may move those criteria to the WHERE clause because it is more efficient to eliminate those rows first. Criteria involving nonaggregate columns actually belong in the WHERE clause, but the query will still work with the criteria appearing in the HAVING clause.

The operators such as equal to (=), less than (<), and BETWEEN that are used in the WHERE clause will work. Here is the syntax:

```
SELECT <aggregate function1>(<col1>),<col2>
FROM <table1>
GROUP BY <col2>
HAVING <aggregate function2>(<col3>) = <value>
```

Like the GROUP BY clause, the HAVING clause will be in aggregate queries only. Listing 7-6 demonstrates the HAVING clause. Be sure to type in and execute the code.

Listing 7-6. Using the HAVING Clause

```
--1
SELECT CustomerID,SUM(TotalDue) AS TotalPerCustomer
FROM Sales.SalesOrderHeader
GROUP BY CustomerID
HAVING SUM(TotalDue) > 5000;

--2
SELECT CustomerID,SUM(TotalDue) AS TotalPerCustomer
FROM Sales.SalesOrderHeader
GROUP BY CustomerID
HAVING COUNT(*) = 10 AND SUM(TotalDue) > 5000;

--3
SELECT CustomerID,SUM(TotalDue) AS TotalPerCustomer
FROM Sales.SalesOrderHeader
GROUP BY CustomerID
HAVING CustomerID > 27858;
```

You can find the results of running this code in Figure 7-8. Query 1 shows only the rows where the sum of the TotalDue exceeds 5,000. The TotalDue column appears within an aggregate expression in the SELECT list. Query 2 demonstrates how an aggregate expression not included in the SELECT list may be used (in this case, the count of the rows) in the HAVING clause. Query 3 contains a nonaggregated column, CustomerID, in the HAVING clause, but it is a column in the GROUP BY clause. In this case, you could have moved the criteria to the WHERE clause instead and received the same results.

	CustomerID	TotalPerCustomer
1	14324	5659.1783
2	15675	7963.05
3	11453	9035.563
4	14155	6622.5524

	CustomerID	TotalPerCustomer
1	29830	38452.4651
2	29842	156413.2374
3	29622	262408.3464
4	29588	17361.1884

	CustomerID	TotalPerCustomer
1	28719	2634.3974
2	28055	83.4054
3	28387	645.2869
4	28032	83.3944

Figure 7-8. The partial results of using the HAVING clause

Developers often struggle when trying to figure out whether the filter criteria belong in the WHERE clause or in the HAVING clause. Here's a tip: you must know the order in which the database engine processes the clauses. First, review the order in which you write the clauses in an aggregate query.

- SELECT
- FROM
- WHERE
- GROUP BY
- HAVING
- ORDER BY

The database engine processes the WHERE clause before the groupings and aggregates are applied. Here is a very simplified version of the order that the database engine actually processes the query:

- FROM
- WHERE
- GROUP BY
- HAVING
- SELECT
- ORDER BY

The database engine processes the WHERE clause before it processes the groupings and aggregates. Use the WHERE clause to completely eliminate rows from the query. For example, your query might eliminate all the orders except those placed in 2011. The database engine processes the HAVING clause after it processes the groupings and aggregates. Use the HAVING clause to eliminate rows based on aggregate expressions or groupings. For example, use the HAVING clause to remove the customers who have placed fewer than ten orders. Practice what you have learned about the HAVING clause by completing Exercise 7-3.

EXERCISE 7-3

Use the AdventureWorks to complete this exercise. You can find the solutions at the end of the chapter.

1. Write a query that returns a count of detail lines in the Sales.SalesOrderDetail table by SalesOrderID. Include only those sales that have more than three detail lines.

2. Write a query that creates a sum of the LineTotal in the Sales.SalesOrderDetail table grouped by the SalesOrderID. Include only those rows where the sum exceeds 1,000.

3. Write a query that groups the products by ProductModelID along with a count. Display the rows that have a count that equals 1.

4. Change the query in question 3 so that only the products with the color blue or red are included.

DISTINCT Keyword

You can use the keyword DISTINCT in any SELECT list. For example, you can use DISTINCT to eliminate duplicate rows in a regular query. This section discusses using DISTINCT and aggregate queries.

Using *DISTINCT* vs. *GROUP BY*

Developers often use the DISTINCT keyword to eliminate duplicate rows from a regular query. Be careful when tempted to do this; using DISTINCT to eliminate duplicate rows may be a sign that there is a problem with the query. Assuming that the duplicate results are valid, you will get the same results by using GROUP BY instead. Type in and execute the code in Listing 7-7 to see how this works.

Listing 7-7. Using DISTINCT and GROUP BY

```
--1
SELECT DISTINCT SalesOrderID
FROM Sales.SalesOrderDetail;

--2
SELECT SalesOrderID
FROM Sales.SalesOrderDetail
GROUP BY SalesOrderID;
```

Queries 1 and 2 return identical results (see Figure 7-9). Even though query 2 contains no aggregate expressions, it is still an aggregate query because GROUP BY has been added. By grouping on SalesOrderID, only the unique values show up in the returned rows. You may be wondering which method is the best. SQL Server will generally use the same execution plan for the two techniques. Some experienced people say that, because you really don't intend to have an aggregate query, you should avoid GROUP BY in this situation. Some say that DISTINCT should always be avoided. Really, in this case, it is up to you.

	SalesOrderID
1	43659
2	43660
3	43661
4	43662

	SalesOrderID
1	43659
2	43660
3	43661
4	43662

Figure 7-9. *The partial results of DISTINCT vs. GROUP BY*

DISTINCT Within an Aggregate Expression

You may also use DISTINCT within an aggregate query to cause the aggregate functions to operate on unique values. For example, instead of the count of rows, you could write a query that counts the number of unique values in a column. Type in and execute the code in Listing 7-8 to see how this works.

Listing 7-8. Using DISTINCT in an Aggregate Expression

```
--1
SELECT COUNT(*) AS CountOfRows,
    COUNT(SalesPersonID) AS CountOfSalesPeople,
    COUNT(DISTINCT SalesPersonID) AS CountOfUniqueSalesPeople
FROM Sales.SalesOrderHeader;

--2
SELECT SUM(TotalDue) AS TotalOfAllOrders,
    SUM(Distinct TotalDue) AS TotalOfDistinctTotalDue
FROM Sales.SalesOrderHeader;
```

Take a look at the results of running this code in Figure 7-10. Query 1 contains three aggregate expressions all using COUNT. The first one counts all rows in the table. The second expression counts the values in SalesPersonID. The expression returns a much smaller value because the data contains many NULL values, which are ignored by the aggregate function. Finally, the third expression returns the count of unique SalesPersonID values by using the DISTINCT keyword.

	CountOfRows	CountOfSalesPeople	CountOfUniqueSalesPeople
1	31465	3806	17

	TotalOfAllOrders	TotalOfDistinctTotalDue
1	123216786.1159	91735344.3814

Figure 7-10. *Using DISTINCT in an aggregate expression*

Query 2 demonstrates that DISTINCT works with other aggregate functions, not just COUNT. The first expression returns the sum of TotalDue for all rows in the table. The second expression returns the sum of unique TotalDue values.

You can use DISTINCT either to return unique rows from your query or to make your aggregate expression operate on unique values in your data. Practice what you have learned by completing Exercise 7-4.

EXERCISE 7-4

Use the AdventureWorks database to complete this exercise. You can find the solutions at the end of the chapter.

1. Write a query using the Sales.SalesOrderDetail table to come up with a count of unique ProductID values that have been ordered.

2. Write a query using the Sales.SalesOrderHeader table that returns the count of unique TerritoryID values per customer.

Aggregate Queries with More Than One Table

So far, the examples have demonstrated how to write aggregate queries involving just one table. You may use aggregate expressions and the GROUP BY and HAVING clauses when joining tables as well; the same rules apply. Type in and execute the code in Listing 7-9 to learn how to do this.

Listing 7-9. Writing Aggregate Queries with Two Tables

```
--1
SELECT c.CustomerID, c.AccountNumber, COUNT(*) AS CountOfOrders,
    SUM(TotalDue) AS SumOfTotalDue
FROM Sales.Customer AS c
INNER JOIN Sales.SalesOrderHeader AS s ON c.CustomerID = s.CustomerID
GROUP BY c.CustomerID, c.AccountNumber
ORDER BY c.CustomerID;


--2
SELECT c.CustomerID, c.AccountNumber, COUNT(*) AS CountOfOrders,
    SUM(TotalDue) AS SumOfTotalDue
FROM Sales.Customer AS c
LEFT OUTER JOIN Sales.SalesOrderHeader AS s ON c.CustomerID = s.CustomerID
GROUP BY c.CustomerID, c.AccountNumber
ORDER BY c.CustomerID;


--3
SELECT c.CustomerID, c.AccountNumber,COUNT(s.SalesOrderID) AS CountOfOrders,
    SUM(COALESCE(TotalDue,0)) AS SumOfTotalDue
FROM Sales.Customer AS c
LEFT OUTER JOIN Sales.SalesOrderHeader AS s ON c.CustomerID = s.CustomerID
GROUP BY c.CustomerID, c.AccountNumber
ORDER BY c.CustomerID;
```

You can see the results of running the code in Listing 7-9 in Figure 7-11. All three queries join the Sales.Customer and Sales.SalesOrderHeader tables together and attempt to count the orders placed and calculate the sum of the total due for each customer.

	CustomerID	AccountNumber	CountOfOrders	SumOfTotalDue
1	11000	AW00011000	3	9115.1341
2	11001	AW00011001	3	7054.1875
3	11002	AW00011002	3	8966.0143
4	11003	AW00011003	3	8993.9155

	CustomerID	AccountNumber	CountOfOrders	SumOfTotalDue
1	1	AW00000001	1	NULL
2	2	AW00000002	1	NULL
3	3	AW00000003	1	NULL
4	4	AW00000004	1	NULL

	CustomerID	AccountNumber	CountOfOrders	SumOfTotalDue
1	1	AW00000001	0	0.00
2	2	AW00000002	0	0.00
3	3	AW00000003	0	0.00
4	4	AW00000004	0	0.00

Figure 7-11. The partial results of using aggregates with multiple tables

Using an INNER JOIN, query 1 includes only the customers who have placed an order. By changing to a LEFT OUTER JOIN, query 2 includes all customers but incorrectly returns a count of 1 for customers with no orders and returns a NULL for the SumOfTotalDue when you probably want to see 0. Query 3 solves the first problem by changing COUNT(*) to COUNT(s.SalesOrderID), which eliminates the NULL values and correctly returns 0 for those customers who have not placed an order. Query 3 solves the second problem by using COALESCE to change the NULL value to 0.

Remember that writing aggregate queries with multiple tables is really not different from doing this for just one table; the same rules apply. You can use your knowledge from the previous chapters, such as how to write a WHERE clause and how to join tables, to write aggregate queries. Practice what you have learned by completing Exercise 7-5.

EXERCISE 7-5

Use the AdventureWorks database to complete this exercise. You can find the solutions at the end of the chapter.

1. Write a query joining the Person.Person, Sales.Customer, and Sales.SalesOrderHeader tables to return a list of the customer names along with a count of the orders placed.

2. Write a query using the Sales.SalesOrderHeader, Sales.SalesOrderDetail, and Production. Product tables to display the total sum of products by Name and OrderDate.

Aggregate Functions and *NULL*

Just as you have had to consider NULL values throughout this book, you will also need to consider NULL with aggregate queries. You have seen that aggregate functions ignore NULL values. It is very important to remember this when using the AVG function. When calculating an average, do you need to consider the NULL rows? There is no right answer; it will depend on the requirements or situation. Listing 7-10 shows the difference.

Listing 7-10. Average and NULL

```
--1
CREATE TABLE #AvgDemo (CustID INT, OrderID INT NOT NULL, Total MONEY NOT NULL,
    DiscountAmt MONEY NULL);
INSERT INTO #AvgDemo (CustID, OrderID, Total, DiscountAmt)
SELECT CustomerID, SOD.SalesOrderID, LineTotal, NULLIF(SUM(UnitPriceDiscount * LineTotal), 0.00)
FROM sales.SalesOrderDetail AS SOD
INNER JOIN Sales.SalesOrderHeader AS SOH ON SOD.SalesOrderID = SOH.SalesOrderID
WHERE CustomerID IN (29648, 30048, 30043, 29716)
GROUP BY CustomerID, SOD.SalesOrderID, LineTotal;

--2
SELECT CustID, AVG(DiscountAmt) AS AvgDiscount,
    AVG(ISNULL(DiscountAmt,0)) AS AvgWithNullRows,
        SUM(DiscountAmt) AS SumOfDiscount,
        COUNT(*) AS CountOfRows,
        COUNT(DiscountAmt) AS NonNullCount
FROM #AvgDemo
GROUP BY CustID;
```

Figure 7-12 shows the results of running this code. Statement 1 creates and populates a temp table with sales information for a handful of customers. Some of the line items have discounts, but others do not. The NULLIF function is used to change zeros in the discount amount to NULL. Query 2 shows what happens when the average is calculated. The AvgDiscount uses the AVG function. Any rows with NULL in the DiscountAmt are ignored in the calculation. To get around this, you can always turn NULLs back into zeros.

	CustID	AvgDiscount	AvgWithNullRows	SumOfDiscount	CountOfRows	NonNullCount
1	30048	15.7206	1.7724	723.1498	408	46
2	29716	226.2739	1.4366	452.5479	315	2
3	29648	97.5864	7.5066	195.1728	26	2
4	30043	58.2258	4.9503	1222.7436	247	21

Figure 7-12. *The results of testing AVG with NULLs*

When you must calculate the average, and there is the possibility of NULL values, be sure to determine if the NULL rows should be ignored.

If you click the Messages tab, you will see the warning *Null value is eliminated by an aggregate or other SET operation.* This warning will appear with any of the aggregate functions, not just AVG. It is possible in some cases for this warning to cause errors in some applications. If this happens, one workaround is to use the SET ANSI_WARNINGS OFF setting for the connection.

Thinking About Performance

The execution plan is a great tool when you are tuning queries to get better performance. In addition, there is another tool that I use very frequently, often along with execution plans, called Statistics IO. This tool is a setting you can toggle on in the query window. Here is the command to turn this on:

```
SET STATISTICS IO ON;
```

When you turn this setting on and run queries, take a look at the Messages tab. The information will look something like that shown in Figure 7-13.

```
Results   Messages

(31465 row(s) affected)
Table 'SalesOrderDetail'. Scan count 1, logical reads 1246, physical reads 0,
read-ahead reads 0, lob logical reads 0, lob physical reads 0, lob read-ahead reads 0.
```

Figure 7-13. *The Statistics IO information*

This option provides information about how much data is read from disk and memory. Table 7-1 explains what each value means.

Table 7-1. *The Output of Statistics IO*

Item	Meaning
Scan count	The number of scans or seeks.
Logical reads	The number of pages read from memory. This is the most useful value.
Physical reads	The number of pages read from disk into memory.
Read-ahead reads	The number of pages placed into cache. This number will often be inflated when an index is fragmented.
Lob logical reads	The number of pages read from memory of large object data types.
Lob physical reads	The number of pages read from disk of large object data types.
Lob read-ahead	The number of pages placed into cache of large object data types reads.

Although it is beyond the scope of this book to cover query processing in depth, it is helpful to know a few basics. Data is stored on disk in a structure called a page. Depending on the size of each row, a page could store more than one row. For example, say that the row you need is on a page with 99 other rows. In order for SQL Server to be able to access the data, the page must be read from disk into memory. The entire page, including the 99 rows you don't care about, must reside in memory before your row can be returned.

The physical reading of pages from disk to memory is usually the most resource-intensive part of the process and often the source of performance bottlenecks, especially if there is not enough random access memory (RAM) on the system to cache, or hold, much data. In that case, the same pages might be read over and over again each time they are needed when it would be more efficient to just hold them in cache. You might guess that among all of the information returned by Statistics IO that physical reads, the number of pages read from disk into memory, would be the most important. Instead, when tuning queries, the logical reads value is actually the one to pay attention to. The logical reads will not change from execution to execution of the identical query, unlike physical reads. This allows a level playing field when comparing two queries for performance.

When comparing the performance of two queries, the query that performs the best will have the lowest number of logical reads. Type in and run Listing 7-11 and then look at the Messages tab to see an example.

Listing 7-11. Using Statistics IO

```
SET STATISTICS IO ON;
GO

SELECT *
FROM Sales.SalesOrderHeader;

SELECT SalesOrderID
FROM Sales.SalesOrderHeader;

SELECT SalesOrderID, OrderDate
FROM Sales.SalesOrderHeader;
```

Figure 7-14 shows the Statistics IO output. You may be wondering why query 1 has 689 logical reads while query 2 has only 57. You may guess that since query 1 returns all the columns, the database engine must read more pages when accessing more columns. But in this case entire rows are stored on the pages, and SQL Server must read the entire page, not just the required columns.

| ▦ Results | ⓑ Messages |

```
(31465 row(s) affected)
Table 'SalesOrderHeader'. Scan count 1, logical reads 689, phys

(31465 row(s) affected)
Table 'SalesOrderHeader'. Scan count 1, logical reads 57, physi

(31465 row(s) affected)
Table 'SalesOrderHeader'. Scan count 1, logical reads 689, phys
```

Figure 7-14. *The Statistics IO output*

■ **Note**   A new way to store data called *column store* was introduced with SQL Server 2012. Individual columns are stored in pages instead of rows. Microsoft also introduced In-Memory OLTP (Online Transaction Processing) with SQL Server 2014. This technology allows entire tables to be loaded into memory automatically for extremely fast data manipulation.

The reason that the first query has 689 logical reads is that it is a scan of the clustered index (table). The database engine must completely read every page in the index because there is no WHERE clause. The second query is a scan of one of the nonclustered indexes. Every nonclustered index automatically includes the cluster key, which is used to find the matching clustered index row. Nonclustered indexes are generally much smaller structures than the table itself, so that is why a much smaller number of pages were read.

Query 3 also requires 689 logical reads. The reason for this is that there is not a nonclustered index containing OrderDate, either as a key or an included column. Just like query 1, the entire clustered index must be scanned.

Summary

If you follow the steps outlined in the preceding sections, you will be able to write aggregate queries. With practice, you will become proficient in doing this. Keep the following rules in mind when writing an aggregate query:

- Any column not contained in an aggregate function in the SELECT list or ORDER BY clause must be part of the GROUP BY clause.

- Once an aggregate function, the GROUP BY clause, or the HAVING clause appears in a query, it is an aggregate query.

- Use the WHERE clause to filter out rows before the grouping and aggregates are applied. The WHERE clause doesn't allow aggregate functions.

- Use the HAVING clause to filter out rows using aggregate functions.

- Don't include anything in the SELECT list or ORDER BY clause that you don't want as a grouping level.

Answers to the Exercises

This section provides solutions to the exercises found on writing aggregate queries.

Solutions to Exercise 7-1: Aggregate Functions

Use the AdventureWorks database to complete this exercise.

1. Write a query to determine the number of customers in the Sales.Customer table.

```
SELECT COUNT(*) AS CountOfCustomers
FROM Sales.Customer;
```

2. Write a query that returns the total number of products ordered. Use the OrderQty column of the Sales.SalesOrderDetail table and the SUM function.

```
SELECT SUM(OrderQty) AS TotalProductsOrdered
FROM Sales.SalesOrderDetail;
```

3. Write a query to determine the price of the most expensive product ordered. Use the UnitPrice column of the Sales.SalesOrderDetail table.

```
SELECT MAX(UnitPrice) AS MostExpensivePrice
FROM Sales.SalesOrderDetail;
```

4. Write a query to determine the average freight amount in the Sales.SalesOrderHeader table.

```
SELECT AVG(Freight) AS AverageFreight
FROM Sales.SalesOrderHeader;
```

5. Write a query using the Production.Product table that displays the minimum, maximum, and average ListPrice.

```
SELECT MIN(ListPrice) AS Minimum,
    MAX(ListPrice) AS Maximum,
    AVG(ListPrice) AS Average
FROM Production.Product;
```

Solutions to Exercise 7-2: The *GROUP BY* Clause

Use the AdventureWorks database to complete this exercise.

1. Write a query that shows the total number of items ordered for each product. Use the Sales.SalesOrderDetail table to write the query.

```
SELECT SUM(OrderQty) AS TotalOrdered, ProductID
FROM Sales.SalesOrderDetail
GROUP BY ProductID;
```

2. Write a query using the Sales.SalesOrderDetail table that displays a count of the detail lines for each SalesOrderID.

```
SELECT COUNT(*) AS CountOfOrders, SalesOrderID
FROM Sales.SalesOrderDetail
GROUP BY SalesOrderID;
```

3. Write a query using the Production.Product table that lists a count of the products in each product line.

```
SELECT COUNT(*) AS CountOfProducts, ProductLine
FROM Production.Product
GROUP BY ProductLine;
```

4. Write a query that displays the count of orders placed by year for each customer using the Sales.SalesOrderHeader table.

```
SELECT CustomerID, COUNT(*) AS CountOfSales,
    YEAR(OrderDate) AS OrderYear
FROM Sales.SalesOrderHeader
GROUP BY CustomerID, YEAR(OrderDate);
```

Solutions to Exercise 7-3: The *HAVING* Clause

Use the AdventureWorks database to complete this exercise.

1. Write a query that returns a count of detail lines in the Sales.SalesOrderDetail table by SalesOrderID. Include only those sales that have more than three detail lines.

```
SELECT COUNT(*) AS CountOfDetailLines, SalesOrderID
FROM Sales.SalesOrderDetail
GROUP BY SalesOrderID
HAVING COUNT(*) > 3;
```

2. Write a query that creates a sum of the LineTotal in the Sales.SalesOrderDetail table grouped by the SalesOrderID. Include only those rows where the sum exceeds 1,000.

```
SELECT SUM(LineTotal) AS SumOfLineTotal, SalesOrderID
FROM Sales.SalesOrderDetail
GROUP BY SalesOrderID
HAVING SUM(LineTotal) > 1000;
```

3. Write a query that groups the products by ProductModelID along with a count. Display the rows that have a count that equals 1.

```
SELECT ProductModelID, COUNT(*) AS CountOfProducts
FROM Production.Product
GROUP BY ProductModelID
HAVING COUNT(*) = 1;
```

4. Change the query in question 3 so that only the products with the color blue or red are included.

```
SELECT ProductModelID, COUNT(*) AS CountOfProducts, Color
FROM Production.Product
WHERE Color IN ('Blue','Red')
GROUP BY ProductModelID, Color
HAVING COUNT(*) = 1;
```

Solutions to Exercise 7-4: *DISTINCT* Keyword

Use the AdventureWorks database to complete this exercise.

1. Write a query using the Sales.SalesOrderDetail table to come up with a count of unique ProductID values that have been ordered.

```
SELECT COUNT(DISTINCT ProductID) AS CountOFProductID
FROM Sales.SalesOrderDetail;
```

2. Write a query using the Sales.SalesOrderHeader table that returns the count of unique TerritoryID values per customer.

```
SELECT COUNT(DISTINCT TerritoryID) AS CountOfTerritoryID,
    CustomerID
FROM Sales.SalesOrderHeader
GROUP BY CustomerID;
```

Solutions to Exercise 7-5: Aggregate Queries with More Than One Table

Use the AdventureWorks database to complete this exercise.

1. Write a query joining the Person.Person, Sales.Customer, and Sales.SalesOrderHeader tables to return a list of the customer names along with a count of the orders placed.

```
SELECT COUNT(*) AS CountOfOrders, FirstName,
    MiddleName, LastName
FROM Person.Person AS P
INNER JOIN Sales.Customer AS C ON P.BusinessEntityID = C.PersonID
INNER JOIN Sales.SalesOrderHeader
    AS SOH ON C.CustomerID = SOH.CustomerID
GROUP BY FirstName, MiddleName, LastName;
```

2. Write a query using the Sales.SalesOrderHeader, Sales.SalesOrderDetail, and Production.Product tables to display the total sum of products by Name and OrderDate.

```
SELECT SUM(OrderQty) SumOfOrderQty, P.Name, SOH.OrderDate
FROM Sales.SalesOrderHeader AS SOH
INNER JOIN Sales.SalesOrderDetail AS SOD
    ON SOH.SalesOrderID = SOD.SalesOrderDetailID
INNER JOIN Production.Product AS P ON SOD.ProductID = P.ProductID
GROUP BY P.Name, SOH.OrderDate;
```

CHAPTER 8

■ ■ ■

Discovering Windowing Functions

The windowing functions, sometimes called window or windowed functions, are the most exciting features added to T-SQL over the past several versions. Starting with SQL Server 2005, the window functions, which have nothing to do with the Windows operating system, enable T-SQL developers to solve complex queries in new and innovative ways. Window functions perform calculations over a "window" or set of rows. They allow the developer to solve problems in easier and frequently better performing ways. This chapter will explain the ranking and window aggregate functions added with SQL Server 2005 and the many enhancements and new analytic functions that are part of SQL Server 2012.

What Is a Windowing Function?

Windowing functions operate on the set of the data that is returned to the client. They might perform a calculation like a SUM over all the rows without losing the details, rank the data, or pull a value from a different row without doing a self-join. For each row of the results of a query, the windowing function will perform a calculation over a window of rows. That window is defined with the OVER clause. The OVER clause is required whenever you use windowing functions.

Windowing functions are allowed only in the SELECT and ORDER BY clauses. It is important to keep this in mind as you use them in your queries. To get around this limitation, you can take advantage of CTEs to separate out the logic and filter in the outer query. The windowing functions can be divided into several types that you will learn about in the sections of this chapter:

- *Ranking functions*: This type of function adds a ranking for each row or divides the rows into buckets.

- *Window aggregates*: This function allows you to calculate summary values in a nonaggregated query.

- *Accumulating aggregates*: Enables the calculation of running totals.

- *Analytic functions*: Several new scalar functions, four of which are almost magical!

Ranking Functions

The ranking functions—ROW_NUMBER, RANK, DENSE_RANK, and NTILE—were added to SQL Server as part of SQL Server 2005. The first three assign a ranking number to each row in the result set. The NTILE function divides a set of rows into buckets.

Defining the Window

As previously mentioned, the OVER clause defines the window for the ranking function. In this case, the OVER clause must specify the order of the rows, which then determines how the function is applied to the data. The ORDER BY inside the OVER clause is not related or linked to an ORDER BY clause for the entire query.

Here is the syntax for the ROW_NUMBER, RANK, and DENSE_RANK functions, respectively:

```
SELECT [<col1>,][<col2>,] ROW_NUMBER() OVER(ORDER BY <col1>[,<col2>]) AS RowNum
FROM <table>;

SELECT [<col1>,][<col2>,] RANK() OVER(ORDER BY <col1>[,<col2>]) AS RankNum
FROM <table>;

SELECT [<col1>,][<col2>,] DENSE_RANK() OVER(ORDER BY <col1>[,<col2>]) AS DenseRankNum
FROM <table>;
```

These functions differ in how they process ties or duplicates in the ORDER BY columns. If the values of the column or combination of columns chosen are unique, then these three functions will return identical results. Type in and run the code in Listing 8-1 to learn how to use these functions.

Listing 8-1. Using the Ranking Functions

```
--1
SELECT CustomerID,
    ROW_NUMBER() OVER(ORDER BY CustomerID) AS RowNum,
    RANK() OVER(ORDER BY CustomerID) AS RankNum,
    DENSE_RANK() OVER(ORDER BY CustomerID) AS DenseRankNum,
    ROW_NUMBER() OVER(ORDER BY CustomerID DESC) AS ReverseRowNum
FROM Sales.Customer
WHERE CustomerID BETWEEN 11000 AND 11200
ORDER BY CustomerID;

--2
SELECT SalesOrderID, CustomerID,
    ROW_NUMBER() OVER(ORDER BY CustomerID) AS RowNum,
    RANK() OVER(ORDER BY CustomerID) AS RankNum,
    DENSE_RANK() OVER(ORDER BY CustomerID) AS DenseRankNum
FROM Sales.SalesOrderHeader
WHERE CustomerID BETWEEN 11000 AND 11200
ORDER BY CustomerID;
```

The ORDER BY option in the OVER clause of query 1 is on the CustomerID column of the Sales.Customer table. Because CustomerID is the primary key and, therefore, unique, the first three functions return the same values. The last function applies the row numbers in reverse order, which brings up an important point. The order specified in the OVER clause does not have to match the ORDER BY of the query itself.

Query 2 also has the CustomerID as the ORDER BY option, but it is not unique in the Sales.SalesOrderHeader table. Notice in Figure 8-1 that when a customer has more than one purchase, in other words the CustomerID is duplicated, the RANK and DENSE_RANK functions produce different values. After the duplicate, RANK catches up with ROW_NUMBER, while DENSE_RANK continues on with the next value.

	CustomerID	RowNum	RankNum	DenseRankNum	ReverseRowNum
1	11000	1	1	1	201
2	11001	2	2	2	200
3	11002	3	3	3	199
4	11003	4	4	4	198

	SalesOrderID	CustomerID	RowNum	RankNum	DenseRankNum
1	43793	11000	1	1	1
2	51522	11000	2	1	1
3	57418	11000	3	1	1
4	43767	11001	4	4	2
5	51493	11001	5	4	2
6	72773	11001	6	4	2
7	43736	11002	7	7	3
8	51238	11002	8	7	3
9	53237	11002	9	7	3
10	43701	11003	10	10	4

Figure 8-1. *The partial results of using the ranking functions*

An interesting thing to note is that ROW_NUMBER will always return a unique value within the window. RANK and DENSE_RANK will also return unique values if the ORDER BY option is unique.

Dividing the Window into Partitions

If you have a window with a view to the outside world near you, it may be divided into two or more panes. You can also divide the window used by your function into sections called *partitions*. This sounds a lot like the GROUP BY clause in aggregate queries, but it is very different. When you are grouping, you end up with one row in the results for each unique group. When partitioning in the OVER clause, you retain all the detail rows in the results.

For the ranking functions, partitioning means that the row or rank number will start over for each partition. When using ROW_NUMBER, the value returned will be unique within the partition. Listing 8-2 demonstrates using the PARTITION BY option of the OVER clause.

Listing 8-2. Using PARTITION BY

```
SELECT SalesOrderID, OrderDate, CustomerID,
    ROW_NUMBER() OVER(PARTITION BY CustomerID ORDER BY OrderDate) AS RowNum
FROM Sales.SalesOrderHeader
ORDER BY CustomerID;
```

Figure 8-2 shows the partial results of running this code. The row numbers start over for each customer.

	SalesOrderID	OrderDate	CustomerID	RowNum
1	43793	2005-07-22 00:00:00.000	11000	1
2	51522	2007-07-22 00:00:00.000	11000	2
3	57418	2007-11-04 00:00:00.000	11000	3
4	43767	2005-07-18 00:00:00.000	11001	1
5	51493	2007-07-20 00:00:00.000	11001	2
6	72773	2008-06-12 00:00:00.000	11001	3
7	43736	2005-07-10 00:00:00.000	11002	1
8	51238	2007-07-04 00:00:00.000	11002	2
9	53237	2007-08-27 00:00:00.000	11002	3
10	43701	2005-07-01 00:00:00.000	11003	1

Figure 8-2. *The partial results of using PARTITION BY*

Using *NTILE*

The NTILE function works differently from other ranking functions. It assigns a number to sections of rows, evenly dividing the data into buckets. Here is the syntax for NTILE:

```
SELECT <col1>,NTILE(<number of buckets>) OVER([PARTITION BY <col2>] ORDER BY <col3>)
FROM <table>;
```

One obvious difference is that there is a required argument, the number of buckets, specified. Otherwise, the OVER clause has the same rules as the other ranking functions. The ORDER BY column is required, and the PARITION BY column is optional. Listing 8-3 shows two examples of the NTILE function.

Listing 8-3. Using the NTILE Function

```
SELECT SP.FirstName, SP.LastName,
    SUM(SOH.TotalDue) AS TotalSales,
    NTILE(4) OVER(ORDER BY SUM(SOH.TotalDue)) AS Bucket
FROM [Sales].[vSalesPerson] SP
JOIN Sales.SalesOrderHeader SOH ON SP.BusinessEntityID = SOH.SalesPersonID
WHERE SOH.OrderDate >= '2007-01-01' AND SOH.OrderDate < '2008-01-01'
GROUP BY FirstName, LastName
ORDER BY TotalSales;

--2
SELECT SP.FirstName, SP.LastName,
        SUM(SOH.TotalDue) AS TotalSales,
        NTILE(4) OVER(ORDER BY SUM(SOH.TotalDue)) * 1000 AS Bonus
FROM [Sales].[vSalesPerson] SP
JOIN Sales.SalesOrderHeader SOH ON SP.BusinessEntityID = SOH.SalesPersonID
WHERE SOH.OrderDate >= '2007-01-01' AND SOH.OrderDate < '2008-01-01'
GROUP BY FirstName, LastName
ORDER BY TotalSales;
```

Listing 8-3 is a very interesting example. It shows that you can use windowing functions in an aggregate query. In fact, an aggregate expression is used as the ORDER BY expression. Query 1 divides the salespeople into four buckets based on the 2007 sales. The salespeople with the lowest sales end up in bucket 1. The salespeople with the highest sales end up in bucket 4.

Query 2 multiplies the bucket number in each row by 1000. In this example, the manager has calculated the bonus due to each salesperson based on sales. Figure 8-3 shows the complete results of query 1 and a few of the rows from query 2. Notice that each bucket has four rows except for bucket 1, which has five rows. The NTILE function divides the data as evenly as it can. If there were 18 rows in the results, bucket 2 would also have an extra row.

	FirstName	LastName	TotalSales	Bucket
1	Syed	Abbas	165622.0321	1
2	Stephen	Jiang	515622.909	1
3	Amy	Alberts	617725.2728	1
4	Lynn	Tsoflias	795341.1682	1
5	Pamela	Ansman-Wolfe	1004700.5413	1
6	Rachel	Valdez	1107155.8886	2
7	Tete	Mensa-Annan	1376371.1384	2
8	David	Campbell	1549495.7049	2
9	Garrett	Vargas	1554236.1881	2
10	José	Saraiva	2075082.0159	3
11	Tsvi	Reiter	2505390.5003	3
12	Ranjit	Varkey Chudukatil	2582651.4735	3
13	Shu	Ito	2641228.7519	3
14	Jillian	Carson	4104089.9192	4
15	Michael	Blythe	4425590.0827	4
16	Linda	Mitchell	4626811.8662	4
17	Jae	Pak	4705252.1691	4

	FirstName	LastName	TotalSales	Bonus
1	Syed	Abbas	165622.0321	1000
2	Stephen	Jiang	515622.909	1000
3	Amy	Alberts	617725.2728	1000
4	Lynn	Tsoflias	795341.1682	1000

Figure 8-3. *The partial results of using NTILE*

Complete Exercise 8-1 to practice what you have learned about the ranking functions.

```
                              EXERCISE 8-1
```

Use the AdventureWorks database to complete this exercise. You can find the solutions at the end of the chapter.

1. Write a query that assigns row numbers to the Production.Product table. Start the numbers over for each ProductSubCategoryID and make sure that the row numbers are in order of ProductID. Display only rows where the ProductSubCategoryID is not null.

2. Write a query that divides the customers into ten buckets based on the total sales for 2005.

Summarizing Results with Window Aggregates

Also introduced with SQL Server 2005, window aggregates allow you to add aggregate expressions to nonaggregate queries. For example, you may want to see an overall total of sales along with the details of those sales.

Window aggregate functions require the OVER clause and support PARTITION BY. They do not, however, support the ORDER BY option. Listing 8-4 demonstrates how to use window aggregates.

Listing 8-4. Using Window Aggregates

```
--1
SELECT SalesOrderID, CustomerID,
    COUNT(*) OVER() AS CountOfSales,
    COUNT(*) OVER(PARTITION BY CustomerID) AS CountOfCustSales,
    SUM(TotalDue) OVER(PARTITION BY CustomerID) AS SumOfCustSales
FROM Sales.SalesOrderHeader
ORDER BY CustomerID;

--2
SELECT SalesOrderID, CustomerID,
    COUNT(*) OVER() AS CountOfSales,
    COUNT(*) OVER(PARTITION BY CustomerID) AS CountOfCustSales,
    SUM(TotalDue) OVER(PARTITION BY CustomerID) AS SumOfCustSales
FROM Sales.SalesOrderHeader
where SalesOrderId > 55000
ORDER BY CustomerID;
```

Figure 8-4 shows the partial results of running this code. Notice that the aggregate functions COUNT and SUM have been added to the query but there is no GROUP BY clause. In addition, the detail rows are returned along with the results of the aggregate functions. The empty OVER clause performs the calculation over the entire set of rows. The window defined by the empty parentheses () is the entire set of results. Notice that query 1 returns 31465 for the count of rows, while query 2 returns only 20123 rows. This is just another reminder that the aggregate functions, and all the windowing functions, operate after the WHERE clause.

	SalesOrderID	CustomerID	CountOfSales	CountOfCustSales	SumOfCustSales
1	43793	11000	31465	3	9115.1341
2	51522	11000	31465	3	9115.1341
3	57418	11000	31465	3	9115.1341
4	51493	11001	31465	3	7054.1875

	SalesOrderID	CustomerID	CountOfSales	CountOfCustSales	SumOfCustSales
1	57418	11000	20123	1	2770.2682
2	72773	11001	20123	1	650.8008
3	57783	11003	20123	1	2674.4757
4	57293	11004	20123	1	2673.0613

Figure 8-4. *The partial results of using window aggregate expressions*

When adding the PARTITION BY option to the OVER clause, the window for each calculation is now defined by the column or columns specified.

Complete Exercise 8-2 to practice what you have learned about window aggregates.

EXERCISE 8-2

Use the AdventureWorks database to complete this exercise. You can find the solutions at the end of the chapter.

1. Write a query returning the SalesOrderID, OrderDate, CustomerID, and TotalDue from the Sales.SalesOrderHeader table. Include the average order total over all the results.

2. Add the average total due for each customer to the query you wrote in question 1.

Defining the Window with Framing

Starting with SQL Server 2012, you can further define the window for certain window functions with frames. You'll see an example of how this is used in the next section. Each row in the results will have a different window for the calculation.

To understand framing, you must first learn the three key phrases UNBOUNDED PRECEDING, UNBOUNDED FOLLOWING, and CURRENT ROW. To understand what these mean and how they work, take a look at the examples in Table 8-1. Imagine that you have 100 rows in the results and you are viewing the rows from the perspective of row 10. Remember that each row in the results has its own window.

Table 8-1. *Framining Examples*

Frame Definition	Rows in Frame for Row 10
ROWS BETWEEN UNBOUNDED PRECEDING AND CURRENT ROW	Rows 1–10
ROWS BETWEEN CURRENT ROW AND UNBOUNDED FOLLOWING	Rows 10–100
ROWS BETWEEN UNBOUNDED PRECEDING AND UNBOUNDED FOLLOWING	Rows 1–100

In each of the examples in Table 8-1, the CURRENT ROW is row 10. The phrase UNBOUNDED PRECEDING means every row up to row 10. The phrase UNBOUNDED FOLLOWING means every row greater than row 10. When using framing, the ORDER BY option of the OVER clause is critical in determining which row is the first row and so on.

You can also specify an *offset*, or the actual number of rows removed from the current row. Table 8-2 shows how this works. Again, these examples are from the perspective of row 10 within a 100 row result set.

Table 8-2. *Using Row Number Offsets*

Frame Definition	Rows in Frame for Row 10
ROWS BETWEEN 3 PRECEDING AND CURRENT ROW	Rows 7–10
ROWS BETWEEN CURRENT ROW AND 5 FOLLOWING	Rows 10–15
ROWS BETWEEN UNBOUNDED PRECEDING AND 5 FOLLOWING	Rows 1–15
ROWS BETWEEN 3 PRECEDING AND 5 FOLLOWING	Rows 7–15

Remember that each row in the results has its own frame. When looking at the frame from the perspective of row 9, the frame will shift to the left one row.

This section covered framing with the keyword ROWS. There is another keyword, RANGE, that can be used in place of ROWS. For the most part, they do the same thing, however, there are some differences. Window functions are part of the ANSI standards for the SQL language. Microsoft has not fully implemented everything that the ANSI standards have come up with for RANGE, so, at this time, it is much better to specify ROWS. See the section "Understanding the Difference Between *ROWS* and *RANGE*" later in the chapter to learn the differences.

Calculating Running Totals

By adding an ORDER BY clause to a window aggregate expression, you can calculate a running total. This functionality was added with SQL Server 2012. If you had tried to add the ORDER BY to a window aggregate function in an earlier version, you would have gotten an error message. The window aggregate functions require a frame, but it is RANGE BETWEEN UNBOUNDED PRECEDING AND CURRENT ROW by default if you don't specify anything different.

Listing 8-5 shows how to calculate running totals using window functions.

Listing 8-5. Using Window Functions to Calculate Running Totals

```
--1
SELECT SalesOrderID, CustomerID, TotalDue,
    SUM(TotalDue) OVER(PARTITION BY CustomerID
        ORDER BY SalesOrderID)
        AS RunningTotal
FROM Sales.SalesOrderHeader
ORDER BY CustomerID, SalesOrderID;

--2
SELECT SalesOrderID, CustomerID, TotalDue,
    SUM(TotalDue) OVER(PARTITION BY CustomerID
        ORDER BY SalesOrderID
        ROWS BETWEEN CURRENT ROW AND UNBOUNDED FOLLOWING)
        AS ReverseTotal
FROM Sales.SalesOrderHeader
ORDER BY CustomerID, SalesOrderID;
```

Figure 8-5 shows the results for the first two customers. By adding ORDER BY to the OVER clause, the window aggregate function now accumulates the totals instead of calculating a discrete total for each row. The results are partitioned by the CustomerID column, so the running total is calculated for each customer. In query 1, the frame is not specified so the default is used. In query 2, a different frame is specified so that the reverse running total is calculated instead.

	SalesOrderID	CustomerID	TotalDue	RunningTotal
1	43793	11000	3756.989	3756.989
2	51522	11000	2587.8769	6344.8659
3	57418	11000	2770.2682	9115.1341
4	43767	11001	3729.364	3729.364
5	51493	11001	2674.0227	6403.3867
6	72773	11001	650.8008	7054.1875

	SalesOrderID	CustomerID	TotalDue	ReverseTotal
1	43793	11000	3756.989	9115.1341
2	51522	11000	2587.8769	5358.1451
3	57418	11000	2770.2682	2770.2682
4	43767	11001	3729.364	7054.1875
5	51493	11001	2674.0227	3324.8235
6	72773	11001	650.8008	650.8008

Figure 8-5. *The partial results of calculating running totals*

Understanding the Difference Between *ROWS* and *RANGE*

As mentioned, frames defined with ROWS and RANGE provide the same results most of the time. Besides not fully implementing RANGE, there is a difference in how these two operators work. ROWS is a physical operator, while RANGE is a logical operator. To see the difference, Listing 8-6 demonstrates how these two operators can return different results when the ORDER BY column is not unique.

Listing 8-6. Demonstrate the Difference Between ROWS and RANGE

```
SELECT SalesOrderID, OrderDate,CustomerID, TotalDue,
    SUM(TotalDue) OVER(PARTITION BY CustomerID
        ORDER BY OrderDate
        ROWS BETWEEN UNBOUNDED PRECEDING AND CURRENT ROW)
        AS ROWS_RT,
        SUM(TotalDue) OVER(PARTITION BY CustomerID
        ORDER BY OrderDate
        RANGE BETWEEN UNBOUNDED PRECEDING AND CURRENT ROW)
        AS RANGE_RT
FROM Sales.SalesOrderHeader
WHERE CustomerID = 29837;
```

Figure 8-6 shows the results of this code. Customer 29837 was chosen because it has multiple orders on the same date. By changing the ORDER BY column in the OVER clause to the nonunique OrderDate, the results of using RANGE are obvious. The ROWS operator returns a running total based on the *physical position* of the rows. The RANGE operator treats duplicate values the same. Because it is calculating based on the *logical value*, the results do not produce a true running total.

	SalesOrderID	OrderDate	CustomerID	TotalDue	ROWS_RT	RANGE_RT
1	51170	2007-07-01 ...	29837	4190.3125	4190.3125	8414.8269
2	51171	2007-07-01 ...	29837	4224.5144	8414.8269	8414.8269
3	55306	2007-10-01 ...	29837	1153.8016	9568.6285	11399.1962
4	55320	2007-10-01 ...	29837	1830.5677	11399.1962	11399.1962
5	61252	2008-01-01 ...	29837	419.7041	11818.9003	12441.8471
6	61262	2008-01-01 ...	29837	622.9468	12441.8471	12441.8471
7	67203	2008-03-31 ...	29837	2746.7906	15188.6377	15188.6377
8	67323	2008-04-01 ...	29837	2036.9284	17225.5661	17225.5661

Figure 8-6. *The difference between ROWS and RANGE*

Notice that on 2007-07-01, two orders were placed. The ROWS_RT column adds the TotalDue as expected. The RANGE_RT treats these as logically the same, so the window for row 1 is the same as the window for row 2.

There are two things to learn from this. First, make sure that you always use a unique column or combination of columns for the ORDER BY option in the OVER clause. You should also understand that, by default, RANGE will be used if no framing option is specified. Second, make sure you always specify ROWS and don't rely on the default value. There is also a performance difference between the two. You'll learn more about this in the "Thinking About Performance" section later in the chapter.

Complete Exercise 8-3 to practice what you have learned about using ROWS and RANGE.

EXERCISE 8-3

Use the AdventureWorks database to complete this exercise. You can find the solutions at the end of the chapter.

1. Write a query that returns the SalesOrderID, ProductID, and LineTotal from Sales. SalesOrderDetail. Calculate a running total of the LineTotal for each ProductID. Be sure to use the correct frame.

2. Explain why you should specify the frame where it is supported instead of relying on the default.

Using Window Analytic Functions

Microsoft added eight new window analytic functions with SQL Server 2012. Four of the functions deal with percentage calculations and the other four allow you to pull data from other rows.

LAG and *LEAD*

The two new functions LAG and LEAD are simply amazing. These functions allow you to "take a peek" at a different row. Previous to SQL Server 2012, you would have had to write poorly performing self-joins to achieve the same results. The LAG function lets you pull any column from a previous row. The LEAD function allows you to pull any column from a following row. The performance of these two functions is fantastic and framing is not supported, but partitioning is. Here is the syntax for LAG and LEAD:

```
SELECT <col1>[,<col2>], LAG(<column to view>) OVER(ORDER BY <col1>[,<col2>]) AS <alias>
FROM <table>;

SELECT <col1>[,<col2>], LAG(<column to view>[,<number of rows>])[,<default value>]
    OVER(ORDER BY <col1>[,<col2>]) AS <alias>
FROM <table>;

SELECT <col1>[,<col2>], LEAD(<column to view>) OVER(ORDER BY <col1>[,<col2>]) AS <alias>
FROM <table>;

SELECT <col1>[,<col2>], LEAD(<column to view>[,<number of rows>])[,<default value>]
    OVER(ORDER BY <col1>[,<col2>]) AS <alias>
FROM <table>;
```

Listing 8-7 demonstrates how to use LAG and LEAD.

Listing 8-7. Using LAG and LEAD

```
--1
SELECT SalesOrderID, OrderDate,CustomerID,
    LAG(OrderDate) OVER(PARTITION BY CustomerID ORDER BY SalesOrderID) AS PrevOrderDate,
    LEAD(OrderDate) OVER(PARTITION BY CustomerID ORDER BY SalesOrderID) AS FollowingOrderDate
FROM Sales.SalesOrderHeader;

--2
SELECT SalesOrderID, OrderDate,CustomerID,
    DATEDIFF(d,LAG(OrderDate,1,OrderDate)
            OVER(PARTITION BY CustomerID ORDER BY SalesOrderID), OrderDate)
            AS DaysSinceLastOrder
FROM Sales.SalesOrderHeader;
```

Figure 8-7 shows the partial results of running this code. Query 1 shows the default behavior of LAG and LEAD. You must specify which column you wish to see as an argument, in this case OrderDate. The ORDER BY option is required; PARTITION BY is optional. When looking at the very earliest order that was placed (Row 1 in the results), the LAG function returns NULL because there is no earlier order.

	SalesOrderID	OrderDate	CustomerID	PrevOrderDate	FollowingOrderDate
1	43793	2005-07-22 ...	11000	NULL	2007-07-22 00:00:00.000
2	51522	2007-07-22 ...	11000	2005-07-22 00:00:00.000	2007-11-04 00:00:00.000
3	57418	2007-11-04 ...	11000	2007-07-22 00:00:00.000	NULL
4	43767	2005-07-18 ...	11001	NULL	2007-07-20 00:00:00.000
5	51493	2007-07-20 ...	11001	2005-07-18 00:00:00.000	2008-06-12 00:00:00.000

	SalesOrderID	OrderDate	CustomerID	DaysSinceLastOrder
1	43793	2005-07-22 00:00:00.000	11000	0
2	51522	2007-07-22 00:00:00.000	11000	730
3	57418	2007-11-04 00:00:00.000	11000	105
4	43767	2005-07-18 00:00:00.000	11001	0
5	51493	2007-07-20 00:00:00.000	11001	732

Figure 8-7. *Using LAG and LEAD*

Query 2 demonstrates how to use the two optional arguments. You can specify how many rows to go backward or forward, with the default of 1. The third argument is a default value to replace any NULL values. In this case, the OrderDate for the current row is specified. Query 2 also nests the LAG function within the DATEDIFF function used to calculate the number of days since the previous order.

FIRST_VALUE and LAST_VALUE

The FIRST_VALUE and LAST_VALUE functions work similarly to LAG and LEAD, but instead pull values from the very first row or very last row of the window. In this case, framing is supported. By default the frame is RANGE BETWEEN UNBOUND PRECEDING AND CURRENT ROW. Be sure to specify ROWS instead of relying on the default. When using LAST_VALUE, while you won't get an error message with the default frame, it will not work as you expect because the default frame only goes up to the current row.

At first, this functionality seems similar to the MAX and MIN aggregate functions. They are very different, however. Instead of finding the maximum or minimum value in a set of results, they retrieve any column from the first or last row. Just like LAG and LEAD, writing a query with older techniques would have required self-joins and performed poorly. Here is the syntax:

```
SELECT <col1>[,<col2>], FIRST_VALUE(<column to view>)
    OVER(ORDER BY <col1>) [frame specification]
FROM <table>;

SELECT <col1>[,<col2>], LAST_VALUE(<column to view>)
    OVER(ORDER BY <col1>) frame specification
FROM <table>;
```

Listing 8-8 demonstrates how to use FIRST_VALUE and LAST_VALUE.

Listing 8-8. Using FIRST_VALUE and LAST_VALUE

```
SELECT SalesOrderID, OrderDate,CustomerID,
    FIRST_VALUE(OrderDate) OVER(PARTITION BY CustomerID ORDER BY SalesOrderID
        ROWS BETWEEN UNBOUNDED PRECEDING AND CURRENT ROW) AS FirstOrderDate,
    LAST_VALUE(OrderDate) OVER(PARTITION BY CustomerID ORDER BY SalesOrderID
        ROWS BETWEEN CURRENT ROW AND UNBOUNDED FOLLOWING) AS LastOrderDate,
```

```
        LAST_VALUE(OrderDate) OVER(PARTITION BY CustomerID ORDER BY SalesOrderID)
            AS DefaultFrame
FROM Sales.SalesOrderHeader
ORDER BY CustomerID, SalesOrderID;
```

Figure 8-8 shows the partial results of running this code. Notice that to get the LAST_VALUE function to work as expected, the frame must be specified. If the frame is not specified, as shown in the DefaultFrame column, the value returned in each row matches the OrderDate value for that row. That is because the default frame doesn't go past the current row and the current row is the last value.

	SalesOrderID	OrderDate	CustomerID	FirstOrderDate	LastOrderDate	DefaultFrame
1	43793	2005-07-22 ...	11000	2005-07-22 00...	2007-11-04 00...	2005-07-22 00...
2	51522	2007-07-22 ...	11000	2005-07-22 00...	2007-11-04 00...	2007-07-22 00...
3	57418	2007-11-04 ...	11000	2005-07-22 00...	2007-11-04 00...	2007-11-04 00...
4	43767	2005-07-18 ...	11001	2005-07-18 00...	2008-06-12 00...	2005-07-18 00...
5	51493	2007-07-20 ...	11001	2005-07-18 00...	2008-06-12 00...	2007-07-20 00...
6	72773	2008-06-12 ...	11001	2005-07-18 00...	2008-06-12 00...	2008-06-12 00...
7	43736	2005-07-10 ...	11002	2005-07-10 00...	2007-08-27 00...	2005-07-10 00...
8	51238	2007-07-04 ...	11002	2005-07-10 00...	2007-08-27 00...	2007-07-04 00...
9	53237	2007-08-27 ...	11002	2005-07-10 00...	2007-08-27 00...	2007-08-27 00...
10	43701	2005-07-01 ...	11003	2005-07-01 00...	2007-11-11 00...	2005-07-01 00...

Figure 8-8. *The partial results of using FIRST_VALUE and LAST_VALUE*

PERCENT_RANK and CUME_DIST

The PERCENT_RANK and CUME_DIST functions are useful for statistical applications. Each of these returns a ranking over the window. For example, remember those standardized tests you took in school? The results usually gave you a ranking that showed how your score compared with the score of other students in your state or country. The ORDER BY clause is required, PARTITION BY is optional, and framing is not supported. Here is the syntax:

```
SELECT <col1>[,<col2>], PERCENT_RANK() OVER(ORDER BY <column or expression>)
FROM <table>;

SELECT <col1>[,<col2>], CUME_DIST() OVER(ORDER BY <column or expression>)
FROM <table>;
```

Type in and run Listing 8-9 to learn how to use these functions.

Listing 8-9. Using PERCENT_RANK and CUME_DIST

```
SELECT COUNT(*) NumberOfOrders, Month(OrderDate) AS OrderMonth,
    PERCENT_RANK() OVER(ORDER BY COUNT(*)) AS PercentRank,
    CUME_DIST() OVER(ORDER BY COUNT(*)) AS CumeDist
FROM Sales.SalesOrderHeader
GROUP BY Month(OrderDate);
```

Figure 8-9 shows the partial results of running this code. Notice that the two functions give slightly different results, how each month compares based on number of sales. Take a look at the sixth row in the results, January. That month had 2483 sales. The month ranked better than 45 percent of the other months. It was actually positioned at 50 percent, in other words its sales were equal to or better than 50 percent of the total sales.

	NumberOfOrders	OrderMonth	PercentRank	CumeDist
1	2094	7	0	0.0833333333333333
2	2282	10	0.0909090909090909	0.166666666666667
3	2298	9	0.181818181818182	0.25
4	2411	8	0.272727272727273	0.333333333333333
5	2474	11	0.363636363636364	0.416666666666667
6	2483	1	0.454545454545455	0.5
7	2686	2	0.545454545454545	0.583333333333333
8	2740	4	0.636363636363636	0.666666666666667
9	2750	3	0.727272727272727	0.75
10	3014	12	0.818181818181818	0.833333333333333
11	3079	6	0.909090909090909	0.916666666666667
12	3154	5	1	1

Figure 8-9. *The results of using PERCENT_RANK and CUME_DIST*

Another example I like to give pertains to my grandson, Thomas. He is a tall seven-year-old at the 90th percentile according to his pediatrician. That means, if I had 100 kids his age lined up by height, he would be at position 90, the cumulative distribution. He is taller than 89 kids, the percentage rank.

PERCENTILE_CONT and PERCENTILE_DISC

The PERCENTILE_CONT and PERCENTILE_DISC functions have the opposite functionality of the previously discussed two. Given a percentage rank, they figure out which value is at that position. There is also an additional clause, WITHIN GROUP, required with these functions. PERCENTILE_CONT stands for percentile continuous and PERCENTILE_DISC stands for percentile discrete. Here is the syntax:

```
PERCENTILE_CONT (<numeric_literal> )
    WITHIN GROUP ( ORDER BY <order_by_expression> [ ASC | DESC ] )
    OVER ( [ <partition_by_clause> ] )

PERCENTILE_DISC ( <numeric_literal> )
    WITHIN GROUP ( ORDER BY <order_by_expression> [ ASC | DESC ] )
    OVER ( [ <partition_by_clause> ] )
```

Another interesting thing to note is that the OVER clause does not contain the ORDER BY option. It is found in the WITHIN GROUP clause. Listing 8-10 shows how to use these functions.

Listing 8-10. Using PERCENTILE_CONT and PERCENTILE_DISC

```
SELECT COUNT(*) NumberOfOrders, Month(OrderDate) AS OrderMonth,
    PERCENTILE_CONT(0.5) WITHIN GROUP(ORDER BY COUNT(*)) OVER() AS PercentileCont,
    PERCENTILE_DISC(0.5) WITHIN GROUP(ORDER BY COUNT(*)) OVER() AS PercentileDisc
FROM Sales.SalesOrderHeader
GROUP BY Month(OrderDate);
```

Figure 8-10 shows the results of running this code. Given a set of values and a rank, these functions return the value at that rank. The difference between the two functions is that PERCENTILE_CONT will calculate the exact value if the actual value is not part of the list. In this example, if one of the months is left out so there is an odd number of rows, PERCENTILE_CONT will return the exact value in the middle of the list. The PERCENTILE_DISC function will always return an actual value from the set, the one that is closest to the rank. The results show which value is at 50 percent.

	NumberOfOrders	OrderMonth	PercentileCont	PercentileDisc
1	2094	7	2584.5	2483
2	2282	10	2584.5	2483
3	2298	9	2584.5	2483
4	2411	8	2584.5	2483
5	2474	11	2584.5	2483
6	2483	1	2584.5	2483
7	2686	2	2584.5	2483
8	2740	4	2584.5	2483
9	2750	3	2584.5	2483
10	3014	12	2584.5	2483
11	3079	6	2584.5	2483
12	3154	5	2584.5	2483

Figure 8-10. *Using PERCENTILE_CONT and PERCENTILE_DISC*

Complete Exercise 8-4 to learn how to use PERCENTILE_CONT and PERCENTILE_DISC.

EXERCISE 8-4

Use the AdventureWorks database to complete this exercise. You can find the solutions at the end of the chapter. Run the following script that creates a table holding stock market data.

```
CREATE TABLE #Stock (Symbol VARCHAR(4), TradingDate DATE,
    OpeningPrice MONEY, ClosingPrice MONEY);
INSERT INTO #Stock(Symbol, TradingDate, OpeningPrice, ClosingPrice)
VALUES ('A','2014/01/02',5.03,4.90),
    ('B','2014/01/02',10.99,11.25),
    ('C','2014/01/02',23.42,23.44),
    ('A','2014/01/03',4.93,5.10),
    ('B','2014/01/03',11.25,11.25),
    ('C','2014/01/03',25.15,25.06),
    ('A','2014/01/06',5.15,5.20),
    ('B','2014/01/06',11.30,11.12),
    ('C','2014/01/06',25.20,26.00);
```

1. Write a query using a window analytic function that calculates the difference in the closing price from the previous day.

2. Modify the query written in question 1 so that the NULL values in the calculation are replaced with zeros. Use an option in the window analytic function.

Applying Windowing Functions

The purposes of most of the functions introduced in this chapter are obvious. When I present this topic at events like PASS Summit or SQL Saturdays, the audience is pretty excited when they see what can be done, especially with LAG, LEAD, FIRST_VALUE, and LAST_VALUE functions. I've heard a few say that they now have a great argument for upgrading to SQL Server 2012 or 2014 sooner rather than later. I'm not exaggerating when I talk about how powerful these functionalities are.

You may be wondering, however, about the ranking functions. Why would you ever need to use a function like ROW_NUMBER? What I have found is that I discover new reasons to use ROW_NUMBER and the other windowing functions all the time. In fact, whenever I have a difficult query to write, I often just add ROW_NUMBER and then look for patterns. Using these functions has helped me approach T-SQL from a set-based mindset instead of an iterative mindset. In this section, I'll show you a couple of examples where these functions can help solve a tricky problem.

Removing Duplicates

One of the applications of ROW_NUMBER is to remove duplicate rows from data. The ROW_NUMBER function returns a unique number for each row in the window or set of rows returned. By adding a row number, you can turn data with duplicates into unique rows temporarily. By partitioning on all the columns, you start the numbering over for each unique combination of columns. That means that each unique row will have a row number of 1, and you can delete the rows with row numbers greater than 1. Listing 8-11 shows how to remove duplicate rows using ROW_NUMBER.

Listing 8-11. Using ROW_NUMBER() to Remove Duplicate Rows

```
--1
CREATE TABLE #Dupes (
    COL1 INT, Col2 INT, Col3 INT);

INSERT INTO #Dupes (Col1, Col2, Col3)
VALUES (1,1,1),(1,1,1),(1,2,3),(1,2,2),(1,2,2),
    (2,3,3),(2,3,3),(2,3,3),(2,3,3);

--2
SELECT Col1, Col2, Col3,
    ROW_NUMBER() OVER(PARTITION BY Col1, Col2, Col3 ORDER BY Col1, Col2, Col3) AS RowNum
FROM #Dupes;

--3
WITH Dupes AS (
        SELECT Col1, Col2, Col3,
            ROW_NUMBER() OVER(PARTITION BY Col1, Col2, Col3 ORDER BY Col1, Col2, Col3) AS RowNum
    FROM #Dupes)
SELECT Col1, Col2, Col3, RowNum
FROM Dupes
WHERE RowNum = 1;
```

```
--4
WITH Dupes AS (
        SELECT Col1, Col2, Col3,
            ROW_NUMBER() OVER(PARTITION BY Col1, Col2, Col3 ORDER BY Col1, Col2, Col3) AS RowNum
    FROM #Dupes)
DELETE Dupes
WHERE RowNum > 1;

--5
SELECT Col1, Col2, Col3
FROM #Dupes;
```

Figure 8-11 shows the results of running this code. Code section 1 creates a table and then populates it with several rows, many are duplicated. Query 2 shows the data along with a row number that is partitioned by the combination of every column. This causes the row numbers to start over for each unique row. Statement 4 removes all of the rows with row numbers over 1. Each unique set of rows has a row number 1. Because we want to keep just one row for each unique combination, deleting the rows with row numbers greater than 1 removes unneeded rows. Because it is not possible to filter on the row number directly, a CTE is used. Finally, query 5 demonstrates that the duplicates were removed.

	Col1	Col2	Col3	RowNum
1	1	1	1	1
2	1	1	1	2
3	1	2	2	1
4	1	2	2	2
5	1	2	3	1
6	2	3	3	1
7	2	3	3	2
8	2	3	3	3
9	2	3	3	4

	Col1	Col2	Col3	RowNum
1	1	1	1	1
2	1	2	2	1
3	1	2	3	1
4	2	3	3	1

	Col1	Col2	Col3
1	1	1	1
2	1	2	3
3	1	2	2
4	2	3	3

Figure 8-11. *Using ROW_NUMBER() to remove duplicates*

Solving an Islands Problem

The *islands problem* is a classic example that is difficult to solve. The purpose is to identify the boundaries of a series of data. For example, say you had the numbers 1, 2, 3, 5, 8, 9, 10, 11. The islands would be 1-3, 5, and 8-11. The gaps in the numbers are the boundaries of the islands. This technique is often used with dates, but to keep it very simple, the following example will use integers instead. Type in and run Listing 8-12 to learn this technique.

Listing 8-12. Solving an Island Problem

```
--1
CREATE TABLE #Island(Col1 INT);

INSERT INTO #Island (Col1)
VALUES(1),(2),(3),(5),(6),(7),(9),(9),(10);

--2
SELECT Col1, DENSE_RANK() OVER(ORDER BY COl1) AS RankNum,
       Col1 - DENSE_RANK() OVER(ORDER BY COl1) AS Diff
FROM #Island;

--3
WITH islands AS (
    SELECT Col1, Col1 - DENSE_RANK() OVER(ORDER BY COl1) AS Diff
    FROM #Island)
SELECT MIN(Col1) AS Begining, MAX(Col1) AS Ending
FROM islands
GROUP BY Diff;
```

Figure 8-12 shows the results of running this code. Code section 1 creates and populates a temp table. Query 2 displays the data along with the DENSE_RANK function. The DENSE_RANK function was used in this case because there are duplicates in the data. Notice that there is a pattern. Within every island, the difference between the rank and the original number is the same. For 1, 2, and 3, the first island, the difference is 0. For 5, 6, and 7, the second island, the difference is 1. Using this pattern, you can then group by the differences. The minimum and maximum values in the groups are the boundaries of the islands.

	Col1	RankNum	Diff
1	1	1	0
2	1	1	0
3	2	2	0
4	3	3	0
5	5	4	1
6	6	5	1
7	7	6	1
8	9	7	2
9	9	7	2
10	10	8	2

	Begining	Ending
1	1	3
2	5	7
3	9	10

Figure 8-12. *Solving an island problem*

Thinking About Performance

Besides making it easier for T-SQL developers to write queries, the windowing functions have been touted as having great performance over more traditional techniques. Unfortunately, you will not always see that performance boost unless you keep a few things in mind. In this section, you will learn what you need to know to get the best performance from these functions.

Indexing

Although index tuning is beyond the scope of this book, be aware that a specific type of index can help the performance of most queries that use windowing functions. This index is composed of the PARTITION BY and OVER BY columns from the OVER clause in that order. Additionally, if there are other columns listed in the SELECT list, add those as included columns to the index. Add any columns listed in the WHERE clause as index keys in front of the PARTITION BY columns.

Of course, you shouldn't add an index to a table for every query you write, but if you do need to tune a query that contains a windowing function, this is the information you will need. The benefit of the index is to eliminate expensive sort operations.

■ **Note** A debt of gratitude from the author is owed to T-SQL guru Itzik Ben-Gan for his work in educating the SQL Server community on how to get the best performance from windowing functions.

The Trouble with Window Aggregates

Window aggregate expressions are great ways to add summary calculations while retaining the details. They are very easy to write. Unfortunately, the performance is worse than when using traditional techniques. Turn on the Actual Execution Plan setting and run Listing 8-13 to see the difference.

Listing 8-13. The Difference Between Using Window Aggregates and Traditional Techniques

```
--1
SELECT CustomerID, SalesOrderID, TotalDue,
    SUM(TotalDue) OVER(PARTITION BY CustomerID) AS CustTotal
FROM Sales.SalesOrderHeader;

--2
;WITH Totals AS (
   SELECT CustomerID, SUM(TotalDue) AS CustTotal
   FROM Sales.SalesOrderHeader
   GROUP BY CustomerID)
SELECT Totals.CustomerID, SalesOrderID, TotalDue, CustTotal
FROM Sales.SalesOrderHeader AS SOH
INNER JOIN Totals ON SOH.CustomerID = Totals.CustomerID;
```

Query 1 uses the window aggregate technique to calculate a total for each customer. Query 2 uses a common table expression to first get a list of all customers and their totals. It then joins to the Sales.SalesOrderHeader table to display the same results as query 1. When you take a look at the execution you'll see that query 1 doesn't perform as well as query 2. While adding an index as described in the previous section can improve performance, the performance will always be worse than that for the technique used in query 2.

You can also turn on Statistics IO to see the difference. Query 1 has over 140,000 logical reads, while query 2 has about 1400 logical reads.

This doesn't mean that you should avoid using window aggregates. It's a fantastic technique that can make your code easy to write and maintain. It is important, however, to keep the performance penalty in mind so they can be avoided when performance is critical.

Framing

In addition to the logical differences described in the section "Understanding the Difference between ROWS and RANGE," there is also a performance difference between ROWS and RANGE. Turn off the Actual Execution Plan, which will be identical for these queries. Run Listing 8-14 to see the differences.

Listing 8-14. Performance Differences Between ROWS and RANGE

```
--1
SET STATISTICS IO ON;
GO
SELECT SalesOrderID, TotalDue, CustomerID,
    SUM(TotalDue) OVER(PARTITION BY CustomerID ORDER BY OrderDate) AS RunningTotal
FROM Sales.SalesOrderHeader;

--2
SELECT SalesOrderID, TotalDue, CustomerID,
    SUM(TotalDue) OVER(PARTITION BY CustomerID ORDER BY OrderDate
            ROWS BETWEEN UNBOUNDED PRECEDING AND CURRENT ROW) AS RunningTotal
FROM Sales.SalesOrderHeader;
```

Query 1 calculates the running total for each customer without specifying the frame. By default, the frame will be RANGE BETWEEN UNBOUNDED PRECEDING AND CURRENT ROW. Because the ORDER BY clause is unique, there will not be any issues with the values returned. Query 2 specifies the framing clause, substituting ROWS instead of RANGE. Figure 8-13 shows the Statistics IO message, which shows that RANGE has much worse performance than ROWS. The difference has to do with how the database engine implements the worktable used to perform the calculations.

```
    Results    Messages

    (31465 row(s) affected)
    Table 'Worktable'. Scan count 50525, logical reads 188673, physi
    Table 'SalesOrderHeader'. Scan count 1, logical reads 689, physi

    (31465 row(s) affected)
    Table 'Worktable'. Scan count 0, logical reads 0, physical reads
    Table 'SalesOrderHeader'. Scan count 1, logical reads 689, physi
```

Figure 8-13. *The performance difference between ROWS and RANGE*

Summary

Beginning with SQL Server 2005, windowing functions have been fantastic additions to the T-SQL language. The more you work with T-SQL, the more frequently you will find reasons to use these functions.

Be sure to keep in mind the lessons found in the "Thinking About Performance" section so you can get the best performance possible from your queries.

In chapter 9 you will learn more about the WHERE clause including pattern matching and full text search.

Answers to the Exercises

This section provides answers to the exercises on writing queries using windowing functions.

Solutions to Exercise 8-1: Ranking Functions

Use the AdventureWorks database to complete this exercise.

1. Write a query that assigns row numbers to the Production.Product table. Start the numbers over for each ProductSubCategoryID and make sure that the row numbers are in order of ProductID. Display only rows where the ProductSubCategoryID is not null.

```
SELECT ProductID, ProductSubcategoryID,
    ROW_NUMBER() OVER(PARTITION BY ProductSubCategoryID
ORDER BY ProductID) AS RowNum
FROM Production.Product
WHERE ProductSubcategoryID IS NOT NULL;
```

2. Write a query that divides the customers into ten buckets based on the total sales for 2005.

```
SELECT CustomerID, SUM(TotalDue) AS TotalSales,
    NTILE(10) OVER(ORDER BY SUM(TotalDue)) AS CustBucket
FROM Sales.SalesOrderHeader
WHERE OrderDate BETWEEN '2005/1/1' AND '2005/12/31'
GROUP BY CustomerID;
```

Solutions to Exercise 8-2: Summarizing Results with Window Aggregates

Use the AdventureWorks database to complete this exercise.

1. Write a query returning the SalesOrderID, OrderDate, CustomerID, and TotalDue from the Sales.SalesOrderHeader table. Include the average order total over all the results.

```
SELECT SalesOrderID, OrderDate, TotalDue, CustomerID,
    AVG(TotalDue) OVER() AS AvgTotalF
FROM Sales.SalesOrderHeader;
```

2. Add the average total due for each customer to the query you wrote in question 1.

```
SELECT SalesOrderID, OrderDate, TotalDue, CustomerID,
    AVG(TotalDue) OVER() AS AvgTotal,
    AVG(TotalDue) OVER(PARTITION BY CustomerID) AS AvgCustTotal
FROM Sales.SalesOrderHeader;
```

Solutions to Exercise 8-3: Understanding the Difference Between *ROWS* and *RANGE*

Use the AdventureWorks database to complete this exercise.

1. Write a query that returns the SalesOrderID, ProductID, and LineTotal from Sales. SalesOrderDetail. Calculate a running total of the LineTotal for each ProductID. Be sure to use the correct frame.

```
SELECT SalesOrderID, ProductID, LineTotal,
    SUM(LineTotal) OVER(PARTITION BY ProductID
        ORDER BY SalesOrderID
    ROWS BETWEEN UNBOUNDED PRECEDING AND CURRENT ROW)
        AS RunningTotal
FROM Sales.SalesOrderDetail;
```

2. Explain why you should specify the frame where it is supported instead of relying on the default.

By default, the frame will be RANGE BETWEEN UNBOUNDED PRECEDING AND CURRENT ROW. This will introduce logic differences when the ORDER BY column is not unique. ROWS also performs much better than RANGE.

Solutions to Exercise 8-4: Using Window Analytic Functions

Use the AdventureWorks database to complete this exercise. Run the following script that creates a table holding stock market data.

```
CREATE TABLE #Stock (Symbol VARCHAR(4), TradingDate DATE,
    OpeningPrice MONEY, ClosingPrice MONEY);
INSERT INTO #Stock(Symbol, TradingDate, OpeningPrice, ClosingPrice)
VALUES ('A','2014/01/02',5.03,4.90),
    ('B','2014/01/02',10.99,11.25),
    ('C','2014/01/02',23.42,23.44),
    ('A','2014/01/03',4.93,5.10),
    ('B','2014/01/03',11.25,11.25),
    ('C','2014/01/03',25.15,25.06),
    ('A','2014/01/06',5.15,5.20),
    ('B','2014/01/06',11.30,11.12),
    ('C','2014/01/06',25.20,26.00);
```

1. Write a query using a window analytic function that calculates the difference in the closing price from the previous day.

```
SELECT Symbol, TradingDate, OpeningPrice, ClosingPrice,
    ClosingPrice - LAG(ClosingPrice)
 OVER(PARTITION BY Symbol ORDER BY TradingDate)
 AS ClosingPriceChange
FROM #Stock;
```

2. Modify the query written in question 1 so that the NULL values in the calculation are replaced with zeros. Use an option in the window analytic function.

```
SELECT Symbol, TradingDate, OpeningPrice, ClosingPrice,
    ClosingPrice - LAG(ClosingPrice,1,ClosingPrice)
    OVER(PARTITION BY Symbol ORDER BY TradingDate)
   AS ClosingPriceChange
FROM #Stock;
```

CHAPTER 9

■ ■ ■

Advanced *WHERE* Clauses

In Chapter 3, you learned how to write queries with SELECT, FROM, WHERE, and ORDER BY clauses. Chapter 3 covered a lot of options for filtering results with the WHERE clause, however, there is still more to learn. This chapter will discuss using the comparison operator LIKE and matching against a partial value or a pattern, full-text search, and WHERE clauses with more than two predicates and the PATINDEX function.

Pattern Matching

Sometimes you know only part of the value that will match the data stored in the table. For example, you may need to search for one word within a description. You can perform searches with pattern matching using wildcards to find one value within another value.

Using *LIKE*

Pattern matching is possible by using the LIKE operator in the expression instead of equal to (=) or one of the other operators. Most of the time, the percent sign (%) is used as a wildcard along with LIKE to represent zero or more characters. You will also see the underscore (_) used as a wildcard to replace exactly one character, but it's not used as often. Type in and run the code from Listing 9-1 to learn how to use LIKE.

Listing 9-1. Using LIKE with the Percent Sign

```
--1
SELECT DISTINCT LastName
FROM Person.Person
WHERE LastName LIKE 'Sand%';

--2
SELECT DISTINCT LastName
FROM Person.Person
WHERE LastName NOT LIKE 'Sand%';

--3
SELECT DISTINCT LastName
FROM Person.Person
WHERE LastName LIKE '%Z%';
```

```
--4
SELECT DISTINCT LastName
FROM Person.Person
WHERE LastName LIKE 'Bec_';
```

The queries in Listing 9-1 contain the keyword DISTINCT to eliminate duplicates in the results shown in Figure 9-1. Query 1 returns all LastName values where the last name starts with *Sand*. Query 2 returns the opposite—it returns all the LastName values not returned by query 1, which are those rows where the last name does not start with *Sand*. Query 3 returns all LastName values that contain a *Z* anywhere in the last name. Query 4 will return only the last name *Beck* or any last name starting with *Bec* and one more character, but not the last name *Becker* because the underscore matches one and only one character.

	LastName
1	Sandberg
2	Sanders
3	Sandidge
4	Sandoval

	LastName
1	Abbas
2	Abel
3	Abercrombie
4	Abolrous

	LastName
1	Alvarez
2	Arbelaez
3	Bacalzo
4	Baltazar

	LastName
1	Beck

Figure 9-1. *The partial results of queries with LIKE*

194

Restricting the Characters in Pattern Matches

The value matching a wildcard may be restricted to a list or range of characters. To do this, surround the possible values or range by square brackets ([]). Alternately, include the caret (^) symbol to list characters or the range of characters that you don't want to use as replacements. Here is the syntax for using brackets as the wildcard:

```
SELECT <column1>,<column2>
FROM <schema>.<table>
WHERE <column> LIKE 'value[a-c]';

SELECT <column1>,<column2>
FROM <schema>.<table>
WHERE <column> LIKE 'value[abc]';

SELECT <column1>,<column2>
FROM <schema>.<table>
WHERE <column> LIKE 'value[^d]';
```

Type in and execute the code from Listing 9-2, which shows some examples. You will probably not encounter the square bracket technique very often, but you should be familiar with the syntax in case you run into it.

Listing 9-2. Using Square Brackets with LIKE

```
--1
SELECT DISTINCT LastName
FROM Person.Person
WHERE LastName LIKE 'Cho[i-k]';

--2
SELECT DISTINCT LastName
FROM Person.Person
WHERE LastName LIKE 'Cho[ijk]';

--3
SELECT DISTINCT LastName
FROM Person.Person
WHERE LastName LIKE 'Cho[^i]';
```

Figure 9-2 displays the results of running Listing 9-2. Queries 1 and 2 could return unique rows with a last name of *Choi*, *Choj*, or *Chok* because the pattern specifies the range *i* to *k*. Only *Choi* is actually found in the data. Query 1 specifies the range of values, while query 2 explicitly lists the allowable values that may be replaced. Query 3 returns unique rows that have a last name beginning with *Cho* and ending with any character except for *i*.

	LastName
1	Choi

	LastName
1	Choi

	LastName
1	Chor
2	Chow

Figure 9-2. *The results of queries restricting characters in matches*

Searching for Wildcards

Occasionally you will need to search for the percent sign, the underscore, or one of the brackets in a string. If you just include them in your search term, the database engine will ignore them. To get around this, always escape these symbols by including them within brackets when you are actually trying to return values that contain them. Table 9-1 shows the strings to use when searching for one of these symbols within a string.

Table 9-1. *Symbols Used in Search Patterns*

Symbol	Search Pattern
Percent %	'%[%]%'
Underscore _	'%[_]%'
Left Bracket [	'%[[]%'
Right Bracket]	'%[]]%'

Combining Wildcards

You may combine wildcards to create even more elaborate patterns. Remember that the percent sign replaces any number of characters, the underscore replaces one character, and the square brackets replace one character based on the values within the brackets. Listing 9-3 demonstrates some examples. Type in and execute the code to see how this works.

Listing 9-3. Combining Wildcards in One Pattern

```
--1
SELECT LastName
FROM Person.Person
WHERE LastName LIKE 'Ber[rg]%';

--2
SELECT LastName
FROM Person.Person
WHERE LastName LIKE 'Ber[^r]%';
```

```
--3
SELECT LastName
FROM Person.Person
WHERE LastName LIKE 'Be%n_';
```

View Figure 9-3 to see the results of running this code. Query 1 returns all rows with a last name beginning with *Ber* followed by either *r* or *g* (which is signified by the characters within the brackets) and then by any number of characters. Query 2 returns all rows with a last name beginning with *Ber* followed by any letter except for *r* and then by any number of characters. Query 3 returns all rows with a last name beginning with *Be* followed by any number of characters, except that the next-to-last character must be an *n*.

	LastName
1	Berg
2	Berge
3	Berge
4	Berger

	LastName
1	Berch
2	Berg
3	Berge
4	Berge

	LastName
1	Bent
2	Berglund
3	Berglund

Figure 9-3. The results of queries with multiple wildcards

You will probably find LIKE used frequently in queries, so it's important to understand how it works. Practice the skills you have just learned by completing Exercise 9-1.

EXERCISE 9-1

Use the AdventureWorks database to complete this exercise. Follow the steps in this exercise to test your knowledge of pattern matching and wildcard queries. You can find the solutions at the end of the chapter.

1. Write a query that displays the product ID and name for each product from the Production. Product table with a name starting with *Chain*.

2. Write a query like the one in question 1 that displays the products with *Paint* in the name.

3. Change the last query so that the products without *Paint* in the name are displayed.

4. Write a query that displays the business entity ID number, first name, middle name, and last name from the Person.Person table for only those rows that include *E* or *B* in the middle name column.

5. Explain the difference between the following two queries:

```
SELECT FirstName
FROM Person.Person
WHERE LastName LIKE 'Ja%es';
```

```
SELECT FirstName
FROM Person.Person
WHERE LastName LIKE 'Ja_es';
```

Using *PATINDEX*

In Chapter 4 you learned to use the CHARINDEX function that returns the position of one string inside another. There is also a function called PATINDEX that works similarly but includes the use of wildcards in the search condition. Here is the syntax:

PATINDEX('%pattern%',expression)

You can use both the percent sign and the underscore and the other patterns used with LIKE. If the pattern is found in the expression, the position where the expression is found is returned. If the pattern is not found, then the function returns 0. Listing 9-4 demonstrates how to use PATINDEX in the SELECT list and the WHERE clause.

Listing 9-4. Using PATINDEX

```
--1
SELECT LastName, PATINDEX('Ber[rg]%', LastName) AS Position
FROM Person.Person
WHERE PATINDEX('Ber[r,g]%', LastName) > 0;

--2
SELECT LastName, PATINDEX('%r%',LastName) Position
FROM Person.Person
WHERE PATINDEX('%[r]%',LastName) > 0;
```

Figure 9-4 shows the partial results of running this code. Query 1 returns any rows where the LastName column starts with *Ber*, either *r* or *g*, and then followed by any number of characters. Query 2 returns all rows where the LastName contains the letter *R*.

	LastName	Position
1	Berg	1
2	Berge	1
3	Berge	1
4	Berger	1

	LastName	Position
1	Abercrombie	4
2	Abercrombie	4
3	Abercrombie	4
4	Abolrous	5
5	Abolrous	5
6	Ackerman	5
7	Ackerman	5
8	Aguilar	7

Figure 9-4. *Using PATINDEX*

Using *WHERE* Clauses with Three or More Predicates

In Chapter 3, you learned how to write a WHERE clause with one or two predicates. A WHERE clause can contain more than two predicates combined by the logical operators AND and OR. If a WHERE clause contains more than two predicates using both AND and OR, you must be careful to ensure that the query returns the expected results. Type in and execute the code in Listing 9-5 to see how the order of the predicates affects the results and how to use parentheses to enforce the correct logic.

Listing 9-5. WHERE Clauses with Three Predicates

```
--1
SELECT BusinessEntityID,FirstName,MiddleName,LastName
FROM Person.Person
WHERE FirstName = 'Ken' AND LastName = 'Myer'
    OR LastName = 'Meyer';


--2
SELECT BusinessEntityID,FirstName,MiddleName,LastName
FROM Person.Person
WHERE LastName = 'Myer' OR LastName = 'Meyer'
    AND FirstName = 'Ken';


--3
SELECT BusinessEntityID,FirstName,MiddleName,LastName
FROM Person.Person
WHERE LastName = 'Meyer'
    AND FirstName = 'Ken' OR LastName = 'Myer';
```

```
--4
SELECT BusinessEntityID,FirstName,MiddleName,LastName
FROM Person.Person
WHERE FirstName = 'Ken' AND (LastName = 'Myer'
    OR LastName = 'Meyer');
```

You can see the results of Listing 9-5 in Figure 9-5. Once both logical operators AND and OR are used in the WHERE clause, things can get complicated. The logical operator AND takes precedence over OR; therefore, the database engine evaluates AND first. For example, suppose you want to find a name in the Person.Person table, *Ken Meyer*, but you can't remember the spelling of the last name. It could be *Myer*. Listing 9-5 shows four attempts to solve this problem, but only the last one is logically correct.

	BusinessEntityID	FirstName	MiddleName	LastName
1	1459	Deanna	NULL	Meyer
2	1455	Eric	B.	Meyer
3	1457	Helen	M.	Meyer
4	2140	Ken	NULL	Meyer
5	1525	Ken	NULL	Myer
6	203	Ken	L	Myer

	BusinessEntityID	FirstName	MiddleName	LastName
1	2140	Ken	NULL	Meyer
2	1523	Dorothy	J.	Myer
3	1525	Ken	NULL	Myer
4	203	Ken	L	Myer
5	2319	Linda	NULL	Myer

	BusinessEntityID	FirstName	MiddleName	LastName
1	2140	Ken	NULL	Meyer
2	1523	Dorothy	J.	Myer
3	1525	Ken	NULL	Myer
4	203	Ken	L	Myer
5	2319	Linda	NULL	Myer

	BusinessEntityID	FirstName	MiddleName	LastName
1	2140	Ken	NULL	Meyer
2	1525	Ken	NULL	Myer
3	203	Ken	L	Myer

Figure 9-5. *The results of queries that force precedence to ensure the correct results*

Query 1 returns the rows with the name *Ken Myer* but also returns any row with the last name *Meyer*. Queries 2 and 3 return identical results—the row with *Ken Meyer* and any rows with the last name *Myer*. Finally, by using the parentheses, query 4 returns the expected results.

When using multiple conditions, you must be very careful about the *precedence*, or order, that the expressions are evaluated. The database engine evaluates the conditions in the WHERE clause from left to right, but AND takes precedence over OR. Rearranging the terms can produce different but possibly still invalid results as in the previous example. To guarantee that the query is correct, always use parentheses to enforce the logic once the logical operator OR is added to the WHERE clause. The code is also more readable with the parentheses in the case where they are not needed. Later when you look at the code, you will know exactly what you had intended.

Using *NOT* with Parentheses

Another interesting twist when using parentheses is that you can negate the meaning of the expression within them by specifying the keyword NOT. For example, you could try to find the rows where the first name is *Ken* and the last name can't be *Myer* or *Meyer*. Type in and execute Listing 9-6 to see two ways to write the query.

Listing 9-6. Using NOT with Parentheses

```
--1
SELECT BusinessEntityID,FirstName,MiddleName,LastName
FROM Person.Person
WHERE FirstName='Ken' AND LastName <> 'Myer'
    AND LastName <> 'Meyer';

--2
SELECT BusinessEntityID,FirstName,MiddleName,LastName
FROM Person.Person
WHERE FirstName='Ken'
    AND NOT (LastName = 'Myer' OR LastName = 'Meyer');
```

Often multiple ways exist to solve the same problem, as in this case. Query 1 contains three expressions. One expression restricts the rows to those where FirstName is *Ken*. The other two expressions compare LastName to a value using not equal to (<>). In query 2, the expressions within the parentheses are evaluated first. Next, that result is negated by the NOT operator to find all last names that are not *Myer* or *Meyer*. Finally, only the rows that also have the first name *Ken* are returned. You can see the results in Figure 9-6.

	BusinessEntityID	FirstName	MiddleName	LastName
1	2300	Ken	NULL	Kwok
2	1726	Ken	NULL	Sánchez
3	1	Ken	J	Sánchez

	BusinessEntityID	FirstName	MiddleName	LastName
1	2300	Ken	NULL	Kwok
2	1726	Ken	NULL	Sánchez
3	1	Ken	J	Sánchez

Figure 9-6. *The identical results of two queries with different techniques*

As a best practice, always employ parentheses whether they are needed or not to enforce precedence when the WHERE clause includes the logical operator OR. Not only will this decrease the possibility of an incorrect WHERE clause, but it will also increase the readability of the query.

Complete Exercise 9-2 to practice the use of these skills.

EXERCISE 9-2

Use the AdventureWorks database to complete this exercise. The solution can be found at the end of the chapter.

1. Write a query that returns any orders that were placed in 2006. The orders must have a total due over $1,000 or have a non-NULL credit card. Display the order ID, order date, total due, and credit card information.

2. Write a query that returns a list of the products where the subcategory or the product name contains the word *Mountain*. Display only those rows where the color is silver. Return the subcategory and product names, the product ID, and the color information.

Performing a Full-Text Search

You have learned how to use LIKE and PATINDEX to find a character match in data. Full-text search provides the ability to search for words or phrases within string or binary data columns similar to a web search such as Google or Bing. You can only use LIKE for pattern matching and not for searching binary data. Full-text search has support for multiple languages and other features such as synonym searches. Full-text search is especially beneficial for documents stored as binary data in the database.

Full-text search must be installed by running the SQL Server installation either during the initial set up or added later. A special full-text index needs to be created on the table. It is beyond the scope of this book to teach you how to set up and manage full-text search, but here you will see how to write some of the basic queries. For more information about full-text search and some of the features not covered here, like CONTAINSTABLE, see the book *Pro Full-Text Search in SQL Server 2008* by Hilary Cotter and Michael Coles (Apress, 2008). There are a number of enhancements to full-text searching introduced with SQL Server 2012 that allow you to search the meta-data, for example, the document author, as well. The AdventureWorks database ships with three full-text indexes already in place. Table 9-2 lists the columns with full-text indexes included by default in AdventureWorks.

Table 9-2. *AdventureWorks Columns with Full-Text Indexes*

Table Name	Column Name	Data Type
Production.ProductReview	Comments	NVARCHAR(3850)
Production.Document	DocumentSummary	NVARCHAR(MAX)
Production.Document	Document	VARBINARY(MAX)
HumanResources.JobCandidate	Resume	XML

Using *CONTAINS*

CONTAINS is one of the functions used to search full-text indexes. The simplest way to use CONTAINS is to search a column for a particular word or phrase. Here is the syntax for CONTAINS:

```
SELECT <column1>,<column2>
FROM <schema>.<tablename>
WHERE CONTAINS(<indexed column>,<searchterm>);
```

Listing 9-7 shows how to use CONTAINS. Notice that the second query has a regular predicate in the WHERE clause as well. Be sure to type in and execute the code to learn how to use CONTAINS.

Listing 9-7. Using CONTAINS

```
--1
SELECT FileName
FROM Production.Document
WHERE CONTAINS(Document,'important');

--2
SELECT FileName
FROM Production.Document
WHERE CONTAINS(Document,' "service guidelines" ')
    AND DocumentLevel = 2;
```

Figure 9-7 displays the results of running this code. Notice how double quotes are used within single quotes to designate a phrase in query 2. Query 2 also demonstrates that both a full-text predicate and a regular predicate can be used in the same query. You may be wondering why the Document column is not part of the results since that is the search term. The document is actually a binary file, such as a Microsoft Word document, that must be opened by the appropriate application.

	FileName
1	Repair and Service Guidelines.doc
2	Crank Arm and Tire Maintenance.doc
3	Lubrication Maintenance.doc

	FileName
1	Repair and Service Guidelines.doc

Figure 9-7. *The results of a full-text search operation*

Using Multiple Terms with *CONTAINS*

You can use CONTAINS to find words in data that are not even next to each other by using AND, OR, and NEAR. You can use the operator AND NOT to find results with one term and not another. Listing 9-8 demonstrates this technique.

Listing 9-8. Multiple Terms in CONTAINS

```
--1
SELECT FileName, DocumentSummary
FROM Production.Document
WHERE CONTAINS(DocumentSummary,'bicycle AND reflectors');
```

```
--2
SELECT FileName, DocumentSummary
FROM Production.Document
WHERE CONTAINS(DocumentSummary,'bicycle AND NOT reflectors');

--3
SELECT FileName, DocumentSummary
FROM Production.Document
WHERE CONTAINS(DocumentSummary,'maintain NEAR bicycle AND NOT reflectors');
```

Figure 9-8 shows the results of running this code. In this case, a regular string data column, DocumentSummary, is searched so you can verify the results.

	FileName	DocumentSummary
1	Front Reflector Bracket Installation.doc	Reflectors are vital safety components of your bi…

	FileName	DocumentSummary
1	Repair and Service Guidelines.doc	It is important that you maintain your bicycle and …
2	Lubrication Maintenance.doc	Guidelines and recommendations for lubricating …
3	Installing Replacement Pedals.doc	Detailed instructions for replacing pedals with Ad…

	FileName	DocumentSummary
1	Repair and Service Guidelines.doc	It is important that you maintain your bicycle and …

Figure 9-8. *The results from using multiple search terms*

Searching Multiple Columns

You can search multiple columns or all full-text indexed columns at once without multiple CONTAINS predicates in the WHERE clause. Use the asterisk to specify that all possible columns are searched, or use a comma-delimited list in parentheses to specify a list of columns. Type in and execute the code in Listing 9-9, which demonstrates these techniques.

Listing 9-9. Using Multiple Columns

```
--1
SELECT FileName, DocumentSummary
FROM Production.Document
WHERE CONTAINS((DocumentSummary,Document),'maintain');

--2
SELECT FileName, DocumentSummary
FROM Production.Document
WHERE CONTAINS((DocumentSummary),'maintain')
      OR CONTAINS((Document),'maintain')

--3
SELECT FileName, DocumentSummary
FROM Production.Document
WHERE CONTAINS(*,'maintain');
```

The list of columns to be searched in query 1 is explicitly listed and contained within an inner set of parentheses. Query 2 is equivalent to query 1 by using two CONTAINS expressions, each searching a different column for the same term. By using the asterisk in query 3 within the CONTAINS expression, all columns with a full-text index are searched.

Using *FREETEXT*

FREETEXT is similar to CONTAINS except that it returns rows that don't exactly match. It will return rows that have terms with similar meanings to your search terms by using a thesaurus. FREETEXT is less precise than CONTAINS, and it is less flexible. The keywords AND, OR, and NEAR can't be used with CONTAINS. Avoid using double quotes that specify an exact phrase with FREETEXT, because then SQL Server won't use the thesaurus and will search only for the exact phrase. The same rules about multiple columns apply. Type in and execute the code in Listing 9-10, which compares FREETEXT to LIKE.

Listing 9-10. Using FREETEXT

```
--1
SELECT FileName, DocumentSummary
FROM Production.Document
WHERE FREETEXT((DocumentSummary),'provides');

--2
SELECT FileName, DocumentSummary
FROM Production.Document
WHERE DocumentSummary LIKE '%provides%'
```

Figure 9-9 displays the results from Listing 9-10. The DocumentSummary values in the rows returned from query 1 do not contain the word *provides*. Query 1 returns the rows anyway because FREETEXT will find similar words as well as exact matches. In each case, the word *provided* can be found in the data. Query 2 doesn't return the rows because the LIKE operator is looking for an exact match.

	FileName	DocumentSummary
1	Repair and Service Guidelines.doc	It is important that you maintain your bicycle and k...
2	Lubrication Maintenance.doc	Guidelines and recommendations for lubricating t...
	FileName	DocumentSummary

Figure 9-9. *The results from using FREETEXT*

Full-text search operations can get much more complicated than the information provided here. This was meant to be an overview of the basic syntax. Be sure to see the book *Pro Full-Text Search in SQL Server 2008* by Hilary Cotter and Michael Coles (Apress, 2008) to learn more about full-text search. Practice what you have just learned about full-text search by completing Exercise 9-3.

EXERCISE 9-3

Use the AdventureWorks database to complete the following tasks. Be sure to take advantage of the full-text indexes in place when writing the queries. You can find the solutions at the end of the chapter.

1. Write a query using the Production.ProductReview table. Use CONTAINS to find all the rows that have the word *socks* in the Comments column. Return the ProductID and Comments columns.

2. Write a query using the Production.Document table. Use CONTAINS to find all the rows that have the word *reflector* in any column that is indexed with full-text search. Display the Title and FileName columns.

3. Change the query in question 2 so that the rows containing *seat* are not returned in the results.

4. Write a query that returns the rows containing any forms of the word *replaced* from the Production.Document table. Return the title, file name, and document summary columns.

Thinking About Performance

You learned in Chapter 4 that using a function on a column in the WHERE clause can decrease performance, especially if that column is the key column of an index that could have been used for the query. If all the columns required for the query are part of a nonclustered index, either as a key column or included column, it is still possible that the optimizer will choose to scan the nonclustered index instead of scanning the table. You may be wondering what the difference is. The nonclustered index will almost always be a smaller structure than the table and will be less work to scan. Imagine that you had to find a particular phrase in a book. It would be easier for you to read the index instead of reading the entire book because the index is smaller. Type and execute Listing 9-11 to see some examples.

Listing 9-11. Comparing LIKE with CHARINDEX

```
--1
SET STATISTICS IO ON;
GO
SELECT Name
FROM Production.Product
WHERE CHARINDEX('Bear',Name) = 1;


--2
SELECT Name
FROM Production.Product
WHERE Name LIKE 'Bear%';


--3
SELECT Name, Color
FROM Production.Product
WHERE CHARINDEX('B',Color) = 1;
```

```
--4
SELECT Name, Color
FROM Production.Product
WHERE Color LIKE 'B%';
```

Query 1 uses the CHARINDEX function to find all rows where the Name value starts with *Bear*. It will return the exact same results as query 2, which uses the LIKE operator. If you take a look at the Messages tab to view the Logical reads, you will see that query 1 takes six logical reads compared to only two logical reads from query 2. The reason for this is that query 1 is scanning the nonclustered index while query 2 is doing a seek against the same index. In this case, a seek of the index is less work.

Queries 3 and 4 do the same test against a non-indexed column, Color. In this case, there is no difference between using a function and LIKE. Both queries take 15 logical reads, the work to scan the entire table. Figure 9-10 shows the Statistics IO information for the four queries.

```
(1 row(s) affected)
Table 'Product'. Scan count 1, logical reads 6, physica

(1 row(s) affected)
Table 'Product'. Scan count 1, logical reads 2, physica

(119 row(s) affected)
Table 'Product'. Scan count 1, logical reads 15, physic

(119 row(s) affected)
Table 'Product'. Scan count 1, logical reads 15, physic
```

Figure 9-10. *The logical reads comparison*

A term you may see that describes the condition where the optimizer can take full advantage of an index is *sargable*. The term *sarg* is short for search argument, which is then turned into the adjective sargable describing the search predicate. Of the four queries in this section, only the predicate in query 2 is sargable.

Summary

This chapter introduced several of the more advanced topics you need to learn to fully take advantage of complex WHERE clauses. In addition, you learned about an optional feature of SQL Server, the full-text index. These indexes are used most often with data containing paragraphs or documents, not the keys and limited values of most databases.

Now that you have learned about all the topics involved with selecting data, it is time to learn how to manipulate data by inserting, updating, and deleting rows in Chapter 10.

Answers to the Exercises

This section provides solutions to the exercises found on writing queries with advanced feature WHERE clauses.

Solutions to Exercise 9-1: Using *LIKE*

Use the AdventureWorks database to complete this exercise.

1. Write a query that displays the product ID and name for each product from the Production.Product table with a name starting with *Chain*.

```
SELECT ProductID, Name
FROM Production.Product
WHERE Name LIKE 'Chain%';
```

2. Write a query like the one in question 1 that displays the products with *Paint* in the name.

```
SELECT ProductID, Name
FROM Production.Product
WHERE Name LIKE '%Paint%';
```

3. Change the last query so that the products without *Paint* in the name are displayed.

```
SELECT ProductID, Name
FROM Production.Product
WHERE Name NOT LIKE '%Paint%';
```

4. Write a query that displays the business entity ID number, first name, middle name, and last name from the Person.Person table for only those rows that include *E* or *B* in the middle name column.

```
SELECT BusinessEntityID,
    FirstName, MiddleName,
    LastName
FROM Person.Person
WHERE MiddleName LIKE '%[EB]%';
```

5. Explain the difference between the following two queries:

```
SELECT FirstName
FROM Person.Person
WHERE LastName LIKE 'Ja%es';
```

```
SELECT FirstName
FROM Person.Person
WHERE LastName LIKE 'Ja_es';
```

The first query will find any rows with a last name that starts with *Ja* and ends with *es*. There can be any number of characters in between. The second query allows only one character in between *Ja* and *es*.

Solution to Exercise 9-2: Using *WHERE* Clauses with Three or More Predicates

Use the AdventureWorks database to complete this exercise.

1. Write a query that returns any orders that were placed in 2006. The orders must have a total due over $1,000 or have a non-NULL credit card. Display the order ID, order date, total due, and credit card information.

```
SELECT SalesOrderID, OrderDate, TotalDue, CreditCardID
FROM Sales.SalesOrderHeader
WHERE OrderDate >= '2006/01/01'
    AND OrderDate < '2007/01/01'
    AND (TotalDue > 1000 OR CreditCardID IS NOT NULL);
```

2. Write a query that returns a list of the products where the subcategory or the product name contains the word *mountain*. Display only those rows where the color is silver. Return the subcategory and product names, the product ID, and the color information.

```
SELECT SUB.Name AS [SubCategory Name],
    P.Name AS [Product Name], ProductID, Color
FROM Production.Product P
JOIN Production.ProductSubcategory SUB
    ON P.ProductSubcategoryID = SUB.ProductSubcategoryID
WHERE (SUB.Name LIKE '%mountain%' OR P.name like '%mountain%')
    AND Color = 'Silver';
```

Solution to Exercise 9-3: Performing a Full-Text Search

Use the AdventureWorks database to solve the exercises.

1. Write a query using the Production.ProductReview table. Use CONTAINS to find all the rows that have the word *socks* in the Comments column. Return the ProductID and Comments columns.

```
SELECT ProductID, Comments
FROM Production.ProductReview
WHERE CONTAINS(Comments,'socks');
```

2. Write a query using the Production.Document table. Use CONTAINS to find all the rows that have the word *reflector* in any column that is indexed with full-text search. Display the Title and FileName columns.

```
SELECT Title, FileName
FROM Production.Document
WHERE CONTAINS(*,'reflector');
```

3. Change the query in question 2 so that the rows containing *seat* are not returned in the results.

```
SELECT Title, FileName
FROM Production.Document
WHERE CONTAINS(*,'reflector AND NOT seat');
```

4. Write a query that returns the rows containing any forms of the word *replaced* from the Production.Document table. Return the title, file name, and document summary columns.

```
SELECT Title, FileName, DocumentSummary
FROM Production.Document
WHERE FREETEXT(*,'replaced');
```

Manipulating Data

The data stored in most databases is not static. The application users are constantly adding data to tables as customers place orders, the company hires employees, and the payroll department writes checks. Automated processes periodically load new data into reporting databases, such as data warehouses, and into production systems. Users and processes also update existing rows or delete rows from tables.

In Chapters 3 through 9, you learned how to retrieve data from SQL Server. These skills are important for generating reports and displaying data, and they will come in handy as you learn to insert new rows, update the values in existing rows, and delete rows from tables. This chapter covers how to manipulate data in many different scenarios, such as by using one table, joins, and subqueries.

Inserting New Rows

There are many ways to add new rows to tables in SQL Server databases. Be aware that there are other tools such as SQL Server Integration Services (SSIS) that you can use to load data into SQL Server, but because this book is about T-SQL, this section only covers the T-SQL statements to insert data. To learn more about SSIS, read *Pro SQL Server 2012 Integration Services* by Francis Rodrigues and Michael Coles (Apress, 2012) and also *SSIS Design Patterns* by Andy Leonard, Tim Mitchell, Jessica Moss, and Michelle Ufford (Apress, 2012).

Run the following code to create a table that you will populate with data in this section:

```
IF OBJECT_ID('dbo.demoCustomer','U') IS NOT NULL BEGIN
    DROP TABLE dbo.demoCustomer;
END;
CREATE TABLE dbo.demoCustomer(CustomerID INT NOT NULL,
    FirstName NVARCHAR(50) NOT NULL, MiddleName NVARCHAR(50) NULL,
    LastName NVARCHAR(50) NOT NULL
    CONSTRAINT PK_demoCustomer PRIMARY KEY (CustomerID));
```

Note   You may notice that I have used two different techniques to check for the existence of a table before dropping it. When using SQL Server Management Studio to create the script, the code checks for the table in the sys.objects table. When I write the code myself, I usually check the results of the OBJECT_ID function. Either technique works and use whichever one you prefer.

Adding One Row with Literal Values

Adding one row with literal values is the simplest way to add data to an existing table. For example, a user may fill out a Windows or web form in an application and click Save. At that point, the application builds and sends a single INSERT statement to SQL Server containing the values that the user entered in the form. To insert new rows, you will use the INSERT statement. The syntax of the INSERT statement, which has two variations, is simple:

```
INSERT [INTO] <table1> [(<col1>,<col2>)] SELECT <value1>,<value2>;

INSERT [INTO] <table1> [(<col1>,<col2>)] VALUES (<value1>,<value2>);
```

The INTO keyword is optional, but I like to include it. Type in and execute the code in Listing 10-1 to learn this technique. The last statement displays the inserted data.

Listing 10-1. Adding One Row at a Time with Literal Values

```
--1
INSERT INTO dbo.demoCustomer (CustomerID, FirstName, MiddleName, LastName)
VALUES (1, N'Orlando', N'N.', N'Gee');

--2
INSERT INTO dbo.demoCustomer (CustomerID, FirstName, MiddleName, LastName)
SELECT 3, N'Donna', N'F.', N'Cameras';

--3
INSERT INTO dbo.demoCustomer
VALUES (4,N'Janet', N'M.', N'Gates');

--4
INSERT INTO dbo.demoCustomer
SELECT 6,N'Rosmarie', N'J.', N'Carroll';

--5
INSERT INTO dbo.demoCustomer (CustomerID, FirstName, MiddleName, LastName)
VALUES (2, N'Keith', NULL, N'Harris');

--6
INSERT INTO dbo.demoCustomer (CustomerID, FirstName, LastName)
VALUES (5, N'Lucy', N'Harrington');

--7
SELECT CustomerID, FirstName, MiddleName, LastName
FROM dbo.demoCustomer;
```

Figure 10-1 shows the results of query 7. The INSERT INTO clause specifies the table name and optionally the column names. Statement 1 inserts the row using the VALUES clause. Notice that parentheses surround the literal values in the statement. Statement 2 uses a slightly different syntax with the keyword SELECT. In this case, you could successfully run the SELECT part of the statement because it is a valid statement by itself. One more thing to note is the letter *N* before each hard-coded string value. This converts the string to an NVARCHAR value to match the data type of the column.

	CustomerID	FirstName	MiddleName	LastName
1	1	Orlando	N.	Gee
2	2	Keith	NULL	Harris
3	3	Donna	F.	Cameras
4	4	Janet	M.	Gates
5	5	Lucy	NULL	Harrington
6	6	Rosmarie	J.	Carroll

Figure 10-1. *The results after inserting six rows*

■ **Note**   This book uses the word *query* for T-SQL commands that return data. It uses the word *statement* for other T-SQL commands.

Both statements 1 and 2 specify the column names in parentheses. The order of the values to be inserted must match the order of the column names. Statements 3 and 4 look very similar to the first two statements, but these statements don't specify the column names. Although not specifying the column names will work some of the time, the best practice is to specify the columns. Not only does this help clarify the code, it often, but not always, keeps the code from breaking if new nonrequired columns are added to the table later.

Notice that statement 5 inserts NULL into the MiddleName column. Statement 6 just leaves MiddleName out of the statement altogether. Both of these statements work because the MiddleName column is optional.

Avoiding Common Insert Errors

The statements in the previous section successfully added six rows to the dbo.demoCustomer table because they were carefully written to avoid breaking any of the constraints and column requirements. Listing 10-2 demonstrates several invalid statements. Type in and execute the code to learn about some of the things that can go wrong when inserting data into tables.

Listing 10-2. Attempting to Insert Rows with Invalid INSERT Statements

```
PRINT '1';
--1
INSERT INTO dbo.demoCustomer (CustomerID, FirstName, MiddleName, LastName)
VALUES (1, N'Dominic', N'P.', N'Gash');

PRINT '2';
--2
INSERT INTO dbo.demoCustomer (CustomerID, MiddleName, LastName)
VALUES (10, N'M.', N'Garza');

GO
PRINT '3';
GO
```

```
--3
INSERT INTO dbo.demoCustomer
VALUES (11, N'Katherine', N'Harding');

GO
PRINT '4';
GO

--4
INSERT INTO dbo.demoCustomer (CustomerID, FirstName, LastName)
VALUES (11, N'Katherine', NULL, N'Harding');

GO
PRINT '5';
GO

--5
INSERT INTO dbo.demoCustomer (CustomerID, FirstName, LastName)
VALUES (N'A', N'Katherine', N'Harding');
```

Figure 10-2 shows the error messages that result from running Listing 10-2. Statement 1 attempts to add another row with the CustomerID value 1. Because a row with CustomerID 1 already exists in the table, the INSERT statement violates the primary key constraint. Because the primary key of a table uniquely identifies a row, you may not insert duplicate values. If the primary key is a composite key, however, you can have duplicate values in any of the columns but not duplicates of the entire key. A primary key may not contain any NULL values in the key columns.

```
Messages
1
Msg 2627, Level 14, State 1, Line 3
Violation of PRIMARY KEY constraint 'PK_demoCustomer'. Cannot insert duplic
The statement has been terminated.
2
Msg 515, Level 16, State 2, Line 8
Cannot insert the value NULL into column 'FirstName', table 'AdventureWorks
The statement has been terminated.
3
Msg 213, Level 16, State 1, Line 3
Column name or number of supplied values does not match table definition.
4
Msg 110, Level 15, State 1, Line 3
There are fewer columns in the INSERT statement than values specified in th
5
Msg 245, Level 16, State 1, Line 3
Conversion failed when converting the nvarchar value 'A' to data type int.
```

Figure 10-2. *The results of attempting to insert rows with invalid INSERT statements*

Statement 2 violates the NOT NULL constraint on the FirstName column. Every row must contain a non-NULL value in the FirstName and LastName columns.

The database engine doesn't discover problems with statements 1 and 2 until the code runs. The problems with statements 3 and 4 are compile errors that cause the entire batch to fail. To show all the error messages for the listing, the word GO separates statements 3 and 4 into their own batches. In fact, even the PRINT statement will not run if it is contained in the same batch as these statements. The intent of statements 3 and 4 is to insert a row with a NULL MiddleName. Because statement 3 doesn't specify the column names, the database engine expects a value for each of the four columns in the table definition. Because the statement supplies only three values, the statement fails. Statement 4 does supply the column names, but the VALUES clause doesn't supply the same number of values. Once again, the statement fails. Statement 5 also contains a compile error. It attempts to insert a string value when the column, CustomerID, accepts only an integer.

Inserting Multiple Rows with One Statement

You will often see code using multiple UNION ALL queries with SELECT statements to insert several rows with one INSERT statement. Starting with SQL Server 2008, you can use a new technique called *row constructors*. The row constructor technique uses the keyword VALUES followed by one or more sets of values. Type in and execute Listing 10-3 to learn how to use both techniques.

Listing 10-3. Inserting Multiple Rows with One INSERT

```
--1
INSERT INTO dbo.demoCustomer (CustomerID, FirstName, MiddleName, LastName)
SELECT 7, N'Dominic', N'P.', N'Gash'
UNION ALL
SELECT 10, N'Kathleen', N'M.', N'Garza'
UNION ALL
SELECT 11, N'Katherine', NULL, N'Harding';

--2
INSERT INTO dbo.demoCustomer (CustomerID, FirstName, MiddleName, LastName)
VALUES (12, N'Johnny', N'A.', N'Capino'),
       (16, N'Christopher', N'R.', N'Beck'),
       (18, N'David', N'J.', N'Liu');

--3
SELECT CustomerID, FirstName, MiddleName, LastName
FROM dbo.demoCustomer
WHERE CustomerID >=7;
```

Figure 10-3 displays the rows inserted by Listing 10-3. Statement 1 uses the UNION ALL query technique. You can successfully select just the five lines that make up the UNION ALL query part of the INSERT statement and run it by itself. Statement 2 demonstrates how to use the row constructor technique. By using row constructors, you can specify multiple lists of values, separated by commas, in one VALUES clause.

	CustomerID	FirstName	MiddleName	LastName
1	7	Dominic	P.	Gash
2	10	Kathleen	M.	Garza
3	11	Katherine	NULL	Harding
4	12	Johnny	A.	Capino
5	16	Christopher	R.	Beck
6	18	David	J.	Liu

Figure 10-3. Inserting multiple rows with one INSERT statement

Inserting Rows from Another Table

So far, you have learned how to insert rows into a table using literal values. Often you will need to insert data from one table or query into another table. For example, you may need to load production data into a data warehouse. Often application programmers think about data in terms of individual rows, so they insert data one row at a time when it is possible, and almost always more efficient, to insert more rows at once. They will often loop through one table, saving the values in variables, and then insert the values in the second table.

My favorite analogy involves a pile of 1,000 car keys. How would you move the keys from one location to another location? Would you pick up one key at a time and move it? No, you would probably grab all the keys if you could and just move them all at once. If you could not pick up all the keys in one trip, you could at least move them in two or three batches. Listing 10-4 shows how to import rows from one table into another all within one statement. This example demonstrates "moving all the car keys at once." Type in and execute the code to see how this works.

Listing 10-4. Inserting Rows from Another Table

```
--1
INSERT INTO dbo.demoCustomer (CustomerID, FirstName, MiddleName, LastName)
SELECT BusinessEntityID, FirstName, MiddleName, LastName
FROM Person.Person
WHERE BusinessEntityID BETWEEN 19 AND 35;


--2
INSERT INTO dbo.demoCustomer (CustomerID, FirstName, MiddleName, LastName)
SELECT DISTINCT s.SalesOrderID, c.FirstName, c.MiddleName, c.LastName
FROM Person.Person AS c
INNER JOIN Sales.SalesOrderHeader AS s ON c.BusinessEntityID = s.SalesPersonID;


--3
SELECT CustomerID, FirstName, MiddleName, LastName
FROM dbo.demoCustomer
WHERE CustomerID > 18;
```

Figure 10-4 shows some of the rows added to the dbo.demoCustomer table by insert statements in Listing 10-4. Statement 1 inserts the rows from the Person.Person table where the BusinessEntityID is between 19 and 35. Statement 2 inserts the rows from a query that joins the Person.Person and Sales.SalesOrderHeader tables. The SELECT parts of the statements are valid queries that you can run without the INSERT clauses. You can use any of the techniques you have learned so far to write SELECT statements to insert data into a table as long as the data selected meets the constraints and requirements of the target table.

	CustomerID	FirstName	MiddleName	LastName
1	19	Mary	A	Dempsey
2	20	Wanida	M	Benshoof
3	21	Terry	J	Eminhizer
4	22	Sariya	E	Harnpadoungsataya
5	23	Mary	E	Gibson
6	24	Jill	A	Williams
7	25	James	R	Hamilton
8	26	Peter	J	Krebs
9	27	Jo	A	Brown
10	28	Guy	R	Gilbert

Figure 10-4. *The partial results of adding rows from another table*

Inserting Missing Rows

You have seen what can happen when you attempt to insert a new row that violates the primary key. You can use the techniques found in Chapter 6 to insert rows into one table that don't exist in the source table. Type in and execute the code in Listing 10-5 to learn how the EXISTS method works.

Listing 10-5. Inserting Missing Rows

```
--1
SELECT COUNT(CustomerID) AS CustomerCount
FROM dbo.demoCustomer;

--2
INSERT INTO dbo.demoCustomer (CustomerID, FirstName, MiddleName, LastName)
SELECT c.BusinessEntityID, c.FirstName, c.MiddleName, c.LastName
FROM Person.Person AS c
WHERE NOT EXISTS (
    SELECT * FROM dbo.demoCustomer a
    WHERE a.CustomerID = c.BusinessEntityID);

--3
SELECT COUNT(CustomerID) AS CustomerCount
FROM dbo.demoCustomer;
```

Figure 10-5 shows the customer count after adding the missing rows. By using NOT EXISTS to find rows in the target table that don't match, the SELECT part of the INSERT statement inserts those rows into the table. As mentioned in the "Inserting Rows from Another Table" section, any valid SELECT statement may be used to insert rows into a table. If you run the same code a second or third time, you will find that the row count doesn't change. Because the code inserted all the missing rows, there are no new rows to insert after the first time.

	CustomerCount
1	3835

	CustomerCount
1	23778

Figure 10-5. The results of checking the row count after adding the missing rows

Creating and Populating a Table in One Statement

The SELECT INTO statement allows you to create a table and populate it with one statement. Developers often use this technique to create temporary tables, or *work tables*. The syntax for this is:

```
SELECT <col1>,<col2>
INTO <table2>
FROM <table1>;
```

Type in and execute the code in Listing 10-6 to learn how to use this technique. The first part of the code drops the dbo.demoCustomer table because the SELECT INTO statement will fail if the table already exists.

Listing 10-6. Using SELECT INTO to Create and Populate a Table

```
IF EXISTS (SELECT * FROM sys.objects
            WHERE object_id = OBJECT_ID(N'[dbo].[demoCustomer]')
                AND type in (N'U'))
DROP TABLE dbo.demoCustomer;

GO

--1
SELECT BusinessEntityID, FirstName, MiddleName, LastName,
    FirstName + ISNULL(' ' + MiddleName,'') + ' ' +  LastName AS FullName
INTO dbo.demoCustomer
FROM Person.Person;

--2
SELECT BusinessEntityID, FirstName, MiddleName, LastName, FullName
FROM dbo.demoCustomer;
```

Figure 10-6 displays the partial results of running this code. Statement 1 lists the columns and an expression along with the word INTO and the name of the table to create. The resulting table contains a column, FullName, that the statement created with the expression. Even though you could write a query that doesn't specify an alias for the expression, you must specify the alias for the expression when writing SELECT INTO statements. The database engine uses the column and alias names when creating the new table.

	BusinessEntityID	FirstName	MiddleName	LastName	FullName
1	285	Syed	E	Abbas	Syed E Abbas
2	293	Catherine	R.	Abel	Catherine R. Abel
3	295	Kim	NULL	Abercrombie	Kim Abercrombie
4	2170	Kim	NULL	Abercrombie	Kim Abercrombie
5	38	Kim	B	Abercrombie	Kim B Abercrombie
6	211	Hazem	E	Abolrous	Hazem E Abolrous
7	2357	Sam	NULL	Abolrous	Sam Abolrous
8	297	Humberto	NULL	Acevedo	Humberto Acevedo
9	291	Gustavo	NULL	Achong	Gustavo Achong
10	299	Pilar	NULL	Ackerman	Pilar Ackerman

Figure 10-6. *The partial results of creating and populating a table with SELECT INTO*

Figure 10-7 shows the table definition of the dbo.demoCustomer table found by navigating to the table in the Object Explorer window of SQL Server Management Studio. You may have to right-click Tables and select Refresh to see the new table. Except for the missing primary key, the column definitions match the columns from the Person.Person table, which was the source of the data. The data in the FullName column can be 152 characters—the three name columns plus the two spaces.

```
□ ▌ AdventureWorks
   ⊞ ▭ Database Diagrams
   □ ▭ Tables
      ⊞ ▭ System Tables
      ⊞ ▭ FileTables
      ⊞ ▭ dbo.AWBuildVersion
      ⊞ ▭ dbo.Customer
      ⊞ ▭ dbo.DatabaseLog
      □ ▭ dbo.demoCustomer
         □ ▭ Columns
               ▤ BusinessEntityID (int, not null)
               ▤ FirstName (Name(nvarchar(50)), not null)
               ▤ MiddleName (Name(nvarchar(50)), null)
               ▤ LastName (Name(nvarchar(50)), not null)
               ▤ FullName (nvarchar(152), not null)
         ⊞ ▭ Keys
```

Figure 10-7. *The dbo.demoCustomer table definition*

Developers often use the SELECT INTO statement to create an empty table by adding 1=2 to the WHERE clause. Because one never equals two, the statement creates the table but doesn't add any rows. Even if you want to create and populate a work table, the performance of the entire system is often better by creating the empty table first and then populating it with a regular INSERT statement when you are working with a very large number of rows. This is because the SELECT INTO statement locks system tables that can cause problems for other connections. Using a CREATE TABLE first and then populating it locks the system tables only momentarily. Using the SELECT INTO syntax locks the tables until the entire statement completes.

Inserting Rows into Tables with Default Column Values

Column definitions often specify a default value, called a *default constraint*, if the INSERT statement doesn't supply a value for the column. This is different from inserting NULL. When inserting NULL, you specify NULL in the INSERT statement, or the NULL value is a result of the SELECT statement used to insert the data. You might also omit the column from the INSERT statement to insert NULL. If the column definition specifies a default constraint, you can just leave that column out of the INSERT statement to automatically insert the default value. Run the code in Listing 10-7 to learn how to insert data into tables when one or more of the columns have a default value. The first part of the code creates the table and two ALTER TABLE statements add the default constraints.

Listing 10-7. Inserting Data with a Column Default Constraint

```
IF  EXISTS (SELECT * FROM sys.objects
           WHERE object_id = OBJECT_ID(N'[dbo].[demoDefault]')
               AND type in (N'U'))
DROP TABLE dbo.demoDefault;
GO

CREATE TABLE dbo.demoDefault(
    KeyColumn int NOT NULL PRIMARY KEY,
    HasADefault1 DATETIME2 (1) NOT NULL,
    HasADefault2 NVARCHAR (50) NULL,
);
GO
ALTER TABLE dbo.demoDefault ADD  CONSTRAINT DF_demoDefault_HasADefault
    DEFAULT (GETDATE()) FOR HasADefault1;
GO
ALTER TABLE dbo.demoDefault ADD  CONSTRAINT DF_demoDefault_HasADefault2
    DEFAULT ('the default') FOR HasADefault2;
GO

--1
INSERT INTO dbo.demoDefault(HasADefault1, HasADefault2, KeyColumn)
VALUES ('2009-04-24', N'Test 1', 1),('2009-10-1', NULL, 2);

--2
INSERT INTO dbo.demoDefault (HasADefault1, HasADefault2, KeyColumn)
VALUES (DEFAULT, DEFAULT, 3), (DEFAULT, DEFAULT, 4);

--3
INSERT INTO dbo.demoDefault (KeyColumn)
VALUES (5),(6);

--4
SELECT HasADefault1,HasADefault2,KeyColumn
FROM dbo.demoDefault;
```

Figure 10-8 shows the results of running this code. Statement 1 inserts literal values into the HasADefault1 and HasADefault2 columns. Even though the two columns have default constraints, you can still override them and insert your own values. Notice that the row inserted with KeyColumn value 2 contains a NULL value in the HasADefault2 column. The statement specified and inserted NULL, not the default value.

	HasADefault1	HasADefault2	KeyColumn
1	2009-04-24 00:00:00.0	Test 1	1
2	2009-10-01 00:00:00.0	NULL	2
3	2014-03-08 13:26:25.5	the default	3
4	2014-03-08 13:26:25.5	the default	4
5	2014-03-08 13:26:25.5	the default	5
6	2014-03-08 13:26:25.5	the default	6

Figure 10-8. *The results of inserting rows into a table with column default constraints*

Statements 2 and 3 take advantage of the default constraints. Statement 2 specifies the keyword DEFAULT instead of a value. Statement 3 just omits the two columns. Whenever using the keyword DEFAULT or omitting the columns, the default definition determines the values to be inserted. The GETDATE function provides default values for the HasDefault1 column. The literal value "the default" is filled in for HasADefault2. If a table has default values defined for every column, you can also insert a row like this:

```
INSERT INTO TableWithAllDefaults
DEFAULT VALUES;
```

Inserting Rows into Tables with Automatically Populating Columns

In addition to default constraints, four types of columns exist that can be auto-populated. In other words, you should not specify values for these columns. The columns types are as follows:

- *Rowversion*: Formerly called TIMESTAMP, this contains a binary number that is unique within a database. Developers generally use ROWVERSION to determine whether changes have been made to a row.

- *Identity*: This contains an auto-incrementing numeric value. Developers often use IDENTITY columns when an ID number is needed for a table.

- *Computed columns*: These have a definition that is usually based on the values of other columns in the same row. The values in a computed column can be stored in the table by specifying the keyword PERSISTED in the column definition. If the table definition doesn't contain PERSISTED, it will be calculated each time it is accessed.

Be sure to always specify the column names, leaving off the automatically populated columns when you write an INSERT statement to avoid causing an error.

■ **Note**   There is an exception to the rule about inserting data into IDENTITY columns. You can change a session-specific setting called IDENTITY_INSERT that will allow you to insert a value into an IDENTITY column. Developers and database administrators often do this when loading data and the IDENTITY values must be preserved. After loading the data, the IDENTITY column will work as it did before once you turn off IDENTITY_INSERT in that session or insert data into the table from a different session.

Type in and execute the code in Listing 10-8. The first part of the code creates a table with the special column types.

Listing 10-8. Inserting Rows into Tables with Autopopulated Columns

```
IF  EXISTS (SELECT * FROM sys.objects
            WHERE object_id = OBJECT_ID(N'[dbo].[demoAutoPopulate]')
                AND type in (N'U'))
DROP TABLE [dbo].[demoAutoPopulate];

CREATE TABLE [dbo].[demoAutoPopulate](
    [RegularColumn] [NVARCHAR](50) NOT NULL PRIMARY KEY,
    [IdentityColumn] [INT] IDENTITY(1,1) NOT NULL,
    [RowversionColumn] [ROWVERSION] NOT NULL,
    [ComputedColumn] AS ([RegularColumn]+CONVERT([NVARCHAR],
    [IdentityColumn],(0))) PERSISTED);
GO

--1
INSERT INTO dbo.demoAutoPopulate (RegularColumn)
VALUES (N'a'), (N'b'), (N'c');

--2
SELECT RegularColumn, IdentityColumn, RowversionColumn, ComputedColumn
FROM demoAutoPopulate;
```

Figure 10-9 shows the results of running this code. Statement 1 specified values for RegularColumn only. The database engine automatically determined the values for the other columns. Notice that the IdentityColumn contains an incrementing value. The ComputedColumn contains the result of the expression RegularColumn + CAST(IdentityColumn AS NVARCHAR).

	RegularColumn	IdentityColumn	RowversionColumn	ComputedColumn
1	a	1	0x00000000000065AF	a1
2	b	2	0x00000000000065B0	b2
3	c	3	0x00000000000065B1	c3

Figure 10-9. *The results of inserting rows into a table with autopopulating columns*

You have learned how to insert new rows into tables by using literal values or data from a query. Before moving on to the next section, where you will learn how to delete data, practice inserting new rows into a table by completing Exercise 10-1.

EXERCISE 10-1

Use the AdventureWorks database to complete this exercise. You can find the solutions at the end of the chapter.

Run the following code to create the required tables. You can also download the code from this book's page at www.apress.com to save typing time.

```
IF  EXISTS (SELECT * FROM sys.objects
            WHERE object_id = OBJECT_ID(N'[dbo].[demoProduct]')
                AND type in (N'U'))
```

```
DROP TABLE [dbo].[demoProduct]
GO

CREATE TABLE [dbo].[demoProduct](
    [ProductID] [INT] NOT NULL PRIMARY KEY,
    [Name] [dbo].[Name] NOT NULL,
    [Color] [NVARCHAR](15) NULL,
    [StandardCost] [MONEY] NOT NULL,
    [ListPrice] [MONEY] NOT NULL,
    [Size] [NVARCHAR](5) NULL,
    [Weight] [DECIMAL](8, 2) NULL,
);
IF  EXISTS (SELECT * FROM sys.objects
            WHERE object_id = OBJECT_ID(N'[dbo].[demoSalesOrderHeader]')
                AND type in (N'U'))
DROP TABLE [dbo].[demoSalesOrderHeader]
GO

CREATE TABLE [dbo].[demoSalesOrderHeader](
    [SalesOrderID] [INT] NOT NULL PRIMARY KEY,
    [SalesID] [INT] NOT NULL IDENTITY,
    [OrderDate] [DATETIME] NOT NULL,
    [CustomerID] [INT] NOT NULL,
    [SubTotal] [MONEY] NOT NULL,
    [TaxAmt] [MONEY] NOT NULL,
    [Freight] [MONEY] NOT NULL,
    [DateEntered] [DATETIME],
    [TotalDue]  AS (ISNULL((([SubTotal]+[TaxAmt])+[Freight],(0))),
    [RV] ROWVERSION NOT NULL);
GO

ALTER TABLE [dbo].[demoSalesOrderHeader] ADD  CONSTRAINT
    [DF_demoSalesOrderHeader_DateEntered]
DEFAULT (getdate()) FOR [DateEntered];

GO
IF  EXISTS (SELECT * FROM sys.objects
    WHERE object_id = OBJECT_ID(N'[dbo].[demoAddress]')
    AND type in (N'U'))
DROP TABLE [dbo].[demoAddress]
GO

CREATE TABLE [dbo].[demoAddress](
    [AddressID] [INT] NOT NULL IDENTITY PRIMARY KEY,
    [AddressLine1] [NVARCHAR](60) NOT NULL,
    [AddressLine2] [NVARCHAR](60) NULL,
    [City] [NVARCHAR](30) NOT NULL,
    [PostalCode] [NVARCHAR](15) NOT NULL
);
```

1. Write a SELECT statement to retrieve data from the Production.Product table. Use these values to insert five rows into the dbo.demoProduct table using literal values. Write five individual INSERT statements.

2. Insert five more rows using literal values into the dbo.demoProduct table. This time write one INSERT statement.

3. Write an INSERT statement that inserts all the rows into the dbo.demoSalesOrderHeader table from the Sales.SalesOrderHeader table. Hint: Pay close attention to the properties of the columns in the dbo.demoSalesOrderHeader table.

4. Write a SELECT INTO statement that creates a table, dbo.tempCustomerSales, inserting every CustomerID from the Sales.Customer along with a count of the orders placed and the total amount due for each customer.

5. Write an INSERT statement that inserts all the products into the dbo.demoProduct table from the Production.Product table that have not already been inserted.

6. Write an INSERT statement that inserts all the addresses into the dbo.demoAddress table from the Person.Address table joined to the Person.StateProvince table. Before running the INSERT statement, type in and run the following command so that you can insert values into the AddressID column:

```
SET IDENTITY_INSERT dbo.demoAddress ON;
```

Deleting Rows

You now know how to add new rows to tables. This section will show you how to do exactly the opposite, how to delete existing rows. This is an important but dangerous task. Many developers and database administrators have accidentally removed the data from an entire table when intending to remove just one row. Care must be taken whenever deleting rows, especially when writing ad hoc delete statements.

Using *DELETE*

The DELETE statement is very simple. At a minimum, you need the word DELETE and the table name. This will remove all rows from the table unless there happens to be foreign keys on the table. Most of the time, your goal will be to remove just a portion of the rows. Here is the syntax:

```
DELETE [FROM] <table1>
[WHERE <condition>]
```

If you omit the WHERE clause, the statement removes every row from the table. The table still exists, just without any rows. When writing ad hoc DELETE statements, always test your WHERE clause with a SELECT statement first to make sure you know exactly which rows you are deleting. Type in and execute the code in Listing 10-9. The listing creates several copies of the main tables from the AdventureWorks database. To avoid typing the table creation portion, you can download the code from the book's page at www.apress.com.

Listing 10-9. Creating Demo Tables

```
IF  EXISTS (SELECT * FROM sys.objects
            WHERE object_id = OBJECT_ID(N'[dbo].[demoProduct]')
                AND type in (N'U'))
DROP TABLE [dbo].[demoProduct];
GO

SELECT * INTO dbo.demoProduct FROM Production.Product;

IF  EXISTS (SELECT * FROM sys.objects
            WHERE object_id = OBJECT_ID(N'[dbo].[demoCustomer]')
                AND type in (N'U'))
DROP TABLE [dbo].[demoCustomer];
GO

SELECT C.*, LastName, FirstName INTO dbo.demoCustomer
FROM Sales.Customer AS C
JOIN Person.Person AS P ON C.CustomerID = P.BusinessEntityID;

IF  EXISTS (SELECT * FROM sys.objects
            WHERE object_id = OBJECT_ID(N'[dbo].[demoAddress]')
                AND type in (N'U'))
DROP TABLE [dbo].[demoAddress];
GO

SELECT * INTO dbo.demoAddress FROM Person.Address;

IF  EXISTS (SELECT * FROM sys.objects
            WHERE object_id = OBJECT_ID(N'[dbo].[demoSalesOrderHeader]')
                AND type in (N'U'))
DROP TABLE [dbo].[demoSalesOrderHeader];
GO

SELECT * INTO dbo.demoSalesOrderHeader FROM Sales.SalesOrderHeader;

IF  EXISTS (SELECT * FROM sys.objects
            WHERE object_id = OBJECT_ID(N'[dbo].[demoSalesOrderDetail]')
                AND type in (N'U'))
DROP TABLE [dbo].[demoSalesOrderDetail];
GO

SELECT * INTO dbo.demoSalesOrderDetail FROM Sales.SalesOrderDetail;
```

You should now have several tables that you can use to practice deleting data. Type in and execute the code in Listing 10-10 to learn how to delete rows from tables.

Listing 10-10. Deleting Rows from Tables

```
--1
SELECT CustomerID
FROM dbo.demoCustomer;
```

```
--2
DELETE dbo.demoCustomer;

--3
SELECT CustomerID
FROM dbo.demoCustomer;

--4
SELECT ProductID
FROM dbo.demoProduct
WHERE ProductID > 900;

--5
DELETE dbo.demoProduct
WHERE ProductID > 900;

--6
SELECT ProductID
FROM dbo.demoProduct
WHERE ProductID > 900;
```

Figure 10-10 shows the rows before and after running the DELETE statements affecting the dbo.demoCustomer and dbo.demoProduct tables. Running a SELECT statement before deleting data is a good idea and it enables you to test your WHERE clause. Make sure you know which rows will be deleted before you delete them. Another thing you can do is to delete rows within a transaction. You can check your results before committing the transaction or roll back in case of a problem. Statement 2 removes every row from dbo.demoCustomer. Statement 5 removes the rows from dbo. demoProduct where the ProductID was greater than 900. The word FROM is optional.

	CustomerID
1	1
2	2
3	3
4	4

	CustomerID

	ProductID
1	901
2	902
3	903
4	904

	ProductID

Figure 10-10. *The partial results before and after rows deleted*

Deleting from a Table Using *EXISTS*

Listing 10-10 demonstrated how to remove rows from a table when the statement contains just one table. You can also remove rows from a table that is involved in a join to restrict which rows the statement deletes. The preferred method is to use a subquery and EXISTS. Here is the syntax:

```
DELETE <alias1>
FROM <table1> AS <alias1>
WHERE [NOT] EXISTS (
    SELECT * FROM <table2> AS <alias2>
    WHERE <alias1>.<Col1> = <alias2>.<Col2>);
```

Type in and execute the code in Listing 10-11 to practice this technique. If you didn't run the code in Listing 10-9 that creates the tables used in these examples and the code in Listing 10-10 that deletes some of the data, do that first.

Listing 10-11. Deleting When Using EXISTS

```
--1
SELECT d.SalesOrderID, SalesOrderNumber
FROM dbo.demoSalesOrderDetail AS d
INNER JOIN dbo.demoSalesOrderHeader AS h ON d.SalesOrderID = h.SalesOrderID
WHERE h.SalesOrderNumber = 'SO71797'

--2
DELETE d
FROM dbo.demoSalesOrderDetail AS d
WHERE EXISTS(
    SELECT *
        FROM dbo.demoSalesOrderHeader AS h
        WHERE h.SalesOrderNumber = 'SO71797'
            AND d.SalesOrderID = h.SalesOrderID);

--3
SELECT d.SalesOrderID, SalesOrderNumber
FROM dbo.demoSalesOrderDetail AS d
INNER JOIN dbo.demoSalesOrderHeader AS h ON d.SalesOrderID = h.SalesOrderID
WHERE h.SalesOrderNumber = 'SO71797'

--4
SELECT SalesOrderID, ProductID
FROM dbo.demoSalesOrderDetail AS SOD
WHERE NOT EXISTS
    (SELECT *
        FROM dbo.demoProduct AS P
        WHERE P.ProductID = SOD.ProductID);
--5
DELETE SOD
FROM dbo.demoSalesOrderDetail AS SOD
WHERE NOT EXISTS
    (SELECT *
        FROM dbo.demoProduct AS P
        WHERE P.ProductID = SOD.ProductID);
```

```
--6
SELECT SalesOrderID, ProductID
FROM dbo.demoSalesOrderDetail
WHERE ProductID NOT IN
    (SELECT ProductID FROM dbo.demoProduct AS P
        WHERE P.ProductID  IS NOT NULL);
```

Figure 10-11 shows the results before and after deleting. Again, write SELECT statements first to test your WHERE clause and to make sure you will delete the correct rows or wrap the delete statements in implicit transactions that you can roll back in case of a mistake. Statement 2 deletes the rows from the dbo.demoSalesOrderDetail table that have a SalesOrderNumber of SO71797 in the dbo.demoSalesOrderHeader table. The value in one table determines which rows in another table will be deleted.

	SalesOrderID	SalesOrderNumber
1	71797	SO71797
2	71797	SO71797
3	71797	SO71797
4	71797	SO71797

	SalesOrderID	SalesOrderNumber

	SalesOrderID	ProductID
1	51081	989
2	51081	990
3	51081	992
4	51081	984

	SalesOrderID	ProductID

Figure 10-11. *The partial results before and after deleting rows using EXISTS*

Statement 4 uses a subquery in the WHERE clause to determine which rows to delete. Statement 5 deletes the rows using NOT EXISTS. Finally, statement 6 checks to make sure the correct rows were deleted.

Another way to delete the rows specifies the table name after the DELETE keyword instead of specifying the alias. Using the alias ensures that the DELETE part of the statement is tied to the SELECT part of the statement. I have seen developers write DELETE statements that inadvertently deleted all rows from a production table because the DELETE part of the statement wasn't really connected to the rest of the statement. I recommend that you always use the technique shown in Listing 10-11 to avoid deleting all the rows in a table by mistake. Here is an example that is really a DELETE statement and a SELECT statement when the intention is just a DELETE statement:

```
--Don't do this!
DELETE dbo.demoSalesOrderDetail
SELECT d.SalesOrderID
FROM dbo.demoSalesOrderDetail AS d
WHERE EXISTS(
    SELECT *
        FROM dbo.demoSalesOrderHeader AS h
        WHERE d.SalesOrderID = h.SalesOrderID
    AND h.SalesOrderNumber = 'SO71797');
```

Truncating

A way to quickly delete all the rows from a table is to use the TRUNCATE TABLE statement. This is a very fast way to empty a large table. Although deleting rows requires that the user account have DELETE permission on the table, truncating a table requires the user be in the dbo or db_ddladmin database roles or the sysadmin server role or have ALTER permission on the table. Here is the syntax:

```
TRUNCATE TABLE <table1>
```

Listing 10-12 demonstrates how to use TRUNCATE. If you didn't run Listing 10-9 to create the tables, do that first before typing and running the code in Listing 10-12.

Listing 10-12. Truncating Tables

```
--1
SELECT SalesOrderID, OrderDate
FROM dbo.demoSalesOrderHeader;

--2
TRUNCATE TABLE dbo.demoSalesOrderHeader;

--3
SELECT SalesOrderID, OrderDate
FROM dbo.demoSalesOrderHeader;
```

Figure 10-12 shows the results before and after truncating the table. One of the reasons that TRUNCATE is so much more powerful than DELETE is because it actually re-creates the table behind the scenes. That is much quicker than deleting all the rows, but no WHERE clause is allowed with TRUNCATE. The TRUNCATE statement can be used only when you intend to empty the table.

	SalesOrderID	OrderDate
1	58054	2007-11-16 00:00:00.000
2	58055	2007-11-16 00:00:00.000
3	58056	2007-11-16 00:00:00.000
4	58057	2007-11-16 00:00:00.000

	SalesOrderID	OrderDate

Figure 10-12. *The results before and after truncating*

Deleting data is a very risky operation. It's why database administrators consider a good backup strategy an important part of their jobs. Practice what you have learned about deleting data by completing Exercise 10-2.

```
                          EXERCISE 10-2
```

Use the AdventureWorks database to complete this exercise. Before starting the exercise, run Listing 10-9 to re-create the demo tables. You can find the solutions at the end of the chapter.

1. Write a query that deletes the rows from the dbo.demoCustomer table where the LastName values begin with the letter *S*.

2. Delete the rows from the dbo.demoCustomer table if the sum of the TotalDue from the dbo. demoSalesOrderHeader table for the customer is less than $1,000.

3. Delete the rows from the dbo.demoProduct table that have never been ordered.

Updating Existing Rows

Updating data is a very important part of T-SQL but it also requires extreme caution. Only deleting rows, which was discussed in the previous section, requires more care. Well, maybe that's not quite true; you could actually drop tables or entire databases accidentally. Within applications, the user will usually be working with one row at a time. For example, they may be viewing a screen that displays and allows editing of one employee, one department, or one order. Automated processes often update data in entire tables or many rows at one time. In this section, you will learn how to use the UPDATE statement to update existing rows in several scenarios, including single tables, joins, and aggregates. Run the code in Listing 10-9 to repopulate the tables you will use for the examples in this section.

Using the *UPDATE* Statement

To update existing rows in a table, use the UPDATE statement. Usually you will add a WHERE clause to make sure you update only the appropriate rows. Often database administrators have to restore backups of databases to get back data that has been accidentally updated because the WHERE clause was incorrect or missing. Here is the syntax of the UPDATE statement:

```
UPDATE <table1>
SET <col1> = <new value1>,<col2> = <new value2>
[WHERE <condition>]
```

You can use expressions, literal values, or other columns to update existing data. Developers often think that updating data must be done one row at a time. I have talked to many developers who insist on updating one row at a time because some of the rows must be updated with one value and some with another. In those cases, maybe they could write an UPDATE statement for each business rule or use the CASE expression but not perform one update for each row. Type in and execute the code in Listing 10-13 to learn how to update data.

Listing 10-13. Updating Data in a Table

```
IF  EXISTS (SELECT * FROM sys.objects
    WHERE object_id = OBJECT_ID(N'[dbo].[demoPerson]')
    AND type in (N'U'))
DROP TABLE [dbo].[demoPerson];
GO
```

```
SELECT *, ' ' Gender INTO dbo.demoPerson
FROM Person.Person
WHERE Title in ('Mr.', 'Mrs.', 'Ms.');


--1
SELECT BusinessEntityID, Title, Gender
FROM dbo.demoPerson
ORDER BY BusinessEntityID;


--2
UPDATE dbo.demoPerson
SET Gender = CASE WHEN Title = 'Mr.' THEN 'M' ELSE 'F' END;


--3
SELECT BusinessEntityID, Title, Gender
FROM dbo.demoPerson
ORDER BY BusinessEntityID;
```

Figure 10-13 shows the results before and after the updates. Query 1 just displays a few rows from the table. Statement 2 updates all the rows in the table, changing the Gender column based on the title.

	BusinessEntityID	Title	Gender
1	5	Ms.	
2	6	Mr.	
3	13	Ms.	
4	24	Ms.	

	BusinessEntityID	Title	Gender
1	5	Ms.	F
2	6	Mr.	M
3	13	Ms.	F
4	24	Ms.	F

Figure 10-13. *The partial results before and after updating*

Updating Data with Expressions and Columns

The statements in the previous section updated the dbo.demoCustomer table with literal values. You can also perform updates using scalar expressions more complex than a literal value or even other columns. Developers and database administrators often must perform large updates to data, sometimes on a periodic basis or to fulfill one-time requests. Here is the syntax for this technique:

```
UPDATE <table1>
SET <col1> = <expression>
[WHERE <condition>]
```

Again, you can use expressions, hard-coded values, or other columns in your statement's SET clause. When multiple rows must be updated, such as batch processing that happens after business hours, whenever possible, you should perform updates in sets, not one row at a time. Type in and execute the code in Listing 10-14 to learn how to perform these updates.

Listing 10-14. Update with Expressions, Columns, or Data from Another Table

```
IF  EXISTS (SELECT * FROM sys.objects
    WHERE object_id = OBJECT_ID(N'[dbo].[demoPersonStore]')
    AND type in (N'U'))
DROP TABLE [dbo].[demoPersonStore];
GO

CREATE TABLE [dbo].[demoPersonStore] (
[FirstName] [NVARCHAR] (60),
[LastName] [NVARCHAR] (60),
[CompanyName] [NVARCHAR] (60)
);

INSERT INTO dbo.demoPersonStore (FirstName, LastName, CompanyName)
SELECT a.FirstName, a.LastName, c.Name
FROM Person.Person a
JOIN Sales.SalesPerson b
ON a.BusinessEntityID = b.BusinessEntityID
JOIN Sales.Store c
ON b.BusinessEntityID = c.SalesPersonID;

--1
SELECT FirstName,LastName, CompanyName,
    LEFT(FirstName,3) + '-' + LEFT(LastName,3) AS NewCompany
FROM dbo.demoPersonStore;

--2
UPDATE dbo.demoPersonStore
SET CompanyName = LEFT(FirstName,3) + '-' + LEFT(LastName,3);

--3
SELECT FirstName,LastName, CompanyName,
    LEFT(FirstName,3) + '-' + LEFT(LastName,3) AS NewCompany
FROM dbo.demoPersonStore;
```

Figure 10-14 shows the results before and after the update. Query 1 displays the data before the update. The NewCompany column contains the expression that will be used in the UPDATE statement. You will find it is useful to display the expression, especially if it is complicated, to make sure your update will do exactly what you expect. Statement 2 updates the data, changing CompanyName in the dbo.demoPersonStore table to the new value derived from the FirstName and LastName columns. Finally, Query 3 displays the updated data. At this point, the CompanyName should be equivalent to the NewCompany expression.

	First Name	Last Name	CompanyName	NewCompany
1	Tsvi	Reiter	Next-Door Bike Store	Tsv-Rei
2	Linda	Mitchell	Professional Sales and Service	Lin-Mit
3	Jillian	Carson	Riders Company	Jil-Car
4	Michael	Blythe	The Bike Mechanics	Mic-Bly

	First Name	Last Name	CompanyName	NewCompany
1	Tsvi	Reiter	Tsv-Rei	Tsv-Rei
2	Linda	Mitchell	Lin-Mit	Lin-Mit
3	Jillian	Carson	Jil-Car	Jil-Car
4	Michael	Blythe	Mic-Bly	Mic-Bly

Figure 10-14. *The results before and after updating with an expression*

You cannot directly perform updates with aggregate functions. You'll learn more about this and how to work around it in Chapter 11.

Updating with a Join

So far, you have seen how to write UPDATE statements with a single table. When joining, you can update only a single table, but by joining with another table, you can limit the rows to be updated or use the second table to provide the value. Here is the syntax:

```
UPDATE <alias>
SET <col1> = <expression>
FROM <table1> AS <alias>
INNER JOIN <table2> on <alias>.<col2>  = <table2>.<col3>
```

The syntax shows an INNER JOIN, but you could perform an OUTER JOIN if that makes sense for the particular update. Type in and execute the code in Listing 10-15 to learn how to perform an update using this technique.

Listing 10-15. Updating with a Join

```
--1
SELECT AddressLine1, AddressLine2
FROM dbo.demoAddress;


--2
UPDATE dA
SET AddressLine1 = P.FirstName + ' ' + P.LastName,
    AddressLine2 = AddressLine1 + ISNULL(' ' + AddressLine2,'')
FROM dbo.demoAddress AS dA
INNER JOIN Person.BusinessEntityAddress BEA ON dA.AddressID = BEA.AddressID
INNER JOIN Person.Person P ON P.BusinessEntityID = BEA.BusinessEntityID;


--3
SELECT AddressLine1, AddressLine2
FROM dbo.demoAddress;
```

Figure 10-15 shows the results before and after the update. In this case, statement 2 uses columns from the second table, the Person.Person table, to build an expression to update AddressLine1. The statement uses another expression to move the original AddressLine1 and AddressLine2, if any, to AddressLine2. The dbo.demoAddress table doesn't join directly to the Person.Person table but must join through an intermediary table, Person.BusinessEntityAddress.

	AddressLine1	AddressLine2
1	1893 Cranbrook Way	NULL
2	7314 El Capitan Lane	NULL
3	4877, rue des Ecoles	NULL
4	6631 Highland Dr.	NULL

	AddressLine1	AddressLine2
1	Jose Young	1893 Cranbrook Way
2	Thomas Young	7314 El Capitan Lane
3	Carl Luo	4877, rue des Ecoles
4	Carl Yuan	6631 Highland Dr.

Figure 10-15. *The results before and after updating with a join*

Like deleting data, you should exercise caution when updating data. Always view the data you are about to change. Look for problems like incorrect joins. You now know how to update data in existing tables with literal values, expressions, and other columns. Now practice what you have learned by completing Exercise 10-3.

EXERCISE 10-3

Use the AdventureWorks database to complete this exercise. Run the code in Listing 10-9 to re-create the tables used in this exercise. You can find the solutions at the end of the chapter.

1. Write an UPDATE statement that changes all NULL values of the AddressLine2 column in the dbo.demoAddress table to *N/A*.

2. Write an UPDATE statement that increases the ListPrice of every product in the dbo.demoProduct table by 10 percent.

3. Write an UPDATE statement that corrects the UnitPrice with the ListPrice of each row of the dbo.demoSalesOrderDetail table by joining the table on the dbo.demoProduct table.

Thinking About Performance

SQL Server performs best when working on sets of data instead of one row at a time. Often developers write code that loops through a record set and performs an update or insert for each pass through the loop. The example code in Listing 10-16 demonstrates the difference in performance between the two techniques. Download and run the code from this book's page on www.apress.com. You may need to stop the code execution after a few minutes.

Listing 10-16. The Difference between the Set-Based and Iterative Approaches

```
SET NOCOUNT ON; -- turns off rows affected message
--Create a work table
IF  EXISTS (SELECT * FROM sys.objects
            WHERE object_id = OBJECT_ID(N'[dbo].[demoPerformance]')
                AND type in (N'U'))
DROP TABLE [dbo].[demoPerformance];
GO

CREATE TABLE [dbo].[demoPerformance](
    [CustomerID] [int] NOT NULL
 CONSTRAINT [PK_demoPerformance] PRIMARY KEY CLUSTERED
(
    CustomerID ASC
)WITH (PAD_INDEX  = OFF, STATISTICS_NORECOMPUTE  = OFF, IGNORE_DUP_KEY = OFF,
    ALLOW_ROW_LOCKS  = ON, ALLOW_PAGE_LOCKS  = ON) ON [PRIMARY]
) ON [PRIMARY]

GO

PRINT 'Insert all rows start';
PRINT SYSDATETIME();

--Insert all rows from the Sales.SalesOrderDetail table at once
INSERT INTO demoPerformance
SELECT CustomerID
FROM Sales.Customer;

PRINT 'Insert all rows end';
PRINT SYSDATETIME();

--Remove all rows from the first insert
TRUNCATE TABLE [dbo].[demoPerformance];

PRINT 'Insert rows one at a time begin';
PRINT SYSDATETIME();

--Set up a loop to insert one row at a time
WHILE EXISTS(

    SELECT *
    FROM Sales.Customer AS c
        WHERE NOT EXISTS(
            SELECT * FROM dbo.demoPerformance AS p
        WHERE c.CustomerID = p.CustomerID)
        ) BEGIN

    INSERT INTO demoPerformance(CustomerID)
        SELECT TOP(1) CustomerID
        FROM Sales.Customer AS c
        WHERE NOT EXISTS(SELECT * FROM dbo.demoPerformance WHERE CustomerID = c.CustomerID);
```

```
END
PRINT 'Insert rows one at a time end';
PRINT SYSDATETIME();
```

After the code executes or you stop execution after a few minutes, click the Messages tab to see the results (Figure 10-16).

```
Insert all rows start
2014-05-11 13:08:08.5415121
Insert all rows end
2014-05-11 13:08:08.5985497
Insert rows one at a time begin
2014-05-11 13:08:08.6045565
Insert rows one at a time end
2014-05-11 13:20:19.6422827
```

Figure 10-16. *The results of comparing one insert vs. a loop with multiple inserts*

Run this statement to see how many rows were actually inserted from the loop:

```
SELECT COUNT(*) FROM dbo.demoPerformance;
```

The loop took about 12 minutes to complete on my laptop with 8GB of RAM and an SSD hard drive! The first INSERT statement, inserting 19,820 rows, took less than a second to run.

Database Cleanup

Run the script in Listing 10-17 to clean up the tables used in this chapter. You can download the script from this book's page at www.apress.com. Alternately, you can reinstall the sample databases by following the instructions in the "Installing the Sample Databases" section in Chapter 1.

Listing 10-17. Deleting Demo Tables

```
IF  EXISTS (SELECT * FROM sys.objects
    WHERE object_id = OBJECT_ID(N'[dbo].[demoPersonStore]')
    AND type in (N'U'))
DROP TABLE [dbo].[demoPersonStore]
GO

IF  EXISTS (SELECT * FROM sys.objects
    WHERE object_id = OBJECT_ID(N'[dbo].[demoPerson]')
    AND type in (N'U'))
DROP TABLE [dbo].[demoPerson];

IF  EXISTS (SELECT * FROM sys.objects
            WHERE object_id = OBJECT_ID(N'[dbo].[demoProduct]')
                AND type in (N'U'))
DROP TABLE [dbo].[demoProduct];
GO
```

```
IF  EXISTS (SELECT * FROM sys.objects
            WHERE object_id = OBJECT_ID(N'[dbo].[demoCustomer]')
              AND type in (N'U'))
DROP TABLE [dbo].[demoCustomer];
GO


IF  EXISTS (SELECT * FROM sys.objects
            WHERE object_id = OBJECT_ID(N'[dbo].[demoAddress]')
              AND type in (N'U'))
DROP TABLE [dbo].[demoAddress];
GO


IF  EXISTS (SELECT * FROM sys.objects
            WHERE object_id = OBJECT_ID(N'[dbo].[demoSalesOrderHeader]')
              AND type in (N'U'))
DROP TABLE [dbo].[demoSalesOrderHeader];
GO


IF  EXISTS (SELECT * FROM sys.objects
            WHERE object_id = OBJECT_ID(N'[dbo].[demoSalesOrderDetail]')
              AND type in (N'U'))
DROP TABLE [dbo].[demoSalesOrderDetail];
GO


IF  EXISTS (SELECT * FROM sys.objects
            WHERE object_id = OBJECT_ID(N'[dbo].[demoDefault]')
              AND type in (N'U'))
DROP TABLE [dbo].[demoDefault];
GO


IF  EXISTS (SELECT * FROM sys.objects
            WHERE object_id = OBJECT_ID(N'[dbo].[demoAutoPopulate]')
              AND type in (N'U'))
DROP TABLE [dbo].[demoAutoPopulate];


IF  EXISTS (SELECT * FROM sys.objects
            WHERE object_id = OBJECT_ID(N'[dbo].[demoPerformance]')
              AND type in (N'U'))
DROP TABLE [dbo].[demoPerformance];
```

Summary

Writing data modification statements is not difficult once you've mastered the basics of selecting data. These tasks do, however, require much more care because it's possible to unintentionally modify and delete rows or even empty entire tables. This type of mistake could cost you your job! Always check the WHERE clause with a SELECT statement first when writing ad hoc statements.

Whenever possible, do modifications on sets of data, not one row at a time. You will often see amazing differences in performance. Many developers learn to operate on one row at a time, but this is not the best way for SQL Server to work.

In Chapter 11 you will learn some advanced query techniques including more ways to use CTEs and paging.

Answers to the Exercises

This section provides solutions to the exercises found on writing statements that modify data.

Solution to Exercise 10-1: Inserting New Rows

Use the AdventureWorks database to complete this exercise. Download the code to create the tables for this exercise from www.apress.com.

1. Write a SELECT statement to retrieve data from the Production.Product table. Use these values to insert five rows into the dbo.demoProduct table using literal values. Write five individual INSERT statements. The rows you choose to insert will vary.

```
INSERT INTO dbo.demoProduct(ProductID,
    Name, Color, StandardCost,
    ListPrice, Size, Weight)
VALUES (680,'HL Road Frame - Black, 58','Black',1059.31,1431.50,'58',1016.04);

INSERT INTO dbo.demoProduct(ProductID, Name,
    Color,StandardCost, ListPrice, Size, Weight)
VALUES (706,'HL Road Frame - Red, 58','Red',1059.31, 1431.50,'58',1016.04);

INSERT INTO dbo.demoProduct(ProductID, Name,
    Color,StandardCost, ListPrice, Size, Weight)
VALUES (707,'Sport-100 Helmet, Red','Red',13.0863,34.99,NULL,NULL);

INSERT INTO dbo.demoProduct(ProductID, Name,
    Color,StandardCost, ListPrice, Size, Weight)
VALUES (708,'Sport-100 Helmet, Black','Black',13.0863,34.99,NULL,NULL);

INSERT INTO dbo.demoProduct(ProductID, Name,
    Color,StandardCost, ListPrice, Size, Weight)
VALUES (709,'Mountain Bike Socks, M', 'White',
    3.3963, 9.50, 'M',NULL);
```

2. Insert five more rows using literal values into the dbo.demoProduct table. This time write one INSERT statement. The rows you choose to insert may vary.

```
INSERT INTO dbo.demoProduct(ProductID, Name,
    Color, StandardCost, ListPrice, Size, Weight)
VALUES (711,'Sport-100 Helmet, Blue','Blue',
    13.0863,34.99,NULL,NULL),
    (712,'AWC Logo Cap','Multi',6.9223,
     8.99,NULL,NULL),
    (713,'Long-Sleeve Logo Jersey,S','Multi',
     38.4923,49.99,'S',NULL),
    (714,'Long-Sleeve Logo Jersey,M','Multi',
     38.4923,49.99,'M',NULL),
    (715,'Long-Sleeve Logo Jersey,L','Multi',
     38.4923,49.99,'L',NULL);
```

3. Write an INSERT statement that inserts all the rows into the dbo.demoSalesOrderHeader table from the Sales.SalesOrderHeader table. Hint: Pay close attention to the properties of the columns in the dbo.demoSalesOrderHeader table.

```
-- Don't insert a value into the SalesID,
-- DateEntered, and RV columns..

INSERT INTO dbo.demoSalesOrderHeader(
    SalesOrderID, OrderDate, CustomerID,
    SubTotal, TaxAmt, Freight)
SELECT SalesOrderID, OrderDate, CustomerID,
    SubTotal, TaxAmt, Freight
FROM Sales.SalesOrderHeader;
```

4. Write a SELECT INTO statement that creates a table, dbo.tempCustomerSales, inserting every CustomerID from the Sales.Customer along with a count of the orders placed and the total amount due for each customer.

```
SELECT COUNT(ISNULL(SalesOrderID,0))
    AS CountOfOrders, c.CustomerID,
    SUM(TotalDue) AS TotalDue
INTO dbo.tempCustomerSales
FROM Sales.Customer AS c
LEFT JOIN Sales.SalesOrderHeader
    AS soh ON c.CustomerID = soh.CustomerID
GROUP BY c.CustomerID;
```

5. Write an INSERT statement that inserts all the products into the dbo.demoProduct table from the Production.Product table that have not already been inserted.

```
INSERT INTO dbo.demoProduct (ProductID, Name,
    Color, StandardCost,
    ListPrice, Size, Weight)
SELECT ProductID, Name, Color, StandardCost,
    ListPrice, Size, Weight
FROM Production.Product AS P
WHERE NOT EXISTS (
    SELECT ProductID
    FROM dbo.demoProduct AS DP
    WHERE DP.ProductID = P.ProductID);
```

6. Write an INSERT statement that inserts all the addresses into the dbo.demoAddress table from the Person.Address table joined to the Person.StateProvince table. Before running the INSERT statement, type in and run the following command so that you can insert values into the AddressID column:

```
SET IDENTITY_INSERT dbo.demoAddress ON;

INSERT INTO dbo.demoAddress(AddressID,
        AddressLine1, AddressLine2,
        City, PostalCode)
    SELECT AddressID, AddressLine1, AddressLine2,
        City, PostalCode
    FROM Person.Address AS A
    JOIN Person.StateProvince AS SP ON A.StateProvinceID = SP.StateProvinceID;
    --to turn the setting off
    SET IDENTITY_INSERT dbo.demoAddress OFF;
```

Solution to Exercise 10-2: Deleting Rows

Use the AdventureWorks database to complete this exercise. Before starting the exercise, run Listing 10-9 to re-create the demo tables. .

1. Write a query that deletes the rows from the dbo.demoCustomer table where the LastName values begin with the letter *S*.

```
DELETE FROM dbo.demoCustomer
WHERE LastName LIKE 'S%';
```

2. Delete the rows from the dbo.demoCustomer table if the sum of the TotalDue from the dbo.demoSalesOrderHeader table for the customer is less than $1,000.

```
DELETE C FROM  dbo.demoCustomer AS C
WHERE NOT EXISTS (
    SELECT *
    FROM dbo.demoSalesOrderHeader AS SOH
    WHERE C.CustomerID = SOH.CustomerID
    GROUP BY SOH.CustomerID
    HAVING SUM(TotalDue) >=1000);
```

3. Delete the rows from the dbo.demoProduct table that have never been ordered.

```
DELETE P FROM dbo.demoProduct AS P
WHERE NOT EXISTS    (
    SELECT *
    FROM dbo.demoSalesOrderDetail AS SOD
    WHERE P.ProductID = SOD.ProductID);
```

Solution to Exercise 10-3: Updating Existing Rows

Use the AdventureWorks database to complete this exercise. Run the code in Listing 10-9 to re-create tables used in this exercise.

1. Write an UPDATE statement that changes all NULL values of the AddressLine2 column in the dbo.demoAddress table to *N/A*.

```
UPDATE dbo.demoAddress SET AddressLine2 = 'N/A'
WHERE AddressLine2 IS NULL;
```

2. Write an UPDATE statement that increases the ListPrice of every product in the dbo. demoProduct table by 10 percent.

```
UPDATE dbo.demoProduct
SET ListPrice =ListPrice *  1.1;
```

3. Write an UPDATE statement that corrects the UnitPrice with the ListPrice of each row of the dbo.demoSalesOrderDetail table by joining the table on the dbo.demoProduct table.

```
UPDATE SOD
SET UnitPrice = P.ListPrice
FROM dbo.demoSalesOrderDetail AS SOD
INNER JOIN dbo.demoProduct AS P
    ON SOD.ProductID = P.ProductID;
```

■ ■ ■

Writing Advanced Queries

In Chapter 10 you learned how to manipulate data. In this chapter you will learn some advanced query techniques. For example, you will learn more about common table expressions (CTEs), how to write a pivot query, and more. As a beginning T-SQL developer, you may or may not need this information right away. This chapter doesn't contain any exercises, but I encourage you to experiment and come up with your own examples for any of the features that you are interested in. Consider the information in this chapter as a head start in becoming an expert T-SQL developer.

Advanced CTE Queries

In Chapter 6 you learned to use CTEs as one of the ways to combine the data from more than one table into one query. CTEs allow you to isolate part of the query logic or do things you could not ordinarily do, such as use an aggregate expression in an update. In these cases, you could use derived tables (see the "Using Derived Tables" section in Chapter 6), but now you will learn that CTEs are much more versatile. You can do several things with CTEs that are not possible with derived tables, such as write a recursive query. This section covers these advanced CTE features.

■ **Caution** The keyword WITH appears in many other statement types. Because of this, a statement containing a CTE must be the first statement in the batch, or the previous statement must end with a semicolon. At this point, Microsoft recommends using semicolons to end T-SQL statements, but it is not required yet. Some developers start all CTE definitions with a semicolon to avoid errors. The semicolon will be required in a future version of SQL Server, so you should start using it now.

Alternate CTE Syntax

Throughout the book when I have demonstrated CTEs, I have shown one particular way to name the columns, within the CTE definition. You can also specify the column names up front in a column list. When you use this method, the specified column names in the column list must be used in the outer SELECT. The list overrides the column names within the CTE definition. Here is the syntax:

```
;WITH <ctename> (<col1>,<col2>)
AS (SELECT <col3>,<col4> FROM <table>
SELECT <col1>,<col2>
FROM <ctename>;
```

Listing 11-1 demonstrates this alternate method. Type in and execute the code to learn more.

Listing 11-1. Naming Columns

```
;WITH myCTE ([First Name], [Last Name], [Full Name])
AS(
    SELECT FirstName, LastName, CONCAT(FirstName, ' ', LastName)
        FROM Person.Person
)
SELECT [First Name], [Last Name], [Full Name]
FROM myCTE;
```

In this example, the column names for the CTE are found in the column list. Notice that the third column is an expression using the CONCAT function. An alias for the expression is not required because the alias will come from the column specification. If the column list was not used, then an alias within the CTE definition would be required.

Using Multiple CTEs

You can use CTEs to organize and isolate query logic in order to write complicated queries efficiently. You can't nest CTEs; that is, one CTE can't contain another CTE. You can, however, add multiple CTEs to one query. You might want to do this just to make your query more readable or possibly because writing the query this way will allow you to avoid temp tables or views. Here is the syntax:

```
WITH <cteName1> AS (SELECT <col1> FROM <table1>),
    <cteName2> AS (SELECT <col2> FROM <table2>),
    <cteName3> AS (SELECT <col3> FROM <table3>)
SELECT <col1>, <col2>, <col3>
FROM <cteName1> INNER JOIN <cteName2> ON <join condition1>
INNER JOIN <cteName3> ON <join condition2>
```

Of course, your CTE definitions can contain just about any valid SELECT statement, and your outer query can use the CTEs in any way you need to use them.

To create example data for the examples in this section, download and execute the code for Listing 11-2 as given on the book's web site page at www.apress.com.

Listing 11-2. Create Data for This Section's Examples

```
USE tempdb;
GO

IF OBJECT_ID('dbo.Employee') IS NOT NULL BEGIN
    DROP TABLE dbo.Employee;
END;
IF OBJECT_ID('dbo.Contact') IS NOT NULL BEGIN
    DROP TABLE dbo.Contact;
END;
IF OBJECT_ID('dbo.JobHistory') IS NOT NULL BEGIN
    DROP TABLE dbo.JobHistory;
END;
```

```
CREATE TABLE [Employee](
        [EmployeeID] [int] NOT NULL,
        [ContactID] [int] NOT NULL,
        [ManagerID] [int] NULL,
        [Title] [nvarchar](50) NOT NULL);

CREATE TABLE [Contact] (
        [ContactID] [int] NOT NULL,
        [FirstName] [nvarchar](50) NOT NULL,
        [MiddleName] [nvarchar](50) NULL,
        [LastName] [nvarchar](50) NOT NULL);

CREATE TABLE JobHistory(
    EmployeeID INT NOT NULL,
    EffDate DATE NOT NULL,
    EffSeq INT NOT NULL,
    EmploymentStatus CHAR(1) NOT NULL,
    JobTitle VARCHAR(50) NOT NULL,
    Salary MONEY NOT NULL,
    ActionDesc VARCHAR(20)
 CONSTRAINT PK_JobHistory PRIMARY KEY CLUSTERED
(
    EmployeeID, EffDate, EffSeq
));

GO


INSERT INTO dbo.Contact (ContactID, FirstName, MiddleName, LastName) VALUES
        (1030,'Kevin','F','Brown'),
        (1009,'Thierry','B','DHers'),
        (1028,'David','M','Bradley'),
        (1070,'JoLynn','M','Dobney'),
        (1071,'Ruth','Ann','Ellerbrock'),
        (1005,'Gail','A','Erickson'),
        (1076,'Barry','K','Johnson'),
        (1006,'Jossef','H','Goldberg'),
        (1001,'Terri','Lee','Duffy'),
        (1072,'Sidney','M','Higa'),
        (1067,'Taylor','R','Maxwell'),
        (1073,'Jeffrey','L','Ford'),
        (1068,'Jo','A','Brown'),
        (1074,'Doris','M','Hartwig'),
        (1069,'John','T','Campbell'),
        (1075,'Diane','R','Glimp'),
        (1129,'Steven','T','Selikoff'),
        (1231,'Peter','J','Krebs'),
        (1172,'Stuart','V','Munson'),
        (1173,'Greg','F','Alderson'),
        (1113,'David','N','Johnson'),
        (1054,'Zheng','W','Mu'),
        (1007, 'Ovidiu', 'V', 'Cracium'),
```

```
        (1052, 'James', 'R', 'Hamilton'),
        (1053, 'Andrew', 'R', 'Hill'),
        (1056, 'Jack', 'S', 'Richins'),
        (1058, 'Michael', 'Sean', 'Ray'),
        (1064, 'Lori', 'A', 'Kane'),
        (1287, 'Ken', 'J', 'Sanchez');

INSERT INTO dbo.Employee (EmployeeID, ContactID, ManagerID, Title) VALUES
        (1, 1209, 16,'Production Technician - WC60'),
        (2, 1030, 6,'Marketing Assistant'),
        (3, 1002, 12,'Engineering Manager'),
        (4, 1290, 3,'Senior Tool Designer'),
        (5, 1009, 263,'Tool Designer'),
        (6, 1028, 109,'Marketing Manager'),
        (7, 1070, 21,'Production Supervisor - WC60'),
        (8, 1071, 185,'Production Technician - WC10'),
        (9, 1005, 3,'Design Engineer'),
        (10, 1076, 185,'Production Technician - WC10'),
        (11, 1006, 3,'Design Engineer'),
        (12, 1001, 109,'Vice President of Engineering'),
        (13, 1072, 185,'Production Technician - WC10'),
        (14, 1067, 21,'Production Supervisor - WC50'),
        (15, 1073, 185,'Production Technician - WC10'),
        (16, 1068, 21,'Production Supervisor - WC60'),
        (17, 1074, 185,'Production Technician - WC10'),
        (18, 1069, 21,'Production Supervisor - WC60'),
        (19, 1075, 185,'Production Technician - WC10'),
        (20, 1129, 173,'Production Technician - WC30'),
        (21, 1231, 148,'Production Control Manager'),
        (22, 1172, 197,'Production Technician - WC45'),
        (23, 1173, 197,'Production Technician - WC45'),
        (24, 1113, 184,'Production Technician - WC30'),
        (25, 1054, 21,'Production Supervisor - WC10'),
        (109, 1287, NULL, 'Chief Executive Officer'),
        (148, 1052, 109, 'Vice President of Production'),
        (173, 1058, 21, 'Production Supervisor - WC30'),
        (184, 1056, 21, 'Production Supervisor - WC30'),
        (185, 1053, 21, 'Production Supervisor - WC10'),
        (197, 1064, 21, 'Production Supervisor - WC45'),
        (263, 1007, 3, 'Senior Tool Designer');

INSERT INTO JobHistory(EmployeeID, EffDate, EffSeq, EmploymentStatus,
    JobTitle, Salary, ActionDesc)
VALUES
    (1000,'07-31-2008',1,'A','Intern',2000,'New Hire'),
    (1000,'05-31-2009',1,'A','Production Technician',2000,'Title Change'),
    (1000,'05-31-2009',2,'A','Production Technician',2500,'Salary Change'),
    (1000,'11-01-2009',1,'A','Production Technician',3000,'Salary Change'),
    (1200,'01-10-2009',1,'A','Design Engineer',5000,'New Hire'),
    (1200,'05-01-2009',1,'T','Design Engineer',5000,'Termination'),
```

```
(1100,'08-01-2008',1,'A','Accounts Payable Specialist I',2500,'New Hire'),
(1100,'05-01-2009',1,'A','Accounts Payable Specialist II',2500,'Title Change'),
(1100,'05-01-2009',2,'A','Accounts Payable Specialist II',3000,'Salary Change');
```

■ **Note** The CTE examples in this chapter create objects in tempdb. Keep in mind that tempdb is re-created each time the SQL service restarts, so if you restart SQL Server, you may need to re-create these objects. Alternatively, create the objects in a different database so that they will be persisted.

Now that you have the data for the example, type in and execute the code for Listing 11-3. This listing demonstrates how to write query with multiple CTEs.

Listing 11-3. A Query with Multiple CTEs

```
USE tempdb;
WITH
Emp AS(
    SELECT e.EmployeeID, e.ManagerID,e.Title AS EmpTitle,
        c.FirstName + ISNULL(' ' + c.MiddleName,'') + ' ' + c.LastName AS EmpName
    FROM dbo.Employee AS e
    INNER JOIN dbo.Contact AS c
    ON e.ContactID = c.ContactID
    ),
Mgr AS(
    SELECT e.EmployeeID AS ManagerID,e.Title AS MgrTitle,
        c.FirstName + ISNULL(' ' + c.MiddleName,'') + ' ' + c.LastName AS MgrName
    FROM dbo.Employee AS e
    INNER JOIN dbo.Contact AS c
    ON e.ContactID = c.ContactID
    )
SELECT EmployeeID, Emp.ManagerID, EmpName, EmpTitle, MgrName, MgrTitle
FROM Emp INNER JOIN Mgr ON Emp.ManagerID = Mgr.ManagerID
ORDER BY EmployeeID;
```

Figure 11-1 shows the partial results of running this code. Each CTE must have a name, followed by the keyword AS and the definition in parentheses. Separate the CTE definitions with a comma. This query, using tables in tempdb, contains a CTE for the employees, Emp, and a CTE for the managers, Mgr. Within each CTE, the Employee table joins the Contact table. By writing the query using CTEs, the outer query is very simple. You join the Mgr CTE to the Emp CTE just as if they were regular tables or views.

	EmployeeID	ManagerID	EmpName	EmpTitle	MgrName	MgrTitle
1	2	6	Kevin F Brown	Marketing Assistant	David M Bradley	Marketing Manager
2	5	263	Thierry B DHers	Tool Designer	Ovidiu V Cracium	Senior Tool Designer
3	6	109	David M Bradley	Marketing Manager	Ken J Sanchez	Chief Executive Officer
4	7	21	JoLynn M Dobney	Production Supervisor - WC60	Peter J Krebs	Production Control Manager
5	8	185	Ruth Ann Ellerbrock	Production Technician - WC10	Andrew R Hill	Production Supervisor - WC10
6	10	185	Barry K Johnson	Production Technician - WC10	Andrew R Hill	Production Supervisor - WC10
7	12	109	Terri Lee Duffy	Vice President of Engineering	Ken J Sanchez	Chief Executive Officer
8	13	185	Sidney M Higa	Production Technician - WC10	Andrew R Hill	Production Supervisor - WC10
9	14	21	Taylor R Maxwell	Production Supervisor - WC50	Peter J Krebs	Production Control Manager
10	15	185	Jeffrey L Ford	Production Technician - WC10	Andrew R Hill	Production Supervisor - WC10
11	16	21	Jo A Brown	Production Supervisor - WC60	Peter J Krebs	Production Control Manager
12	17	185	Doris M Hartwig	Production Technician - WC10	Andrew R Hill	Production Supervisor - WC10

Figure 11-1. *The partial results of multiple CTEs in one statement*

Referencing a CTE Multiple Times

Just as you can have multiple CTE definitions within one statement, you can reference a CTE multiple times within one statement. This is not possible with a derived table, which can be used only once within a statement. (See Chapter 6 for more information about derived tables.) A CTE could be used in a self-join, in a subquery, or in any valid way of using a table within a statement. Here are two syntax examples:

```
--self-join
WITH <cteName> AS (SELECT <col1>, <col2> FROM <table1>)
SELECT a.<col1>, b.<col1>
FROM <cteName> AS a
INNER JOIN <cteName> AS b ON <join condition>;


--subquery
WITH <cteName> AS (SELECT <col1>, <col2> FROM <table1>)
SELECT <col1>
FROM <cteName>
WHERE <col2> IN (SELECT <col2>
    FROM <cteName> INNER JOIN <table1> ON <join condition>);
```

Type in and execute Listing 11-4 to see some examples. The self-join produces the same results as those in the previous section. It uses tables created in Listing 11-2.

Listing 11-4. Calling a CTE Multiple Times Within a Statement

```
USE tempdb;
GO
;WITH
Employees AS(
    SELECT e.EmployeeID, e.ManagerID,e.Title,
        c.FirstName + ISNULL(' ' + c.MiddleName,'') + ' ' +  c.LastName AS EmpName
    FROM dbo.Employee AS e
```

```
    INNER JOIN dbo.Contact AS c
    ON e.ContactID = c.ContactID
    )
SELECT emp.EmployeeID, emp.ManagerID, emp.EmpName, emp.Title AS EmpTitle,
    mgr.EmpName as MgrName, mgr.Title as MgrTitle
FROM Employees AS Emp INNER JOIN Employees AS Mgr
ON Emp.ManagerID = Mgr.EmployeeID;
```

Figure 11-2 shows the partial results of running this code. The query defines just one CTE, joining Employee to Contact. The outer query calls the CTE twice, once with the alias Emp and once with the alias Mgr.

	EmployeeID	ManagerID	EmpName	EmpTitle	MgrName	MgrTitle
1	2	6	Kevin F Brown	Marketing Assistant	David M Bradley	Marketing Manager
2	5	263	Thierry B DHers	Tool Designer	Ovidiu V Cracium	Senior Tool Designer
3	6	109	David M Bradley	Marketing Manager	Ken J Sanchez	Chief Executive Officer
4	7	21	JoLynn M Dobney	Production Supervisor - WC60	Peter J Krebs	Production Control Manager
5	8	185	Ruth Ann Ellerbrock	Production Technician - WC10	Andrew R Hill	Production Supervisor - WC10
6	10	185	Barry K Johnson	Production Technician - WC10	Andrew R Hill	Production Supervisor - WC10
7	12	109	Terri Lee Duffy	Vice President of Engineering	Ken J Sanchez	Chief Executive Officer
8	13	185	Sidney M Higa	Production Technician - WC10	Andrew R Hill	Production Supervisor - WC10

Figure 11-2. *The partial results of using a CTE twice in one statement*

Joining a CTE to Another CTE

Another very interesting feature of CTEs is the ability to call one CTE from another CTE definition. This is not recursion, which you will learn about in the "Writing a Recursive Query" section. Calling one CTE from within another CTE definition allows you to base one query on a previous query. Here is a syntax example:

```
WITH <cteName1> AS (SELECT <col1>, <col2> FROM <table1>),
     <cteName2> AS (SELECT <col1>, <col2>, <col3>
         FROM <table3> INNER JOIN <cteName1> ON <join condition>)
SELECT <col1>, <col2>, <col3> FROM <cteName2>
```

The order in which the CTE definitions appear is very important. You can't call a CTE before it is defined. Type in and execute the code in Listing 11-5 to learn more.

Listing 11-5. Joining a CTE to Another CTE

```
USE tempdb;
GO

--1
DECLARE @Date DATE = '05-02-2009';

--2
WITH EffectiveDate AS (
        SELECT MAX(EffDate) AS MaxDate, EmployeeID
        FROM dbo.JobHistory
```

```
        WHERE EffDate <= @Date
        GROUP BY EmployeeID
    ),
    EffectiveSeq AS (
        SELECT MAX(EffSeq) AS MaxSeq, j.EmployeeID, MaxDate
        FROM dbo.JobHistory AS j
        INNER JOIN EffectiveDate AS d
            ON j.EffDate = d.MaxDate AND j.EmployeeID = d.EmployeeID
        GROUP BY j.EmployeeID, MaxDate)
SELECT j.EmployeeID, EmploymentStatus, JobTitle, Salary
FROM dbo.JobHistory AS j
INNER JOIN EffectiveSeq AS e ON j.EmployeeID = e.EmployeeID
    AND j.EffDate = e.MaxDate AND j.EffSeq = e.MaxSeq;
```

Figure 11-3 shows the results of running this code. I based this example on a system I worked with for several years. Many of the tables in this system contain history information with an effective date and an effective sequence. The system adds one row to these tables for each change to the employee's data. For a particular effective date, the system can add more than one row along with an incrementing effective sequence. To display information valid on a particular date, you first have to figure out the latest effective date before the date in mind and then figure out the effective sequence for that date. At first glance, you might think that just determining the maximum date and maximum sequence in one aggregate query should work. This doesn't work because the maximum sequence in the table for an employee may not be valid for a particular date. For example, the employee may have four changes and, therefore, four rows for an earlier date and only one row for the latest date.

	EmployeeID	Employment Status	Job Title	Salary
1	1000	A	Intern	2000.00
2	1100	A	Accounts Payable Specialist II	3000.00
3	1200	T	Design Engineer	5000.00

Figure 11-3. *The results of calling one CTE from another CTE definition*

The JobHistory table was created in tempdb including a primary key composed of EmployeeID, EffDate, and EffSeq in Listing 11-2. Notice that the insert statement inserts one row for each change even if the changes happen on the same date. Statement 1 of Listing 11-5 declares and initializes a variable, @Date, which will be used in the WHERE clause in statement 2. You can change the value of this variable to validate the results for different dates.

Statement 2 contains the SELECT statement. The first CTE, EffectiveDate, just determines the maximum EffDate from the JobHistory table for each employee that is valid for the @Date value. The second CTE, EffectiveSeq, joins the JobHistory table to the EffectiveDate CTE to find the maximum EffSeq for each employee for the date determined in the previous CTE, EffectiveDate. Finally, the outer query joins the JobHistory table on the EffectiveSeq CTE to display the valid data for each employee on the date stored in @Date.

Writing a Recursive Query

Recursive code, in any programming language, is code that calls itself. Programmers use this technique to follow paths in tree or directory structures, for example, an organization chart or family tree. When following the paths in these structures, the code must start at the root, follow each path to the end, and back up again to the next path repeatedly. In T-SQL, you can use the same technique in a CTE. Recursion, while somewhat fun to write for developers, is rarely needed. Before you decide to try recursion, make sure the problem you are trying to solve is actually a good fit. Let's use the same Employee table created in tempdb at the beginning of the chapter to demonstrate how to use a recursive CTE. The self-join found in that table represents a hierarchical structure, the organizational chart. To view the entire hierarchy, you must start at the root, the CEO of the company, and follow every possible manager-employee path down to the lowest person. Here is the syntax for writing a recursive CTE:

```
WITH <cteName> (<col1>, <col2>, <col3>, level)
AS
(
    --Anchor member
    SELECT <primaryKey>,<foreignKey>,<col3>, 0 AS level
    FROM <table1>
    WHERE <foreignKey> = <startingValue>
    UNION ALL
    --Recursive member
    SELECT a.<primaryKey>,a.<foreignKey>,a.<col3>, b.level + 1
    FROM <table1> AS a
    INNER JOIN <cteName> AS b
        ON a.<foreignKey>  = b.<primaryKey>
)
SELECT <col1>,<col2>,<col3>,level
FROM <cteName> [OPTION (MAXRECURSION <number>)]
```

To write the recursive CTE, you must have an anchor member, which is a statement that returns the top of your intended results. This is like the root of the directory. Following the anchor member, you will write the recursive member. The recursive member actually joins the CTE that contains it to the same table used in the anchor member. The results of the anchor member and the recursive member join in a UNION ALL query. Type in and execute the code in Listing 11-6 to see how this works.

Listing 11-6. A Recursive CTE

```
;WITH OrgChart (EmployeeID, ManagerID, Title, Level,Node)
    AS (SELECT EmployeeID, ManagerID, Title, 0,
            CONVERT(VARCHAR(30),'/') AS Node
        FROM dbo.Employee
        WHERE ManagerID IS NULL
        UNION ALL
        SELECT Emp.EmployeeID, Emp.ManagerID, Emp.Title, OrgChart.Level + 1,
            CONVERT(VARCHAR(30), OrgChart.Node +
            CONVERT(VARCHAR(30), Emp.ManagerID) + '/')
        FROM dbo.Employee AS Emp
        INNER JOIN OrgChart  ON Emp.ManagerID = OrgChart.EmployeeID
    )
SELECT EmployeeID, ManagerID, SPACE(Level * 3) + Title AS Title, Level, Node
FROM OrgChart
ORDER BY Node;

--2 Incorrectly written Recursive CTE
;WITH OrgChart (EmployeeID, ManagerID, Title, Level,Node)
    AS (SELECT EmployeeID, ManagerID, Title, 0,
            CONVERT(VARCHAR(30),'/') AS Node
        FROM dbo.Employee
        WHERE ManagerID IS NOT NULL
```

```
        UNION ALL
        SELECT Emp.EmployeeID, Emp.ManagerID,Emp.Title, OrgChart.Level + 1,
            CONVERT(VARCHAR(30),OrgChart.Node +
                CONVERT(VARCHAR,Emp.ManagerID) + '/')
        FROM dbo.Employee AS Emp
        INNER JOIN OrgChart  ON Emp.EmployeeID = OrgChart.EmployeeID
    )
SELECT EmployeeID, ManagerID, SPACE(Level * 3) + Title AS Title, Level, Node
FROM OrgChart
ORDER BY Node OPTION (MAXRECURSION 10);
```

Figure 11-4 shows the partial results of query 1. Query 2 will generate an error message. Query 1 is a correctly written recursive query. The anchor member selects the EmployeeID, ManagerID, and Title from the Employee table for the CEO. The CEO is the only employee with a NULL ManagerID. The level is zero. The node column, added to help sorting, is just a slash. To get this to work, the query uses the CONVERT function to change the data type of the slash to a VARCHAR(30) because the data types in the columns of the anchor member and recursive member must match exactly. The recursive member joins Employee to the CTE, OrgChart. The query is recursive because the CTE is used inside its own definition. The regular columns in the recursive member come from the table, and the level is one plus the value of the level returned from the CTE. To sort in a meaningful way, the Node shows the ManagerID values used to get to the current employee surrounded with slashes.

	EmployeeID	ManagerID	Title	Level	Node
1	109	NULL	Chief Executive Officer	0	/
2	6	109	Marketing Manager	1	/109/
3	12	109	Vice President of Engineering	1	/109/
4	148	109	Vice President of Production	1	/109/
5	3	12	Engineering Manager	2	/109/12/
6	4	3	Senior Tool Designer	3	/109/12/3/
7	9	3	Design Engineer	3	/109/12/3/
8	11	3	Design Engineer	3	/109/12/3/
9	263	3	Senior Tool Designer	3	/109/12/3/
10	5	263	Tool Designer	4	/109/12/3/263/
11	21	148	Production Control Manager	2	/109/148/
12	7	21	Production Supervisor - WC60	3	/109/148/21/

Figure 11-4. The partial results of a recursive query

The query runs the recursive member repeatedly until all possible paths are selected; that is, until the recursive member no longer returns results.

Query 2 is written incorrectly. The JOIN condition joining the anchor to the recursive member is incorrect. An incorrectly written recursive query could run in an endless loop. The recursive member will run only 100 times by default unless you specify the MAXRECURSION option to limit how many times the query will run. If the MAXRECURSION option is set to 0, it is possible to create a query that will run until you stop it. If the query will run more times than the MAXRECURSION option, an error message condition will result.

Data Manipulation with CTEs

You learned how to insert, update, and delete data in Chapter 10. You can use CTEs when modifying data, but the syntax may not be obvious at first. You perform the data modifications in the outer query whenever a CTE is used. It may be surprising, but you can also update the CTE itself. Listing 11-7 demonstrates how to use CTEs to perform inserts, updates, and deletes.

Listing 11-7. Using CTEs to Manipulate Data

```
--1
USE tempdb;
GO
CREATE TABLE dbo.CTEExample(CustomerID INT, FirstName NVARCHAR(50),
    LastName NVARCHAR(50), Sales Money);

--2
;WITH Cust AS(
        SELECT CustomerID, FirstName, LastName
        FROM AdventureWorks.Sales.Customer AS C
        JOIN AdventureWorks.Person.Person AS P ON C.CustomerID = P.BusinessEntityID
)
INSERT INTO dbo.CTEExample(CustomerID, FirstName, LastName)
SELECT CustomerID, FirstName, LastName
FROM Cust;

--3
;WITH Totals AS (
        SELECT CustomerID, SUM(TotalDue) AS CustTotal
        FROM AdventureWorks.Sales.SalesOrderHeader
        GROUP BY CustomerID)
UPDATE C SET Sales = CustTotal
FROM CTEExample AS C
INNER JOIN Totals ON C.CustomerID = Totals.CustomerID;

--4
;WITH Cust AS(
        SELECT CustomerID, Sales
        FROM CTEExample)
DELETE Cust
WHERE Sales < 10000;
```

Statement 1 creates a table for the example. The table contains the CustomerID, FirstName, LastName, and a Sales column. Statement 2 inserts rows from an AdventureWorks query within the CTE supplying the CustomerID and names. Usually when inserting data from a query, the word INSERT is first. When using a CTE, the statement begins with the CTE and then it is used in the outer query as any other table.

Statement 3 updates the table with an aggregate expression, SUM(TotalDue). It is important to note that it is not possible to update directly with an aggregate, so you must come up with some way to isolate the aggregate query. This is just one way to do it. You could create a temporary work table or use a derived table instead.

Statement 4 is very interesting. Not only is it using a CTE to delete some rows, it is actually deleting rows from the CTE itself.

Isolating Aggregate Query Logic

Several techniques exist that allow you to separate an aggregate query from the rest of the statement. Sometimes this is necessary because the grouping levels and the columns that must be displayed are not compatible. For example, you may need to show details along with summary expressions. This section will demonstrate these techniques.

Correlated Subqueries in the SELECT list

You may see correlated subqueries used within the SELECT list. I really don't recommend this technique because if the query contains more than one correlated subquery, performance deteriorates quickly. You will learn about better options to use later in this section. Here is the syntax for the SELECT list correlated subquery:

```
SELECT <select list>,
    (SELECT <aggregate function>(<col1>)
     FROM <table2> WHERE <col2> = <table1>.<col3>) AS <alias name>
FROM <table1>
```

The subquery must produce only one row for each row of the outer query, and only one expression may be returned from the subquery. The subquery executes once for each row of the outer query. Listing 11-8 shows two examples of this query type.

Listing 11-8. Using a Correlated Subquery in the SELECT List

```
USE AdventureWorks;
GO
SELECT CustomerID, C.StoreID, C.AccountNumber,
    (SELECT COUNT(*)
     FROM Sales.SalesOrderHeader AS SOH
     WHERE SOH.CustomerID = C.CustomerID) AS CountOfSales
FROM Sales.Customer AS C
ORDER BY CountOfSales DESC;

--2
SELECT CustomerID, C.StoreID, C.AccountNumber,
    (SELECT COUNT(*) AS CountOfSales
     FROM Sales.SalesOrderHeader AS SOH
     WHERE SOH.CustomerID = C.CustomerID) AS CountOfSales,
    (SELECT SUM(TotalDue)
     FROM Sales.SalesOrderHeader AS SOH
     WHERE SOH.CustomerID = C.CustomerID) AS SumOfTotalDue,
    (SELECT AVG(TotalDue)
     FROM Sales.SalesOrderHeader AS SOH
     WHERE SOH.CustomerID = C.CustomerID) AS AvgOfTotalDue
FROM Sales.Customer AS C
ORDER BY CountOfSales DESC;
```

You can see the partial results of running this code in Figure 11-5. Query 1 demonstrates how the correlated subquery returns one value per row. Notice the WHERE clause in the subquery. The CustomerID column in the subquery must be equal to the CustomerID in the outer query. The alias for the column must be added right after the subquery definition, not the column definition.

	CustomerID	StoreID	AccountNumber	CountOfSales
1	11091	NULL	AW00011091	28
2	11176	NULL	AW00011176	28
3	11185	NULL	AW00011185	27
4	11200	NULL	AW00011200	27

	CustomerID	StoreID	AccountNumber	CountOfSales	SumOfTotalDue	AvgOfTotalDue
1	11091	NULL	AW00011091	28	1314.2103	46.936
2	11176	NULL	AW00011176	28	1458.6118	52.0932
3	11185	NULL	AW00011185	27	1786.0233	66.149
4	11200	NULL	AW00011200	27	1617.0356	59.8902

Figure 11-5. *Using a correlated subquery in the SELECT list*

Normally, when working with the same column name from two tables, both must be qualified. Within the subquery, if the column is not qualified, the column is assumed to be from the table within the subquery. As a best practice, always qualify both tables in a correlated subquery.

Notice that query 2 contains three correlated subqueries because three values are required. Although one correlated subquery doesn't usually cause a problem, performance quickly deteriorates as additional correlated subqueries are added to the query. Luckily, other techniques exist to get the same results with better performance.

Using Derived Tables

In Chapter 6 you learned about derived tables. You can use derived tables to isolate the aggregate query from the rest of the query. Here is the syntax:

```
SELECT <col1>,<col4>,<col3> FROM <table1> AS a
INNER JOIN
    (SELECT <aggregate function>(<col2>) AS <col4>,<col3>
     FROM <table2> GROUP BY <col3>) AS <ALIAS> ON a.<col1> = b.<col3>
```

Listing 11-9 shows how to use this technique. Type in and execute the code.

Listing 11-9. *Using a Derived Table*

```
SELECT c.CustomerID, c.StoreID, c.AccountNumber, s.CountOfSales,
    s.SumOfTotalDue, s.AvgOfTotalDue
FROM Sales.Customer AS c INNER JOIN
    (SELECT CustomerID, COUNT(*) AS CountOfSales,
        SUM(TotalDue) AS SumOfTotalDue,
        AVG(TotalDue) AS AvgOfTotalDue
     FROM Sales.SalesOrderHeader
     GROUP BY CustomerID) AS s
ON c.CustomerID = s.CustomerID;
```

You can see the partial results of running this code in Figure 11-6. This query has much better performance than the second query in Listing 11-8, but it produces the same results. Remember that any column required in the outer query must be listed in the derived table. You must also supply an alias for the derived table.

	CustomerID	StoreID	AccountNumber	CountOfSales	SumOfTotalDue	AvgOfTotalDue
1	11000	NULL	AW00011000	3	9115.1341	3038.378
2	11001	NULL	AW00011001	3	7054.1875	2351.3958
3	11002	NULL	AW00011002	3	8966.0143	2988.6714
4	11003	NULL	AW00011003	3	8993.9155	2997.9718
5	11004	NULL	AW00011004	3	9056.5911	3018.8637
6	11005	NULL	AW00011005	3	8974.0698	2991.3566
7	11006	NULL	AW00011006	3	8971.5283	2990.5094
8	11007	NULL	AW00011007	3	9073.1551	3024.385
9	11008	NULL	AW00011008	3	8957.4726	2985.8242
10	11009	NULL	AW00011009	3	8940.9197	2980.3065

Figure 11-6. *The partial results of using a derived table*

Besides the increase in performance, the derived table may return more than one row for each row of the outer query in some situations, and multiple aggregates may be included.

Common Table Expressions

A CTE also allows you to isolate the aggregate query from the rest of the statement. The CTE is not stored as an object; it just makes the data available during the query. You can think of it as a temporary view. Here is the syntax:

```
WITH <cteName> AS (SELECT <aggregate function>(<col2>) AS <col4>, <col3>
    FROM <table2> GROUP BY <col3>)
SELECT <col1>,<col4>,<col3>
FROM <table1> INNER JOIN b ON <cteName>.<col1> = <table1>.<col3>;
```

Type in and execute the code in Listing 11-10 to learn how to use a CTE with an aggregate query.

Listing 11-10. Using a Common Table Expression

```
;WITH s AS
    (SELECT CustomerID, COUNT(*) AS CountOfSales,
        SUM(TotalDue) AS SumOfTotalDue,
        AVG(TotalDue) AS AvgOfTotalDue
    FROM Sales.SalesOrderHeader
    GROUP BY CustomerID)
SELECT c.CustomerID, c.StoreID, c.AccountNumber, s.CountOfSales,
    s.SumOfTotalDue, s.AvgOfTotalDue
FROM Sales.Customer AS c INNER JOIN s
ON c.CustomerID = s.CustomerID;
```

Figure 11-7 displays the results of running this code. This query looks a lot like the one in Listing 11-9. The only difference is that this query uses a CTE instead of a derived table. At this point, there is no real advantage to the CTE over the derived table, but it is easier to read, in my opinion.

	CustomerID	StoreID	AccountNumber	CountOfSales	SumOfTotalDue	AvgOfTotalDue
1	11000	NULL	AW00011000	3	9115.1341	3038.378
2	11001	NULL	AW00011001	3	7054.1875	2351.3958
3	11002	NULL	AW00011002	3	8966.0143	2988.6714
4	11003	NULL	AW00011003	3	8993.9155	2997.9718
5	11004	NULL	AW00011004	3	9056.5911	3018.8637
6	11005	NULL	AW00011005	3	8974.0698	2991.3566
7	11006	NULL	AW00011006	3	8971.5283	2990.5094
8	11007	NULL	AW00011007	3	9073.1551	3024.385
9	11008	NULL	AW00011008	3	8957.4726	2985.8242
10	11009	NULL	AW00011009	3	8940.9197	2980.3065

Figure 11-7. *Using a common table expression*

Using *CROSS APPLY* and *OUTER APPLY*

The CROSS APPLY and OUTER APPLY techniques were originally intended to enable joining to table-valued functions (see Chapter 14). They can, however, be used similarly to join to a derived table. The function or subquery on the right will be called once for every row from the table on the left. Use OUTER APPLY like a LEFT OUTER JOIN to return a row from the left even if there is nothing returned from the right. Listing 11-11 shows an example.

Listing 11-11. Using CROSS APPLY

```
--1
SELECT SOH.CustomerID, SOH.OrderDate, SOH.TotalDue, CRT.RunningTotal
FROM Sales.SalesOrderHeader AS SOH
CROSS APPLY(
    SELECT SUM(TotalDue) AS RunningTotal
        FROM Sales.SalesOrderHeader RT
        WHERE RT.CustomerID = SOH.CustomerID
            AND RT.SalesOrderID <= SOH.SalesOrderID) AS CRT
ORDER BY SOH.CustomerID, SOH.SalesOrderID;

--2
SELECT Prd.ProductID, S.SalesOrderID
FROM Production.Product AS Prd
OUTER APPLY (
  SELECT TOP(2) SalesOrderID
  FROM Sales.SalesOrderDetail AS SOD
  WHERE SOD.ProductID = Prd.ProductID
  ORDER BY SalesOrderID) AS S
 ORDER BY Prd.ProductID;
```

Query 1 returns a list of customers and their orders along with a running total (see Figure 11-8). The inner query joins to the outer query on the CustomerID and the OrderID where the OrderID is less than or equal to the OrderID from the outer query. The inner query will run once for each row of the outer query. As you may guess, this technique generally does not perform well for large tables. See Chapter 8 to see a much better way to get the same results if you are using SQL Server 2012 or later.

	CustomerID	OrderDate	TotalDue	RunningTotal
1	11000	2005-07-22 00:00:00.000	3756.989	3756.989
2	11000	2007-07-22 00:00:00.000	2587.8769	6344.8659
3	11000	2007-11-04 00:00:00.000	2770.2682	9115.1341
4	11001	2005-07-18 00:00:00.000	3729.364	3729.364

	ProductID	SalesOrderID
210	680	NULL
211	706	NULL
212	707	43665
213	707	43668
214	708	43661
215	708	43668
216	709	43659
217	709	43665

Figure 11-8. *The partial results of CROSS APPLY and OUTER APPLY*

Query 2 returns a list of the products along with the OrderID of the first two orders placed, if any, for that product. Because it uses OUTER APPLY, all products are returned even if no order has been placed. Figure 11-8 shows the partial results of running this code.

The *OUTPUT* Clause

You learned how to manipulate data in Chapter 10. The OUTPUT clause allows you to see or even save the modified values when you perform a data manipulation statement. The interesting thing about OUTPUT is that data manipulation statements don't normally return data except for a message stating the number of rows affected. By using OUTPUT, you can retrieve a result set of the data in the same statement that updates the data. You can see the result set in the query window results or return the result set to a client application.

Using *OUTPUT* to View Data

When using OUTPUT, you can view the data using the special tables DELETED and INSERTED. Triggers also use DELETED and INSERTED tables. You may wonder why there is not an UPDATED table. Instead of an UPDATED table, you will find the old values in the DELETED table and the new values in the INSERTED table. Here are the syntax examples for using the OUTPUT clause for viewing changes when running data manipulation statements:

```
--Update style 1
UPDATE a SET <col1> = <value>
OUTPUT deleted.<col1>,inserted.<col1>
FROM <table1> AS a
```

```
--Update style 2
UPDATE <table1> SET <col1> = <value>
OUTPUT deleted.<col1>, inserted.<col1>
WHERE <criteria>

--Insert style 1
INSERT [INTO] <table1> (<col1>,<col2>)
OUTPUT inserted.<col1>, inserted.<col2>
SELECT <col1>, <col2>
FROM <table2>

--Insert style 2
INSERT [INTO] <table1> (<col1>,<col2>)
OUTPUT inserted.<col1>, inserted.<col2>
VALUES (<value1>,<value2>)

--Delete style 1
DELETE [FROM] <table1>
OUTPUT deleted.<col1>, deleted.<col2>
WHERE <criteria>

--DELETE style 2
DELETE [FROM] a
OUTPUT deleted.<col1>, deleted.<col2>
FROM <table1> AS a
```

Probably the trickiest thing about using OUTPUT is figuring out where in the statement to include it. Type in and execute the code in Listing 11-12 to learn more about OUTPUT.

Listing 11-12. Viewing the Manipulated Data with OUTPUT

```
--1
USE tempdb;
GO
IF OBJECT_ID('dbo.Customers') IS NOT NULL BEGIN
    DROP TABLE dbo.Customers;
END;

CREATE TABLE dbo.Customers (CustomerID INT NOT NULL PRIMARY KEY,
    Name VARCHAR(150),PersonID INT NOT NULL);
GO

--2
INSERT INTO dbo.Customers(CustomerID,Name,PersonID)
OUTPUT inserted.CustomerID,inserted.Name
SELECT c.CustomerID, p.FirstName + ' ' + p.LastName, c.PersonID
FROM AdventureWorks.Sales.Customer AS c
INNER JOIN AdventureWorks.Person.Person AS p
ON c.PersonID = p.BusinessEntityID;
```

```
--3
UPDATE c SET Name = p.FirstName +
    ISNULL(' ' + p.MiddleName,'') + ' ' + p.LastName
OUTPUT deleted.CustomerID,deleted.Name AS OldName, inserted.Name AS NewName
FROM dbo.Customers AS c
INNER JOIN AdventureWorks.Person.Person AS p on c.PersonID = p.BusinessEntityID;

--4
DELETE FROM dbo.Customers
OUTPUT deleted.CustomerID, deleted.Name, deleted.PersonID
WHERE CustomerID = 11000;
```

Figure 11-9 shows the partial results of running this code. Unfortunately, for the demo, you can't add an ORDER BY clause to OUTPUT, and the INSERT statement, on my machine, returns the rows in a different order than the UPDATE statement. Code section 1 creates the dbo.Customers table in tempdb. Statement 2 inserts all the rows when joining the Sales.Customer table to the Person.Person table in the AdventureWorks database. You may have to adjust the name of the database if yours has the version number appended. The OUTPUT clause, located right after the INSERT clause, returns the CustomerID and Name. Statement 3 modifies the value in the Name column by including the MiddleName in the expression. The DELETED table displays the Name column data before the update. The INSERTED table displays the Name column after the update. The UPDATE clause includes aliases to differentiate the values. Statement 4 deletes one row from the table. The OUTPUT clause displays the deleted data.

	CustomerID	Name
1	11000	Jon Yang
2	11001	Eugene Huang
3	11002	Ruben Torres
4	11003	Christy Zhu

	CustomerID	OldName	NewName
1	29485	Catherine Abel	Catherine R. Abel
2	29486	Kim Abercrombie	Kim Abercrombie
3	29487	Humberto Acevedo	Humberto Acevedo
4	29484	Gustavo Achong	Gustavo Achong

	CustomerID	Name	PersonID
1	11000	Jon V Yang	13531

Figure 11-9. The partial results of viewing the manipulated data with OUTPUT

Saving *OUTPUT* Data to a Table

Instead of displaying or returning the rows from the OUTPUT clause, you might need to save the information in another table. For example, you may need to populate a history table or save the changes for further processing. Here is a syntax example showing how to use INTO along with OUTPUT:

```
INSERT [INTO] <table1> (<col1>, <col2>)
OUTPUT inserted.<col1>, inserted.<col2>
    INTO <table2>
SELECT <col3>,<col4>
FROM <table3>
```

Type in and execute the code in Listing 11-13 to learn more.

Listing 11-13. Saving the Results of OUTPUT

```
Use tempdb;
GO
--1
IF OBJECT_ID('dbo.Customers') IS NOT NULL BEGIN
    DROP TABLE dbo.Customers;
END;

IF OBJECT_ID('dbo.CustomerHistory') IS NOT NULL BEGIN
    DROP TABLE dbo.CustomerHistory;
END;

CREATE TABLE dbo.Customers (CustomerID INT NOT NULL PRIMARY KEY,
    Name VARCHAR(150),PersonID INT NOT NULL);

CREATE TABLE dbo.CustomerHistory(CustomerID INT NOT NULL PRIMARY KEY,
    OldName VARCHAR(150), NewName VARCHAR(150),
    ChangeDate DATETIME);
GO

--2
INSERT INTO dbo.Customers(CustomerID, Name, PersonID)
SELECT c.CustomerID, p.FirstName + ' ' + p.LastName,PersonID
FROM AdventureWorks.Sales.Customer AS c
INNER JOIN AdventureWorks.Person.Person AS p
ON c.PersonID = p.BusinessEntityID;

--3
UPDATE c SET Name = p.FirstName +
    ISNULL(' ' + p.MiddleName,'') + ' ' + p.LastName
OUTPUT deleted.CustomerID,deleted.Name, inserted.Name, GETDATE()
INTO dbo.CustomerHistory
FROM dbo.Customers AS c
INNER JOIN AdventureWorks.Person.Person AS p on c.PersonID = p.BusinessEntityID;

--4
SELECT CustomerID, OldName, NewName,ChangeDate
FROM dbo.CustomerHistory
ORDER BY CustomerID;
```

Figure 11-10 shows the partial results of running this code. Code section 1 creates the two tables used in this example in tempdb. Statement 2 inserts data from AdventureWorks into the new Customer table. Statement 3 updates the Name column for all of the rows. By including OUTPUT INTO, the CustomerID along with the previous and current Name values are saved into the CustomerHistory table. The statement also populates the ChangeDate column by using the GETDATE function. Statement 4 returns the rows that have been saved.

	CustomerID	OldName	NewName	ChangeDate
1	11000	Jon Yang	Jon V Yang	2014-04-24 18:22:10.433
2	11001	Eugene Huang	Eugene L Huang	2014-04-24 18:22:10.433
3	11002	Ruben Torres	Ruben Torres	2014-04-24 18:22:10.433
4	11003	Christy Zhu	Christy Zhu	2014-04-24 18:22:10.433
5	11004	Elizabeth Johnson	Elizabeth Johnson	2014-04-24 18:22:10.433
6	11005	Julio Ruiz	Julio Ruiz	2014-04-24 18:22:10.433
7	11006	Janet Alvarez	Janet G Alvarez	2014-04-24 18:22:10.433
8	11007	Marco Mehta	Marco Mehta	2014-04-24 18:22:10.433
9	11008	Rob Verhoff	Rob Verhoff	2014-04-24 18:22:10.433
10	11009	Shannon Carlson	Shannon C Carlson	2014-04-24 18:22:10.433

Figure 11-10. The partial results of saving the OUTPUT data into a table

The *MERGE* Statement

The MERGE statement, also known as *upsert*, allows you to bundle INSERT, UPDATE, and DELETE operations into a single statement to perform complex operations such as synchronizing the contents of one table with another. For example, you would normally need to perform at least one UPDATE, one INSERT, and one DELETE statement to keep the data in one table up to date with the data from another table. By using MERGE, you can perform the same work more efficiently (assuming that the tables have the proper indexes in place) with just one statement. The drawback is that MERGE is more difficult to understand and write than the three individual statements. One potential use for MERGE—where taking the time to write the MERGE statements really pays off—is loading data warehouses and data marts. Here is the syntax for a simple MERGE statement:

```
MERGE <target table>
USING <source table name>|<query> AS alias [(column names)]
ON (<join criteria>)
WHEN MATCHED [AND <other criteria>]
THEN UPDATE SET <col> = alias.<value>
WHEN NOT MATCHED BY TARGET [AND <other criteria>]
THEN INSERT (<column list>) VALUES (<values>) -- row is inserted into target
WHEN NOT MATCHED BY SOURCE [AND <other criteria>]
THEN DELETE -- row is deleted from target
[OUTPUT $action, DELETED.*, INSERTED.*];
```

At first glance, the syntax may seem overwhelming. Basically, it defines an action to perform if a row from the source table matches the target table (WHEN MATCHED), an action to perform if a row is missing in the target table (WHEN NOT MATCHED BY TARGET), and an action to perform if an extra row is in the target table (WHEN NOT MATCHED BY SOURCE). The actions to perform on the target table can be anything you need to do. For example, if the source table is missing a row that appears in the target table (WHEN NOT MATCHED BY SOURCE), you don't have to delete the target row. You could, in fact, leave out that part of the statement or perform another action. In addition to the join criteria, you can also specify any other criteria in each match specification. You can include an optional OUTPUT clause along with the $action option. The $action option shows you which action is performed on each row. Include the DELETED and INSERTED tables in the OUTPUT clause to see the before and after values. The MERGE statement must end with a semicolon. Type in and execute the code in Listing 11-14 to learn how to use MERGE.

Listing 11-14. Using the MERGE Statement

```
USE tempdb;
GO
--1
IF OBJECT_ID('dbo.CustomerSource') IS NOT NULL BEGIN
    DROP TABLE dbo.CustomerSource;
END;
IF OBJECT_ID('dbo.CustomerTarget') IS NOT NULL BEGIN
    DROP TABLE dbo.CustomerTarget;
END;

CREATE TABLE dbo.CustomerSource (CustomerID INT NOT NULL PRIMARY KEY,
    Name VARCHAR(150) NOT NULL, PersonID INT NOT NULL);
CREATE TABLE dbo.CustomerTarget (CustomerID INT NOT NULL PRIMARY KEY,
    Name VARCHAR(150) NOT NULL, PersonID INT NOT NULL);

--2
INSERT INTO dbo.CustomerSource(CustomerID,Name,PersonID)
SELECT CustomerID,
    p.FirstName + ISNULL(' ' + p.MiddleName,'') + ' ' + p.LastName,
    c.PersonID
FROM AdventureWorks.Sales.Customer AS c
INNER JOIN AdventureWorks.Person.Person AS p ON c.PersonID = p.BusinessEntityID
WHERE c.CustomerID IN (29485,29486,29487,20075);

--3
INSERT INTO dbo.CustomerTarget(CustomerID,Name,PersonID)
SELECT c.CustomerID, p.FirstName  + ' ' + p.LastName, PersonID
FROM AdventureWorks.Sales.Customer AS c
INNER JOIN AdventureWorks.Person.Person AS p ON c.PersonID = p.BusinessEntityID
WHERE c.CustomerID IN (29485,29486,21139);

--4
SELECT CustomerID, Name, PersonID
FROM dbo.CustomerSource
ORDER BY CustomerID;

--5
SELECT CustomerID, Name, PersonID
FROM dbo.CustomerTarget
ORDER BY CustomerID;

--6
MERGE dbo.CustomerTarget AS t
USING dbo.CustomerSource AS s
```

```
ON (s.CustomerID = t.CustomerID)
WHEN MATCHED AND s.Name <> t.Name
THEN UPDATE SET Name = s.Name
WHEN NOT MATCHED BY TARGET
THEN INSERT (CustomerID, Name, PersonID) VALUES (CustomerID, Name, PersonID)
WHEN NOT MATCHED BY SOURCE
THEN DELETE
OUTPUT $action, DELETED.*, INSERTED.*;--semi-colon is required

--7
SELECT CustomerID, Name, PersonID
FROM dbo.CustomerTarget
ORDER BY CustomerID;
```

Figure 11-11 shows the results of running this code. Code section 1 creates the dbo.CustomerSource and dbo.CustomerTarget tables in tempdb. They have the same column names, but this is not a requirement. Statement 2 populates the dbo.CustomerSource table with four rows. It creates the Name column using the FirstName, MiddleName, and LastName columns. Statement 3 populates the dbo.CustomerTarget table with three rows. Two of the rows contain the same customers as the dbo.CustomerSource table. Query 4 displays the data from dbo.CustomerSource, and query 5 displays the data from dbo.CustomerTarget.

	CustomerID	Name	PersonID
1	20075	Aaron A Allen	17561
2	29485	Catherine R. Abel	293
3	29486	Kim Abercrombie	295
4	29487	Humberto Acevedo	297

	CustomerID	Name	PersonID
1	21139	Alex Adams	16724
2	29485	Catherine Abel	293
3	29486	Kim Abercrombie	295

	$action	CustomerID	Name	PersonID	CustomerID	Name	PersonID
1	INSERT	NULL	NULL	NULL	20075	Aaron A Allen	17561
2	DELETE	21139	Alex Adams	16724	NULL	NULL	NULL
3	UPDATE	29485	Catherine Abel	293	29485	Catherine R. Abel	293
4	INSERT	NULL	NULL	NULL	29487	Humberto Acevedo	297

	CustomerID	Name	PersonID
1	20075	Aaron A Allen	17561
2	29485	Catherine R. Abel	293
3	29486	Kim Abercrombie	295
4	29487	Humberto Aceve...	297

Figure 11-11. The results of using MERGE

262

Statement 6 synchronizes dbo.CustomerTarget with dbo.CustomerSource, correcting the Name column, inserting missing rows, and deleting extra rows by using the MERGE command. The statement will update dob.CustomerTarget with data from dbo.CustomerSource. The rows are matched on CustomerID. The WHEN MATCHED clause specifies what to do when there is a match between the two tables. If the Name values do not match, then change the value to the value of the Name from the source. The WHEN NOT MATCHED BY TARGET clause specifies what to do when there is a row in the source that doesn't match the target. In this case, a row will be inserted into the target. Finally, the WHEN NOT MATCHED BY SOURCE clause specifies what to do when a row in the target doesn't have a match in the source. In this case, the row is removed from the target table. Because the query includes the OUTPUT clause, you can see the action performed on each row. Query 7 displays the dbo.CustomerTarget with the changes. The target table now matches the source table.

GROUPING SETS

You learned all about aggregate queries in Chapter 7. Another option, GROUPING SETS, when added to an aggregate query, allows you to combine different grouping levels within one statement. This is equivalent to combining multiple aggregate queries with UNION. For example, suppose you want the data summarized by one column combined with the data summarized by a different column. Just like MERGE, this feature is very valuable for loading data warehouses and data marts. When using GROUPING SETS instead of UNION, you can see increased performance, especially when the query includes a WHERE clause and the number of columns specified in the GROUPING SETS clause increases. Here is the syntax:

```
SELECT <col1>,<col2>,<aggregate function>(<col3>)
FROM <table1>
WHERE <criteria>
GROUP BY GROUPING SETS (<col1>,<col2>)
```

Listing 11-15 compares the equivalent UNION query to a query using GROUPING SETS. Type in and execute the code to learn more.

Listing 11-15. Using GROUPING SETS

```
USE AdventureWorks;
GO
--1
SELECT NULL AS SalesOrderID, SUM(UnitPrice)AS SumOfPrice, ProductID
FROM Sales.SalesOrderDetail
WHERE SalesOrderID BETWEEN 44175 AND 44178
GROUP BY ProductID
UNION ALL
SELECT SalesOrderID,SUM(UnitPrice), NULL
FROM Sales.SalesOrderDetail
WHERE SalesOrderID BETWEEN 44175 AND 44178
GROUP BY SalesOrderID;

--2
SELECT SalesOrderID, SUM(UnitPrice) AS SumOfPrice,ProductID
FROM Sales.SalesOrderDetail
WHERE SalesOrderID BETWEEN 44175 AND 44178
GROUP BY GROUPING SETS(SalesOrderID, ProductID);
```

Figure 11-12 shows the results of running this code. Query 1 is a UNION query that calculates the sum of the UnitPrice. The first part of the query supplies a NULL value for SalesOrderID. That is because SalesOrderID is just a placeholder. The query groups by ProductID, and SalesOrderID is not needed. The second part of the query supplies a NULL value for ProductID. In this case, the query groups by SalesOrderID, and ProductID is not needed. The UNION query combines the results. Query 2 demonstrates how to write the equivalent query using GROUPING SETS.

	SalesOrderID	SumOfPrice	ProductID
1	NULL	3578.27	751
2	NULL	3578.27	752
3	NULL	3578.27	753
4	NULL	3374.99	777
5	44175	3578.27	NULL
6	44176	3578.27	NULL
7	44177	3374.99	NULL
8	44178	3578.27	NULL

	SalesOrderID	SumOfPrice	ProductID
1	NULL	3578.27	751
2	NULL	3578.27	752
3	NULL	3578.27	753
4	NULL	3374.99	777
5	44175	3578.27	NULL
6	44176	3578.27	NULL
7	44177	3374.99	NULL
8	44178	3578.27	NULL

Figure 11-12. *The results of comparing UNION to GROUPING SETS*

CUBE and ROLLUP

You can add subtotals to your aggregate queries by using CUBE or ROLLUP in the GROUP BY clause. CUBE and ROLLUP are very similar, but there is a subtle difference. CUBE will give subtotals for every possible combination of the grouping levels. ROLLUP will give subtotals for the hierarchy. For example, if you are grouping by three columns, CUBE will provide subtotals for every grouping column. ROLLUP will provide subtotals for the first two columns but not the last column in the GROUP BY list. Here is the syntax:

```
SELECT <col1>, <col2>, <aggregate expression>
    FROM <table>
GROUP BY <CUBE or ROLLUP>(<col1>,<col2>)
```

The following example demonstrates how to use CUBE and ROLLUP. Run the code in Listing 11-16 to see how this works.

Listing 11-16. Using CUBE and ROLLUP

```
--1
SELECT COUNT(*) AS CountOfRows,
    ISNULL(Color, CASE WHEN GROUPING(Color)=0 THEN 'UNK' ELSE 'ALL' END) AS Color,
        ISNULL(Size,CASE WHEN GROUPING(Size) = 0 THEN 'UNK' ELSE 'ALL' END) AS Size
FROM Production.Product
GROUP BY CUBE(Color,Size)
ORDER BY Size, Color;

--2
SELECT COUNT(*) AS CountOfRows,
    ISNULL(Color, CASE WHEN GROUPING(Color)=0 THEN 'UNK' ELSE 'ALL' END) AS Color,
        ISNULL(Size,CASE WHEN GROUPING(Size) = 0 THEN 'UNK' ELSE 'ALL' END) AS Size
FROM Production.Product
GROUP BY ROLLUP(Color,Size)
ORDER BY Size, Color;
```

Figure 11-13 shows the partial results of running this code. Query 1 returns 98 rows while query 2 returns only 79 rows. Notice that query 1 has subtotal rows for size 38 and 40 while query 2 does not, denoted by the word ALL in the Color column. These queries use the GROUPING function, which returns a 1 if it is a summary row or 0 if it is not. This is combined with the ISNULL function so that it is only applied on the rows with actual null values or the summary rows. Scroll down in the data to find the rows where the color column is summarized.

	CountOfRows	Color	Size
1	12	ALL	38
2	5	Black	38
3	5	Silver	38
4	2	Yellow	38
5	11	ALL	40
6	4	Black	40

	CountOfRows	Color	Size
1	5	Black	38
2	5	Silver	38
3	2	Yellow	38
4	4	Black	40
5	4	Silver	40
6	3	Yellow	40

Figure 11-13. *The partial results of CUBE and ROLLUP*

Pivoted Queries

Normally a query displays the data in a way that is similar to how it looks in a table, often with the column headers being the actual names of the columns within the table. A pivoted query displays the values of one column as column headers instead. For example, you could display the sum of the sales by month so that the month names are column headers. Each row would then contain the data by year with the sum for each month displayed from left to right. This section shows how to write pivoted queries with two techniques: CASE and PIVOT.

Pivoting Data with *CASE*

Many developers still use the CASE function to create pivoted results. (See "The Case Expression" section in Chapter 4 to learn more about CASE.) Essentially, you use several CASE expressions in the query, one for each pivoted column header. For example, the query could have a CASE expression checking to see whether the month of the order date is January. If the order does occur in January, it returns the total sales value. If not, it supplies a zero. For each row, the data ends up in the correct column where it can be aggregated. Here is the syntax for using CASE to pivot data:

```
CASE <col1>,SUM(CASE <col3> WHEN <value1> THEN <col2> ELSE 0 END) AS <alias1>,
    SUM(CASE <col3> WHEN <value2> THEN <col2> ELSE 0 END) AS <alias2>,
    SUM(CASE <col3> WHEN <value3> THEN <col2> ELSE 0 END) AS <alias3>
FROM <table1>
GROUP BY <col1>
```

Type in and execute Listing 11-17 to learn how to pivot data using CASE.

Listing 11-17. Using CASE to Pivot Data

```
SELECT YEAR(OrderDate) AS OrderYear,
ROUND(SUM(CASE MONTH(OrderDate) WHEN 1 THEN TotalDue ELSE 0 END),0)
    AS Jan,
ROUND(SUM(CASE MONTH(OrderDate) WHEN 2 THEN TotalDue ELSE 0 END),0)
    AS Feb,
ROUND(SUM(CASE MONTH(OrderDate) WHEN 3 THEN TotalDue ELSE 0 END),0)
    AS Mar,
ROUND(SUM(CASE MONTH(OrderDate) WHEN 4 THEN TotalDue ELSE 0 END),0)
    AS Apr,
ROUND(SUM(CASE MONTH(OrderDate) WHEN 5 THEN TotalDue ELSE 0 END),0)
    AS May,
ROUND(SUM(CASE MONTH(OrderDate) WHEN 6 THEN TotalDue ELSE 0 END),0)
    AS Jun
FROM Sales.SalesOrderHeader
GROUP BY YEAR(OrderDate)
ORDER BY OrderYear;
```

Figure 11-14 shows the results of running this code. To save space in the results, the statement calculates the totals only for the months January through June and uses the ROUND function. The GROUP BY clause contains just the YEAR(OrderDate) expression. You might think that you need to group by month as well, but this query doesn't group by month. It just includes each TotalDue value in a different column depending on the month.

	OrderYear	Jan	Feb	Mar	Apr	May	Jun
1	2005	0.00	0.00	0.00	0.00	0.00	0.00
2	2006	1462449.00	2749105.00	2350568.00	1727690.00	3299799.00	1920507.00
3	2007	1968647.00	3226056.00	2297693.00	2660724.00	3866365.00	2852210.00
4	2008	3359927.00	4662656.00	4722358.00	4269365.00	5813557.00	6004156.00

Figure 11-14. *The results of using CASE to create a pivot query*

Using the *PIVOT* Function

Microsoft introduced the PIVOT function with SQL Server 2005. In my opinion, the PIVOT function is more difficult to understand than using CASE to produce the same results. Just like CASE, you have to hard-code the column names. This works fine when the pivoted column names will never change, such as the months of the year. When the query bases the pivoted column on data that changes over time, such as employee or department names, the query must be modified each time that data changes. Here is the syntax for PIVOT:

```
SELECT <groupingCol>, <pivotedValue1> [AS <alias1>], <pivotedValue2> [AS <alias2>]
FROM (SELECT <groupingCol>, <value column>, <pivoted column>) AS <queryAlias>
PIVOT
( <aggregate function>(<value column>)
FOR <pivoted column> IN (<pivotedValue1>,<pivotedValue2>)
) AS <pivotAlias>
[ORDER BY <groupingCol>]
```

The SELECT part of the query lists any non-pivoted columns along with the values from the pivoted column. These values from the pivoted column will become the column names in your query. You can use aliases if you want to use a different column name than the actual value. For example, if the column names will be the month numbers, you can alias with the month names.

This syntax uses a derived table, listed after the word FROM, as the basis of the query. See the "Using Derived Tables" section in Chapter 6 to review derived tables. Make sure that you only list columns that you want as grouping levels, the pivoted column, and the column that will be summarized in this derived table. Adding other columns to this query will cause extra grouping levels and unexpected results. The derived table must be aliased, so don't forget this small detail.

■ **Tip**   It is possible to use a CTE to write this query instead of a derived table. See the article "Create Pivoted Tables in 3 Steps" in *SQL Server Magazine*'s July 2009 issue to learn this alternate method.

Follow the derived table with the PIVOT function. The argument to the PIVOT function includes the aggregate expression followed by the word FOR and the pivoted column name. Right after the pivoted column name, include an IN expression. Inside the IN expression, list the pivoted column values. These will match up with the pivoted column values in the SELECT list. The PIVOT function must also have an alias. Finally, you can order the results if you want. Usually this will be by the grouping level column, but you can also sort by any of the pivoted column names. Type in and execute Listing 11-18 to learn how to use PIVOT.

Listing 11-18. Pivoting Results with PIVOT

```
--1
SELECT OrderYear, [1] AS Jan, [2] AS Feb, [3] AS Mar,
    [4] AS Apr, [5] AS May, [6] AS Jun
FROM (SELECT YEAR(OrderDate) AS OrderYear, TotalDue,
    MONTH(OrderDate) AS OrderMonth
    FROM Sales.SalesOrderHeader) AS MonthData
PIVOT (
    SUM(TotalDue)
    FOR OrderMonth IN ([1],[2],[3],[4],[5],[6])
    ) AS PivotData
ORDER BY OrderYear;

--2
SELECT OrderYear, ROUND(ISNULL([1],0),0) AS Jan,
    ROUND(ISNULL([2],0),0) AS Feb, ROUND(ISNULL([3],0),0) AS Mar,
    ROUND(ISNULL([4],0),0) AS Apr, ROUND(ISNULL([5],0),0) AS May,
    ROUND(ISNULL([6],0),0) AS Jun
FROM (SELECT YEAR(OrderDate) AS OrderYear, TotalDue,
    MONTH(OrderDate) AS OrderMonth
    FROM Sales.SalesOrderHeader) AS MonthData
PIVOT (
    SUM(TotalDue)
    FOR OrderMonth IN ([1],[2],[3],[4],[5],[6])
    ) AS PivotData
ORDER BY OrderYear;
```

Figure 11-15 shows the results of running this code. First, take a look at the derived table aliased as MonthData in query 1. The SELECT statement in the derived table contains an expression that returns the year of the OrderDate, the OrderYear, and an expression that returns the month of the OrderDate, OrderMonth. It also contains the TotalDue column. The query will group the results by OrderYear. The OrderMonth column is the pivoted column. The query will sum up the TotalDue values. The derived table contains only the columns and expressions needed by the pivoted query.

	OrderYear	Jan	Feb	Mar	Apr	May	Jun
1	2005	NULL	NULL	NULL	NULL	NULL	NULL
2	2006	1462448.8986	2749104.6546	2350568.1264	1727689.5793	3299799.233	1920506.6177
3	2007	1968647.184	3226056.1486	2297692.9898	2660723.7481	3866365.1263	2852209.8283
4	2008	3359927.2196	4662655.6183	4722357.5175	4269365.0103	5813557.453	6004155.7672

	OrderYear	Jan	Feb	Mar	Apr	May	Jun
1	2005	0.00	0.00	0.00	0.00	0.00	0.00
2	2006	1462448.90	2749104.65	2350568.13	1727689.58	3299799.23	1920506.62
3	2007	1968647.18	3226056.15	2297692.99	2660723.75	3866365.13	2852209.83
4	2008	3359927.22	4662655.62	4722357.52	4269365.01	5813557.45	6004155.77

Figure 11-15. *The results of using PIVOT*

The PIVOT function specifies the aggregate expression SUM(TotalDue). The pivoted column is OrderMonth. The IN expression contains the numbers 1 to 6, each surrounded by brackets. The IN expression lists the values for OrderMonth that you want to show up in the final results. These values are also the column names. Because columns starting with numbers are not valid column names, the brackets surround the numbers. You could also quote these numbers. The IN expression has two purposes: to provide the column names and to filter the results.

The outer SELECT list contains OrderYear and the numbers 1 to 6 surrounded with brackets. These must be the same values found in the IN expression. Because you want the month abbreviations instead of numbers as the column names, the query uses aliases. Notice that the SELECT list does not contain the TotalDue column. Finally, the ORDER BY clause specifies that the results will sort by OrderYear.

The results of query 2 are identical to the results from the pivoted results using the CASE technique in the previous section. This query uses the ROUND and ISNULL functions to replace NULL with zero and round the results.

Using the *UNPIVOT* Function

The opposite of pivoting data is unpivoting data. With this function you can turn the column headings into row data. Like the PIVOT function, the UNPIVOT function requires knowing the column list up front and hard coding it in the query. Here is the syntax:

```
SELECT <regular columns>, <summary column>, <unpivoted column>
FROM (
     SELECT <regular columns>,<col header 1>, <col header 2>, [<col header N>]
     FROM <table to unpivot>) <ALIAS>
UNPIVOT (
     <summary column> FOR <unpivoted column> IN
               (<col header 1>, <col header 2>, [<col header N>])
) AS <ALIAS>;
```

Listing 11-19 demonstrates how to use this function. Type in and execute the code to learn more.

Listing 11-19. Using UNPIVOT

```
--1
CREATE TABLE #pivot(OrderYear INT, Jan NUMERIC(10,2),
    Feb NUMERIC(10,2), Mar NUMERIC(10,2),
        Apr NUMERIC(10,2), May NUMERIC(10,2),
        Jun NUMERIC(10,2));

--2
INSERT INTO #pivot(OrderYear, Jan, Feb, Mar,
    Apr, May, Jun)
VALUES (2006, 1462449.00, 2749105.00, 2350568.00, 1727690.00, 3299799.00, 1920507.00),
       (2007, 1968647.00, 3226056.00, 2297693.00, 2660724.00, 3866365.00, 2852210.00),
       (2008, 3359927.00, 4662656.00, 4722358.00, 4269365.00, 5813557.00, 6004156.00);

--3
SELECT * FROM #pivot;
```

```
--4
SELECT OrderYear, Amt, OrderMonth
FROM (
    SELECT OrderYear, Jan, Feb, Mar, Apr, May, Jun
        FROM #pivot) P
UNPIVOT (
    Amt FOR OrderMonth IN
                (Jan, Feb, Mar, Apr, May, Jun)
        ) AS unpvt;
```

Figure 11-16 shows the partial results of running this code. Statement 1 creates a temp table called #pivot. Statement 2 populates the table so that the data looks like the pivoted data from the previous section. Query 3 returns the data so that you can look at it before it is unpivoted. Query 4 is the actual unpivot query.

	OrderYear	Jan	Feb	Mar	Apr	May	Jun
1	2006	1462449.00	2749105.00	2350568.00	1727690.00	3299799.00	1920507.00
2	2007	1968647.00	3226056.00	2297693.00	2660724.00	3866365.00	2852210.00
3	2008	3359927.00	4662656.00	4722358.00	4269365.00	5813557.00	6004156.00

	OrderYear	Sales	OrderMonth
1	2006	1462449.00	Jan
2	2006	2749105.00	Feb
3	2006	2350568.00	Mar
4	2006	1727690.00	Apr
5	2006	3299799.00	May
6	2006	1920507.00	Jun
7	2007	1968647.00	Jan
8	2007	3226056.00	Feb
9	2007	2297693.00	Mar

Figure 11-16. *The partial results of UNPIVOT*

You will unpivot the month columns, Jan through Jun. The SELECT part of the query contains any regular columns, in this case OrderYear. Next you list the name for the values in the columns to unpivot, Sales. The final column is the name of your unpivoted columns, Order Month. The list of columns is followed by the FROM clause containing a derived table, just the data to unpivot. The derived table must be aliased.

Now add the UNPIVOT function. The argument to the function contains a phrase consisting of the numeric column followed by FOR and the unpivot column. Then you must supply a hard-coded list of the columns. Finally, supply an alias. Figure 11-17 shows where OrderMonth and Sales originate.

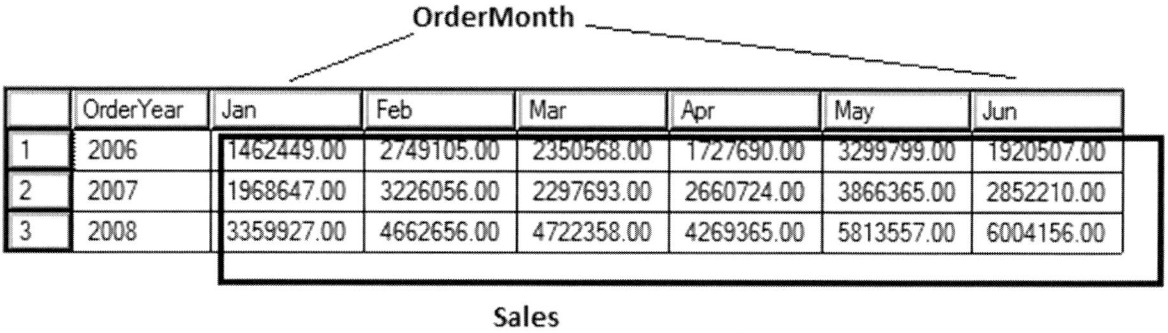

Figure 11-17. *The origination of the columns*

Paging

Imaging that you are performing a search on your favorite e-commerce web site and several hundred products will be returned from your search. Instead of displaying all of the products at once, the site will display 10 or 20 products at a time. Hopefully, you will find what you need on the first or second page that is displayed and can complete the purchase.

The technique of displaying a page of data at a time is called *paging*. There are two ways that this is commonly done with T-SQL. The first method takes advantage of the ROW_NUMBER function. The second method uses the OFFSET/FETCH NEXT functionality added with SQL Server 2008.

To keep the following examples simple, assume that the data to be paged is static. Type in Listing 11-20 to learn these two techniques.

Listing 11-20. Paging with T-SQL

```
--1
DECLARE @PageSize INT = 5;
DECLARE @PageNo INT = 1;

;WITH Products AS(
    SELECT ProductID, P.Name, Color, Size,
        ROW_NUMBER() OVER(ORDER BY P.Name, Color, Size) AS RowNum
    FROM Production.Product AS P
    JOIN Production.ProductSubcategory AS S
        ON P.ProductSubcategoryID = S.ProductSubcategoryID
        JOIN Production.ProductCategory AS C
            ON S.ProductCategoryID = C.ProductCategoryID
        WHERE C.Name = 'Bikes'
)
SELECT TOP(@PageSize) ProductID, Name, Color, Size
FROM Products
WHERE RowNum BETWEEN (@PageNo -1) * @PageSize + 1
    AND @PageNo * @PageSize
ORDER BY Name, Color, Size;
```

```
--2
SELECT ProductID, P.Name, Color, Size
FROM Production.Product AS P
JOIN Production.ProductSubcategory AS S
    ON P.ProductSubcategoryID = S.ProductSubcategoryID
JOIN Production.ProductCategory AS C
    ON S.ProductCategoryID = C.ProductCategoryID
WHERE C.Name = 'Bikes'
ORDER BY P.Name, Color, Size
    OFFSET @PageSize * (@PageNo -1) ROWS FETCH NEXT @PageSize ROWS ONLY;
```

Figure 11-18 shows the results. Query 1 uses a CTE so that it can filter on the RowNum column. The TOP expression is used to control how many rows are returned. In this case, the @PageSize variable is used. In this example, five rows are returned per page and the first page is returned. When substituting the values for the variables in the WHERE clause expressions, rows 1 to 5 are returned.

```
(1 - 1) * 5 + 1 = Row 1
1 * 5 = Row 5
```

	ProductID	Name	Color	Size
1	775	Mountain-100 Black, 38	Black	38
2	776	Mountain-100 Black, 42	Black	42
3	777	Mountain-100 Black, 44	Black	44
4	778	Mountain-100 Black, 48	Black	48
5	771	Mountain-100 Silver, 38	Silver	38

	ProductID	Name	Color	Size
1	775	Mountain-100 Black, 38	Black	38
2	776	Mountain-100 Black, 42	Black	42
3	777	Mountain-100 Black, 44	Black	44
4	778	Mountain-100 Black, 48	Black	48
5	771	Mountain-100 Silver, 38	Silver	38

Figure 11-18. *The paging results*

Query 2 uses the newer syntax that is an enhancement of the ORDER BY clause. The value following the word OFFSET specifies how many rows to skip. The value following FETCH NEXT specifies how many rows to return. When substituting the values for the variables, 0 rows are skipped and 5 rows are returned.

```
5 * (1 - 1) = 0 Rows skipped
5 = 5 Rows to return
```

The OFFSET keyword can be used without FETCH NEXT. In that case, all possible rows after the offset are returned. Modify the values of the variables to perform additional tests of the two solutions.

Summary

This chapter covered how to write advanced queries using some T-SQL features supported in SQL Server. Starting with Chapter 6, you saw how CTEs can help you solve query problems without resorting to temporary tables or views. In this chapter, you learned several other ways to use CTEs, including how to display hierarchical data with a recursive CTE. With the OUTPUT clause, you can return or store the data involved in data manipulation statements. If you will be involved with loading data warehouses, you can use the MERGE and GROUPING SET, CUBE, and ROLLUP features. You learned two ways to write pivot queries, using CASE and using the PIVOT function. You also learned how to UNPIVOT data. Finally, you learned how to return data a page at a time.

Although the material in this chapter is not required knowledge for beginning T-SQL developers, it will be very beneficial to you to keep these techniques in mind. As you gain more experience, you will often find ways to take advantage of these features.

In Chapter 12 you will learn about T-SQL programming logic.

CHAPTER 12

■ ■ ■

Understanding T-SQL Programming Logic

Even though the primary purpose of T-SQL is to retrieve and manipulate data, like other programming languages, it also contains logic elements. Most of the time you will write T-SQL statements that retrieve or update data, but you can also set up loops and write code with conditional flow. Often database administrators write scripts in T-SQL to perform maintenance tasks that require more than just retrieving or updating data. For example, you might need to write a script that checks the last backup date of all databases on the server or checks the free space of all the databases. Although most administrative tasks are beyond the scope of this book, you may find many uses in your environment for the techniques you will learn in this chapter.

Variables

If you have programmed in any other language, you have probably used *variables* in your programs. Variables hold temporary values used to help you in designing programming logic. For example, you might use a variable to hold the results of a calculation, the results of a string concatenation, or to control the number of times a loop executes.

Declaring and Initializing a Variable

To use a variable, you must first *declare* it. SQL Server also gives you the option to *initialize* a variable, that is, assign a value to the variable at the same time you declare it. By default, the variable will be assigned the value NULL if you don't assign an explicit value. Versions earlier than SQL Server 2008 required that you assign a value on a separate line. Here is the syntax for declaring a variable and assigning a value at the same time and later in the code:

```
DECLARE @variableName <type> = <value1>
SET @variableName = <value2>
```

You assign a value to a variable after you declare it by using the SET statement or by using the SELECT statement. The SET statement lets you work with only one variable at a time. The SELECT statement allows multiple variables to be modified in the same statement. Using a SELECT statement to assign values to multiple variables is more efficient than individual SET statements. You can also assign a value to a variable from a column within a query. When using SELECT to assign the value of a variable from a query, make sure that the query returns only one row. Otherwise, when doing so, that will be the only thing the query can do; the query can't return a result set. Type in and execute Listing 12-1 to learn how to declare and assign variables.

Listing 12-1. Declaring and Using Variables

```
--1
DECLARE @myNumber INT = 10;
PRINT 'The value of @myNumber';
PRINT @myNumber;
SET @myNumber = 20;
PRINT 'The value of @myNumber';
PRINT @myNumber;
GO


--2
DECLARE @myString VARCHAR(100), @myBit BIT;
SELECT @myString = 'Hello, World', @myBit = 1;
PRINT 'The value of @myString';
PRINT @myString;
PRINT 'The value of @myBit';
PRINT @myBit;
GO


--3
DECLARE @myUnicodeString NVARCHAR(100);
SET @myUnicodeString = N'This is a Unicode String';
PRINT 'The value of @myUnicodeString';
PRINT @myUnicodeString;
GO


--4
DECLARE @FirstName NVARCHAR(50), @LastName NVARCHAR(50);
SELECT @FirstName  = FirstName, @LastName = LastName
FROM Person.Person
WHERE BusinessEntityID = 1;

PRINT 'The value of @FirstName';
PRINT @FirstName;
PRINT 'The value of @LastName';
PRINT @LastName;
GO


--5
PRINT 'The value of @myString';
PRINT @myString;
```

Figure 12-1 shows the results of running this code. The script in Listing 12-1 consists of five batches separated by the word GO. Batch 1 declares and initializes the local variable @myNumber in one line to the value 10. Local variables in T-SQL begin with the at (@) symbol and are in scope within the current connection and the current batch. Another line in the batch sets the value of the variable to 20 using the SET command. The SET command will set the value of only one variable at a time. Using the PRINT command, you can print the value of a variable.

```
Messages
 The value of @myNumber
 10
 The value of @myNumber
 20
 The value of @myString
 Hello, World
 The value of @myBit
 1
 The value of @myUnicodeString
 This is a Unicode String
 The value of @FirstName
 Ken
 The value of @LastName
 Sánchez
 Msg 137, Level 15, State 2, Line 4
 Must declare the scalar variable "@myString".
```

Figure 12-1. *The results of declaring and initializing a variable*

Batch 2 demonstrates how you can declare more than one variable on the same line. The batch uses a SELECT statement to assign values to both variables in the same statement. Batch 3 demonstrates that you set the value of an NVARCHAR string a bit differently. You should begin the string with the uppercase letter *N*. By doing so, SQL Server converts the string to Unicode. If you don't begin the string with *N*, you may lose any special characters.

In batch 4, the SELECT statement assigns the value of the FirstName and LastName columns to two variables from one row of the Person.Person table. In this case, the WHERE clause restricts the SELECT statement to just one row. If the statement didn't have a WHERE clause or a less restrictive one, the value from every row would be assigned to the variable. Eventually, the variable will contain the final value assigned from the query. Because SQL Server doesn't guarantee the order of the results returned, this could be any value in the results.

Batch 5 demonstrates that the variable declared in batch 2 is no longer in scope. Variables go out of scope when the batch completes. Even if there is only one batch in the script, once the code completes, the variable goes out of scope and is no longer in memory.

Using Expressions and Functions with Variables

The previous example demonstrated how to declare and assign a literal value or a value from a query. You can also use any expression and function to assign a value to a variable. For example, you may need to save the count of the rows of a query for later in the script, or you may need to save the value of a file name concatenated to a file path for a maintenance script. Type in and execute the code in Listing 12-2 to learn more about variables.

Listing 12-2. Using Expressions and Functions to Assign Variable Values

```
--1
DECLARE @myINT1 INT = 10, @myINT2 INT = 20, @myINT3 INT;
SET @myINT3 = @myINT1 * @myINT2;
PRINT 'Value of @myINT3: ' + CONVERT(VARCHAR(30),@myINT3);
GO
```

```
--2
DECLARE @myString VARCHAR(100);
SET @myString = 'Hello, ';
SET @myString += 'World';
PRINT 'Value of @myString: ' + @myString;
GO

--3
DECLARE @CustomerCount INT;
SELECT @CustomerCount = COUNT(*)
FROM Sales.Customer;
PRINT 'Customer Count: ' + CAST(@CustomerCount AS VARCHAR(30));

--4
DECLARE @FullName NVARCHAR(152);
SELECT @FullName = FirstName + ISNULL(' ' + MiddleName,'') + ' ' + LastName
FROM Person.Person
WHERE BusinessEntityID = 1;
PRINT 'FullName: ' + @FullName;
```

Figure 12-2 shows the results of running this code. Batch 1 declares three integer variables and assigns a value to two of them. The next line uses the SET statement to assign the product of the two variables to the third one. Finally, to print the label explaining the value and the value on the same line, the code converts the value of the @myINT3 variable to a string.

```
 Messages
  Value of @myINT3: 200
  Value of @myString: Hello, World
  Customer Count: 19820
  FullName: Ken J Sánchez
```

Figure 12-2. *The results of using variables with expressions*

Batch 2 assigns the value Hello (with a space after it) to the @myString variable. The next line uses the += operator to concatenate another string, *World*, to the variable. The += operator is available in many programming languages as a shorter way to write an assignment. Without the shortcut, the code would look like this:

```
SET @myString = @myString + 'World';
```

Batch 3 assigns the result of the expression COUNT(*) to the variable @CustomerCount. When assigning a value to a variable from a query, you will assign only one value to a variable. Make sure that only one row is returned when you use this technique. In this case, the query returns only one value, the count of all the rows from the table. The query in batch 4 also returns one row because of the criteria in the WHERE clause. The query assigns a value to the @FullName variable for one row only.

Using Variables in *WHERE* and *HAVING* Clauses

So far, the examples in this book have used literal values in the expressions, also known as *predicates*, in WHERE and HAVING clauses. You will often not know ahead of time what values will be needed, so it makes sense to use variables. Type in and execute the code in Listing 12-3 to learn more about using a variable instead of a literal value in a WHERE or HAVING clause.

Listing 12-3. Using a Variable in a WHERE or HAVING Clause Predicate

```
--1
DECLARE @ID INT;
SET @ID = 1;

SELECT BusinessEntityID, FirstName, LastName
FROM Person.Person
WHERE BusinessEntityID = @ID;
GO


--2
DECLARE @FirstName NVARCHAR(50);
SET @FirstName = N'Ke%';

SELECT BusinessEntityID, FirstName, LastName
FROM Person.Person
WHERE FirstName LIKE @FirstName
ORDER BY BusinessEntityID;
GO


--3
DECLARE @ID INT = 1;
--3.1
SELECT BusinessEntityID, FirstName, LastName
FROM Person.Person
WHERE @ID = CASE @ID WHEN 0 THEN 0 ELSE BusinessEntityID END;

SET @ID = 0;

--3.2
SELECT BusinessEntityID, FirstName, LastName
FROM Person.Person
WHERE @ID = CASE @ID WHEN 0 THEN 0 ELSE BusinessEntityID END;

GO


--4
DECLARE @Amount INT = 10000;

SELECT SUM(TotalDue) AS TotalSales, CustomerID
FROM Sales.SalesOrderHeader
GROUP BY CustomerID
HAVING SUM(TotalDue) > @Amount;
```

Figure 12-3 shows the results of running this code. Batch 1 declares a variable @ID and assigns the value 1. The query uses the variable in the WHERE clause to restrict the results to just the row from the Person.Person table where the BusinessEntityID is 1. Batch 2 demonstrates how pattern matching with LIKE can be used. The variable contains the wildcard %. The query returns all rows where the FirstName begins with *Ke*.

	BusinessEntityID	FirstName	LastName
1	1	Ken	Sánchez

	BusinessEntityID	FirstName	LastName
1	1	Ken	Sánchez
2	17	Kevin	Brown
3	58	Kendall	Keil
4	105	Kevin	Homer

	BusinessEntityID	FirstName	LastName
1	1	Ken	Sánchez

	BusinessEntityID	FirstName	LastName
1	285	Syed	Abbas
2	293	Catherine	Abel
3	295	Kim	Abercrombie
4	2170	Kim	Abercrombie

	TotalSales	CustomerID
1	68644.5658	30030
2	93888.441	29784
3	302061.1054	30076
4	76266.9402	29538

Figure 12-3. *The partial results of using a variable in the WHERE and HAVING clauses*

Batch 3 uses the variable @ID within a CASE expression in the WHERE clause. The variable starts out with the value 1. Query 3.1 returns only the row in which BusinessEntityID equals 1. Take a closer look at the CASE expression. The variable does not equal 0, so the CASE expression returns the column BusinessEntityID. The variable @ID equals the BusinessEntityID in only one row. Use caution with this technique. Remember that embedding a column in a function causes the index to be scanned. In query 3.2, the value of @ID is 0. The CASE expression returns 0 because @ID is equal to 0. Because @ID is equal to 0 and the CASE expression returns 0, the query returns every row. Zero is always equal to zero.

Batch 4 demonstrates that the variables can also be used in the HAVING clause of an aggregate query. Recall from Chapter 7 that you use the HAVING clause to filter the rows after the database engine processes the GROUP BY clause. The query returns only the rows from the Sales.SalesOrderHeader table where the TotalSales value by CustomerID exceeds the value stored in @Amount.

Now that you understand some of the things you can do with variables, practice working with them by completing Exercise 12-1.

```
┌────────────────────────────────────────────────────────────────────────┐
│                             EXERCISE 12-1                                │
└────────────────────────────────────────────────────────────────────────┘
```

Use the AdventureWorks database to complete this exercise. You can find the solutions at the end of the chapter.

1. Write a script that declares an integer variable called @myInt. Assign 10 to the variable, and then print it.

2. Write a script that declares a VARCHAR(20) variable called @myString. Assign 'This is a test' to the variable, and print it.

3. Write a script that declares two integer variables called @MaxID and @MinID. Use the variables to print the highest and lowest SalesOrderID values from the Sales.SalesOrderHeader table.

4. Write a script that declares an integer variable called @ID. Assign the value 70000 to the variable. Use the variable in a SELECT statement that returns all the rows from the Sales.SalesOrderHeader table that have a SalesOrderID greater than the value of the variable.

5. Write a script that declares three variables, one integer variable called @ID, an NVARCHAR(50) variable called @FirstName, and an NVARCHAR(50) variable called @LastName. Use a SELECT statement to set the value of the variables with the row from the Person.Person table with BusinessEntityID = 1. Print a statement in the "BusinessEntityID: FirstName LastName" format.

6. Write a script that declares an integer variable called @SalesCount. Set the value of the variable to the total count of sales in the Sales.SalesOrderHeader table. Use the variable in a SELECT statement that shows the difference between the @SalesCount and the count of sales by customer.

The *IF ... ELSE* Construct

Use IF along with the optional ELSE keyword to control code flow in your T-SQL scripts. Use IF just as you would in any other programming language to execute a statement or group of statements based on an expression that must evaluate to TRUE or FALSE. For example, you might need to display an error message if the count of the rows in a table is too low. If the count exceeds a given value, your code repopulates a production table.

Using *IF*

Always follow the keyword IF with a condition that evaluates to TRUE or FALSE. You can follow the condition with the next statement to run on the same line or on the next line. If the condition applies to a group of statements, you will use BEGIN and END to designate which statements are within the IF block. Here is the syntax:

```
IF <condition> <statement>

IF <condition> BEGIN
    <statement1>
    [<statement2>]
END
```

To make my code more readable and avoid mistakes, I generally use the second method. You can actually put the statement to execute on a new line. For example, I might decide later to add a PRINT statement before the line to execute when the condition is true. In that case, I might accidentally cause the IF to apply just to the PRINT statement by forgetting to go back and add BEGIN and END. Type in and execute the code in Listing 12-4 to learn how to use IF.

Listing 12-4. Using IF to Control Code Execution

```
--1
DECLARE @Count INT;

SELECT @Count = COUNT(*)
FROM Sales.Customer;

IF @Count > 500 BEGIN
    PRINT 'The customer count is over 500.';
END;
GO

--2
DECLARE @Name VARCHAR(50);

SELECT @Name = FirstName + ' ' + LastName
FROM Person.Person
WHERE BusinessEntityID = 1;

--2.1
IF CHARINDEX('Ken',@Name) > 0 BEGIN
    PRINT 'The name for BusinessEntityID = 1 contains "Ken"';
END;
--2.2
IF CHARINDEX('Kathi',@Name) > 0 BEGIN
    PRINT 'The name for BusinessEntityID = 1 contains "Kathi"';
END;
```

Figure 12-4 shows the results of running this code. Batch 1 retrieves the count of the rows in the Sales.Customer table. If the count exceeds 500, then the PRINT statement executes. You can use any valid statements within the IF block. These code examples use PRINT statements so that you can easily see the results. Batch 2 assigns the value returned by the expression FirstName + ' ' + LastName to the variable. The 2.1 IF block executes the PRINT statement if the value contains *Ken*. The 2.2 IF block executes the PRINT statement if the value contains *Kathi*. Because the value doesn't contain *Kathi*, nothing prints.

```
Messages
  The customer count is over 500.
  The name for BusinessEntityID = 1 contains "Ken"
```

Figure 12-4. The results of using IF

Using *ELSE*

Often you will need to perform an alternate option if the condition you are checking is false. If you are using the BEGIN and END keywords in the IF block, you must close the block first before adding ELSE. Just like IF, you can use BEGIN and END to designate the ELSE block. You can also type the statement on the same line or the next line if you choose. Here are some syntax examples for many of the ways you can use ELSE:

```
IF <condition> <statement>
ELSE <statement>

IF <condition> BEGIN
    <statement1>
    [<statement2>]
END
ELSE <statement>

IF <condition> BEGIN
    <statement1>
    [<statement2>]
END
ELSE BEGIN
    <statement1>
    [<statement2>
END
```

The syntax examples show some of the ways you can use ELSE along with IF. You can use BEGIN and END with both or either parts of the construct. Type in and execute Listing 12-5 to learn how to use ELSE.

Listing 12-5. Using ELSE

```
--1
DECLARE @Count INT;

SELECT @Count = COUNT(*)
FROM Sales.Customer;

IF @Count < 500 PRINT 'The customer count is less than 500.';
ELSE PRINT 'The customer count is 500 or more.';
GO

--2
DECLARE @Name NVARCHAR(101);

SELECT @Name = FirstName + ' ' + LastName
FROM Person.Person
WHERE BusinessEntityID = 1;

--2.1
IF CHARINDEX('Ken', @Name) > 0 BEGIN
    PRINT 'The name for BusinessEntityID = 1 contains "Ken"';
END;
```

```
ELSE BEGIN
    PRINT 'The name for BusinessEntityID = 1 does not contain "Ken"';
    PRINT 'The name is ' + @Name;
END;
--2.2
IF CHARINDEX('Kathi', @Name) > 0 BEGIN
    PRINT 'The name for BusinessEntityID = 1 contains "Kathi"';
END;
ELSE BEGIN
    PRINT 'The name for BusinessEntityID = 1 does not contain "Kathi"';
    PRINT 'The name is ' + @Name;
END;
```

Figure 12-5 shows the results of running this code. This listing looks almost like the code in Listing 12-4 except that it contains the ELSE blocks. Batch 1 saves the count of the customers in a variable. This time, if the count is less than 500, the PRINT statement in the IF block executes. In this case, the count exceeds 500, so the PRINT statement in the ELSE block executes. Batch 2 executes the PRINT statement in the IF block of the 2.1 section of code because the value of the variable contains *Ken*. The 2.2 section of code executes the PRINT statement in the ELSE block because the value of the variable does not contain *Kathi*.

```
 Messages
  The customer count is 500 or more.
  The name for BusinessEntityID = 1 contains "Ken"
  The name for BusinessEntityID = 1 does not contain "Kathi"
  The name is Ken Sánchez
```

Figure 12-5. *The results of using ELSE*

Using Multiple Conditions

So far, theexamples have shown only one condition along with each IF or ELSE. You can include multiple conditions along with AND and OR just like within a WHERE clause. You can also control the logic with parentheses. For example, you may need to execute a statement only if the current day is Monday and the count of the rows in a table exceeds a certain value. Type in and execute the code in Listing 12-6.

Listing 12-6. Using Multiple Conditions with IF and ELSE

```
--1
DECLARE @Count INT;

SELECT @Count = COUNT(*)
FROM Sales.Customer;

IF @Count > 500 AND DATEPART(dw,getdate()) = 2 BEGIN
    PRINT 'The count is over 500.';
    PRINT 'Today is Monday.';
END;
ELSE BEGIN
    PRINT 'Either the count is too low or today is not Monday.';
END;
```

```
--2
IF @Count > 500 AND (DATEPART(dw,getdate()) = 2 OR DATEPART(m,getdate())= 3) BEGIN
    PRINT 'The count is over 500.';
    PRINT 'It is either Monday or the month is March.';
END;
```

Figure 12-6 shows the results of running this code. This listing contains just one batch after setting the database context. The IF block in code section 1 checks to see whether the count exceeds 500 and whether the current day of the week is Monday. You may get different results depending on the day of the week you run the code. The IF block in code section 2 checks first to see whether the day of the week is Monday or whether the current month is March. The block then checks the count, which must exceed 500. Because both the count exceeds 500 and I executed the code in March, the statements print. Again, you may get different results depending on when you run the code example.

```
Messages
 Either the count is too low or today is not Monday.
 The count is over 500.
 It is either Monday or the month is March.
```

Figure 12-6. *The results of using multiple conditions with IF*

Nesting *IF ... ELSE*

You can nest IF and ELSE blocks inside other IF and ELSE blocks to create even more complex logic. For example, you may need to check to make sure the current date is not a Sunday and execute a statement. Then within the IF block, check to make sure the table has at least a certain number of rows before executing another statement. The BEGIN and END keywords are sometimes optional, but I suggest you include them to make sure that the code is correct and readable. Here are two of the possible syntax examples:

```
IF <condition> BEGIN
    [<statement1>]
    IF <condition> BEGIN
        <statement2>
    END
END

IF <condition> BEGIN
    <statement1>
END
ELSE BEGIN
    [statement2]
    IF <condition> BEGIN
        <statement3>
        [<statement4>]
    END
    ELSE <statement5>
END
```

As you can probably tell, nesting IF blocks can cause your code to become complex. Be sure to use comments and consistent formatting to aid in your understanding of the code when you come back to it a few months or years after you write it. Type in and execute the code in Listing 12-7 to learn how to nest IF blocks.

Listing 12-7. Using a Nested IF Block

```
DECLARE @Count INT;

SELECT @Count = COUNT(*)
FROM Sales.Customer;

IF @Count > 500 BEGIN
    PRINT 'The count is over 500.';
    IF DATEPART(dw,getdate())= 2 BEGIN
        PRINT 'Today is Monday.';
    END;
    ELSE BEGIN
        PRINT 'Today is not Monday.';
    END;
END;
```

Figure 12-7 shows the results. Because the count exceeds 500, the code executes the first PRINT statement. Then, depending on the day that you execute the code, one of the statements inside the nested IF ... ELSE block will print. When writing nested IF blocks, make sure that the logic actually acts in the way you intended.

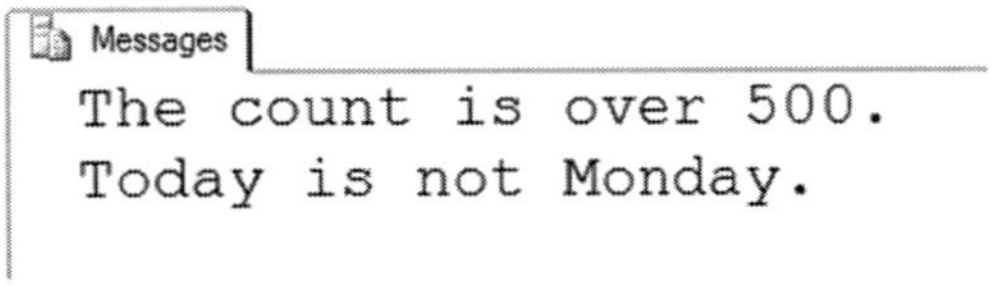

Figure 12-7. *The results of using a nested IF block*

Using *IF* with a Query

You can use IF with a query either to check for the existence of rows with EXISTS or to check the results of one value from one row. For example, you could check to see whether a certain part number is listed in the parts table. If it is, then based on the results, you can choose to begin or end the script or raise an error. You may have noticed IF EXISTS being used throughout the book to check the system tables to make sure a table exists before dropping it. Here is the syntax:

```
IF [NOT] EXISTS(SELECT * FROM <TABLE1> [WHERE <condition>]) BEGIN
    <statement1>
    [<statement2>]
END

IF (SELECT <expression> FROM <table>) = <value> BEGIN
    <statements>
END
```

Using EXISTS is one case where using the asterisk (*) is perfectly acceptable. You could also substitute a 1 or any value in place of the asterisk. The database engine just checks to see whether the query will return even one row but doesn't return any rows at all. The EXISTS function returns only TRUE or FALSE. Type in and execute Listing 12-8 to learn how to use IF with subqueries.

Listing 12-8. Using IF EXISTS

```
--1
IF EXISTS(SELECT * FROM Person.Person WHERE BusinessEntityID = 1) BEGIN
   PRINT 'There is a row with BusinessEntityID = 1';
END;
ELSE BEGIN
   PRINT 'There is not a row with BusEntityID = 1';
END;

--2
IF (SELECT COUNT(*) FROM Person.Person WHERE FirstName = 'Kathi') = 0 BEGIN
   PRINT 'There is not a person with the first name "Kathi".';
END;
```

Figure 12-8 shows the results of running this code. The IF block in code section 1 checks to see whether there is a row in the Person.Person table with BusinessEntityID = 1. You can also use ELSE along with IF EXISTS. The IF block in code section 2 checks the value of the expression, the count of the rows, to make sure there isn't a row with the FirstName of *Kathi* and executes the PRINT statements because there isn't a row with that name.

```
Messages
 There is a row with BusinessEntityID = 1
 There is not a person with the first name "Kathi".
```

Figure 12-8. *The results of using IF EXISTS*

You should now know how to use IF and ELSE in a number of situations. Practice what you have learned by completing Exercise 12-2.

EXERCISE 12-2

Use the AdventureWorks database to complete this exercise. You can find the solutions at the end of the chapter.

1. Write a batch that declares an integer variable called @Count to save the count of all the Sales.SalesOrderDetail records. Add an IF block that prints "Over 100,000" if the value exceeds 100,000. Otherwise, print "100,000 or less."

2. Write a batch that contains nested IF blocks. The outer block should check to see whether the month is October or November. If that is the case, print "The month is" and the month name. The inner block should check to see whether the year is even or odd and print the result. You can modify the month to check to make sure the inner block fires.

3. Write a batch that uses IF EXISTS to check to see whether there is a row in the Sales.SalesOrderHeader table that has SalesOrderID = 1. Print "There is a SalesOrderID = 1" or "There is not a SalesOrderID = 1" depending on the result.

WHILE

Use the WHILE construct to set up *loops*, or sections of code that execute a number of times, in T-SQL. For example, you might have a script that updates 10,000 rows each time within the loop because updating 10,000 rows at a time is more efficient than updating millions of rows at once. Updating the very large number of rows in one transaction could cause excessive locking and logging and impact the performance of the application. Although it is definitely better to update sets of data, not a row at a time, it is often necessary to update smaller batches.

Using a *WHILE* Loop

The WHILE loop uses a *Boolean* expression (an expression that evaluates to true or false) to determine when the looping should stop. If you don't specify an expression or the expression never evaluates to false, the loop will run until you stop it manually or some error condition causes it to stop. Here is the syntax:

```
WHILE <boolean expression> BEGIN
    <statement1>
   [<statement2>]
END
```

You can use several different techniques to create the Boolean expression that the database engine checks to determine when to exit the loop. One technique is to declare a variable, usually an integer, to be used as a counter. At the beginning of the loop, the code compares the variable to a value. Inside the loop, the code increments the variable. Another common way to control the loop is by using the EXISTS keyword with a query or to check the value of a column from a query. This might be used if a statement within the loop modifies data in the table used in the EXISTS condition. Type in and execute Listing 12-9 to learn how to use WHILE.

Listing 12-9. Using WHILE

```
--1
DECLARE @Count INT = 1;

WHILE @Count < 5 BEGIN
    PRINT @Count;
    SET @Count += 1;
END;
GO


--2
IF  EXISTS (SELECT * FROM sys.objects
            WHERE object_id = OBJECT_ID(N'dbo.demoContactType')
                AND type in (N'U'))
DROP TABLE dbo.demoContactType;
GO
CREATE TABLE dbo.demoContactType(ContactTypeID INT NOT NULL PRIMARY KEY,
    Processed BIT NOT NULL);
GO
INSERT INTO dbo.demoContactType(ContactTypeID,Processed)
SELECT ContactTypeID, 0
FROM Person.ContactType;
DECLARE @Count INT = 1;
```

```
WHILE EXISTS(SELECT * From dbo.demoContactType  WHERE Processed = 0) BEGIN
    UPDATE dbo.demoContactType SET Processed = 1
    WHERE ContactTypeID = @Count;
    PRINT 'Executed loop #' + CAST(@Count AS VARCHAR(10));
    SET @Count += 1;
END;
PRINT 'Done!';
```

Figure 12-9 shows the partial results of running this code. Batch 1 declares a variable and sets the value to 1 to use as a counter. Once the value of @Count reached 5, the execution exited the loop. It is very important that you set the value of the counter before the WHILE statement. If the value is NULL, then the loop will not run at all because comparing NULL to 5 will return UNKNOWN.

```
 Messages

1
2
3
4

(20 row(s) affected)

(1 row(s) affected)
Executed loop #1

(1 row(s) affected)
Executed loop #2

(1 row(s) affected)
Executed loop #3
```

Figure 12-9. *The partial results of using a WHILE loop*

The code prints the value of the counter each time through the loop of code section 1 followed by the messages and row counts from code section 2.

The second example contains more than one batch because it creates and populates a table to be updated within the loop. This example also contains a variable called @Count, but the value of @Count doesn't control the execution. This WHILE loop checks to see whether any rows in table dbo.demoContactType have a zero value in the Processed column. Each time through the loop, the code updates any rows with a ContactTypeID equal to the current value of @Count. (I removed all but two of the statements reporting that one row has been updated to save space in Figure 12-9.) When no more rows exist with Processed = 0, the code completes, and the PRINT statement executes. I purposely chose a small table for this example because processing a table row by row is very inefficient.

Nesting *WHILE* Loops

Just as you can nest IF blocks, you can also create WHILE loops within WHILE loops. You can also nest IF blocks within WHILE loops and WHILE loops within IF blocks. The important thing to remember when your T-SQL scripts become more complex is to keep your formatting consistent and add comments to your code. You may understand what your code does when you write it, but you may have a hard time figuring it out months or years later when you need to troubleshoot a problem or make a change. Type in and execute Listing 12-10 to learn how to nest WHILE loops.

Listing 12-10. Using a Nested WHILE Loop

```
DECLARE @OuterCount INT = 1;
DECLARE @InnerCount INT;

WHILE @OuterCount < 10 BEGIN
    PRINT 'Outer Loop';
    SET @InnerCount = 1;
    WHILE @InnerCount < 5 BEGIN
        PRINT '    Inner Loop';
        SET @InnerCount += 1;
    END;
    SET @OuterCount += 1;
END;
```

Figure 12-10 shows the partial results of running this code. The PRINT statements show which loop is executing at the time. Make sure you reset the value of the inner loop counter in the outer loop right before the inner loop. Otherwise, the inner loop will not run after the first time because the counter is already too high.

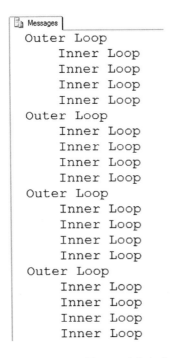

Figure 12-10. *The partial results of running a nested WHILE loop*

Exiting a Loop Early

Most of the time a WHILE loop continues until the Boolean expression returns false. You can also cause code execution to exit early by using the BREAK statement. Usually you will include a nested IF statement that controls when the BREAK statement will execute. One reason you might want to use BREAK is if you decide not to include a controlling condition at the top of the loop and include the expression in an IF block instead. The condition may be a query checking to see whether any rows remain to be updated. Type in and execute the code in Listing 12-11 to learn how to use BREAK.

Listing 12-11. Using BREAK

```
DECLARE @Count INT = 1;

WHILE @Count < 50  BEGIN
    PRINT @Count;
    IF @Count = 10 BEGIN
        PRINT 'Exiting the WHILE loop';
        BREAK;
    END;
    SET @Count += 1;
END;
```

Figure 12-11 shows the results of running this code. If the code didn't include the BREAK statement, the loop would print the numbers from 1 to 49. Instead, the loop exits when it reaches 10.

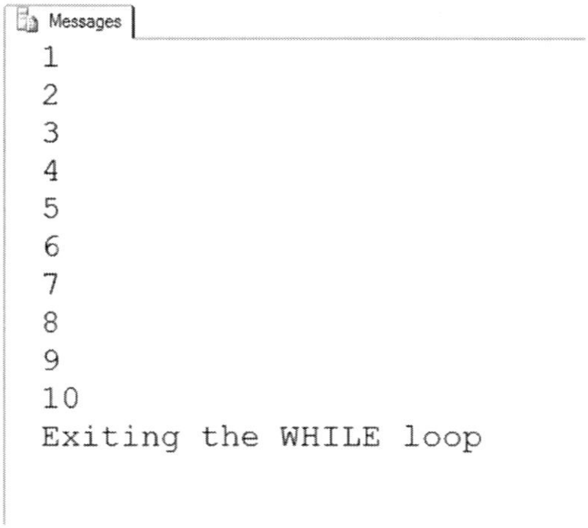

Figure 12-11. *The results of using the BREAK command*

Using *CONTINUE*

The CONTINUE command causes the loop to continue at the top. In other words, the code following the CONTINUE statement doesn't execute. Generally, you will find the CONTINUE within an IF block nested inside the WHILE loop. Use caution when writing a loop with CONTINUE to make sure you fully understand why you need this and are not creating an infinite loop. Type in and execute Listing 12-12 to learn how to use CONTINUE.

Listing 12-12. Using CONTINUE in a WHILE Loop

```
DECLARE @Count INT = 1;

WHILE @Count < 10 BEGIN
    PRINT @Count;
    SET @Count += 1;
    IF @Count = 3 BEGIN
        PRINT 'CONTINUE';
        CONTINUE;
    END;
    PRINT 'Bottom of loop';
END;
```

Figure 12-12 shows the results of running this code. Each time though the loop, the PRINT statement at the bottom of the loop executes except for the time when the counter equals 3. Notice that the counter increments before the IF block. If the counter incremented at the bottom of the loop, then the loop would execute indefinitely.

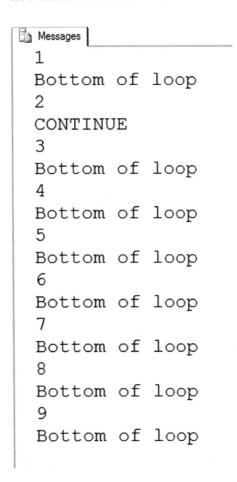

Figure 12-12. *The results of using CONTINUE in a WHILE loop*

Now that you know how to write code with a WHILE loop, practice what you have learned by completing Exercise 12-3.

EXERCISE 12-3

Use the AdventureWorks database to complete this exercise. You can find the solutions at the end of the chapter.

1. Write a script that contains a WHILE loop that prints out the letters *A* to *Z*. Use the function CHAR to change a number to a letter. Start the loop with the value 65. Here is an example that uses the CHAR function:

   ```
   DECLARE @Letter CHAR(1);
   SET @Letter = CHAR(65);
   PRINT @Letter;
   ```

2. Write a script that contains a WHILE loop nested inside another WHILE loop. The counter for the outer loop should count up from 1 to 100. The counter for the inner loop should count up from 1 to 5. Print the product of the two counters inside the inner loop.

3. Change the script in question 2 so the inner loop exits instead of printing when the counter for the outer loop is evenly divisible by 5.

4. Write a script that contains a WHILE loop that counts up from 1 to 100. Print "Odd" or "Even" depending on the value of the counter.

Temporary Tables and Table Variables

Temporary, or *temp*, tables and table variables allow you to save data in short-lived table structures that you can use in your scripts. For example, you may need to save the results of complicated calculations for further processing. The use of temp tables and table variables is controversial. You can find many articles and newsgroup discussions stating that no one should ever use these structures. In my opinion, temp tables and table variables are just more tools that you can use if you need them. I have found that they often allow me to break extremely complicated queries into smaller, more manageable pieces—sometimes with better performance.

You can create two kinds of temp tables: local and global. When creating a local temp table, you can access the table only within the connection where it was created. When the connection closes, the database engine destroys the temp table. When creating a global temp table, any connection can see the table. When the last connection to the temp table closes, the database engine destroys the temp table.

Creating Local Temp Tables

Local temp tables look and behave just like regular tables except that they live in the tempdb database instead of a user database like AdventureWorks. The tempdb database is one of the system databases required for SQL Server. SQL Server also uses tempdb as a work area for sorting and other behind-the-scene tasks.

To create a local temp table, preface the table name with the number sign (#). Only the connection in which the table was created can see a local temp table. Chapter 14 covers creating tables with the CREATE TABLE command, but you have learned how to use the SELECT INTO syntax to create a table. You have also typed in numerous CREATE TABLE statements to create work tables for examples and exercises in Chapter 11. Here is the minimum syntax to create a local temp table using the CREATE TABLE command:

```
CREATE TABLE #tableName (<col1> <data type>,<col2> <data type>)
```

Temp tables can have anything that a regular table has, such as primary keys, defaults, and indexes. Type in and execute the code from Listing 12-13 to learn how to create a temp table.

Listing 12-13. Creating and Populating Local Temp Table

```
CREATE TABLE #myCustomers(CustomerID INT, FirstName VARCHAR(25),
    LastName VARCHAR(25));
GO

INSERT INTO #myCustomers(CustomerID,FirstName,LastName)
SELECT C.CustomerID, FirstName, LastName
FROM Person.Person AS P INNER JOIN Sales.Customer AS C
ON P.BusinessEntityID = C.PersonID;

SELECT CustomerID, FirstName, LastName
FROM #myCustomers;

DROP TABLE #myCustomers;
```

Figure 12-13 shows the results of running this code. The code first uses the CREATE TABLE command to create the table, #myCustomers. This example is very simple. The command could define a primary key, CustomerID, and define that the FirstName and LastName columns should not contain NULL values. The script could include an ALTER TABLE command to add an index. The script populates the table with a regular insert statement, inserting the rows from a join on two tables. The SELECT statement looks like any other SELECT statement. Finally, the DROP TABLE command destroys the table. Even though the table will drop automatically when the connection closes, it's a good practice to drop temp tables when you are done using them. The order in which your data is returned may differ from my results.

	CustomerID	FirstName	LastName
1	18265	Trisha	Cai
2	19469	Valerie	Cai
3	11757	Vincent	Cai
4	24918	Warren	Cai
5	17643	Wesley	Cai
6	25960	Willie	Cai
7	29614	Ryan	Calafato
8	29615	Mari	Caldwell
9	29616	Barbara	Calone
10	29617	Lindsey	Camacho

Figure 12-13. *The partial results of creating and populating a temp table*

Creating Global Temp Tables

Global temp tables begin with two number signs (##). Type in and execute the code from Listing 12-14 to learn how to create a global temp table. Don't close the query window when you're done.

Listing 12-14. Creating and Populating a Global Temp Table

```
CREATE TABLE ##myCustomers(CustomerID INT, FirstName VARCHAR(25),
    LastName VARCHAR(25));
GO

INSERT INTO ##myCustomers(CustomerID,FirstName,LastName)
SELECT C.CustomerID, FirstName,LastName
FROM Person.Person AS P INNER JOIN Sales.Customer AS C
ON P.BusinessEntityID = C.PersonID;

SELECT CustomerID, FirstName, LastName
FROM ##myCustomers;

--Run the drop statement when you are done
--DROP TABLE ##myCustomers;
```

By using ## in the name, you create a global temp table. Open another query window and type the same SELECT statement to see that you can access the table from another connection. The results will look the same as those shown in Figure 12-13. Be sure to drop temp tables, especially global temp tables, when you no longer need them.

You won't find many reasons to use global temp tables. For example, suppose that an application creates a global temp table. If another user runs the same code to create the global temp table with the same name while the first temp table exists, an error will occur. I have actually seen this error happen in a commercially available application!

Creating Table Variables

Table variables became available in SQL Server 2000. At that time, many T-SQL developers decided they should always use table variables instead of temp tables because of a myth about them. Many developers believe that table variables exist in memory instead of tempdb, but that is not the case. Table variables do live in tempdb. Here is the syntax for creating a table variable:

```
DECLARE @tableName TABLE (<col1> <data type> [Primary Key],<col2> <data type>)

DECLARE @tableName TABLE (<col1> <data type> [Primary Key],
    <col2> <data type>, <col3> <data type> [INDEX <indexName> (<col2>,<col3> )]
```

Because a table variable is a variable, it follows the same scoping rules as other variables. Table variables go out of scope at the end of the batch, not when the connection closes. Prior to SQL Server 2014 you couldn't have nonclustered indexes in a table variable because you couldn't perform an ALTER TABLE command, which would change the table variable once it was declared. Starting with SQL Server 2014, you can add nonclustered indexes as part of the declaration, as shown in the second example. Table variables are fine for small tables that you won't need after running the batch. Table variables do not contain statistics. Statistics help the optimizer come up with a good query plan. Temp tables are the better choice for tables with large numbers of rows that could benefit from statistics or when you need to use the table after the batch is done.

Starting with SQL Server 2014, memory-optimized table variables are available with the new In-Memory OLTP features. These features are beyond the scope of this book.

Type in and execute Listing 12-15 to learn how to use a table variable.

Listing 12-15. Creating and Populating Table Variable

```
DECLARE @myCustomers TABLE (CustomerID INT, FirstName VARCHAR(25),
    LastName VARCHAR(25))

INSERT INTO @myCustomers(CustomerID,FirstName,LastName)
SELECT C.CustomerID, FirstName,LastName
FROM Person.Person AS P INNER JOIN Sales.Customer AS C
ON P.BusinessEntityID = C.PersonID;

SELECT CustomerID, FirstName, LastName
FROM @myCustomers;
```

The results are identical to those shown in Figure 12-14. Again, if you need to save a large number of rows temporarily, you may find that a temporary table is a better choice. Another reason you might want to use a temp table is that you can create it with a SELECT INTO statement, which is not possible with a table variable. The advantage of a SELECT INTO is that you don't need to know the column names and data types up front. See the "Creating and Populating a Table in One Statement" section in Chapter 10 for more information.

Using a Temp Table or Table Variable

You may be wondering why you might need to use a temporary table. For example, in many human resource system databases, most of the tables have history and future rows. The tables have effective dates and effective sequences. The effective sequences determine the valid row for a given date for a given employee. Instead of figuring out the effective date and effective sequence for each employee over and over in my scripts, I create a temporary table to hold that information. When using this technique, also check to see if a common table expression might be more efficient.

Another way I use temp tables is to store a list of a small number of values for filtering queries. For example, suppose a user can select one or more values to filter a report. The reporting application sends a comma-delimited list of values to a stored procedure. You can add each value from the comma-delimited list to a temp table or table variable and then use that table to filter the report results. You will learn about stored procedures in Chapter 14. Listing 12-16 shows how to use a table variable populated from a list of values. Type in and execute the code.

Listing 12-16. Using a Temp Table to Solve a Query Problem

```
--1
DECLARE @IDTable TABLE (ID INT);
DECLARE @IDList VARCHAR(2000);
DECLARE @ID INT;
DECLARE @Loc INT;

--2
SET @IDList = '16496,12506,11390,10798,2191,11235,10879,15040,3086';

--3
SET @Loc = CHARINDEX(',',@IDList);
```

```
--4
WHILE @Loc > 0 BEGIN
    --4.1
    SET @ID = LEFT(@IDList,@Loc-1);
    --4.2
    SET @IDList = SUBSTRING(@IDList,@Loc +1,2000);
    --4.3
    INSERT INTO @IDTable(ID)
    VALUES (@ID);
    --4.4
    SET @Loc = CHARINDEX(',',@IDList);
END;
--5
IF LEN(@IDList) > 0 BEGIN
    SET @ID = @IDList;
    INSERT INTO @IDTable(ID)
    VALUES (@ID);
END;

--6
SELECT BusinessEntityID, FirstName, LastName
FROM Person.Person AS p
WHERE BusinessEntityID IN (SELECT ID FROM @IDTable);
```

Figure 12-14 shows the results of running this code. Code section 1 declares four variables: @IDTable, which is a table variable; @IDList to hold the comma-delimited list sent from the application; @ID to hold one individual value from the list; and @Loc to hold the location of the comma. Statement 2 sets the value of @IDList, which represents the list of values sent by the application.

	BusinessEntityID	FirstName	LastName
1	16496	Gabriel	Mitchell
2	12506	Alejandro	Liang
3	11390	Christy	Tang
4	10798	Katherine	Smith
5	2191	Alfredo	Fuentes Espinosa
6	11235	Isabella	Martin
7	10879	Jenna	Hall
8	15040	Eduardo	Bell
9	3086	Stephanie	Ward

Figure 12-14. *The results of using a table variable*

The code finds each ID value from the comma-delimited string and stores the value in the table variable. Statement 3 finds the location of the first comma in the list and stores the location in @Loc. Code section 4 is a WHILE loop. Inside the WHILE loop, statement 4.1 stores the first value in the @ID variable, and statement 4.2 removes that value along with the comma from @IDList based on the value of @Loc. Statement 4.3 inserts the value stored in @ID into the table variable, @IDTable. Finally, at the bottom of the loop, statement 4.4 locates the next comma, resetting the value of @Loc. The loop continues as long as the code continues to find a comma in @IDList. Once the loop completes, the last value is most likely still in @IDList. Code section 5 checks the length of @IDList and inserts the last value into the table variable. This technique should only be used on a small number of values. Chapter 15 will demonstrate another method to parse the string using XML. Query 6 uses @IDTable in a subquery to filter the Person.Person table.

Using a Temp Table or Table Variable Like an Array

An *array* is a collection of values used in many programming languages. T-SQL doesn't have an array structure, but programmers sometimes use temp tables or table variables in the same manner as arrays. I often use this method in my administrative scripts to perform a backup or check the space used on each database on a server, for example. Listing 12-17 demonstrates how you might use a table variable like an array. Type in and execute the code to learn how to use this technique.

Listing 12-17. Using an Array

```
--1
SET NOCOUNT ON;
GO

--2
DECLARE @IDTable TABLE([Index] INT NOT NULL IDENTITY,
    ID INT);
DECLARE @RowCount INT;
DECLARE @ID INT;
DECLARE @Count INT = 1;

--3
INSERT INTO @IDTable(ID)
VALUES(500),(333),(200),(999);

--4
SELECT @RowCount = COUNT(*)
FROM @IDTable;

--5
WHILE @Count <= @RowCount BEGIN
    --5.1
    SELECT @ID = ID
    FROM @IDTable
    WHERE [Index] = @Count;
    --5.2
    PRINT CAST(@COUNT AS VARCHAR) + ': ' + CAST(@ID AS VARCHAR);
    --5.3
    SET @Count += 1;
END;
```

Figure 12-15 shows the results of running this code. Statement 1 sets the NOCOUNT property to ON. This will remove the messages showing how many each statement affects. In this case, the messages just get in the way. Code section 2 declares the variables used in this example. The table variable, @IDTable, contains an identity column called ArrayIndex. See Chapter 10 for more information about identity columns. Statement 3 populates @IDTable with several values. Because the database engine populates the INDEX column automatically, you now have a two-dimensional "array." Statement 4 populates the @RowCount variable with the number of rows in @IDTable. Code section 5 is a WHILE loop that runs once for each row in @IDTable. During each iteration of the loop, statement 5.1 sets the value of @ID with the ID column from @IDTable corresponding to the ArrayIndex column matching @Count. Statement 5.2 prints the @Count and @ID values, but you could do whatever you need to do instead of just printing the values. Statement 5.3 increments the @Count.

```
Messages
 1:  500
 2:  333
 3:  200
 4:  999
```

Figure 12-15. *The results of using an array*

Temp tables and table variables are just more tools in your T-SQL tool belt, but use them wisely.

Using a Cursor

Another way to loop through a result set is by using a cursor. This is a very controversial topic, especially for beginners. Developers frequently overuse cursors and end up writing poorly performing code, because when writing procedural code, you expect to go row by row. I'll cover cursors so that you are familiar with them and so that you understand the example in the "Thinking About Performance" section. Type in and execute the code from Listing 12-18, which shows a simple example.

Listing 12-18. Using a Cursor

```
--1
DECLARE @ProductID INT;
DECLARE @Name NVARCHAR(25);

--2
DECLARE products CURSOR FAST_FORWARD FOR
    SELECT ProductID, Name
    FROM Production.Product;

--3
OPEN products;

--4
FETCH NEXT FROM products INTO @ProductID, @Name;
```

```
--5
WHILE @@FETCH_STATUS = 0 BEGIN
    --5.1
    PRINT @ProductID;
    PRINT @Name;
    --5.2
    FETCH NEXT FROM products INTO @ProductID, @Name;
END

--6
CLOSE products;
DEALLOCATE products;
```

Figure 12-16 shows the results of running this code. Code section 1 declares variables that will be used later in the code. Statement 2 declares the cursor. The cursor must have a name and a SELECT statement. I included the option FAST_FORWARD to improve the performance. This option means that the cursor is read-only and you can only go forward in the data, not backward. See Books Online if you are interested in learning more about cursor options.

```
Messages
 1
 Adjustable Race
 879
 All-Purpose Bike Stand
 712
 AWC Logo Cap
 3
 BB Ball Bearing
 2
 Bearing Ball
 877
 Bike Wash - Dissolver
 316
 Blade
 843
 Cable Lock
```

Figure 12-16. *The partial results of using a cursor*

Statement 3 opens the cursor so that it is ready for access. Statement 4 reads the first row from the cursor into the variables. There must be one variable for each column selected in the cursor definition. The WHILE loop checks the status of the last read of the cursor. As long as the value is zero, the loop continues. Section 5.1 prints out the variables, but you could do anything you need to do at this point. Statement 5.2 is very important; it reads the next row. Without statement 5.2, the WHILE loop would continue indefinitely. Finally, section 6 cleans up the cursor. Cursors are another tool at your disposal, but use them only when another better-performing option is not available. Developers often use cursors to update one row at a time, which is usually a very bad idea.

Complete Exercise 12-4 to practice what you have learned about temporary tables and table variables.

EXERCISE 12-4

Use the AdventureWorks database to complete this exercise. You can find the solutions at the end of the chapter.

1. Create a temp table called #CustomerInfo that contains CustomerID (INT), FirstName, and LastName columns (NVARCHAR(50) for each one). Include CountOfSales (INT) and SumOfTotalDue (MONEY) columns. Populate the table with a query using the Sales.Customer, Person.Person, and Sales.SalesOrderHeader tables.

2. Change the code written in question 1 to use a table variable instead of a temp table.

3. Create a table variable with two integer columns, one of them an IDENTITY column. Use a WHILE loop to populate the table with 1,000 random integers using the following formula. Use a second WHILE loop to print the values from the table variable one by one.

```
CAST(RAND() * 10000 AS INT) + 1
```

Thinking About Performance

This chapter focuses on the logic features available in T-SQL instead of retrieving or updating data. Depending on the task at hand, you may or may not need to use this functionality. Often you may need to write or support very complex T-SQL scripts that run once each night. The performance of these scripts is not as critical as that of the performance of T-SQL code in an application or a report, but over time you may have to rewrite several to perform better. For example, a programmer from a software vendor writes a custom program that creates a denormalized table of information from a financial system. That table is needed by many other systems in the enterprise. The program as originally written takes more than an hour to run. Luckily, you have access to the original source code and find that the program populated this table one row and one column at a time. Another way of writing the code and having it run much faster is by using a set-based approach and inserting or updating all the rows at once from each source table instead of one row at a time.

The following example compares two ways to solve a typical problem. The first uses a cursor solution and the second a set-based approach. The requirements are to calculate sales totals by order year, order month, and TerritoryID. The report must also show the total sales for the previous month in the same row. Every territory, year, and month possible must appear on the report even if there are no sales for a particular combination. To save typing, you might want to download the code from this book's page at www.apress.com. Listing 12-19 uses a cursor and two nested WHILE loops to create a temp table with the totals. On my laptop, the code took 19 seconds to run.

Listing 12-19. Using a Cursor to Populate a Report

```
DECLARE @Year INT;
DECLARE @Month INT;
DECLARE @TerritoryID INT;
DECLARE @Total MONEY;
DECLARE @PreviousTotal MONEY;
DECLARE @FirstYear INT;
DECLARE @LastYear INT;
DECLARE @BeginDate DATETIME;
DECLARE @EndDate DATETIME;
```

```
--Create a table to hold the results
CREATE TABLE #Totals(OrderYear INT, OrderMonth INT,
    TerritoryID INT, TotalSales MONEY,
    PreviousSales MONEY);

--Grab the first and last years from the sales
SELECT @FirstYear = MIN(YEAR(OrderDate)),
    @LastYear = MAX(YEAR(OrderDate))
FROM Sales.SalesOrderHeader;

--Here we declare the cursor
DECLARE Territory CURSOR FAST_FORWARD FOR
    SELECT TerritoryID
    FROM Sales.SalesTerritory;

--Open the cursor
OPEN Territory;
--Save the values of the first row in variables
FETCH NEXT FROM Territory INTO @TerritoryID;
WHILE @@FETCH_STATUS = 0 BEGIN
    SET @Year = @FirstYear;
    --loop once for every year
    WHILE @Year <= @LastYear BEGIN
        --loop once for each month
        SET @Month = 1;
        WHILE @Month <= 12 BEGIN
            --find the beginning or end of the month
            SET @BeginDate = CAST(@Year AS VARCHAR) + '/' +
                CAST(@Month AS VARCHAR) + '/1';
            SET @EndDate = DATEADD(M,1,@BeginDate);
            --reset the total
            SET @Total = 0;
            --save the current value in the variable
            SELECT @Total = SUM(LineTotal)
            FROM Sales.SalesOrderDetail AS SOD
            INNER JOIN Sales.SalesOrderHeader AS SOH
            ON SOD.SalesOrderID = SOH.SalesOrderID
            WHERE TerritoryID = @TerritoryID
                AND OrderDate >= @BeginDate AND OrderDate < @EndDate;
            --set variables for this month
            SET @PreviousTotal = 0;
            SET @EndDate = @BeginDate;
            SET @BeginDate = DATEADD(M,-1,@BeginDate);

            --save the previous total
            SELECT @PreviousTotal = SUM(LineTotal)
            FROM Sales.SalesOrderDetail AS SOD
            INNER JOIN Sales.SalesOrderHeader AS SOH
            ON SOD.SalesOrderID = SOH.SalesOrderID
            WHERE TerritoryID = @TerritoryID
                AND OrderDate >= @BeginDate AND OrderDate < @EndDate;
```

```
        --insert the values
        INSERT INTO #Totals(TerritoryID, OrderYear,
        OrderMonth,TotalSales, PreviousSales)
        SELECT @TerritoryID, @Year, @Month,
        ISNULL(@Total,0), ISNULL(@PreviousTotal,0);

            SET @Month +=1;
        END; -- Month loop
        SET @Year += 1;
    END; -- Year Loop
    FETCH NEXT FROM Territory INTO @TerritoryID;
END; -- Territory cursor
CLOSE Territory;
DEALLOCATE Territory;

SELECT OrderYear, OrderMonth, TerritoryID,
    TotalSales, PreviousSales
FROM #Totals
WHERE TotalSales <> 0
ORDER BY OrderYear, OrderMonth, TerritoryID;

DROP TABLE #Totals;
```

The code in Listing 12-19 uses a cursor-based approach to populate a temp table for the report. The code creates a cursor that loops through the TerritoryID values. Inside the cursor loop, a WHILE loop of months is nested inside a WHILE loop of possible years. The code performs the calculations and inserts a row within the innermost loop. Finally, after the loops complete, a statement displays the results. This code actually performs better than some other code I have seen. It is not unusual to see code that not only loops through the territories but also loops through all the individual sales. Now try the example in Listing 12-20, which produces the same results much faster using a technique you learned in Chapter 8.

Listing 12-20. Producing the Report Without a Cursor

```
SELECT YEAR(OrderDate) AS OrderYear,
    MONTH(OrderDate) AS OrderMonth,
        TerritoryID,
        SUM(LineTotal) AS TotalSales,
        LAG(SUM(TotalDue),1,0)
            OVER(PARTITION BY TerritoryID
            ORDER BY YEAR(OrderDate),MONTH(OrderDate)) AS PreviousSales
FROM Sales.SalesOrderHeader AS SOH
JOIN Sales.SalesOrderDetail AS SOD
ON SOH.SalesOrderID = SOD.SalesOrderID
GROUP BY YEAR(OrderDate),
    MONTH(OrderDate), TerritoryID
    ORDER BY OrderYear, OrderMonth, TerritoryID;
```

Listing 12-20 uses the LAG function introduced to you in Chapter 8.

The point of this example is to show that most of the time a set-based approach can be found and is more efficient. It may take more practice and experience before you come up with this solution, but the more you work with T-SQL, the better you will get.

Summary

If you know one programming language, you will probably find the second and third languages even easier to learn because the logic is very similar. You will generally have ways to execute or avoid executing lines of code based on certain criteria. You will have ways to repeatedly execute lines code of code by looping. Whether or not you decide to implement this logic in T-SQL scripts will depend on the design of your application, the standards in your shop, or what works best for the problem at hand.

This chapter covered using variables, conditional logic, looping, and temporary table structures. In Chapter 13, you will use some of what you learned to trap errors in transactions. In Chapter 14, you will use what you have learned in this chapter to create stored procedures, user-defined functions, and more.

Answers to the Exercises

This section provides solutions to the exercises found on programming logic.

Solutions to Exercise 12-1: Variables

Use the AdventureWorks database to complete this exercise.

1. Write a script that declares an integer variable called @myInt. Assign 10 to the variable, and then print it.

   ```
   DECLARE @myInt INT = 10;
   PRINT @myInt;
   ```

2. Write a script that declares a VARCHAR(20) variable called @myString. Assign 'This is a test' to the variable, and print it.

   ```
   DECLARE @myString VARCHAR(20) = 'This is a test';
   PRINT @myString;
   ```

3. Write a script that declares two integer variables called @MaxID and @MinID. Use the variables to print the highest and lowest SalesOrderID values from the Sales.SalesOrderHeader table.

   ```
   DECLARE @MaxID INT, @MinID INT;
   SELECT @MaxID = MAX(SalesOrderID),
       @MinID = MIN(SalesOrderID)
   FROM Sales.SalesOrderHeader;
   PRINT CONCAT('Max: ', @MaxID);
   PRINT CONCAT('Min: ', @MinID);
   ```

4. Write a script that declares an integer variable called @ID. Assign the value 70000 to the variable. Use the variable in a SELECT statement that returns all the rows from the Sales.SalesOrderHeader table that have a SalesOrderID greater than the value of the variable.

   ```
   DECLARE @ID INT = 70000;
   SELECT SalesOrderID
   FROM Sales.SalesOrderHeader
   WHERE SalesOrderID > @ID;
   ```

5. Write a script that declares three variables, one integer variable called @ID, an NVARCHAR(50) variable called @FirstName, and an NVARCHAR(50) variable called @LastName. Use a SELECT statement to set the value of the variables with the row from the Person.Person table with BusinessEntityID = 1. Print a statement in the "BusinessEntityID: FirstName LastName" format.

```
DECLARE @ID INT, @FirstName NVARCHAR(50),
    @LastName NVARCHAR(50);

SELECT @ID = BusinessEntityID,
    @FirstName = FirstName,
    @LastName = LastName
FROM Person.Person
WHERE BusinessEntityID = 1;

PRINT CONVERT(NVARCHAR,@ID) + ': ' + @FirstName + ' ' + @LastName;
```

6. Write a script that declares an integer variable called @SalesCount. Set the value of the variable to the total count of sales in the Sales.SalesOrderHeader table. Use the variable in a SELECT statement that shows the difference between the @SalesCount and the count of sales by customer.

```
DECLARE @SalesCount INT;
SELECT @SalesCount = COUNT(*)
FROM Sales.SalesOrderHeader;

SELECT @SalesCount - COUNT(*) AS CustCountDiff,
    CustomerID
FROM Sales.SalesOrderHeader
GROUP BY CustomerID;
```

Solutions to Exercise 12-2: The *IF … ELSE* Construct

1. Write a batch that declares an integer variable called @Count to save the count of all the Sales.SalesOrderDetail records. Add an IF block that prints "Over 100,000" if the value exceeds 100,000. Otherwise, print "100,000 or less."

```
DECLARE @Count INT;
SELECT @Count = COUNT(*)
FROM Sales.SalesOrderDetail;

IF @Count > 100000 BEGIN
    PRINT 'Over 100,000';
END
ELSE BEGIN
    PRINT '100,000 or less.';
END;
```

2. Write a batch that contains nested IF blocks. The outer block should check to see whether the month is October or November. If that is the case, print "The month is " and the month name. The inner block should check to see whether the year is even or odd and print the result. You can modify the month to check to make sure the inner block fires.

```
IF MONTH(GETDATE()) IN (10,11) BEGIN
    PRINT 'The month is ' +
        DATENAME(mm, GETDATE());
    IF YEAR(GETDATE()) % 2 = 0 BEGIN
        PRINT 'The year is even.';
    END
    ELSE BEGIN
        PRINT 'The year is odd.';
    END
END;
```

3. Write a batch that uses IF EXISTS to check to see whether there is a row in the Sales. SalesOrderHeader table that has SalesOrderID = 1. Print "There is a SalesOrderID = 1" or "There is not a SalesOrderID = 1" depending on the result.

```
IF EXISTS(SELECT * FROM Sales.SalesOrderHeader
        WHERE SalesOrderID = 1) BEGIN
    PRINT 'There is a SalesOrderID = 1';
END
ELSE BEGIN
    PRINT 'There is not a SalesOrderID = 1';
END;
```

Solutions to Exercise 12-3: *WHILE*

Use the AdventureWorks database to complete this exercise.

1. Write a script that contains a WHILE loop that prints out the letters *A* to *Z*. Use the function CHAR to change a number to a letter. Start the loop with the value 65.

```
DECLARE @Letter CHAR(1);
SET @Letter = CHAR(65);
PRINT @Letter;

DECLARE @Count INT = 65;
WHILE @Count < 91 BEGIN
    PRINT CHAR(@Count);
    SET @Count += 1;
END;
```

2. Write a script that contains a WHILE loop nested inside another WHILE loop. The counter for the outer loop should count up from 1 to 100. The counter for the inner loop should count up from 1 to 5. Print the product of the two counters inside the inner loop.

```
DECLARE @i INT = 1;
DECLARE @j INT;
```

```
WHILE @i <= 100 BEGIN
    SET @j = 1;
    WHILE @j <= 5 BEGIN
        PRINT @i * @j;
        SET @j += 1;
    END;
    SET @i += 1;
END;
```

3. Change the script in question 2 so the inner loop exits instead of printing when the counter for the outer loop is evenly divisible by 5.

```
DECLARE @i INTEGER = 1;
DECLARE @j INTEGER;
WHILE @i <= 100 BEGIN
    SET @j = 1;
    WHILE @j <= 5 BEGIN
        IF @i % 5 = 0 BEGIN
            PRINT 'Breaking out of loop.'
            BREAK;
        END;
        PRINT @i * @j;
        SET @j += 1;
    END;
    SET @i += 1;
END;
```

4. Write a script that contains a WHILE loop that counts up from 1 to 100. Print "Odd" or "Even" depending on the value of the counter.

```
DECLARE @Count INT = 1;
WHILE @Count <= 100 BEGIN
    IF @Count % 2 = 0 BEGIN
        PRINT 'Even';
    END
    ELSE BEGIN
        PRINT 'Odd';
    END
    SET @Count += 1;
END;
```

Solutions to Exercise 12-4: Temporary Tables and Table Variables

Use the AdventureWorks database to complete this exercise. You can find the solutions at the end of the chapter.

1. Create a temp table called #CustomerInfo that contains CustomerID (INT), FirstName, and LastName columns (NVARCHAR(50) for each one). Include CountOfSales (INT) and SumOfTotalDue (MONEY) columns. Populate the table with a query using the Sales. Customer, Person.Person, and Sales.SalesOrderHeader tables.

```
CREATE TABLE #CustomerInfo(
    CustomerID INT, FirstName NVARCHAR(50),
    LastName NVARCHAR(50),CountOfSales INT,
    SumOfTotalDue MONEY);
```

```
GO
INSERT INTO #CustomerInfo(CustomerID,FirstName,LastName,
    CountOfSales, SumOfTotalDue)
SELECT C.CustomerID, FirstName, LastName,COUNT(*),SUM(TotalDue)
FROM Sales.Customer AS C
INNER JOIN Person.Person AS P ON C.CustomerID = P.BusinessEntityID
INNER JOIN Sales.SalesOrderHeader
    AS SOH ON C.CustomerID = SOH.CustomerID
GROUP BY C.CustomerID, FirstName, LastName;
```

2. Change the code written in question 1 to use a table variable instead of a temp table.

```
DECLARE @CustomerInfo TABLE (
    CustomerID INT, FirstName VARCHAR(50),
    LastName VARCHAR(50),CountOfSales INT,
    SumOfTotalDue MONEY);
INSERT INTO @CustomerInfo(CustomerID,
    FirstName, LastName,
    CountOfSales, SumOfTotalDue)

SELECT C.CustomerID, FirstName,
    LastName,COUNT(*),SUM(TotalDue)
FROM Sales.Customer AS C
INNER JOIN Person.Person AS P
    ON C.CustomerID = P.BusinessEntityID
INNER JOIN Sales.SalesOrderHeader
    AS SOH ON C.CustomerID = SOH.CustomerID
GROUP BY C.CustomerID, FirstName, LastName;
```

3. Create a table variable with two integer columns, one of them an IDENTITY column. Use a
    WHILE loop to populate the table with 1,000 random integers using the following formula.
    Use a second WHILE loop to print the values from the table variable one by one.

```
CAST(RAND() * 10000 AS INT) + 1
```

Here's a possible solution:

```
DECLARE @test TABLE (ID INTEGER NOT NULL IDENTITY, Random INT)
DECLARE @Count INT = 1;
DECLARE @Value INT;

WHILE @Count <= 1000 BEGIN
    SET @Value = CAST(RAND()*10000 AS INT) + 1;
    INSERT INTO @test(Random)
    VALUES(@Value);
    SET @Count += 1;
END;
SET @Count = 1;
WHILE @Count <= 1000 BEGIN
    SELECT @Value = Random
    FROM @test
    WHERE ID = @Count;
    PRINT @Value;
    SET @Count += 1;
END;
```

CHAPTER 13

■ ■ ■

Managing Transactions

In Chapter 10, you learned how to manipulate data using T-SQL statements. In this chapter, you will learn about a very important aspect of manipulating data: transactions. A *transaction* is a unit of work in SQL Server. Most of the time, a transaction is one statement that inserts, updates, or deletes data. It is possible, however, to define an explicit transaction that includes one or more statements. You can also include SELECT statements in a transaction. A transaction can be committed or rolled back as a unit.

The classic example involves a bank ATM where a customer can transfer money from a savings account to a checking account. Imagine the problems created if an error occurred after the system subtracted the money from the savings account but before the money showed up in the checking account! By using an explicit transaction, any error between the two updates can cause a roll back of both of them. If an error occurred, the money would just go back to the savings account like nothing had happened. This chapter covers writing multiple statements within explicit transactions, how to commit or roll back transactions, and what happens when transactions last longer than needed.

ACID Properties

One of the most common questions at an interview for a DBA or database developer job is to explain the ACID (atomicity, consistency, isolation, durability) properties of a database system. These properties guarantee the reliability of the data in a database. Imagine that you have deposited your check at the bank. I'm sure you don't want record of that check to disappear when the bank reboots its servers! Table 13-1 lists the ACID properties and what they mean.

Table 13-1. *The ACID Properties*

Property	Purpose
Atomicity	A transaction is one unit of work.
Consistency	A transaction must leave the database in a consistent state. A transaction must follow the rules, like constraints, defined in the database.
Isolation	A transaction cannot affect other transactions.
Durability	Once a transaction has been committed, it will not be lost, even after a reboot or power outage.

These properties are not important for every database. You may have heard about database systems like NoSQL and MySQL that are not generally ACID compliant.

Writing an Explicit Transaction

The important thing to remember when working with SQL Server is to keep transactions as short as they can be and still do the work. Once a transaction starts, the database engine puts locks on rows or tables involved within the transaction so that the rows usually may not be accessed by another query when the default settings are in place. Here is the syntax for a simple transaction:

```
BEGIN TRAN|TRANSACTION
    <statement 1>
    <statement 2>
COMMIT [TRAN|TRANSACTION]
```

Listing 13-1 demonstrates what happens when a transaction fails for some types of errors. Type in and execute the code.

Listing 13-1. Explicit Transactions

```
IF  EXISTS (SELECT * FROM sys.objects
            WHERE object_id = OBJECT_ID(N'[dbo].[demoTransaction]')
                AND type in (N'U'))
DROP TABLE [dbo].[demoTransaction];
GO

CREATE TABLE dbo.demoTransaction (col1 INT NOT NULL);
GO

--1
BEGIN TRAN
    INSERT INTO dbo.demoTransaction (col1) VALUES (1);
    INSERT INTO dbo.demoTransaction (col1) VALUES (2);
COMMIT TRAN;

--2
BEGIN TRAN
    INSERT INTO dbo.demoTransaction (col1) VALUES (3);
    INSERT INTO dbo.demoTransaction (col1) VALUES ('a');
COMMIT TRAN;

GO
--3
SELECT col1
FROM dbo.demoTransaction;
```

Figure 13-1 shows the results of running this code. After running the batch, the query window will display the Messages tab first with an error message. You will have to click the Results tab to see the inserted rows. Transaction block 1 successfully inserts two rows with integer values into the table. Transaction block 2 inserts the value 3 and the value a. Because you can't insert the string value a into a column of type INT, the statement fails. In this case, the entire transaction fails. Query 3 returns the inserted rows, which are only the rows inserted in the first transaction. In reality, not all error types will cause the entire transaction to fail. You must add error handling, which you will learn about later in the chapter.

	col1
1	1
2	2

Figure 13-1. *The results of using explicit transactions to insert data*

Rolling Back a Transaction

You can purposely roll a transaction back before it is committed by issuing a ROLLBACK command even without an error condition. For example, when transferring money from your savings account to your checking account, what if the bank ATM added the money to the checking account before removing it from the savings account and didn't check the savings account balance first? The transaction could roll back the transaction once the balance was checked but before the transaction was committed. Here is the syntax for rolling back a transaction:

```
BEGIN TRAN|TRANSACTION
    <statement 1>
    <statement 2>
ROLLBACK [TRAN|TRANSACTION]
```

Before rolling back a transaction, you can also check the value of the @@TRANCOUNT variable. This is a count of the BEGIN TRAN statements and it resets to 0 after a COMMIT or ROLLBACK. Later in this chapter you will learn how to trap errors and use conditional logic that will allow your code to COMMIT or ROLLBACK based on certain conditions. For now, type in and execute Listing 13-2 to learn how to use the ROLLBACK command.

Listing 13-2. Using a ROLLBACK Command

```
IF  EXISTS (SELECT * FROM sys.objects
            WHERE object_id = OBJECT_ID(N'[dbo].[demoTransaction]')
              AND type in (N'U'))
DROP TABLE [dbo].[demoTransaction];
GO

CREATE TABLE dbo.demoTransaction (col1 INT NOT NULL);
GO

--1
BEGIN TRAN
    INSERT INTO dbo.demoTransaction (col1) VALUES (1);
    INSERT INTO dbo.demoTransaction (col1) VALUES (2);
COMMIT TRAN

--2
BEGIN TRAN
    INSERT INTO dbo.demoTransaction (col1) VALUES (3);
    INSERT INTO dbo.demoTransaction (col1) VALUES (4);
ROLLBACK TRAN
```

```
GO
--3
SELECT col1
FROM dbo.demoTransaction;

DROP TABLE dbo.demoTransaction;
```

Figure 13-2 shows the results of running this code. Transaction block 1 completes successfully and inserts the two rows in the table. Transaction block 2 contains two valid statements, but because it contains the ROLLBACK command instead of the COMMIT command, the transaction doesn't complete. Query 3 shows that the batch inserts only values 1 and 2 into the table.

	col1
1	1
2	2

Figure 13-2. The results of a rolled-back transaction

Using the *XACT_ABORT* Setting

The XACT_ABORT setting automatically rolls back transactions and stops the batch in the case of runtime errors such as violating primary or foreign keys. Listing 13-3 is an example that shows the default behavior, the setting is turned off.

Listing 13-3. Using XACT_ABORT with the Setting Off

```
--1
CREATE TABLE #Test_XACT_OFF(COL1 INT PRIMARY KEY, COL2 VARCHAR(10));

--2
--What happens with the default?
BEGIN TRANSACTION
    INSERT INTO #Test_XACT_OFF(COL1,COL2)
    VALUES(1,'A');

    INSERT INTO #Test_XACT_OFF(COL1,COL2)
        VALUES(2,'B');

    INSERT INTO #Test_XACT_OFF(COL1,COL2)
        VALUES(1,'C');
COMMIT TRANSACTION;

--3
SELECT * FROM #Test_XACT_OFF;
```

Figure 13-3 shows that only two rows have been inserted. The second insert has failed, but the other two insert statements succeeded in adding the two rows. If you take a look at the Messages tab, you'll see that the primary key has been violated.

	COL1	COL2
1	1	A
2	2	B

Figure 13-3. *The results of using the default XACT_ABORT behavior*

To see what happens when the setting is turned on, run Listing 13-4.

Listing 13-4. Testing XACT_ABORT with the Setting On

```
--1
CREATE TABLE #Test_XACT_ON(COL1 INT PRIMARY KEY, COL2 VARCHAR(10));

--2
--Turn on the setting
SET XACT_ABORT ON;
GO

--3
BEGIN TRANSACTION
    INSERT INTO #Test_XACT_ON(COL1,COL2)
    VALUES(1,'A');

    INSERT INTO #Test_XACT_ON(COL1,COL2)
        VALUES(2,'B');

    INSERT INTO #Test_XACT_ON(COL1,COL2)
        VALUES(1,'C');
COMMIT TRANSACTION;

GO
--4
SELECT * FROM #Test_XACT_ON;
GO

--5
SET XACT_ABORT OFF;
```

Statement 2 turns on the XACT_ABORT setting. Statement 3 is identical to the transaction in Listing 13-3. In this case, because the setting is turned on, none of the rows are inserted. The entire transaction is rolled back. Finally, statement 5 turns the setting back off. When using this setting, it is only in effect within the current connection or until it is toggled off. Practice what you have learned by completing Exercise 13-1.

EXERCISE 13-1

Use the AdventureWorks database to complete this exercise. Run the following script to create a table for this exercise. You can find the solutions at the end of the chapter.

```
IF OBJECT_ID('dbo.Demo') IS NOT NULL BEGIN
    DROP TABLE dbo.Demo;
END;
GO
CREATE TABLE dbo.Demo(ID INT PRIMARY KEY, Name VARCHAR(25));
```

1. Write a transaction that includes two INSERT statements to add two rows to the dbo.Demo table.

2. Write a transaction that includes two INSERT statements to add two more rows to the dbo. Demo table. Attempt to insert a letter instead of a number into the ID column in one of the statements. Select the data from the dbo.Demo table to see which rows made it to the table.

Error Handling

Applications must gracefully handle errors, especially those occurring within the context of a transaction. T-SQL has two ways to deal with errors, one of which you will learn about in this section in detail. The legacy way to handle errors was by checking the value of the @@ERROR function. This older method was messy and inefficient. In this section, you will learn the modern way to handle errors. If you are writing T-SQL code within an application (for example, with a .NET language), your program will probably deal with the errors. If, however, you are writing a T-SQL script, you can handle errors at the T-SQL level. You can and should do both; you can handle errors within T-SQL and decide what you want sent back to the calling application.

Using *TRY...CATCH*

The TRY . . . CATCH error handling method is similar to the error handling in other programming languages such as C# and VB.NET. Along with this newer method, you use several functions that provide information about the error. You can also avoid sending an error message to the client if you choose. Here is the syntax:

```
BEGIN TRY
    <statements that might cause an error>
END TRY
BEGIN CATCH
    <statements to access error information and deal with the error>
END CATCH
```

Table 13-2 lists the functions you use along with TRY . . . CATCH. One benefit is that the functions retain their values while in the CATCH block. You can access the values as many times as needed. Once outside the CATCH block, the values of the error functions revert to NULL.

Table 13-2. *The Error Functions*

Function	Purpose
ERROR_NUMBER()	Provides the error number. This was the only information you could get in previous releases.
ERROR_SEVERITY()	Provides the severity of the error. The severity must exceed 10 in order to be trapped.
ERROR_STATE()	Provides the state code of the error. This refers to the cause of the error.
ERROR_PROCEDURE()	Returns the name of a stored procedure or trigger that caused the error.
ERROR_LINE()	Returns the line number that caused the error.
ERROR_MESSAGE()	Returns the actual text message describing the error.

Listing 13-5 demonstrates how to use TRY . . . CATCH. Type in and execute the code to learn how to use it.

Listing 13-5. Using TRY . . . CATCH

```
--1
BEGIN TRY
    PRINT 1/0;
END TRY
BEGIN CATCH
    PRINT 'Inside the Catch block';
    PRINT ERROR_NUMBER();
    PRINT ERROR_MESSAGE();
    PRINT ERROR_NUMBER();
END CATCH
PRINT 'Outside the catch block';
PRINT CASE WHEN ERROR_NUMBER() IS NULL THEN 'NULL'
    ELSE CAST(ERROR_NUMBER() AS VARCHAR(10)) END;
GO

--2
BEGIN TRY
    DROP TABLE testTable;
END TRY
BEGIN CATCH
    PRINT 'An error has occurred.'
    PRINT ERROR_NUMBER();
    PRINT ERROR_MESSAGE();
END CATCH;
```

Figure 13-4 shows the results of running this code. One difference between TRY . . . CATCH and @@ERROR is that you can print the error numbers and messages multiple times within the CATCH block. The values reset to NULL once execution leaves the CATCH block. When using TRY . . . CATCH, the error will not print at all unless you purposely print it. It is possible to just ignore the error, but most of the time you will want to do something else. You might want to record the error in a log table or retry the transaction.

```
 Messages
 Inside the Catch block
 8134
 Divide by zero error encountered.
 8134
 Outside the catch block
 NULL
 An error has occurred.
 3701
 Cannot drop the table 'testTable', because it does not exist
```

Figure 13-4. *The results of using TRY...CATCH*

Viewing Untrappable Errors

TRY . . . CATCH can't trap some errors. For example, if the code contains an incorrect table or column name or a database server is not available, the entire batch of statements will fail, and the error will not be trapped. One interesting way to work around this problem is to encapsulate calls within stored procedures and then call the stored procedure inside the TRY block. You will learn about stored procedures in Chapter 14. Database administrators might use the stored procedure technique for management jobs, for example, checking the job history on each server. If one server is down, the database administrator would want the code to continue to check the other servers. Type in and execute Listing 13-6 to see some examples.

Listing 13-6. Untrappable Errors

```
--1
PRINT 'Syntax error.';
GO
BEGIN TRY
    SELECT FROM Sales.SalesOrderDetail;
END TRY
BEGIN CATCH
    PRINT ERROR_NUMBER();
END CATCH;
GO

--2
PRINT 'Invalid column.';
GO
BEGIN TRY
    SELECT ABC FROM Sales.SalesOrderDetail;
END TRY
BEGIN CATCH
    PRINT ERROR_NUMBER();
END CATCH;
```

Figure 13-5 shows the results of running this code. I put the PRINT statements before each TRY . . . CATCH block in separate batches because they wouldn't print along with these incorrect statements. Example 1 is a syntax error; the SELECT list is empty. Example 2 contains an invalid column name.

```
 Messages
  Syntax error.
  Msg 156, Level 15, State 1, Line 2
  Incorrect syntax near the keyword 'FROM'.
  Invalid column.
  Msg 207, Level 16, State 1, Line 2
  Invalid column name 'ABC'.
```

Figure 13-5. *The results of running untrappable errors*

Using *RAISERROR*

By using TRY . . . CATCH, you can avoid having an error message return to the client application, basically "trapping" the error. Sometimes you might want to return a different error or return an error to the client when one doesn't exist. For example, you might want to return an error message to a client when the code tries to update a nonexistent row. This wouldn't cause a database error, but you might want to cause an error to fire anyway from SQL Server to the client application. You can use the RAISERROR function to raise an error back to the client. Here is the syntax:

```
RAISERROR(<message>,<severity>,<state>)
```

The RAISERROR function has several other optional parameters that provide additional functionality, but for a first look, these three parameters may be all you need. You can create reusable custom error messages by using the sp_addmessage stored procedure or just use a variable or hard-coded string with RAISERROR. Type in and execute Listing 13-7 to learn how to use RAISERROR.

Listing 13-7. Using RAISERROR

```
USE master;
GO

--1 This code section creates a custom error message
IF EXISTS(SELECT * FROM sys.messages where message_id = 50002) BEGIN
    EXEC sp_dropmessage 50002;
END;
GO
PRINT 'Creating a custom error message.'
EXEC sp_addmessage 50002, 16,
   N'Customer missing.';
GO

USE AdventureWorks;
GO
--2
IF NOT EXISTS(SELECT * FROM Sales.Customer
        WHERE CustomerID = -1) BEGIN
   RAISERROR(50002,16,1);
END;
GO
```

```
--3
BEGIN TRY
    PRINT 1/0;
END TRY
BEGIN CATCH
    IF ERROR_NUMBER() = 8134 BEGIN
        RAISERROR('A bad math error!',16,1);
    END;
END CATCH;
```

Figure 13-6 shows the results of running this code. You can provide either a message number or a message string for the message parameter. Batch 1 sets up a custom error message that you can use later when raising an error, as in batch 2. Batch 3 returns a different error message to the client than the one that actually happened. Because the code returned an ad hoc error message, the database engine supplied the default number, 50000. The second parameter, severity, ranges from 1 to 25. When under 11, the message is a warning or information. You might want to build a dynamic error based on what happened in your code. If you would like to do this, make sure you save the message in a variable. You can't build the message dynamically inside the RAISERROR function, you can only use a variable or literal value. See the Books Online article "Database Engine Error Severities" to learn more about error severities, but you will generally use 16 for errors correctable by the user. The state parameter is an integer between 1 and 255. You can use state to define where in the code the error occurred.

```
Messages
Creating a custom error message.
Msg 50002, Level 16, State 1, Line 4
Customer missing.
Msg 50000, Level 16, State 1, Line 8
A bad math error!
```

Figure 13-6. *The results of using RAISERROR*

Using *TRY…CATCH* with Transactions

You can use TRY . . . CATCH to make sure that explicit transactions complete successfully so the transaction may be rolled back if necessary. Include the transaction in the TRY block. Type in and execute Listing 13-8, which shows a simple example.

Listing 13-8. Using TRY…CATCH with a Transaction

```
--1
CREATE TABLE #Test (ID INT NOT NULL PRIMARY KEY);
GO


--2
BEGIN TRY
    --2.1
    BEGIN TRAN
        --2.1.1
        INSERT INTO #Test (ID)
        VALUES (1),(2),(3);
```

```
        --2.1.2
        UPDATE #Test SET ID = 2 WHERE ID = 1;
    --2.2
    COMMIT
END TRY

--3
BEGIN CATCH
    --3.1
    PRINT ERROR_MESSAGE();
    --3.2
    PRINT 'Rolling back transaction';
    IF @@TRANCOUNT > 0 BEGIN
        ROLLBACK;
    END;
END CATCH;
```

Figure 13-7 shows the error message and the transaction rolled back. Statement 2.1.2 attempts to set the value ID to 2 in the row where it equals 1. This violates the primary key; you can't have two rows with the value 2. If the entire transaction had been successful, the COMMIT statement would have committed the transaction. Instead, the CATCH block fired, giving you the chance to handle the error.

```
 Messages

 (3 row(s) affected)

 (0 row(s) affected)
 Violation of PRIMARY KEY constraint 'PK__#Test_____3214EC27AE98F49C'.
 Cannot insert duplicate key in object 'dbo.#Test'. The duplicate
 key value is (2).
 Rolling back transaction
```

Figure 13-7. *The results of using TRY . . . CATCH with a transaction*

Using *THROW* Instead of *RAISERROR*

New in SQL Server 2012 is the THROW statement. You'll find using THROW to be much simpler than using RAISERROR. For example, the error number in the THROW statement doesn't have to exist in sys.messages. Here is the syntax:

```
THROW [ { error_number | message | state } ] [ ; ]
```

Any statement prior to the THROW command must end with a semicolon. Any error occurring in the THROW statement will cause the batch execution to end. Listing 13-9 shows a basic THROW command. The severity will always be 16. Figure 13-8 shows the output.

Listing 13-9. Simple THROW Statement

```
THROW 999999, 'This is a test error.', 1;
```

```
 Messages
 Msg 999999, Level 16, State 1, Line 1
 This is a test error.
```

Figure 13-8. *Results of THROW statement*

Now let's see how to use the THROW statement in a TRY CATCH block. For this example, you'll attempt to insert a duplicate row into the Person.PersonPhone table. Run the script in Listing 13-10. Figure 13-9 shows the output. Feel free to change the error message to anything you want.

Listing 13-10. Using THROW in a transaction

```
BEGIN TRY
INSERT INTO Person.PersonPhone (BusinessEntityID, PhoneNumber, PhoneNumberTypeID)
VALUES (1, '697-555-0142', 1);
END TRY
BEGIN CATCH
THROW 999999, 'I will not allow you to insert a duplicate value.', 1;
END CATCH;
```

```
 Messages

 (0 row(s) affected)
 Msg 999999, Level 16, State 1, Line 6
 I will not allow you to insert a duplicate value.
```

Figure 13-9. *Results of THROW statement in a transaction*

As you can see, the THROW statement is easy to use and extremely customizable. The command is especially useful for those unusual application errors that SQL Server may not be aware of or may not explain with a clearly expressive message indicating the content of the error. As always, though, try to keep your error messages easily understandable and detailed enough to help diagnose the error.

Trapping and handling errors is a very important part of T-SQL. If anything can go wrong, it often will. Practice what you have learned by completing Exercise 13-2.

EXERCISE 13-2

Use AdventureWorks to complete this exercise. You can find the solutions at the end of the chapter.

1. Write a statement that attempts to insert a duplicate row into the HumanResources.Department table. Use TRY . . . CATCH to trap the error. Display the error number, message and severity.

2. Change the code you wrote in question 1 to raise a custom error message instead of the actual error message.

Thinking About Performance

The old programming joke is that a transaction includes waiting for the end user to click an OK button. But instead of clicking the button, the end user goes to lunch, effectively locking up the application for the rest of the users until he gets back to his desk. Make sure that explicit transactions only update data that must be updated as a unit, not just because you have a batch of statements that go together. Transactions should be kept as short as possible to decrease performance issues caused by excessive blocking in your applications.

SQL Server has several *isolation levels* to control how transactions from one connection affect statements from another connection. This section will demonstrate the default behavior and then compare it to another isolation level that is sometimes used to increase performance, but with unfortunate side effects. The default SQL Server isolation level is called *Read Committed*. This means that while a transaction happens, other connections cannot see the data that the transaction has locked. Although looking at transaction levels at a deep level is beyond the scope of this book, I recommend reading *SQL Server Concurrency: Locking, Blocking and Row Versioning* by Kalen Delaney (Redgate, 2013) to learn more.

For this example, you will use two query windows, so follow the instructions carefully.

From query window 1, run this code:

```
IF  EXISTS (SELECT * FROM sys.objects
            WHERE object_id = OBJECT_ID(N'[dbo].[demoTransaction]')
              AND type in (N'U'))
DROP TABLE [dbo].[demoTransaction];
GO


CREATE TABLE dbo.demoTransaction (col1 INT NOT NULL);
GO


BEGIN TRAN
    INSERT INTO dbo.demoTransaction (col1) VALUES (1);
    INSERT INTO dbo.demoTransaction (col1) VALUES (2);
```

Switch to window 2, and run this code:

```
SELECT col1 FROM dbo.demoTransaction;
```

At this point, you will see nothing returned from the code from step 2 as it waits for the transaction in window 1 to complete. The code in window 2 is blocked by the transaction in window 1. Switch to window 1, and run this code:

```
COMMIT TRAN;
```

Switch back to window 2 to view the results.

Once you committed the transaction, the SELECT statement in window 2 could complete. Obviously, this isolation level will affect the performance of your application, and the application must be written to keep transactions short and have retry logic.

To get around the isolation aspect of the ACID properties and eliminate blocking, some shops use another isolation level called *Read Uncommitted*, the least restrictive level available. Before using this isolation level, it is important to understand just how this can cause incorrect results as uncommitted data, called *dirty reads*, is returned.

This isolation can be enabled in two ways. First, the SET TRANSACTION ISOLATION LEVEL command can be used. This changes the isolation level for the connection. The second way is to use the NOLOCK hint in a query. Follow the instructions carefully to see how this works. Run this code in window 1:

```
--1
IF  EXISTS (SELECT * FROM sys.objects
            WHERE object_id = OBJECT_ID(N'[dbo].[demoTransaction]')
               AND type in (N'U'))
DROP TABLE [dbo].[demoTransaction];
GO

CREATE TABLE dbo.demoTransaction (col1 INT NOT NULL);
GO
--2
INSERT INTO dbo.demoTransaction (col1) VALUES (1);
INSERT INTO dbo.demoTransaction (col1) VALUES (2);

--3
BEGIN TRANSACTION
UPDATE dbo.demoTransaction SET Col1 = 100;
```

Now switch to window 2 and run this code:

```
SET TRANSACTION ISOLATION LEVEL READ UNCOMMITTED;
GO
SELECT col1 FROM dbo.demoTransaction;
```

Even though the transaction to update the rows has not committed in window 1, the change can be seen in window 2. This update has not been committed in the database, but the second connection still returns the change.

Go back to window 1 and run this code to undo the change:

```
ROLLBACK;
```

Rerun the code in window 2. Now the correct results are displayed, the data is back to the original values. Obviously, this isolation level can be very dangerous. It can cause invalid results to be returned. Starting with SQL Server 2005, Microsoft introduced a new type of isolation level called *Snapshot* that creates copies of the data in tempdb before the data is changed. This is called *row versioning*. Any reads of the data during the transaction comes from the row version copies. That way updates to the data do not block reads of the data.

Summary

When manipulating data, you are performing transactions. These transactions are either implicit, each statement is a transaction, or explicit, one or more statements marked by BEGIN TRANSACTION and COMMIT TRANSACTION or ROLLBACK TRANSACTION statements. Be sure to know, based on the requirements of your application, when explicit transactions should be used.

Answers to the Exercises

This section provides solutions to the exercises found on using transactions.

Solutions to Exercise 13-1: Writing an Explicit Transaction

Use the AdventureWorks database to complete this exercise. Run the following script to create a table for this exercise.

```
IF OBJECT_ID('dbo.Demo') IS NOT NULL BEGIN
    DROP TABLE dbo.Demo;
END;
GO
CREATE TABLE dbo.Demo(ID INT PRIMARY KEY, Name VARCHAR(25));
```

1. Write a transaction that includes two INSERT statements to add two rows to the dbo.Demo table.

    Here's a possible solution:

    ```
    BEGIN TRAN
        INSERT INTO dbo.Demo(ID,Name)
        VALUES (1,'Test1');

        INSERT INTO dbo.Demo(ID,Name)
        VALUES(2,'Test2');
    COMMIT TRAN;
    ```

2. Write a transaction that includes two INSERT statements to add two more rows to the dbo. Demo table. Attempt to insert a letter instead of a number into the ID column in one of the statements. Select the data from the dbo.Demo table to see which rows made it to the table.

    Here's a possible solution:

    ```
    BEGIN TRAN
        INSERT INTO dbo.Demo(ID,Name)
        VALUES(3,'Test3');
        INSERT INTO dbo.Demo(ID,Name)
        VALUES('a','Test4');
    COMMIT TRAN;
    GO
    SELECT ID,Name
    FROM dbo.Demo;
    ```

Solutions to Exercise 13-2: Error Handling

Use AdventureWorks to complete this exercise.

1. Write a statement that attempts to insert a duplicate row into the HumanResources. Department table. Use TRY . . . CATCH to trap the error. Display the error number, message and severity.

```
BEGIN TRY
    INSERT INTO
        HumanResources.Department
        (Name, GroupName, ModifiedDate)
    VALUES ('Engineering','Research and Development', GETDATE());
END TRY
BEGIN CATCH
    SELECT ERROR_NUMBER() AS
        ErrorNumber,ERROR_MESSAGE()
            AS ErrorMessage,
        ERROR_SEVERITY() AS ErrorSeverity;
END CATCH;
```

2. Change the code you wrote in question 1 to raise a custom error message instead of the actual error message.

```
BEGIN TRY
    INSERT INTO
        HumanResources.Department
            (Name, GroupName, ModifiedDate)
    VALUES ('Engineering',
        'Research and Development',
        GETDATE());
END TRY
BEGIN CATCH
    IF ERROR_NUMBER() = 2627 BEGIN
        RAISERROR(
            'You attempted to insert a duplicate!',
            16, 1);
    END;
END CATCH;
```

Implementing Logic in the Database

So far you have worked exclusively with tables by using Data Manipulation Language (DML) statements. You have learned to manipulate data by inserting new rows and updating or deleting existing rows. You can use many other objects in a SQL Server database to make your database applications more efficient and secure. You have also used control flow language. This chapter teaches you how to add restrictions to tables and to create other objects that help to enforce key business rules. In this chapter, you will learn about Data Definition Language (DDL) statements and constraints on tables, views, stored procedures, user-defined functions, and user-defined types. Because SQL Server provides so many choices for creating these objects, this chapter doesn't attempt to explore every possible option. The chapter does, however, provide enough detail to teach you most of what you will encounter on your journey to becoming an expert T-SQL developer.

Tables

SQL Server and other database systems store data in tables. You have learned how to retrieve data from tables as well as how to insert, update, and delete data. Specifically, you learned how to create temporary tables in Chapter 12 and how to create tables using the SELECT INTO and CREATE TABLE syntax in Chapter 10. You have already started to define business rules when you chose a data type and nullability. You can enforce even more business rules based on the constraints you can add to the table definition.

As a beginner T-SQL developer, you will most likely write T-SQL code against a database already in place, possibly from a software vendor or one created by a design team using data-modeling software to create the tables. Although your job description may not include writing scripts to create tables, you do need to understand how the table definition controls the data you can insert into a table and how you can update the data. This section covers many options available when creating or altering tables such as computed columns, primary keys, foreign keys, and other constraints. The point of this section is not to encourage you to memorize how to add keys and constraints but rather to give you an understanding of the implications of having them in place.

Tip By using SQL Server Management Studio, you can script the commands to create existing tables and other objects in the database. This is a great way to learn how to write scripts and learn the syntax. To script the definition of a table, right-click the object and select the Script table as menu. Then select the Create to option.

Adding Check Constraints to a Table

As you already know, each column in a table must have a specific data type and usually a maximum size that controls what data can be inserted or updated and whether a column may contain NULL values. For example, you can't add a non-numeric string to an INT column. It is also possible to further control what data you can add by defining check constraints. For example, you may want to restrict the values of a column to a particular range of values.

■ **Note**   The NULL and NOT NULL options are also commonly referred to as *constraints*.

Here is the syntax to add a check constraint to a table when creating the table and later with an ALTER TABLE command:

```
--Adding during CREATE TABLE
CREATE TABLE <table name> (<col1> <data type>,<col2> <data type>,
    CONSTRAINT <constraint name> CHECK (<condition>))

--Adding during ALTER TABLE
CREATE TABLE <table name> (<col1> <data type>, <col2> <data type>)
ALTER TABLE <table name> ADD CONSTRAINT <constraint name> CHECK (<condition>)
```

The condition looks much like the criteria in a WHERE clause. If you try to insert or update data that would return false, the change will not succeed. Although the constraint name is optional, the name will appear in any error messages when the constraint is violated, therefore helping you troubleshoot. Type in and execute the code in Listing 14-1 to learn how to add a constraint.

Listing 14-1. Adding a Check Constraint

```
USE tempdb;
GO
--1
IF OBJECT_ID('table1') IS NOT NULL BEGIN
    DROP TABLE table1;
END;

--2
CREATE TABLE table1 (col1 SMALLINT, col2 VARCHAR(20),
    CONSTRAINT ch_table1_col2_months
    CHECK (col2 IN ('January','February','March','April','May',
        'June','July','August','September','October',
        'November','December')
    )
 );

--3
ALTER TABLE table1 ADD CONSTRAINT ch_table1_col1
    CHECK (col1 BETWEEN 1 and 12);
PRINT 'January';

--4
INSERT INTO table1 (col1,col2)
VALUES (1,'Jan');
```

```
PRINT 'February';

--5
INSERT INTO table1 (col1,col2)
VALUES (2,'February');

PRINT 'March';

--6
INSERT INTO table1 (col1,col2)
VALUES (13,'March');

PRINT 'Change 2 to 20';
--7
UPDATE table1 SET col1 = 20;
```

Figure 14-1 shows the results of running this code. Code section 1 drops the table in case it already exists. Statement 2 creates table1 along with a constraint specifying that the exact months of the year may be entered into col2. Statement 3 adds another constraint to the table, specifying values for col1. Statements 4 to 6 insert new rows into table1. Only statement 5 succeeds because the values in statements 4 and 6 each violate one of the constraints. If the constraints had not been added to the table, these inserts would have worked. Statement 7 attempts to update the one successful row with an invalid col1. You can see all the error messages in Figure 14-1.

```
🔲 Messages

January
Msg 547, Level 16, State 0, Line 21
The INSERT statement conflicted with the CHECK constraint "ch_table1_col2_months".
The conflict occurred in database "tempdb", table "dbo.table1", column 'col2'.
The statement has been terminated.
February

(1 row(s) affected)
March
Msg 547, Level 16, State 0, Line 29
The INSERT statement conflicted with the CHECK constraint "ch_table1_col1".
The conflict occurred in database "tempdb", table "dbo.table1", column 'col1'.
The statement has been terminated.
Change 2 to 20
Msg 547, Level 16, State 0, Line 33
The UPDATE statement conflicted with the CHECK constraint "ch_table1_col1".
The conflict occurred in database "tempdb", table "dbo.table1", column 'col1'.
The statement has been terminated.
```

Figure 14-1. *The results of attempting to violate check constraints*

Adding *UNIQUE* Constraints

You can specify that a column or columns in a table contain unique values. Unlike primary keys, which you will learn more about in the next section, unique columns may contain one NULL value. In the case of multiple columns, you must decide whether to have a constraint on each column or a constraint that covers several columns. In the first case, each column value must be unique; in the second case, the combination of the column values must be unique. You can add UNIQUE constraints to tables when you create them or later with an ALTER TABLE statement. Here is the syntax:

```
--Adding a unique constraints to individual columns
CREATE TABLE <table name> (<col1> <data type> UNIQUE, <col2> <data type> UNIQUE)

--Adding a unique constraint, but including constrait names
CREATE TABLE <table name> (<col1> <data type>, <col2> <data type>
    CONSTRAINT <constraint name1> UNIQUE (<col1>),
    CONSTRAINT <constraint name2> UNIQUE (<col2>))

--Adding a combination constraint
CREATE TABLE <table name> (<col1> <data type>, <col2> <data type>,
    CONSTRAINT <constraint name> UNIQUE (<col1>,<col2>))

--Add a constraint with ALTER TABLE
CREATE TABLE <table name> (<col1> <data type>, <col2> <data type>)
ALTER TABLE ADD CONSTRAINT <constraint name> UNIQUE (<col1>,<col2>)
```

The first syntax example creates a separate constraint on each column within the CREATE TABLE statement, but SQL Server will come up with the constraint names. The second example shows the same thing except that constraints are named. The other two examples each create one constraint on a combination of the columns. If you don't specify a constraint name as in the first syntax example, SQL Server will come up with a name for you. Listing 14-2 contains example code showing how to create UNIQUE constraints. Type in and execute the code to learn more.

Listing 14-2. Creating Tables with UNIQUE Constraints

```
USE tempdb;
GO
--1
IF OBJECT_ID('table1') IS NOT NULL BEGIN
    DROP TABLE table1;
END;

--2
CREATE TABLE table1 (col1 INT NULL UNIQUE,
    col2 VARCHAR(20) NULL, col3 DATE NULL);
GO

--3
ALTER TABLE table1 ADD CONSTRAINT
    unq_table1_col2_col3 UNIQUE (col2,col3);

--4
PRINT 'Statement 4'
INSERT INTO table1(col1,col2,col3)
VALUES (1,2,'2009/01/01'),(2,2,'2009/01/02');
```

```
--5
PRINT 'Statement 5'
INSERT INTO table1(col1,col2,col3)
VALUES (3,2,'2009/01/01');

--6
PRINT 'Statement 6'
INSERT INTO table1(col1,col2,col3)
VALUES (1,2,'2009/01/01');

--7
PRINT 'Statement 7'
UPDATE table1 SET col3 = '2009/01/01'
WHERE col1 = 1;
```

Figure 14-2 shows the results. Code section 1 drops the table in case it already exists. Statement 2 creates table1 with three columns. It creates a UNIQUE constraint on col1. Statement 3 adds another UNIQUE constraint on the combination of columns col2 and col3. Statement 4 adds two rows to the table successfully. Statement 5 violates the constraint on col2 and col3. Statement 6 violates the constraint on col1. Statement 7 violates the constraint on col2 and col3 with an UPDATE to the table.

```
 Messages
 Statement 4

 (2 row(s) affected)
 Statement 5
 Msg 2627, Level 14, State 1, Line 13
 Violation of UNIQUE KEY constraint 'unq_table1_col2_col3'.
 Cannot insert duplicate key in object 'dbo.table1'. The duplicate
 key value is (2, Jan  1 2009 12:00AM).
 The statement has been terminated.
 Statement 6
 Msg 2627, Level 14, State 1, Line 18
 Violation of UNIQUE KEY constraint 'UQ__table1__357D0D3FF8333B22'.
 Cannot insert duplicate key in object 'dbo.table1'. The duplicate
 key value is (1).
 The statement has been terminated.
 Statement 7
 Msg 2627, Level 14, State 1, Line 23
 Violation of UNIQUE KEY constraint 'unq_table1_col2_col3'.
 Cannot insert duplicate key in object 'dbo.table1'. The duplicate
 key value is (2, Jan  2 2009 12:00AM).
 The statement has been terminated.
```

Figure 14-2. *The results of adding UNIQUE constraints*

Another interesting thing about UNIQUE constraints is that you will not see them in the Constraints section in SQL Server Management Studio. Instead, you will find them in the Indexes and Keys sections. When creating a unique constraint, you are actually creating a unique index. Figure 14-3 shows the constraints, as indexes and keys, added to table1.

```
tempdb
    Tables
        System Tables
        dbo.table1
            Columns
            Keys
                unq_table1_col2_col3
                UQ_table1__357D0D3FC0F025DC
            Constraints
            Triggers
            Indexes
                unq_table1_col2_col3 (Unique, Non-Clustered)
                UQ_table1__357D0D3FC0F025DC (Unique, Non-Clustered)
            Statistics
```

Figure 14-3. *The unique constraints defined on table1 are indexes and keys*

Adding a Primary Key to a Table

Throughout this book, you have read about primary keys. You can use a primary key to uniquely define a row in a table. A primary key must have the following characteristics:

- A primary key may be made of one column or multiple columns, called a *composite key*.

- A table can have only one primary key.

- The values of a primary key must be unique.

- If the primary key is a composite key, the combination of the values must be unique.

- None of the columns making up a primary key can contain NULL values.

I once received a call from a developer asking me to remove the primary key from a table because it was preventing him from inserting rows into a table in one of our enterprise systems. He insisted that the table definition must be wrong. I spent ten minutes explaining that the primary key was preventing him from making a mistake and helped him figure out the correct statements. After this developer moved on to another company, I received almost the identical phone call from his replacement. *Primary keys and other constraints are there to ensure data consistency, not to make your job harder.*

You can add a primary key to a table when you create the table using the CREATE TABLE statement or later by using the ALTER TABLE statement. Like other constraints, explicitly naming the constraint will help you read error messages. Here is the syntax:

```
--Single column key
CREATE TABLE <table name> (<column1> <data type> NOT NULL PRIMARY KEY
    [CLUSTERED|NONCLUSTERED] <column2> <data type>)


--Single column key with name
CREATE TABLE <table name> (<column1> <data type> NOT NULL
    [CLUSTERED|NONCLUSTERED] <column2> <data type>
    CONSTRAINT <constraint name> PRIMARY KEY [CLUSTERED|NONCLUSTERED] (<column1>)
```

```
--Composite key
CREATE TABLE <table name>(<column1> <data type> NOT NULL,
    <column2> <data type> NOT NULL, <column3> <data type>,
    CONSTRAINT <constraint name> PRIMARY KEY [CLUSTERED|NONCLUSTERED]
    (<column1>,<column2>)
)

--Using ALTER TABLE
CREATE TABLE <table name>(<column1> <data type> NOT NULL,
    <column2> <data type>)

ALTER TABLE <table name> ADD CONSTRAINT <primary key name>
    PRIMARY KEY [CLUSTERED|NONCLUSTERED] (<column1>)
```

Take a look at the keys and indexes of the HumanResources.Department table in the AdventureWorks database (see Figure 14-4). When you create a primary key, the database engine automatically creates an index composed of that key. One of the indexes, PK_Department_DepartmentID, is also the primary key composed of the DepartmentID column. There is also a unique index on the department name column. In this case, the index was explicitly created and a unique constraint was not added to the table. 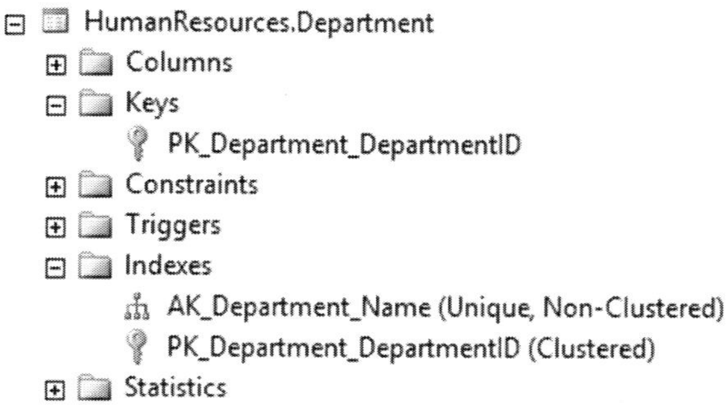

Figure 14-4. *The indexes of the HumanResources.Department table*

Listing 14-3 contains some examples that create tables with primary keys, either during the CREATE command or later with the ALTER command. Type in and execute the code to learn more.

Listing 14-3. Creating Primary Keys

```
USE tempdb;
GO


--1
IF OBJECT_ID('table1') IS NOT NULL BEGIN
    DROP TABLE table1;
END;

IF OBJECT_ID('table2') IS NOT NULL BEGIN
    DROP TABLE table2;
END;
```

```
IF OBJECT_ID('table3') IS NOT NULL BEGIN
    DROP TABLE table3;
END;

--2
CREATE TABLE table1 (col1 INT NOT NULL,
    col2 VARCHAR(10)
    CONSTRAINT PK_table1_Col1 PRIMARY KEY (col1));

--3
CREATE TABLE table2 (col1 INT NOT NULL,
    col2 VARCHAR(10) NOT NULL, col3 INT NULL,
    CONSTRAINT PK_table2_col1col2 PRIMARY KEY
    (col1, col2)
);

--4
CREATE TABLE table3 (col1 INT NOT NULL,
    col2 VARCHAR(10) NOT NULL, col3 INT NULL);

--5
ALTER TABLE table3 ADD CONSTRAINT PK_table3_col1col2
    PRIMARY KEY NONCLUSTERED (col1,col2);
```

Figure 14-5 shows the resulting tables. Code section 1 drops the tables if they already exist in the database. Statement 2 creates table1 with a primary key made of col1. The code doesn't contain the optional keyword CLUSTERED. The keyword CLUSTERED specifies that the primary key is also a clustered index. (See Chapter 2 for more information about clustered and nonclustered indexes.) By default, if no clustered index already exists on the table, as in this case, the primary key will become a clustered index.

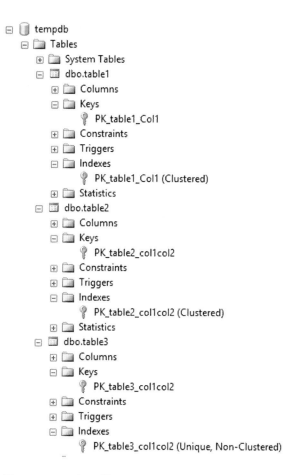

Figure 14-5. *The tables created with primary keys*

Statement 3 creates a composite primary key composed of col1 and col2. You actually don't have to specify NOT NULL when defining the primary key, because SQL Server will change the primary key columns to NOT NULL for you. I prefer to specify the NOT NULL constraint in the CREATE TABLE statement for clarity, especially if I am saving the script. Again, because there is no other clustered index, the primary key will also be a clustered index on table2.

Statement 4 creates table3 without specifying a primary key. Statement 5, an ALTER TABLE statement, adds the primary key, in this case a nonclustered index. The primary key is often a clustered index, but that is not a requirement. You will often see the clustered index composed of a smaller column, such as an INT column, if the primary key contains several large columns. The reason is that the clustered index is automatically part of every other index, so having a "narrow" clustered index saves space in the database. Keep in mind the wider the index the more reads SQL Server will need to perform to retrieve the data, and this can have a negative impact on performance.

Creating Foreign Keys

You have seen how to join tables on the primary key of one table to the foreign key of another table beginning with Chapter 5. Having foreign keys defined on tables is not a requirement to join tables but, in addition to performance implications, explicitly defined foreign keys can help enforce what is called *referential integrity*. Referential integrity means that data consistency between tables is maintained. For example, no orders may exist without a valid customer for that order.

Just like primary keys, you can define a foreign key within the CREATE TABLE command or later in an ALTER TABLE statement. Here is the syntax for creating simple foreign keys:

```
--On one column in the CREATE TABLE
CREATE TABLE <table1> (<col1> <data type>
    CONSTRAINT <foreign key name> FOREIGN KEY REFERENCES <table2> (<col3>))

--On two columns in the CREATE TABLE
CREATE TABLE <table1> (<col1> <data type>, <col2> <data type>,
    CONSTRAINT <foreign key name> FOREIGN KEY (<col1>,<col2>)
    REFERENCES <table2> (<col3>,<col4>))

--Adding with ALTER table
CREATE TABLE <table1> (<col1> <data type>, <col2> <data type>)
ALTER TABLE <table1> ADD CONSTRAINT <foreign key name> FOREIGN KEY (<col1>)
    REFERENCES <table2> (<col3>))
```

The foreign key refers to the table specified before the keyword REFERENCES. For example, if you were defining the foreign key on the orders table, table2 would be the customers table. The column or columns specified after the REFERENCES keyword generally will be the primary key of that table. If the column or columns referred to are not the primary key, they at least have to be defined as UNIQUE or have a unique index defined on the column. Type in and execute Listing 14-4, which shows a simple example.

Listing 14-4. Adding a Foreign Key

```
--1
IF OBJECT_ID('table1') IS NOT NULL BEGIN
    DROP TABLE table1;
END;
IF OBJECT_ID('table2') IS NOT NULL BEGIN
    DROP TABLE table2;
END;

--2
CREATE TABLE table1 (col1 INT NOT NULL,
    col2 VARCHAR(20), col3 DATETIME
    CONSTRAINT PK_table1_Col1 PRIMARY KEY(col1));

--3
CREATE TABLE table2 (col4 INT NULL,
    col5 VARCHAR(20) NOT NULL,
    CONSTRAINT pk_table2 PRIMARY KEY (col5),
    CONSTRAINT fk_table2_table1 FOREIGN KEY (col4) REFERENCES table1(col1)
    );
GO

--4
PRINT 'Adding to table1';
INSERT INTO table1(col1,col2,col3)
VALUES(1,'a','2014/01/01'),(2,'b','2014/01/01'),(3,'c','1/3/2014');
```

```
--5
PRINT 'Adding to table2';
INSERT INTO table2(col4,col5)
VALUES(1,'abc'),(2,'def');

--6
PRINT 'Violating foreign key with insert';
INSERT INTO table2(col4,col5)
VALUES (7,'aaa');

--7
PRINT 'Violating foreign key with update';
UPDATE table2 SET col4 = 6
WHERE col4 = 1;
```

Figure 14-6 shows the results of adding the foreign key and then violating it. Code section 1 drops table1 and table2 if they exist. Notice that the code drops table2 first. If the drop statements are reversed and you run the code multiple times, it will fail. Note that table1 may not be dropped while the foreign key pointing to it exists. To eliminate this problem, drop table2 first. You can also drop foreign keys by using the ALTER TABLE statement, but if you are dropping tables, be sure to drop the referencing table first.

```
Adding to table1

(3 row(s) affected)
Adding to table2

(2 row(s) affected)
Violating foreign key with insert
Msg 547, Level 16, State 0, Line 14
The INSERT statement conflicted with the FOREIGN KEY
constraint "fk_table2_table1". The conflict occurred in databa
The statement has been terminated.
Violating foreign key with update
Msg 547, Level 16, State 0, Line 19
The UPDATE statement conflicted with the FOREIGN KEY
constraint "fk_table2_table1". The conflict occurred in databa
The statement has been terminated.
```

Figure 14-6. *The results of adding a foreign key*

Statement 2 creates table1. Statement 3 creates table2 with the foreign key. Statement 4 adds three rows to table1. Statement 5 inserts two valid rows to table2. Any value for col4 must already exist in col1 of table1. Statement 6 attempts to insert a row with the value 7. Because the value 7 doesn't exist in col1 of table1, the statement fails. Statement 7 attempts to update an existing row with an invalid value. The statement fails because the value, 6, doesn't exist in col1 of table1.

Creating Foreign Keys with Delete and Update Rules

You saw in the previous section that foreign keys ensure that only valid values from the referenced table are used. For example, if you have an order table, only valid CustomerID values from the customer table may be used. You can also define what should happen if a customer with orders is deleted from the database. Will all orders also be deleted at the same time? Should SQL Server prevent the customer from being deleted? What about changing the CustomerID in the customer table? Will that change also change the CustomerID in the order table or prevent the change? You can define all that behavior within the foreign key definition. A rule may be set up for deletions and for updates. Here are the possible values:

- NO ACTION: Prevents the deletion or update and rolls back the transaction.

- CASCADE: Applies the same action to the foreign key table.

- SET NULL: Sets the value of the foreign key columns to NULL.

- SET DEFAULT: Sets the value of the foreign key columns to the default values or NULL if no default is defined.

Here is the syntax for creating foreign keys with update and delete rules:

```
CREATE TABLE <table1> (<col1> <data type>,<col2> <data type>,
    CONSTRAINT <foreign key name> FOREIGN KEY (<col1>) REFERENCES <table2> (<col3>)
    [ON DELETE [NO ACTION|CASCADE|SET NULL|SET DEFAULT]]
    [ON UPDATE [NO ACTION|CASCADE|SET NULL|SET DEFAULT]])
```

By default, the NO ACTION option applies if no rule is defined. In this case, if you attempt to delete a customer who has placed one or more orders, SQL Server will return an error message and roll back the transaction. To use SET NULL, the columns making up the foreign key must allow NULL values. The other requirement is that the default values must be a valid value that satisfies the foreign key. The example in Listing 14-5 is fairly long. You may want to download the code from the book's web site at www.apress.com instead of typing it. Execute the code in Listing 14-5 to learn how these rules work.

Listing 14-5. Using Update and Delete Rules

```
USE tempdb;
GO
SET NOCOUNT ON;
GO
--1
IF OBJECT_ID('Child') IS NOT NULL BEGIN
    DROP TABLE Child;
END;

IF OBJECT_ID('Parent') IS NOT NULL BEGIN
    DROP TABLE Parent;
END;

--2
CREATE TABLE Parent (col1 INT NOT NULL PRIMARY KEY,
    col2 VARCHAR(20), col3 DATE);

--3 default rules
PRINT 'No action by default';
CREATE TABLE Child (col4 INT NULL DEFAULT 7,
    col5 VARCHAR(20) NOT NULL,
    CONSTRAINT pk_Child PRIMARY KEY (col5),
    CONSTRAINT fk_Child_Parent FOREIGN KEY (col4) REFERENCES Parent(col1)
    );
```

```
--4
PRINT 'Adding to Parent';
INSERT INTO Parent(col1,col2,col3)
VALUES(1,'a','2014/01/01'),(2,'b','2014/02/01'),(3,'c','2014/01/03'),
    (4,'d','2014/01/04'),(5,'e','2014/01/06'),(6,'g','2014/01/07'),
    (7,'g','2014/01/08');

--5
PRINT 'Adding to Child';
INSERT INTO Child(col4,col5)
VALUES(1,'abc'),(2,'def'),(3,'ghi'),
    (4,'jkl');

--6
SELECT col4, col5 FROM Child;

--7
PRINT 'Delete from Parent'
DELETE FROM Parent WHERE col1 = 1;

--8
ALTER TABLE Child DROP CONSTRAINT fk_Child_Parent;

--9
PRINT 'Add CASCADE';
ALTER TABLE Child ADD CONSTRAINT fk_Child_Parent
    FOREIGN KEY (col4) REFERENCES Parent(col1)
    ON DELETE CASCADE
    ON UPDATE CASCADE;

--10
PRINT 'Delete from Parent';
DELETE FROM Parent WHERE col1 = 1;

--11
PRINT 'Update Parent';
UPDATE Parent SET col1 = 10 WHERE col1 = 4;

--12
ALTER TABLE Child DROP CONSTRAINT fk_Child_Parent;

--13
PRINT 'Add SET NULL';
ALTER TABLE Child ADD CONSTRAINT fk_Child_Parent
    FOREIGN KEY (col4) REFERENCES Parent(col1)
    ON DELETE SET NULL
    ON UPDATE SET NULL;

--14
DELETE FROM Parent WHERE col1 = 2;
```

337

```
--15
ALTER TABLE Child DROP CONSTRAINT fk_Child_Parent;

--16
PRINT 'Add SET DEFAULT';
ALTER TABLE Child ADD CONSTRAINT fk_Child_Parent
    FOREIGN KEY (col4) REFERENCES Parent(col1)
    ON DELETE SET DEFAULT
    ON UPDATE SET DEFAULT;

--17
PRINT 'Delete from Parent';
DELETE FROM Parent WHERE col1 = 3;

--18
SELECT col4, col5 FROM Child;
```

Figure 14-7 shows the information and error messages that result from running the script. Code section 1 drops the Parent and Child tables if they exist. Statement 2 creates Parent. Statement 3 creates Child with a foreign key referencing Parent with the default NO ACTION rules. In my experience, most of the time, the default NO ACTION is in effect, which prevents updates and deletions from the referenced table, as in statement 3. Statements 4 and 5 add a few rows to the tables. Statement 7 deletes a row from Parent. Because that deletion violates the foreign key rules, the statement rolls back and produces an error.

```
No action by default
Adding to Parent
Adding to Child
Delete from Parent
Msg 547, Level 16, State 0, Line 40
The DELETE statement conflicted with the
REFERENCE constraint "fk_Child_Parent". The conflict
The statement has been terminated.
Add CASCADE
Delete from Parent
Update Parent
Add SET NULL
Add SET DEFAULT
Delete from Parent
```

Figure 14-7. *The results of applying foreign key rules*

Statement 8 drops the foreign key constraint so that statement 9 can re-create the foreign key with the CASCADE options. Statement 10, which deletes the row from Parent with col1 equal to 1, succeeds. The CASCADE rule also automatically deletes the matching row from Child. (Figure 14-8 shows how Child looks after population and at the end of the script.) Statement 11 changes the value of col1 in Parent to 10 where the value is equal to 4. The CASCADE rule automatically updates the matching row in Child.

	col4	col5
1	1	abc
2	2	def
3	3	ghi
4	4	jkl

	col4	col5
1	NULL	def
2	7	ghi
3	10	jkl

Figure 14-8. *The results of changes based on foreign key options*

Statement 12 drops the foreign key constraint so that statement 13 can re-create the foreign key with the SET NULL option. Statement 14 deletes a row from Parent. The SET NULL rule automatically changes the matching value in Child to NULL.

Statement 15 drops the foreign key constraint so that statement 16 can re-create the foreign key with the SET DEFAULT option. Statement 17 deletes a row from Parent. The SET DEFAULT rule automatically changes the matching value in Child to the default value 7. Finally, statement 18 displays the rows after all the automatic changes. Review the script again. Except for the INSERT statement, the script contains no other explicit changes to the data in the Child table. The rule in effect at the time of each data change to Parent automatically made changes to the data in Child.

Defining Automatically Populated Columns

You have seen automatically populated columns used in the "Inserting Rows into Tables with Automatically Populating Columns" section in Chapter 10. This section will show you how to define IDENTITY columns, ROWVERSION columns, COMPUTED columns, and columns with DEFAULT values. Here are the syntax examples:

```
--IDENTITY
CREATE TABLE <table name> (<col1> INT NOT NULL IDENTITY[(<seed>,<increment>)],
    <col1> <data type>)

--ROWVERSION, originally TIMESTAMP
CREATE TABLE <table name> (<col1> <data type>,<col2> ROWVERSION)

--COMPUTED column
CREATE TABLE <table name> (<col1> <data type>,<col2> AS <computed column definition>
    [PERSISTED])

--DEFAULT column
CREATE TABLE <table name> (<col1> <data type> DEFAULT <default value or function>)
```

Several rules apply to using these column types. Review the following to learn more.

The rules for IDENTITY columns are:

- A table may contain only one IDENTITY column.

- By default, IDENTITY columns begin with the value 1 and increment by 1.

- You can specify different values by specifying seed and increment values.

- You may not insert values into IDENTITY columns unless the IDENTITY_INSERT setting is turned on for the current session.

The rules for ROWVERSION data type are:

- The ROWVERSION value will be unique within the database.
- A table may contain only one ROWVERSION column.
- You may not insert values into ROWVERSION columns.
- Each time you update the row, the ROWVERSION value changes.

The rules for COMPUTED columns are:

- A table may contain multiple COMPUTED columns.
- Do not specify a data type for COMPUTED columns.
- You may not insert values into COMPUTED columns.
- By specifying the option PERSISTED, the database engine stores the value in the table.
- You can define indexes on deterministic COMPUTED columns.
- You can specify other non-COMPUTED columns, literal values, and scalar functions in the COMPUTED column definition.

The rules for DEFAULT columns are:

- When inserting rows, you do not need to specify a value for a column with a DEFAULT value defined.
- You can use expressions with literal values and scalar functions, but not other column names with DEFAULT value columns.
- When inserting rows, if a value is specified for a column with a DEFAULT, the specified value applies.
- If a column with a DEFAULT value specified allows NULL values, you can still specify NULL for the column.
- You can use the new SEQUENCE object and the NEXT VALUE FOR function as a default to insert incrementing values.

■ **Note**   Although a sequence does enable you to auto populate values in a table, it is a database object and is not dependent upon the table. You create SEQUENCE objects apart from tables and reference them in your INSERT statements or use them as a default value.

Listing 14-6 demonstrates creating and populating tables with these automatically populating columns. Type in and execute the code to learn more.

Listing 14-6. Defining Tables with Automatically Populating Columns

```
USE tempdb;
GO
--1
IF OBJECT_ID('MySequence') IS NOT NULL BEGIN
```

```
        DROP SEQUENCE MySequence;
END;

CREATE SEQUENCE MySequence START WITH 1;

--2
IF OBJECT_ID('table3') IS NOT NULL BEGIN
    DROP TABLE table3;
END;

--2
CREATE TABLE table3 (col1 CHAR(1),
    idCol INT NOT NULL IDENTITY,
    rvCol ROWVERSION,
    defCol DATETIME2 DEFAULT GETDATE(),
    SeqCol INT DEFAULT NEXT VALUE FOR dbo.MySequence,
    calcCol1 AS DATEADD(m,1,defCol),
    calcCol2 AS col1 + ':' + col1
    );
GO

--3
INSERT INTO table3 (col1)
VALUES ('a'), ('b'), ('c'), ('d'), ('e'), ('g');

--4
INSERT INTO table3 (col1, defCol)
VALUES ('h', NULL),('i','2014/01/01');

--5
SELECT col1, idCol, rvCol, defCol, calcCol1, calcCol2, SeqCol
FROM table3;
```

Figure 14-9 shows the results of running this code. Statement 1 drops and creates the sequence object. Statement 2 drops and creates table3 with one regular column, col1, and several other columns that may be automatically populated. Statement 3 inserts several rows into table3, specifying values only for col1. Statement 4 inserts two more rows, specifying values for col1 and the column with a DEFAULT value, defCol. Notice that the first row inserted in statement 4 specifies NULL for defCol. Statement 5 just returns the results.

	col1	idCol	rvCol	defCol	calcCol1	calcCol2	SeqCol
1	a	1	0x000000000000F245	2014-05-26 18:38:12.6970000	2014-06-26 18:38:12.6970000	a:a	1
2	b	2	0x000000000000F246	2014-05-26 18:38:12.6970000	2014-06-26 18:38:12.6970000	b:b	2
3	c	3	0x000000000000F247	2014-05-26 18:38:12.6970000	2014-06-26 18:38:12.6970000	c:c	3
4	d	4	0x000000000000F248	2014-05-26 18:38:12.6970000	2014-06-26 18:38:12.6970000	d:d	4
5	e	5	0x000000000000F249	2014-05-26 18:38:12.6970000	2014-06-26 18:38:12.6970000	e:e	5
6	g	6	0x000000000000F24A	2014-05-26 18:38:12.6970000	2014-06-26 18:38:12.6970000	g:g	6
7	h	7	0x000000000000F24B	NULL	NULL	h:h	7
8	i	8	0x000000000000F24C	2014-01-01 00:00:00.0000000	2014-02-01 00:00:00.0000000	i:i	8

Figure 14-9. *The results of populating a table with automatically populating columns*

If you run the script more than once, you will see that the ROWVERSION column, rvCol, contains different values each time. Notice, also, that in the row where col1 equals h, both devCol and calcCol1 also contain NULL. That is because statement 4 explicitly inserted a NULL value into defCol. Because the value for calcCol1 is based on defCol and any operation on NULL returns NULL, calcCol1 also contains a NULL in that row. Statement 4 inserts a row with another explicit value for defCol, and calcCol1 reflects that as well.

Even though the main purpose of database tables is to store data, you can enforce many business rules by the table definition. Practice what you have learned by completing Exercise 14-1.

EXERCISE 14-1

Use the tempdb database to complete this exercise. You can find the solutions at the end of the chapter.

1.   Create a table called dbo.testCustomer. Include a CustomerID that is an identity column primary key. Include FirstName and LastName columns. Include an Age column with a check constraint specifying that the value must be less than 120. Include an Active column that is one character with a default of Y and allows only Y or N. Add some rows to the table.

2.   Create a table called dbo.testOrder. Include a CustomerID column that is a foreign key pointing to dbo.testCustomer. Include an OrderID column that is an identity column primary key. Include an OrderDate column that defaults to the current date and time. Include a ROWVERSION column. Add some rows to the table.

3.   Create a table called dbo.testOrderDetail. Include an OrderID column that is a foreign key pointing to dbo.testOrder. Include an integer ItemID column, a Price column, and a Qty column. The primary key should be a composite key composed of OrderID and ItemID. Create a computed column called LineItemTotal that multiplies Price times Qty. Add some rows to the table.

Views

SQL Server stores data in tables, but you can create objects, called *views*, that you query just like tables. Views don't store data; they are just saved query definitions. Developers can use views to simplify coding. Another reason to use views is security. You can give the end user permission to select from a view without giving permission to the underlying tables.

In the AdventureWorks database, the Person.Person table defines the attributes of a person for several other tables. You could create views to join the Person.Person table to the other tables so that you would always have the name columns available, therefore simplifying queries for reports.

You can also simplify security by using views. You can give a user permission to select data from a view when the user doesn't have permission to select data from the tables comprising the view. This keeps users from seeing or modifying data they should not access.

■ **Note**   An indexed view, also known as a *materialized view*, actually does contain data. To create an indexed view, add a clustered index to the view. See Books Online for more information about creating and using indexed views.

Creating Views

Creating views is easy. You can create views using most SELECT statements, including those made with common table expressions. For example, you might want to create a view that lists all the customers in the Sales.Customer table from the AdventureWorks database along with their names from the Person.Person table. You could use that view instead of the Sales.Customer table in other queries. Here is the syntax to create, alter, and drop views:

```
CREATE VIEW <view name> AS SELECT <col1>, <col2> FROM <table>

ALTER VIEW <view name> AS SELECT <col1>, <col2> FROM <table>

DROP VIEW <view name>
```

Type in and execute the code in Listing 14-7 to learn how to create and use views.

Listing 14-7. Creating and Using a View

```
--1
USE AdventureWorks;
GO
IF OBJECT_ID('dbo.vw_Customer') IS NOT NULL BEGIN
    DROP VIEW dbo.vw_Customer;
END;
GO


--2
CREATE VIEW dbo.vw_Customer AS
    SELECT c.CustomerID, c.AccountNumber, c.StoreID,
        c.TerritoryID, p.FirstName, p.MiddleName,
        p.LastName
    FROM Sales.Customer AS c
    INNER JOIN Person.Person AS p ON c.PersonID = p.BusinessEntityID;
GO


--3
SELECT CustomerID,AccountNumber,FirstName,
    MiddleName, LastName
FROM dbo.vw_Customer;

GO


--4
ALTER VIEW dbo.vw_Customer AS
    SELECT c.CustomerID,c.AccountNumber,c.StoreID,
        c.TerritoryID, p.FirstName,p.MiddleName,
        p.LastName, p.Title
    FROM Sales.Customer AS c
    INNER JOIN Person.Person AS p ON c.PersonID = p.BusinessEntityID;

GO
```

```
--5
SELECT CustomerID,AccountNumber,FirstName,
    MiddleName, LastName, Title
FROM dbo.vw_Customer
ORDER BY CustomerID;
```

Figure 14-10 shows the results of running this code. Code section 1 drops the view if it already exists. Code section 2 creates the view. Notice that the GO statements surround the CREATE VIEW code so that it has its own batch. Any time you create or alter a view, the code must be contained within a batch that has no other code except for comments. Notice that the view begins with the characters vw_, designating that it is a view, not a table. This is not a requirement, just a suggestion. Often companies will have naming conventions such as this; be sure to find out whether your company requires special naming for views. Statement 3 selects several of the columns from the view. At this point, you can treat the view like a table and the query could include a WHERE clause, an ORDER BY clause, or involve the view in an aggregate query if you wanted. Basically, you can treat the view like a table in a SELECT statement. Statement 4 alters the view by adding a column. Statement 5 is another SELECT statement, which includes the new column and an ORDER BY clause.

	CustomerID	AccountNumber	FirstName	MiddleName	LastName
1	29485	AW00029485	Catherine	R.	Abel
2	29486	AW00029486	Kim	NULL	Abercrombie
3	29487	AW00029487	Humberto	NULL	Acevedo
4	29484	AW00029484	Gustavo	NULL	Achong

	CustomerID	AccountNumber	FirstName	MiddleName	LastName	Title
1	11000	AW00011000	Jon	V	Yang	NULL
2	11001	AW00011001	Eugene	L	Huang	NULL
3	11002	AW00011002	Ruben	NULL	Torres	NULL
4	11003	AW00011003	Christy	NULL	Zhu	NULL

Figure 14-10. *The results of creating and using a view*

To see the view in SQL Server Management Studio, navigate to the Views section of the AdventureWorks database. You will see the newly created view along with several views that ship with the database. Notice that each of the preexisting views belongs to one of the schemas in the database. Just like tables, you can script out the definition or bring up a graphical designer. Figure 14-11 shows the graphical designer for the view.

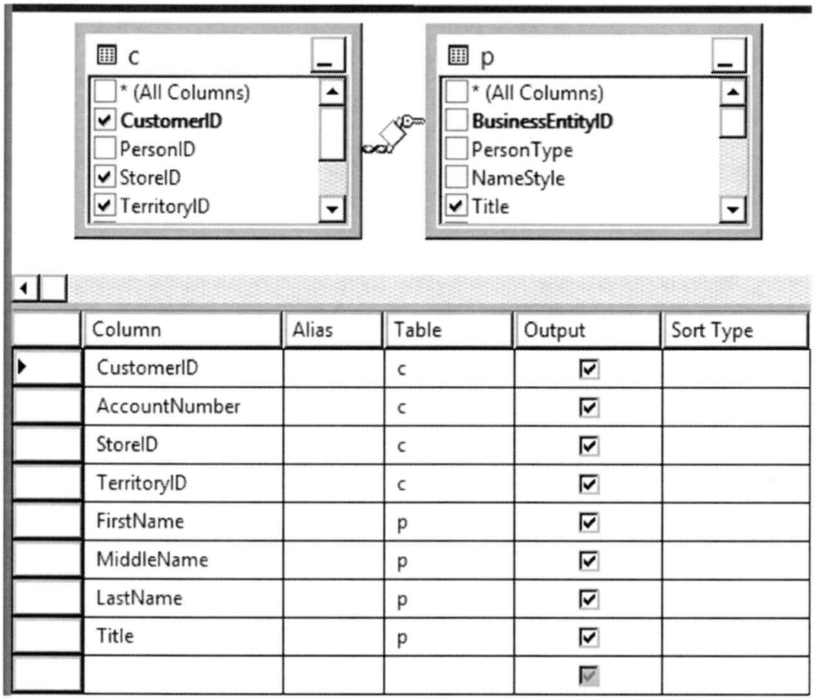

Figure 14-11. *The graphical designer for views*

Avoiding Common Problems with Views

You may decide that you should set up views joining all the tables in the database and just write queries against those views, but there are often problems associated with using views as the main strategy for database development. One problem is the confusion that can result from views created on top of other views on top of other views. Tracking down logic errors becomes difficult when they are buried in layers of views. If the underlying table structure changes, the view may produce strange results, as shown in Listing 14-8. To avoid this problem, you can define a view with the SCHEMABINDING option, which prevents the underlying table from being changed.

Listing 14-8. Common Problems Using Views

```
--1
IF OBJECT_ID('vw_Dept') IS NOT NULL BEGIN
    DROP VIEW dbo.vw_Dept;
END;
IF OBJECT_ID('demoDept') IS NOT NULL BEGIN
    DROP TABLE dbo.demoDept;
END;

--2
SELECT DepartmentID,Name,GroupName,ModifiedDate
INTO dbo.demoDept
FROM HumanResources.Department;
```

```
GO

--3
CREATE VIEW dbo.vw_Dept AS
    SELECT *
    FROM dbo.demoDept;
GO

--4
SELECT DepartmentID, Name, GroupName, ModifiedDate
FROM dbo.vw_Dept;

--5
DROP TABLE dbo.demoDept;
GO

--6
SELECT DepartmentID, GroupName, Name, ModifiedDate
INTO dbo.demoDept
FROM HumanResources.Department;
GO

--7
SELECT DepartmentID, Name, GroupName, ModifiedDate
FROM dbo.vw_Dept;
GO

--8
DROP VIEW dbo.vw_Dept;
GO

--9
CREATE VIEW dbo.vw_Dept AS
    SELECT TOP(100) PERCENT DepartmentID,
        Name, GroupName, ModifiedDate
    FROM dbo.demoDept
    ORDER BY Name;
GO

--10
SELECT DepartmentID, Name, GroupName, ModifiedDate
FROM dbo.vw_Dept;
```

Make sure you don't use views in a way that will negatively impact performance. For example, suppose you created a view containing the customers, customer addresses, sales, and sales details tables. If you just wanted a list of customers, you could query the view, but you would be also accessing tables you didn't need to view at that time. Multiple layers of views can also make it difficult for SQL Server to come up with a good execution plan.

Developers often want to add an ORDER BY clause to a view definition. This is actually disallowed except under specific conditions and doesn't make sense because you can always add the ORDER BY clause to the outer query. (To add an ORDER BY to a view definition, you must add the TOP specifier to the view. Chapter 11 discussed TOP in more detail.) In fact, the database engine doesn't guarantee that the data will be returned in the order specified in the view definition according to the CREATE VIEW topic in SQL Server Books Online. Type in and execute the code in Listing 14-8 to learn more about two common problems with views.

Figure 14-12 shows the results of running this code. Code section 1 drops the view and a work table in case they already exist. Statement 2 creates the table dbo.demoDept from the HumanResources.Department table. Statement 3 creates a view, dbo.vw_Dept, using the asterisk (*) syntax against the dbo.demoDept table. Statement 4 selects all the rows from the view, and the results look as expected in the first result set.

	DepartmentID	Name	GroupName	ModifiedDate
1	1	Engineering	Research and Development	2002-06-01 00:00:00.000
2	2	Tool Design	Research and Development	2002-06-01 00:00:00.000
3	3	Sales	Sales and Marketing	2002-06-01 00:00:00.000
4	4	Marketing	Sales and Marketing	2002-06-01 00:00:00.000

	DepartmentID	Name	GroupName	ModifiedDate
1	1	Research and Development	Engineering	2002-06-01 00:00:00.000
2	2	Research and Development	Tool Design	2002-06-01 00:00:00.000
3	3	Sales and Marketing	Sales	2002-06-01 00:00:00.000
4	4	Sales and Marketing	Marketing	2002-06-01 00:00:00.000

	DepartmentID	Name	GroupName	ModifiedDate
1	1	Engineering	Research and Development	2002-06-01 00:00:00.000
2	2	Tool Design	Research and Development	2002-06-01 00:00:00.000
3	3	Sales	Sales and Marketing	2002-06-01 00:00:00.000
4	4	Marketing	Sales and Marketing	2002-06-01 00:00:00.000

Figure 14-12. *The results of demonstrating some common problems with views*

Statement 5 drops the dbo.demoDept table, and statement 6 creates and populates the table again but with the columns in a different order. Statement 7 selects the rows from the view, but this time with surprising results. Because the table was dropped and re-created differently, the columns in the view are now mismatched, as shown in the second result set. The Name and GroupName columns are reversed. To fix this problem you would have to refresh the view definition with the ALTER VIEW command.

Statement 8 drops the view, and statement 9 creates it while attempting to enforce a specific order in the view definition. Statement 10 shows within the final set of results that the ORDER BY clause within the view definition didn't make any difference.

Manipulating Data with Views

So far you have seen how you can use views to select data. You can also modify the data of a table by updating a view as long as the view meets several requirements:

- Modifying the data of a view by inserting or updating may affect only one base table.

- You may not delete data from a view that consists of more than one table.

- The columns updated must be directly linked to updateable table columns; in other words, you can't update a view column based on an expression or an otherwise non-updateable column.

- Inserts into views are possible only if all columns that require a value are exposed through the view.

As you can see, modifying data through views can be much more complicated than through tables, especially if the view is made up of more than one table. Type in and execute the code in Listing 14-9 to learn how to update data using views.

Listing 14-9. Modifying Data Through Views

```
--1
IF OBJECT_ID('dbo.demoCustomer') IS NOT NULL BEGIN
    DROP TABLE dbo.demoCustomer;
END;
IF OBJECT_ID('dbo.demoPerson') IS NOT NULL BEGIN
    DROP TABLE dbo.demoPerson;
END;
IF OBJECT_ID('dbo.vw_Customer') IS NOT NULL BEGIN
    DROP VIEW dbo.vw_Customer;
END;

--2
SELECT CustomerID, TerritoryID, StoreID, PersonID
INTO dbo.demoCustomer
FROM Sales.Customer;

SELECT BusinessEntityID, Title, FirstName, MiddleName, LastName
INTO dbo.demoPerson
From Person.Person;
GO

--3
CREATE VIEW vw_Customer AS
    SELECT CustomerID, TerritoryID, PersonID, StoreID,
        Title, FirstName, MiddleName, LastName
    FROM dbo.demoCustomer
    INNER JOIN dbo.demoPerson ON PersonID = BusinessEntityID;
GO

--4
SELECT CustomerID, FirstName, MiddleName, LastName
FROM dbo.vw_Customer
WHERE CustomerID IN (29484,29486,29489,100000);

--5
PRINT 'Update one row';
UPDATE dbo.vw_Customer SET FirstName = 'Kathi'
WHERE CustomerID = 29486;

--6
GO
PRINT 'Attempt to update both sides of the join'
GO
UPDATE dbo.vw_Customer SET FirstName = 'Franie',TerritoryID = 5
WHERE CustomerID = 29489;
```

```
--7
GO
PRINT 'Attempt to delete a row';
GO
DELETE FROM dbo.vw_Customer
WHERE CustomerID = 29484;

--8
GO
PRINT 'Insert into dbo.demoCustomer';
INSERT INTO dbo.vw_Customer(TerritoryID,
    StoreID, PersonID)
VALUES (5,5,100000);

--9
GO
PRINT 'Attempt to insert a row into demoPerson';
GO
INSERT INTO dbo.vw_Customer(Title, FirstName, LastName)
VALUES ('Mrs.','Lady','Samoyed');

--10
SELECT CustomerID, FirstName, MiddleName, LastName
FROM dbo.vw_Customer
WHERE CustomerID IN (29484,29486,29489,100000);

--11
SELECT CustomerID, TerritoryID, StoreID, PersonID
FROM dbo.demoCustomer
WHERE PersonID = 100000;
```

Because this code will produce some errors, view the error messages and then click the Results tab (see Figure 14-13). Code section 1 drops the two tables and the view involved in this script if they exist. Code section 2 creates the two tables, dbo.demoPerson and dbo.demoCustomer, using SELECT INTO statements. Because the two tables must be in place before the view is created, the code to create dbo.vw_Customer is in a separate batch. Statement 4 shows how three of the rows look before the data is manipulated and is the first result set in Figure 14-13. Statement 5 changes the first name of one row from *Kim* to *Kathi*. This statement succeeds because the update affects only one of the tables.

	CustomerID	FirstName	MiddleName	LastName
1	29484	Gustavo	NULL	Achong
2	29486	Kim	NULL	Abercrombie
3	29489	Frances	B.	Adams

	CustomerID	FirstName	MiddleName	LastName
1	29484	Gustavo	NULL	Achong
2	29486	Kathi	NULL	Abercrombie
3	29489	Frances	B.	Adams

	CustomerID	TerritoryID	StoreID	PersonID
1	30119	5	5	100000

Figure 14-13. *The results of manipulating data through a view*

Statement 6 attempts to update two of the columns. Because the FirstName column is from one base table and TerritoryID is from a different base table, the update fails. Statement 7 attempts to delete a row from the view but fails. Deletions will work only if the view consists of one base table.

Statement 8 successfully inserts one row into the dbo.demoCustomer table through the view. Statement 9 attempts to insert a row into dbo.demoPerson but fails because the view does not expose the non-NULL column, BusinessEntityID, and there is no way to add a valid value. Statements 10 and 11 show the results of the script. The script updated only one row and added one row to dbo.demoCustomer through the view.

Another problem you may encounter is updating a view with a WHERE clause filter. You can create the view with the WITH CHECK OPTION to prevent any updates that violate the filter. Developers can use views to simplify database programming, but care must be taken to avoid performance and logic problems. Practice what you have learned by completing Exercise 14-2.

EXERCISE 14-2

Use the AdventureWorks database to complete this exercise. You can find the solutions at the end of the chapter.

1. Create a view called dbo.vw_Products that displays a list of the products from the Production.Product table joined to the Production.ProductCostHistory table. Include columns that describe the product and show the cost history for each product. Test the view by creating a query that retrieves data from the view.

2. Create a view called dbo.vw_CustomerTotals that displays the total sales from the TotalDue column per year and month for each customer. Test the view by creating a query that retrieves data from the view.

User-Defined Functions

You learned about the built-in functions available in SQL Server in Chapter 4 You can also create your own T-SQL user-defined functions (UDFs) that can be used in the same ways as the built-in functions. You will learn about two types of UDFs in this section: *scalar valued*, which return one value, and *table valued*, which return sets of data.

By using UDFs, you can reuse code to simplify development and hide complex logic. Use caution when using UDFs. They can negatively affect performance due to the overhead of calling the function for each row. Although not as elegant, performance is generally better with a complex expression.

Creating User-Defined Scalar Functions

A scalar function returns one value and may take one or more parameters. You can create your own scalar functions to simplify your code. For example, your application may have a complex calculation that appears in many queries. Instead of including the formula in every query, you can create and include the function in your queries instead. Keep these facts about scalar UDFs in mind:

- They can be used almost anywhere in a T-SQL statement.
- They can accept one or more parameters.
- They return one value.
- They can use logic such as IF blocks and WHILE loops.
- They can access data, though this is sometimes not a good idea.
- They can't update data.
- They can call other functions.
- Their definition must include a return value.

You may have noticed that scalar-valued UDFs can access data, but this is not always a good use of UDFs. UDFs should generally not be dependent on the tables in a particular database. They should be reusable as much as possible. Another problem with UDFs that access data is that the performance can be very poor, especially when used within a T-SQL query. The queries within the function run for each row in the outer query. Here is the syntax for creating, altering, and deleting user-defined scalar functions:

```
CREATE FUNCTION <scalar function Name> (<@param1> <data type1>,
    <@param2> <data type2>)
RETURNS <data type> AS
BEGIN
    <statements>
    RETURN <value>
END

ALTER FUNCTION <scalar function Name> ([<@param1> <data type>,
    <@param2> <data type>])
RETURNS <data type> AS
BEGIN
    <statements>
    RETURN <value>
END

DROP FUNCTION <scalar function name>
```

Listing 14-10 demonstrates how to create and use user-defined functions. Type in and execute the code to learn more.

Listing 14-10. Creating and Using User-Defined Scalar Functions

```
--1
IF OBJECT_ID('dbo.udf_Product') IS NOT NULL BEGIN
    DROP FUNCTION dbo.udf_Product;
END;
IF OBJECT_ID('dbo.udf_Delim') IS NOT NULL BEGIN
    DROP FUNCTION dbo.udf_Delim;
END;
GO

--2
CREATE FUNCTION dbo.udf_Product(@num1 INT, @num2 INT) RETURNS INT AS
BEGIN

    DECLARE @Product INT;
    SET @Product = ISNULL(@num1,0) * ISNULL(@num2,0);
    RETURN @Product;

END;
GO

--3
CREATE FUNCTION dbo.udf_Delim(@String VARCHAR(100),@Delimiter CHAR(1))
    RETURNS VARCHAR(200) AS
BEGIN
    DECLARE @NewString VARCHAR(200) = '';
    DECLARE @Count INT = 1;

    WHILE @Count <= LEN(@String) BEGIN
        SET @NewString += SUBSTRING(@String,@Count,1) + @Delimiter;
        SET @Count += 1;
    END

    RETURN @NewString;
END
GO

--4
SELECT StoreID, TerritoryID,
    dbo.udf_Product(StoreID, TerritoryID) AS TheProduct,
    dbo.udf_Delim(FirstName,',') AS FirstNameWithCommas
FROM Sales.Customer AS c
INNER JOIN Person.Person AS p ON c.PersonID= p.BusinessEntityID;
```

Figure 14-14 shows the results of running this code. Code section 1 drops the UDFs in case they already exist. Code section 2 creates the UDFs dbo.udf_Product and dbo.udf_Delim. The dbo.udf_Product UDF takes two INT parameters. Inside the UDF, the two parameters are multiplied together after correcting for NULL values. The code saves the product in a variable, @Product, which is returned.

	StoreID	TerritoryID	TheProduct	FirstNameWithCommas
1	294	4	1176	C,a,t,h,e,r,i,n,e,
2	296	3	888	K,i,m,
3	298	2	596	H,u,m,b,e,r,t,o,
4	292	5	1460	G,u,s,t,a,v,o,
5	300	9	2700	P,i,l,a,r,
6	NULL	4	0	A,a,r,o,n,
7	NULL	4	0	A,d,a,m,
8	NULL	1	0	A,l,e,x,
9	NULL	4	0	A,l,e,x,a,n,d,r,a,
10	NULL	7	0	A,l,l,i,s,o,n,

Figure 14-14. *The partial results of using two user-defined scalar functions*

The second UDF, dbo.udf_Delim, takes two parameters: @String, which is a VARCHAR(100), and @Delimiter, which is a one-character string. Inside the definition, a loop builds a new string inserting the delimiter after each character in the original string. The function returns the new string. Query 4 uses the new functions in the SELECT list, multiplying the StoreID by the TerritoryID and adding commas to the FirstName column. Each of these functions is database agnostic; you could add them to any database.

Using Table-Valued User-Defined Functions

The second type of UDF returns a set of rows instead of one value. You can't use this type of UDF in the SELECT list within a query, but you can use it in place of a table or save the results into a temp table or table variable for use later in your script.

There are two types of table-valued UDFs. One type, sometimes called an inline table-valued UDF, contains only a SELECT statement. The other contains multiple statements.

The AdventureWorks database contains one example of a table-valued UDF. This function accepts a @PersonID value and returns information about the contact. Using SQL Server Management Studio, navigate to the AdventureWorks database, and drill down to the dbo.ufnGetContactInformation function via Programmability ➤ Functions ➤ Table-valued Functions. Once you reach the function, right-click and choose Script Function as ➤ Create to ➤ New Query Editor Window. You can see why this is a function instead of a view. Because the Person.Person table contains information about contacts from many different tables, the function uses logic to figure out which query to run to pull the information. You can't define logic like that in a view, so that is why the AdventureWorks developers chose to create the table-valued UDF. This function is fine if an application calls it to get the information about one person. If it is used in a query that returns many rows, the performance would be terrible.

To work with a table-valued UDF, you can select from it like a table or use the CROSS APPLY operator to join the function to another table. Here is the syntax:

```
SELECT <col1>,<col2> FROM <schema>.<udf name>(<@param>)
```

```
SELECT <col1>,<col2> FROM <table1> CROSS APPLY <udf name>(<table1>.<col3>)
```

Listing 14-11 demonstrates using the dbo.ufnGetContactInformation function. Type in and execute to learn more.

Listing 14-11. Using a Table-Valued UDF

```
--1
SELECT PersonID,FirstName,LastName,JobTitle,BusinessEntityType
FROM dbo.ufnGetContactInformation(1);


--2
SELECT PersonID,FirstName,LastName,JobTitle,BusinessEntityType
FROM dbo.ufnGetContactInformation(7822);


--3
SELECT e.BirthDate, e.Gender, c.FirstName,c.LastName,c.JobTitle
FROM HumanResources.Employee as e
CROSS APPLY dbo.ufnGetContactInformation(e.BusinessEntityID ) AS c;


--4
SELECT sc.CustomerID,sc.TerritoryID,c.FirstName,c.LastName
FROM Sales.Customer AS sc
CROSS APPLY dbo.ufnGetContactInformation(sc.PersonID) AS c;
```

Figure 14-15 shows the partial results of running this code. Query 1 calls the UDF with the parameter 1. The logic inside the UDF determines that BusinessEntityID 1 belongs to an employee and returns that information. Query 2 calls the UDF with parameter 7822. The logic inside the UDF determines that this BusinessEntityID belongs to a customer and returns the appropriate information. Query 3 uses the CROSS APPLY operator to join the HumanResources.Employee table to the UDF. Instead of supplying an individual value to find one name, the query supplies the BusinessEntityID column of the HumanResources.Employee table to the function. Columns from the UDF and the table appear in the SELECT list. Query 4 uses CROSS APPLY to join the UDF on the Sales.Customer table. Another option, OUTER APPLY, returns rows even if a NULL value is passed to the UDF, similar to an OUTER JOIN. The APPLY operator calls the function one time for each row of the table on the left. A join will generally be more efficient, so use a join over APPLY when possible.

	PersonID	FirstName	LastName	JobTitle	BusinessEntityType
1	1	Ken	Sánchez	Chief Executive Officer	Employee

	PersonID	FirstName	LastName	JobTitle	BusinessEntityType
1	7822	Faith	Hughes	NULL	Consumer

	BirthDate	Gender	FirstName	LastName	JobTitle
1	1963-03-02	M	Ken	Sánchez	Chief Executive Officer
2	1965-09-01	F	Terri	Duffy	Vice President of Engineering
3	1968-12-13	M	Roberto	Tamburello	Engineering Manager
4	1969-01-23	M	Rob	Walters	Senior Tool Designer

	CustomerID	TerritoryID	FirstName	LastName
1	11000	9	Jon	Yang
2	11001	9	Eugene	Huang
3	11002	9	Ruben	Torres
4	11003	9	Christy	Zhu

Figure 14-15. *The partial results of using a table-valued UDF*

You will probably find many reasons to write scalar-valued user-defined functions. Table-valued UDFs are not as common. Always consider the performance implications of using either type of UDF. You can also create user-defined functions with a .NET language, but this is beyond the scope of this book. Practice what you have learned about UDFs by completing Exercise 14-3.

EXERCISE 14-3

Use the AdventureWorks database to complete this exercise. You can find the solutions at the end of the chapter.

1. Create a user-defined function called dbo.fn_AddTwoNumbers that accepts two integer parameters. Return the value that is the sum of the two numbers. Test the function.

2. Create a user-defined function called dbo.Trim that takes a VARCHAR(250) parameter. This function should trim off the spaces from both the beginning and the end of the string. Test the function.

3. Create a function dbo.fn_RemoveNumbers that removes any numeric characters from a VARCHAR(250) string. Test the function. Hint: The ISNUMERIC function checks to see whether a string is numeric. Check Books Online to see how to use it.

4. Write a function called dbo.fn_FormatPhone that takes a string of ten numbers. The function will format the string into this phone number format: "(###) ###-####." Test the function.

Stored Procedures

Stored procedures (sometimes shortened to procs) are the workhorses of T-SQL. Developers and database administrators use them to increase security as well as encapsulate logic. Stored procedures can contain programming logic, update data, create other objects, and more. Essentially, stored procedures are just saved scripts, and they can do anything that the stored-procedure owner can do. Like views, the user of the stored procedure doesn't usually need to have permissions on the tables used within the stored procedure.

▪ **Tip** Stored procedures are often used to prevent SQL injection attacks. Hackers employing SQL injection techniques insert SQL commands into web forms that build SQL statements dynamically. Eventually the hacker takes over databases, servers, and networks. This problem is not unique to SQL Server; other database systems have been attacked as well.

Stored procedures and UDFs have many similarities but they also have some distinct differences. Table 14-1 shows some of the differences between stored procedures and UDFs as well as views.

Table 14-1. *The Differences Between Stored Procedures and User-Defined Functions*

Feature	SP	Scalar UDF	Table UDF	View
Return tabular data	Yes	No	Yes	Yes
Return multiple sets of results	Yes	N/A	No	No
Update data	Yes	No	No	No
Create other objects	Yes	No	No	No

(continued)

Table 14-1. (*continued*)

Feature	SP	Scalar UDF	Table UDF	View
Call from a procedure	Yes	Yes	Yes	Yes
Can call a procedure	Yes	No	No	No
Can call a function	Yes	Yes	Yes	Yes
Can call within a SELECT list	No	Yes	No	No
Use to populate multiple columns in a table	Yes	No	Yes	Yes
Return value required	No	Yes	Yes (table)	N/A
Return value optional	Yes	No	No	N/A
Takes parameters	Yes	Yes	Yes	No
Output parameters	Yes	No	No	No

You will find that creating stored procedures is easy. Here's the syntax to create, alter, drop, and execute a stored procedure:

```
CREATE PROC[EDURE] <proc name> [<@param1> <data type>,<@param2> <data type>] AS
    <statements>
    [RETURN <INT>]

ALTER PROC[EDURE] <proc name> [<@param1> <data type>,<@param2> <data type>] AS
    <statements>
    [RETURN <INT>]

EXEC <proc name> <param values>

DROP PROC[EDURE] <proc name>
```

Some shops require that developers use stored procedures for all database calls from their applications. I have also heard of shops that don't allow stored procedures at all. Chances are you will work with stored procedures at some point in your career. Listing 14-12 shows how to create a stored procedure. Type in and execute the code to learn more.

Listing 14-12. Creating and Using a Stored Procedure

```
--1
IF OBJECT_ID('dbo.usp_CustomerName') IS NOT NULL BEGIN
    DROP PROC dbo.usp_CustomerName;
END;
GO

--2
CREATE PROC dbo.usp_CustomerName AS
    SET NOCOUNT ON;
```

```
    SELECT c.CustomerID,p.FirstName,p.MiddleName,p.LastName
    FROM Sales.Customer AS c
    INNER JOIN Person.Person AS p on c.PersonID = p.BusinessEntityID
    ORDER BY p.LastName, p.FirstName,p.MiddleName ;

    RETURN 0;
GO

--3
EXEC dbo.usp_CustomerName
GO

--4
ALTER PROC dbo.usp_CustomerName @CustomerID INT AS
    SET NOCOUNT ON;

    IF @CustomerID > 0 BEGIN

        SELECT c.CustomerID,p.FirstName,p.MiddleName,p.LastName
        FROM Sales.Customer AS c
        INNER JOIN Person.Person AS p on c.PersonID = p.BusinessEntityID
        WHERE c.CustomerID = @CustomerID;

        RETURN 0;
    END
    ELSE BEGIN
        RETURN -1;
    END;

GO

--5
EXEC dbo.usp_CustomerName @CustomerID = 15128;
```

Figure 14-16 shows the results of running this code. Code section 1 drops the stored procedure if it already exists. Code section 2 creates the stored procedure, dbo.usp_CustomerName. You can have many statements in a stored procedure. This procedure has two statement and a return value. The SET NOCOUNT ON statement keeps the rows' affected messages from being returned. The procedure simply joins the Sales.Customer table to the Person.Person table and returns several columns from those tables. Notice that the query includes the ORDER BY clause. Unlike views, the ORDER BY clause will actually return the rows in the order specified. Statement 3 calls the procedure with the EXEC command. Code section 4 changes the stored procedure by adding a parameter and using that parameter in a WHERE clause. By using the ALTER PROC statement instead of dropping and re-creating the procedure, the security is retained.

	CustomerID	FirstName	MiddleName	LastName
1	29485	Catherine	R.	Abel
2	29486	Kim	NULL	Abercrombie
3	29487	Humberto	NULL	Acevedo
4	29484	Gustavo	NULL	Achong

	CustomerID	FirstName	MiddleName	LastName
1	15128	Angelica	NULL	Barnes

Figure 14-16. *The partial results of using a stored procedure*

Statement 5 calls the modified procedure, supplying a value for the @CustomerID parameter. You could have left out the name of the parameter when you called the stored procedure in this case. Supplying the name of the parameter makes the code easier to read and understand.

Using Default Values with Parameters

SQL Server requires that you supply a value for each parameter unless you define a default value for the parameter. When a parameter has a default value, you can skip the parameter when you call the stored procedure. In that case, you will have to name the other parameters, not just rely on the position in the list. Once you use a named parameter when calling the stored procedure, you must continue naming parameters. You may want to get in the habit of naming the parameters anyway because it makes your code easier to understand. Here is the syntax for creating a stored procedure with default value parameters:

```
CREATE PROC[EDURE] <proc name> <@param1> <data type> = <default value> AS
    <statements>
    [return <value>]
```

Listing 14-13 shows how to use default value parameters. Type in and execute the code to learn more.

Listing 14-13. Using Default Value Parameters

```
--1
IF OBJECT_ID('dbo.usp_CustomerName') IS NOT NULL BEGIN
    DROP PROC dbo.usp_CustomerName;
END;
GO


--2
CREATE PROC dbo.usp_CustomerName @CustomerID INT = -1 AS
    SELECT c.CustomerID,p.FirstName,p.MiddleName,p.LastName
    FROM Sales.Customer AS c
    INNER JOIN Person.Person AS p on c.PersonID = p.BusinessEntityID
    WHERE @CustomerID = CASE @CustomerID WHEN -1 THEN -1 ELSE c.CustomerID END;

    RETURN 0;
GO
```

```
--3
EXEC dbo.usp_CustomerName 15128;

--4
EXEC dbo.usp_CustomerName ;
```

Figure 14-17 shows the results of running this code. Code section 1 drops the stored procedure if it exists. Code section 2 creates the stored procedure along with the parameter @CustomerID and the default value –1. In this case, if the user calls the stored procedure without a value for @CustomerID, the stored procedure will return all the rows. Statement 3 calls the stored procedure with a value, and the stored procedure returns the one matching row. Statement 4 calls the stored procedure without the parameter value, and the stored procedure returns all the rows.

	CustomerID	FirstName	MiddleName	LastName
1	15128	Angelica	NULL	Barnes

	CustomerID	FirstName	MiddleName	LastName
1	11012	Lauren	M	Walker
2	11013	Ian	M	Jenkins
3	11014	Sydney	NULL	Bennett
4	11021	Destiny	NULL	Wilson

Figure 14-17. *The partial results of using a default value parameter*

Using the *OUTPUT* Parameter

You can use an OUTPUT parameter to get back a value from a stored procedure directly into a variable. This is one of those gray areas where you may decide to use a scalar-value UDF with a return value instead unless there are other reasons to use a procedure such as data modifications. In my opinion, if the logic is not portable to any database, use a stored procedure. Save scalar-valued UDFs for truly database-agnostic uses. Here is the syntax for creating and using an OUTPUT parameter with a stored procedure:

```
CREATE PROC[EDURE] <proc name> <@param> <data type> OUTPUT AS
    <statements>
    [return <value>]
GO

DECLARE <@variable> <data type>
EXEC <proc name> [<@param> =] <@variable> OUTPUT
PRINT <@variable>
```

You can include as many parameters as you need, and your OUTPUT parameter can pass a value to the stored procedure as well as return a value. Type in and execute Listing 14-14 to learn how to use an OUTPUT parameter.

Listing 14-14. Using an OUTPUT Parameter

```
--1
IF OBJECT_ID('dbo.usp_OrderDetailCount') IS NOT NULL BEGIN
    DROP PROC dbo.usp_OrderDetailCount;
END;
GO

--2
CREATE PROC dbo.usp_OrderDetailCount @OrderID INT,
    @Count INT OUTPUT AS

    SELECT @Count = COUNT(*)
    FROM Sales.SalesOrderDetail
    WHERE SalesOrderID = @OrderID;

    RETURN 0;
GO

--3
DECLARE @OrderCount INT;

--4
EXEC usp_OrderDetailCount 71774, @OrderCount OUTPUT;

--5
PRINT @OrderCount;
```

Code section 1 drops the stored procedure if it exists. Code section 2 creates the stored procedure, dbo.usp_ OrderDetailCount, along with two parameters, @OrderID and @Count. The first parameter accepts a SalesOrderID value. The second parameter is the OUTPUT parameter, which returns the count of the orders for that SalesOrderID. Statement 3 creates a variable, @OrderCount, to be used as the OUTPUT parameter. Statement 4 calls the stored procedure with the value for @OrderID and the variable for the @Count parameter. In statement 5, the final value of @Count from inside the stored procedure saved to the variable @OrderCount prints in the Message window. The call to the stored procedure could also have looked like this:

```
EXEC dbo.usp_OrderDetailCount @OrderID = 71774, @Count = @OrderCount OUTPUT.
```

One mistake that developers often make is to forget to use the OUTPUT keyword when calling the stored procedure. To get the modified parameter value back, you must use OUTPUT.

Saving the Results of a Stored Procedure in a Table

One very popular use of a stored procedure is to save the results in a temp or work table for later processing. When saving the results of a stored procedure in a table, define the table ahead of time. All the columns must be in place and of compatible data types. If the procedure returns multiple sets of results, the first set will populate the table. Here is the syntax for inserting the rows returned from a stored procedure into a table:

```
INSERT [INTO] <table name> EXEC <stored proc> [<@param value>]
```

Listing 14-15 shows how to save the results of a procedure into a table. Type in and execute the code to learn more.

Listing 14-15. Inserting the Rows from a Stored Procedure into a Table

```
--1
IF OBJECT_ID('dbo.tempCustomer') IS NOT NULL BEGIN
    DROP TABLE dbo.tempCustomer;
END;
IF OBJECT_ID('dbo.usp_CustomerName') IS NOT NULL BEGIN
    DROP PROC dbo.usp_CustomerName;
END;
GO

--2
CREATE TABLE dbo.tempCustomer(CustomerID INT, FirstName NVARCHAR(50),
    MiddleName NVARCHAR(50), LastName NVARCHAR(50));
GO

--3
CREATE PROC dbo.usp_CustomerName @CustomerID INT = -1 AS
    SELECT c.CustomerID,p.FirstName,p.MiddleName,p.LastName
    FROM Sales.Customer AS c
    INNER JOIN Person.Person AS p on c.PersonID = p.BusinessEntityID
    WHERE @CustomerID = CASE @CustomerID WHEN -1 THEN -1 ELSE c.CustomerID END;

    RETURN 0;
GO

--4
INSERT INTO dbo.tempCustomer EXEC dbo.usp_CustomerName;

--5
SELECT CustomerID, FirstName, MiddleName, LastName
FROM dbo.tempCustomer;
```

Figure 14-18 shows the results of running this code. Code section 1 drops the table and stored procedure if they exist. Statement 2 creates the table dbo.tempCustomer, matching up columns and data types. They don't need to have the same names as the stored procedure, but they should have the same number of columns, in the same order, and of compatible data types. Alternately, you can specify the column names instead. In this case, the list of columns must match the columns returned from the procedure. Code section 3 creates the stored procedure. Statement 4 calls the stored procedure while at the same time storing the results in dbo.tempCustomer. Query 5 returns the results.

	CustomerID	FirstName	MiddleName	LastName
1	29485	Catherine	R.	Abel
2	29486	Kim	NULL	Abercrombie
3	29487	Humberto	NULL	Acevedo
4	29484	Gustavo	NULL	Achong
5	29488	Pilar	NULL	Ackerman
6	28866	Aaron	B	Adams
7	13323	Adam	NULL	Adams
8	21139	Alex	C	Adams
9	29170	Alexandra	J	Adams
10	19419	Allison	L	Adams

Figure 14-18. *The partial results of saving the results of a stored procedure into a table*

Using a Logic in Stored Procedures

So far you have seen stored procedures that don't do much more than run queries, but stored procedures are capable of so much more. You can include conditional code, loops, error trapping, object creation statements, and more within stored procedures. Listing 14-16 shows an example. Type in and execute the code to learn more.

Listing 14-16. Using Logic in a Stored Procedure

```
USE tempdb;
GO

--1
IF OBJECT_ID('usp_ProgrammingLogic') IS NOT NULL BEGIN
    DROP PROC usp_ProgrammingLogic;
END;
GO

--2
CREATE PROC usp_ProgrammingLogic AS
    --2.1
    CREATE TABLE #Numbers(number INT NOT NULL);
    --2.2
    DECLARE @count INT;
    SET @count = ASCII('!');

    --2.3
    WHILE @count < 200 BEGIN
        INSERT INTO #Numbers(number) VALUES (@count);
        SET @count = @count + 1;
    END;
```

```
    --2.4
    ALTER TABLE #Numbers ADD symbol NCHAR(1);
    --2.5
    UPDATE #Numbers SET symbol = CHAR(number);

    --2.6
    SELECT number, symbol FROM #Numbers;
GO

--3

EXEC usp_ProgrammingLogic;
```

Figure 14-19 shows the results of running this code. This stored procedure creates a table of numbers and the ASCII symbol for each number. This is a simple example just to give you an idea of what you can do. Anything you have learned in this book can be encapsulated within a stored procedure.

	number	symbol
1	33	!
2	34	"
3	35	#
4	36	$
5	37	%
6	38	&
7	39	'
8	40	(
9	41	)
10	42	*

Figure 14-19. *The partial results of using a stored procedure with programming logic*

Now that you have seen many of the possibilities of using stored procedures, complete Exercise 14-4 to practice what you have learned.

EXERCISE 14-4

Use the AdventureWorks database to complete this exercise. You can find the solutions at the end of the chapter.

1. Create a stored procedure called dbo.usp_CustomerTotals instead of a view from question 2 in Exercise 14-2. Test the stored procedure.

2. Modify the stored procedure created in question 1 to include a parameter @CustomerID. Use the parameter in the WHERE clause of the query in the stored procedure. Test the stored procedure.

3. Create a stored procedure called dbo.usp_ProductSales that accepts a ProductID for a parameter and has an OUTPUT parameter that returns the total number sold for the product. Test the stored procedure.

User-Defined Data Types

Within a database, you can create user-defined data types (UDTs), which are nothing more than native data types that you have given a specific name or alias. This enables you to make sure that a particular type of column is consistently defined throughout the database. These are not used very often, but I have seen them used in a production system, and there are several in the AdventureWorks database. For example, databases often contain ZIP code and phone number columns as UDTs.

Take a look at the UDTs defined for the AdventureWorks database by navigating to Programmability ➤ Types ➤ User-Defined Data Types. If you double-click the Phone data type, you can see the graphical editor for the type (see Figure 14-20).

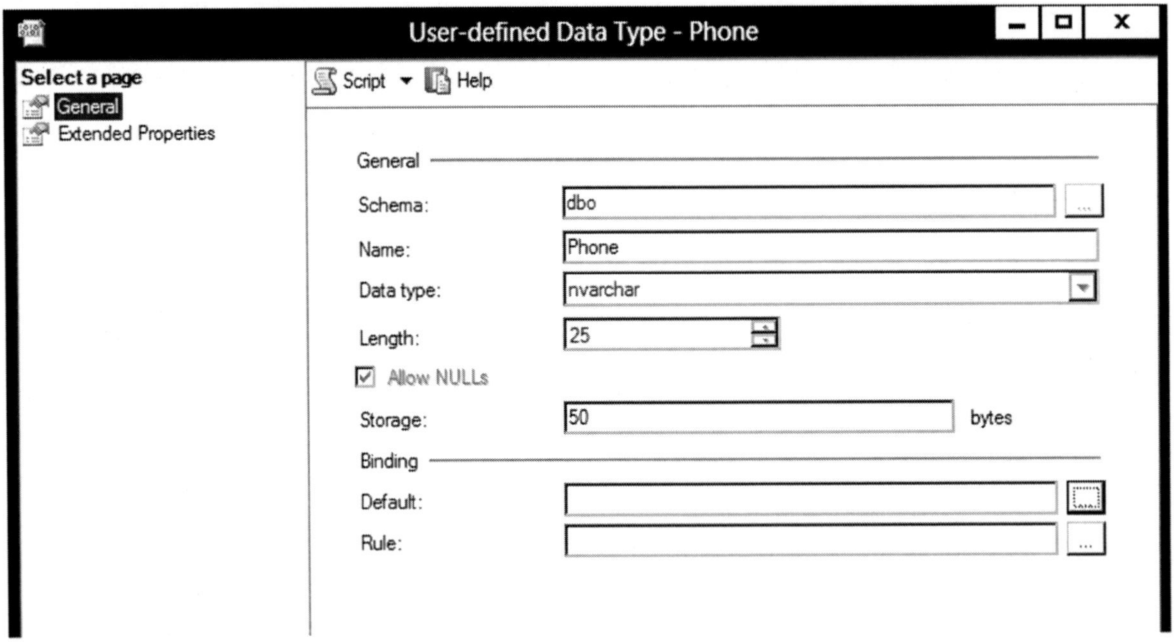

Figure 14-20. *The properties of the Phone user defined data type*

The Phone data type is an NVARCHAR(25) that allows NULL values. The Binding section for Default and Rule are blank. In previous versions of SQL Server, you had to create defaults and rules that were then applied to columns or UDTs, but the binding features have been deprecated and should not be used. Once you have the data type defined, you can use it when defining columns in tables as any other data type. Here is the syntax for creating a UDT:

```
CREATE TYPE <type name> FROM <native type and size> [NULL|NOT NULL]
```

Listing 14-17 shows how to create a UDT. Type in and execute the code to learn more.

Listing 14-17. Creating a User-Defined Data Type

```
IF  EXISTS (
    SELECT * FROM sys.types st
    JOIN sys.schemas ss ON st.schema_id = ss.schema_id
    WHERE st.name = N'CustomerID' AND ss.name = N'dbo') BEGIN

    DROP TYPE dbo.CustomerID;
END;
GO

CREATE TYPE dbo.CustomerID FROM INT NOT NULL;
```

Now that the new UDT exists, you can use it when defining new tables. Another type of object is called a *user-defined type*. This type must be created with a .NET language called a CLR data type. CLR types can contain multiple properties and can contain methods. Beginning with SQL Server 2008, Microsoft has included several complex data types created with the CLR. You will learn about these data types in Chapter 16.

Table Types

A special type of user-defined type object is the *table type*. A table type allows you to pass tabular data to a stored procedure in the form of a table variable. Before this feature became available, it was difficult, but not impossible, to send multiple rows of data to a stored procedure in one call. One workaround was to send the data in a variable, but then you would have to implement logic in the stored procedure to parse out the columns and rows. This is a big issue when sending data to SQL Server to be processed from a .NET application when multiple rows are involved. Usually, the solution was to create the stored procedure to accept one parameter for each column. Then the application would send the data for one row at a time.

Starting with SQL Server 2008, the table type is available to enable stored procedures to accept multiple rows at one time and treat the variable inside the procedure as a table that can be used to join to other tables, insert rows, or update existing data.

■ **Note** As part of the In-Memory OLTP features available with SQL Server 2014, the table types can be configured to reside in memory only. Traditional table variables are actually created on disk in tempdb. The In-Memory OLTP features, codenamed Hekaton, are beyond the scope of this book.

A table type is just a definition, similar to a UDT. Here is the syntax for creating a table type:

```
CREATE TYPE <schema>.<tableName> AS TABLE(
    <col1> <dataType1>, <col2> <dataType2> );
```

Type in and execute the code in Listing 14-18 to create a table type.

Listing 14-18. Create a Table Type

```
--Clean up objects for this section if they exist
IF EXISTS(SELECT * FROM sys.procedures WHERE name = 'usp_TestTableVariable') BEGIN
        DROP PROCEDURE usp_TestTableVariable;
END;
```

```
IF EXISTS(SELECT * FROM sys.types WHERE name = 'CustomerInfo') BEGIN
        DROP TYPE dbo.CustomerInfo;
END;

CREATE TYPE dbo.CustomerInfo AS TABLE
(
    CustomerID INT NOT NULL PRIMARY KEY,
        FavoriteColor VARCHAR(20) NULL,
        FavoriteSeason VARCHAR(10) NULL
);
```

Once dbo.CustomerInfo is created, you can see it in the Programmability section of SQL Server Management Studio, as shown in Figure 14-21.

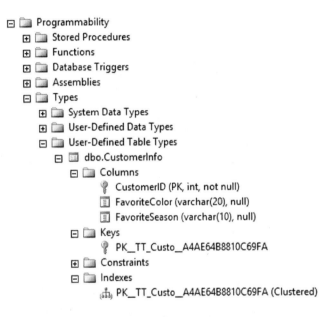

Figure 14-21. *The CustomerInfo type*

Although you can view the properties of the CustomerInfo type, you can't add data to it or query it. A variable must be created based on the type. Listing 14-19 demonstrates how to create and populate the table variable.

Listing 14-19. Create and Populate Table Variable Based on the Type

```
DECLARE @myTableVariable [dbo].[CustomerInfo];

INSERT INTO @myTableVariable(CustomerID, FavoriteColor, FavoriteSeason)
VALUES(11001, 'Blue','Summer'),(11002,'Orange','Fall');

SELECT CustomerID, FavoriteColor, FavoriteSeason
FROM @myTableVariable;
```

The @myTableVariable variable has the same definition as the dbo.CustomerInfo type. It could be used to send multiple rows to a stored procedure for further processing. This is called a *table-valued parameter.* Listing 14-20 creates a stored procedure and then executes it, passing in a table variable as an argument.

Listing 14-20. Create a Stored Procedure and Use a Table Variable

```
GO
--1
CREATE PROC dbo.usp_TestTableVariable @myTable CustomerInfo READONLY AS
    SELECT c.CustomerID, AccountNumber, FavoriteColor, FavoriteSeason
    FROM AdventureWorks.Sales.Customer AS C INNER JOIN @myTable MT
        ON C.CustomerID = MT.CustomerID;

GO
--2
DECLARE @myTableVariable [dbo].[CustomerInfo]
INSERT INTO @myTableVariable(CustomerID, FavoriteColor, FavoriteSeason)
VALUES(11001, 'Blue','Summer'),(11002,'Orange','Fall');

--3
EXEC usp_TestTableVariable @myTableVariable;
```

Code section 1 creates a stored procedure that accepts a variable of type CustomerInfo. Inside the stored procedure the table variable is read-only, and that must be specified in the stored procedure definition. Inside the procedure, the table variable is used to join on the Sales.Customer table. Code section 2 declares and populates a table variable. Code section 3 calls the stored procedure with the table-valued parameter. Figure 14-22 shows the results.

	CustomerID	AccountNumber	FavoriteColor	FavoriteSeason
1	11001	AW00011001	Blue	Summer
2	11002	AW00011002	Orange	Fall

Figure 14-22. *The results of using a table-valued parameter*

Triggers

Triggers are a very powerful feature of SQL Server. As with most powerful things, they can also cause many problems. Triggers are like a special type of stored procedure that runs whenever data is modified. You can also create triggers at the database level that fire when any object definition is modified or at the server level when a login to the database is attempted. You can define triggers on tables that fire when new rows are inserted or when existing rows are updated or deleted. Triggers can insert data into auditing tables, roll back the current update, or even modify the row that caused the trigger to fire in the first place. Obviously, they can have an impact on performance, and care must be taken so that triggers are not used in a way that causes them to fire repeatedly because of one update.

Any code within a trigger must be very efficient. The transaction that caused the trigger to fire can't complete until the trigger is successfully completed. One common use of triggers is to enforce *referential integrity,* or the primary key to foreign key relationships between tables. For example, a trigger that fires when a customer is deleted from the customer table might delete all the orders for that customer. In actuality, this use of triggers is not necessary. Database designers can use foreign key constraints to take care of situations like this.

Because this is a beginners book, it doesn't cover creating triggers. Just be aware that triggers often exist in databases and are frequently the cause of performance or logic problems that are difficult to track down.

CLR Integration

In addition to creating stored procedures, triggers, functions, and user-defined types using T-SQL, you can also create these objects in a .NET language. This is called CLR, or common language runtime, integration. Although it is an excellent way to extend the functionality of SQL Server, it has never been very popular with database administrators. For retrieving and updating data, T-SQL is the best choice. For complex string manipulation or calculations, you may benefit from a CLR object instead of T-SQL. Once the CLR object is created and added to the SQL Server instance, you use it just like a native object.

Microsoft has taken advantage of CLR to create the XML, HierarchyID, and spatial data types. These data types not only have properties, they also have methods. You will learn about the XML data type in Chapter 15 and the other two in Chapter 16.

Because creating CLR integrated objects requires .NET code, such as C# or VB.NET, it is not covered in this book. To see an end-to-end example, read this Books Online article at http://msdn.microsoft.com/en-us/library/ms131043.aspx.

Thinking About Performance

This chapter covers many ways you can add logic to the database to enforce business rules or make development easier. One common problem is using UDFs that access data within a query. The database engine will have to execute the function for each row of the query. Listing 14-21 illustrates this point. Run the first part of the code to create the objects. Then run query 3 and see how long it takes. Run query 4 and see how long that query takes.

Listing 14-21. Performance Issues with UDFs

```
--RUN THIS FIRST
USE AdventureWorks;
GO

IF OBJECT_ID('dbo.udf_ProductTotal') IS NOT NULL BEGIN
    DROP FUNCTION dbo.udf_ProductTotal;
END;
GO

CREATE FUNCTION dbo.udf_ProductTotal(@ProductID INT,@Year INT) RETURNS MONEY AS
BEGIN

    DECLARE @Sum MONEY;

    SELECT @Sum = SUM(LineTotal)
    FROM Sales.SalesOrderDetail AS sod
    INNER JOIN Sales.SalesOrderHeader AS soh
            ON sod.SalesOrderID = soh.SalesOrderID
    WHERE ProductID = @ProductID AND YEAR(OrderDate) = @Year;

    RETURN ISNULL(@Sum,0);

END;
GO
--TO HERE


--3 Run this by itself to see how long it takes
SELECT ProductID, dbo.udf_ProductTotal(ProductID, 2004) AS SumOfSales
```

```
FROM Production.Product
ORDER BY SumOfSales DESC;

--4 Run this by itself to see how long it takes
WITH Sales AS (
    SELECT SUM(LineTotal) AS SumOfSales, ProductID,
        YEAR(OrderDate) AS OrderYear
    FROM Sales.SalesOrderDetail AS sod
    INNER JOIN Sales.SalesOrderHeader AS soh
        ON sod.SalesOrderID = soh.SalesOrderID
    GROUP BY ProductID, YEAR(OrderDate)
)
SELECT p.ProductID, ISNULL(SumOfSales,0) AS SumOfSales
FROM Production.Product AS p
LEFT OUTER JOIN Sales ON p.ProductID = Sales.ProductID
    AND OrderYear = 2004
ORDER BY SumOfSales DESC;
```

On my laptop with 8GB of RAM and a solid-state drive, query 3 takes about two seconds to run, and query 4 executes immediately. Because the user-defined function must access the Sales.SalesOrderDetail table once for every product, it takes a lot of resources. Unfortunately, the execution plans, if you choose to compare them, don't accurately reflect the difference. On my computer, query 4 takes 100 percent of the resources in the execution plans, but I know that is not true since query 4 runs so much faster.

Database Cleanup

You have created quite a few objects during this chapter. You can either run the script in Listing 14-22 (also available on the book's web page at www.apress.com) to clean up the objects from the examples or reinstall the sample databases according to the instructions in the "Installing the Sample Databases" section in Chapter 1.

Listing 14-22. Database Cleanup

```
USE AdventureWorks;
GO
IF OBJECT_ID('vw_Customer') IS NOT NULL BEGIN
    DROP VIEW vw_Customer;
END;

IF OBJECT_ID('vw_Dept') IS NOT NULL BEGIN
    DROP VIEW dbo.vw_Dept;
END;

IF OBJECT_ID('demoDept') IS NOT NULL BEGIN
    DROP TABLE dbo.demoDept;
END;

IF OBJECT_ID('dbo.demoCustomer') IS NOT NULL BEGIN
    DROP TABLE dbo.demoCustomer;
END;

IF OBJECT_ID('dbo.demoPerson') IS NOT NULL BEGIN
    DROP TABLE dbo.demoPerson;
END;
```

```
IF OBJECT_ID('dbo.udf_Product') IS NOT NULL BEGIN
    DROP FUNCTION dbo.udf_Product;
END;

IF OBJECT_ID('dbo.udf_Delim') IS NOT NULL BEGIN
    DROP FUNCTION dbo.udf_Delim;
END;

IF OBJECT_ID('dbo.usp_CustomerName') IS NOT NULL BEGIN
    DROP PROC dbo.usp_CustomerName;
END;

IF OBJECT_ID('dbo.usp_OrderDetailCount') IS NOT NULL BEGIN
    DROP PROC dbo.usp_OrderDetailCount;
END;

IF OBJECT_ID('dbo.tempCustomer') IS NOT NULL BEGIN
    DROP TABLE dbo.tempCustomer;
END;

IF OBJECT_ID('usp_ProgrammingLogic') IS NOT NULL BEGIN
    DROP PROC usp_ProgrammingLogic
END;

IF OBJECT_ID('dbo.udf_ProductTotal') IS NOT NULL BEGIN
    DROP FUNCTION dbo.udf_ProductTotal;
END;

IF OBJECT_ID('dbo.vw_Products') IS NOT NULL BEGIN
    DROP VIEW dbo.vw_Products;
END;

IF OBJECT_ID('dbo.vw_CustomerTotals') IS NOT NULL BEGIN
    DROP VIEW dbo.vw_CustomerTotals;
END;

IF OBJECT_ID('dbo.fn_AddTwoNumbers') IS NOT NULL BEGIN
    DROP FUNCTION dbo.fn_AddTwoNumbers;
END;

IF OBJECT_ID('dbo.Trim') IS NOT NULL BEGIN
    DROP FUNCTION dbo.Trim;
END

IF OBJECT_ID('dbo.fn_RemoveNumbers') IS NOT NULL BEGIN
     DROP FUNCTION dbo.fn_RemoveNumbers;
END;

IF OBJECT_ID('dbo.fn_FormatPhone') IS NOT NULL BEGIN
    DROP FUNCTION dbo.fn_FormatPhone;
END;
```

```
IF OBJECT_ID('dbo.usp_CustomerTotals') IS NOT NULL BEGIN
    DROP PROCEDURE dbo.usp_CustomerTotals;
END;

IF OBJECT_ID('dbo.usp_ProductSales') IS NOT NULL BEGIN
    DROP PROCEDURE dbo.usp_ProductSales;
END;

IF EXISTS(SELECT * FROM sys.procedures WHERE name = 'usp_TestTableVariable') BEGIN
        DROP PROCEDURE usp_TestTableVariable;
END;

IF EXISTS(SELECT * FROM sys.types WHERE name = 'CustomerInfo') BEGIN
        DROP TYPE dbo.CustomerInfo;
END;

IF OBJECT_ID('MySequence') IS NOT NULL BEGIN
        DROP SEQUENCE MySequence;
END;
```

Summary

SQL Server contains many ways to enforce business rules and ensure data integrity. You can set up primary and foreign keys, constraints, and defaults in table definitions. You can create user-defined functions, stored procedures, views, and user-defined data types to add other ways to enforce business rules. You have many options that you can use to make development simpler and encapsulate logic.

Each new version of SQL Server adds new data types and functions. Chapter 16 covers some of the newer data types added with SQL Server 2008. The new updates to data types related to geography and geometry are especially interesting. Chapter 15 covers the XML data type.

Answers to the Exercises

This section provides solutions to the exercises found on creating database objects.

Solutions to Exercise 14-1: Tables

Use the AdventureWorks database to complete the exercises.

1. Create a table called dbo.testCustomer. Include a CustomerID that is an identity column primary key. Include FirstName and LastName columns. Include an Age column with a check constraint specifying that the value must be less than 120. Include an Active column that is one character with a default of Y and allows only Y or N. Add some rows to the table.

    Here's a possible solution:

    ```
    IF OBJECT_ID ('dbo.testCustomer') IS NOT NULL BEGIN
        DROP TABLE dbo.testCustomer;
    END;
    ```

```
GO
CREATE TABLE dbo.testCustomer (
    CustomerID INT NOT NULL IDENTITY,
    FirstName VARCHAR(25), LastName VARCHAR(25),
    Age INT, Active CHAR(1) DEFAULT 'Y',
    CONSTRAINT ch_testCustomer_Age
        CHECK (Age < 120),
    CONSTRAINT ch_testCustomer_Active
        CHECK (Active IN ('Y','N')),
    CONSTRAINT PK_testCustomer PRIMARY KEY (CustomerID)

);
GO
INSERT INTO dbo.testCustomer(FirstName, LastName,Age)
VALUES ('Kathy','Morgan',35),
    ('Lady B.','Kellenberger',14),
    ('Dennis','Wayne',30);
```

2. Create a table called dbo.testOrder. Include a CustomerID column that is a foreign key pointing to dbo.testCustomer. Include an OrderID column that is an identity column primary key. Include an OrderDate column that defaults to the current date and time. Include a ROWVERSION column. Add some rows to the table.

```
IF OBJECT_ID('dbo.testOrder') IS NOT NULL BEGIN
    DROP TABLE dbo.testOrder;
END;
GO
CREATE TABLE dbo.testOrder
    (CustomerID INT NOT NULL,
        OrderID INT NOT NULL IDENTITY,
        OrderDate DATETIME DEFAULT GETDATE(),
        RW ROWVERSION,
        CONSTRAINT fk_testOrders
            FOREIGN KEY (CustomerID)
        REFERENCES dbo.testCustomer(CustomerID),
        CONSTRAINT PK_TestOrder PRIMARY KEY (OrderID)
    );
GO
INSERT INTO dbo.testOrder (CustomerID)
VALUES (1),(2),(3);
```

3. Create a table called dbo.testOrderDetail. Include an OrderID column that is a foreign key pointing to dbo.testOrder. Include an integer ItemID column, a Price column, and a Qty column. The primary key should be a composite key composed of OrderID and ItemID. Create a computed column called LineItemTotal that multiplies Price times Qty. Add some rows to the table.

```
IF OBJECT_ID('dbo.testOrderDetail') IS NOT NULL BEGIN
    DROP TABLE dbo.testOrderDetail;
END;
```

```
GO
CREATE TABLE dbo.testOrderDetail(
    OrderID INT NOT NULL, ItemID INT NOT NULL,
    Price Money NOT NULL, Qty INT NOT NULL,
    LineItemTotal AS (Price * Qty),
    CONSTRAINT pk_testOrderDetail
        PRIMARY KEY (OrderID, ItemID),
    CONSTRAINT fk_testOrderDetail
        FOREIGN KEY (OrderID)
        REFERENCES dbo.testOrder(OrderID)
);
GO
INSERT INTO dbo.testOrderDetail(OrderID,ItemID,Price,Qty)
VALUES (1,1,10,5),(1,2,5,10);
```

Solution to Exercise 14-2: Views

Use the AdventureWorks database to complete the exercises.

1. Create a view called dbo.vw_Products that displays a list of the products from the Production.Product table joined to the Production.ProductCostHistory table. Include columns that describe the product and show the cost history for each product. Test the view by creating a query that retrieves data from the view.

```
IF OBJECT_ID('dbo.vw_Products') IS NOT NULL BEGIN
   DROP VIEW dbo.vw_Products;
END;
GO
CREATE VIEW dbo.vw_Products AS (
    SELECT P.ProductID, P.Name, P.Color,
        P.Size, P.Style,
        H.StandardCost, H.EndDate, H.StartDate
    FROM Production.Product AS P
    INNER JOIN Production.ProductCostHistory AS H
        ON P.ProductID = H.ProductID);
GO
SELECT ProductID, Name, Color, Size, Style,
    StandardCost, EndDate, StartDate
FROM dbo.vw_Products;
```

2. Create a view called dbo.vw_CustomerTotals that displays the total sales from the TotalDue column per year and month for each customer. Test the view by creating a query that retrieves data from the view.

```
IF OBJECT_ID('dbo.vw_CustomerTotals') IS NOT NULL BEGIN
   DROP VIEW dbo.vw_CustomerTotals;
END;
GO
CREATE VIEW dbo.vw_CustomerTotals AS (
    SELECT C.CustomerID,
        YEAR(OrderDate) AS OrderYear,
        MONTH(OrderDate) AS OrderMonth,
```

```
            SUM(TotalDue) AS TotalSales
        FROM Sales.Customer AS C
        INNER JOIN Sales.SalesOrderHeader
            AS SOH ON C.CustomerID = SOH.CustomerID GROUP BY C.CustomerID,
            YEAR(OrderDate), MONTH(OrderDate));
    GO
    SELECT CustomerID, OrderYear,
        OrderMonth, TotalSales
    FROM dbo.vw_CustomerTotals;
```

Solution to Exercise 14-3: User-Defined Functions

Use the AdventureWorks database to complete this exercise.

1. Create a user-defined function called dbo.fn_AddTwoNumbers that accepts two integer
    parameters. Return the value that is the sum of the two numbers. Test the function.

```
IF OBJECT_ID('dbo.fn_AddTwoNumbers')
    IS NOT NULL BEGIN
    DROP FUNCTION dbo.fn_AddTwoNumbers;
END;
GO
CREATE FUNCTION dbo.fn_AddTwoNumbers
    (@NumberOne INT, @NumberTwo INT)
RETURNS INT AS BEGIN
    RETURN @NumberOne + @NumberTwo;
END;
GO
SELECT dbo.fn_AddTwoNumbers(1,2);
```

2. Create a user-defined function called dbo.Trim that takes a VARCHAR(250) parameter.
    This function should trim off the spaces from both the beginning and the end of the string.
    Test the function.

```
IF OBJECT_ID('dbo.Trim') IS NOT NULL BEGIN
    DROP FUNCTION dbo.Trim;
END
GO
CREATE FUNCTION dbo.Trim
    (@Expression VARCHAR(250))
RETURNS VARCHAR(250) AS BEGIN
    RETURN LTRIM(RTRIM(@Expression));
END;
GO
SELECT '*' + dbo.Trim('  test  ') + '*';
```

3. Create a function dbo.fn_RemoveNumbers that removes any numeric characters from a VARCHAR(250) string. Test the function. Hint: The ISNUMERIC function checks to see whether a string is numeric. Check Books Online to see how to use it.

```
IF OBJECT_ID('dbo.fn_RemoveNumbers')
    IS NOT NULL BEGIN
    DROP FUNCTION dbo.fn_RemoveNumbers;
END;
GO
CREATE FUNCTION dbo.fn_RemoveNumbers
    (@Expression VARCHAR(250))
RETURNS VARCHAR(250) AS BEGIN
    RETURN REPLACE( REPLACE (REPLACE (REPLACE( REPLACE( REPLACE( REPLACE( REPLACE(
        REPLACE( @Expression,'1', ''),'2', ''),'3', ''),'4', ''),'5', ''),'6', ''),'7', ''),
            '8', ''),'9', ''),'0', '');
END;
GO
SELECT dbo.fn_RemoveNumbers
    ('abc 123 this is a test');
```

4. Write a function called dbo.fn_FormatPhone that takes a string of ten numbers. The function will format the string into this phone number format: "(###) ###-####." Test the function.

```
IF OBJECT_ID('dbo.fn_FormatPhone') IS NOT NULL
BEGIN
    DROP FUNCTION dbo.fn_FormatPhone;
END;
GO
CREATE FUNCTION dbo.fn_FormatPhone
    (@Phone VARCHAR(10))
RETURNS VARCHAR(14) AS BEGIN
    DECLARE @NewPhone VARCHAR(14);
    SET @NewPhone = '(' + SUBSTRING(@Phone,1,3)
        + ') ';
    SET @NewPhone = @NewPhone +
        SUBSTRING(@Phone, 4, 3) + '-';
    SET @NewPhone = @NewPhone +
        SUBSTRING(@Phone, 7, 4);
    RETURN @NewPhone;
END;
GO
SELECT dbo.fn_FormatPhone('5555551234');
```

Solution to Exercise 14-4: Stored Procedures

Use the AdventureWorks database to complete this exercise.

1. Create a stored procedure called dbo.usp_CustomerTotals instead of a view from question 2 in Exercise 14-2. Test the stored procedure.

```
IF OBJECT_ID('dbo.usp_CustomerTotals')
    IS NOT NULL BEGIN
    DROP PROCEDURE dbo.usp_CustomerTotals;
END;
GO
CREATE PROCEDURE dbo.usp_CustomerTotals AS
    SELECT C.CustomerID,
        YEAR(OrderDate) AS OrderYear,
        MONTH(OrderDate) AS OrderMonth,
        SUM(TotalDue) AS TotalSales
    FROM Sales.Customer AS C
    INNER JOIN Sales.SalesOrderHeader
        AS SOH ON C.CustomerID = SOH.CustomerID
    GROUP BY C.CustomerID, YEAR(OrderDate),
        MONTH(OrderDate);
GO
EXEC dbo.usp_CustomerTotals;
```

2. Modify the stored procedure created in question 1 to include a parameter @CustomerID. Use the parameter in the WHERE clause of the query in the stored procedure. Test the stored procedure.

```
IF OBJECT_ID('dbo.usp_CustomerTotals')
    IS NOT NULL BEGIN
    DROP PROCEDURE dbo.usp_CustomerTotals;
END;
GO
CREATE PROCEDURE dbo.usp_CustomerTotals
    @CustomerID INT AS
    SELECT C.CustomerID,
        YEAR(OrderDate) AS OrderYear,
        MONTH(OrderDate) AS OrderMonth,
        SUM(TotalDue) AS TotalSales
    FROM Sales.Customer AS C
    INNER JOIN Sales.SalesOrderHeader
        AS SOH ON C.CustomerID = SOH.CustomerID
    WHERE C.CustomerID = @CustomerID
    GROUP BY C.CustomerID,
        YEAR(OrderDate), MONTH(OrderDate);
GO
EXEC dbo.usp_CustomerTotals 17910;
```

3. Create a stored procedure called dbo.usp_ProductSales that accepts a ProductID for
a parameter and has an OUTPUT parameter that returns the total number sold for the
product. Test the stored procedure.

```
IF OBJECT_ID('dbo.usp_ProductSales')
    IS NOT NULL BEGIN
    DROP PROCEDURE dbo.usp_ProductSales;
END;
GO
CREATE PROCEDURE dbo.usp_ProductSales
    @ProductID INT,
    @TotalSold INT = NULL OUTPUT AS

    SELECT @TotalSold = SUM(OrderQty)
    FROM Sales.SalesOrderDetail
    WHERE ProductID = @ProductID;
GO
DECLARE @TotalSold INT;
EXEC dbo.usp_ProductSales @ProductID = 776,
    @TotalSold =  @TotalSold OUTPUT;
PRINT @TotalSold;
```

■ ■ ■

Working with XML

Beginning with SQL Server 2005, Microsoft added the XML data type, the XQuery language, and several new functions for working with XML data in addition to the functionality found in SQL Server 2000. XML stands for Extensible Markup Language, and it looks a lot like HTML except that it generally contains data while HTML is used to create web pages. Companies often use XML to exchange data between incompatible systems or with their vendors and customers. SQL Server also extensively uses XML data to store query plans.

Fully covering XML support in SQL Server would take another complete book, so I'll just briefly discuss it here. In the past, to work with XML, databases stored the XML data in string columns. The database was just a storage place for the XML data. There was nothing to validate the XML data or to query just part of the XML data. To learn about SQL Server support for XML in depth, check out the book *Pro SQL Server 2008 XML* by Michael Coles (Apress, 2008).

The Parts of XML

An XML document is often said to be self-describing. That is, the tags tell you what is in the document. It is generally easy to read an XML document and have an idea about what it contains.

The document itself begins with an optional XML declaration followed by the markup and content. The *markup* consists of tags that start and end with pointed brackets (< >). Within the tags, you will find descriptions of the data. The *content* is the data itself.

Here is a sample XML document:

```
<?xml version="1.0" encoding="UTF-8"?>
<Products>
<Product ProductID="32565451" ProductName="Bicycle Pump">
    <Order ProductID="32565451" SalesID="5" OrderDate="2011-07-04T00:00:00">
        <OrderDetail OrderID="10248" CustomerID="22" Quantity="12"/>
        <OrderDetail OrderID="10248" CustomerID="11" Quantity="10"/>
    </Order>
</Product>
<Product ProductID="57841259" ProductName="Bicycle Seat">
    <Order ProductID="57841259" SalesID="3" OrderDate="2011-015-16T00:00:00">
        <OrderDetail OrderID="54127" CustomerID="72" Quantity="3"/>
    </Order>
</Product>
</Products>
```

The declaration states that this is version 1.0, the only option available at this time. Then the name of the code set, UTF-8, is specified. It is the most common set to use and can represent all the Unicode characters. This document is organized by Product. Within the Product, you will find one or more Orders, and each Order has one or more OrderDetails. Notice that each tag that is opened has a closing tag. If a tag has no child elements, the tag can be closed at the end of the same tag with a slash and closing pointed bracket (/>).

In the previous example, Products, Product, Order, and OrderDetail are *elements* and the values ProductID, ProductName, SalesID, OrderDate, OrderID, CustomerID, and Quantity are called *attributes*. The next is an element-centric example.

```xml
<?xml version="1.0" encoding="UTF-8"?>
<Products>
<Product>
    <ProductID>32565451</ProductID>
    <ProductName>Bicycle Pump</ProductName>
        <Order>
            <ProductID>32565451</ProductID>
            <SalesID>5</SalesID>
            <OrderDate>2011-07-04T00:00:00</OrderDate>
            <OrderDetail>
                <OrderID>10248</OrderID>
                <CustomerID>22</CustomerID>
                <Quantity>12</Quantity>
            </OrderDetail>
            <OrderDetail>
                <OrderID>10248</OrderID>
                <CustomerID>11</CustomerID
                <Quantity>10</Quantity>
            </OrderDetail>
        </Order>
</Product>
<Product>
    <ProductID>57841259</ProductID>
    <ProductName>Bicycle Seat</ProductName>
        <Order>
            <ProductID>57841259</ProductID>
            <SalesID>3</SalesID>
            <OrderDate>2011-015-16T00:00:00</OrderDate>
            <OrderDetail>
                <OrderID>54127</OrderID>
                <CustomerID>72</CustomerID>
                <Quantity>3</Quantity>
            </OrderDetail>
        </Order>
</Product>
</Products>
```

Converting XML Using *OPENXML*

There are primarily two ways of handling XML. Either you need to convert an XML document into a rowset (table) or you have a rowset and want to convert it into an XML document. Converting an XML document into a rowset is called *shredding*, and this is the purpose of the OPENXML command introduced with SQL Server 2000. OPENXML must also be used in conjunction with two other commands: sp_xml_preparedocument and sp_xml_removedocument.

The first command loads the XML document into memory; this process is expensive and takes up to one-eighth of SQL Server's total memory. The command sp_xml_removedocument removes the XML from SQL Server memory and should always be executed at the very end of the script. Listing 15-1 shows how this is done, and Figure 15-1 shows the results from the query.

Listing 15-1. OPENXML Query

```
--1
DECLARE @hdoc int;
DECLARE @doc varchar(1000) = N'
<Products>
<Product ProductID="32565451" ProductName="Bicycle Pump">
    <Order ProductID="32565451" SalesID="5" OrderDate="2011-07-04T00:00:00">
        <OrderDetail OrderID="10248" CustomerID="22" Quantity="12"/>
        <OrderDetail OrderID="10248" CustomerID="11" Quantity="10"/>
    </Order>
</Product>
<Product ProductID="57841259" ProductName="Bicycle Seat">
    <Order ProductID="57841259" SalesID="3" OrderDate="2011-015-16T00:00:00">
        <OrderDetail OrderID="54127" CustomerID="72" Quantity="3"/>
    </Order>
</Product>
</Products>';

--2
EXEC sp_xml_preparedocument @hdoc OUTPUT, @doc;

--3
SELECT *
FROM OPENXML(@hdoc, N'/Products/Product');

--4
EXEC sp_xml_removedocument @hdoc;
```

	id	parentid	nodetype	localname	prefix	namespaceuri	datatype	prev	text
1	2	0	1	Product	NULL	NULL	NULL	NULL	NULL
2	3	2	2	ProductID	NULL	NULL	NULL	NULL	NULL
3	28	3	3	#text	NULL	NULL	NULL	NULL	32565451
4	4	2	2	ProductName	NULL	NULL	NULL	NULL	NULL
5	29	4	3	#text	NULL	NULL	NULL	NULL	Bicycle Pump
6	5	2	1	Order	NULL	NULL	NULL	NULL	NULL
7	6	5	2	ProductID	NULL	NULL	NULL	NULL	NULL
8	30	6	3	#text	NULL	NULL	NULL	NULL	32565451
9	7	5	2	SalesID	NULL	NULL	NULL	NULL	NULL
10	31	7	3	#text	NULL	NULL	NULL	NULL	5
11	8	5	2	OrderDate	NULL	NULL	NULL	NULL	NULL
12	32	8	3	#text	NULL	NULL	NULL	NULL	2011-07-04T00:00:00

Figure 15-1. *Partial results of the OPENXML query*

Statement block 1 declares two variables to be used in the script. The first variable, @hdoc, is a number referring to the XML document in memory. The @doc variable is the document itself. In statement 2, the document is loaded into memory with the sp_xml_preparedocument command. In statement 3, the OPENXML command is called with the @hdoc parameter and the rowpattern. The rowpattern, /Products/Product, identifies the nodes in the XML document. Finally, statement 4 removes the XML from memory.

Notice that SQL Server predefines the columns in the results. These column names are based on the XML *edge table format*. This format is the default structure for XML represented in table format. Luckily, you can modify the column output in order to customize your rowset definitions. You accomplish this by specifying the optional WITH clause in your select statement. Listing 15-2 runs the same OPENXML query but includes the WITH clause, and Figure 15-2 shows the results of the OPENXML query.

Listing 15-2. OPENXML Query Using the WITH Clause

```
--1
DECLARE @hdoc int;
DECLARE @doc varchar(1000) = N'
<Products>
<Product ProductID="32565451" ProductName="Bicycle Pump">
   <Order ProductID="32565451" SalesID="5" OrderDate="2011-07-04T00:00:00">
      <OrderDetail OrderID="10248" CustomerID="22" Quantity="12"/>
      <OrderDetail OrderID="10248" CustomerID="11" Quantity="10"/>
   </Order>
</Product>
<Product ProductID="57841259" ProductName="Bicycle Seat">
   <Order ProductID="57841259" SalesID="3" OrderDate="2011-015-16T00:00:00">
      <OrderDetail OrderID="54127" CustomerID="72" Quantity="3"/>
   </Order>
</Product>
</Products>';

--2
EXEC sp_xml_preparedocument @hdoc OUTPUT, @doc;

--3
SELECT *
FROM OPENXML(@hdoc, N'/Products/Product/Order/OrderDetail')
WITH (CustomerID int '@CustomerID',
      ProductID int '../@ProductID',
      ProductName varchar(30) '../../@ProductName',
      OrderID int '@OrderID',
      Orderdate varchar(30) '../@OrderDate');

--4
EXEC sp_xml_removedocument @hdoc;
```

	CustomerID	ProductID	ProductName	OrderID	Orderdate
1	22	32565451	Bicycle Pump	10248	2011-07-04T00:00:00
2	11	32565451	Bicycle Pump	10248	2011-07-04T00:00:00
3	72	57841259	Bicycle Seat	54127	2011-08-16T00:00:00

Figure 15-2. *Using the WITH clause with OPENXML*

This example differs from Listing 15-1 because it uses the WITH clause of the OPENXML function. Within the WITH clause, a table specification is provided along with a mapping to the attributes. The attribute at the innermost level can be specified by using the name preceded by an at symbol (@). For each level up in the hierarchy, add two periods and a slash (../).

Retrieving Data as XML Using the *FOR XML* Clause

As mentioned, XML is normally handled in one of two ways. The first way is when you have an XML document and you need to shred it into a table format. For this method, use the OPENXML command. The other way to work with XML is to convert table data into an XML document using FOR XML.

The FOR XML clause, added with SQL Server 2000, is actually part of a SELECT statement. A SELECT statement returns data from a table in rowset format. Adding the FOR XML clause at the end converts the rowset data into XML format. The command has four modes and each mode provides a different level of control. The modes determine how much control you want when converting rowset data containing columns and rows into an XML document consisting of elements and attributes. The four modes are RAW, AUTO, EXPLICIT, and PATH. Each one provides certain advantages and disadvantages. Table 15-1 gives a brief summary of each.

Table 15-1. *FOR XML Modes*

MODE	Description
RAW	Easiest to use but provides the least flexibility. Each row creates a single element.
AUTO	Similar to RAW but provides more flexibility. Each column returned is an element and each referenced table with a column in the SELECT clause is an element.
EXPLICIT	Difficult to use but provides improved granularity for creating complex XML documents. Allows you to mix attributes and elements but requires specific syntax structure in the SELECT clause.
PATH	It is recommended to use the PATH mode instead of EXPLICIT. This mode provides similar functionality but with less complexity.

FOR XML RAW

The RAW mode is the simplest mode but provides the least flexibility when generating XML from rowsets. Listing 15-3 shows an example; this mode is an excellent means to quickly generate XML documents from tables. Figure 15-3 shows the initial output.

Listing 15-3. Generating XML Using the FOR XML RAW Command

```
SELECT TOP(5) FirstName
FROM Person.Person
FOR XML RAW;
```

	XML_F52E2B61-18A1-11d1-B105-00805F49916B
1	<row FirstName="Syed"/><row FirstName="Catherine"/><row FirstName="Kim"/><row FirstName="Kim"/><ro...

Figure 15-3. *Using the FOR XML RAW command*

When you click the XML hyperlink you can see the XML document:

```
<row FirstName="Syed" />
<row FirstName="Catherine" />
<row FirstName="Kim" />
<row FirstName="Kim" />
<row FirstName="Kim" />
```

As you can tell from the output, RAW mode produces a single node "row" for each row returned and each element has a column-based attribute. By default, RAW mode produces an attribute-centric XML document. Remember that attribute-centric XML consists of inline attributes. Also, each node is named row, which is not very helpful when describing the contents of the XML data. To create an element-centric XML document with a friendlier node name, you will need to include the ELEMENTS option along with a node definition. Listing 15-4 shows an example.

Listing 15-4. Creating Element-Centric XML Using XML RAW

```
SELECT TOP(5) FirstName, LastName
FROM Person.Person
FOR XML RAW ('NAME'), ELEMENTS;
```

The following is some of the output:

```
<NAME>
  <FirstName>Syed</FirstName>
  <LastName>Abbas</LastName>
</NAME>
<NAME>
  <FirstName>Catherine</FirstName>
  <LastName>Abel</LastName>
</NAME>
<NAME>
  <FirstName>Kim</FirstName>
  <LastName>Abercrombie</LastName>
</NAME>
<NAME>
  <FirstName>Kim</FirstName>
  <LastName>Abercrombie</LastName>
</NAME>
<NAME>
  <FirstName>Kim</FirstName>
  <LastName>Abercrombie</LastName>
</NAME>
```

In Listing 15-4, the FOR XML RAW clause takes NAME as an input. This defines the node name. The ELEMENTS option converts the columns from attributes to elements within the NAME node.

■ **Note**   It is possible to mix attribute-centric mapping with element-centric mapping using FOR XML. To do so requires using nested FOR XML queries. Nested FOR XML queries are beyond the scope of this book. Actually, using the PATH option, that you will learn about later in the "FOR XML PATH" section, with nested FOR XML is considered better practice than using the EXPLICIT option. You can get more information at http://msdn.microsoft.com/en-us/library/bb510436(v=SQL.120).aspx.

Keep in mind that even with the ability to use FOR XML RAW to create attribute-centric XML or element-centric XML, the mode still limits your ability to form complex XML documents. FOR XML RAW is well suited for testing or creating simple XML documents. For more complex XML documents, you will want to work with the other available modes.

FOR XML AUTO

Another option is AUTO mode. This mode is similar to RAW (and just as easy to use) but produces a more complex XML document based on your SELECT query. AUTO creates an element for each table in the FROM clause that has a column in the SELECT clause. Each column in the SELECT clause is represented as an attribute in the XML document. Look at Listing 15-5 to see an example of FOR XML in use.

Listing 15-5. Using AUTO Mode

```
SELECT TOP(5) CustomerID, LastName, FirstName, MiddleName
FROM Person.Person AS Person
INNER JOIN Sales.Customer AS Customer ON Person.BusinessEntityID = Customer.PersonID
ORDER BY CustomerID
FOR XML AUTO;
```

The following is an example of the output that you'll get from executing the query in Listing 15-5:

```
<Customer CustomerID="11000">
  <Person LastName="Yang" FirstName="Jon" MiddleName="V" />
</Customer>
<Customer CustomerID="11001">
  <Person LastName="Huang" FirstName="Eugene" MiddleName="L" />
</Customer>
<Customer CustomerID="11002">
  <Person LastName="Torres" FirstName="Ruben" />
</Customer>
<Customer CustomerID="11003">
  <Person LastName="Zhu" FirstName="Christy" />
</Customer>
<Customer CustomerID="11004">
  <Person LastName="Johnson" FirstName="Elizabeth" />
</Customer>
```

Listing 15-6 shows how AUTO mode converts the tables Customer and Person into elements. SQL Server was intelligent enough to link the corresponding columns as attributes in the respective elements. For example, CustomerID is a column in the Sales.Customer table, so AUTO mode created CustomerID as an attribute in the

Customer element. The AUTO mode would continue to expand the XML document for each table and column you add to the query.

Now add the ELEMENTS option in Listing 15-6 like you did with RAW mode to see how it affects the XML output.

Listing 15-6. Using AUTO Mode with the ELEMENTS Option

```
SELECT TOP(3) CustomerID, LastName, FirstName, MiddleName
FROM Person.Person AS Person
INNER JOIN Sales.Customer AS Customer ON Person.BusinessEntityID = Customer.PersonID
ORDER BY CustomerID
FOR XML AUTO, ELEMENTS;
```

The following is the output from Listing 15-6:

```
<Customer>
  <CustomerID>11000</CustomerID>
  <Person>
    <LastName>Yang</LastName>
    <FirstName>Jon</FirstName>
    <MiddleName>V</MiddleName>
  </Person>
</Customer>
<Customer>
  <CustomerID>11001</CustomerID>
  <Person>
    <LastName>Huang</LastName>
    <FirstName>Eugene</FirstName>
    <MiddleName>L</MiddleName>
  </Person>
</Customer>
<Customer>
  <CustomerID>11002</CustomerID>
  <Person>
    <LastName>Torres</LastName>
    <FirstName>Ruben</FirstName>
  </Person>
</Customer>
```

Just as in the example using RAW mode, the ELEMENTS option displays columns as elements for each node instead of the default attribute mapping. One difference is the exclusion of the ElementName option that you saw in the previous RAW mode (RAW(NAME)). You can leave this out because AUTO mode automatically names the nodes after the name of each table; in fact, you will receive a syntax error if you try to use the option.

FOR XML EXPLICIT

The most complicated means to convert table data into XML is by using the FOR XML EXPLICIT mode, but with complexity comes flexibility and control. The complexity lies in the rigorous requirement that you structure your SELECT clause so the output forms a *universal table*.

As you can see from previous examples, XML is based on hierarchies. Listing 15-7 shows a Customer element or node and under Customer is a subelement called Person. Person is a child element of Customer. In order to create a similar XML document using the EXPLICIT mode, you need to define this relationship in the universal table.

This is done by creating two columns called Tag and Parent. Think of this as the relationship between manager and employee. A manager would have a tag ID of 1 and the employee would have a tag ID of 2. Because you are only concerned about the manager level in the hierarchy, the manager would have a parent of 0 (NULL) but the employee would have a parent of 1. Listing 15-7 shows a simple example.

Listing 15-7. Using XML FOR EXPLICIT

```
SELECT 1 AS Tag,
       NULL      AS Parent,
       CustomerID AS [Customer!1!CustomerID],
       NULL       AS [Name!2!FName],
       NULL       AS [Name!2!LName]
FROM Sales.Customer AS C
INNER JOIN Person.Person AS P
ON  P.BusinessEntityID = C.PersonID
UNION ALL
SELECT 2 AS Tag,
       1 AS Parent,
       CustomerID,
       FirstName,
       LastName
FROM Person.Person P
INNER JOIN Sales.Customer AS C
ON P.BusinessEntityID = C.PersonID
ORDER BY [Customer!1!CustomerID], [Name!2!FName]
FOR XML EXPLICIT;
```

The partial results are as follows:

```
<Customer CustomerID="11000">
  <Name FName="Jon" LName="Yang" />
</Customer>
<Customer CustomerID="11001">
  <Name FName="Eugene" LName="Huang" />
</Customer>
<Customer CustomerID="11002">
  <Name FName="Ruben" LName="Torres" />
</Customer>
<Customer CustomerID="11003">
  <Name FName="Christy" LName="Zhu" />
</Customer>
<Customer CustomerID="11004">
  <Name FName="Elizabeth" LName="Johnson" />
</Customer>
<Customer CustomerID="11005">
  <Name FName="Julio" LName="Ruiz" />
</Customer>
```

By using the UNION ALL operator, you can define different Tag and Parent values in each SELECT clause. This allows you to nest the XML and create hierarchies. In this case, you assigned to Customer a tag of 1 and Parent as NULL. In the next SELECT statement, you assigned Name a tag of 2 and Parent a tag of 1. Table 15-2 shows what the universal table looks like for CustomerID 11008 in Listing 15-7.

Table 15-2. *Example Universal Table for the EXPLICIT Mode*

Tag	Parent	Customer!1!CustomerID	Name!2!FName	Name!2!LName
1	NULL	11008	NULL	NULL
2	1	NULL	"Rob"	"Verhoff"

In addition to the Tag and Parent values, the ElementName!TagNumber!Attribute defines where in the hierarchy each column exists. The value Customer!1!CustomerID tells you the value belongs with the Customer element, the !1! tells you it is tag 1 and CustomerID is the attribute.

■ **Note** There is an optional value called Directive when creating the universal table. The format is ElementName!TagNumber!Attribute!Directive. This allows you to control how to encode values (ID, IDREF, IDREFS) and how to map string data to XML (hide, element, elementxsinil, xml, xmltext, and cdata). The details of each can be found at http://msdn.microsoft.com/en-us/library/ms189068(v=SQL.120).aspx or in Pro SQL Server 2008 XML (Apress 2008) by Michael Coles.

As you can readily see, using the EXPLICIT mode can quickly become cumbersome. So for complex XML documents that mix and match attributes and elements, you will want to use the FOR XML PATH mode with nested XML.

FOR XML PATH

As mentioned previously, if you need to develop complex XML documents from table data, the best tool to use is the FOR XML PATH mode. This is primarily because PATH mode takes advantage of the XPath standard. XPath is a W3C standard for navigating XML hierarchies. XPath includes other useful tools such as XQuery and XPointer.

■ **Note** W3C, or World Wide Web Consortium (www.w3.org), is a group of professionals (both volunteer and paid) who help to define Internet standards. Without a central organization developing standards, it would be difficult for the Internet to exist and thrive. XPath is a standard developed for navigating XML documents. This is just one of the items that makes XML such a powerful tool for sharing data between systems around the world running on differing platforms.

Listing 15-8 demonstrates a simple example of the PATH mode. This example runs a SELECT statement against the Production.Product table.

Listing 15-8. Simple FOR XML PATH Query

```
SELECT TOP(3) p.FirstName,
       p.LastName,
       s.Bonus,
       s.SalesYTD
FROM Person.Person p
JOIN Sales.SalesPerson s
ON p.BusinessEntityID = s.BusinessEntityID
ORDER BY s.SalesYTD DESC
FOR XML PATH;
```

The output from the query in Listing 15-8 will appear as follows:

```
<row>
  <FirstName>Linda</FirstName>
  <LastName>Mitchell</LastName>
  <Bonus>2000.0000</Bonus>
  <SalesYTD>4251368.5497</SalesYTD>
</row>
<row>
  <FirstName>Jae</FirstName>
  <LastName>Pak</LastName>
  <Bonus>5150.0000</Bonus>
  <SalesYTD>4116871.2277</SalesYTD>
</row>
<row>
  <FirstName>Michael</FirstName>
  <LastName>Blythe</LastName>
  <Bonus>4100.0000</Bonus>
  <SalesYTD>3763178.1787</SalesYTD>
</row>
```

Without any modification, the XML PATH mode will create a simple element-centric XML document. Listing 15-8 produces an element for each row. As always, you may want to enhance the format of the output. Listing 15-9 demonstrates how you can easily mix and match element- and attribute-centric XML document styles.

Listing 15-9. Defining XML Hierarchy Using PATH Mode

```
SELECT TOP(3) p.FirstName "@FirstName",
       p.LastName "@LastName",
           s.Bonus "Sales/Bonus",
           s.SalesYTD "Sales/YTD"
FROM Person.Person p
JOIN Sales.SalesPerson s
ON p.BusinessEntityID = s.BusinessEntityID
ORDER BY s.SalesYTD DESC
FOR XML PATH;
```

The following is the output:

```
<row FirstName="Linda" LastName="Mitchell">
  <Sales>
    <Bonus>2000.0000</Bonus>
    <YTD>4251368.5497</YTD>
  </Sales>
</row>
<row FirstName="Jae" LastName="Pak">
  <Sales>
    <Bonus>5150.0000</Bonus>
    <YTD>4116871.2277</YTD>
  </Sales>
</row>
<row FirstName="Michael" LastName="Blythe">
  <Sales>
    <Bonus>4100.0000</Bonus>
    <YTD>3763178.1787</YTD>
  </Sales>
</row>
```

If you think the SELECT statement in Listing 15-9 looks familiar, you're right. A similar query was used in Listing 15-2 when navigating an XML document in the OPENXML command using the WITH statement. Keep in mind when mapping columns to an XML document that any column defined with an at (@) sign becomes an attribute of the node, and any column defined with a slash (/) becomes a separate element. Similar to the OPENXML example, if you add a name value to the PATH mode (FOR XML PATH ('Product')), you can rename the root node from "row" to "Product." Listing 15-10 shows what this looks like.

Listing 15-10. Simple FOR XML PATH Query with NAME Option

```
SELECT TOP(5) ProductID "@ProductID",
       Name "Product/ProductName",
       Color "Product/Color"
FROM Production.Product
ORDER BY ProductID
FOR XML PATH ('Product');
```

The query output is as follows:

```
<Product ProductID="1">
  <Product>
    <ProductName>Adjustable Race</ProductName>
  </Product>
</Product>
<Product ProductID="2">
  <Product>
    <ProductName>Bearing Ball</ProductName>
  </Product>
</Product>
<Product ProductID="3">
  <Product>
```

```
      <ProductName>BB Ball Bearing</ProductName>
  </Product>
</Product>
<Product ProductID="4">
  <Product>
      <ProductName>Headset Ball Bearings</ProductName>
  </Product>
</Product>
<Product ProductID="316">
  <Product>
      <ProductName>Blade</ProductName>
  </Product>
</Product>
```

When choosing from the FOR XML methods, the PATH mode is the preferred means to generate complex XML documents. It allows for granular control of structuring the document but is not overly complicated as is the EXPLICIT mode. Beyond the previous legacy modes, Microsoft has developed even more robust methods of generating and handling XML in SQL Server.

The XML Data Type

Beginning with SQL 2005, you can define a column as XML when creating a table object. Doing so specifically tells SQL Server to treat the data in the column as XML. You can also use the XML built-in data type when defining variables. Data types are discussed in more detail in Chapter 16. Listing 15-11 creates a sample table with a column defined as a built-in XML data type.

Listing 15-11. Built-in XML Data Type

```
USE tempdb;
GO

CREATE TABLE dbo.ProductList (ProductInfo XML);
```

You'll find XML data types scattered throughout the AdventureWorks database. For example, the Person.Person table has two columns defined as XML: AdditionalContactInfo and Demographics. The AdditionalContactInfo column is NULL but is useful for working with XML inserts and updates, while the Demographics column shows how the data is, in fact, stored as XML. In the past, this data would be stored one of the string data types. Keep in mind the following rules around a column with the XML data type:

- It can't be used as a primary or foreign key.

- You can't convert or cast the column to a text or ntext. It is recommended to use varchar(max) or nvarchar(max). Text and ntext will be deprecated in future versions of SQL Server.

- Column can't be used in a GROUP BY statement.

- The data can't be greater than 2GB.

Let's create another table with an XML column and populate it with some data. Type in and execute the code in Listing 15-12.

Listing 15-12. Using XML as a Data Type

```
--1
CREATE TABLE #CustomerList (CustomerInfo XML);

--2
DECLARE @XMLInfo XML;

--3
SET @XMLInfo = (SELECT CustomerID, LastName, FirstName, MiddleName
FROM Person.Person AS p
INNER JOIN Sales.Customer AS c ON p.BusinessEntityID = c.PersonID
FOR XML PATH);

--4
INSERT INTO #CustomerList(CustomerInfo)
VALUES(@XMLInfo);

--5
SELECT CustomerInfo FROM #CustomerList;
DROP TABLE #CustomerList;
```

Figure 15-4 shows the results of running this code. Statement 1 creates a table with an XML column. Statement 2 declares a variable with the XML data type. Statement 3 saves the information in XML format about each customer from the Sales.Customer and Person.Person tables into a variable. The data comes from the same query that you saw in the previous section. Statement 4 inserts a row into the #CustomerList table using the variable. Query 5 returns the CustomerInfo column from the table without using the FOR XML clause. Because the table stores the data in XML format, the statement looks just like a regular SELECT statement yet returns the data as XML.

	CustomerInfo
1	<row><CustomerID>29485</CustomerID><LastName>Abel</LastName><FirstName>Catherine</FirstName><MiddleName>R.</Middl...

Figure 15-4. *The results of using the XML data type*

XML Methods

XML methods provide ways to handle XML in the XML data type. They allow you to update the XML, convert the XML to rowsets, check whether the XML has nodes, and many other useful options. They provide many of the same functionalities you saw with the legacy XML commands. Table 15-3 summarizes these methods and I'll discuss each of them.

Table 15-3. *XML Data Type Methods*

Method	Description
query(xquery)	Executes an XQuery against the XML data type. Returns an XML type.
value(xquery, sqltype)	Executes an XQuery against the XML data type and returns an SQL scalar value.
exist(xquery)	Executes an XQuery against the XML data type and returns a bit value representing a criteria of 1 if there is at least one node, 0 if there are no nodes, and NULL if the XML data type in the XQuery is NULL.
modify(xml_dml)	Used to update XML stored as the XML data type.
nodes()	Used to convert (shred) an XML data type into a rowset (table). If you want to convert XML into a relational form, use this method.

The *QUERY* Method

Use the QUERY method when you need to extract elements from an XML column or variable. You have the capability to extract specific elements and create new XML documents. Listing 15-13 creates and populates a temp table with an XML column. You will use this table for the rest of the examples in this section.

Listing 15-13 Create a Temp Table with an XML Column

```
--1
CREATE TABLE #Bikes(ProductID INT, ProductDescription XML);

--2
INSERT INTO #Bikes(ProductID, ProductDescription)
SELECT ProductID,
        (SELECT ProductID, Product.Name, Color, Size, ListPrice, SC.Name AS BikeSubCategory
        FROM Production.Product AS Product
        JOIN Production.ProductSubcategory SC
                ON Product.ProductSubcategoryID = SC.ProductSubcategoryID
        JOIN Production.ProductCategory C
                ON SC.ProductCategoryID = C.ProductCategoryID
        WHERE Product.ProductID = Prod.ProductID
        FOR XML RAW('Product'), ELEMENTS) AS ProdXML
FROM   Production.Product AS Prod
        JOIN Production.ProductSubcategory SC
                ON Prod.ProductSubcategoryID = SC.ProductSubcategoryID
        JOIN Production.ProductCategory C
                ON SC.ProductCategoryID = C.ProductCategoryID
WHERE C.Name = 'Bikes';

--3
SELECT *
FROM #Bikes;
```

Figure 15-5 shows the partial results of running this code. Statement 1 creates the temp table, #Bikes, with just a ProductID and the ProductDescription columns. The ProductDescription column is the XML data type. Statement 2 inserts data from AdventureWorks into the temp table. A correlated subquery is used to populate the ProductDescription column using a technique you learned earlier in this chapter, FOR XML.

	ProductID	Product Description
1	749	\<Product>\<ProductID>749\</ProductID>\<Name>Road-150 Red, 62\</Name>\<Color>Red\</Color>\<Size>62\</Size>\<ListPrice>3578.2700\</ListPrice...
2	750	\<Product>\<ProductID>750\</ProductID>\<Name>Road-150 Red, 44\</Name>\<Color>Red\</Color>\<Size>44\</Size>\<ListPrice>3578.2700\</ListPrice...
3	751	\<Product>\<ProductID>751\</ProductID>\<Name>Road-150 Red, 48\</Name>\<Color>Red\</Color>\<Size>48\</Size>\<ListPrice>3578.2700\</ListPrice...
4	752	\<Product>\<ProductID>752\</ProductID>\<Name>Road-150 Red, 52\</Name>\<Color>Red\</Color>\<Size>52\</Size>\<ListPrice>3578.2700\</ListPrice...
5	753	\<Product>\<ProductID>753\</ProductID>\<Name>Road-150 Red, 56\</Name>\<Color>Red\</Color>\<Size>56\</Size>\<ListPrice>3578.2700\</ListPrice...
6	754	\<Product>\<ProductID>754\</ProductID>\<Name>Road-450 Red, 58\</Name>\<Color>Red\</Color>\<Size>58\</Size>\<ListPrice>1457.9900\</ListPrice...
7	755	\<Product>\<ProductID>755\</ProductID>\<Name>Road-450 Red, 60\</Name>\<Color>Red\</Color>\<Size>60\</Size>\<ListPrice>1457.9900\</ListPrice...
8	756	\<Product>\<ProductID>756\</ProductID>\<Name>Road-450 Red, 44\</Name>\<Color>Red\</Color>\<Size>44\</Size>\<ListPrice>1457.9900\</ListPrice...
9	757	\<Product>\<ProductID>757\</ProductID>\<Name>Road-450 Red, 48\</Name>\<Color>Red\</Color>\<Size>48\</Size>\<ListPrice>1457.9900\</ListPrice...
10	758	\<Product>\<ProductID>758\</ProductID>\<Name>Road-450 Red, 52\</Name>\<Color>Red\</Color>\<Size>52\</Size>\<ListPrice>1457.9900\</ListPrice...
11	759	\<Product>\<ProductID>759\</ProductID>\<Name>Road-650 Red, 58\</Name>\<Color>Red\</Color>\<Size>58\</Size>\<ListPrice>782.9900\</ListPrice...
12	760	\<Product>\<ProductID>760\</ProductID>\<Name>Road-650 Red, 60\</Name>\<Color>Red\</Color>\<Size>60\</Size>\<ListPrice>782.9900\</ListPrice>...
13	761	\<Product>\<ProductID>761\</ProductID>\<Name>Road-650 Red, 62\</Name>\<Color>Red\</Color>\<Size>62\</Size>\<ListPrice>782.9900\</ListPrice>...
14	762	\<Product>\<ProductID>762\</ProductID>\<Name>Road-650 Red, 44\</Name>\<Color>Red\</Color>\<Size>44\</Size>\<ListPrice>782.9900\</ListPrice>...
15	763	\<Product>\<ProductID>763\</ProductID>\<Name>Road-650 Red, 48\</Name>\<Color>Red\</Color>\<Size>48\</Size>\<ListPrice>782.9900\</ListPrice>...
16	764	\<Product>\<ProductID>764\</ProductID>\<Name>Road-650 Red, 52\</Name>\<Color>Red\</Color>\<Size>52\</Size>\<ListPrice>782.9900\</ListPrice>...

Figure 15-5. The partial #Bikes temp table data

Up to this point in the book, the columns and variables of the data types you have used have had values. You can retrieve or modify the values, but nothing else. The XML data type also has methods. Type in Listing 15-14 to learn how to use the QUERY method to retrieve an element. Note that the method name is case sensitive and must be lower case.

Listing 15-14. Using the QUERY method

```
SELECT ProductID,
    ProductDescription.query('Product/ListPrice') AS ListPrice
FROM #Bikes;
```

Figure 15-6 shows the results of running this code. The QUERY method takes the path to the element as an argument. Notice that it returns XML.

	ProductID	ListPrice
1	749	\<ListPrice>3578.2700\</ListPrice>
2	750	\<ListPrice>3578.2700\</ListPrice>
3	751	\<ListPrice>3578.2700\</ListPrice>
4	752	\<ListPrice>3578.2700\</ListPrice>
5	753	\<ListPrice>3578.2700\</ListPrice>
6	754	\<ListPrice>1457.9900\</ListPrice>
7	755	\<ListPrice>1457.9900\</ListPrice>
8	756	\<ListPrice>1457.9900\</ListPrice>
9	757	\<ListPrice>1457.9900\</ListPrice>
10	758	\<ListPrice>1457.9900\</ListPrice>
11	759	\<ListPrice>782.9900\</ListPrice>
12	760	\<ListPrice>782.9900\</ListPrice>

Figure 15-6. The partial results of using the QUERY method

The *VALUE* Method

Although the QUERY method allowed you to extract a particular element in XML format, the VALUE method extracts a scalar value instead. Type in and execute Listing 15-15 to see how to use the VALUE method. This example also uses the temp table created in Listing 15-13.

Listing 15-15. Using the VALUE Method

```
SELECT ProductID,
    ProductDescription.value('(/Product/ListPrice)[1]', 'MONEY') AS ListPrice
FROM #Bikes;
```

Figure 15-7 shows the partial results of running this code. This example is a bit more complex than the QUERY method example. A second argument specifying the SQL data type is required. Because this is a scalar function, only one value can be returned. To ensure that only the first value is returned, the index [1] is appended to the element path. This is similar to an array syntax. In this case, there is only one possible value, but you are still required to specify it. Because there is only one ListPrice in each document, if you change the index to a different number, nothing will be returned.

	ProductID	List Price
1	749	3578.27
2	750	3578.27
3	751	3578.27
4	752	3578.27
5	753	3578.27
6	754	1457.99
7	755	1457.99
8	756	1457.99
9	757	1457.99
10	758	1457.99

Figure 15-7. *The partial results of using the VALUE method*

If the XML document you are working with contains attributes, you can specify the attribute with the at (@) symbol. Listing 15-16 shows an example.

Listing 15-16. Using the VALUE Method with an Attribute

```
DECLARE @test XML = '
<root>
<Product ProductID="123" Name="Road Bike"/>
<Product ProductID="124" Name="Mountain Bike"/>
</root>';

SELECT @test.value('(/root/Product/@Name)[2]','NVARCHAR(25)');
```

This script returns the value "Mountain Bike" because it has requested the Name attribute of the second Product.

The *EXIST* Method

The EXIST method allows you to search for specific values in the XML. It returns a 1 if the value is found or a 0 if it is not. Similar to the VALUE method, you must specify the particular instance of the element you are looking for. Listing 15-17 demonstrates how to use the *EXIST* method in the WHERE clause.

Listing 15-17. Using the EXIST method

```
SELECT ProductID,
    ProductDescription.value('(/Product/ListPrice)[1]', 'MONEY') AS ListPrice
FROM #Bikes
WHERE ProductDescription.exist('/Product/ListPrice[text()[1] lt 3000]') = 1;
```

Figure 15-8 shows the partial results of running this code. This example locates the rows with XML documents where the ListPrice is less than 3,000. The text value of the first ListPrice element is compared to 3,000. You can also use eq for equal to and gt for greater than.

	ProductID	List Price
1	754	1457.99
2	755	1457.99
3	756	1457.99
4	757	1457.99
5	758	1457.99
6	759	782.99
7	760	782.99
8	761	782.99
9	762	782.99
10	763	782.99

Figure 15-8. *The partial results of using EXIST*

When working with dates in XML along with EXIST, you must cast the XML value to a date. Type in and execute Listing 15-18, which has two examples:

Listing 15-18. Using EXIST with Dates

```
--1
DECLARE @test1 XML = '
<root>
    <Product ProductID="123" LastOrderDate="2014-06-02"/>
</root>';

--2
DECLARE @test2 XML = '
<root>
    <Product>
            <ProductID>123</ProductID>
```

```
                    <LastOrderDate>2014-06-02</LastOrderDate>
          </Product>
</root>';

--3
SELECT @test1.exist('/root/Product[(@LastOrderDate cast as xs:date?)
    eq xs:date("2014-06-02")]'),
@test2.exist('/root/Product/LastOrderDate[(text()[1] cast as xs:date?)
    eq xs:date("2014-06-02")]');
```

Both expressions from statement 3 return 1. This example shows how to work with both attributes and elements.

The *MODIFY* Method

You will use the MODIFY method if you want to modify data stored as an XML data type. The MODIFY method is similar to using update, insert, and delete commands. One primary difference is that the *MODIFY* method can only be used in a SET clause of an UPDATE statement or the SET statement. Listing 15-19 shows the different ways to use the MODIFY method to change data in an XML document assigned to a variable.

Listing 15-19. Using the MODIFY method

```
--1
DECLARE @x xml =
'<Product ProductID = "521487">
  <ProductType>Paper Towels</ProductType>
  <Price>15</Price>
  <Vendor>Johnson Paper</Vendor>
  <VendorID>47</VendorID>
  <QuantityOnHand>500</QuantityOnHand>
</Product>';

--2
SELECT @x;

--3
/* inserting data into xml with the modify method */
SET @x.modify('
insert <WarehouseID>77</WarehouseID>
into (/Product)[1]');

--4
SELECT @x;

--5
/* updating xml with the modify method */
SET @x.modify('
replace value of (/Product/QuantityOnHand[1]/text())[1]
with "250"');
```

```
--6
SELECT @x;

--7
/* deleting xml with the modify method */
SET @x.modify('
delete (/Product/Price)[1]');

--8
SELECT @x;
```

The original XML looked like the following:

```
<Product ProductID="521487">
  <ProductType>Paper Towels</ProductType>
  <Price>15</Price>
  <Vendor>Johnson Paper</Vendor>
  <VendorID>47</VendorID>
  <QuantityOnHand>500</QuantityOnHand>
</Product>
```

Statement 3 inserted the Warehouse element into the XML. Statement 5 changed the QuantityOnHand to 250. Finally, statement 7 removed the Price element. After all of the modifications have been completed, the XML looks like this:

```
<Product ProductID="521487">
  <ProductType>Paper Towels</ProductType>
  <Vendor>Johnson Paper</Vendor>
  <VendorID>47</VendorID>
  <QuantityOnHand>250</QuantityOnHand>
  <WarehouseID>77</WarehouseID>
</Product>
```

The *NODES* Method

You can use the NODES method along with the VALUE method to shred XML into relational data. In this case, you can expand the individual elements. Listing 15-20 is an example.

Listing 15-20. Using the NODES method

```
--1
DECLARE @XML XML = '
<Product>
        <ProductID>749</ProductID>
        <ProductID>749</ProductID>
        <ProductID>750</ProductID>
        <ProductID>751</ProductID>
        <ProductID>752</ProductID>
        <ProductID>753</ProductID>
        <ProductID>754</ProductID>
```

```
          <ProductID>755</ProductID>
          <ProductID>756</ProductID>
          <ProductID>757</ProductID>
          <ProductID>758</ProductID>
</Product>';

--2
SELECT P.ProdID.value('.', 'INT') as ProductID
FROM @XML.nodes('/Product/ProductID') P(ProdID);
```

Figure 15-9 shows the results of running this code. The XML in this example contains several ProductID numbers. By using the NODE method and specifying the path, the list of ProductID values can be returned using the VALUE method. The table of values returned is aliased as "P" with the column ProdID. The table name plus the column named joined with a period along with the VALUE function is used in the SELECT list to return the results.

	ProductID
1	749
2	749
3	750
4	751
5	752
6	753
7	754
8	755
9	756
10	757
11	758

Figure 15-9. *The results of using the NODE method*

Namespaces

Namespaces can be confusing when first learning XML, but the concept is simple. XML uses namespaces to uniquely define element and attribute names in an XML document. The classic example is the element <table>. If the XML document is used by a furniture company, <table> would mean a piece of furniture. If the XML document is used by a company writing data modeling software, <table> would mean a database table. In this case, the furniture company and the data modeling company will use different namespaces. In order to facilitate data transfers and communication, all furniture companies may use the same namespace so that <table> always refers to the same thing.

XML data can be typed or untyped. So far in this chapter, you have worked with untyped XML data. XML data that is typed is associated with a schema, an explicit definition for that document. All of the XML columns in the AdventureWorks database are typed.

If you take a look at any of the XML data in AdventureWorks, you will see that each document begins with the namespace. Run this query and then click the XML to see an example:

```
SELECT Demographics FROM Sales.Store;
```

The XML for one of the rows looks like this:

```
<StoreSurvey xmlns="http://schemas.microsoft.com/sqlserver/2004/07/adventure-works/StoreSurvey">
  <AnnualSales>800000</AnnualSales>
  <AnnualRevenue>80000</AnnualRevenue>
  <BankName>United Security</BankName>
  <BusinessType>BM</BusinessType>
  <YearOpened>1996</YearOpened>
  <Specialty>Mountain</Specialty>
  <SquareFeet>21000</SquareFeet>
  <Brands>2</Brands>
  <Internet>ISDN</Internet>
  <NumberEmployees>13</NumberEmployees>
</StoreSurvey>
```

When writing a query using any of the XML methods against the Demographics column, you will refer to the namespace found at http://schemas.microsoft.com/sqlserver/2004/07/adventure-works/StoreSurvey. This namespace was defined for you in the stored XML. The namespace must be included in your query because the XML data includes it.

Within the query, you declare the required namespace. You can then refer to the XML elements using the namespace prefix. In the following example, you use the prefix /ss to refer to each element. For example, /ss:StoreSurvey/ ss:AnnualSales grabs the AnnualSales element from the XML. The braces symbol {} tell the QUERY method to insert a value into the output. Listing 15-21 demonstrates how to use the namespace along with the QUERY method.

Listing 15-21. Using a Namespace

```
SELECT Demographics.query('declare namespace ss = "http://schemas.microsoft.com/sqlserver/2004/07/
adventure-works/StoreSurvey";
<Store AnnualSales = "{ /ss:StoreSurvey/ss:AnnualSales }"
      BankName = "{ /ss:StoreSurvey/ss:BankName }" />
') AS Result
FROM Sales.Store;
```

Splitting a String

Splitting a delimited string into its individual elements is an interesting use of the XML methods. For example, imagine that you have a comma-delimited list of values that have been supplied as an argument to a stored procedure. In order to work with the values, the string must be separated into the individual values. Type in and execute Listing 15-22 to learn this method.

Listing 15-22. Splitting a String Using XML

```
--1
DECLARE @values NVARCHAR(30) = N'Bike,Seat,Pedals,Basket';

--2
DECLARE @XML XML
```

```
--3
SELECT @XML = '<item>' + REPLACE(@values,',','</item><item>') + '</item>';

--4
SELECT @XML;

--5
SELECT I.Product.value('.','NVARCHAR(10)') AS Item
FROM @XML.nodes('/item') AS I(Product);
```

Figure 15-10 shows the results of running this code. Statement 1 saves the list of items into a variable. Statement 2 declares a variable to hold the list once it is converted into XML. Statement 3 uses the REPLACE function to replace the commas with closing and opening item tags; an opening tag is required at the beginning of the string and a closing tag is required at the end. Statement 4 displays the XML. This is just to verify that statement 3 is correct. Finally, the NODES method is used to shred the XML into a list.

	(No column name)
1	<item>Bike</item><item>Seat</item><item>Pedals</item><item>Basket</item>

	Item
1	Bike
2	Seat
3	Pedals
4	Basket

Figure 15-10. *Splitting a string into individual elements*

Summary

This chapter only scratches the surface of SQL Server's capabilities in handling XML data. The XML data and its associated methods allow much greater flexibility and control than the legacy OPENXML command. I strongly suggest using the new methods of VALUE, MODIFY, EXIST and NODES over the legacy commands, especially when implementing the XML data type.

In the next chapter you will learn more about the data types available with SQL Server.

■ ■ ■

Expanding on Data Type Concepts

You have learned how to retrieve data from SQL Server tables in a number of ways: through simple queries, through joins, with functions, and more. You have learned to manipulate data, write scripts, and create database objects. Essentially, you have learned the T-SQL basics. Not only have you learned the mechanics of T-SQL, but you have also learned to think about the *best* way to solve a problem, not just the easy way.

This chapter introduces some of the more interesting and complex data types available in SQL Server. You will learn about sparse columns, built-in complex types (HIERARCHYID, GEOMETRY, and GEOGRAPHY), enhanced date and time data types, large-value data types (MAX), and FILESTREAM data. Some of these, such as the complex data types, are nothing like the traditional data types you have been using throughout this book. They are based on the CLR (Common Language Runtime). New data types similar to these built-in complex types can be created with a .NET language. You will not learn to create new data types from this book, but you will learn how to use the built-in CLR types.

Chapters 1 through 14 covered the important skills you need to become a proficient T-SQL developer. Chapter 15 covered working with XML in SQL Server. Because this chapter covers "bonus material," it doesn't contain exercises. I encourage you to practice working with any of the new data types that interest you or that you think will be beneficial in your job.

Large-Value String Data Types (MAX)

Older versions of SQL Server used NTEXT and TEXT data types to represent large values. Microsoft has deprecated those types, which means that in some future release of SQL Server, NTEXT and TEXT will no longer work. For now, however, the deprecated data types still work in SQL Server 2014. Going forward, you should replace these data types with VARCHAR(MAX) and NVARCHAR(MAX).

The TEXT and NTEXT data types have many limitations. For example, you can't declare a variable of type TEXT or NTEXT, use them with most functions, or use them within most search criteria. The MAX data types represent the benefits of both the regular string data types and the TEXT and NTEXT data types when storing large strings. They allow you to store large amounts of data and offer the same functionality of the traditional data types.

When creating string data types, you supply a number of characters. Instead of supplying a number, use the word MAX when the data is going to surpass the maximum normally allowed. Table 16-1 lists the differences between the string value data types.

Table 16-1. *The String Data Types*

Name	Type	Maximum Characters	Character Set
CHAR	Fixed width	8,000	ASCII
NCHAR	Fixed width	4,000	Unicode
VARCHAR	Variable width	8,000	ASCII
NVARCHAR	Variable width	4,000	Unicode
TEXT	Variable width	$2^{31} - 1$	ASCII
NTEXT	Variable width	$2^{30} - 1$	Unicode
VARCHAR(MAX)	Variable width	$2^{31} - 1$	ASCII
NVARCHAR(MAX)	Variable width	$2^{30} - 1$	Unicode

■ **Note** One difference between CHAR/VARCHAR and NCHAR/NVARCHAR when specifying a literal string is that the NCHAR/NVARCHAR types should be preceded by the letter *N*. This tells the query processor to interpret the string as Unicode. If you don't precede the literal string with the letter *N*, the code will usually still work.

You work with the MAX string data types just like you do with the traditional types for the most part. Type in and execute Listing 16-1 to learn how to work with the MAX types.

Listing 16-1. Using VARCHAR(MAX)

```
--1
CREATE TABLE #maxExample (maxCol VARCHAR(MAX),
    line INT NOT NULL IDENTITY PRIMARY KEY);
GO

--2
INSERT INTO #maxExample(maxCol)
VALUES ('This is a varchar(max)');

--3
INSERT INTO #maxExample(maxCol)
VALUES (REPLICATE('aaaaaaaaaa',9000));

--4
INSERT INTO #maxExample(maxCol)
VALUES (REPLICATE(CONVERT(VARCHAR(MAX),'bbbbbbbbbb'),9000));

--5
SELECT LEFT(MaxCol,10) AS Left10,LEN(MaxCol) AS varLen
FROM #maxExample;

GO
DROP TABLE #maxExample;
```

Figure 16-1 shows the results of running this code. Statement 1 creates a temp table, #maxExample, with a VARCHAR(MAX) column. Statement 2 inserts a row into the table with a short string. Statement 3 inserts a row using the REPLICATE function to create a very large string. If you look at the results, the row inserted by statement 3 contains only 8,000 characters. Statement 4 also inserts a row using the REPLICATE function. This time the statement explicitly converts the string to be replicated to a VARCHAR(MAX). That is because, without explicitly converting it, the string is just a VARCHAR. The REPLICATE function, like most string functions, returns the same data types as supplied to it. To return a VARCHAR(MAX), the function must receive a VARCHAR(MAX). Statement 5 uses the LEFT function to return the first ten characters of the value stored in the maxCol column, demonstrating that you can use string functions with VARCHAR(MAX). Attempting to use LEFT on a TEXT column will just produce an error. It uses the LEN function to see how many characters the column stores in each row. Only 8,000 characters of the row inserted in statement 3 made it to the table because the value wasn't explicitly converted to VARCHAR(MAX) before the REPLICATE function was applied.

	Left10	varLen
1	This is a	22
2	aaaaaaaaaa	8000
3	bbbbbbbbbb	90000

Figure 16-1. *The results of using the VARCHAR(MAX) data type*

If you get a chance to design a database, you may be tempted to make all your string value columns into MAX columns. Microsoft recommends that you use the MAX data types only when it is likely that you will exceed the 8,000- or 4,000-character limits. To be most efficient, size your columns to the expected data.

Large-Value Binary Data Types

You probably have less experience with the data types that store binary data. You can use BINARY, VARBINARY, and IMAGE to store binary data including files such as images, movies, and Word documents. The BINARY and VARBINARY data types can hold up to 8,000 bytes. The IMAGE data type, which is deprecated like the TEXT and NTEXT types, holds data that exceeds 8,000 bytes, up to 2GB. In SQL Server versions 2005 and greater, always use the VARBINARY(MAX) data type, which can store up to 2GB of binary data, instead of IMAGE.

Creating *VARBINARY(MAX)* Data

To store data into a VARBINARY(MAX) column, or any of the binary data columns, you can use the CONVERT or CAST function to change string data into binary data. If you have data that is already in hexadecimal format, you can add 0x in front of it instead of casting. Using a program written in a .NET language or any language type that supports working with SQL Server, you can save actual files into VARBINARY(MAX) columns. In this simple demonstration, you will add data by converting string data. Type in and execute Listing 16-2 to learn more.

Listing 16-2. *Using VARBINARY(MAX) Data*

```
--1
CREATE TABLE #BinaryTest (DataDescription VARCHAR(50),
    BinaryData VARBINARY(MAX));
--2
INSERT INTO #BinaryTest (DataDescription,BinaryData)
VALUES ('Test 1', CONVERT(VARBINARY(MAX),'this is the test 1 row')),
    ('Test 2', CONVERT(VARBINARY(MAX),'this is the test 2 row'));
```

```
--3
SELECT DataDescription, BinaryData, CONVERT(VARCHAR(MAX), BinaryData)
FROM #BinaryTest;
```

```
--4
DROP TABLE #BinaryTest;
```

Figure 16-2 shows the results of running this code. Statement 1 creates the #BinaryTest table containing the BinaryData column of type VARBINARY(MAX). corStatement 2 inserts two rows. To insert data into the BinaryData column, it must be converted into a binary type. Query 3 displays the data. To read the data, the statement converts it back into a string data type.

	DataDescription	BinaryData	Converted
1	Test 1	0x746869732069732074686520746573742031206F77	this is the test 1 row
2	Test 2	0x746869732069732074686520746573742032206F77	this is the test 2 row

Figure 16-2. *The results of using a VARBINARY(MAX) column*

Using FILESTREAM

Often database applications involving files, such as images or Word documents, store just the path to the file in the database and store the actual file on a share in the network. This can be more efficient than storing large files within the database because the file system works more efficiently than SQL Server with streaming file data. This solution also poses some problems. Because the files live outside the database, you have to make sure they are secure. You can't automatically apply the security as set up in the database to the files. Another issue is backups. When you back up a database, how do you make sure that the backups of the documents in the file shares are done at the same time so the data is consistent in case of a restore?

The FILESTREAM object solves these issues by storing the files on the file system but making the files become part of the database. This is the recommended solution if the files are over 1MB in size. To add and manipulate files, you must use T-SQL commands. In addition, an API is available for modifying the files, although this solution is rather cumbersome.

To set up a FILESTREAM object, add the word FILESTREAM to the VARBINARY(MAX) column when creating the table. The SQL Server instance must be configured to allow FILESTREAM data, and the database must have a filegroup defined for FILESTREAM data. To configure the SQL Server instance to allow FILESTREAM data, follow these instructions:

1. Launch the SQL Server Configuration Manager utility as shown in Figure 16-3.

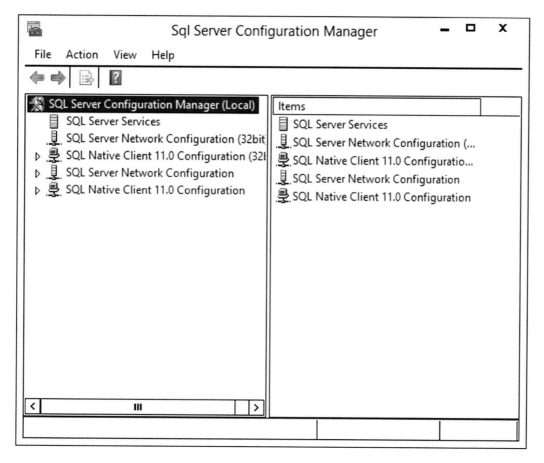

Figure 16-3. *The SQL Server Configuration Manager*

2. Select SQL Server Services and locate the SQL Server instance as shown in Figure 16-4.

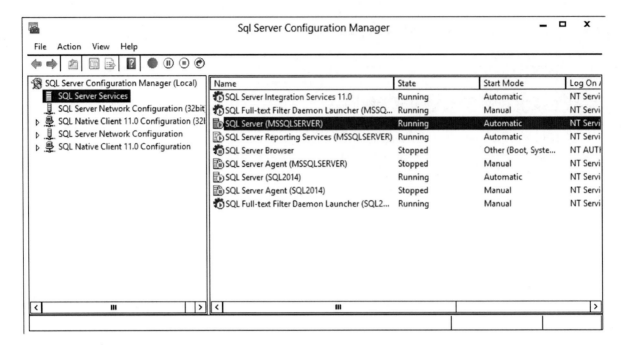

Figure 16-4. *The SQL Server Instance*

3. Double-click the Instance and select the FILESTREAM tab as shown in Figure 16-5. Make sure that all options are enabled. By checking Enable FILESTREAM for file I/O access you will turn on the FileTable functionality (discussed in the next section). Allowing remote access lets users from other systems access the files.

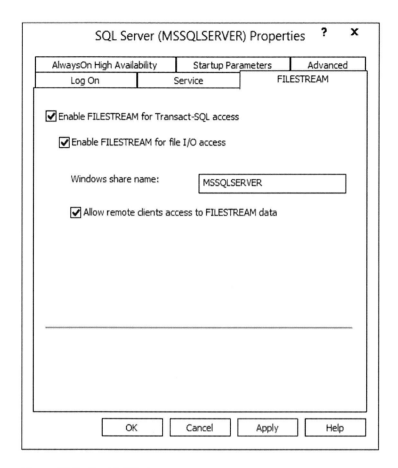

Figure 16-5. Enable Filestream

4. Click OK. If changes were made, restart the SQL Server.

SQL Server databases have a minimum of two files: the data file and the log file. To use the Filestream functionality in a database, you will add a special filegroup and add a file to the filegroup. To add Filestream to AdventureWorks, follow these instructions:

1. Right-click the AdventureWorks database and select Properties.

2. Select Filegroups.

3. In the FILESTREAM section, click Add Filegroup. A new row will appear in the FILESTREAM section.

4. Type FileStream in the name as shown in Figure 16-6.

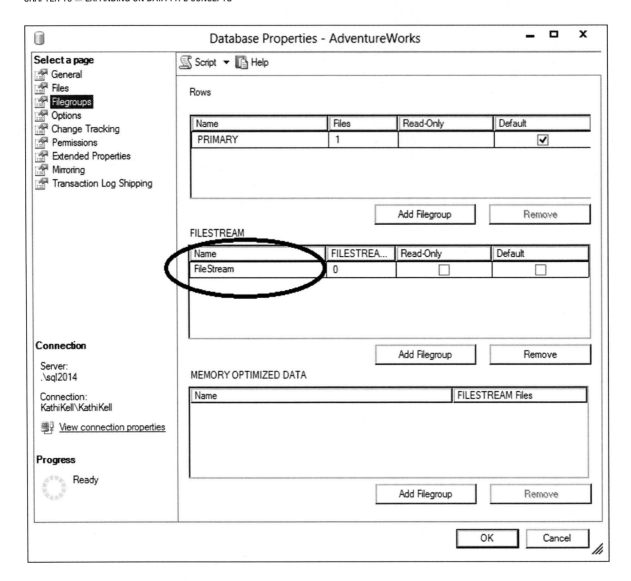

Figure 16-6. *Adding a filegroup*

5. Select the Files page.

6. Click Add, and then type in AWFS in the Logical Name property in the new row.

7. Under File Type, select FILESTREAM Data as shown in Figure 16-7.

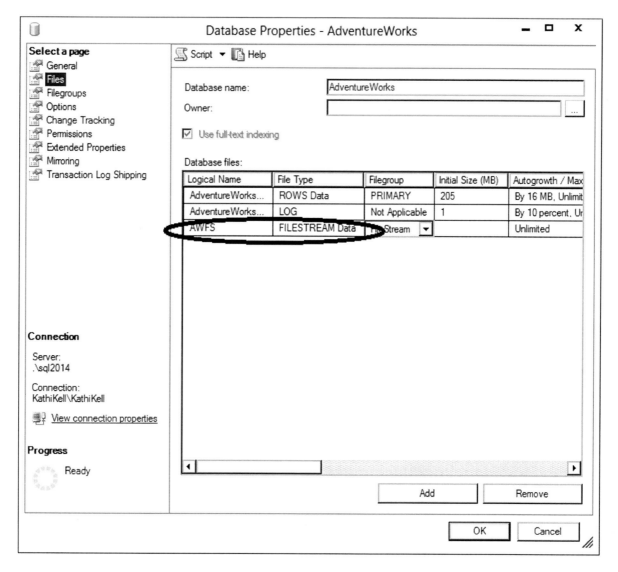

Figure 16-7. *Add the File Type property*

8. Scroll to the right and locate the Path property of the AWFS logical file. Click the ellipsis button to set the location of the new file. Make a note of the Path property so you will have it available later in the chapter.

9. Click OK. Now the AdventureWorks database is set up for FILESTREAM data.

To create a FILESTREAM column, you just add the word FILESTREAM to the VARBINARY(MAX) column definition when it is created. Listing 16-3 creates and populates a FILESTREAM type column.

Listing 16-3. Working with a FILESTREAM Column

```
--1
IF OBJECT_ID('dbo.NotepadFiles') IS NOT NULL BEGIN
    DROP TABLE dbo.NotepadFiles;
END;

--2
CREATE table dbo.NotepadFiles(Name VARCHAR(25),
    FileData VARBINARY(MAX) FILESTREAM,
    RowID UNIQUEIDENTIFIER ROWGUIDCOL
        NOT NULL UNIQUE DEFAULT NEWSEQUENTIALID());

--3
INSERT INTO dbo.NotepadFiles(Name,FileData)
VALUES ('test1', CONVERT(VARBINARY(MAX),'This is a test')),
    ('test2', CONVERT(VARBINARY(MAX),'This is the second test'));

--4
SELECT Name,FileData,CONVERT(VARCHAR(MAX),FileData) TheData, RowID
FROM dbo.NotepadFiles;
```

Figure 16-8 shows the results of running this code. Code section 1 drops the NotepadFiles table in case it already exists. Statement 2 creates the NotepadFiles table. The Name column contains a value to help identify the row. The FileData column is the FILESTREAM column. To create the FILESTREAM column, specify the FILESTREAM keyword when creating a VARBINARY(MAX) column. The RowID column has a special setting ROWGUIDCOL, which specifies that the column is automatically updated with a unique global identifier. The NEWSEQUENTIALID function populates the RowID column. This function creates a unique value for each row, which is required when using FILESTREAM data.

	Name	FileData	TheData	RowID
1	test1.txt	0x54686973206973206120746573374	This is a test	ED074F72-54C3-E311-BE90-9917FCEA92B6
2	test2.txt	0x546869732069732074686520736563 6F6E642074657374	This is the second test	EE074F72-54C3-E311-BE90-9917FCEA92B6

Figure 16-8. *The results of populating a FILESTREAM column*

Statement 3 inserts two rows into the table. The data to be inserted into the FileData column must be of type VARBINARY(MAX) so the statement converts it. Statement 4 shows the results. The FileData column displays the binary data. By converting it to VARCHAR(MAX), you can read the data. Navigate to the appropriate folder on your system through the path you saved when setting up the FileStream filegroup. You should see an AWFS folder. You will get a warning saying you don't have permission to access the folder. You can click Continue to view the contents.

Inside the AWFS folder is a folder with a unique identifier name; this folder corresponds to the dbo.NotepadFiles table you created in the last demo because it has a FILESTREAM column. Figure 16-9 shows the AWFS folder on my system.

☐	Name	▲	Date modified	Type		Size
	📁 SFSGC		4/13/2014 4:42 PM	File folder		
	📁 SFSLOG		4/13/2014 4:42 PM	File folder		
	📁 0edd03bd-0b2b-4c4a-b50c-b40f7dc3a...		4/13/2014 4:42 PM	File folder		
	📄 filestream.hdr		4/13/2014 4:42 PM	HDR File		

Figure 16-9. *The ASFS folder*

If you navigate further down in the unique identifier named folder to the actual files, you will see two files that can be opened in Notepad. The text inside those files will match the data demonstrated in Listing 16-3. When working with a production database, the user would have an application that opens the file through calls to SQL Server with the appropriate program, not by navigating to the actual file. In a non-laboratory environment, do not open the files directly.

When you delete a row from the NotepadFiles table, the corresponding file on disk will also disappear. If you drop the table, the entire folder will disappear. Run this code, and then check the Documents folder once again:

```
DROP TABLE NotepadFiles;
CHECKPOINT;
```

The database engine doesn't delete the folder until the database commits all transactions to disk, called a *checkpoint*. By running the CHECKPOINT command, you force the checkpoint.

FileTables

Building on the FILESTREAM technology, SQL Server 2012 introduced an exciting new feature called FileTables. FileTables allow you to store files like movies, documents, or music in an SQL Server table but still allows access to them through Windows Explorer or through another application. The fact that these files are stored in the file system but controlled by SQL Server is transparent to the user but, because they are part of the database, you get many of the benefits of a relational database, such as the ability to query file properties using T-SQL and security.

Because the data stored in a FileTable is not your normal data, you will need to first tell SQL Server to treat the data differently. You do this by telling SQL Server the data is non-transactional. A FileTable requires a directory name so you create one in your ALTER DATABASE statement. I chose the name FileTableDocuments. After running the ALTER DATABASE script, you are now able to create a FileTable. In my example, I created a FileTable name MyDocuments that points to a directory called Misc Documents. As you'll see later, the Misc Documents folder will be created under the FileTableDocuments folder. Listing 16-4 shows both queries.

Listing 16-4. Creating a FileTable

```
USE MASTER;
GO
ALTER DATABASE AdventureWorks
    SET FILESTREAM ( NON_TRANSACTED_ACCESS = FULL, DIRECTORY_NAME = 'FileTableDocuments');
GO

USE AdventureWorks;
GO
```

413

```
CREATE TABLE MyDocuments AS FileTable
    WITH (
            FileTable_Directory = 'Misc Documents',
            FileTable_Collate_Filename = SQL_Latin1_General_CP1_CI_AS
          );
GO
```

If the command doesn't work in a couple of seconds, you may need to close all connections to the database first. One thing to note is when creating the FileTable, I needed to specify the collation. In some cases, the AdventureWorks database download is case sensitive and FileTables can't be created with a case-sensitive collation. The collation I specified in the CREATE TABLE statement is case insensitive. Also note I did not include any column names in my CREATE TABLE statement. This is because a FileTable has a default set of columns that can't be altered. These columns refer to key metadata information on the file stored in the table.

Now that you have the FileTable created, you get to the fun part. There are two ways to get to the directory, or contents, of the table. The first way is through SQL Server Management Studio. If you navigate to the Tables folder under the AdventureWorks database, you will notice an additional folder called FileTables. If you expand the folder, you will see the table created in Listing 16-4. Figure 16-10 shows where the FileTable object can be found in SQL Server Management Studio.

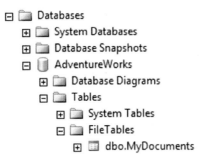

Figure 16-10. *FileTable in SQL Server Management Studio*

Right-click the file table and select Explore FileTable Directory. Once the folder opens, notice the full path to the directory in the address bar. In my case, the full path is \\Kathikell\sql2014\FileTableDocuments\Misc Documents. This leads to the second method of getting to the folder. You can access this folder by typing the UNC path in the run bar under your Windows Start menu. This is also the path you can share with other users who need to place files in the directory.

Right now the FileTable is empty, as is the folder. You can confirm this by executing a SELECT statement against the table and noticing that no rows are returned. So let's put a file in the folder. You can either create a new file like a .txt file or you can copy an existing file into the directory. In my example, I will right-click the empty directory and create a blank text file called FileTableTest.txt. After the file is created, run a SELECT statement against the table. Figure 16-11 shows the partial results of my SELECT statement.

	stream_id	file_stream	name	path_locator	parent_path_locator	file_type
1	C207F01E-5AC3-E311-BE90-9917FCEA92B6	0x	FileTableTest.txt	0xFC287442EE0FA18FCD1077AD799118FBCBE43506A0	NULL	txt

Figure 16-11. *Viewing a document in a FileTable*

You now have a text document stored in a database table, but it can be viewed through Windows Explorer as if it were stored on a file system. If you delete the file from the folder, the row will be removed from the table. If you delete the row from the table, the file will be removed from the folder. This means you get many of the benefits of a relational database including all the backup, recovery, and security options SQL Server offers but with the simplicity of Windows file navigation.

You can also use T-SQL statements to create and delete files by inserting rows into the MyDocuments table. Type in and run the following statement and then take a look at the share again. You can open the file with Wordpad to see the contents.

```
INSERT INTO [dbo].[MyDocuments]
          ([file_stream]
          ,[name])
     VALUES
          (cast('hello' as varbinary(max)),'MyNewFile.txt');
GO
```

Enhanced Date and Time

Previous versions of SQL Server have the DATETIME and SMALLDATETIME data types for working with temporal data. One big complaint by developers has been that there wasn't an easy way to store just dates or just time. SQL Server contains several temporal data types. You have a choice of using the DATE and TIME data types as well as the DATETIME2 and DATETIMEOFFSET data types.

Using *DATE, TIME,* and *DATETIME2*

You can store just a date or time value by using the new DATE and TIME data types. The traditional DATETIME and SMALLDATETIME data types default to 12 a.m. when you don't specify the time. You can also specify a precision, from zero to seven decimal places, when using the TIME and DATETIME2 data types. Type in and execute Listing 16-5 to learn how to use the new types.

Listing 16-5. Using DATE and TIME

```
USE tempdb;

--1
IF OBJECT_ID('dbo.DateDemo') IS NOT NULL BEGIN
    DROP TABLE dbo.DateDemo;
END;

--2
CREATE TABLE dbo.DateDemo(JustTheDate DATE, JustTheTime TIME(1),
    NewDateTime2 DATETIME2(3), UTCDate DATETIME2);

--3
INSERT INTO dbo.DateDemo (JustTheDate, JustTheTime, NewDateTime2,
    UTCDate)
VALUES (SYSDATETIME(), SYSDATETIME(), SYSDATETIME(), SYSUTCDATETIME());

--4
SELECT JustTheDate, JustTheTime, NewDateTime2, UTCDate
FROM dbo.DateDemo;
```

Figure 16-12 shows the results of running this code. Code section 1 drops the dbo.DateDemo table if it already exists. Statement 2 creates the dbo.DateDemo table with a DATE, a TIME, and two DATETIME2 columns. Notice that the TIME and DATETIME2 columns have the precision specified. The default is seven places if a precision is not specified. Statement 3 inserts a row into the table using the SYSDATETIME function. This function works like the GETDATE function except that it has greater precision than GETDATE. The statement populates the UTCDate column with the SYSUTCDATETIME function, which provides the Coordinated Universal Time (UTC). Statement 4 shows the results. The JustTheDate value shows that even though the SYSDATETIME function populated it, it stored only the date. The JustTheTime values stored only the time with one decimal place past the seconds. The NewDateTime2 column stored both the date and time with three decimal places. The UTCDate column stored the UTC date along with seven decimal places. Because the computer running this demo is in Central time, the time is five hours different.

	Just The Date	Just The Time	New Date Time2	UTCDate
1	2014-04-13	17:26:20.6	2014-04-13 17:26:20.568	2014-04-13 22:26:20.5677047

Figure 16-12. *The results of using the new date and time data types*

Most business applications won't require the default precision of seven places found with the TIME and DATETIME2 types. Be sure to specify the required precision when creating tables with columns of these types to save space in your database.

Using *DATETIMEOFFSET*

The new DATETIMEOFFSET data type contains, in addition to the date and time, a time zone offset for working with dates and times in different time zones. This is the difference between the UTC date/time and the stored date. Along with the new data type, several new functions for working with DATETIMEOFFSET are available. Type in and execute Listing 16-6 to learn how to work with this new data type.

Listing 16-6. Using the DATETIMEOFFSET Data Type

```
USE tempdb;

--1
IF OBJECT_ID('dbo.OffsetDemo') IS NOT NULL BEGIN
    DROP TABLE dbo.OffsetDemo;
END;

--2
CREATE TABLE dbo.OffsetDemo(Date1 DATETIMEOFFSET);

--3
INSERT INTO dbo.OffsetDemo(Date1)
VALUES (SYSDATETIMEOFFSET()),
    (SWITCHOFFSET(SYSDATETIMEOFFSET(),'+00:00')),
    (TODATETIMEOFFSET(SYSDATETIME(),'+05:00'));

--4
SELECT Date1
FROM dbo.OffsetDemo;
```

Figure 16-13 shows the results of running this code. Code section 1 drops the dbo.OffsetDemo table if it exists. Statement 2 creates the table with a DATETIMEOFFSET column, Date1. Statement 3 inserts three rows into the table using the new functions for working with the new data types. The SYSDATETIMEOFFSET function returns the date and time on the server along with the time zone offset. The computer I am using is five hours behind UTC, so the value −05:00 appears after the current date and time. Using the SWITCHOFFSET function, you can switch a DATETIMEOFFSET value to another time zone. Notice that by switching to +00:00, the UTC time, the date, and time values adjust. By using the TODATETIMEOFFSET function, you can add a time zone to a regular date and time.

	Date1
1	2014-04-13 17:28:20.6735238 -05:00
2	2014-04-13 22:28:20.6735238 +00:00
3	2014-04-13 17:28:20.6735238 +05:00

Figure 16-13. *The results of using DATETIMEOFFSET*

The DATETIMEOFFSET type and functions may be useful to you if you work with data in different time zones. When time changes go into effect, such as Daylight Saving Time, the offsets don't adjust. Keep that in mind if you choose to work with DATETIMEOFFSET.

HIERARCHYID

The HIERARCHYID data type is used to represent hierarchical relationships in data, for example, family trees, which means that it can contain multiple properties instead of just one value. The HIERARCHYID column also has methods, which means that columns and variables of this type can "do something" and not just contain a value. The HIERARCHYID data type originally shipped with SQL Server 2008, and you can use it even if you don't want to create any custom types.

You learned about joining a table to itself in the "Self-Joins" section in Chapter 5. In older versions of AdventureWorks, the ManagerID column points back to the EmployeeID column in the HumanResources.Employee table. To follow the organizational chart from this table, you must recursively follow the chain of command from the CEO down each manager-employee path to the lowest employee, which is pretty difficult to do with T-SQL. Chapter 11 covered how to do this in the "Writing a Recursive Query" section. The 2012 AdventureWorks database replaces the self-join with OrganizationalNode, a HIERARCHYID column, which is much easier to query.

Viewing *HIERARCHYID*

If you just write a query to view the OrganizationalNode in the HumanResources.Employee table, you will see binary data. That is because CLR data types are stored as binary values. To view the data in readable form, you must use the ToString method of the type. The OrganizationalLevel column in the table is a computed column based on OrganizationalNode using the GetLevel method. Type in and execute Listing 16-7 to view the data.

Listing 16-7. Viewing the OrganizationalNode

```
USE AdventureWorks;
GO
SELECT BusinessEntityID,
    SPACE((OrganizationLevel) * 3) + JobTitle AS Title,
    OrganizationNode, OrganizationLevel,
    OrganizationNode.ToString() AS Readable
FROM HumanResources.Employee
ORDER BY Readable;
```

Figure 16-14 shows the partial results of running this code. As mentioned, the OrganizationalNode data is meaningless unless you use the ToString method as in the Readable column. By using the SPACE function to indent the JobTitle column from the table to produce the Title column in the results and by sorting on the Readable column, you can see the relation between the job titles in the data.

	BusinessEntityID	Title	OrganizationNode	OrganizationLevel	Readable
1	1	Chief Executive Officer	0x	0	/
2	2	Vice President of Engineering	0x58	1	/1/
3	3	Engineering Manager	0x5AC0	2	/1/1/
4	4	Senior Tool Designer	0x5AD6	3	/1/1/1/
5	5	Design Engineer	0x5ADA	3	/1/1/2/
6	6	Design Engineer	0x5ADE	3	/1/1/3/
7	7	Research and Development Manager	0x5AE1	3	/1/1/4/
8	8	Research and Development Engineer	0x5AE158	4	/1/1/4/1/
9	9	Research and Development Engineer	0x5AE168	4	/1/1/4/2/
10	10	Research and Development Manager	0x5AE178	4	/1/1/4/3/
11	11	Senior Tool Designer	0x5AE3	3	/1/1/5/
12	12	Tool Designer	0x5AE358	4	/1/1/5/1/
13	13	Tool Designer	0x5AE368	4	/1/1/5/2/
14	14	Senior Design Engineer	0x5AE5	3	/1/1/6/

Figure 16-14. *The partial results of querying the HumanResources.Employee table*

The very first node in the hierarchy is the CEO (chief executive officer) of the company, represented as a slash (/) in the Readable column. The level for the CEO is 0, which you can see in the computed column OrganizationLevel. Several employees have an OrganizationLevel of 1; these employees report directly to the CEO. If you scroll down through all the results, you will see that these have a value, 1 through 6, in between two slashes. The vice president of engineering is the first node in level 1. The marketing manager is the second node in level 1. Each of these employees has other employees reporting to them. Those employees have a level of 2. For example, the engineering manager reports to the vice president of engineering and has a Readable value of /1/1/. Four employees report to the engineering manager. These employees all have Readable values that begin with /1/1/ along with an additional value, 1 through 4.

Creating a Hierarchy

As you can see from the previous example, querying hierarchical data using HIERARCHYID is not difficult. Maintaining the data, however, is much more challenging. To add a new value or update existing values, you must use the built-in methods of the data type. If you have worked with nodes and pointers in other programming languages, you will find this to be very similar. To learn how to insert nodes using these methods to create hierarchical data, download or type in and execute the code in Listing 16-8.

Listing 16-8. Creating a Hierarchy with HIERARCHYID

```
Use tempdb;

--1
IF OBJECT_ID('SportsOrg') IS NOT NULL BEGIN
    DROP TABLE SportsOrg;
END;

--2
CREATE TABLE SportsOrg
    (DivNode HIERARCHYID NOT NULL PRIMARY KEY CLUSTERED,
    DivLevel AS DivNode.GetLevel(), --Calculated column
    DivisionID INT NOT NULL,
    Name VARCHAR(30) NOT NULL);

--3
INSERT INTO SportsOrg(DivNode,DivisionID,Name)
VALUES(HIERARCHYID::GetRoot(),1,'State');

--4
DECLARE @ParentNode HIERARCHYID, @LastChildNode HIERARCHYID;

--5
SELECT @ParentNode = DivNode
FROM SportsOrg
WHERE DivisionID = 1;

--6
SELECT @LastChildNode = max(DivNode)
FROM SportsOrg
WHERE DivNode.GetAncestor(1) = @ParentNode;

--7
INSERT INTO SportsOrg(DivNode,DivisionID,Name)
VALUES (@ParentNode.GetDescendant(@LastChildNode,NULL),
2,'Madison County');

--8
SELECT DivisionID,DivLevel,DivNode.ToString() AS Node,Name
FROM SportsOrg;
```

Figure 16-15 shows the results of running this code. You might be surprised how much code was required just to insert two rows! Code section 1 drops the SportsOrg table if it already exists. Statement 2 creates the SportsOrg table with the DivisionID and Name columns to identify each division or team. The DivNode column is a HIERARCHYID column, and the DivLevel is a computed column. Statement 3 inserts the first row, the root, into the table. Take a close look at the INSERT statement. Instead of inserting a value into DivNode, the statement uses the name of the data type along with the GetRoot method. Of course, because DivLevel is a computed column, you don't insert anything into it.

	DivisionID	DivLevel	Node	Name
1	1	0	/	State
2	2	1	/1/	Madison County

Figure 16-15. *The results of creating a hierarchy*

To insert the second and subsequent nodes, you have to use the GetDescendant method of the parent node. You also have to determine the last child of the parent. Statement 4 declares two variables needed to accomplish this. Statement 5 saves the parent into a variable. Statement 6 saves the last child of the parent into a variable. In this case, there are no children just yet. Statement 7 inserts the row using the GetDescendant method. If the second argument is NULL, the method returns a new child that is greater than the child node in the first argument. Finally, query 8 displays the data.

Using Stored Procedures to Manage Hierarchical Data

Working with HIERARCHYID can be pretty complicated, as shown in the previous section. If you decide to use this data type in your applications, I recommend that you create stored procedures to encapsulate the logic and make coding your application much easier. Listing 16-9 contains a stored procedure to add new rows to the table. There is a lot of code to type so you may want to download the code from the book's web site (www.apress.com) instead of typing it in. Execute the code to learn more.

Listing 16-9. Using a Stored Procedure to Insert New Nodes

```
USE tempdb;
GO


--1
IF OBJECT_ID('dbo.usp_AddDivision') IS NOT NULL BEGIN
    DROP PROC dbo.usp_AddDivision;
END;
IF OBJECT_ID('dbo.SportsOrg') IS NOT NULL BEGIN
    DROP TABLE dbo.SportsOrg;
END;
GO


--2
CREATE TABLE SportsOrg
    (DivNode HierarchyID NOT NULL PRIMARY KEY CLUSTERED,
    DivLevel AS DivNode.GetLevel(), --Calculated column
    DivisionID INT NOT NULL,
    Name VARCHAR(30) NOT NULL);
GO


--3
INSERT INTO SportsOrg(DivNode,DivisionID,Name)
VALUES(HIERARCHYID::GetRoot(),1,'State');
GO
```

```
--4
CREATE PROC usp_AddDivision @DivisionID INT,
    @Name VARCHAR(50),@ParentID INT AS
    SET TRANSACTION ISOLATION LEVEL SERIALIZABLE;

    DECLARE @ParentNode HierarchyID, @LastChildNode HierarchyID;

    --Grab the parent node
    SELECT @ParentNode = DivNode
    FROM SportsOrg
    WHERE DivisionID = @ParentID;

    BEGIN TRANSACTION
        --Find the last node added to the parent
        SELECT @LastChildNode = max(DivNode)
        FROM SportsOrg
        WHERE DivNode.GetAncestor(1) = @ParentNode;
        --Insert the new node using the GetDescendant function
        INSERT INTO SportsOrg(DivNode,DivisionID,Name)
        VALUES (@ParentNode.GetDescendant(@LastChildNode,NULL),
            @DivisionID,@Name);
    COMMIT TRANSACTION;
GO


--5
EXEC usp_AddDivision 2,'Madison County',1;
EXEC usp_AddDivision 3,'Macoupin County',1;
EXEC usp_AddDivision 4,'Green County',1;
EXEC usp_AddDivision 5,'Edwardsville',2;
EXEC usp_AddDivision 6,'Granite City',2;
EXEC usp_AddDivision 7,'Softball',5;
EXEC usp_AddDivision 8,'Baseball',5;
EXEC usp_AddDivision 9,'Basketball',5;
EXEC usp_AddDivision 10,'Softball',6;
EXEC usp_AddDivision 11,'Baseball',6;
EXEC usp_AddDivision 12,'Basketball',6;
EXEC usp_AddDivision 13,'Ages 10 - 12',7;
EXEC usp_AddDivision 14,'Ages 13 - 17',7;
EXEC usp_AddDivision 15,'Adult',7;
EXEC usp_AddDivision 16,'Preschool',8;
EXEC usp_AddDivision 17,'Grade School League',8;
EXEC usp_AddDivision 18,'High School League',8;

--6
SELECT DivNode.ToString() AS Node,
    DivisionID, SPACE(DivLevel * 3) + Name AS Name
FROM SportsOrg
ORDER BY DivNode;
```

Figure 16-16 shows the results of running this code. Code section 1 drops the stored procedure and table if they already exist. Statement 2 creates the table, and statement 3 inserts the root as in the previous section. Code section 4 creates the stored procedure to insert new nodes. The stored procedure requires the new DivisionID and Name values along with the DivisionID of the parent node. Inside the stored process, an explicit transaction contains the code to grab the last child node and perform the insert. If this were part of an actual multiuser application, it would be very important to make sure that two users didn't accidentally insert values into the same node position. By using an explicit transaction with serializable isolation, you avoid that problem. Code section 5 calls the stored procedure to insert each node. Finally, query 6 retrieves the data from the SportsOrg table. The query uses the same technique from the previous section utilizing the SPACES function to format the Name column results.

	Node	DivisionID	Name
1	/	1	State
2	/1/	2	Madison County
3	/1/1/	5	Edwardsville
4	/1/1/1/	7	Softball
5	/1/1/1/1/	13	Ages 10 - 12
6	/1/1/1/2/	14	Ages 13 - 17
7	/1/1/1/3/	15	Adult
8	/1/1/2/	8	Baseball
9	/1/1/2/1/	16	Preschool
10	/1/1/2/2/	17	Grade School League
11	/1/1/2/3/	18	High School League
12	/1/1/3/	9	Basketball
13	/1/2/	6	Granite City
14	/1/2/1/	10	Softball
15	/1/2/2/	11	Baseball
16	/1/2/3/	12	Basketball
17	/2/	3	Macoupin County
18	/3/	4	Green County

Figure 16-16. *The results of using a stored procedure to insert new rows*

Deleting a node is easy; you just delete the row. Unfortunately, there is nothing built into the HIERARCHYID data type to ensure that the children of the deleted nodes are also deleted or moved to a new parent. You will end up with orphaned nodes if the deleted node was a parent node. You can also move nodes, but you must make sure that you move the children of the moved parent nodes as well. If you decide to include the HIERARCHYID in your applications, be sure to learn about this topic in depth before you design your application. See Books Online for more information about how to work with HIERARCHYID.

Spatial Data Types

In the previous section, you learned about the CLR data type HIERARCHYID. SQL Server has two other CLR data types, GEOMETRY and GEOGRAPHY, also known as the *spatial* data types. The GEOMETRY data type might be used for a warehouse application to store the location of each product in the warehouse. The GEOGRAPHY data type can be used to store data that can be used in mapping software. You may wonder why two types that both store locations exist. The GEOMETRY data type follows a "flat Earth" model, with basically X, Y, and Z coordinates. The GEOGRAPHY data type represents the "round Earth" model, storing longitude and latitude. These data types implement international standards for spatial data.

Using *GEOMETRY*

By using the GEOMETRY type, you can store points, lines, and polygons. You can calculate the difference between two shapes, determine whether they intersect, and much more. Just like HIERARCHYID, the database engine stores the data as a binary value. GEOMETRY also has many built-in methods for working with the data. Type in and execute Listing 16-10 to learn how to use the GEOMETRY data type with some simple examples.

Listing 16-10. Using the GEOMETRY Data Type

```
USE tempdb;
GO

--1
IF OBJECT_ID('dbo.GeometryData') IS NOT NULL BEGIN
    DROP TABLE dbo.GeometryData;
END;

--2
CREATE TABLE dbo.GeometryData (
    Point1 GEOMETRY, Point2 GEOMETRY,
    Line1 GEOMETRY, Line2 GEOMETRY,
    Polygon1 GEOMETRY, Polygon2 GEOMETRY);

--3
INSERT INTO dbo.GeometryData (Point1, Point2, Line1, Line2, Polygon1, Polygon2)
VALUES (
    GEOMETRY::Parse('Point(1 4)'),
    GEOMETRY::Parse('Point(2 5)'),
    GEOMETRY::Parse('LineString(1 4, 2 5)'),
    GEOMETRY::Parse('LineString(4 1, 5 2, 7 3, 10 6)'),
    GEOMETRY::Parse('Polygon((1 4, 2 5, 5 2, 0 4, 1 4))'),
    GEOMETRY::Parse('Polygon((1 4, 2 7, 7 2, 0 4, 1 4))'));

--4
SELECT Point1.ToString() AS Point1, Point2.ToString() AS Point2,
    Line1.ToString() AS Line1, Line2.ToString() AS Line2,
    Polygon1.ToString() AS Polygon1, Polygon2.ToString() AS Polygon2
FROM dbo.GeometryData;

--5
SELECT Point1.STX AS Point1X, Point1.STY AS Point1Y,
    Line1.STIntersects(Polygon1) AS Line1Poly1Intersects,
    Line1.STLength() AS Line1Len,
    Line1.STStartPoint().ToString() AS Line1Start,
    Line2.STNumPoints() AS Line2PtCt,
    Polygon1.STArea() AS Poly1Area,
    Polygon1.STIntersects(Polygon2) AS Poly1Poly2Intersects
FROM dbo.GeometryData;
```

Figure 16-17 shows the results of running this code. Code section 1 drops the dbo.GeometryData table if it already exists. Statement 2 creates the table along with six GEOMETRY columns each named for the type of shape it will contain. Even though this example named the shape types, a GEOMETRY column can store any of the shapes; it is

423

not limited to one shape. Statement 3 inserts one row into the table using the Parse method. Query 4 displays the data using the ToString method so that you can read the data. Notice that the data returned from the ToString method looks just like it does when inserted. Query 5 demonstrates a few of the methods available for working with GEOMETRY data. For example, you can display the X and Y coordinates of a point, determine the length or area of a shape, determine whether two shapes intersect, and count the number of points in a shape.

	Point1	Point2	Line1	Line2	Polygon1	Polygon2
1	POINT (1 4)	POINT (2 5)	LINESTRING (1 4, 2 5)	LINESTRING (4 1, 5 2, 7 3, 10 6)	POLYGON ((1 4, 2 5, 5 2, 0 4, 1 4))	POLYGON ((1 4, 2 7, 7 2, 0 4, 1 4))

	Point1X	Point1Y	Line1Poly1Intersects	Line1Len	Line1Start	Line2PtCt	Poly1Area	Poly1Poly2Intersects
1	1	4	1	1.4142135623731	POINT (1 4)	4	4	1

Figure 16-17. *The results of using the GEOMETRY type*

Using *GEOGRAPHY*

The GEOGRAPHY data type is even more interesting than the GEOMETRY type. With the GEOGRAPHY type, you can store longitude and latitude values for actual locations or areas. Just like the GEOMETRY type, you can use several built-in methods to work with the data. These data types are used extensively with SQL Server Reporting Services.

The AdventureWorks database contains one GEOMETRY column in the Person.Address table. Type in and execute the code in Listing 16-11 to learn more.

Listing 16-11. *Using the GEOGRAPHY Data Type*

```
USE AdventureWorks;
GO

--1
DECLARE @OneAddress GEOGRAPHY;

--2
SELECT @OneAddress = SpatialLocation
FROM Person.Address
WHERE AddressID = 91;

--3
SELECT AddressID,PostalCode, SpatialLocation.ToString(),
    @OneAddress.STDistance(SpatialLocation) AS DiffInMeters
FROM Person.Address
WHERE AddressID IN (1,91, 831,11419);
```

Figure 16-18 shows the results of running this code. Statement 1 declares a variable, @OneAddress, of the GEOGRAPHY type. Statement 2 assigns one value to the variable. Query 3 displays the data including the AddressID, the PostalCode, and the SpatialLocation.ToString method. The DiffInMeters column displays the distance between the location saved in the variable to the stored data. Notice that the difference is zero when comparing a location to itself.

	AddressID	PostalCode	(No column name)	DiffInMeters
1	1	98011	POINT (-122.164646615406 47.7869921906598)	25366.6874166672
2	91	98104	POINT (-122.391164430965 47.6176669267707)	0
3	831	06510	POINT (-72.9550181450784 41.3589413896096)	3924885.39255556
4	11419	98366	POINT (-122.72771089643 47.575135985628)	25748.07917586

Figure 16-18. *The results of using the GEOGRAPHY data type*

Viewing the Spatial Results Tab

When you select GEOMETRY or GEOGRAPHY data in the native binary format, another tab shows up in the results. This tab displays a visual representation of the spatial data. Type in and execute Listing 16-12 to see how this works.

Listing 16-12. Viewing Spatial Results

```
--1
DECLARE @Area GEOMETRY;

--2
SET @Area = geometry::Parse('Polygon((1 4, 2 5, 5 2, 0 4, 1 4))');

--3
SELECT @Area AS Area;
```

After running the code, click the Spatial Results tab. Figure 16-19 shows how this should look. This tab will show up whenever you return spatial data in the binary format in a grid.

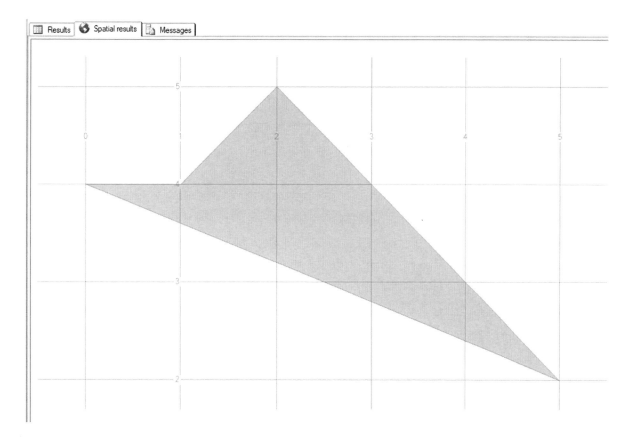

Figure 16-19. *The Spatial results tab*

Although the spatial data types are very interesting, they also require specialized knowledge to take full advantage of them. I encourage you to learn more about this if you think your applications can benefit from these new data types.

Circular Arcs

SQL Server 2012 included a number of enhancements to both the geography and the geometry features. These new features demonstrate the increasing need for advanced spatial capabilities in relational databases. One of these new features is the introduction of circular arcs. Simply put, *circular arcs* allow for curved lines between any two points. You can also combine straight and curved lines for even more complex shapes. Figure 16-20 shows some examples.

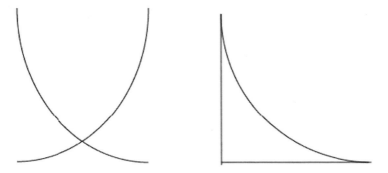

Figure 16-20. *Example shapes using curved and straight lines*

To create these shapes, you will use the `CIRCULARSTRING` command. This command requires you to define at least three points along the circular arc: a beginning, a point anywhere along the segment, and an end. The total amount of points along the arc will always be odd, and you are allowed to have the last point be the same as the first. Listing 16-13 shows how you would use the `CIRCULARSTRING` command to create a single curved line. You can combine multiple curved or straight lines using the `COMPOUNDCURVE` command. When combining lines, whether curved or straight, the beginning of the next line must always be the endpoint of the previous line. Figure 16-21 shows the output from the two `SELECT` statements in the listing.

Listing 16-13. Example of Curved Lines Using CIRCULARSTRING and COMPOUNDCURVE

```
DECLARE @g geometry;

SET @g = geometry:: STGeomFromText('CIRCULARSTRING(1 2, 2 1, 4 3)', 0);
SELECT @g.ToString();

SET @g = geometry::STGeomFromText('
COMPOUNDCURVE(
CIRCULARSTRING(1 2, 2 1, 4 3),
CIRCULARSTRING(4 3, 3 4, 1 2))', 0);
SELECT @g AS Area;
```

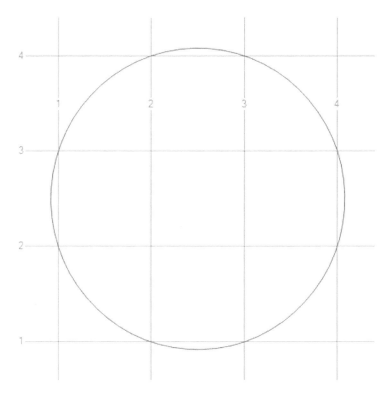

Figure 16-21. *Results of using CIRCULARSTRING and COMPOUNDCURVE*

The COMPOUNDCURVE command allows you to simply combine multiple curved arcs or create more complicated shapes by combining curved and straight lines. The CIRCULARSTRING command defines each circular arc while the straight lines are defined with only the points along the line. Remember that lines are defined with only two points, but curved lines are defined with three. The endpoint of one arc is the starting point of the next. Listing 16-14 shows examples of each. The shape the query generates is shown in Figure 16-22.

Listing 16-14. Example of Mixing Straight and Curved Lines Using COMPOUNDCURVE

```
DECLARE @g geometry = 'COMPOUNDCURVE(CIRCULARSTRING(2 0, 0 2, -2 0), (-2 0, 2 0))';
SELECT @g;
```

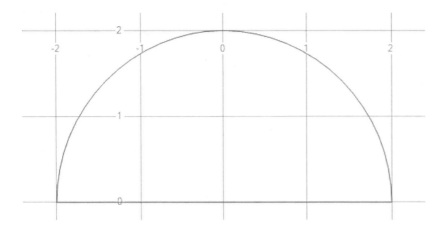

Figure 16-22. *Using COMPOUNDCURVE to mix lines and curved segments*

■ **Note**   This chapter only scratches the surface of the available features included in SQL Server for the geography and geometry data types. SQL Server includes a large number of additional methods and performance improvement for these data types such as FULLGLOBE and GEOGRAPHY_AUTO_GRID. If your job requires you to understand more on this subject or if you are simply curious, I suggest you go to http://msdn.microsoft.com/en-us/library/ff848797(v=SQL.120).aspx for more information.

Sparse Columns

Whenever you store fixed-length data, such as any of the numeric data types and some of the string data types, the data takes up the same amount of space in the database even when storing NULL values. By using the new sparse option, you can significantly reduce the amount of storage for NULL values. The tradeoff is that the non-NULL values of sparse columns take up slightly more space than values stored in regular columns, and there is a small performance decrease when retrieving the non-NULL values. To use sparse columns, the option must be specified when creating the table. You can also include a special type of column, called a *column set*, to return all the sparse columns as XML. Type in and execute Listing 16-15 to learn more.

Listing 16-15. Using Sparse Columns

```
USE tempdb;
GO

--1
IF OBJECT_ID('dbo.SparseData') IS NOT NULL BEGIN
    DROP TABLE dbo.SparseData;
END;
GO
```

```
--2
CREATE TABLE dbo.SparseData
    (ID INT NOT NULL PRIMARY KEY,
    sc1 INT SPARSE NULL,
    sc2 INT SPARSE NULL,
    sc3 INT SPARSE NULL,
    cs XML COLUMN_SET FOR ALL_SPARSE_COLUMNS);
GO

--3
INSERT INTO dbo.SparseData(ID,sc1,sc2,sc3)
VALUES  (1,1,NULL,3),(2,NULL,1,1),(3,NULL,NULL,1);

--4
INSERT INTO SparseData(ID,cs)
SELECT 4,'<sc2>5</sc2>';

--5
SELECT * FROM dbo.SparseData;

--6
SELECT ID, sc1, sc2, sc3, cs FROM SparseData;
```

Figure 16-23 shows the results of running this code. Code section 1 drops the dbo.SparseData table if it exists. Statement 2 creates the table with a primary key column, ID; three sparse integer columns; and the XML column, cs. Statement 3 inserts three rows into the table, leaving out the cs column. Statement 4 inserts a row, but this time only providing values for ID and cs. Query 5 uses the asterisks to return all the columns and rows with surprising results. Instead of returning the individual sparse columns, the cs column provides the sparse data. Query 6 shows that you can still retrieve these columns individually if you need to and validates the cs column. Statement 4 provides a value only for the cs column and not the sparse columns. Query 6 proves that statement 4 inserted the data correctly into the sparse column.

	ID	cs
1	1	<sc1>1</sc1><sc3>3</sc3>
2	2	<sc2>1</sc2><sc3>1</sc3>
3	3	<sc3>1</sc3>
4	4	<sc2>5</sc2>

	ID	sc1	sc2	sc3	cs
1	1	1	NULL	3	<sc1>1</sc1><sc3>3</sc3>
2	2	NULL	1	1	<sc2>1</sc2><sc3>1</sc3>
3	3	NULL	NULL	1	<sc3>1</sc3>
4	4	NULL	5	NULL	<sc2>5</sc2>

Figure 16-23. *The results of using sparse columns*

Because there is increased overhead when using sparse columns and because non-NULL values of sparse columns take a bit more space, Microsoft suggests that you use this feature only when the data will contain mostly NULL values. SQL Server Books Online contains a table in the "Using Sparse Columns" article showing the percentage of NULL values the data should contain in order to make using the sparse columns beneficial.

To make it easier to work with the new sparse columns, Microsoft introduced a type of index called a *filtered index*. By using a filtered index, you can filter out the NULL values from the sparse columns right in the index.

Thinking About Performance

SQL Server provides a multitude of data types including the special data types covered in this chapter. Choosing the correct data types can directly affect performance and storage efficiency of the database. I once had to troubleshoot issues with a database that had one data type in the entire database—VARCHAR(MAX). Just because that data type could store all the data in the database did not mean that it was a good idea.

One area in particular that can cause difficult-to-track-down performance problems is comparing expressions of different data types. The database engine sometimes must convert one side of the expression so that the values can be compared. For example, a string cannot be compared to a number without converting the string to a number. When the conversion is part of a query, it is called an *explicit conversion*. Otherwise it is called an *implicit conversion*. Either way, converting a column can cause an index to be scanned as any other function can do.

You can see the implicit conversion in the execution plan. Listing 16-16 shows an example. Be sure to turn on the Include Actual Execution Plan setting before running statements 2 and 3.

Listing 16-16. Implicit Conversions

```
USE AdventureWorks;
GO

--1
CREATE TABLE #Test(ID VARCHAR(20) PRIMARY KEY, LastName VARCHAR(25), FirstName VARCHAR(25));
CREATE INDEX ndxTest ON #Test(LastName);

INSERT INTO #Test(ID, LastName, FirstName)
SELECT BusinessEntityID, LastName, FirstName
FROM Person.Person;

--2
SELECT ID
FROM #Test
WHERE ID = 285;

--3
SELECT ID
FROM #Test
WHERE ID = '285';
```

When you look at the execution plans for statements 2 and 3, you will see that statement 2 performs an index scan and statement 3 performs an index seek. Hold the mouse cursor over the index scan operator to see the properties (Figure 16-24). The Predicate property shows the implicit conversion that causes the problem. SQL Server implicitly converted the ID value in every row to a number before comparing it to the number 285.

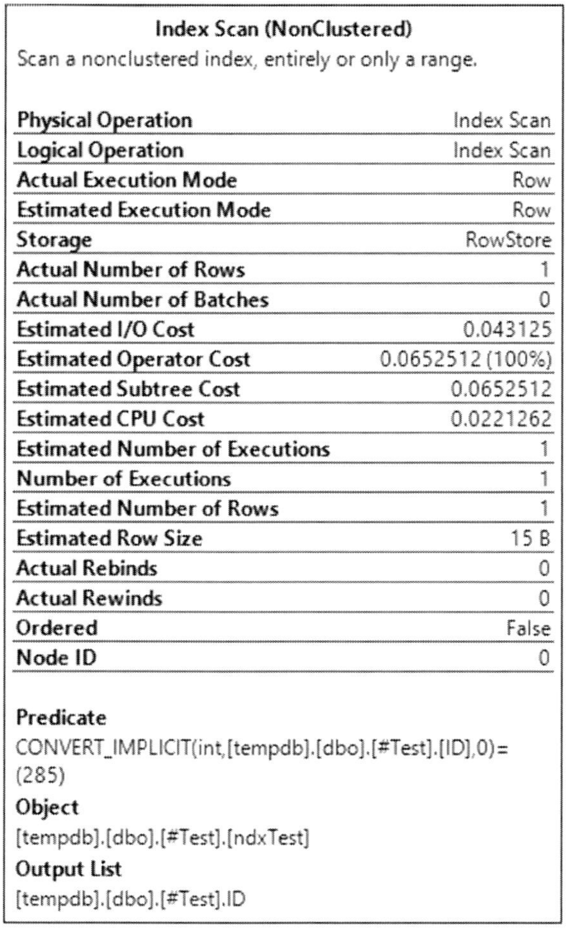

Index Scan (NonClustered)
Scan a nonclustered index, entirely or only a range.

Physical Operation	Index Scan
Logical Operation	Index Scan
Actual Execution Mode	Row
Estimated Execution Mode	Row
Storage	RowStore
Actual Number of Rows	1
Actual Number of Batches	0
Estimated I/O Cost	0.043125
Estimated Operator Cost	0.0652512 (100%)
Estimated Subtree Cost	0.0652512
Estimated CPU Cost	0.0221262
Estimated Number of Executions	1
Number of Executions	1
Estimated Number of Rows	1
Estimated Row Size	15 B
Actual Rebinds	0
Actual Rewinds	0
Ordered	False
Node ID	0

Predicate
CONVERT_IMPLICIT(int,[tempdb].[dbo].[#Test].[ID],0) = (285)
Object
[tempdb].[dbo].[#Test].[ndxTest]
Output List
[tempdb].[dbo].[#Test].ID

Figure 16-24. *The properties of the scan*

Keep data type incompatibilities in mind when troubleshooting performance issues.

Summary

By practicing the skills taught in Chapters 1 through 15, you should become a very proficient T-SQL developer. This chapter introduced you to advanced data types available in SQL Server and how to work with them. You now know that you should not use TEXT, NTEXT, and IMAGE types going forward and that the new MAX data types should be used for very large columns. If you must store files, such as Microsoft Word documents or video, you know about the FILESTREAM and FILETABLE options. The new HIERARCHYID type and the spatial types of GEOGRAPHY and GEOMETRY are available for special-purpose applications. You also have a new way to save space when working with tables that have many columns containing mostly NULLs. You now know what these types can do as well as the downsides of using these types. Armed with this knowledge, you can come up with solutions to challenging problems that may not occur to others on your team.

In Chapter 17 you will learn how to run SQL Server in the cloud!

■ ■ ■

Running SQL Server in the Cloud

I must confess that when I hear the phrase "in the cloud" I immediately picture white fluffy clouds with desktop computers, complete with monitors and keyboards strewn about. I'm not sure where this image originated because I know that Microsoft has datacenters worldwide that are situated firmly on the ground consisting of thousands of commodity servers in racks that look nothing like desktop computers. Microsoft's cloud services are branded *Microsoft Azure.*

The enterprise computing landscape is ever evolving, and right now, companies are taking advantage of cloud services, like Microsoft Azure, to save money and be more flexible. Large companies are using cloud services for many purposes. Some are obvious, such as secondary backup locations. Companies are moving their web-based applications entirely to the cloud. In the case of Microsoft Azure SQL Database, it is possible to scale up and down quickly as needs change over time. The beauty of this, over traditional onsite datacenters, is that you just pay for what you use.

Imagine buying and configuring the hardware for an application that is used mainly during the holiday season. You would have to buy hardware good enough to handle the load during the busiest time. During the other 9 or 10 months of the year, that hardware would be sitting mostly idle. If the application and database were built instead in Azure, you could scale out during the busy months and scale back during the slow months. You would pay more during the busy months and save a lot of money during the slow months.

The world moves quickly in the cloud. Microsoft makes frequent announcements about new services, enhanced features, and pricing changes. Microsoft has been releasing a new version of SQL Server approximately every two years since 2008. You will see feature announcements much more frequently with Microsoft Azure SQL Database.

There are two ways to run SQL Server in the cloud. The first is very similar to how you do it today on your own servers, however, you do not purchase and provision the hardware. You can create Azure virtual machines (VMs) and run the desired version and edition of SQL Server on the VM. Once you have SQL Server running in the VM, you can create your databases. The second method is by creating a Microsoft Azure SQL Database. In this case, you create just the database; you do not spin up a VM.

This chapter will discuss the advantages and how to get started with each method.

Procuring a Microsoft Azure Account

I have an MSDN (Microsoft Developer Network) subscription. The level of my subscription gives me $150 worth of Azure services to use each month. This allows me to create VMs and databases for development, learning, experimenting, and teaching only. If I wanted to create a production database or application, I would have to use a paid account.

If you have an MSDN subscription, be sure to activate your free Azure benefits. One nice thing about this benefit is that if you accidently use the entire allowance during a given month, the services will just stop. You won't be charged unless you configure the account to do so.

If you are not lucky enough to have an MSDN subscription, you can still sign up for a free trial of Azure. At the time of this writing, you can get a one-month trial consisting of $200 worth of services (http://azure.microsoft.com/en-us/pricing/free-trial/).

If you decide that you will need an account for longer than a month or one that is licensed for production workloads, there are several options. You can "pay as you go" with no commitment. You will pay for only the services you enable. There are also two prepay options. You can sign up for $500 or $1000 worth of services per month. By doing so, you get additional discounts and unused services rollover. See http://azure.microsoft.com/en-us/pricing/purchase-options/ for information about paid plans.

The Azure Dashboard

Microsoft provides a web-based dashboard for provisioning and managing your Windows Azure services. Figure 17-1 shows my dashboard with my service names blurred out.

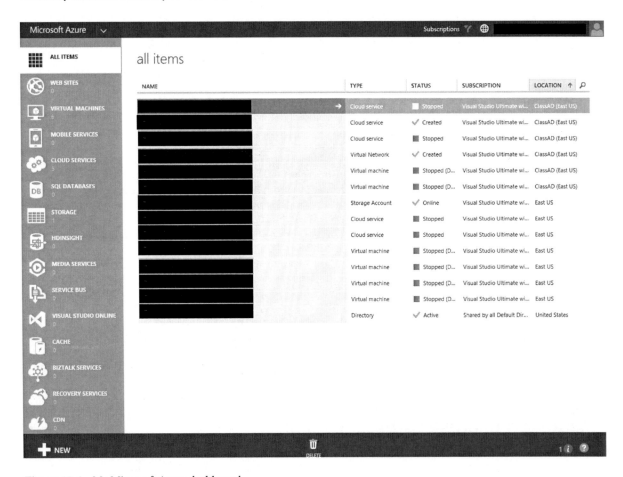

Figure 17-1. *My Microsoft Azure dashboard*

The possible services are listed along the left side of the screen. In addition to VMs and Microsoft Azure SQL Databases, you can create web sites, mobile services, storage, HDInsight for analyzing big data, and more. This chapter will just focus on VMs and Microsoft Azure SQL Database.

Clicking one of the service types on the left will filter your list of services on the right. You can then manage each service.

Windows Azure Virtual Machines

Virtual Machines is my favorite Azure feature. I love how I can create a new VM in just a few minutes. As long as I keep the VM stopped while I am not using it, the charges are minimal. There are still charges for the storage, but the VM itself doesn't generate charges when it is not running. Obviously, this isn't usually possible for production servers, but for learning and experimenting it is a great option.

Many companies take advantage of virtual machines in their own data centers. In fact, your production SQL Servers could be running on VMs today and you wouldn't even know it. The idea is that powerful servers running special software for virtualization, called a *hypervisor*, would then host many individual guest servers. The benefits of this arrangement include the ability to flexibly reassign resources as the VMs need them, increased availability because it is possible to quickly move a VM to another host, decreased procurement time, and cost savings.

You have the ability to upload an existing VM, create a blank VM and install everything, or create one using a template. To create your Windows Azure VM, you must first make some decisions. Which operating system will you need? Do you want SQL Server to be preinstalled? Do you want a SharePoint VM? You can even create a Linux VM from a template. In this example, let's take advantage of the templates by following these steps:

1. Click the Virtual Machines link on the left side of the dashboard.

2. If you have any existing VMs, you will see them listed. Click the +New icon at the bottom of the screen (Figure 17-2).

Figure 17-2. *Click to create a new VM*

3. Select Compute ➤ Virtual Machine ➤ From Gallery, as shown in Figure 17-3.

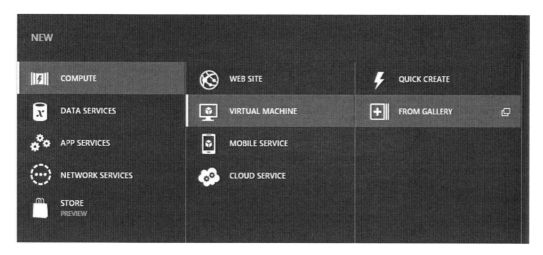

Figure 17-3. *Create a VM from a template*

CHAPTER 17 ■ RUNNING SQL SERVER IN THE CLOUD

4. The next step is to select the image. Notice that there are many options for non-Microsoft servers as well as for the expected Windows Servers. Because this book is about SQL Server, select SQL Server from the list to filter the list of templates available. If you are familiar with the Windows 8 operating system, select SQL Server 2014 RTM Enterprise, as shown in Figure 17-4. If you are still used to the traditional Windows 7 operating system, you should probably select one of the images using Windows Server 2008 R2 instead. After selecting an image, click the arrow at the bottom right.

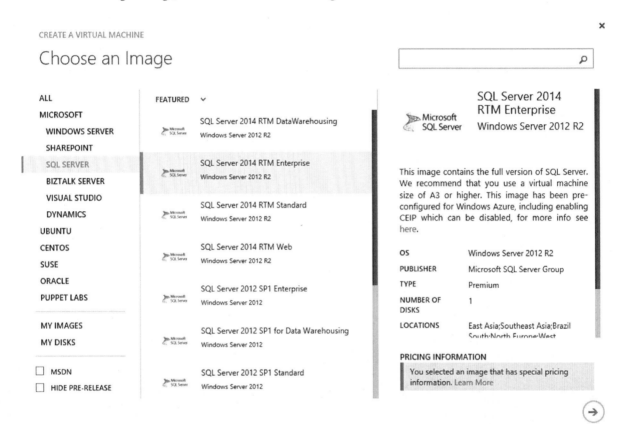

Figure 17-4. *Select SQL Server 2014 RTM Enterprise*

5. On the Virtual machine configuration page, type in a name for your new VM.

6. Select the Tier, either Basic or Standard. Basic is fine for a test machine, but you will probably want Standard for production servers to take advantage of several features such as load balancing.

7. Select a machine size. This will directly affect both your performance and the price you pay. For this example, select A3.

8. Enter a User Name. This name will be the administrator account for the server. Be sure to write down the name.

9. Finally, enter a password for the administrator account and write it down. Figure 17-5 shows how my screen looks. Click the right arrow when your page is complete.

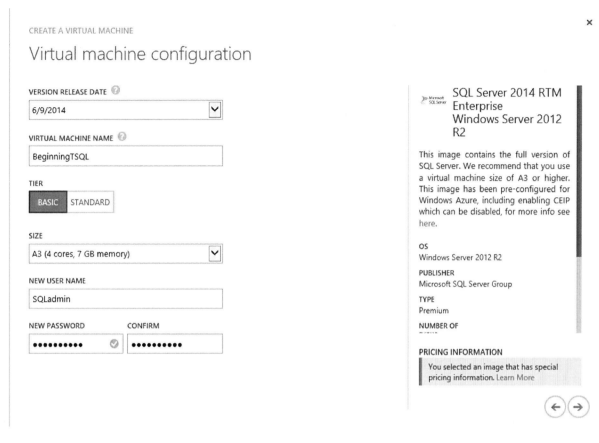

Figure 17-5. *The Virtual machine configuration*

10. The next screen is also called Virtual machine configuration, but it has a different set of questions. If this is your first VM, you will need to create a new cloud service. Otherwise, you could select an existing service from the list.

11. Your new cloud service name will be automatically filled in for you.

12. In the Region/Affinity Group/Virtual Network box, select a region that is close to you geographically.

13. Leave the Storage Account set to automatically generate an account or select an existing one from the list if this is not your first VM.

14. For practice VMs, you can leave the Availability Set at (none). Figure 17-6 shows how you may have this set up. Click the right arrow when you are done.

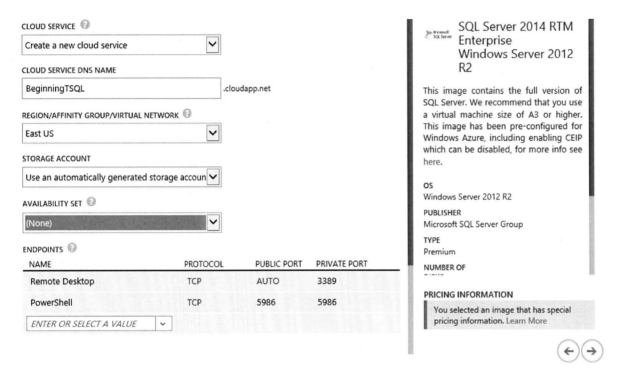

Figure 17-6. *Setting up the cloud service*

15. Another screen provides several options for the VM. These options allow you to manage administration and security of the VMs. Make sure that Install the VM agent is selected and click the checkbox.

After following the steps, you will see the dashboard once again. Your new VM will be listed, but it will take a few minutes before it is available for you to use. Compare that to the amount of time it would take if you had to order hardware, put everything together, and then install the operating system.

Make sure that the VM status says Running as shown in Figure 17-7 before trying to connect to the VM. Click the Status column next to the server name and then click the Connect button at the bottom of the screen.

virtual machines

INSTANCES   IMAGES   DISKS

Figure 17-7. *The new VM is ready*

If you are asked if you want to save or open the file, select Open. You will be using Remote Desktop to connect to your server, as shown in Figure 17-8. Check "Don't ask me again for connections to this computer" and click Connect.

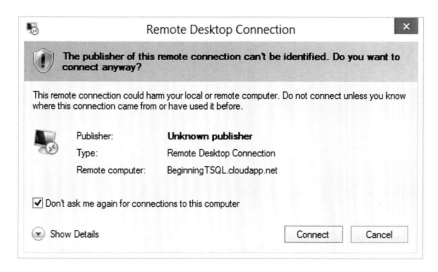

Figure 17-8. *The Remote Desktop Connection*

When prompted, use the admin account and password you set up earlier in steps 8 and 9 to log into the server, as shown in Figure 17-9.

Figure 17-9. *Enter the credentials*

Congratulations! You are now remote controlling your first Azure VM.

SQL Server is installed on this server just waiting for you to add user databases. You can add the AdventureWorks databases or create a new one if you wish.

When you are done with the VM, be sure to shut it down using the menu on the Azure dashboard. The next time you want to use your VM, just start it up again. This will prevent the meter from running when you don't need the VM.

The Windows Azure Virtual Machines feature is a great way to set up "playgrounds" for learning and experimenting. I have created several for writing articles and technical editing of other book projects. I have also created Azure VMs for writing this book.

Azure SQL Database

The previous section described how to set up servers in the cloud running SQL Server. This section will explain a strictly cloud-based database called Windows Azure SQL Database, or SQL Database for short. To make the meaning clear, I will use the term Azure SQL Database in this chapter. Notice that the word "server" is missing from the name. That's because you don't actually have control of a server, just databases.

Part of the appeal of Azure SQL Database is that you can provision a database in seconds and never have to worry about reboots, upgrades, or backups. Microsoft automatically performs most of the maintenance for you. Another interesting thing about Azure SQL Database is the pricing. The monthly rate is calculated based on the database size and prorated based on the day.

Luckily, the majority of T-SQL DML and DDL commands are exactly the same as those used in traditional SQL Server. Microsoft is adding new features regularly to Azure SQL Database, and it is possible that some features will appear in the cloud before the traditional versions of SQL Server.

Because the features can change rapidly, I won't attempt to list all the differences. To see up-to-date information, review the current official information found at `http://msdn.microsoft.com/en-us/library/ee336250.aspx`. You should also visit the Azure SQL Database Transact-SQL Reference found at `http://msdn.microsoft.com/en-us/library/ee336281.aspx`. As a beginning T-SQL developer, the majority of features you probably care about are supported.

To get started with SQL Database, follow these instructions:

1. Log on to your Windows Azure Dashboard.

2. Select SQL Databases.

3. Click +New found in the bottom menu.

4. Select Data Services ➤ SQL Database ➤ Quick Create, as shown in Figure 17-10.

Figure 17-10. *Create a SQL Database*

5. Fill in a name for the database.

6. In the Server selection, if this is your first Azure SQL Database, choose New SQL database server. Otherwise, select a previous server from the drop-down list. You won't actually have control of a server; this is more of a way to organize your databases.

7. Select a region that is close to you.

8. Create a login and password. Be sure to write these down.

9. Click the check mark next to Create SQL Database at the bottom of the form.

It took less than 10 seconds for my database's status to change to Online after clicking the check mark. There is still some configuration to do. To increase security, only connections from known IP addresses are allowed. Make sure your database is selected and click Manage. When you do, a message will pop up asking to include your current IP address in the firewall rules. Click Yes to continue and then Yes again when asked if you want to manage the database. Enter the username and password from step 8 above and click Log On.

You should now see the Azure SQL Database dashboard, which allows you to create tables and write queries. This dashboard can also change frequently as Microsoft adds new functionality. At the time of this writing, it looked like Figure 17-11.

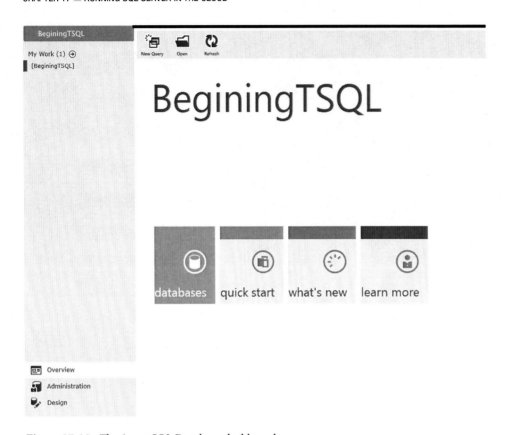

Figure 17-11. *The Azure SQL Database dashboard*

To create a table, click the Design link and then New Table. Fill out the form with column names and data types as shown in Figure 17-12 and then click Save.

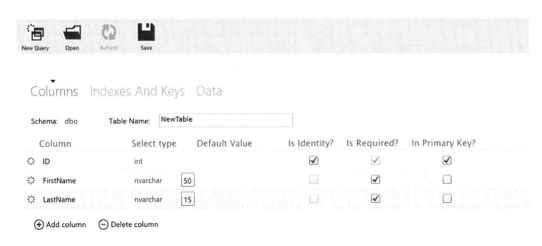

Figure 17-12. *Create a new table*

Click New Query to open a query window. In this window you can type in and run Listing 17-1 if you created the table shown in Figure 17-12.

Listing 17-1. Create a Table in SQL Database

```
--1
INSERT INTO dbo.NewTable(FirstName, LastName)
VALUES('Ken','Sanchez'),('Terri','Duffy'),('Roberto','Tamburello');

--2
SELECT ID, FirstName, LastName
FROM NewTable;
```

Figure 17-13 shows the results of running this code.

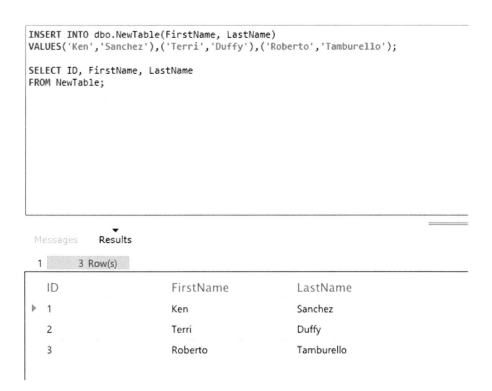

Figure 17-13. *The results of populating a table in SQL Database*

At the time of this writing, no IntelliSense was available. It is, however, possible to see the execution plan. Select just query 2 and click the Actual Plan icon. After the query runs, click the Query Plan link. Figure 17-14 shows the execution plan.

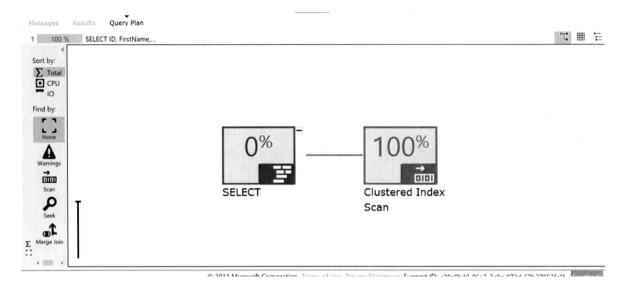

Figure 17-14. *The execution plan*

Although the interface for working with your SQL Databases is improving over time as Microsoft adds new features, it still might be easier to work with the database through SQL Server Management Studio (SSMS). Follow these steps to connect using SSMS:

1. Log on to the Microsoft Azure dashboard.

2. Click the name of your database, as shown in Figure 17-15.

sql databases

Figure 17-15. *Find your SQL Database*

3. You will now see a page with many tasks you can perform to manage this database. Near the bottom of the page, copy the connection string, as shown in Figure 17-16.

beginingtsql

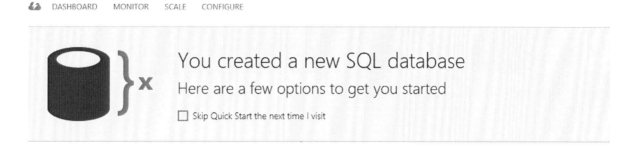

Get Microsoft database design tools ⊚
Install Microsoft SQL Server Data Tools

Design your SQL database ⊚
Download a starter project for your SQL database   Set up Windows Azure firewall rules for this IP address

Connect to your database ⊚
Design your SQL database   Run Transact-SQL queries against your SQL database   View SQL Database connection strings for ADO .Net, ODBC, PHP, and JDBC

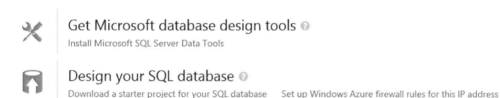

Figure 17-16. *Copy the connection string*

4. Start up SSMS.

5. When prompted to connect, paste in the connection string you copied from the Azure page.

6. Change the Authentication to SQL Server Authentication.

7. Type in the username and password you used to create the database and click Connect.

You should be able to see the table you created and use the Query Window to write queries. This may be a more comfortable environment to work in; however, at the time of this writing, you are still missing features such as IntelliSense.

Even though most T-SQL statements are compatible, there are some things to keep in mind when working with Azure SQL Database. First, some of the database administration-type tasks are taken care of by Microsoft, such as fault tolerance or high-availability and Database Console Commands (DBCC) to check for database consistency.

For fault tolerance, Microsoft automatically creates three replicas of each database. You don't have access to the replicas, but one of the replicas will become active in case of a problem. This is seamless; there is no change to the connection properties when a replica takes over. To set up something similar in your own data center is expensive and requires the efforts of highly skilled database and network professionals.

Throttling

Another thing to keep in mind is the concept of *multitenancy*. This means that your database is hosted on a server with databases belonging to other customers. You can only see your databases, and no one else can see your database. Except for the master database, you cannot see any system databases. Even within master, most system tables don't exists or at least you don't have permission to run them. Try running Listing 17-2 in both your Azure database and an on-premises SQL Server database.

Listing 17-2. Querying System Tables

```
--1
SELECT * FROM sys.databases;

--2
SELECT * FROM sys.database_files;
```

After running the statements in both types of databases, you'll find that statement 1 will run in both, but statement 2 will work only against the traditional SQL Server.

Because multiple customers will have databases on the same servers, what happens if one customer runs a query that takes the majority of the resources on the server? In a case like that, and I'm sure it happens often, the offending connections are throttled, preventing writing and sometimes reading to the database. It is possible to upgrade your databases to the Premium edition, in preview at the time of this writing, for a higher price so that your databases are immune to throttling.

Database Size Limitations

From the beginning of Azure SQL Database availability, the database size has been limited. Frequently, however, Microsoft will announce new, larger sizes. At the time of this writing, an Azure SQL Database can be up to 150GB, which can be relatively constricting in today's database world. To get around this limitation, applications can be designed to split the data over several databases.

Another benefit to this is called *elasticity*. Elasticity is the ability to scale out to multiple databases in times of heavy activity. For example, imagine that you have an application that collects information during elections. You can increase the number of databases on election day and roll the data back into a smaller number of databases once the election is complete. This would also improve performance because the transactions would be spread over many databases.

There are two ways to accomplish this scale out. The first method is called *sharding*. When you decide to use sharding, you will provision multiple databases, and it is up to you when you create your application to direct the inserts into the appropriate databases. The second method is called *federation*. Federation works automatically to spread the data over the federated database. Unfortunately, Microsoft is discontinuing this functionality and recommends using the custom sharding method.

Pricing

You pay for Azure SQL Databases based on the size and service tier of the database. At the time of this writing, there are two service tiers available, Basic and Standard. Microsoft has announced that these tiers will be retired in April 2015 and will be replaced with Basic, Standard, and Premium tiers. The Premium version will allow you to avoid throttling and also has advanced business continuity features including point in time restores.

The charge for databases is prorated by the day that the database exists. If you create a database and then delete it a few seconds later, you will pay for one day. This is another reason that scaling out when needed has such great cost benefits. Scale out when your requirements increase, and scale back when your requirements decrease. Be sure to delete any databases that you create just to experiment when you are done using them to minimize charges.

There is one more thing to keep in mind about pricing. You are also charged for data leaving the data center. The results from a query that you run in the Management Portal or from an Azure web application do not leave the data center. The results from a query that you run from SSMS or from a non-Azure hosted web application do leave the data center. For more information about pricing, see http://azure.microsoft.com/en-us/pricing/details/sql-database/.

AZURE SQL DATABASE REAL-WORLD EXPERIENCE

By Kim Tessereau

SQL Azure can be quite a mystery until you actually begin to work with it. And even then, there is so much that is unknown and unpublished that even the experienced database administrator finds it hard to transverse over the new terrain called Azure SQL Database.

When I was first assigned the task of moving one of our flagship applications into Azure, I was excited that I was going to finally get experience working with Azure. So like any good database administrator, I started my research by trying to hunt down a good book so I could get some basic knowledge on using Azure. Well that search ended abruptly when I couldn't find a book on Azure that was more than a high-level introduction to a rather elusive product. To save time, I found a two-day hands-on class that had you create a small Azure database along with a small application to show how Azure works. Everything went great during the labs and everything seemed so straightforward. Unfortunately, that wasn't the case in the real world. Once I returned to work, I started to play around with Azure and found some things that were really limiting, such as not being able to run certain types of DBCC. Then I slowly started to realize that I didn't need to be able to run some of these commands because Microsoft took care of a lot administration overhead. And disaster recovery in Azure was taken care of by the "cloud."

The main lesson that we learned was you have to pick the right type of application to put into the Azure cloud. There is a rather exhaustive list of features that are not supported in Azure SQL Database including things like SQL Agent Jobs and Replication. The design of your application is very dependent on what is available to you in Azure. There are, however, some definite benefits to the cloud for the right type of application.

Summary

The cloud is the future of enterprise computing. There is no turning back now. This chapter has provided a glimpse of what is possible. One thing to keep in mind is that things move fast in the Azure world. Microsoft frequently makes announcements about feature and pricing changes.

Now that you have a good background in T-SQL and some special topics like XML, special data types, and Azure SQL Database, it's time to think about other ways to advance your knowledge. Chapter 18 helps you figure out where to go next.

CHAPTER 18

■ ■ ■

Where to Go Next?

I hope you have enjoyed learning about T-SQL as much as I have enjoyed writing about it. Not everyone is cut out to be a T-SQL developer; it helps to really enjoy writing code. Programming is not something you can just learn and be done with it. You will continue to learn new techniques as long as you are programming T-SQL. The other thing you can count on is that Microsoft will continue to add new features to SQL Server, including new T-SQL features, giving you more to learn about. In fact, this book describes numerous, T-SQL enhancements only found in SQL Server 2012 and later versions.

You may have read this book from cover to cover, typing in all the sample code and performing the exercises found in most of the chapters. If you are like me, you may have just skipped around looking for specific knowledge as you needed it, using the book as a reference. Either way, you would have found simple examples that showed you how to use a specific feature or solve a particular problem. Each chapter used techniques from the previous chapters to solve more complex query problems as the book progressed.

I began writing T-SQL queries 17 years ago. I had a book that was about four inches thick on my desk that contained just about everything I needed to know about SQL Server at the time, including T-SQL. I remember constantly looking up how to join tables, write aggregate queries, or perform updates until, eventually, I just knew the syntax. As I learned even more techniques, the syntax I knew continued to grow. Since then, Microsoft has introduced several new versions of SQL Server, expanding the feature set each time. I would probably need four or five books the size of my old reference to cover everything offered with SQL Server today. The T-SQL I used 17 years ago looks much the same as it does today but it has evolved in tremendous ways. And that is just the T-SQL language. SQL Server is far more than just a relational engine with many components used to make businesses run smoothly and help executives make the correct decisions.

The world of databases never stops changing. The buzzwords of today, like cloud and big data, may be the norm tomorrow. There is always more to learn. If you are like me, you find that pretty exciting!

Online Resources

Besides having a great reference book in your hands, what other ways can you learn? A wealth of knowledge is available for free on the Web. You can post questions on newsgroups and forums; read articles, blogs, and white papers; and even view videos explaining how to write T-SQL code. Someone else has already posted an answer, blog, or article that covers just about anything you could ever want to know. Here are some of my favorite sites featuring SQL Server information:

- `www.sqlservercentral.com`

- `www.sqlteam.com`

- `www.microsoft.com/sqlserver/en/us/community.aspx`

- `www.sql-server-performance.com`

- `sqlblog.com`

- sqlserverpedia.com

- www.sqlshare.com

- www.mssqltips.com

- blogs.msdn.com/b/sqlcat

- www.simple-talk.com

At the time of this writing, social networking sites such as Facebook, LinkedIn, and Twitter make the news every day. These sites provide yet another way to get answers to questions by discussing the issues with colleagues across the world. For example, if you send a SQL Server question on Twitter and use hashtag #sqlhelp, you'll get professionals from around the world willing to answer your question.

Because of printing and shipping costs and the impact of online resources, publishers are moving print magazines to online services only. I suspect that over time we will see less and less paper and even more online subscription resources. You'll also want to take advantage of e-books, which can be quickly downloaded onto your e-reader and are much less expensive to purchase this way than physical books.

Conferences

If you get the chance, attend a conference such as the Professional Association for SQL Server (PASS) Summit, PASS SQL Rally, SQL Connections, SQL Bits, and SQL Saturday, to name a few. The beauty of attending conferences is that you get a chance to talk with the gurus and experts as well as listen to the presentations. You also get to meet other people who face many of the same issues you do and learn about the solutions they have developed. Conferences can get you out of your day-to-day environment, get you refreshed, and get you excited about the future.

Just as more and more traditionally printed material now appears on the Internet, you can also attend virtual conferences via the Web. The PASS organization hosts several free online conferences each year called 24 Hours of PASS. The advantages to virtual conferences over in-person conferences are in cost savings and lack of travel. The disadvantage, of course, is not getting to meet the speakers and other attendees face to face. Either way, attending conferences is a great way to learn about SQL Server.

User Groups

Many metropolitan areas have user groups dedicated to programming languages or using certain software. These groups often provide pizza, prizes, and educational presentations at meetings held on a scheduled basis. To find a list of user groups that are associated with PASS, go to www.sqlpass.org. User group membership is usually free. A few dedicated volunteers run most user groups, and sponsors, such as recruiting firms or software vendors, often pay for the food and provide prizes. Not only is attending user group meetings a great way to learn T-SQL and other SQL Server topics, but you may also meet your next employer at a user group meeting!

Also keep an eye out for SQL Saturday events. These events are part of PASS but are arranged by local user groups and volunteers. They occur throughout the year in various locations around the world. A SQL Saturday event is an entire Saturday of SQL Server presentations and—the best part—it's free! To see if there is a SQL Saturday scheduled near you, go to www.sqlsaturday.com/ and check it out.

Vendors

Even though they may have an ulterior motive, such as getting you to buy a product, vendors creating software for SQL Server developers and database administrators often provide a wealth of information. Vendors have educational web sites, webinars, newsletters, and online books all for free. Some of the software vendors employ high-profile SQL Server experts who speak at user group meetings and conferences to provide education to the SQL Server community.

Books

Even though there are many online resources available to you, nothing beats a great book that you can carry with you on an airplane or a bus. You now have the choice to buy the physical book, download the book as a computer file, or read the book on a subscription device such as a Kindle or Nook. The great thing about books by Apress authors, regardless of how you access the books, is that they are written by developers and database administrators who have worked at real jobs—just like you. Apress authors can pass along the benefit of their experience as well as their knowledge.

If you need to get started learning a language or need to really focus on a particular area, a well-organized book will save you a lot of time vs. hunting down resources on the Web. When learning a new programming language, follow the examples from cover to cover at first. Then, once you are familiar with the language, save your book as a reference for when you need more information about a particular topic.

Classes

If you live in a metropolitan area, many training centers offer SQL Server courses. These classes are a great way to get you started with a new language, especially if you learn better in person than with a book or video. Another benefit is being able to ask the instructor questions, often even after the class is over by e-mail. Like conferences, getting out of the regular work environment helps you focus and learn. I encourage you to attend training classes, especially if your employer is willing to foot the bill.

SQL Server Documentation

Refer to SQL Server Books Online (`http://technet.microsoft.com/en-us/library/ms130214.aspx`) often. I am constantly surprised to learn new ways to use T-SQL features from taking a look at Books Online when I thought I already knew all there was to know about a feature. I often use Books Online as a starting point and then see how someone else explains the same concept in a book or article.

One thing that I don't like about Books Online is how the syntax is presented. The syntax examples include every possible option, making it, in my opinion, difficult to understand. I usually skip down to the example code to figure it out. I hope you learned a lot by the way this book presented the syntax examples, showing only what you needed to see to learn the particular topic at hand.

Practice, Practice, and More Practice

The only way to really learn T-SQL is by doing it. You can have an entire bookshelf filled with T-SQL books, attend conferences and classes, ask questions, and surf the Web, but you won't learn T-SQL without practicing it yourself. I am reminded of a recent television episode of *The Big Bang Theory* where one of the characters thought he could learn to swim by just reading about swimming on the Web. The more you practice and experiment, the faster you will learn.

This book is full of examples and exercises that you can use to experiment. What will happen if you tweak this query, or how can you change that query so that it runs more efficiently? Keep working at it; keep learning.

Teach Someone Else

I am always amazed at how much I learn when I must explain a concept to another developer or write about a T-SQL topic. To use a feature, you have to understand it or at least successfully follow an example, but to teach it, you have to know it at an entirely different level. I have learned so much by writing this book, not only about the process of writing a book, but also about writing T-SQL code. I have been surprised that writing a query one way didn't really give me the performance increase I expected. I have also learned about using optional parameters or perhaps a different way to use a particular feature. To explain a concept to you, I had to really think about how the query works, not just how to make it work.

I have learned a lot writing this book. Thank you for learning along with me.

Index

▦ A

ABS function, 82
Accumulating aggregates, 169
    ROWS *vs.* RANGE, 177
    total calculations, 176–177
Administrative functions, 89–90
Advanced queries, 241
    aggregate query, 252
        CROSS APPLY technique, 255
        derived tables, 253
        OUTER APPLY technique, 255
        SELECT list, 252–253
        table expressions, 254–255
    CTEs (*see* Common table expressions (CTEs))
    CUBE and ROLLUP, 264
    GROUPING SETS clause, 263
    MERGE statement
        coding, 261
        output, 262
        syntax, 260
    OUTPUT clause, 256
        data manipulation, 257–258
        INTO keyword, 259
        save OUTPUT data, 259
        syntax, 256
    paging
        definition, 271
        OFFSET/FETCH NEXT
          method, 272
        WHERE clause, 272
        with T-SQL, 271
    pivoted queries (*see* Pivoted queries)
AdventureWorks databases, 14–15, 28, 33
Aggregate functions, 147, 165
Aggregate queries, 147
    aggregate functions, 147, 165
    AVG and NULL function, 162

DISTINCT Keyword, 167
    aggregate expression, 159
    vs. GROUP BY clause, 158
GROUP BY clause, 166
    coding, 150
    grouping expressions, 151–152
    SELECT list, 150
    syntax, 149
HAVING clause, 166
    aggregate expression, 156
    coding, 156
    definition, 155
    syntax, 155
    WHERE clause, 157
joining tables, 160–161, 168
ORDER BY clause
    coding, 153
    error message, 153
    syntax, 153
Statistics IO tool
    nonclustered indexes, 164
    output of, 163
    RAM, 163
    usage, 162
WHERE clause, 154
Alias, 36
Analytic functions, 169, 190
    FIRST_VALUE and LAST_VALUE, 180–181
    LAG and LEAD, 179
    PERCENTILE_CONT and PERCENTILE_DISC, 182–183
    PERCENT_RANK and CUME_DIST, 181–182
AND and OR logical operators, 199–200
Arrays, 298
    ArrayIndex, 299
    NOCOUNT property, 299
Asterisk (*) technique, 65
Atomicity, 309
AVG function, 147, 162

Azure SQL Database, 440
    administrator, 447
    creation, 441
    dashboard, 442
    execution plan, 444
    instructions, 440
    limitations, 446
    multi tenancy, 446
    Premium version, 446
    SSMS, 444–445
    table creation, 442

■ B

BETWEEN operator, 40
BIGINT, 67
BinaryData column, 406
Books Online, 451

■ C

Cancel Executing Query icon, 103
Cartesian product, 103, 115
CASCADE rule, 336, 338
CASE function
    listing a column as the return value, 87
    overview, 85
    searched CASE, 86
    simple CASE, 85
CAST function, 63, 405
CHARINDEX function, 69
CHAR string data type, 404
Checkpoints, 413
CHOOSE function, 71
CIRCULARSTRING command, 426–427
Cloud services, 433
    Azure SQL Database, 440
        administrator, 447
        creation, 441
        dashboard, 442
        execution plan, 444
        instructions, 440
        limitations, 446
        multi tenancy, 446
        Premium version, 446
        SSMS, 444–445
        table creation, 442–443
    Microsoft Azure dashboard, 434
    MSDN, 433
    VM (see Virtual Machines (VM))
CLR Integration, 368
Clustered index, 27
COALESCE, 62, 89
CodePlex samples, 14
Column sets, 428

Common table expressions (CTEs)
    data manipulation with, 251
    derived tables, 241
    joining, 247
    multiple
        creation, 242
        partial results, 246
        query with, 245
        SELECT statement, 242
        syntax, 242
    overview, 138–139
    recursive code
        definition, 248
        partial results of, 250
        UNION ALL query, 249
    self-join, 246
    syntax, 241
    using to solve complicated join problem, 139–141
Composite key, 330
COMPOUNDCURVE command, 426–427
Computed columns, 221
CONCAT function, 242
CONCAT statement, 61
Conferences, 450
Consistency, 309
CONTAINS function, 203–204
CONVERT function, 63, 79, 405
COUNT function, 147
CROSS JOIN, 115–116

■ D

Database Engine Configuration, 7
Database schemas, 28
Data Definition Language (DDL) statements, 325
DATALENGTH function, 69
Data manipulation, 211
    database cleanup, 236–237
    row deletion, 224, 240
        DELETE statement, 224, 226
        demo table creation, 225
        EXISTS statement, 227
        truncate, 229
    row insertion, 238–239
        another table, 216–217
        autopopulated columns, 222–223
        computed columns, 221
        dbo.demoCustomer table, 219
        default constraint, 220–221
        error messages, 214
        identity column, 221
        INSERT statement, 212
        INTO keyword, 212
        Invalid INSERT statements, 213–214
        NOT EXISTS method, 217

NOT NULL constraint, 215
overview, 211
primary key constraint, 214
Rowversion column, 221
SELECT INTO statement, 218–219
table creation, 211
UNION ALL queries, 215
VALUES clause, 212
row updation, 230, 240
CASE expression, 230
expressions, 231–233
partial results, 231
UPDATE statement, 230, 232
with Join, 233
set-based *vs.* iterative approaches, 235–236
transactions (*see* Transactions)
Data Manipulation Language (DML) statements, 325
Data types
DATE, 415
DATETIME2, 415
DATETIMEOFFSET, 416
HIERARCHYID
hierarchy creation, 418
HumanResources.Employee table, 417
OrganizationalNode, 417
stored procedures, hierarchical data
management, 420
viewing, 417
large-value binary data types
FILESTREAM (*see* FILESTREAM)
FileTables, 413
VARBINARY(MAX) data, 405
large-value string data types, 404
NTEXT and TEXT data types, 403
VARCHAR(MAX), 404
sparse columns, 428
spatial
circular arcs, 426
GEOGRAPHY, 424
GEOMETRY, 423
results tab, 425
TIME, 415
DATEADD function, 75
DATEDIFF, 77
Date and Time function
CONVERT, 79–80
DATEADD, 75–76
DATEDIFF, 77
DATEFROMPARTS, 81
DATENAME, 77–78
DATEPART, 77–78
DAY, MONTH, and YEAR, 78–79
EOMONTH, 81
FORMAT, 80–81
GETDATE and SYSDATETIME, 75

DATENAME function, 77
DATEPART function, 77, 79
DATETIME2 data type, 415
DATETIMEOFFSET data types, 416
DAY function, 78
dbo.BinaryTest table, 406
Derived tables, 137
DiffInMeters column, 424
DivLevel, 419
DivNode column, 419
Durability, 309

■ **E**

Elasticity, 446
Error handling, 324
RAISERROR function, 317–318
THROW statement, 319
TRY CATCH method, 314–316, 318
untrappable errors, 316–317
Execution plan icon, 54
EXISTS statement, 227
Explicit transaction, 323, 422
Expression using operators
COALESCE, 62
CONCAT, 61
concatenating other data types to strings, 63
concatenating strings and NULL, 60
ISNULL, 62
mathematical operators, 65
string concatenation, 59

■ **F**

Federation, 446
FETCH clauses, 63, 93
FILESTREAM, 7
CHECKPOINT command, 413
column populating, 412
Documents folder, 412
FileData column, 412
NEWSEQUENTIALID function, 412
ROWGUIDID, 412
VARBINARY(MAX) column, 406
working with column, 412
FileTables, 413
FileTableTest.txt, 414
Filtered index, 430
Folding tables, 132
Foreign keys, 101
coding, 334–335
delete and update rules, 336
referential integrity, 333
result, 335
syntax, 334

FORMAT, 80
FOR XML AUTO mode, 385
FOR XML clause
    AUTO mode, 385
    EXPLICIT mode, 386
    modes, 383
    PATH mode, 388
    RAW mode, 383
    SELECT statement, 383
FOR XML EXPLICIT mode, 386
FOR XML PATH mode, 388
FOR XML RAW mode, 383
FREETEXT function, 205
FROM clause, 33, 101–102, 116
FULLGLOBE data type, 428
FULL OUTER JOIN, 114–115
Full-text search, 209
Functions
    date functions (*see* Date and Time function)
    mathematical functions, 82
    nesting functions, 74
    ORDER BY clause, 90
    performance, 93
    string functions (*see* String function)
    system functions (*see* System function)
    WHERE clauses, 90

■ **G**

GEOGRAPHY_AUTO_GRID data type, 428
GEOGRAPHY data type, 422, 424
GEOMETRY data types, 422–423
GETDATE function, 75, 416
GetDescendant method, 420
GetLevel method, 417
GetRoot method, 419
GROUP BY clause, 166
    coding, 150
    grouping expressions, 151–152
    SELECT list, 150
    syntax, 149
GROUPING SETS clause, 263

■ **H**

HIERARCHYID data type, 117
    hierarchy creation, 418
    HumanResources.Employee table, 417
    OrganizationalNode, 417
    stored procedures, hierarchical data
        management, 420
    viewing, 417

■ **I**

Identity column, 221
IIF statement, 88
IMAGE data type, 405
IN list, subqueries in, 127
INNER JOINS, 233
    avoiding incorrect join
        condition, 103–104
    joining on different column name, 104
    joining on more than one column, 105
    joining three or more
        tables, 106–108, 124
    joining two tables, 101, 103
    overview, 101
IN Operator, 47
INT, 67
IntelliSense, 14
ISNULL function, 62, 265
Isolation, 309

■ **J**

Joins, 101
JustTheDate value, 416
JustTheTime values, 416

■ **K**

Kindle, 451

■ **L**

Large-value binary data types
    FILESTREAM (*see* FILESTREAM)
    FileTables, 413
    VARBINARY(MAX) data, 405
Large-value string data types, 404
    NTEXT and TEXT data types, 403
    VARCHAR(MAX), 404
LEFT function, 68, 405
LEFT OUTER JOIN, 108–109
    adding table to left side of, 113
    adding table to right
        side of, 111, 113
LEN function, 69, 405
LIKE operator, 208
    PATINDEX, 198–199
    percent sign (%), 193–194
    square brackets ([]), 195–196
    wildcards, 196
LOWER function, 72
LTRIM functions, 67

■ M

Many-to-many relationship, 106
MAX function, 147
MERGE statement
    coding, 261
    output, 262
    syntax, 260
Microsoft Developer Network (MSDN), 433
Microsoft Help Viewer, 11
MIN function, 147
minus symbol (–), 65
Misc Documents, 413
modulo (%), 65
MONTH function, 78

■ N

NCHAR string data type, 404
NEWSEQUENTIALID function, 412
NO ACTION rule, 336, 338
Nonclustered index, 27
NOT BETWEEN operator, 42
NotepadFiles table, 412
NOT EXISTS statement, 228
NOT IN
    subqueries containing NULL with, 129–130
    using subqueries with, 128
NOT operator
    subqueries and, 128
NTEXT data type, 403
NTEXT string data type, 404
NTILE function, 172
NULL function, 162
    in the SalesOrderID column, 111
    in the Sales.SalesOrderHeader column, 111
    subqueries containing with NOT IN, 129–130
NULL values, 49
NVARCHAR(MAX) string data type, 404
NVARCHAR string data type, 277, 404

■ O

OFFSET clauses, 63, 93
Online resources, 449
OPENXML
    partial results of, 381
    rowset, 380
    shredding, 380
    WITH clause, 382
ORDER BY clause, 50–51, 346–347
    coding, 153
    error message, 153
    syntax, 153
    using functions in, 90

OrganizationalLevel column, 417
OrganizationalNode, 417
OUTER JOINS, 108, 233
    adding table to left side of, 114
    adding table to right side of, 112
    CROSS JOIN, 115–116
    FULL OUTER JOIN, 114–115
    LEFT OUTER JOIN, 108–109
        adding table to left side of, 113
        adding table to right side of, 111, 113
    overview, 108
    RIGHT OUTER JOIN, 109–110
    self-joins, 117–118
    using to find rows with
        no match, 110–111
OUTPUT parameter, 377

■ P

Paging
    definition, 271
    OFFSET/FETCH NEXT method, 272
    WHERE clause, 272
    with T-SQL, 271
Pattern matching
    LIKE operator
        PATINDEX, 198–199
        percent sign (%), 193–194
        square brackets ([]), 195–196
        wildcards, 196
    predicates, 209
Person.Person table, 104
Pivoted queries
    CASE function, 266
    PIVOT function
        aggregate expression, 267
        IN expression, 269
        SELECT statement, 268
        syntax, 267
    ROUND function, 266
    UNPIVOT function, 269
plus symbol (+), 65
POWER function, 82
Primary key
    characteristics, 330
    clustered index, 333
    CLUSTERED keyword, 332
    creation, 331, 333
    HumanResources.Department table, 331
    NOT NULL constraint, 333
    syntax, 330
Production.ProductColor table, 115
Production.Product table, 114
Professional Association for SQL
        Server (PASS), 450

■ Q

Querying multiple tables, 101
 common table expressions (CTEs)
  overview, 138–139
  using to solve complicated join
   problem, 139–141
 derived tables, 136–137
 EXCEPT and INTERSECT queries, 135
 hash match, 122
  join type, 123
  Sales.SalesOrderHeader table, 122
 INNER JOINS
  avoiding incorrect join condition, 103–104
  joining on different column name, 104
  joining on more than one column, 105
  joining three or more tables, 106–108, 124
  joining two tables, 101, 103
  overview, 101
 merge join, 119
  nested loop, 120
  seek index properties, 121
  working, 120
 OUTER JOINS, 108
  adding table to left side of, 113–114
  adding table to right side of, 111–113
  CROSS JOIN, 115–116
  FULL OUTER JOIN, 114–115
  LEFT OUTER JOIN, 108–109
  overview, 108
  RIGHT OUTER JOIN, 109–110
  self-joins, 117–118
  using to find rows with no match, 110–111
 overview, 101
 subqueries, 130
  containing NULL with NOT IN, 129–130
  CROSS APPLY and OUTER APPLY, 131
  EXISTS, 130
  NOT EXISTS technique, 131
  using in IN list, 127
  using with NOT IN, 128
 UNION queries, 132–135
  CTE, 143
  UNION to UNION ALL, 142
 virtual table, 138

■ R

RAND function, 84
Random access memory (RAM), 163
Ranking functions, 169, 189
 coding, 170
 NTILE function, 172
 ORDER BY, 170
 PARTITION BY option, 171
 syntax, 170

Readable values, 418
REPLACE function, 72
REPLICATE function, 405
REVERSE function, 71
RIGHT function, 68
RIGHT OUTER JOIN, 109–110
ROUND function, 83
Row constructors, 215
ROWGUIDID, 412
Rowversion column, 221
RTRIM function, 67

■ S

Sales.SalesOrderDetail table, 102, 119, 142
Sales.SalesOrderHeader table, 102, 122
Sales.SalesSpecialOfferProduct table, 105
Sample databases installation
 AdventureWorks databases, 14
 books online, 10
 CodePlex samples, 14
 Microsoft Help Viewer, 11
Scripted SELECT statement, 35
SELECT list, 102
SELECT statement
 execution plans, 54
 filtering data
  adding a WHERE clause (see WHERE clause)
  date and time, 43
  using BETWEEN operator, 40
  using NOT BETWEEN operator, 42
  using the IN operator, 47
 index properties, 52–53
 mixing literals and column names, 35
 retrieving from a table, 32
 running first T-SQL statement, 32
 scripted SELECT statement, 35
 sorting data, ORDER BY clause, 50–51
 statements returning literal values, 32
 working with nothing, 48
Self-joins, 117
Service Configuration screen, 6
SET DEFAULT rule, 336, 339
SET NULL rule, 336, 339
Setup Support Rules, 3
Sharding, 446
slash (/), 65
SPACE function, 418, 422
Sparse columns, 428
Spatial data types
 circular arcs, 426
 GEOGRAPHY, 424
 GEOMETRY, 423
 Spatial results tab, 425
SpatialLocation.ToString method, 424
SportsOrg table, 419, 422

SQL Server
    clustered index, 27
    database as container, 21
    database schemas, 28
    data in tables, 23
    data types, 23
        HumanResources.Employee table, 24
        phone user-defined data type, 24
    denormalized database, 26
    nonclustered index, 27
    normalization process, 25
    normalized database, 27
    service *vs.* application, 20
    SQL sever files, 22
SQL server books online, 451
SQL Server Business Intelligence Edition, 19
SQL Server Compact Edition, 19
SQL Server Developer Edition, 19
SQL Server Enterprise Edition, 19
SQL Server Express Edition, 1, 19
    Database Engine Configuration, 7
    FILESTREAM configuration, 7
    Hardware and Software Requirements link, 3
    Installation pane, 3–4
    planning pane, 2
    report, 9
    Service Configuration screen, 6
    Setup Support Rules, 2–3
    Space Requirements screen, 10
SQL Server Installation Center, 10
SQL Server Integration Services (SSIS), 211
SQL Server Management Studio (SSMS), 444–445
    automatically generated code, 16
    commented code, 18
    definition, 12
    file icon results, 17
    HumanResources.Employee table, 16
    IntelliSense, 14
    Object Explorer, 13
    server dialog box connection, 12
SQL Server Standard Edition, 19
SQRT function, 83
SQUARE function, 83
Stored procedures
    ALTER PROC statement, 357
    creation, 356, 376
    default value parameters, 358
    definition, 355
    modification, 376
    OUTPUT parameter, 360, 377
    row insertion, 361–362
    SET NOCOUNT ON statement, 357
    syntax, 356
    vs. user-defined functions, 355
    using programming logic, 362–363

String function
    CHARINDEX, 69
    CHOOSE, 71
    LEFT and RIGHT, 68
    LEN and DATALENGTH, 69
    REPLACE, 72
    REVERSE, 71
    RTRIM and LTRIM, 67
    SUBSTRING, 70
    UPPER and LOWER, 72
Subqueries
    containing NULL with NOT IN, 129–130
    using in IN list, 127
    using with NOT IN, 128
SUBSTRING function, 70
SUM function, 147
SWITCHOFFSET function, 417
SYSDATETIME function, 75, 416
SYSDATETIMEOFFSET function, 417
System function
    admin function, 89
    CASE Function (*see* CASE function)
    COALESCE, 89
    IIF, 88
SYSUTCDATETIME function, 416

■ T

Tables, 325
    automatically populating columns coding, 340
    check constraints
        ALTER TABLE command, 326
        coding, 326
        error messages, 327
    COMPUTED columns, 340
    creation, 371–372
    data-modeling software, 325
    DEFAULT columns, 339–340
    foreign keys
        coding, 334–335
        delete and update rules, 336
        referential integrity, 333
        result, 335
        syntax, 334
    IDENTITY columns, 339
    primary key
        characteristics, 330
        clustered index, 333
        CLUSTERED keyword, 332
        creation, 331, 333
        HumanResources.Department table, 331
        NOT NULL constraint, 333
        syntax, 330
    querying multiple, overview of, 101
    ROWVERSION data type, 339–340

Tables (*cont.*)
UNIQUE constraints, 329
ALTER TABLE statement, 328
creation, 328
indexes and keys, 330
TEXT data type, 403
TEXT string data type, 404
The Big Bang Theory, 451
TODATETIMEOFFSET function, 417
TOP keyword, 92
ToString method, 418, 424
Transactions
ACID properties, 309
dirty reads, 321
error handling
RAISERROR function, 317–318
THROW statement, 319
TRY CATCH method, 314–316, 318
untrappable errors, 316–317
explicit transaction
coding, 310
data insertion, 311
ROLLBACK command, 311–312
syntax, 310
XACT_ABORT setting, 312–313
isolation levels, 321
overview, 309
SELECT statement, 321
Snapshot, 322
Triggers, 367
Truncate, 229
T-SQL, 275
IF...ELSE construct, 281
ELSE block, 283
IF block, 281
IF EXISTS, 286
multiple conditions, 284
nesting IF...ELSE, 285
performance, 301
cursor-based approach, 301, 303
set-based approach, 303
table variables, 293
application, 297
array, 298
creation, 295
cursors, 299
scoping rules, 295
SELECT INTO statement, 296
temporary tables, 293
ALTER TABLE command, 294
application, 296
array, 298
CREATE TABLE command, 293
cursors, 299

global creation, 293, 295
local creation, 293
variables, 275
declaring and initializing, 275, 277
expressions and functions, 277
SELECT statement, 275, 277
SET statement, 275
WHERE/HAVING clause predicate, 279
WHILE construct, 288
BREAK statement, 290–291
CONTINUE command, 291
nesting WHILE loops, 289
WHILE loop, 288
T-SQL classes, 451
T-SQL, definition, 1
T-SQL teaching, 452

■ U

Unary relationship, 117
UNION queries, 132–135
UPPER function, 72
User-defined data types (UDTs), 364
creation, 365
properties, 364
syntax, 364
table type
creation, 365
CustomerInfo type, 366
definition, 365
stored procedure creation, 367
syntax, 365
table-valued parameter, 367
User-defined functions (UDFs), 350, 374
creation, 351
database cleanup, 369
performance issues, 368
scalar functions, 351
table-valued function
CROSS APPLY operator, 353–354
dbo.ufnGetContactInformation function, 353–354
result, 354
types, 353
User groups, 450

■ V

VARCHAR(MAX) string data type, 404
VARCHAR string data type, 404
Vendors, 451
Views, 373
ALTER VIEW, 343
common problems, 347
CREATE VIEW, 343

data manipulation
  data modification, 348–349
  requirements, 347
  SELECT INTO statements, 349
  WITH CHECK OPTION, 350
definition, 342
DROP VIEW, 343
GO statements, 344
graphical designer for, 345
Virtual Machines (VM), 438
  advantage, 435
  configuration, 437
  creation, 435
  hypervisor, 435
  Remote Desktop Connection, 439
  setup, 438
  SQL Server 2014 RTM Enterprise, 436

PERCENTILE_CONT and
    PERCENTILE_DISC, 182–183
  PERCENT_RANK and CUME_DIST, 181–182
framing, 175
island problem, 186
performance
  indexing, 187
  ROWS *vs.* RANGE, 188, 190
  window aggregates *vs.* traditional techniques, 187
ranking functions (*see* Ranking functions)
ROW_NUMBER() function, 184
Row Number Offsets, 176
types, 169
window aggregate functions, 174
Windows Azure Virtual Machines. *See* Virtual
    Machines (VM)
WITH keyword, 139

■ W

WHERE clause, 154, 157, 193
  derived tables and, 137
  Full-text search
    adventure works database, 202
    CONTAINS function, 203–204
    definition, 202
    FREETEXT function, 205
    multiple columns, 204
  how to use, 37
  LIKE *vs.* CHARINDEX, 206–207
  pattern matching (*see* Pattern matching)
  predicates
    AND and OR logical
      operators, 199–200
    NOT with parentheses, 201
  predicates expressions, 37
  results of using, 38
  subqueries, 127, 130
  syntax, 37
  using functions in, 90
  with alternate operators, 38
  with two predicates, 45–46
Wildcards, 196
Window aggregate functions, 169, 174, 189
Windowing functions, 169
  accumulating aggregates, 169
    ROWS *vs.* RANGE, 177
    total calculations, 176–177
  analytic functions, 169
    FIRST_VALUE and LAST_VALUE, 180–181
    LAG and LEAD, 179

■ X

XML, 379
  content, 379
  data retrieval, FOR XML clause
    AUTO mode, 385
    EXPLICIT mode, 386
    modes, 383
    PATH mode, 388
    RAW mode, 383
    SELECT statement, 383
  data type
    built-in table, 391
    execution code, 392
    EXIST method, 393, 396
    MODIFY method, 393, 397–398
    NODES method, 393, 398–399
    query() method, 393
    results, 392
    rules, 391
    VALUE method, 393, 395
  element-centric example, 380
  namespaces, 399–400
  OPENXML
    partial results of, 381
    rowset, 380
    shredding, 380
    WITH clause, 382
  splitting, 400–401

■ Y, Z

YEAR function, 78

Get the eBook for only $10!

Now you can take the weightless companion with you anywhere, anytime. Your purchase of this book entitles you to 3 electronic versions for only $10.

This Apress title will prove so indispensible that you'll want to carry it with you everywhere, which is why we are offering the eBook in **3 formats** for only $10 if you have already purchased the print book.

Convenient and fully searchable, the PDF version enables you to easily find and copy code—or perform examples by quickly toggling between instructions and applications. The MOBI format is ideal for your Kindle, while the ePUB can be utilized on a variety of mobile devices.

Go to www.apress.com/promo/tendollars to purchase your companion eBook.

Manufactured by Amazon.ca
Acheson, AB

13610787R00273